PUBLIC RIGHTS OF WAY AND ACCESS TO LAND

SECOND EDITION

PUBLIC RIGHTS OF WAY AND ACCESS TO LAND

SECOND EDITION

Angela Sydenham
*Consultant with Birketts
Solicitors, Ipswich, Suffolk*

JORDANS
2003

Published by
Jordan Publishing Limited
21 St Thomas Street
Bristol BS1 6JS

British Library Cataloguing-in-Publication Data
A catalogue record for this book is available from the British Library.

ISBN 0 85308 842 X

Typeset by Mendip Communications Ltd, Frome, Somerset
Printed in Great Britain by MPG Books Ltd, Bodmin, Cornwall

DEDICATION

To Nigel Farthing

Polished, polite and persuasive advocate

PREFACE TO THE FIRST EDITION

The aim of the first part of this book is to set out as clearly as possible the law relating to public rights of way, as amended by the Countryside and Rights of Way Act 2000. It is hoped that it is written without bias and will be useful for all those involved in public rights of way: landowners, farmers, users, local authorities, inspectors, lawyers, land agents, academics and students.

Public rights of way are often seen as a source of conflict and confrontation. Part of this is due to lack of knowledge of the arcane and often archaic nature of highway law. To most people the word 'highway' conjures up a picture of a metalled road with motor cars speeding along it. Farmers understandably may find it difficult to appreciate that in law the dusty footpath across their field is also a highway.

Perhaps the three most difficult things from a landowner's point of view to accept are that: (a) the surface of a publicly maintainable footpath (or other public right of way) is vested in the Highway Authority; (b) a public right of way continues to have legal existence even if it has not been used for many years; and (c) the recorded rights on the definitive map are only the starting point. Greater or additional rights may exist and be legally valid, even if not recorded.

This is not to underestimate the practical problems which some landowners and farmers have in relation to rights of way. This book will suggest solutions to those problems as well as explaining the law.

It is difficult to draw a clear dividing line between the law relating to public rights of way and highway law generally. The scope of this book is limited to setting out the law as it relates to highways which may be entered on the definitive map; that is byways open to all traffic, roads used as public paths, restricted byways, bridleways and footpaths. It does not include those other highways which form part of the road network or rivers (although rivers are treated as highways for some purposes).

In writing Chapters 1 to 10 of this book, I have been greatly stimulated by the *Rights of Way Law Review*. Everyone involved in public rights of way should subscribe to this publication which gives full coverage to the law in this area.

However, this book is not just an exercise in plagiarism. It is written from the personal experience of giving advice to landowners on public rights of way during my years as Chief Legal Adviser to the Country Landowners Association, and subsequently. It also benefits from my more sharp-end practice as a consultant with Birketts, acting for landowners and County Councils.

Chapters 11 to 16 of this book deal with the access provisions of the Countryside and Rights of Way Act 2000. Although the Act has received Royal Assent, the main provisions, which give the public a right of access, are not yet in force. Much of the detail of the legislation will be in regulations. Therefore, how the Act will work in practice remains to be seen. Chapters 11 to 16 therefore concentrate on explaining the sections of the Act in the light of the background papers and the *Hansard* reports as the Bill progressed through Parliament. It is intended to publish a supplement to the book when the main regulations have been promulgated.

I would like to acknowledge the help and criticism I have received from Nigel Farthing (litigation partner at Birketts) in writing this book and the lessons learnt by watching his eloquent and successful advocacy at numerous public inquiries.

My attempts to understand the often opaque provisions of the new legislation amending the law relating to public rights of way have been greatly assisted by the insights and background knowledge of Dr Karen Jones. However, any mistakes are mine. Unfortunately, I cannot blame anyone else.

Heartfelt thanks are due to Peggy Alexander who typed and retyped, more times than either of us care to remember, the contents of this book.

Finally, I am grateful to Martin West of Jordans who has, as always, been supportive of the project, its concept and execution.

ANGELA SYDENHAM
April 2001

PREFACE TO THE SECOND EDITION

This second edition comes close astern of the first edition. The reason a new edition was deemed necessary is because of the spate of regulations which have gushed forth under the CROW Act 2000. Of course the flood has not yet abated. Many more regulations are to come. But guidance is required now on the many issues relating to the mapping of open country. Chapter 12 has therefore been expanded and the statutory instruments relating to draft, provisional, and conclusive maps, as well as appeals, have been included in the appendices.

Also in the appendices are the new regulations relating to local access forums in England and Wales. The forums are important not only in relation to open land but also to rights of way. The provisions of the CROW Act relating to Rights of Way Improvement Plans are now in force and highway authorities are required by the legislation to consult local access forums.

The first part of the book, dealing with public rights of way, has been amended to take into account new case-law. The case of most significance, though, relates to private rights of way. Since *Hanning v Top Deck Travel Group* it has been considered by the author, amongst others, that most claimed prescriptive easements for vehicles must be void. The recent case of *Massey v Boulden* has now held this view to be correct. The ill-thought through regulations for statutory easements under s 68 of the CROW Act 2000 are likely to result in many a dispute. They too are included in the appendices.

My thanks to Martin West of Jordans for allowing me to develop the work in a new edition rather than just having a reprint of the first, and also to Gary Hill for his careful and patient editing.

The law is stated as at 31 December 2002.

ANGELA SYDENHAM
Aldeburgh
Candlemas 2003

CONTENTS

TABLE OF CASES

References are to paragraph numbers.

TABLE OF STATUTES

References are to paragraph numbers.

TABLE OF STATUTORY INSTRUMENTS

References are to paragraph numbers.

TABLE OF INTERNATIONAL MATERIAL

References are to paragraph numbers.

TABLE OF CIRCULARS, GUIDANCE ETC

References are to paragraph numbers.

TABLE OF ABBREVIATIONS

AONB	Area of Outstanding Natural Beauty
BOATs	Byways open to all traffic
CA 1968	Countryside Act 1968
CROW Act 2000	Countryside and Rights of Way Act 2000
DEFRA	Department of the Environment, Food and Rural Affairs
GLA road	Greater London Authority road
NPACA 1949	National Parks and Access to the Countryside Act 1949
RUPP	Road used as a public path
RWA 1932	Rights of Way Act 1932
RWA 1990	Rights of Way Act 1990
SSSI	Site of Special Scientific Interest
WLCA 1981	Wildlife and Countryside Act 1981

Chapter 1

DEFINITIONS AND CLASSES OF PUBLIC RIGHTS OF WAY AND ANALOGOUS RIGHTS

1.1 DEFINITION

A highway is a public right of way over a defined linear route. The term 'highway' and 'public right of way' are used interchangeably, although sometimes the term 'highway' is used to denote the physical route, rather than the right itself. Roads normally used by motor vehicles are seldom described as public rights of way.

1.1.1 Right of passage

The legal consequence of land being a highway is that the public have a right to pass and repass along the route. Any other activity, unless it is incidental to the right of passage, will be a trespass.

Permitted incidental activities include parking a car on a vehicular highway, resting, stopping for refreshments, taking photographs or making a sketch. However, interfering with a game drive[1] or observing the performance of race horses on adjoining land[2] has been held to be a trespass. Metal detecting would also be a trespass.[3]

The previous two paragraphs state the law as understood before *DPP v Jones and Another*.[4] Three out of the five Law Lords held that an assembly on a highway, even though it was not ancillary to the exercise of a right of passage, was a reasonable use of the highway provided it did not interfere with other users and was not a public or private nuisance. This decision implies that the right of the public on public rights of way has been greatly increased. It is no longer limited to a right to pass and repass and incidental activities. It should be noted, however, that this case was concerned with whether a criminal offence had been committed under s 14A of the Public Order Act 1986.

---

1   *Harrison v Rutland* [1893] 1 QB 142.
2   *Hickman v Maisey* [1900] 1 QB 752.
3   *Waverley Borough Council v Fletcher* [1995] 4 All ER 756. Metal detecting on a scheduled site is an offence. Ancient Monuments and Archaeological Areas Act 1979, s 42.
4   [1999] 2 WLR 625. See *Rights of Way Law Review (RWLR)* Michael Doherty 'Public's right of access to the highway', RWLR 4.3, p 39.

1.1.2   The public

For a highway to exist, there must be a right of passage for the public at large, not a section of the public.[1]

A highway may be contrasted with a private right of way, or easement for the benefit of some nearby land. Sometimes there are accommodation roads for several adjoining landowners. There are also churchways or local roads, available for parishioners of a particular parish or manor, which do not amount to highways.

1.1.3   Defined route

The right of passage must exist over a defined route. A route may be sufficiently defined if it varies from time to time.[2] There cannot be a public right to wander (*ius spatiendi*) at common law.[3] Although such a right may be created by statute or agreement, it will not create highway rights.

The defined route does not have to lead anywhere. It can be a cul-de-sac.[4] However, when considering evidence as to whether or not a highway exists, it will be relevant to consider the purpose of such a highway. If it does not connect to another highway, or a place of popular resort, such as a river,[5] the sea[6] or a beauty spot,[7] this may strengthen an argument against the existence of a highway,[8] or that the highway continued further.

1.2   CLASSES OF PUBLIC HIGHWAY

There are three main categories of a highway:

(1) a carriageway, including a byway open to all traffic;
(2) a bridleway; and
(3) a footpath.

For the purposes of the definitive map,[9] there is a further category:

(4) a road used as a public path (RUPP) (or in the future a restricted byway).

---

1   *Poole v Huskinson* (1843) 11 M&W 827.
2   *Fernlee Estates v City and Council of Swansea and National Assembly for Wales* [2001] P&CR 19; see also *Wimbledon & Putney Commons Conservators v Dixon* [1875] 1 Ch 368 (way across open land divided into parallel routes).
3   *A G Antrobus* [1905] 2 Ch 188.
4   *Rugby Charity Trustees v Merryweather* (1790) 11 East 375n (see discussion at **7.6**).
5   *R v St Issey Inhabitants* (1849) 14 LT(OS) 176.
6   *Williams-Ellis v Cobb* [1935] 1 KB 310.
7   *Eyre v New Forest Highway Board* (1892) 56 JP 517; *Moser v Ambleside UDC* (1925) 89 JP 118.
8   *Roberts v Webster* (1967) 66 LGR 298.
9   See Chapter 5.

There is a duty imposed on the highway authority to reclassify RUPPs into one of the three main categories.[1] When s 47 of the Countryside and Rights of Way Act 2000 (CROW Act 2000) comes into force, all RUPPs will automatically become restricted byways. Section 54 of the Wildlife and Countryside Act 1981 (WLCA 1981), which imposes the duty on a surveying authority to reclassify RUPPs, will cease to have effect.

1.2.1   Carriageways and Byways Open to All Traffic

Carriageways and Byways Open to All Traffic (BOATs) give the public a right of passage with vehicles. As there is a general principle of law that the greater includes the lesser right, the public may also use a carriageway on horse and on foot.[2] This rule is subject to specific statutory exceptions, for example the rules governing use of motorways.

Although there is a presumption that carriageways include a right to drive animals along them, the presumption may be rebutted.[3]

BOATs are a special sub-category of carriageways which are recorded on definitive maps. The definition is as follows:

> ' "byway open to all traffic" means a highway over which the public have a right of way for vehicular and all other kinds of traffic, but which is used by the public mainly for the purposes for which footpaths and bridleways are so used.'[4]

1.2.2   Bridleways

Bridleways are defined as:

> 'a highway over which the public have the following, but no other, rights of way, that is to say, a right of way on foot and a right of way on horseback or leading a horse, with or without a right to drive animals of any description along the highway.'[5]

'Horse' is defined to include pony, ass or mule,[6] but not a llama.

Whether or not driftway rights (ie a right to drive animals) exist will depend on the evidence.

The rights have been extended by the Countryside Act 1968 to include the right to ride a bicycle but not 'a mechanically propelled vehicle intended or

---

1   Wildlife and Countryside Act 1981, s 54.
2   *R v Hatfield (Inhabitants)* (1736) Lee Temp Hard 315; *Wells v London, Tilbury and Southend Rail Co* (1877) 5 Ch D 126.
3   *Ballard v Dyson* (1808) 1 Taunt 279.
4   WLCA 1981, s 66(1). The term was first introduced in the Countryside Act 1968.
5   WLCA 1981, s 66(1); Highways Act 1980, s 329(1).
6   Ibid.

adapted for use on roads'.[1] In exercising their rights, cyclists must give way to pedestrians and horse riders.[2] Cycle riding may be forbidden by local orders or bylaws.[3]

1.2.3 Footpaths

The public have a right of way on foot only over a footpath.[4]

Questions which often arise over footpaths are what the walker can take with him. It was said in *R v Mathias*[5] that a person may take:

> 'such things as are usual accompaniments of a large class of foot passengers, being so small and light, as neither to be a nuisance to other passengers nor injurious to the soil.'

In that case the jury decided that a perambulator was a usual accompaniment. However, it is suggested that a bicycle would not be, unless it were carried.[6]

Dogs, on the other hand, are regarded as a usual accompaniment, although this has not been tested by the courts.[7]

1.2.4 Road used as a public path

The term 'road used as a public path' (RUPP) was introduced by the National Parks and Access to the Countryside Act 1949 (NPACA 1949).[8] RUPPs were defined as:

> 'highways, other than public paths, used by the public mainly for the purposes for which footpaths and bridleways are so used.'

Until reclassified, they have the same status as bridleways.[9] Use by motorised vehicles will be an offence unless it can be proved by documentary evidence or by user evidence pre-dating the Road Traffic Act 1930 that vehicular rights exist.[10] Only specified categories of persons are entitled to produce evidence rebutting the presumption that motorised vehicular rights do not exist.[11] RUPPs will become restricted byways as explained below.

---

1   Road Traffic Act 1988, Sch 3, para 5.
2   Countryside Act 1968, s 30. The reference to bicycle, rather than cycle, seems to restrict it to two-wheeled cycles.
3   Local Government Act 1972, s 235.
4   WLCA 1981, s 66(1).
5   (1861) 2 F&F 570 NP.
6   Bruce Monnington 'Cyclists Rights of Way', RWLR 3.2, p 1.
7   Riddall and Trevelyan, *Rights of Way*, 3rd edn, p 29. See also Peter Carty 'Dogs with Walkers', RWLR 3.2, p 11.
8   Section 27(2).
9   WLCA 1981, s 56(1)(d).
10   Road Traffic Act 1988, s 34. *Stevens v Secretary of State for the Environment* (1998) 76 P&CR 503.
11   For a discussion of prosecutions under the Road Traffic Act 1988, s 34, see **9.8.2**.

1.2.5   Restricted byways

When s 47 of the CROW Act 2000 comes into force, all RUPPs will automatically become restricted byways. The public will have restricted byway rights over these routes:

(a)   a right of way on foot;
(b)   a right of way on horseback or leading a horse; and
(c)   a right of way for vehicles other than mechanically propelled vehicles.[1]

These are the minimum rights. A restricted byway may also include the right to drive animals. Restricted byway rights are:

> 'without prejudice to any question whether the public have over any way, in addition to restricted byway rights, a right of way for mechanically propelled vehicles or any other right.'[2]

1.2.6   Cycle tracks

The Cycle Tracks Act 1984 enables footpaths to be converted into cycle tracks. These are a statutory creation which confer a right of way for pedal cycles (not confined to two-wheeled cycles) and usually on foot.

1.2.7   Long-distance paths

The provision for long-distance paths is found in NPACA 1949.[3] The Countryside Agency (originally the National Parks Commission) make proposals for the route to the Secretary of State. The proposals include new paths and ferries where necessary, and the provision of accommodation and refreshments.

If the Secretary of State gives his approval, highway authorities implement the proposals through creation agreements and orders and diversion orders.

1.3   PUBLIC RIGHTS OF WAY CONTRASTED WITH OTHER RIGHTS OF WAY

1.3.1   Easements

A private right of way is an easement (ie a right over land for the benefit of other land). However, the right must be attached to a particular piece of land and cannot be used by the public generally.[4] A public footpath or bridleway may also carry private vehicular rights. These rights may be vested in a third party as an easement or reserved to the landowner.

---

1   CROW Act 2000, s 48(4).
2   Ibid, s 48(6).
3   Sections 50A–55.
4   On easements generally, see Megarry and Wade *Law of Real Property* (Sweet & Maxwell, 5th edn), para 18–042 et seq.

It is generally accepted that where a public footpath or bridleway is dedicated the landowner is able by implication to reserve for himself vehicular rights. Where the surface is vested in the highway authority the reservation must amount to an easement.

1.3.2   Licences and permissive paths

A landowner may allow one or more specified persons to use a route across his land. If the way is used by permission, it will not, even after 20 years' use, amount to dedication of a right of way. The permission may be withdrawn in accordance with the terms of the licence or, if it is not for a specified period and there is no provision for termination, on reasonable notice.

A landowner may also allow the public, as distinct from specified persons, to use a path by licence. This is known as a permissive path. It is important from a landowner's point of view that the public should be made aware that they do not use the route by right. In order to rebut any claim that there has been a deemed dedication, the landowner should lodge a Statement and Declaration with the highway authority[1] as well as erecting notices informing the public that it is a permissive path only.

Often a landowner will enter into an agreement with a highway authority setting out in a document the agreed terms for the use of the path.

The general law relating to public rights of way does not apply to permissive paths. There is, however, a requirement to cut back overhanging vegetation on any road or path to which the public have access.[2] There are also other statutory provisions, in particular, road traffic offences, which apply 'to any road to which the public have access'.[3]

1.3.3   Occupation road

Occupation roads may be laid out for the use and occupation of the occupier of particular lands. Private roads within an estate may be used by local inhabitants. For example, there may have been cottages for farm workers which were subsequently sold off and the right of the owners to use the adjoining lane may amount to an easement in common with the other cottage owners. These roads will not be highways[4] unless there is also use by the general public.

1.3.4   Church ways

In order to be a highway, the use must be by the public at large and not merely the local inhabitants. In many parishes, there may be church ways which have been used by the parishioners to gain access to the church.[5]

---

1   Highways Act 1980, s 31(6).
2   Ibid, s 154(1).
3   For example, Road Traffic Act 1988, ss 2 and 3.
4   *Selby v Crystal Palace Gas Co* (1862) 4 De GF & J 246.
5   See J Harte 'Churchyards and Coffin Ways', RWLR 11, p 17.

1.3.5 Green lanes

A green lane is not a legal term. It is a physical description of an unsurfaced track. Usually the track will be between hedges, ditches or walls. However, the term does not indicate whether the track carries public or private rights or any rights at all. It cannot therefore be argued without further evidence that a green lane is a public right of way for vehicles.

1.3.6 Railways

Although there may be a right of way across a railway line, either on a level crossing or on a bridge or under a tunnel, the railway track itself is not a public right of way. The right to travel along the tracks in a train is a contractual right. The Railways Clauses Consolidation Act 1845[1] imposes a duty on railway companies to maintain proper approaches and gates and stiles in lineside fences. Where the Act applies, the duties can be enforced by an application to the magistrates' court. There may also be liability in negligence where there are not proper safeguards preventing access to the line.[2]

Where a railway company purchased land to develop a railway which had the effect of severing land in one ownership, it often provided accommodation works, such as a bridge or a tunnel to enable the landowner to reach the land on the other side. The rights over the accommodation will be private rights, although public rights may subsequently be acquired by long use.

1.3.7 Towpaths

Towpaths along canals or rivers are not public rights of way unless such rights have been dedicated either expressly or by long use.[3] If a right of way is dedicated, it will be subject to the primary needs of navigation.[4]

The CROW Act 2000 provides that restricted byway rights can exist on towpaths.[5]

1.3.8 Rivers

Rivers for some purposes are considered to be highways. However, it has been held that a right of way over a river is not covered by the deemed dedication provisions of the Rights of Way Act 1932.[6]

1.3.9 Fords

The definition section[7] of the Highways Act 1980 states that 'land' includes land covered by water and this has been held to refer to fords. The highway still runs

---

1   Sections 61 and 65.
2   *Thomas v British Railway Board* [1976] 2 WLR 761.
3   *Ball v Herbert* (1789) 3 TR 253.
4   *Grand Junction Canal Co v Petty* (1888) 21 QBD 273.
5   Section 48(5).
6   *Attorney-General (ex rel Yorkshire Derwent Trust) v Brotherton* [1992] AC 425.
7   Section 329.

over the land. This is in contrast to rivers where the public right of way is over the water as distinct from the land.

1.3.10   Foreshore

There is no public right to walk on the foreshore: that is the land between medium high and medium low water. The rights of the public are limited to navigation and fishing. Incidental to the right of fishing is the right to collect lugworms for non-commercial purposes.[1]

A public right of way may be dedicated expressly or by implication over the foreshore. The foreshore is generally owned by the Crown, which is not bound by s 31 of the Highways Act 1980. So any claim to a deemed dedication would have to be made at common law.

However, the Crown may have conveyed the foreshore to a local authority or The National Trust. It is also possible that the foreshore may have vested in the Lord of the Manor pre-Magna Carta.

1.3.11   Ferries

Ferries may in the past have linked highways separated by water. Today, many ferries, being unprofitable, have fallen into disuse. The NPACA 1949[2] empowers highway authorities to provide and operate ferries.

---

1   *Anderson v Alnwick District Council* [1993] 1 WLR 1156. *Adair v The National Trust* [1998] NI 33. See W Howarth 'Access to the Foreshore', RWLR 11, p 11; P Carty 'Rights over the Foreshore', RWLR 11, p 49. The Land Registration Act 2002, s 79, enables the Crown to register the foreshore.
2   Section 53.

Chapter 2

THE LEGAL INTERESTS AND RIGHTS OF HIGHWAY AUTHORITIES, LANDOWNERS, USERS AND UTILITY COMPANIES

2.1 INTRODUCTION

One of the characteristics of real property law is that several interests can exist in the same piece of land. This is especially so where there is a public right of way.

2.2 THE HIGHWAY AUTHORITY

2.2.1 Public maintainable highways

Where a highway is publicly maintainable, the surface is vested in the highway authority.[1] Section 263(1) of the Highways Act 1980[2] provides:

> 'every highway maintainable at the public expense, together with the materials and scrapings thereof, vests in the highway authority who are for the time being the highway authority for the highway.'

The question of whether or not a highway is maintainable at public expense is discussed in Chapter 8. The answer is complex. But as a guiding principle, public rights of way will be publicly maintainable if they are created formally or if they were created before 16 December 1949.

2.2.2 The extent of the public maintainable highway

The highway authority has a statutory form of determinable fee simple in that its interest lasts until the highway is stopped up or diverted. However, that interest does not extend up to the sky and down to the centre of the earth. The interest in the airspace and below the surface is limited to that which is required by the authority for the exercise of its powers and the performance of its statutory duties. In the words of Lord Herschell in *Tunbridge Wells Corporation v Baird*:[3]

> 'The interest of the highway authority is that which is necessary for its control, protection and maintenance as a highway for public use.'

---

1   For definition, see Highways Act 1980, s 1.
2   This provision was first introduced by the Public Health Act 1848, s 68.
3   [1896] AC 634.

There is no statutory definition of the extent required. Lord Denning in *Tithe Redemption Commissioners v Runcorn Urban District Council*[1] referred to:

'the top spit, or perhaps, I should say the top two spits of the road ...'

The question most often arises in connection with the laying of pipes, wires, cables and other apparatus in the highway. This is discussed under Utility Companies (see **2.5**). It has also arisen in relation to possession proceedings. In *Wiltshire County Council v Frazer*,[2] it was held that the highway authority's ownership of the surface enabled it to bring an action for possession against squatters who had set up their caravans on the highway.

The width of the highway is also an important issue. Where rights of way are entered on the definitive map, the width may be specified in the statement accompanying the map. If not, the width may be ascertained from other documents. Failing that, the width will be the historic use of the route.[3]

There are also presumptions in relation to highways which may be relevant, depending on whether there is:

(a) a metalled road;
(b) fences or dykes;
(c) ditches;
(d) no defined track.

(a) The public are not confined to using only the metalled road. It may be that the verges of the road have also been dedicated to the public use. But where a metalled road crosses unenclosed land, and there is no indication of the limits of the highway by fences, ditches, etc then the presumption is that the public right of way is limited to the metal track.[4]

(b) If it is established that fences adjoining a highway were put up in order to separate it from the adjoining land, there is a presumption that the public are entitled to a right of passage over the whole space beween the hedges and dykes unless there is evidence to the contrary. However, there is no presumption that the fences were put up to separate the adjoining land from the highway. In the words of Chadwick LJ in *Hale v Norfolk County Council*:[5]

'It seems to me much less clear that there is any foundation for a presumption of law that a fence or hedge which does, in fact, separate land over part of which there is an undoubted public highway from land enjoyed by the landowner has been erected or established for that purpose. It must, in my view, be a question of fact in each case.'

1   [1954] 2 WLR 518.
2   (1984) 47 P&CR 69.
3   *Easton v Richmond Highway Board* (1871) LR 7 QB 69.
4   *Belmore (Countess) v Kent County Council* [1901] 1 Ch 873.
5   *Hale v Norfolk County Council* [2001] 2 WLR 1481, qualifying *Attorney General v Beynon* [1970] 1 Ch 1; see Ross Crail 'The fence to fence presumption' RWLR 2.2, p 41.

The fence may have nothing to do with the highway.[1] For instance, the fence may be so far away from the road that it cannot have any connection with it; or the fence may have been put up for the purpose of separating farmland from waste.

(c) Ditches, such as those normally made by owners on the boundaries of their property, are not presumed to be part of the highway.[2] However, it is possible for ditches to be piped and filled in and dedicated as part of the highway. Moreover, ditches are sometimes made specifically for draining the highway.[3]

(d) Where there is a public right of passage over a field or open space but no defined track then the right is probably confined to a strip of reasonable width running between specified points.

Sometimes highways are created as a result of statute or by orders or agreements made under statutes. These may specify the widths.

The Rights of Way Act 1990 introduced statutory widths in relation to the restoration of paths after cultivation, but these are not relevant for other purposes.

2.2.3 Non-publicly maintainable highways

If a highway is not publicly maintainable, the surface as well as the subsoil will remain vested in the landowner. However, the highway authority has powers of control over the highway and could therefore be liable in nuisance for obstruction.

2.2.4 Statutory rights

Highway authorities are given various statutory powers in relation to highways which do not depend on any property interest. An example is the right to use vehicles and appliances on footpaths and bridleways.[4]

2.2.5 Statutory functions

Local highway authorities have numerous statutory functions relating to public rights of way. These include the making of improvement plans, public path and definitive map orders, the maintenance of a publicly maintainable highway, and taking action to prevent or remove obstructions. The main functions are discussed under the relevant chapter headings.

The Secretary of State, for England, and the National Assembly, for Wales, have power to make regulations by statutory instrument (subject to annulment by

---

1   *Hinds and Diplock v Breconshire County Council* [1938] 4 All ER 24.
2   *Hanscombe v Bedfordshire County Council* [1938] 1 Ch 944.
3   *Chorley Corporation v Nightingale* [1907] 2 KB 637.
4   Highways Act 1980, s 300, as amended by the CROW Act 2000, s 70(4).

resolution of either House) requiring local highway authorities to publish reports on the performance of their functions relating to public rights of way.[1]

2.3   LANDOWNERS

2.3.1   Publicly maintainable highways

Even where the surface is vested in the highway authority, the landowner usually retains an interest in the subsoil. He also owns the airspace above the highway. This enables him to build cellars or tunnels under the road, or where he owns property on both sides, a building or bridge over the road.

Landowners do not own the subsoil under many major roads. Often the highway authority will have purchased the land on which the road is built either by a compulsory purchase order or agreement.

Adjoining landowners have, subject to planning control, a right of access to the highway from any point of their land[2] and may do repairs to their property from the highway.[3]

2.3.2   Non-publicly maintainable highways

The landowner retains the entire legal interest in the land but it is subject to the right of passage of members of the public and the rights of control vested in the highway authority.

2.3.3   Statutory restrictions

Although the landowner retains title to the land, his use of the land over which the highway runs may be restricted. For example, without the consent of the highway authority, he may not construct buildings over or under the highway.[4]

2.3.4   The presumption *usque ad medium filum*

Where a right of way separates land in different ownership, there is a presumption that the adjoining landowner owns the land up to the centre point of the track adjoining his property.[5] The presumption extends to any waste land between the adjoining land and the highway.[6]

This presumption may be rebutted by evidence that ownership of the soil of the track is vested in one adjoining landowner alone or in a third party. However, it will not be rebutted where there is a description in a conveyance that the

---

1   CROW Act 2000, s 71.
2   *Lyon v Fishmongers' Co* (1876) 1 App Cas 662.
3   *Cobb v Saxby* [1914] 3 KB 822.
4   Highways Act 1980, ss 176–179.
5   *Central London Railway Co v City of London Land Tax Commissioners* [1911] 2 Ch 467.
6   *Doe d' Pring and Another v Pearsey* [1824–34] All ER Rep 164.

property is bounded by a road nor where the property is described by reference to red edging on a plan and the plan does not include the road.[1]

Whether or not the presumption applies to highways set out under inclosure awards depends on the construction of the award. The presumption rests on the argument that each of the adjoining owners contributed land to the formation of the highway. Where it is a new road, this argument would not be relevant. It may be that the road would remain vested in the Lord of the Manor unless he was compensated for loss of his rights in the soil.[2]

In new developments, roads are often retained by the developer and do not pass with a sale of the plots.

2.3.5   Reservation of implied rights

It is generally accepted that, where a landowner dedicates a public right of way, that dedication is limited to granting the public a right of passage. The landowner is therefore able to use the land over which the right of way exists for his own purposes and to grant others rights insofar as those uses do not derogate from the dedication. Where the public right of way is publicly maintainable so that the surface vests in the highway authority, the legal nature of those implied rights will be reserved easements.

2.4   USERS

The right of the user is to pass and repass as explained in **1.1.1**. The public have no legal interest in the land itself. The right of passage, however, is a legal right which has legal protection.

2.5   UTILITY COMPANIES

2.5.1   Position contrasted with highway authority

The highway authority has rights in the soil of the highway for purposes connected with the highway maintenance. This would include putting in drains or culverts. It would not include the power to authorise the laying of pipes or cables by other bodies.[3]

The right to lay and keep such apparatus under the track or in the highway verge has been awarded to utility companies by statutes without any obligation to pay compensation. However, the extent of their powers varies according to the particular statute.

Each of the utility statutes incorporates, and varies, the definition of 'street' set out in Part III of the New Roads and Streets Works Act 1991:

---

1   *Micklethwait v Newlay Bridge Co* (1886) 33 ChD 133.
2   *Neaverson v Peterborough RC* [1901] Ch 22.
3   *Salt Union Ltd and Droitwich Salt Co Ltd v Harvey & Co* (1897) 13 TLR 297.

'"street" means the whole or any part of the following, irrespective of whether it is a thoroughfare –
(a) any highway, road, land, footway, alley or passage,
(b) any square or court, and
(c) any land laid out as a way whether it is for the time being formed as a way or not.
Where a street passes over a bridge or through a tunnel, references in this Part to the street include that bridge or tunnel.'[1]

In every case, the obligation to pay compensation for the installation of pipes and other apparatus in private land and the extent to which the definition of 'street' is restricted are set out in each Act. On the other hand, it is clear that the power to install apparatus in a 'street' does not carry any obligation to pay compensation to the owner of the subsoil nor to the owner or occupier of the surface of a private street or a public right of way. In effect, the statutes treat the public highway as a route for the conveying of both traffic and public services.

2.5.2   Telecommunications Act 1984

The right to install (and keep, maintain, repair, replace, etc) apparatus in a street extends only to a highway which is maintainable at the public expense but there is a specific exclusion (in Sch 2, para 1 to the Telecommunications Act 1984) of footpaths and bridleways which cross, or form part of, any agricultural land or any land which is being brought into use for agriculture. Where apparatus is to be installed in or under any private street or an agricultural footpath or bridleway, the consent of the occupier or manager must be obtained or the agreement of the county court must be secured and, in either case, the terms, including payment, must be fixed.

2.5.3   Gas Act 1986

Under Sch 3 to the Gas Act 1986, the Secretary of State can authorise a public gas transporter (usually BG Transco) to acquire land or rights in land for the laying of transmission pipes. Schedule 4 gives power to public gas transporters to break up any 'street' to install pipes and undertake any associated works but in the case of a street which is not dedicated to public use, the right is limited only to the giving of a supply to a property which abuts that street.

2.5.4   Electricity Act 1989

Paragraph 1 of Sch 4 to the Electricity Act 1989 gives a power to install apparatus in any street which is maintainable at the public expense. The consent of the Secretary of State is required before a street which is not dedicated to public use can be used, and notice of the application must be served on the person whose consent would otherwise be required. Paragraph 6 of the same Schedule lays down the procedure to be followed to acquire

---

1   Section 48(1).

wayleaves and para 7 specifies the compensation due to owners and occupiers for the rights exercised under para 6.

2.5.5 Water Industry Act 1991 and Water Resources Act 1991

The Water Industry Act 1991 and the Water Resources Act 1991 give a power to install pipes in or under any 'street' and the definition in the New Roads and Streets Works Act 1991 is unqualified. The right extends to any street, whether dedicated to public use or not, whether in agricultural land or not. There is a separate power to install apparatus in land which is not a street on the service of notice.

2.5.6 Extinguishment and diversion orders

The Secretary of State must not make or confirm a public path extinguishment or diversion order, nor the council confirm an unopposed order, where there is any apparatus of a statutory undertaker relating to their undertaking in, upon, over, along or across the land of the path, unless the consent of the undertaker has been confirmed.[1] The consent must not be unreasonably withheld but the statutory undertakers are entitled to provisions protecting their equipment. The appropriate minister will determine whether or not the withholding of consent was unreasonable.[2]

There are also different provisions in the various statutes relating to gas, electricity, water, sewerage and telecommunications.

The details on notice, relocation of apparatus, expenses and compensation are outside the scope of this book.

---

1   Highways Act 1980, s 121(4).
2   Ibid, s 121(5).

Chapter 3

CREATION OF PUBLIC RIGHTS OF WAY

3.1 INTRODUCTION

Highways may be created by statute or by dedication and acceptance, either at common law or by statutory presumption. Statute provides for highways to be created on construction, by declaration, by agreement and by order. The principal statute under which highways are constructed today is the Highways Act 1980. The normal procedure is for the highway authority to acquire the land by agreement or under compulsory powers.[1] Once constructed, the way automatically becomes a highway without any dedication or acceptance.[2]

Private carriageways, whether in existence or to be constructed, may also be adopted so that they become highways. An agreement is made by the persons who have the capacity to dedicate the highway and the highway authority.[3] Where the road is to be constructed the agreement will provide that it should be constructed to a specified standard. Once adopted, the road becomes maintainable by the public.

Section 34 of the Highways Act 1980 enables a county council, a metropolitan district council, a London Borough Council or the Common Council to make a declaration that a street which is not a highway and land treated as a street shall become a highway. Footpaths and bridleways are usually created by agreements or orders or by dedication and acceptance.

3.2 IMPROVEMENT PLANS

3.2.1 Introduction

In 1999, the Countryside Commission, as it then was, published a document, *Rights of Way in the 21st Century*.[4] It recommended, amongst other things, that highway authorities should review the adequacy of the rights of way network in their areas at periodic intervals, and prepare and implement programmes of new creations to fulfil the needs identified in the review. The CROW Act 2000

---

1   Highways Act 1980, Part XII. Acquisition of Land Act 1981.
2   *R v Lyon* (1825) 5 Dow & Ry KB 497.
3   Highways Act 1980, s 38.
4   Countryside Commission, 1999. See also *Improving Rights of Way in England and Wales* (DETR Consultation Paper, 1999).

responds to the first part of the recommendation in its provision for improvement plans.

In preparing and revising improvement plans, local authorities must have regard to any guidance given to them by the Secretary of State or the National Assembly for Wales.[1] Regulations may require highway authorities to publish reports on the performance of their functions relating to rights of way,[2] including the implementation of improvement plans.

3.2.2   Initial plan

Every local highway authority, other than an Inner London authority (that is, Transport for London, the council of an inner London borough or the Common Council of the City of London[3]), is required to prepare and publish a rights of way improvement plan within 5 years of the commencement of s 60 of the CROW Act 2000.[4] This section came into force on 21 November 2001.[5] The local highway authority may make arrangements for its functions to be carried out jointly with any relevant district council or National Park authority.[6]

The plan must contain the authority's assessment of:

(a)   the extent to which the local rights of way meet the present and likely future needs of the public;
(b)   the opportunities which local rights of way provide for exercise and other forms of open air recreation and enjoyment of the authority's area;
(c)   the accessibility of local rights of way for the blind or partially sighted and others with mobility problems; and
(d)   such other matters relating to local rights of way as the Secretary of State or the National Assembly may direct.

The plan must also contain a statement of action which the authority proposes to take for the management of local rights of way and for seeking an improved local network, taking into account the matters dealt with in the assessment.

The Secretary of State and National Assembly have power to require other material to be included in the improvement plan. They may also give guidance from time to time on the preparation and publication of improvement plans to which the highway authorities must pay due regard in carrying out their functions.

Local rights of way are defined as footpaths, cycle tracks (other than those at the side of or in a made up carriageway), bridleways and restricted byways (whether shown on the definitive map or not) and ways which are shown on

---

1   CROW Act 2000, s 61(4).
2   Ibid, s 71.
3   Ibid, s 60(5).
4   Ibid, s 60(1).
5   The Countryside and Rights of Way Act 2000 (Commencement No 2) Order, SI 2002/ 2833 (C.89).
6   CROW Act 2000, s 61(5).

the definitive map as restricted byways or byways open to all traffic.[1] Until the coming into force of s 47, designating all RUPPs as restricted byways, RUPPs will be included within the definition of local rights of way.[2]

3.2.3 Reviews

An authority must make, within 10 years of the publication of the initial plan and subsequently at intervals of not more than 10 years, a new assessment of the local needs, review the plan and decide whether or not to amend it. If it decides to amend the plan, it must publish it in its amended form. If it decides not to amend it, it must publish a report of its decisions with reasons.[3]

3.2.4 Consultation

Before preparing or reviewing an improvement plan and in making an assessment, a local authority must consult:

(a) each local highway authority which adjoins its area;
(b) each parish and community council within its area and, where relevant:
(c) the National Park authority;
(d) the Broads Authority;
(e) any local access forum established in its area;
(f) the Countryside Agency or the Countryside Council for Wales;
(g) such persons as are prescribed by the Secretary of State or National Assembly for Wales;
(h) such persons as the local authority considers appropriate.[4]

3.2.5 Publication, notice, inspection

A local highway authority must publish a draft of the initial, and any subsequently revised, plan and give notice in two or more newspapers circulating in its area where the plan can be inspected or obtained and how representations can be made. It is under a duty to consider any representations which are made.[5]

A copy of the draft plan (and any report of the decision not to amend the initial plan) must be available for inspection free of charge at all reasonable times at the principal offices of the authority. A copy must be supplied to anyone who requests it, either free or on payment of a reasonable charge.[6]

3.2.6 Inner London

Although not under a duty to prepare an improvement plan, the council of an inner London borough or the Common Council of the City of London may

---

1   CROW Act 2000, s 60(5).
2   Ibid, s 60(6).
3   Ibid, s 60(3).
4   Ibid, s 61(1).
5   Ibid, s 61(2).
6   Ibid, s 61(3).

adopt by resolution the provisions relating to improvement plans.[1] If the council does so, the plan should be prepared and published within 5 years of the resolution.

3.2.7   Implementation of plans

Although the plans have to show the action the authorities propose to take, there is no obligation to take any. In its consultation paper[2] the former Department of the Environment, Transport and the Regions (DETR) stated:

> 'The government does not ... consider that it would be appropriate to place a specific duty on authorities to implement the findings of their reviews within a particular timescale. It would be for the authority to decide how and when to take forward the results, in line with their other priorities and taking account of local circumstances.'

3.2.8   Statutory guidance to local highway authorities

The provisions relating to improvement plans[3] came into force on 21 November 2002.[4] The Secretary of State has produced guidance[5] to highway authorities in England. The guidance does not apply to the council of an inner London borough or the Common Council of the City of London unless they adopt by resolution ss 60 and 61 of the Act. The National Assembly for Wales is responsible for giving guidance to local highway authorities in Wales. The Secretary of State intends to review the guidance in consultation with the Countryside Agency and other interested bodies after the first plans have been published.

In preparing improvement plans, local authorities should take into account other plans and strategies in related areas of work. They should consult, among others, representatives of those who are likely to use public rights of way.[6]

Local authorities are reminded of their general duties in exercising their functions to take into account the environment[7] and, in particular, the purpose of conserving and enhancing natural beauty in AONBs.[8]

Guidance is given on assessing users' needs, minimising conflicts between different classes of users and accommodating the interests of land managers. Local Access Forums will have an important part to play.[9]

---

1   CROW Act 2000, s 62.
2   *Improving Rights of Way in England and Wales* (1999) at 2.5.
3   CROW Act 2000, ss 60–61.
4   The Countryside and Rights of Way Act 2000 (Commencement No 2) Order, SI 2002/2833 (C.89).
5   Under powers contained in s 61(4).
6   See general duties under Local Government Act 1999, s 3.
7   European Directive 2001/42/EC.
8   CROW Act 2000, s 85.
9   See CROW Act 2000, ss 94 and 95. The Local Access Forums (England) Regulations, SI 2002/1836.

The Guidance also covers the process of making the assessment, preparing a statement of action, publishing the draft plan and understanding the needs of those with mobility problems.

3.3 PUBLIC PATH CREATION AGREEMENTS

3.3.1 Local authority agreements

Footpaths and bridleways may be created by the landowner and local authority. 'Local authority' is defined to include unitary authorities, county councils, district councils, National Park authorities, the Broads Authority, the Common Council and the Greater London Council.[1]

The agreement may provide for payments to be made to the landowner and for the dedication of the public path to be subject to limitations or conditions.[2]

Before entering into the agreement, the local authority should consult any other local authorities in whose area the land is situated. It does not have to consult parish councils or the public. It is also the duty of the local authority to have due regard to the needs of agriculture and forestry and the desirability of conserving flora, fauna and geographical and physiographical features. 'Agriculture' includes the breeding and keeping of horses.[3]

Once the agreement has been made, the local authority is obliged to take all necessary steps to ensure that the bridleway or footpath is dedicated in accordance with the agreement. After the path is dedicated, the local authority must publish notice of the dedication in at least one local newspaper circulating in the area.

The path automatically becomes maintainable at public expense.

3.3.2 Parish and community council agreements

Parish and community councils have power to enter into agreements for the creation of footpaths or bridleways, with those who have the capacity to dedicate public rights of way, over land in the parish or community or an adjoining parish or community.[4]

The dedication must, in the opinion of the council, be beneficial to the inhabitants of the parish or community. The council is under no obligation to take into account the needs of agriculture or forestry or conservation issues when agreeing a path.

There is no power for the parish or community to make a payment for the paths to be dedicated. However, there is power for the councils to carry out works including works of maintenance or improvement, or to contribute to the

---

1   Highways Act 1980, s 25(2). Norfolk and Suffolk Broads Act 1988.
2   Ibid, s 25.
3   Ibid, s 29, as amended by the CROW Act 2000, Sch 6, Part 1, para 2.
4   Highways Act 1980, s 30.

expense of carrying out such works, but the path is not automatically maintainable at public expense.

There is no obligation to see that the path is set out physically or to publish its existence.

3.4   PUBLIC PATH CREATION ORDERS

3.4.1   Orders for public right of way purposes

Unitary authorities, district and county councils, National Park authorities, London borough councils and the Common Council have power to make orders for the creation of footpaths and bridleways.

It must appear to the council that there is a need for the new path and it must be satisfied that it is expedient to create a new path having regard to:

(a) the extent to which it would add to the convenience or enjoyment of a substantial section of the public or of local residents; and

(b) the effect which the creation order would have on the rights of those with an interest in the land taking into account the provisions for compensation.[1]

The council must consult with other local authorities in whose area the land is situated.

The Secretary of State may also make creation orders, provided they comply with the tests set out above. He must consult with the relevant local authorities. The Secretary of State, when deciding whether to make or confirm an order, and the local authority, when deciding whether to confirm an unopposed order, must have regard to the rights of way improvement plan for the area.[2]

The public path order may create a public path unconditionally or subject to conditions or limitations. The procedure which must be followed is set out in the Highways Act 1980.[3] The order must be in the form prescribed by regulations.[4] As with creation agreements, the local authority must have due regard to the needs of agriculture and forestry and the desirability of conserving flora, fauna and geological and physiographical features in making the order.[5]

The order made by the authority must subsequently be confirmed by the authority or, where objections are made, by the Secretary of State. The Secretary of State, in deciding whether or not to make or confirm an order, and

---

1   Highways Act 1980, ss 26, 28.
2   Ibid, s 26(3A), inserted by the CROW Act 2000, Sch 6.
3   Ibid.
4   Public Path Orders Regulations 1993, SI 1993/11. See also Circular 2/93.
5   Highways Act 1980, s 29, as amended by the CROW Act 2000, Sch 6, Part 1, para 2.

the local authority, in deciding whether to confirm an unopposed order, must take into account any improvement plan for the area.[1]

New paths may be created as part of the reorganisation of the network. Concurrent orders relating to creation, diversion and extinguishment of paths are discussed together with the procedure for the making and confirmation of public path orders in Chapters 4 and 6. The highway authority must do what is necessary to make up the new path or arrange that the order-making authority does so.[2]

Compensation is payable to the landowner if the value of his land has been depreciated or if he has suffered damage by being disturbed in his enjoyment of land, by the coming into effect of the creation order. Disputes on the amount of compensation are decided by the Lands Tribunal.[3]

3.4.2 Applications for purposes of access to open and registered common land

The Countryside Agency may make an application to the Secretary of State for a public path creation order to enable the public to obtain access, or of facilitating such access, to access land within the meaning of Part 1 of the CROW Act 2000. In Wales, the application is made by the Countryside Council for Wales to the National Assembly for Wales.[4]

Before the Countryside Agency or the Countryside Council for Wales makes the request, it must have regard to any rights of way improvement plan prepared by the local highway authority for the relevant area.[5]

3.5 DEDICATION AND ACCEPTANCE

3.5.1 Expressed or implied

A landowner may expressly dedicate a right of way. The dedication must be in perpetuity.[6] It cannot be for a term of years. The dedication may be made subject to limitations. For example, a right of way may be dedicated subject to gates or the right to hold fairs or markets.[7] There must also be acceptance by the public.[8] The historical reason for this is that, before 1835, all highways were repairable by the inhabitants of the parish. It was therefore considered that a landowner, by dedicating a route, should not impose liability on the local inhabitants unless the route was shown to be of use to them.

---

1   Highways Act 1980, s 26 as amended by the CROW Act 2000, Sch 6, Part 1, para 1. See also s 85(1) (special considerations to be taken into account in AONBs).
2   Highways Act 1980, s 27.
3   Ibid, s 28. See **4.6.5**.
4   CROW Act 2000, s 58(1).
5   Ibid, s 58(2).
6   *Dawes v Hawkins* (1860) 8 CB NS 848.
7   *Attorney General v Horner* (1885) 11 App Cas 66.
8   *R v Mellor* (1830) 1 Lew CC 158; *Cubitt v Maxse* (1873) LR 8 CP 704.

A highway authority has power to accept a highway on behalf of the public. Acceptance by the highway authority is capable therefore of amounting to proof of acceptance by the public. Examples are where a highway authority agrees in writing to accept a dedication or where an appropriate committee of the highway authority agrees to do so.[1]

Although new highways are today normally created under statutory provisions, recourse to the common law rules is necessary to establish whether disputed rights of way were dedicated in the past.

Use by the public may not only be evidence of acceptance of a dedicated route, but also evidence of dedication itself. Long use may give rise to an inferred dedication at common law or a statutory deemed dedication.

3.5.2   User as of right

In order for there to be an inferred dedication at common law or deemed dedication under the Highways Act 1980, the user must be as of right. This means that the user must be without force, secrecy or permission.[2] This is similar to the requirement for obtaining a private right of way by prescription.

The user will not be without force if it is necessary to break locks or fences or if the user is contentious or subject to protest.[3] It will be secret if the route is used only at night or when it is known that the landowner or his agent is away. The user will be permissive as far as employees and invitees are concerned or where tolls are paid.[4] User was held to be permissive where a landowner had executed a deed under s 193 of the Law of Property Act 1925, giving the public a right of access for air and access to certain tracks, even though the public were unaware of the deed.[5]

The requirement of user as of right was summed up by Lord Blackburn in *Mann v Brodie*.[6] He said:

> 'Where there has been evidence of a user by the public so long and in such a manner that the owner of the field, whoever he was, must have been aware that the public were acting under the belief that the way had been dedicated, and has taken no steps to disabuse them of their belief, it is not conclusive evidence, but evidence on which those who have to find a fact may find that there was a dedication by the owner whoever he was.'

---

1   *Secretary of State for the Environment, Transport and the Regions v Baylis (Gloucester) Ltd* [2000] EGLR 92.
2   *Earl De la Warr v Miles* (1881) 17 Ch D 535, 596; *Gardner v Hodgsons's Kingston Brewery Ltd* [1903] AC 229, 239.
3   *Eaton v Swansea Waterworks Co* (1851) 17 QB 267; *Dalton v Angus & Co* (1881) 6 App Cas 740, 786.
4   *R v Secretary of State for the Environment ex parte Cowell* [1993] JPL 851.
5   *R v Secretary of State for the Environment, Transport and the Regions ex parte Billson* [1999] QB 374.
6   (1885) 10 App Cases 378, 386.

The subjective belief of the users themselves is immaterial. This point has been firmly established by the House of Lords in the case of *R v Oxfordshire County Council and Anor ex parte Sunningwell Parish Council.*[1]

Lord Hoffmann said:

> 'A person who believes he has the right to use a footpath will use it in the way in which a person having such a right would use it. But user which is apparently as of right cannot be discounted merely because, as will often be the case, many of the users over a long period were subjectively indifferent as to whether a right existed, or even had private knowledge that it did not.'

3.5.3 The public at large

The dedication of a way must be to the public at large, not to a particular class of persons. Some paths, such as church paths, may be available for a particular purpose and their use may be limited, say, to the parishioners. However, the acceptance does not have to be by all members of the public. It is sufficient for a highway to be created if it is used by a section of the public.

In *R v Broke*[2] the court decided that use by seafarers of a path amounted to use by the public. There is a distinction between a grant to the public, when the path must be made available for all Her Majesty's subjects, and user by the public. User can therefore be established for the purposes of common law dedication even if the route has been used only by local inhabitants, as long as there is nothing to prevent it being used by anyone. This point was made by Coleridge CJ in *R v Inhabitants of Southampton*,[3] where he explained that user by the public 'must not be taken in its widest sense; it cannot mean that it is a user by all the subjects of the Queen, for it is common knowledge that in many cases it is only the residents in the neighbourhood who ever use a particular road or bridge'.

Often, a public right of way may have been established for a purpose which no longer exists. For instance, it may have provided a route for people to get to a village shop which has subsequently been converted into a house or to a place of work which has been closed. Provided there was a genuine public right of way, rather than merely a permissive route, the right of way continues to have legal existence. It matters not that the route is used for recreational purposes only.

The laying out of estate roads for the use of those living on the estate will not amount to dedication. Although the road may be used by postmen, meter readers, tradesmen and so on, they will be using the road not as members of the general public but as invitees or licensees.[4]

---

1   [1999] 3 WLR 160, 171.
2   (1859) 1 F&F 514. See also *R v Inhabitants of Southampton* (1887) 19 QBD 590.
3   (1887) 19 QBD 590.
4   *Selby v Crystal Palace Gas Co* (1862) 4 DeGF&J 246.

It is possible that a road which was originally used as an estate road may subsequently be used by the public. However, the courts will look more closely at the degree of user where the route started off as a private road.[1]

3.5.4 Illegal user

There cannot be user as of right if the user is contrary to statute.[2] Since the Road Traffic Act 1930, it has been an offence to drive a motor car without lawful authority:

(a) on to or upon any common land, moorland or land of any other description,[3] not being land forming part of a road; or

(b) on any road being a footpath or bridleway.[4]

This means that long use by motor vehicles cannot give rise to an implied dedication for public vehicular use of a footpath, bridleway[5]or road used as a public path (RUPP).[6] A RUPP is conclusive evidence as to bridleway rights only. Therefore, it is an offence to drive on a RUPP unless it can be shown that there was sufficient vehicular user evidence pre-dating 1930 or there is documentary evidence supporting a vehicular right.

The CROW Act 2000[7] has amended s 34 of the Road Traffic Act 1988 by redefining motor car as a mechanically propelled vehicle and making it an offence to drive such a vehicle on a restricted byway, as well as on a footpath or bridleway.

User may also be illegal where the use would give rise to a public nuisance. An example is where the route is so physically narrow that use by vehicles would endanger other classes of user.[8]

3.5.5 User which may upgrade footpaths and bridleways

Use by horse riders of a footpath is a trespass against the landowner, but not a criminal offence. Therefore, it is possible that bridleway rights may be acquired over a footpath by long use. Nor is it a criminal offence to drive a horse and cart on a footpath or bridleway. Long use is capable of converting a footpath or bridleway into a byway open to all traffic. Once that right is acquired for

---

1   See Neville J in *Holloway v Egham UDC* (1908) 72 JP 433, 434.

2   *Cargill v Gotts* [1981] 1 WLR 441; *Hanning v Top Deck Travel Group* (1993) 68 P&CR 14 and *Bakewell Management Ltd v Brandwood* (2002) 14 EG 124; but see CROW Act 2000, s 68 for the acquisition of a prescriptive statutory private right of way where user is contrary to statute.

3   For meaning of and of any other description see *Massey and Drew v Boulden* [2002] EWCA Civ 1634, [2002] TLR 496.

4   See Road Traffic Act 1988, s 34.

5   *Robinson v Adair* [1995] NPC 30.

6   *Stevens v Secretary of State for the Environment* (1998) 76 P&CR 503.

7   Section 67, Sch 7, para 5.

8   *Sheringham UDC v Holsey* (1904) 68 JP 395; *Hereford & Worcester County Council v Pick* (1996) 71 P&CR 231.

vehicles, it can be used by motor vehicles, since the method of propulsion is immaterial.[1]

3.5.6 Bicycles

Bicycles are allowed on bridleways by virtue of the Countryside Act 1968.[2] However, in exercising that right, cyclists must give way to pedestrians and persons on horseback. The right may be prohibited or restricted by bylaws or local authority orders. Highway authorities are not under any obligation to make or maintain bridleways so that they are suitable for bicycles.

There is no right to ride a bicycle on a footpath. Anyone doing so would be committing a trespass against the landowner. However, it is not a criminal offence. As bicycles are not a natural accompaniment of a walker, pushing a bicycle would be a trespass. Carrying a bicycle should not be a trespass as there is no physical contact with the ground and the burden on the path is not increased.

Were a sufficient number of people to ride a bicycle over a defined route or on a public footpath, theoretically it could amount to a deemed dedication of a byway open to all traffic. (A bicycle is treated as a vehicle for some offences under the Road Traffic Act 1988[3] and the Local Government Act 1888[4] declared bicycles to be carriages within the meaning of the Highways Acts.) However, this proposition has not been tested in the courts and there are arguments based, amongst other things, on the additional burden on the soil why this should not be so.[5]

Section 3 of the Cycle Tracks Act 1984 enables a footpath to be converted into a cycle track by a conversion order. The procedure for making a conversion order is set out in regulations.[6] The Act provides that any person having a legal interest in agricultural land, which the footpath crosses, must have consented in writing to the order.[7] There is a duty before making the order to consult with the organisations which represent persons using the footpath, other parochial authorities, any statutory undertakers whose property is crossed by the footpath and the chief police officer for the area. Compensation is payable if the land is depreciated by the creation of the track or damage is caused by the conversion work.[8]

---

1   *Lock v Abercester Ltd* [1939] Ch 861; cf restricted byways, where a distinction has been made between mechanically propelled vehicles and other vehicles.
2   Countryside Act 1968, s 30.
3   For example, s 36.
4   Ibid, s 35.
5   Bruce Monington 'Cyclists' Rights of Way', RWLR 3.2, p 1.
6   Cycle Tracks Regulations 1984, SI 1984/1431.
7   Cycle Tracks Act 1984, s 4.
8   Ibid, s 5.

3.5.7   Inferred dedication at common law

(1)   Intention

A landowner must have an intention to dedicate a right of way over his land. Public user may be evidence from which that intention may be inferred. This reflects the policy of the courts to uphold long use and assume it has a lawful origin. This is shown in other areas of law, such as the prescriptive right to easements and the upholding of customary rights. However, mere use does not create the highway, dedication is required.[1]

On the other hand, the courts have in some instances refused to imply dedication where they can find that the use has been as a result of the tolerance of land owners:

> 'It is the wise policy of the law, not to construe acts of charity, though continued and repeated for never so many years, in such a manner as to make them the foundation of legal obligations' per Heath J in *Steel v Houghton*.[2]

It is possible that what was originally tolerance, over the years, may turn into intention to dedicate.

Where the public has deviated onto adjoining land because of the poor condition of the right of way this will not usually create a new route.[3]

(2)   Burden of proof

Where there is a claim that a public right of way has been dedicated, it is for the claimant to prove that it can be inferred by the landowner's conduct that he had actually dedicated the route as a public right of way.[4] User of right is not of itself necessarily sufficient. It is still possible that the use was due to the landowner's tolerance rather than his intention to dedicate the route, or that there is evidence of the landlord's lack of intention to dedicate.[5]

(3)   Length and quality of user

The length of enjoyment which must be shown depends on the circumstances. In one case, 18 months was held to be sufficient.[6]

The amount of user, that is the number of people who have used a route, also has not been defined and will be considered in the light of the particular facts. The essential element is that it should be obvious to the landowner that a route was being used by the public.

---

1   *Attorney-General v Esher Linoleum Company Ltd* [1901] 2 Ch 647.
2   (1788) 1 HyBl 51, 60. See also *R v Oxfordshire County Council ex parte Sunningwell Parish Council* [1999] 3 WLR 160 for the distinction between tolerance and permission.
3   *Dawes v Hawkins* (1860) 8 CB NS 848.
4   *Jaques v Secretary of State for the Environment* [1995] JPEL 1031. See also *R v Lloyd* (1808) 1 Camp 260, 170 ER 1191 and *Folkestone Corporation v Brockman* [1914] AC 338.
5   *Folkestone Corporation v Brockman* [1914] AC 338.
6   *North London Rail Co v St Mary, Islington Vestry* (1827) 27 LT 672.

(4)   *Rebutting dedication*

A landowner, or a tenant,[1] may prevent a right of way being established across his land. He can put up physical barriers, erect notices indicating that the route is private, turn people back, and lodge statements and declarations with the highway authority.

In *Poole v Huskinson*, Park B said:

'A single act of interruption by a landowner is of much more weight, upon the question of intention, than many acts of enjoyment.'[2]

Gates put across a route may indicate that the landowner has no intention to dedicate a right of way. However, other interpretations are possible. The purpose of the gates may be to control stock, not deter the public; or the right of way may have been dedicated subject to the gate or other obstruction.[3]

Shutting the path for at least one day a year has been accepted as a standard method of showing an intention not to dedicate.[4] The fact that the path is to be closed should be brought to the attention of the public.

What is needed to rebut dedication are overt and contemporaneous acts by the landowner to show that he had no intention to dedicate. It is not sufficient for him merely to state that he had no such intention.

In the words of Lord Denning:[5]

'In my opinion a landowner cannot escape the effect of 20 years' prescription by saying that, locked in his own mind, he had no intention to dedicate it: or by telling a stranger to the locality (who had no reason to dispute it) that he had no intention to dedicate. In order for there to be "sufficient evidence that there was no intention" to dedicate the way, there must be evidence of some overt acts on the part of the landowner such as show the public at large – the public who use the path, in this case the villagers – that he had no intention to dedicate. He must, in Lord Blackburn's words, take steps to disabuse those persons of any belief that there was a public right: see *Mann v Brodie*, 10 App Cas 378, 386 . . .'

Although Lord Denning refers to the 20-year period under what is now the Highways Act 1980, his words would equally apply to dedication at common law.

Recent cases have held that the overt acts do not have to be directed towards the public which use the way. The dicta of Lord Denning to the contrary are no longer considered good law. In *R v Secretary of State ex parte Billson*,[6] Sullivan J reviewed the authorities and stated, albeit obiter, that it was unnecessary for

---

1   *Rowley v Secretary of State for Transport, Local Government and the Regions* [2002] EWHC 1040.
2   (1843) 11 M&W 827, 830.
3   *Barraclough v Johnson* (1838) SA&E 99.
4   *Rugby Charity Trustees v Merryweather* (1790) 11 East 375n; *British Museum Trustees v Finnis* (1833) 4 C&P 460.
5   *Fairey v Southampton County Council* [1956] 2 QB 439, 458.
6   [1998] 2 All ER 587.

the landowner to publicise his intention not to dedicate. This view was accepted by Dyson J in *R v Secretary of State ex parte Dorset County Council*.[1] A landowner's objection to the revision of the definitive map made to the Department of the Environment was sufficient even though the public were unaware of the objection. Although it is necessary that a challenge which brings a right of way into question for the purposes of s 31(1) of the Highways Act 1980 must be brought home to the public, this is not essential in order to show lack of intention to dedicate.

The Rights of Way Act 1932 (RWA 1932), which introduced the statutory presumption of dedication, also provided additional statutory ways of rebutting deemed dedication. These statutory provisions are effective to rebut dedication at common law as well as the statutory deemed dedication.

As stated above, notices, provided they are absolutely clear, may rebut deemed dedication. Sometimes notices have been held not to be effective as they were interpreted as indicating merely that the adjoining land is private. However, cases which pre-date the *Dorset* case should be viewed with caution. Notices, even though not absolutely clear to the public, may be an overt and contemporaneous act by the landowner, that he had no intention to dedicate the route. Problems arose because sometimes these notices were taken down. The RWA 1932 introduced the provision that, where the notice is subsequently torn down or defaced, the landowner may lodge with the highway authority a notice stating that the way is not dedicated as a highway.[2]

Another provision introduced by the RWA 1932 was that, if the land is let on either a fixed-term tenancy or a periodic yearly tenancy, the person entitled to the reversion has the right, notwithstanding the existence of the tenancy, to put up a notice. However, in doing so, he must not injure the business or occupation of the tenant.[3] The lessee, being in exclusive possession of the land, needs no statutory authority to erect any notices.

The most important method of rebutting deemed dedication, also introduced by the RWA 1932, was the lodging of a map and statement indicating what ways, if any, the landowner admits to having dedicated as highways. The map should be of a scale of not less than 6 inches to the mile. It is not, however, the statement, but the subsequent declaration which 'in the absence of proof of a contrary intention, [is] sufficient evidence to negative the intention of the owner or his successors in title to dedicate any such additional way as a highway'.[4]

The statement and declaration should be made by the owner. 'Owner' is defined as the person who is for the time being entitled to dispose of the fee simple of the land.[5] The declaration has to be made within 6 years from the date of

---

1   *R v Secretary of State for the Environment, Transport and the Regions ex parte Dorset County Council* [2000] JPL 396.
2   See now Highways Act 1980, s 31(3)(5).
3   Ibid, s 31(4).
4   Ibid, s 31(6).
5   Ibid, s 31(7).

deposit or within 6 years from the date on which the last declaration was made. This period will be altered to 10 years when Sch 6 to the CROW Act 2000 comes into force. As it is the declaration which rebuts the deemed dedication, it should be lodged as soon as the highway authority gives an official date for the lodging of the statement. This may be several days after the posting of the statement by the landowner or his advisers. Landowners should remember to lodge a further declaration before 6 years (or 10 years once the relevant provision of the CROW Act 2000 is in force) have elapsed from the original declaration.

It is important to stress that this procedure rebuts any intention of dedication in the future only. It cannot take away any claims which are based on past user. Nor will it overcome any claims based on documentary evidence.

The appropriate council is required to keep a register of deposited maps and statements and declarations lodged with that council. Regulations may provide for the format and contents of the register and the circumstances when entries relating to a map, statement or declaration may be removed. The register must be available for inspection free of charge at all reasonable hours.[1]

(5) Capacity

Although a person may have an expressed or implied intention to dedicate, such a dedication will be ineffective if that person does not have the legal capacity to do so. Generally speaking, it will be the fee simple owner, that is the person with the legal estate, who will be able to dedicate a right of way.

(i) Tenant for life under strict settlement
Although new strict settlements cannot be created, except in limited circumstances, existing strict settlements will continue.[2] Moreover, in investigating whether public rights of way were dedicated in the past, it may be necessary to consider strict settlements which have terminated.

Before 1926, a tenant for life could not dedicate a highway as he did not have the legal estate, which might be divided between several beneficiaries or vested in other trustees, nor did he have any statutory power to dedicate.[3] After 1926, a tenant for life under a strict settlement may dedicate a public right of way, provided it is for the general benefit of the residents of the settled land or there is a specific power in the trust instrument.[4] In other circumstances, all the beneficiaries must agree to the dedication, either expressly or by implication. In order to be a valid agreement, the beneficiaries must be of full age and capacity.

---

1   Highways Act 1980, s 31A, inserted by the CROW Act 2000, Sch 6, para 4.
2   Trusts of Land and Appointment of Trustees Act 1996, s 2(1).
3   See Megarry and Wade *Law of Real Property* 6th edn, pp 374–376; *Eyre v New Forest Highway Board* (1892) 56 JP 517.
4   Settled Land Act 1925, s 56.

This obviously causes problems where a claim to a right of way is based on long user. However, the onus of proving that the land was subject to a strict settlement lies on the person so alleging.[1]

Even if it is shown that the land was subject to a strict settlement, there may be an implied dedication. This is illustrated by the case of *Farquhar v Newbury Rural District Council*,[2] where the remaindermen were in possession, managing the property on behalf of the tenant for life. The court held that, by implication, both the tenant for life and the remaindermen had agreed to the dedication of a public right of way. On the other hand, where some of the beneficiaries are infants or cannot be ascertained, such a dedication cannot be implied at common law.

RWA 1932[3] introduced a provision enabling a person entitled in remainder or reversion on the determination of a tenancy for life or *pur autre vie* to bring actions for trespass or an injunction to prevent the acquisition by the public of a right of way as if they were in possession of land.

(ii)   *Trustees of trust for sale*
Before the coming into force of the Trusts of Land and Appointment of Trustees Act 1996, land conveyed to trustees on trust for sale or to co-owners[4] would be held by them on trust for sale. As trustees they would hold the legal estate and have all the powers of a tenant for life and trustees of a strict settlement.[5] They could therefore dedicate a public right of way for the benefit of the residents of the land subject to the trust. If the trust instrument gave them the powers of absolute owners, they could dedicate even if a public right of way was not for the benefit of the trust land. Moreover, the trustees and beneficiaries could together dedicate either expressly or by implication a public right of way.

(iii)   *Trustees of the trust of land*
After the coming into force of the Trusts of Land and Appointment of Trustees Act 1996, it is now no longer possible to create strict settlements. All existing and future trusts for sale will be trusts of land.[6] Such trusts, whether there is a duty to sell or not, will vest the legal estate in trustees. The trustees have the powers of absolute owners and so are able to dedicate public rights of way.[7]

(iv)   *Mortgagors*
Pre-1926 mortgages were created by conveying the legal estate to the mortgagee.[8] If the mortgagor was in possession, no dedication could be inferred against the mortgagee as he would not normally be in a position to know about user. The mortgagor would not have the capacity to dedicate as he would not have the legal estate. Nowadays, although the legal estate remains

---

1   *R v Petrie* (1855) 4 El & Bl 737; *Powers v Bathurst* (1880) 49 LJ Ch 294.
2   [1909] 1 Ch 12.
3   Section 74.
4   Law of Property Act 1925, ss 34–36.
5   Ibid, s 28.
6   Trusts of Land and Appointment of Trustees Act 1996, s 1(1).
7   Ibid, s 6(1).
8   See Megarry and Wade *Law of Real Property* 6th edn, 19–009.

with the mortgagor, the consent of the mortgagee will be necessary to any dedication. This is because the value of the mortgagee's security could be reduced. Both the mortgagor and the mortgagee need to agree to dedicate. It is only in exceptional circumstances that it will be possible to infer such consent.

(v) Lessees

Rights of way must be dedicated in perpetuity. Therefore, lessees cannot dedicate a public right of way without the concurrence of the freehold owner. It may be possible that such concurrence may be implied, especially where user began before the grant of the lease, or where there have been several successive tenancies.[1]

Moreover, since 1932 the reversioner has been able to place notices on the let land indicating that the route is not a public right of way.[2] If he has not availed himself of this statutory provision it may be difficult for him to rebut any deemed dedication.

(vi) Possessory title holder

Where title is based on adverse possession, the ability of the landowner to dedicate depends on whether the title is registered or unregistered. If the title is unregistered, the squatter obtains the fee simple as soon as he takes possession and excludes the owner with the documentary title. After 12 years (subject to exceptions where, for example, the landowner is a reversioner or the Crown), the right of the paper owner to recover the property is barred by statute.[3]

Long user can therefore give rise to an implied dedication against the squatter where the title is unregistered. This is provided there are no third-party rights which preclude such dedication. A squatter's title is subject to any third-party rights which exist when he takes possession.

Where the title is registered, a squatter does not obtain title until his name is entered on the register.[4] It is therefore the registered proprietor, rather than the squatter, who has the capacity to dedicate a right of way.

(vii) Public bodies

A public body must operate within the powers conferred by the statute which created it. If it acts outside those powers, any rights or obligations entered into will be void. Where a statutory body has power to hold and alienate land, it will generally have incidental powers which would include dedicating public rights of way. Some 19th-century Railway and Canal Acts prevent dedication of a right of way as does the British Transport Commission Act 1949, over certain land belonging to the Commission.

---

1   See *Davies v Stephens* (1836) Car & P 570; *Corsellis v London County Council* [1907] 1 Ch 704.
2   Highways Act 1980, s 31(4).
3   Limitation Act 1980, s 15.
4   Land Registration Act 2002, s 97 and Sch 6.

An implied dedication will not arise if the existence of a highway would be incompatible with the purposes of a corporation or other body or person in possession of land for public or statutory purposes.[1]

(viii)   The church

Difficulties arise where a public right of way is claimed through a churchyard. An incumbent cannot expressly dedicate any public right of way over a consecrated churchyard. This is because the fee simple is in abeyance and the control of the churchyard is vested in the Chancellor of the Diocese. For there to be any dealings with the churchyard a faculty is needed. It is probable that the most the faculty can authorise is a licence to use a route as if it were a highway. For this reason, there cannot be a deemed dedication arising from long use.[2]

(ix)   Charities

Before 1993, s 29 of the Charities Act 1960 required the consent of the Charity Commissioners to the disposition of any interest in land forming part of the permanent endowment of the charity or of land which was or had been occupied for purposes of the charity. Any disposition without such consent was void. Ownership by a charity may therefore prevent implied dedication of a public right of way before 1993.

3.5.8   Statutory deemed dedication

(1)   *Difference from common law*

The RWA 1932, now replaced by s 31 of the Highways Act 1980, simplifies the proof of implied dedication by long use. A right of way can be established if there has been 20 years' use of the way over land by the public as of right, without interruption, unless the landowner can show that during that period there was no intention to dedicate.

There may be circumstances where it is not possible to rely on what is now s 31 of the Highways Act 1980. The Act does not apply to the Crown, the Duchies of Lancaster and Cornwall, the Forestry Commission and Government Departments, which count as the Crown; or there may be less than 20 years' use, or the use which is relied on may not immediately pre-date the event which brings the right of way into question. In such circumstances, reliance will have to be placed on common law dedication. Section 31(9) provides:

> 'Nothing in this section operates to prevent the dedication of a way as a highway being presumed on use for less than 20 years, or being presumed or proved in any circumstances in which it might have been presumed or proved immediately before the commencement of this Act.'

---

1   The common law position is preserved by the Highways Act 1980, s 31(8). Cf *British Transport Commission v Westmoreland County Council* [1958] AC 126: dedication possible if not incompatible with purposes of railway undertaking.
2   See J Harte 'Churchyards and Coffin Ways', RWLR 11, p 17.

Section 31 is retrospective and applies to user both before and after the Act came into force. In *Fairey v Southampton County Council*,[1] a right of way was brought into question in 1931. Twenty years' user was shown before that date and it was held that the path could validly be shown on the definitive map.

Section 31 does not apply to rivers.[2] Rights of navigation may still be claimed by long use at common law.

The main difference between implied dedication at common law and under the Highways Act 1980 is the burden of proof. At common law, the claimant has to show that the landowner intended, or could be presumed to have intended, to dedicate a public right of way. Under the statute, it is for the landowner to rebut the presumption.

The statutory presumption will preclude any argument that the user was attributable to tolerance. In addition, it may, in some situations, counter any argument that the landowner, lacking capacity, could not have dedicated a public right of way. The position is far from clear and in order to understand the arguments it is necessary to consider the Prescription Act 1832, on which the RWA 1932 was based.

The Prescription Act 1832 has been held to be one of the worst-drafted Acts on the statute books. This Act introduced two periods of user for claiming easements such as private rights of way.[3] The shorter period merely shortens the time needed for prescription. User no longer has to be from time immemorial as at common law; 20 years will suffice. However, a claim may be defeated by showing that there was no person with a capacity to make the grant. User as at common law is based on the theory of a presumed grant, the user being evidence of such a grant.

User for the longer period of 40 years, on the other hand, makes any right claimed absolute and indefeasible. Therefore, it makes no difference that the fee simple owner was in no position to contest the user (subject to specific provisions relating to leases). It may also be that, because of the wording of the Act, the right will exist even if there is no person with the capacity to make the grant. It seems, although the authorities are conflicting, that 40 years' user actually creates the right, rather than being evidence of the presumed grant as it is where there is 20 years' use. However, deducted from calculating the 40-year period are periods when the land over which the right has been claimed is held under a term of over 3 years or for life. Moreover, if a lease existed at the beginning of the 40-year period and continued throughout, there can be no prescriptive claim.

Section 1 of the RWA 1932 provided as follows:

'(i) Where a way ... upon or over any land has actually been enjoyed by the public as of right and without interruption for a full period of 20 years, such way shall be

---

1   [1956] 2 QB 439.
2   *Attorney General (ex rel Yorkshire Derwent Trust) v Brotherton* [1992] AC 425.
3   Sections 1 and 2.

deemed to have been dedicated as a highway unless there is sufficient evidence to show that there was no intention during that period to dedicate such a way, or unless during such period of 20 years there was not at any time any person in possession of such land capable of dedicating such a way.

(ii) Where any such way has been enjoyed as aforesaid for a full period of 40 years, such way shall be deemed conclusively to have been dedicated as a highway unless there is sufficient evidence that there is no intention during such period to dedicate such a way.'

In other words, the RWA 1932, in the same way as the Prescription Act 1832 provided that 20-year and 40-year periods of user should have different legal effects. Twenty-year user merely gave use to a statutory presumption of evidence, but 40-year user positively created a new right.

However, the National Parks and Access to the Countryside Act 1949 repealed s 1(2) and amended s 1(1) by deleting the words 'or unless during such period of 20 years there was not at any time any person in possession of such land capable of dedicating such a way'. The amendments followed a recommendation in the Hobson Report:[1]

'We think however that it would be regarded as reasonable today if the Rights of Way Act 1932 were amended in a single respect with a view to simplifying the existing machinery for establishing proof of the dedication of rights of way. We recommend that after 20 years' use of a way by the public "as of right and without interruption", that way shall be deemed in all cases to have been dedicated as a highway. This will cover the case of entailed estates and would do away with the existing requirement that in such cases proof of 40 years' public use must be adduced. This uniform period of 20 years should apply to all cases immediately on alteration of the law so that this new provision can be used in determining disputed cases in the survey.'

Introducing the Bill at second reading the Minister, Lord Silkin, said:[2]

'There is also a very useful provision for ensuring that in future there is a presumption of dedication of a right of way after 20 years user in all cases. I think that will remove a great many doubts about the law and make it very much easier to establish a dedication of a right of way.'

Section 1(ii) of the RWA 1932 provides that where there was 40 years' use, a way was deemed *conclusively* to have been dedicated. On the other hand, s 1(i), which dealt with 20 years' use, merely provided that 'such way shall be deemed to have been dedicated'. It is unlikely, however, that very much turns on this slightly different wording.

The result appears to be that, where s 31 of the Highways Act 1980 applies, it will be no argument against dedication that, at the time of the deemed dedication, the property was subject to a strict settlement or a trust for sale. This is reinforced by s 33, which enables reversioners under settlements and trusts to bring actions for trespass and injunctions to prevent the acquisition by the public of rights of way as if they were in possession of the land.

---

1   Cmnd 7208, para 56.
2   *Hansard*, 31 March 1949, vol 463.

The provision enabling a landlord to rebut deemed dedication by placing a notice on that land will also make it difficult for a landlord to allege that there has not been a statutory deemed dedication.

A leading textbook[1] states that a statutory dedication cannot take place where the property is mortgaged unless the consent of both mortgagor and mortgagee can be implied. No authorities are given for this proposition and it is suggested that, where the mortgagor has the legal estate and is in possession, deemed dedication could be implied under the statutory presumption. However, the presumption could be rebutted. For instance, if there was anything in the mortgage deed that precluded dedication, then the mortgagor would be liable to the mortgagee, and, it could be argued, on the basis of *R v Secretary of State for the Environment, Transport and the Regions ex parte Dorset County Council*,[2] that it was a contemporaneous and overt act showing lack of intention to dedicate a public right of way.

The position of public bodies is specifically left unaltered. Section 31(8) provides:

> 'Nothing in this section affects any incapacity of a corporation or other body or person in possession of land for public and statutory purposes to dedicate a way over land as a highway if the existence of a highway would be incompatible with those purposes.'

The difficulties of the church dedicating a right of way expressly or by implication apply equally to the statutory presumption as they do to dedication at common law.[3] It is arguable that s 31 would not cure the problem of charities. The section is aimed at curing lack of capacity of the landowner not dispensing with the need for the consent of an outside official body.

The statutory presumption does not apply to the Crown as public Acts of Parliament do not bind the Crown unless there is a provision to the contrary.

At common law, no time-limits are set for establishing implied dedication. The statutory provision requires 20 years' use.

Although the RWA 1932 provided additional statutory methods of rebutting statutory deemed dedication, these methods are equally effective for rebuttal of common law dedication.

The differences between common law and statutory dedication are set out below in chart form.

1   Pratt & Mackenzie p 30. *Halsbury's Laws of England* vol 21, para 73.
2   [2000] JPL 396.
3   See **3.5.7(5)**(viii) above.

Common Law	Section 31
1. *Proof* Burden of proof on applicant to show that it can be inferred from landowner's conduct that he dedicated a right of way.	1. *Proof* Statutory presumption that landowner intended to dedicate.
2. *Intention* User may be attributable to tolerance.	2. *Intention* No argument on tolerance should prevail where there is no evidence of rebuttal.
3. *Capacity* Capacity to dedicate is needed. If landowner can show title would preclude dedication, no dedication will be inferred.	3. *Capacity* The statutory presumption should make lack of capacity irrelevant in case of strict settlements, trusts for sale, leases and possibly mortgages.[1]
4. *Time* No time stipulated. It depends on all the circumstances.	4. *Time* 20 years' use required.

(2) Calculation of 20 years' use

The Highways Act 1980[2] provides:

> 'The period of 20 years ... is to be calculated retrospectively from the date when the right of the public to use the way is brought into question, whether by a notice ... or otherwise.'

The statutory presumption, as explained, was first introduced by the RWA 1932. However, it has been held that the 20-year period can begin and end before the RWA 1932 came into force.[3]

The period must, however, end at the time when the right of way is brought into question. It may be brought into question by physical obstructions such as a locked gate, by notices inconsistent with the dedication of a right of way or by stopping people using the path. Court actions for trespass or declarations would also bring the right of way into question. However, in *Owen v Buckinghamshire County Council*,[4] it was held that the ploughing up of a path was not sufficient.

---

1   Cf *Jaques v Secretary of State for the Environment* [1995] JPL 1031. Section 31 did not apply as the land was requisitioned, therefore no-one had capacity to dedicate during user period.
2   Section 31(2).
3   *Fairey v Southampton County Council* [1956] 2 QB 439.
4   *Owen v Buckinghamshire County Council* (1957) 55 LGR 373.

This is not an exhaustive list. The essential requirement is that the challenge to the existence of a right of way must be brought home to the public. In *Fairey v Southampton County Council*[1] it was held that in order to bring into question the right of the public to use a way, a landowner must indicate 'by some means sufficient to bring home to the public that he is challenging their right to use the way, so that they may be apprised of the challenge and have a reasonable opportunity of meeting it'. So in *R v Secretary of State for the Environment, Transport and the Regions ex parte Dorset County Council*,[2] a right of way was not brought into question when landowners wrote to the DETR objecting to the inclusion of a bridleway on the revision of the definitive map. Although the DETR passed on the information to the council, the challenge was not made known to the public and, in the event, the review was abandoned. The landowner's letter was, however, sufficient evidence to amount to a contemporaneous and overt act showing a lack of intention to dedicate.[3]

There may be several dates when the way is brought into question. Those claiming a right of way will succeed if they can show an interrupted use for 20 years, ending on one of those dates.

'Without interruption' means some actual and physical stopping of the enjoyment.[4] Use was interrupted where a gate across a path was locked, even though people continued to use the route by going around the side of the gate.[5] Merely challenging the right of the public is not enough. 'Without interruption' does not mean that the public must use the route continuously. In other words, it does not refer to the activity of the user, but of the landowner.

The RWA 1932, and now s 31 of the Highways Act 1980, does not state that a public right of way comes into existence after 20 years' use. As explained above, the requirement is that the user must be for 20 years before the right of way is brought into question. Until that time, there is no statutory dedication, however long the user. The right remains merely inchoate until that time. Indeed, until the question has been resolved, either by confirmation of the definitive map order or court action, the right cannot be finally established.

The same argument applies where claims are made for a private right of way under the Prescription Act 1832. The right has to be established by action and the 20 years must be 'next before suit or action'.[6]

In *De Rothschild v Buckinghamshire County Council*,[7] the public used a path across the De Rothschilds' land for 26 years from 1914 to 1940. The land was requisitioned and, during that time, there was no evidence of public use. The public's right of way was challenged in 1948, but a claim to a public right of way

---

1   [1956] 2 QB 439.
2   [2000] JPL 396.
3   See Louise Davies 'Ex parte Dorset County Council', RWLR 6.2, p 69.
4   *Merstham Manor v Coulsdon and Purley UDC* [1937] 2 KB 77.
5   *R v Secretary of State for the Environment ex parte Blake* [1984] JPL 101.
6   See Megarry and Wade *Law of Real Property* 6th edn, para 18–143.
7   (1957) 55 LGR 595.

failed because there had been no use during the 20 years immediately preceding 1948.

This principle has important implications where, for example, vehicular use is claimed over a footpath. If the right of way were brought into question, say, in 1972, 20 years' user before that date could not be established. This is because the Road Traffic Act 1930 made it illegal to drive a motor vehicle on a footpath. Illegal user cannot give rise to legal right.[1] Although it might be possible to establish 20 years' vehicular user before 1930, that would not make the user after that date legal. This is because no right is established until the right of way is brought into question. Any claim based on long use would have to be established at common law, not on statutory deemed dedication.

(3)   Way of such a character

Section 31 stipulates that the statutory presumption will not apply where there is 'a way of such a character that use of it by the public could not give rise at common law to any presumption of dedication'.

The meaning of this phrase is obscure. It may cover situations such as paths through churchyards. As it has been held that the use of the word 'way' in the section refers to the physical way[2] and not the legal right of way, it does not appear to cover any lack of capacity of landowners with limited interest. It is possible that it would cover situations where a deemed dedication, being contrary to statute, could not arise; for instance, driving with a motor vehicle on a footpath or bridleway contrary to the Road Traffic Act 1988, or claiming a right over land belonging to British Rail on which it is a criminal offence to trespass. What is clear is that s 31 does not apply to right of navigation over rivers. Although the Act defines 'land' to include land covered with water, this has been interpreted to mean fords, not rivers where the right is over water rather than land.[3]

3.6   LIMITED DEDICATION

3.6.1   General principles

A landowner may dedicate a public right of way subject to physical obstructions such as gates, or the right to plough. The practical difficulty may be in establishing whether the obstruction pre- or post-dated the dedication.

Even where the right of way was originally dedicated subject to a limitation, use of the way for 20 years after the removal of the limitation may amount to re-dedication without the obstruction. So, if a highway was dedicated subject to gates, but the gates were subsequently removed, then after 20 years there would be an unlimited dedication. In *Gloucestershire County Council v*

---

1   *Cargill v Gotts* [1981] 1 WLR 441; *Robinson v Adair* [1995] NPC 30 but see CROW Act
      2000, s 68 for statutory provisions on prescriptive private rights of way.
2   *Attorney General v Brotherton* [1992] AC 425.
3   Ibid.

Farrow,[1] it was held that the Lord of the Manor had lost his right to obstruct the highway with market stalls after he had failed to do so for a period of over 20 years.

The dedication may also be subject to the rights of the landowner, or third parties, to carry on activities on land adjacent to the path which would otherwise amount to a nuisance. A farmer may have dedicated a path subject to his right to plough or carry on other agricultural activities. However, the limitations must not be incompatible with the existence of a right of way. They should, moreover, be entered on the statement attached to the definitive map. If they are not, it will be more difficult for the landowner to prove the limited dedication.

It is assumed that, where a landowner dedicates a public right of way, that dedication is subject to his right to use the path for his own purposes. For example, although it is an offence for a member of the public to use a motor vehicle on a footpath or bridleway, a landowner could do so by virtue of his ownership. If the path is publicly maintainable, the legal analysis is that an easement is reserved over the surface, the legal estate of which is vested in the local authority.

3.6.2 Restricted byways

The CROW Act 2000[2] provides that any restricted byway rights are subject to any conditions or limitations which existed immediately before the section creating restricted byways came into force.

It also provides that any owner or lessee of premises adjoining or adjacent to a restricted byway shall, so far as is necessary for the reasonable enjoyment and occupation of the premises, have vehicular access over the relevant highway. 'Relevant highway' means a highway which became maintainable at public expense on the automatic reclassification of a RUPP as a restricted byway and which had previously been owned by the owner of the premises or included in the lease of the premises.

3.7 PRIVATE AND PUBLIC RIGHTS

It is possible for private and public rights to exist over the same route.[3] For instance, the public may have a right on foot and a third party may have a private right of way, or easement, for use with vehicles.

If there is a public right of way for vehicles, the landowner will not be able to grant any private vehicular rights because he will have parted with his interest. However, private vehicular rights may have pre-dated the public right and, should the public rights be extinguished, the person entitled to the benefit of the easement will continue to be able to use the route.

---

1   [1985] 1 WLR 741.
2   Section 50.
3   See Colin Sydenham 'Greater Rights over Minor Highways', RWLR 3.3, p 1.

Private vehicular rights may be expressly or impliedly granted or reserved by a landowner. Such a grant may have pre-dated the public dedication or, if the public right is limited to pedestrian or horse use, be granted afterwards provided it does not derogate from the public right already granted. A prescriptive private vehicular right,[1] however, must be claimed before the public footpath or bridleway was dedicated. This is because there can be no claim based on unlawful use and it is an offence to drive on a footpath or bridleway without lawful permission.

There is a strong argument, not so far accepted by the courts, that prescription, being evidence of a presumed grant, should constitute lawful authority.[2] In the same way, deemed dedication is based on a theory that there must have once been a dedication and the subsequent use is evidence of that dedication. Long use for both prescription and deemed dedication does not of itself create the right, but is evidence that there was a legal origin for the use.

---

1   On the difficulties of obtaining prescriptive rights for vehicles, see *Massey v Boulden* [2002] EWCA Civ 1634, [2002] TLR 496.
2   See the CROW Act 2000, s 68 for an attempt to deal with the problems caused by claims to prescriptive rights for private rights of way across commons based on user contrary to the Road Traffic Act 1988, s 34(1)(a).

Chapter 4

EXTINGUISHMENT AND DIVERSION ORDERS

4.1 INTRODUCTION

There is a legal adage, 'Once a highway always a highway'.[1] This means that, even though a highway has not been used for many years and even though it may not be visible on the ground, it will continue to have legal existence.[2] It also means that it is not possible to establish title by adverse possession to a highway if the effect would be to restrict the public's right of passage.[3]

In order for a highway to be extinguished or diverted, there must be an order made under statutory provision. There is an exception where the highway has ceased to exist physically. The obvious example is a footpath along a cliff which is eroded and falls into the sea.[4] It is sometimes difficult to ascertain whether a path running, say, by a river can be repaired or has ceased to exist entirely. In *R v Secretary of State for the Environment, Transport and the Regions ex parte Gloucestershire County Council*,[5] it was held that the erosion of the river bank destroyed the path and did not give a right to deviate inland. On the other hand, where a landslip destroyed a metalled road, it was held that the highway continued to exist along the line of the old road.[6] There is another possible exception where a public right of way is inaccessible. In *Bailey v Jamieson*,[7] a public footpath became inaccessible due to the stopping up of the highway at either end. Denman J said:

'I think we are compelled to hold that this is a case where that which formerly was a highway, but which, though it has not been stopped up by statutory process, has, by reason of legal acts at either end, ceased to be a place which the Queen's subjects can have access, loses its character of a highway.'

Public rights of way may be stopped up or diverted under public, private or local Acts of Parliament. This chapter deals with the public Acts under which most orders are made.

---

1   See eg *R v Inhabitants of St James, Taunton* (1315) Selwyn's NSR; *Harvey v Truro RDC* [1903] 2 Ch 638.
2   *Attorney General v Stokesley RDC* (1928) 26 LGR 440.
3   *Gerring v Barfield* (1864) 16 CB (NS) 597.
4   *R v The Inhabitants of the Parish of Paul in Cornwall* (1840) 2 Mood and R 307 (wall carrying right of way washed into the sea); *R v The Inhabitants of Hornsea in the East Riding of Yorkshire* (1854) Dears CC 291 (part of road eroded). See M Orlik 'Once a highway always a highway', RWLR 2.1, p 5.
5   [2000] EGCS 150.
6   *R v The Inhabitants of Greenhow in the North Riding of Yorkshire* (1876) 1 QBD 703.
7   (1876) 1 CPD 329.

4.2   EFFECT OF ORDERS

4.2.1   Stopping up

The effect of a stopping-up order is that the right of the public to pass and repass is extinguished. Where the surface of the path is publicly maintainable, the determinable fee simple which was vested in the highway authority will cease.[1] The fee simple will therefore revest in the landowner free of the public rights. However, any private rights will continue.[2]

It is also possible for some, rather than all, of the rights to be extinguished. Vehicular rights could be extinguished, but bridleway and pedestrian rights retained.[3]

4.2.2   Diversions

A diversion is an alteration of the route of the path. This usually means that the old route will be closed and a new route created. There is some conflicting case-law on whether the diversion needs to be to an entirely or partially new route or to an existing route which is improved in some way.[4] Much depends on the statutory provision under which the diversion is being made.[5]

4.3   JUDICIAL OR ADMINISTRATIVE ORDERS

Historically, highway matters were dealt with at Quarter Sessions. The jurisdiction of the magistrates' court has been retained in relation to a limited number of issues, including the diversion and extinguishment of highways.[6] However, there is also an administrative procedure for extinguishing and diverting bridleways and footpaths,[7] but not vehicular routes.

The Department of the Environment, Transport and the Regions (as it was then known) in its Consultation Paper[8] made the following proposal for reform:

'Proposal 16
In addition to their powers to divert to close footpaths and bridleways, highway authorities should be empowered to make orders diverting or closing rights of way which carry vehicular rights and which are recorded on definitive maps. There should be reserve powers for the Secretary of State and the National Assembly for Wales. Magistrates' current powers to close or divert footpaths, bridleways or Byways Open to All Traffic should be withdrawn.'

---

1   *Tunbridge Wells Corporation v Baird* [1896] AC 434; *Rolls v St George the Martyr Southwark, Vestry* (1880) 14 Ch D 785.
2   *Walsh v Oates* [1953] 1 QB 578.
3   An example is under the Highways Act 1980, s 116(4).
4   *Welch v Nash* (1807) 8 East 394; *De Ponthieu v Pennyfeather* (1814) 5 Taunt 634; *R v Phillips* (1866) LR 1 QB 648.
5   See Stephen Sauvain *Highway Law* (Sweet & Maxwell 2nd edn), p 203. Under the Town and Country Planning Act 1990, s 257(2)(a) diversions may be made to existing highways.
6   Highways Act 1980, s 116.
7   Ibid, ss 118, 119.
8   *Improving Rights of Way in England and Wales* (1999).

This proposal has not been enacted in the CROW Act 2000. However, the new sections in the Act enabling special extinguishment and diversion orders, and diversion orders for the protection of Sites of Special Scientific Interest, do cover certain forms of vehicular highway.

4.4   EXTINGUISHMENT AND DIVERSION ORDERS UNDER SECTION 116

4.4.1   Use of section 116

Orders for stopping up and diversions may be made for all kinds of highways other than trunk roads and special roads, under this section. This is in contrast to orders (other than special extinguishment and diversion orders) under ss 118 and 119 which can be made only in relation to footpaths and bridleways. It is also possible to extinguish vehicular rights subject to the reservation of a restricted byway, bridleway or footpath.[1] It is not possible to do this directly under s 118. However, a bridleway could be extinguished and concurrently a new right created for walkers.[2]

Where bridleways and footpaths are concerned, local authorities are encouraged by the Secretary of State for Transport and for Wales to use ss 118 and 119 rather than s 116.

> 'Whilst it is recognised that there may be circumstances where it is appropriate to use the Magistrates' Court procedure, for example the extinguishment or diversion of a footpath or bridleway (or to retain such rights) simultaneously with the extinguishment of a vehicular right of way, the Secretaries of State consider that authorities should make use of the other powers available unless there are good reasons for not doing so.'[3]

Nor are the Ramblers' Association and Open Spaces Society in favour of magistrates being involved in diversion and extinguishment of public rights of way.

> 'The prospect of appearing in court is a deterrent to potential witnesses, the prospect of facing costs if an objection is lodged to a s 116 application is very worrying to small and relatively impoverished organisations concerned about the proposals of a highway authority backed by public funds; there is no requirement on magistrates to give reasons for their decisions.'[4]

All the same, there may be situations when there would be advantages for the landowner or local authority proceeding under s 116. It was used by some local authorities when there was a limit on the amount of expenses which could be

---

1   Highways Act 1980, s 116(4), as amended by the CROW Act 2000, Sch 5, Pt 11, para 15. In considering whether any public right of way should be reserved any access land is to be disregarded, CROW Act 2000, s 59.
2   Eg under the Highways Act 1980, s 26.
3   Circular No 2/93; Welsh Circular 5/93.
4   John Riddall and John Trevelyan *Rights of Way: A Guide to Law and Practice* (Commons, Open Spaces and Footpaths Preservation Society and Ramblers' Association, 1992, 3rd edn), p 189.

reclaimed from the applicant under ss 118 and 119. Application to the magistrates' court is likely to be quicker than orders under ss 118 and 119. However, it should be noted that the district and parish councils have a right to veto s 116 applications.[1]

4.4.2　Stopping up

A public right of way may be stopped up if it appears to the magistrate that the way is unnecessary. 'Unnecessary' means unnecessary for the public.[2] What is or is not unnecessary depends on the facts in a particular case. Use does not of itself indicate that the highway is necessary, although it will obviously be an important factor to take into account. The existence of an alternative route may be relevant,[3] but access land under the CROW Act 2000 is not to be taken into account in considering whether the existing highway is unnecessary or whether any public right of way should be reserved.[4] Section 116 may be used to reduce the width of a highway.

However, even if the magistrates consider the route unnecessary they still have a discretion on whether or not to order that the highway be stopped up.

In *Maile v Manchester City Council*[5] Laws J said:

> 'Section 116(1) confers, of course, no more nor less than a discretion in the court to authorise the stopping-up of a highway. The discretion only arises if the Court concludes that the highway is unnecessary. That being the position the court is not, in my judgment, limited to the bare question whether the highway is necessary or not necessary when it comes to exercise the discretion.'

No compensation is payable for loss suffered by anyone as a result of the stopping up of the highway.

4.4.3　Diversion

In order for a diversion to be made the new route must be nearer or more commodious for the public. The convenience of the landowner is not relevant. 'Commodious' has been interpreted to mean 'a flavour of convenience, roominess and spaciousness'.[6]

Although it seems that the diversion can be to an existing route[7] if that route is to be extended or enlarged, where there is no such alteration to the route, the proper course would be to apply for a stopping-up order rather than a diversion.

1　Highways Act 1980, s 116(3).
2　*Ramblers' Association v Kent County Council* (1990) 60 P&CR 464, but see *Westley v Hertfordshire County Council* [1995] CL 846: parking not a relevant use of the highway.
3　See unreported case *Stevens v Dorset County Council* (16 March 1999) – use by Trail Riders Fellowship not necessary where 140 miles of unpaved country road including 10 miles of byways in Dorset.
4　CROW Act 2000, s 59.
5　(1997) 74 P&CR 451.
6　*Gravesham Borough Council v Wilson and Straight* [1983] JPL 607.
7　See **4.2.2**, footnote 4 above.

Where a diversion is made, the new route should carry the same rights as the old route.[1] If lesser rights are to be diverted, there must be a stopping-up order for the greater rights. For example, the vehicular rights could be stopped up on a byway open to all traffic and the remaining bridleway and footpath rights diverted.

The consent of the owner of the land, over which the diverted way will run, is required, but there is no provision for compensation.

Where a diversion order is made, it should not take effect until the new route has been completed and a certificate signed by two justices that it has been completed to their satisfaction. Until that is done, the order is not effective.[2]

4.4.4 Costs of application

An individual may request the highway authority to make an application for a stopping-up or diversion order. The authority may require that person to pay the reasonable costs in making the application for the order, as a condition of granting the request.[3]

4.4.5 Procedure

Before making an application by means of a complaint to the magistrates' court, notice must be given to the district and parish councils. If, within 2 months of receiving notice, either council refuses in writing its consent to the application, the application cannot go ahead.[4] There is no requirement that consent should not reasonably be withheld, which means that the councils have the power of veto.

Where the application is for a diversion order, the consent of every owner of land over which the route is to run must be obtained and produced to the court.[5]

At least 28 days before the application, notice must be given to the owners and occupiers of all the lands which adjoin the highway. Notices must also be served on any statutory undertakers with apparatus in, over, along or across the path. In addition, notices embodying the plan must be displayed in prominent positions at the ends and intersections of the path.[6] This is generally taken to mean that the plan should be displayed on the site. However, a reference to a plan which can be inspected at the council's office was upheld in the unreported case of *Stevens v Dorset County Council*.[7]

---

1   *Ramblers' Association v Kent CC* (1990) 60 P&CR 464.
2   Highways Act 1980, s 116(8); *Stockwell v Southgate Corporation* [1936] 2 All ER 1343.
3   Ibid, s 117.
4   Ibid, s 116(8).
5   Ibid.
6   Ibid, Sch 12. See *Ramblers' Association v Kent CC* (1990) 60 P&CR 464, on importance of notices not to be misleading and what amounts to 'ends of the highway'.
7   16 March 1999, Co/2149/98.

The notices must specify the time and place for the hearing, the terms of the proposed order, and must also include a plan showing the effect of the order.

The justices must be satisfied before making an order that all the notices have been given and that the consents of the owners over whose land the diverted highway will run have been lodged with the court. Recipients of the notices, users of the highway and aggrieved persons are entitled to be heard.

The order, accompanied by a plan, when made, must be signed by the chairman and sent to the authority which made the application.

4.4.6   Appeals

A right of appeal to the Crown Court against an order made by the magistrates' court is given to the highway authority or anyone who was or claimed to be entitled to be heard at the magistrates' court.[1]

There is a more limited appeal on a point of law only by way of case stated to the High Court.

4.5   EXTINGUISHMENT ORDERS UNDER SECTION 118

4.5.1   The tests

Bridleways and footpaths, but not vehicular routes, may be extinguished under s 118. This is achieved by a two-stage process: first of all, the making of an order and, secondly, the confirmation. There are separate criteria which must be fulfilled at each stage.

In making the order it must *appear* to the local authority:

> 'that it is expedient that the path or way should be stopped up on the ground that it is not needed for public use.'

In deciding this question, the highway authority must not consider any access land under the CROW Act 2000 as reducing the need.[2] It must have due regard to the needs of agriculture, forestry and nature conservation.[3]

In confirming the order the local authority must be *satisfied*:

> 'that it is expedient to do so having regard to the extent (if any) to which it appears ... that the path or way would, apart from the order, be likely to be used by the public and having regard to the effect which the extinguishment of the right of way would have as respects the land served by the path or way, account being taken as to the provisions for compensation.'

The difference in wording between 'appears' and 'is satisfied' may reflect the difference in procedure. An order is made without a full inquiry into

---

1   Highways Act 1980, s 317.
2   CROW Act 2000, s 59 (2).
3   Highways Act 1980, ss 121(3), 29 as amended by the CROW Act 2000, Sch 6, Pt 1, para 14(4).

objections. If objections are made, usually there is a public inquiry and opportunity for the inspector to weigh up the evidence on both sides.

The difference between the test of 'not needed for public use' at the order-making stage and the extent that the path is 'likely to be used by the public' at the confirmation stage is significant. The Secretary of State or local authority may confirm the order even if the path was used to something more than a minimal extent provided it was not needed, because for instance there was a convenient alternative path.[1] However, in considering the question of the extent to which the highway is likely to be used, where it is on or near access land, he must have regard to its use at any time when the right of entry to the access land is not exercisable.[2]

The question of need is decided by the order-making authority. That question does not come to the inspector by way of appeal. The inspector, however, in deciding whether it is expedient to confirm the order, can take into account additional considerations as well as use by the public.

When making or confirming an order, any temporary circumstances preventing or diminishing the use of the path by the public are ignored.[3] 'Temporary circumstances' include substantial buildings such as electricity sub-stations, trees and high hedges. There is an obvious judicial reluctance to allow highways to be extinguished on the basis that they had previously been improperly obstructed.[4]

In deciding whether or not to confirm an extinguishment order, the Secretary of State or, where the order is unopposed, the council, must have regard to any improvement plan which includes the area in which the path lies.[5]

In making the order, the authority must have due regard to the needs of agriculture, forestry and nature conservation.[6]

4.5.2 Concurrent orders

Section 118(5) envisages that there will be concurrent orders involving creation and diversion orders and extinguishment orders. In making and confirming an extinguishment order, the local authority or Secretary of State 'may have regard to the extent to which the public path creation order or the public path diversion order would provide an alternative path'.

There is, however, no similar provision which provides that, when deciding whether there is a need for a footpath or bridleway, extinguishment or

---

1   Highways Act 1980, s 118(5). *R v Secretary of State for the Environment ex parte Stewart* [1980] JPL 175; *R v Secretary of State for the Environment ex parte Cheshire County Council* [1991] JPL 537. See also Michael Orlik 'A power or duty to make path orders', RWLR 7.2, p 29.
2   CROW Act 2000, s 59(3).
3   Highways Act 1980, s 118(6).
4   CROW Act 2000, ss 118(6). *Wood v Secretary of State for the Environment* [1977] JPL 307; *R v Secretary of State for the Environment ex parte Stewart* [1980] JPL 175.
5   Highways Act 1980, s 118(6A), as inserted by the CROW Act 2000, Sch 6, Pt 1, para 6.
6   Highways Act, ss 121(3) and 29, as amended by the CROW Act 2000, Sch 6, para 14(4).

diversion orders should be taken into account. From this, it seems that the need test must be satisfied on its own.

If this is right, on a reorganisation of public rights of way the first question must be whether there is a need for new rights.

In considering whether a path is needed for public use, 'any temporary circumstances preventing or diminishing the use of a path or way by the public' are to be disregarded. Temporary circumstances do not mean temporary structures. Case-law has established that some substantial obstructions such as buildings have to be disregarded if they could legally and physically be removed.[1]

Concurrent orders may be useful when the tests for a diversion order cannot be satisfied. A creation and an extinguishment order could be made. Another example is where an authority might want to divert two paths onto a single new route. It could extinguish one route and divert the other. As there is no power under s 118 to downgrade a bridleway to a footpath, an extinguishment order could be made and an order made to create a footpath over the same route.[2]

4.5.3   Applications relating to agricultural land

Although an owner, lessee or occupier might request an extinguishment order, many local authorities have been reluctant to make orders unless they are concurrent with orders for the creation or diversion of other rights of way. Even if the tests for making and confirming an order are satisfied, the authority is not under a duty to make an order. It may, in exercising its discretion, decide that it is not expedient to do so. There will often be opposition to the closure of paths and local authorities are therefore sometimes reluctant to use their limited resources to make orders. They are specifically directed not to make orders which result in cul-de-sac paths.[3]

Although there is provision for the Secretary of State to use his reserve powers should a local authority refuse to make an order,[4] these powers are seldom used.

The position of an owner, lessee or occupier of any land used for agriculture, forestry or the breeding or keeping of horses has been strengthened by the CROW Act 2000.[5] They are given a formal right of application for an extinguishment order with a right of appeal against the authorities' refusal to make an order.

An application must be made on a prescribed form and be accompanied by a map on a scale to be prescribed. The map must show the land over which the

---

1   See **4.5.1**, footnote 4.
2   See Riddal and Trevelyan *Rights of Way: A Guide to Law and Practice* 3rd edn, pp 169–170.
3   DOE Circular 2/93, *Public Rights of Way*.
4   Highways Act 1980, s 120(3).
5   Ibid, s 118ZA; CROW Act 2000, Sch 6, Pt 1, para 7.

right of way will be extinguished. Regulations may prescribe any fees payable for making the application and any further charges if the application is granted.

The council must determine the application as soon as reasonably practicable. If the council does not make its decision within 4 months, the applicant may apply to the Secretary of State, who, after consulting with the council, may direct the council to make the order before the end of a specified period.[1]

Before making an order, the council may require the applicant to pay any compensation due to a third party whose land has been depreciated, or who has suffered damage by being disturbed in his enjoyment of land, by the order.[2]

After an application has been determined, the council must give the applicant notice of the decision with reasons for it and a copy of the notice must be given to prescribed persons.

Although the new procedures should mean that orders will be made more readily, it will still be necessary to satisfy the council, or the Secretary of State, that the path is not needed for public use. It will often not be possible to do this. Where landowners have compelling reasons for wanting a right of way extinguished, they will have to give serious consideration to creating new rights of way where the public want them. They may then be able to show that the existing path is not needed. Otherwise they should concentrate on managing the right of way and seeking other solutions to perceived problems.

4.5.4 Special extinguishment orders for crime prevention and school security[3]

Local highway authorities may make orders stopping up certain highways for purposes of preventing or reducing crime, which would otherwise disrupt the life of the community, in areas designated by the Secretary of State. The powers extend to footpaths, bridleways, restricted byways (whether on the definitive map or not) and such paths if shown on the definitive map but over which the public have a right of way for vehicular and all other kinds of traffic. The highway authority may also stop up highways shown on the definitive map as byways open to all traffic, but there is no power to stop up a trunk or special road.

Before the power can be exercised, it must be shown that premises adjoining or adjacent to the highway are affected by high levels of crime and the existence of the highway is enabling persistent commission of criminal offences.

An order will not be confirmed unless the Secretary of State, or the highway authority for uncontested orders, is satisfied that those conditions have been fulfilled and that it is expedient to confirm the order. In particular, regard must be paid to any strategy for the reduction of crime and disorder prepared under s 6 of the Crime and Disorder Act 1998, any alternative routes and the

---

1   Highways Act 1980, s 118ZA(7), inserted by the CROW Act 2000, Sch 6, para 7.
2   Ibid.
3   CROW Act 2000, Sch 6, para 8; Highways Act 1980, s 118B.

possibility of a diversion rather than a stopping-up order, and the effect that the extinguishment will have on other land served by the highway, taking into account the compensation provisions.[1]

The highway authority may also stop up the highways specified above which cross land occupied for the purposes of a school, in order to protect pupils and staff from:

(1) violence;
(2) harassment;
(3) alarm or distress arising from unlawful activity; or
(4) any other risk to their health or safety arising from such activity.

The proprietor of the school may make an application to the highway authority for a special extinguishment order. The provisions set out at **4.5.3** above, relating to applications by owners of agricultural land, will apply.[2]

An order will not be confirmed unless it is expedient to do so, having regard to any other security measures which could have been taken, whether the order will achieve a substantial improvement in that security, the availability of an alternative route and the possibility of a diversion rather than a stopping-up order and the effect that the closure will have on any other land served by the highway, taking into account provisions for compensation.

Before making a special extinguishment order, either for crime prevention or school security, the council must consult the police authority for the area in which the highway lies.

The form of special extinguishment orders and the scale of the map which is required will be prescribed by regulations. Schedule 6 to the Highways Act 1980 will govern the making, confirmation, validity and date of operation of the orders.

4.6   DIVERSION ORDERS UNDER SECTION 119

4.6.1   The tests

Bridleways and footpaths may be diverted under s 119. In the same way as for extinguishments, the procedure for a diversion is for an order to be made and then confirmed. Where there are objections, the order must be referred to the Secretary of State for confirmation or otherwise.

In deciding whether to make an order, the council must consider that it is expedient 'in the interests of the owner, lessee or occupier of land crossed by the path or way or of the public' that the path should be diverted. No limitation is placed on the interests of owners, lessees or occupiers and diversions could therefore be obtained on grounds of security or privacy.[3]

---

1   See Highways Act 1980, ss 121(2), 28.
2   Ibid, s 118C.
3   *Robertson v Secretary of State for the Environment* [1976] 1 WLR 371 (diversion of path across the Chequers Estate).

However, an order must not alter a point of termination if that point is not on a highway. In other words, a highway authority has no power to divert a cul-de-sac end of a route. Where the termination point is on a highway, the diversion must be to another point on the same highway or a highway connected with it and it must be as substantially convenient to the public.[1]

In making the order, the highway authority must have regard to agriculture, forestry and nature conservation.[2]

For an order to be confirmed, the highway authority or the Secretary of State must be satisfied not only that it is expedient, but also that the diverted path will not be substantially less convenient. In particular, regard must be had to the effect the diversion would have on:

(1) public enjoyment of the path;
(2) other land served by the existing right of way, taking into account the provision for compensation; and
(3) the land over which the new route will pass.[3]

In deciding whether or not to confirm the order, the material provisions of any improvement plan for the area must be considered.[4]

4.6.2 Diversion on to an existing highway

A diverted route may include part of an existing highway. Section 119(7)(b), which is concerned with maps to be attached to public path diversion orders, states that the map should indicate 'whether a new right of way is created by the order over the whole of the new site or whether some part of it is already comprised in a footpath or bridleway'. Section 119(2)(b), dealing with the requirement that where a route terminates on a highway the diverted route should terminate on the same highway or one connected to it, also envisages that the diversion may be to an existing route.

However, it would not appear that a diversion order could be made to an existing route without any new route being provided.[5] The appropriate order in such circumstances would be an extinguishment order.

4.6.3 Diversion with limitations or conditions

The diversion order may specify that the diverted route be subject to limitations or conditions even if the original route which is extinguished by the order was not so subject.[6] These limitations or conditions should be recorded in the order.

---

1   Highways Act 1980, s 119(2).
2   Ibid, ss 121(3), 29 as amended by the CROW Act 2000, Sch 6, Pt 1, para 14(4). See also Highways Act 1980, s 85(1) – special considerations in AONBs.
3   Ibid, s 119(6).
4   Ibid, s 119(6A).
5   *R v Lake District Planning Board ex parte Bernstein* (1982) *The Times*, February 3.
6   Highways Act 1980, s 119(4).

4.6.4   Costs

Applicants may be liable to pay the costs of making an order. The Local Authorities (Recovery of Costs of Public Path Orders) Regulations 1993 provide that the costs which local authorities may recover must not exceed the costs actually incurred.

Local authorities may waive all or part of the costs. They are likely to do so if the order benefits the public, as where an extra path is created. The fact that an order is not confirmed does not give the applicant an automatic right to a refund. Costs must be refunded, however, where the authority decides not to proceed with an order or the order is invalid.

Local authorities are encouraged to publish details of their policy on charging.

The authority can require the applicant to enter into an agreement to pay, or contribute towards the costs of making up the new path and any compensation that may be payable, before it will make a diversion order.

4.6.5   Compensation

Compensation is payable to anyone whose property can be shown to have been adversely affected by public path orders under the Highway Act 1980.[1] For example, compensation could be claimed by a landowner where a path is created over or diverted on to his land. An application should be made in writing to the local authority which made the order, or the authority nominated by the Secretary of State where he made the order, within 6 months of the coming into operation of the order.[2] Disputes as to the amount of compensation are decided by the Lands Tribunal.[3] An action to recover the money must be brought within 6 years from the date when the claim for compensation was lodged.[4]

4.6.6   Physical setting out of path

Works may be necessary to create the new path on the diverted route. Until such time as the authority certifies that the work has been done, the old route will continue to exist.[5]

4.6.7   The practicalities

There are differing perceptions about the making and confirmation of diversion orders. Landowners consider that applications for diversions are very rarely successful, while ramblers have statistics to prove that diversion orders are usually confirmed.

---

1   Highways Act 1980, ss 121(2) and 28.
2   Public Path Order Regulations 1993, SI 1998/11, reg 5.
3   Highways Act 1980, ss 307, 309.
4   Limitation Act 1980, s 9; *Rotherwick v Oxfordshire County Council* (2002) 28 EG 144.
5   Highways Act 1980, s 119(3), as amended by the CROW Act 2000, Sch 6, Pt 1,
     para 9(3).

What is clear is that much homework is necessary before an application is made. A person who wants a diversion should make sure that the diversion achieves what he wants, fulfils the tests set out in s 119 and gives some extra advantage to the public.

Important considerations include the effect the diversion will have on other paths in the neighbourhood, and whether the new route will be easier to walk, or provide better views.

The applicant should consult all the possible interested parties. These include the landowner, the tenant, the highway authority, the parish council and local user groups.

Although there is no specific provision that temporary circumstances preventing the use of the existing path should be taken into account when considering a diversion order, local authorities may refuse to make a diversion order if there are obstructions on the original route.

It is recommended that the Rights of Way Review Committee Practice Guidance Note 4, 'Securing Agreement to Public Path Orders', be studied before an application is made. Local authorities should consult Practice Guidance Note 1, 'Code of Practice on Consultation', over changes to rights of way before making any order.

A local authority is not under a duty to make a diversion order and may in its discretion decide not to do so even though the tests under s 119 have been fulfilled. Where an order is not made but an owner, lessee or occupier of land crossed by a footpath or bridleway satisfies the Secretary of State that it is expedient to make diversion order, the Secretary of State may himself make an order, provided that he has powers to confirm any order so made.[1] He must consult with the appropriate authority before doing so. In practice, these reserve powers are seldom used.

The position of an owner, lessee or occupier of any land used for agriculture, forestry or the breeding or keeping of horses has been strengthened by the CROW Act 2000.[2] They are given a formal right of application for a diversion order with a right of appeal against the authorities' refusal to make an order.

Where the diverted route would link to a classified road, a special road, a Greater London Authority road or any other highway for which the Minister is responsible, the consent of the relevant highway authority is required.[3] The consent of any statutory undertaker is required where the diverted route will pass over land covered by its works or the curtilage of such land.[4]

An application must be made on a prescribed form and be accompanied by a map on a scale to be prescribed. The map must show the line of the existing path and the proposed new route. The map must indicate whether it is

---

1   Highways Act 1980, s 120(3).
2   Ibid, s 119ZA; CROW Act 2000, Sch 6, Pt 1, para 7.
3   Ibid, s 119ZA(2).
4   Ibid, s 119ZA(3).

proposed to create a new right of way over the whole of the new site or whether some of it is already comprised in a footpath or bridleway.

Regulations may prescribe any fees payable for making the application and any further charges if a diversion order is made.

The council must determine the application as soon as reasonably practicable. If the council does not make its decision within 4 months, the applicant may apply to the Secretary of State, who, after consulting with the council, may direct the council to make the order before the end of a specified period.

Before making an order, the council may require the applicant to pay any compensation due to a third party whose land has been depreciated, or who has suffered damage by being disturbed in his enjoyment of land, by the order.

After an application has been determined, the council must give the applicant notice of the decision with reasons for it and a copy of the notice must be given to prescribed persons.

Although the new procedures should mean that orders will be made more readily, it will still be necessary to satisfy the council, or the Secretary of State, that the tests for the making and confirmation of the order have been satisfied.

4.6.8   Special diversion orders for crime prevention and school security[1]

Local highway authorities may make orders diverting certain highways for purposes of preventing or reducing crime, which would otherwise disrupt the life of the community, in areas designated by the Secretary of State. The powers extend to footpaths, bridleways, restricted byways (whether on the definitive map or not) and such paths if shown on the definitive map but over which the public have a right of way for vehicular and all other kinds of traffic. The highway authority may also divert highways shown on the definitive map as byways open to all traffic, but not a highway which is a trunk or special road.

Before the power can be exercised, it must be shown that premises adjoining or adjacent to the highway are affected by high levels of crime and the existence of the highway is enabling persistent commission of criminal offences.

An order will not be confirmed unless the Secretary of State, or the highway authority for uncontested orders, is satisfied that those conditions have been fulfilled and that it is expedient to confirm the order. In particular, regard must be paid to any strategy for the reduction of crime and disorder prepared under s 6 of the Crime and Disorder Act 1998, and the effect that the diversion will have on land served by the existing right of way and the land over which the new route will run, taking into account the compensation provisions under s 28 of the Highways Act 1980.

---

1   CROW Act 2000, Sch 6; Highways Act 1980, s 118B.

The highway authority may also divert the highways specified above which cross land occupied for the purposes of a school, in order to protect pupils and staff from:

(1) violence;
(2) harassment;
(3) alarm or distress arising from unlawful activity; or
(4) any other risk to their health or safety arising from such activity.

The proprietor of the school may make an application to the highway authority for a special diversion order. The provisions set out at **4.6.7** above relating to applications by owners of agricultural land will apply.

Where the diverted route would link to a classified road, a special road, a GLA road or any other highway for which the Minister is responsible, the consent of the relevant highway authority is required.[1]

Before deciding to make the order, the council may require the applicant to pay or make a contribution to any compensation payable to a third party, costs which may be incurred in bringing the new route into a condition fit for public use, and any costs due to another highway authority for work carried out.

An application must be made on a prescribed form and be accompanied by a map on a scale to be prescribed. The map must show the line of the existing path and the proposed new route. The map must indicate whether it is proposed to create a new right of way over the whole of the new site or whether some of it is already comprised in a footpath or bridleway. Schedule 6 to the Highways Act 1980 will govern the making, confirmation, validity and date of operation of the orders.

An order will not be confirmed unless it is expedient to do so, having regard to any other security measures which could have been taken, whether the order will achieve a substantial improvement in that security, and the effect that the diversion will have on any other land served by the existing right of way and the land over which the new route will run, taking into account provisions for compensation.

Before making a special diversion order either for crime prevention or school security, the council must consult the police authority for the area in which the highway lies.

A special diversion order must not divert the cul-de-sac end of a highway nor, where the termination is on a highway, otherwise than to another point on the same highway or a highway connected with it.

The new route may be unconditional or subject to limitations and conditions even if the old route was not. The new route will come into existence, and the old route will be extinguished on the date specified in the order. However, where work is necessary on the new route, the old route will not be extinguished until the council certifies that the work has been carried out.

---

1   Highways Act 1980, s 119ZA(2), inserted by the CROW Act 2000, Sch 6, para 10.

There is no obligation imposed on a highway authority to provide, on any highway created by a special diversion order, a metalled carriageway.

4.6.9   SSSI diversion orders

English Nature or the Countryside Council for Wales may apply to the local highway authority for a diversion order for the protection of Sites of Special Scientific Interest (SSSIs).[1] The council's powers to make a diversion order extend to footpaths, bridleways, restricted byways (whether on the definitive map or not) and such paths if shown on the definitive map but over which the public have a right of way for vehicular and all other kinds of traffic. The highway authority may also divert highways shown on the definitive map as byways open to all traffic, but not a highway which is a trunk or special road.

The highway must be in, or form part of, or be adjacent to, or contiguous with an SSSI. The test for making the order is that the public use of the highway is causing or is likely to cause significant damage to the flora, fauna or geological or physiographical features which caused the area to be designated an SSSI and it is expedient in order to prevent such damage that the whole or part of the path should be diverted.

An SSSI diversion order must not divert the cul-de-sac end of a highway nor, where the termination is on a highway, otherwise than to another point on the same highway or a highway connected with it.

Before deciding to make the order, the council may require English Nature or the Countryside Council for Wales to pay or make a contribution to any compensation payable to a third party, or costs which may be incurred in bringing the new route into a condition fit for public use, or any costs due to another highway authority for work carried out.

An application must be made on a prescribed form and be accompanied by a map on a scale to be prescribed. The map must show the line of the existing path and the proposed new route. The map must indicate whether it is proposed to create a new right of way over the whole of the new site or whether some of it is already comprised in a footpath or bridleway. The application must also have an assessment in the prescribed form of the effects of the public right of way on the SSSI.

At least 14 days before an application is made, notice in the prescribed form must be given by English Nature or the Countryside Council for Wales to any owner, lessee or occupier of land over which the old or new route would run, to persons who may be prescribed, and to the Countryside Agency (where the application is made by English Nature).

Schedule 6 to the Highways Act 1980 will govern the making, confirmation, validity and date of operation of the orders.

The council, in deciding whether it is expedient to make, and the council or Secretary of State, whether it is expedient to confirm, an order, must consider

---

1   Highways Act 1980, s 119D, introduced by the CROW Act 2000, Sch 6, para 12.

whether the damage could be prevented by the council making a road traffic regulation order and whether such an order would cause less inconvenience to the public than a diversion order. Where an SSSI diversion order is made by the Secretary of State, on the failure of the council to do so, he must have regard to the same considerations.

An order will not be confirmed unless the Secretary of State, or the council for an unopposed order, is satisfied that the tests for making the order have been fulfilled and that it is expedient to confirm the order having regard to the effect the diversion will have on the enjoyment of the public right of way as a whole, and the effect that the diversion will have on any other land served by the existing right of way and the land over which the new route will run, taking into account provisions for compensation.

The new route may be unconditional or subject to limitations and conditions, even if the old route was not.

The new route will come into existence, and the old route will be extinguished, on the date specified in the order. However, where work is necessary on the new route, the old route will not be extinguished until the council certifies that the work has been carried out. There is no obligation imposed on a highway authority to provide, on any highway created by an SSSI diversion order, a metalled carriageway.

4.7   RAIL CROSSING ORDERS

4.7.1   Tests for making the order

In order to improve public safety, the Transport and Works Act 1992 introduced into the Highways Act 1980[1] new powers for closing and diverting footpaths and bridleways over railway crossings.

Before making the order, the highway authority must be satisfied that it is expedient to do so in the interests of the safety of members of the public who use, or are likely to use, the crossing.[2]

A rail crossing diversion order must not alter the point of the termination of a path unless that point is on a highway over which there is at least a similar right of way or, where the point of termination is on such a highway, to another point on the same highway or one connected with it.

A stopping-up order may stop up the public right of way over the rail crossing alone or it may in addition stop up the route on one or both sides of the crossing until its junction with another highway.

When confirming the order, the authority or the Secretary of State must be satisfied that it is expedient to do so in all the circumstances and, in particular,

---

1   Highways Act 1980, ss 118A and 119A.
2   See DoE Circular 2/93, *Public Rights of Way*, which suggests factors which should be taken into account.

whether it is reasonably practicable to make the crossing safe and, if the order is to be confirmed, what arrangements have been made for barriers and signs to be erected and maintained.

The Secretary of State has power to require the operator to provide a tunnel or bridge, or to improve an existing tunnel or bridge to take the path under or over the railway instead of making the order.[1]

4.7.2   Procedure

An application for a stopping-up or diversion order must be made by the railway operator in the form prescribed by regulations.[2] The railway operator is the company responsible for maintaining the track. If a separate company operates the trains it has no right to apply. The applicant must provide information on the need for the order and other alternative measures such as safety improvements to the crossing.

The Secretary of State has special reserve powers. If the authority has not made and confirmed an order, or submitted an opposed order for confirmation within 6 months of receiving a valid application, he may intervene and make an order himself.

The Health and Safety Executive has produced guidelines on the safety requirements for footpaths and bridleways at level crossings.

4.8   PROCEDURE FOR MAKING PUBLIC PATH ORDERS UNDER THE HIGHWAYS ACT 1980

4.8.1   General principles

Public path orders under the Highways Act 1980 consist of creation orders, stopping-up orders and diversion orders. The procedures for making and confirming the orders are the same for each form of order.[3] Powers of entry are given to survey the land in connection with orders and claims for compensation.[4]

---

1   Transport and Works Act 1992, s 48(2).
2   Rail Crossing Extinguishment and Diversion Orders Regulations 1993, SI 1993/9.
3   Highways Act 1980, ss 118–121, Sch 6; Public Path Orders Regulations 1993, SI 1993/11, as amended by the Rail Crossing Extinguishment and Diversion Orders, the Public Path Orders and Definitive Map and Statements (Amendment) Regulations 1995, SI 1995/451.
4   Highways Act 1980, s 293 as amended by the CROW Act 2000, Sch 6, para 17.

4.8.2 Who can initiate the process

The authority[1] may make an order on its own initiative or a request for an order may be made by local residents, path users, farmers, landowners and anyone else. The CROW Act 2000 has given owners and occupiers of land used for agriculture, forestry or the breeding or keeping of horses a right to make a formal application for an order.[2]

It is important where an application or a request is made, for the person who wants the order to have spoken to all those who might be affected by it. For instance, a farmer who wants a path closed or diverted should speak to the parish council and local user groups. Unless they are consulted and approve of the proposals, they are likely to object to the order. Preliminary discussions should also be held with the highway authority's rights of way officer.

A school proprietor can make an application where an order is sought for the purpose of protecting staff and children.[3]

4.8.3 Applications by landowners and school proprietors

The Secretary of State is given power to make regulations where applications are made under the new provisions. These may cover, amongst other things, certificates giving details of the interests and rights in the land to which the application relates, the giving of notices, publication of the application and the payment of charges. Any person who deliberately or recklessly gives a false or misleading certificate will be guilty of an offence.[4]

The council is required to keep a register of applications and keep them available for inspection at all reasonable hours free of charge. Regulations will specify the form and content of the register.[5]

A council may decline to determine an application where, within the last 3 years, the Secretary of State has refused to make an order on appeal or confirm an order on a similar application or order. Before declining to make an order for school security reasons, the council must consider whether the risks have substantially increased since the Secretary of State made his previous decision.[6]

A council may also decline to determine an application where an application or order similar to the current application or relating to the same land has not finally been determined.

Where a council has refused to:

---

1   The authority, for this purpose, is a county council, unitary authority, district council, London Borough Council, the Common Council, Council of Welsh County or County Borough, National Park Authority. Highways Act 1980, s 329(1), Local Government Act 1992, ss 17–23, Local Government (Wales) Act 1994, Environment Act 1995.
2   Schedule 6, paras 7 and 10, inserting ss 118ZA and 119ZA into the Highways Act 1980.
3   CROW Act 2000, Sch 6, paras 8 and 12, inserting ss 118C and 119C into the Highways Act 1980.
4   Ibid, Sch 6, para 15, inserting s 121A into the Highways Act 1980.
5   Highways Act 1980, s 121B.
6   Ibid, s 121C.

(a) make an order on an application;
(b) confirm as an unopposed order an order which was made as a result of an application;
(c) submit an opposed order made on an application to the Secretary of State,

the applicant may appeal to the Secretary of State. There will be no right of appeal, however, in any case where the consent of another person is required and that consent has not been obtained.[1]

Nor will there be a right to appeal against the refusal to make an order where the applicant has refused to enter into an agreement to pay or make a contribution to any compensation payable to third parties or, where there is a diversion, any expenses which may be incurred in bringing the new path into a fit condition for use by the public.

On an appeal from the refusal of a council to make an order, the Secretary of State will make a draft order, give notice of it and, provided the consent of any statutory undertakers with equipment on or under the path has been obtained, determine the order taking into account any objections.[2] Where an appeal is lodged after an order has been made, the Secretary of State will treat the order as if it had been submitted to him for confirmation.

The Secretary of State may not make or confirm a diversion order where work is necessary on the new path which cannot be carried out without consent of another person or statutory authorisation, and such consent or authorisation has not been obtained. Nor can he make or modify a diversion order so as to create a public right of way over land on which a statutory undertaker has works unless its consent is obtained.

The Secretary of State has powers to make regulations governing appeal procedures, compensation and charges. Any person who deliberately or recklessly gives false or misleading information in any certificates required by the regulations will be guilty of an offence.

The provisions of Sch 6 to the Highways Act 1980 relating to objections, hearings and public inquiries will apply.

4.8.4   Refusal to make order where no right of application

Only the people specified above are entitled to make an application for an order. Others may request an order but, if the council refuse to make an order, the appeal procedures discussed above will not apply. Where the Secretary of State considers it expedient, he can make an extinguishment or diversion order himself provided that if an order were made he would have power to confirm it.[3] In the case of a diversion, it is for the owner, lessee or occupier of the land crossed by the footpath or bridleway to satisfy the Secretary of State that a

---

1   Highways Act 1980, s 121D.
2   Ibid, s 121E.
3   Ibid, s 120(3).

diversion is expedient. These powers of the Secretary of State are seldom exercised.

4.8.5 Special provisions for SSSI diversions

The Secretary of State may make a diversion order, even though the conservation authority (English Nature or the Countryside Council for Wales) has not made an application for an order to the highway authority.[1] Where it does make an application but the council has neither confirmed the order nor submitted it to the Secretary of State for confirmation within 6 months of receiving the application, the Secretary of State may make the diversion order without consulting the council.[2] Before making an order, the Secretary of State may require the conservation body to enter into an agreement with the council to pay or contribute to any compensation payable or any expenses in relation to making up the new path.[3]

4.8.6 Consultation

Before making an order, the authority has to consult any other local authority for the area (including the National Parks Planning Board, if there is one). There is no obligation to consult parish councils, the landowner, nor user groups. However, the authority is encouraged to do so. The Lake District and Peak District National Parks and the Norfolk and Suffolk Broads Authority have power to make applications. It must consult county and district councils.

4.8.7 Deciding whether to make the order

The authority must be sure that the tests set out in the relevant Act for making the order are fulfilled. Even where they are, the authority has a discretion. It may decide not to make the order. There is no appeal against the authority's decision not to make an order, but the applicant can ask the Secretary of State to make the order. He will only do so in exceptional circumstances. The decisions about whether to make public path orders are usually made by a sub-committee of the Highway Department or the Leisure and Recreation Department.

Members of the public are entitled to attend meetings unless confidential or exempt information would be disclosed to the public.[4]

Notice of meetings must be given at least 5 days before the meeting or, if the meeting is convened at shorter notice, at the time that it is convened.[5]

---

1   Highways Act 1980, s 120(3C).
2   Ibid, s 120(3D).
3   Ibid, s 120(7).
4   Local Government Act 1972, s 100(k).
5   Ibid, s 100A(6). The Local Authorities (Access to Meetings and Documents) (Period of Notice) (England) Order 2002, SI 2002/715.

The agenda and papers for the meeting must be available at and before the meeting unless they relate to items during which the meeting is not likely to be open to the public.[1]

The minutes, a summary of the proceedings, agenda and reports must be available for inspection for 6 years after the date of the meeting.[2]

Background papers to the reports must be available for inspection for 4 years after the date of the meeting.[3]

Authorities must maintain a register of council members with their names and addresses. They must also maintain a register of powers delegated to council officers.[4]

4.8.8 The order

The form of the order is set out in regulations. The order should contain a plan to a scale of not less than 1:2500 or to the scale of the largest published map for the area. It must be accompanied by a notice which:

(1) briefly describes the effect of the order;
(2) states where the order may be inspected free of charge and where a copy can be purchased:
(3) gives the address to which objections can be sent; and
(4) gives the date by which any objections must be made.

This must be at least 28 days after the notice of the order is first published.

4.8.9 Giving notice of a path order

The notice must be published in a local newspaper, sent to anyone who has formally requested and paid for notice of such an order and prominently displayed at council offices in the locality and at any other places the authority considers appropriate.

In addition, the notice and plan must be displayed at the ends of the path affected by the order. The plan must show the effect of the order on the path.

The notice, plan and order must be sent to:

(1) any other local authorities in the area, including the parish council or meeting;
(2) the owners, occupiers and lessees of any land affected by the order and the bodies prescribed in the regulations.

These bodies are, for all orders in England – British Horse Society, Byways and Bridleways Trust, Cyclists Touring Club, Open Spaces Society, Ramblers'

---

1   Local Government Act 1972, s 100B.
2   Ibid, s 100C.
3   Ibid, s 100C.
4   Ibid, s 100G.

Association; in addition, where the path is in the relevant area, the Chiltern Society or Peak and Northern Footpath Society.

The Auto Cycle Union and British Driving Society are prescribed bodies to receive copies of notices and orders, except those affecting footpaths and bridleways over which no public vehicular rights are claimed or suspected to exist.

4.8.10　Statement of reasons

There is no statutory requirement obliging the authority to give reasons for making an order. However, the rights of way review committee[1] has recommended that a statement should accompany the order to:

(a) explain the authority's reason for making the order, indicating why it is believed to be both necessary and fair;
(b) explain why in the authority's view the order complies with the tests laid down in the Act; and
(c) indicate who will receive objections and representations to the order and be available to discuss any concerns.

4.8.11　Objections

Objections should be made in writing before the date set out in the notice. Objections may be made on the grounds that the tests set out in the Act have not been satisfied, that there are reasons why a path should not be created, diverted or extinguished or that the details of the order are unacceptable.

4.8.12　Unopposed orders

If there are no objections or the objections are withdrawn to the order, it can be confirmed by the local authority.[2] It should determine whether to do so or whether to submit the order to the Secretary of State as soon as reasonably practicable after the time for making representations has expired. Notice of the decision, with reasons, should be given to the applicant and any prescribed persons as soon as practicable after the decision has been made.[3]

Where a determination has not been made within 2 months, beginning with the expiry of the time for making representations, the Secretary of State may, at the request of the person on whose application the order was made, direct the authority to determine the question before the time specified in the direction.[4]

Should the authority want to change the order, it must start the process again and make a new order or submit the order to the Secretary of State (even where there are no objections). He has power to confirm the order with modifications.

1　Rights of Way Review Committee Practice Guidance No 1, Code of Practice on Consultation Over Changes to Rights of Way.
2　Highways Act 1980, Sch 6, para 2(1).
3　Ibid, Sch 6, para 2ZA(1)(2).
4　Ibid, Sch 6, para 2ZA(3).

However, where an application has been made by an owner or occupier of agricultural land, or a school proprietor, the authority may not submit the order to the Secretary of State for confirmation with any modification of the map contained in the order.[1]

4.8.13 Opposed orders

If there are objections to the order, the authority may decide by formal resolution not to proceed with the order.[2] The usual procedure, however, is to refer the order to the Secretary of State for confirmation. The authority should determine whether to submit the order to the Secretary of State as soon as reasonably practicable after the time for making representations has expired. Notice of the decision, with reasons, should be given to the applicant and any prescribed persons as soon as practicable after the decision has been made.[3]

Where a determination has not been made within 2 months, beginning with the expiry of the time for making representations, the Secretary of State may, at the request of the person on whose application the order was made, direct the authority to determine the question before the time specified in the direction.[4]

Where the order is submitted to the Secretary of State, the authority may, in the light of objections received, ask the Secretary of State to modify the order.

The Secretary of State will appoint an inspector to hold a public inquiry or hearing or deal with the matter by written representations.[5] These procedures are discussed in Chapter 6.

The inspector may confirm the order, refuse to confirm it or confirm the order with modifications. If the modifications are not of a minor nature, but, say, affect land not within the original order, the modified order must be re-advertised. If objections are received, a second inquiry may be necessary.

Modifications cannot be made to correct serious legal errors or discrepancies. A new order will have to be made regardless of the merits of the defective order.

4.8.14 Protection of statutory undertakers

The Secretary of State must not make, nor must he or the council confirm, an extinguishment or diversion order where a statutory undertaker has apparatus in the path to be extinguished unless that undertaker consents.[6] The consent must not be unreasonably withheld, but conditions may be imposed for the protection of the equipment.[7] The Minister may determine any question on

---

1   Highways Act 1980, Sch 6, para 2ZB.
2   There is no statutory authority for this power. However, the DOE took the view in Circular 1/83, Annex B, para 4 that this could be done. In *R (Hargrave) v Stroud District Council* [2001] NPC 180, the Court of Appeal upheld this view.
3   Highways Act 1980, Sch 6, para 2ZA(1)(2).
4   Ibid, Sch 6, para 2ZA(3).
5   Ibid, s 302. Local Government Act 1972, s 250.
6   Highways Act 1980, s 121(4).
7   Ibid, s 121(5).

consent and may hold a hearing or inquiry. He must do so if a request is made by the statutory undertakers or by the applicant, where an order has been made on his application, or by the appellant, where the order is to be made on appeal.[1]

4.8.15 Notice of confirmation

Notice of a confirmed order must be given by the authority in the same way as it gave notice of the making of the order.

If the order is not confirmed, the persons and organisations who were given notice of the making of the order must be informed. The authority does not have to publish the decision in the press or put up notices on the path.

4.8.16 Statutory review

The decision to confirm an order made by the inspector may be challenged only where he has exceeded his powers or where the proper procedures have not been followed. This provision has been interpreted to include mistakes of law.

An application to the High Court must be made within 42 days of the decision. The court may quash the decision. The order may not be challenged in any other legal proceedings whatsoever.[2]

4.8.17 Judicial review

Where an inspector decides not to confirm the order the decision may be challenged on the grounds of illegality, irrationality or procedural impropriety,[3] amongst other things. An application for leave for judicial review should be made without delay and in any event within 3 months of the decision.

4.8.18 Effect of the confirmed order

The order may specify when it will come into operation. This may be when the order is confirmed, at a stated time after the confirmation of the order or when certain works have been completed. This applies particularly in development cases. Because of the delay that can arise, a further notice of the coming into operation of the order has to be published to inform the public of the change. If the development is not carried out or the new path is not certified as completed, an order, although confirmed, may never come into operation.

The definitive map and statement is amended after the path order is brought into operation. A legal events modification order is made. Because the order merely records what has already taken place it does not have to be advertised, nor is there any scope for objections.

---

1   Highways Act 1980, s 121(5A), (5B), Sch 12ZA, inserted by the CROW Act 2000, Sch 6.
2   Ibid, Sch 6.
3   *Council of Civil Service Unions v Minister for the Civil Service* [1984] 3 All ER 935, at pp 949–951.

The Ordnance Survey has to be notified of the confirmed order and the date it comes into operation. The alteration will be made to the Ordnance Survey map on the next revision.

Even though it is purely an administrative procedure, there can sometimes be a delay of several years after the public path order is in operation before the legal event order is made. There is a new power, introduced by the CROW Act 2000,[1] whereby joint public path and definitive map orders may be made, thus cutting down delay and bureaucracy.

It is the responsibility of the authority for the area to see that any new path created by order is properly signposted and waymarked. There is no legal obligation to put up notices stating that paths have been closed by orders, although sometimes it would be helpful to do so.

4.9   PLANNING PURPOSES

4.9.1   General principles

Planning permission is generally needed for development. This is defined as:

> 'The carrying out of building, engineering, mining or other operations in, on, over or under land, or the making of any material change in the use of any buildings or other land.'[2]

Certain classes of development covered by a general or special development order do not require planning permission.

The grant of planning permission, whether outline or detailed, does not extinguish or divert any existing public rights of way. Nor does it preclude a modification order being made to add additional public rights of way to the definitive map if their legal existence can be proved.

In the past, the existence of a public right of way may not have been taken into account on an application for planning permission. However, Circular 2/93, 'Public Rights of Way', issued by the former Department of the Environment states:

> 'The Secretaries of State take the view that the effect of development on a public right of way is a material consideration in the determination of applications for planning permission and ask local authorities to ensure that the effect on the right of way is taken into account whenever such applications are considered.'

In addition, the Town and Country Planning General Development Order 1988 requires that a development affecting a public right of way must be advertised in a local newspaper and by posting a notice on the site.

Once planning permission has been obtained, the developer will need to obtain a diversion or extinguishment order before proceeding with the development.

---

1   Schedule 5, para 2, inserting s 53A into the Wildlife and Countryside Act 1981.
2   Town and Country Planning Act 1990, s 55.

He cannot assume that, because he has obtained planning permission, an order will automatically be made and confirmed.

It is possible for a planning permission to be made conditional on a diversion or stopping-up order.[1] However, this is discouraged in Circular 2/93:

> 'Authorities have on occasions granted planning permission on the condition that an order to stop-up or divert a right of way is obtained before the development commences. The Secretaries of State take the view that such a condition is unnecessary in that it duplicates the separate statutory procedure that exists for diverting or stopping up the right of way, and would require the developer to do something outside his or her control.'

Where there is a confirmed diversion order, it will be for the developer to construct any new path. The highway authority or order-making authority must certify that the diverted path has been constructed to a satisfactory standard. Until that certificate is issued, there is no legal change in the right of way even though there is a confirmed order.

4.9.2 Order made by the Secretary of State under s 247 of the Town and Country Planning Act 1990

The Secretary of State has powers to authorise by order[2] the stopping up or diversion of any highway (vehicular routes, bridleways, footpaths), if he is satisfied it is necessary to enable development to be carried out in accordance with planning permission or under a general development order or where permission is not needed (eg where the development is by a government department).

A developer who seeks to persuade the Secretary of State to make the order may be required to meet the expenses incurred by the Secretary of State or the highway authority in making alternative routes or paying compensation to third parties.

An order cannot generally be made unless planning permission has first been obtained. The order must be necessary to enable the development to be carried out. The development must therefore not have been completed before the application is made. It can, however, have been begun and have already blocked the highway.[3]

There are exceptions to the rule that planning permission must be obtained before an order is made. Under s 253, the Secretary of State may make an order in anticipation of planning permission where the application for permission is before him on a call-in[4] or appeal. He may also make an order where the application is made by a local authority, statutory undertaker or British Coal.

---

1   *Grampion Regional Council v City of Aberdeen Council* [1984] JPL 590, see also Circular 11/95: The Use of Conditions in Planning Permissions para 38.
2   The terminology differs. A local authority makes an order and it is confirmed by the authority or the Secretary of State. The Secretary of State proposes to make an order and then makes (rather than confirms) the order.
3   *Ashby v Secretary of State for the Environment* [1980] 1 WLR 673.
4   Under the Town and Country Planning Act 1990, s 77.

4.9.3   Orders made by the local planning authority under s 257 of the Town and Country Planning Act 1990

Although any highway may be diverted or extinguished by the Secretary of State under s 247, orders in respect of footpaths or bridleways may also be made by local planning authorities under s 257. Indeed, in Circular 2/93, the Department of the Environment encourages local planning authorities to make the order.

> 'Orders under section 247 of the 1990 Act can be made by the Secretary of State in appropriate cases, for example, where an application for planning permission is before him, either on appeal or following call-in, and it is considered expedient to invoke the concurrent procedure under section 253 of the Act in anticipation of planning permission. Otherwise, it is only in exceptional circumstances, for example, in relation to development of strategic or national importance, that the Secretaries of State would expect to be asked to exercise this power. It should not be regarded by planning authorities as an alternative to the exercise by them of their Order-making powers under section 257 of the Act. In such circumstances the Secretaries of State expect the authority to make the Order.'

Before making an order under s 257 to divert or close a path, the authority, in making the order, and the Secretary of State, when confirming an order, must be satisfied that it is necessary to do so to enable the development to be carried out and that the development is:

(1) in accordance with a planning permission that has been granted; or
(2) permitted development under a general or special development order; or
(3) to be undertaken by a government department.

Orders are made by the planning authority which granted the permission. No other authority has to be consulted.[1]

4.9.4   The tests

Both the Secretary of State and the planning authority have a discretionary power to stop up or divert paths. They are not under a duty to do so. There are no statutory guidelines as to how they should exercise their discretion. But case-law has made it clear that there is no power to reconsider the merits of the planning permission. Also, the Secretary of State has to take into account the effect the order would have on those entitled to the rights which would be extinguished if the order was made.

4.9.5   The moral

Developers should ascertain what rights of way cross the site at the earliest opportunity. Solutions to the problems they could cause should be sought before a planning application is submitted, otherwise the development may be delayed or, worse, be thwarted completely.

---

1   Procedure is governed by the Town and Country Planning Act 1990, Sch 14 and the Town and Country Planning (Public Path Orders) Regulations 1993, SI 1993/10.

4.9.6 Orders extinguishing or diverting public rights of way crossing or entering proposed highway under s 248 of the Town and Country Planning Act 1990

The Secretary of State may make an order stopping up or diverting a highway which crosses or enters the route of a proposed or improved highway. The Secretary of State must be satisfied that it is expedient to make the order in the interests of the safety of users of the proposed highway or to facilitate the movement of traffic.

This section can be used where ss 14 and 18 of the Highways Act 1980 is not available as the highway is not a special or classified road. See **4.9.1**.

4.9.7 Orders extinguishing vehicular use under s 249 of the Town and Country Planning Act 1990

The local planning authority may apply to the Secretary of State for converting a carriageway to a footpath or bridleway to improve the amenity of the area. Certain classes of vehicle or vehicles belonging to specified persons may be permitted to continue to use the route.

4.9.8 Orders extinguishing public rights of way over land held for planning purposes under ss 251 and 258 of the Town and Country Planning Act 1990

The Secretary of State, for all highways, and the planning authority, for bridleways and byways, may extinguish public rights of way over land which has been acquired or appropriated by a local authority for planning purposes.

The Secretary of State or planning authority must be satisfied that there is or will be an alternative right of way or that one is not required.

4.9.9 Temporary stopping up and diversions for mineral workings under s 261 of the Town and Country Planning Act 1990

Mining comes within the definition of planning and orders to close or divert paths for a specified period may be made under the Town and Country Planning Act 1990. After the minerals have been worked, the route must be restored to a condition not substantially less convenient to the public.

There are special provisions for open-cast coal mining under the Open Cast Coal Act 1958. The Secretary of State may suspend a public right of way if it is a footpath or bridleway. He must be satisfied that an alternative route will be provided or that one is not necessary.

4.10   EXTINGUISHMENTS AND DIVERSIONS FOR OTHER PURPOSES

4.10.1   Road construction

The Secretary of State and highway authorities have power to construct new and improved highways under the Highways Act 1980.[1] This may involve stopping up or diverting existing roads and public rights of way. Orders will be made under s 18 for special roads (motorways) and for trunk and classified roads under s 14.

Orders may authorise a highway authority to stop up, divert, improve, raise, lower or otherwise alter a highway which crosses or enters the new road or is affected by its construction or improvement. A Minister must neither make nor confirm an order, where the original order has been made by the highway authority, unless he is satisfied that another reasonably convenient route is available or will be provided before the road is actually stopped up.

4.10.2   Reservoirs

The Environment Agency and water undertakers are given powers to enable them to carry out works to reservoirs and if necessary to apply to the Secretary of State for an order to stop up or divert public rights of way.[2] Public notice of proposal has to be given with a plan showing the effect the order sought would have on any footpath or bridleways and inquiries may be held by the Secretary of State if there are objections.

4.10.3   Civil aviation

The Secretary of State may stop up or divert any highway if he is satisfied that it is necessary to do so to secure the safe and efficient use of land for civil aviation purposes.[3] The Civil Aviation Authority must own the land or intend to acquire it. The making of the order is subject to special parliamentary procedure.[4] If there are objections, a public local inquiry must be held unless the Secretary of State is satisfied that a public inquiry is unnecessary.

4.10.4   Local authority-owned land

There is provision under the Acquisition of Land Act 1981[5] for an authority acquiring land by compulsory purchase or by agreement where compulsory purchase powers are available to extinguish any footpath or bridleway across the land. Where bridleways or footpaths are extinguished, the local authority

---

1   Highways Act 1980, ss 24 and 62.
2   Water Resources Act 1991, s 168, Sch 10.
3   Civil Aviation Act 1982, s 48. Section 59 of the Airports Act 1986 applies s 48 to land vested in or proposed to be acquired by any relevant airport operator.
4   Statutory Orders (Special Procedure) Act 1945, Sch 1.
5   Section 21.

must secure that an alternative route exists or will be provided or be satisfied that an alternative is not needed.

4.10.5 Urban development

The Secretary of State or local highway authority may make orders extinguishing any highway over land vested in, or acquired by, an urban development corporation,[1] new town development corporation[2] or the Urban Regeneration Agency.[3] The same power exists where the highway authority owns the land, but holds it for new town or urban development corporation purposes.

There is no power for the Secretary of State to make a diversion order.

4.10.6 Housing action trust

Housing action trusts may apply to the Secretary of State for an order extinguishing a right of way.[4]

4.10.7 Slum clearance areas

A housing authority may extinguish a public right of way over land acquired or proposed to be acquired by the authority for slum clearance purposes, subject to approval by the Secretary of State.[5]

4.10.8 Military land

Public rights of way may be closed under the Defence Act 1842[6] and the Defence Act 1860[7] and there is no right of objection. Under the 1842 Act, an alternative route must be provided; under the 1860 Act, there is a power but not a duty to do so.

The Military Lands Act 1892[8] applies s 116 of the Highways Act 1980 to enable the stopping up or diverting of a footpath on the ground that the highway crosses or runs inconveniently or dangerously near to military land. However, the magistrates' court must not make an order authorising the stopping up or diversion of the footpath unless it is satisfied that a new footpath will be substituted or that the diverted footpath will be as convenient for the public.

Paths may also be stopped up and diverted, on a temporary or permanent basis, under the Land Powers (Defence) Act 1958 where land is to be used by the Secretary of State for defence purposes, or is to be used by a manufacturer of

---

1   Local Government and Planning Act 1980, Sch 28, para 11.
2   New Towns Act 1981, s 23.
3   Housing and Urban Development Act 1993.
4   Housing Act 1988, Sch 10.
5   Housing Act 1985, s 294.
6   Section 16.
7   Section 40.
8   Section 13 as amended by the Highways Act 1959, Sch 22, London Government Act 1963, s 16(2), Highways Act 1980, Sch 24.

aircraft as an airfield, wholly or mainly in connection with the manufacture of aircraft for defence purposes. The Secretary of State has to be satisfied that the highway should be stopped up or diverted so that the land may be used efficiently without danger to the public. The powers used for such stopping-up or diversion orders are those contained in the Town and Country Planning Act 1990.

4.11   TEMPORARY DIVERSIONS AND CLOSURES

4.11.1   Temporary diversions and engineering work

Statutes allow for temporary diversions for specific purposes. These include diversions of footpaths and bridleways for up to 3 months in connection with any excavation or engineering operation that is reasonably necessary for agricultural purposes. The highway authority will make an order, but it does not have to be advertised, nor is there any opportunity for objections to be made. A notice and plan must be displayed at either end of the diversion whilst it is in force.[1]

4.11.2   Traffic regulations for road works

Temporary diversions or closures may be made under traffic regulation orders by a highway authority to enable works to be carried out on or near the road or because of danger to the public.[2] There is a power to make temporary diversions where a highway is about to be repaired or widened.[3]

4.11.3   Animal disease and plant health

The Department of the Environment, Food and Rural Affairs (DEFRA) may prohibit entry to a notified area infected by certain animal diseases, such as foot and mouth disease, or plant diseases like rhizomania.[4] Public rights of way in the notified area may not be used. Contravention of any orders made by DEFRA will be an offence carrying a fine.

4.11.4   Dangerous works

The CROW Act 2000 introduces a new power to make temporary diversions.[5] An occupier of land may divert on a temporary basis that part of a footpath or bridleway where works, of a kind to be specified in regulations, are likely to cause danger to users of a right of way. In order to give effect to the diversion,

---

1   Highways Act, s 135, as amended by the Rights of Way Act 1990.
2   Road Traffic Regulation Act 1984, s 24.
3   Highways Act 1980, s 122.
4   Animal Health Act 1981, s 23. Foot and Mouth Disease Order 1983; SI 1983/1950 as amended; Plant Health (Great Britain) Order 1987, SI 1987/1758; Plant Health (Great Britain) Amendment Order 1989, SI 1989/553.
5   Schedule 6, para 16, inserting ss 135A and 135B into the Highways Act 1980.

he may divert other parts of the path, in so far as it passes over other land occupied by him.

The occupier may not divert any part of the path for more than 14 days in any one calendar year. If different parts of the same path are diverted, the diversions in total must not exceed 14 days.

The diversion must be reasonably convenient for the exercise of the right of way and the line of the path must be indicated on the ground to not less than the minimum width. The minimum width for footpaths is one metre for a crossfield path and 1.5 metres for a field edge path. For a bridleway, it is 2 metres for a crossfield path and 3 metres for any other bridleway.

A right of way cannot be diverted onto land occupied by that other person without that person's consent and the consent of any other person whose consent is necessary to obtain access to it. The diversion of a footpath cannot be onto another highway unless that highway is a footpath or a bridleway. A bridleway may not be diverted onto a highway other than a bridleway.

The occupier must give the local highway authority, and where the footpath or bridleway passes over or is contiguous with access land, the Countryside Agency or the Countryside Council for Wales, at least 14 days' notice in the prescribed form of the proposed diversion. Notice of the diversion must be published in a local paper at least 7 days before it takes effect. The occupier must also display notices in the places, manner and for the periods which are to be specified in regulations.

It is an offence to make a false statement in a notice, to display a notice falsely indicating that the diversion is an authorised diversion, or to make a diversion which is not reasonably convenient for public use or which does not indicate the line on the ground to the required minimum width.

Before the end of the period authorised by the diversion, the occupier must make good any damage to the original path and remove any obstructions caused by the prescribed works. It is an offence not to comply with these requirements. On default by the occupier, the highway authority has power to do the work and to recover from him their expenses in so doing. It has power to authorise anyone to enter the land with vehicles, machinery and other equipment necessary to do the work. The authority should give the occupier at least 24 hours' notice of their proposed entry together with details of the path to which the notice relates, the work to be done, equipment to be used, route to be taken to access the path, and the date and time of the proposed entry.

An occupier remains liable for anything done on the footpath or bridleway, other than the authorised works. He is not authorised to interfere with the apparatus or works of any statutory undertakers.

It is the duty of the highway authority to enforce these provisions, but this is without prejudice to its general duty to assert and protect the rights of the public to the use and enjoyment of the highway.

Sections 135A and 135B do not apply in the Isles of Scilly unless an order is made by the Secretary of State after consultation with the Council of the Isles.[1]

---

1   Schedule 5, para 2, inserting s 53A into the Wildlife and Countryside Act 1981.

Chapter 5

RECORDING RIGHTS OF WAY

5.1 THE DEFINITIVE MAP AND STATEMENT

5.1.1 Purpose

The definitive map and statement is a record maintained by the county council of the public rights of way within its area. The purpose is to make sure that public rights of way are properly identified and do not disappear through neglect.

The recording of rights of way must be distinguished from public path orders which are made under the Highways Act 1980. The definitive map is concerned with recording existing rights, rather than creating new ones.

5.1.2 The map

The definitive map is based on an Ordnance Survey map which may be drawn to a scale of 1:10,000 or to a smaller scale of 2½ inches to the mile. It will show by special designation footpaths, bridleways, roads used as public paths and byways open to all traffic.[1]

The CROW Act 2000 gives the Secretary of State or National Assembly for Wales power to prescribe the scale of the definitive map for any purpose under Part III of the Wildlife and Countryside Act 1981 (WLCA 1981).[2]

5.1.3 The statement

The statement which accompanies the definitive map may contain particulars relating to the position and width of the path or any limitations or conditions affecting the right of way. Some of the statements are based on information supplied by the parish council surveys. It is sometimes difficult to establish whether the parish council was merely recording the physical features on the ground or was stating that a right of way was dedicated subject to a particular obstruction. There may be similar problems with width. The statement may indicate a legal width or merely describe the features on the ground at particular points.

---

1   WLCA 1981, s 57(2). Wildlife and Countryside Act 1981 (Definitive Maps and Statements) Regulations 1993, SI 1993/12.
2   Section 51, Sch 5, para 7.

5.1.4   Conflict between the map and the statement

There may be a conflict between the position of the path shown on the map and its description in the statement. There is no case-law which decides which is to prevail. However, on general principles, the statement should prevail.[1] This is particularly so where a small-scale map is used. For instance, an Ordnance Survey map of a scale of 1:10,560 means that 0.474 millimetres on the map is 5 metres on the ground.

5.2   HISTORY OF THE DEFINITIVE MAP

5.2.1   National Parks and Access to the Countryside Act 1949

The National Parks and Access to the Countryside Act 1949 (NPACA 1949) introduced the system for registering public footpaths and bridleways and roads used as public paths on county definitive maps made and maintained by the county councils as highway authorities.[2] The NPACA 1949 provided for surveys of paths by county councils after consultation with parish councils and district councils. The survey was followed by the preparation of draft maps to which objections could be made.[3] After the objections and appeals had been settled, provisional maps had to be published. It was open to owners, occupiers and lessees to challenge them by way of an application to Quarter Sessions with a further right of appeal to the Crown Court.[4] After all appeals had been determined, or the time for making such appeals had lapsed, a definitive map and statement had to be published. Thereafter there was a 6-week period when the map or statement could be challenged on the ground that the powers contained in the NPACA 1949 had been exceeded or the proper procedures had not been followed.[5]

The survey was optional in London and the county boroughs. County councils were also able to omit built-up areas from their surveys.

The NPACA 1949 provided that the county definitive maps should be reviewed at least every 5 years by county councils. The review had to be for the whole county at the same time. The maps would be altered if public rights of way had been created or extinguished since the preparation of the map or last review.[6] It was also possible to add paths which had been mistakenly omitted from the original draft map, but there was no provision for removing paths which had been incorrectly included. Nor was there any requirement that a landowner be given notice that rights were to be recorded across his land, either when the map was originally published or on its review.

---

1   See Paul Coughlan 'Definitive Map and Statement', RWLR 8.1.
2   Section 27.
3   Section 28. National Parks and Access to the Countryside Regulations 1950, SI 1950/1066.
4   NPACA 1949, s 31; Public Rights of Way (Applications to Quarter Sessions) Regulations 1952, SI 1952/55, as amended.
5   NPACA 1949, Schedule 1, Pt III, para 10.
6   Ibid, s 33.

5.2.2 Countryside Act 1968

The Countryside Act 1968 (CA 1968) made some important changes concerning the preparation and revision of definitive maps. It became possible to amend the definitive map to delete paths where there was new evidence discovered by the authority or evidence not previously considered that there was no public right of way of the status shown on the definitive map.[1] These new powers of revision applied only to reviews carried out after the commencement of the CA 1968 and were subject to an important limitation. No evidence could be taken into account which the surveying authority was satisfied could have been produced by the person prejudiced at the time of the preparation of the original map, unless there was a reasonable excuse for failing to do so. This is an important point when considering why a landowner may not have taken some steps to rectify the definitive map under the CA 1968. The review process was also revised so that it was no longer necessary to go through the three-stage process of draft, provisional and definitive map.[2]

One of the most important changes introduced by the CA 1968 was the provision for a special review to reclassify roads used as a public path so that they became either footpaths, bridleways or byways open to all traffic. This could be part of the normal review process or a limited special review dealing solely with reclassification of RUPPs.[3]

5.2.3 Local Government Act 1972

The Local Government Act 1972 abolished county boroughs and reorganised many county boundaries. Many new county councils found that there were within their boundaries areas which had reached different stages in the production of definitive maps and statements.

The new county councils were required to continue any survey or review in progress on 1 April 1974 and to abandon and start again any review for which no revised draft map had been published. They had the option of abandoning and starting again a survey or a review in which a draft map or a revised draft map, but not a provisional or revised provisional map, had been published by 1 April 1974. Once the council had definitive maps for the entire area, a review of the whole of the county had to be carried out.[4]

5.2.4 Wildlife and Countryside Act 1981

The preparation and revision of definitive maps was a very slow process. Although the revision of maps had been speeded up by the simpler procedures introduced by CA 1968, the preparation of maps which had begun before the 1968 Act came into force was still subject to the three-stage process of NPACA 1949. WLCA 1981 therefore introduced a system of continuous review.

---

1   Countryside Act 1968, s 31, Sch 3, Pt I.
2   Ibid, Sch 3, Pt II.
3   Ibid, Sch 3, Pt III.
4   Local Government Act 1972, Sch 17, Pt II.

WLCA 1981 for the first time imposed an obligation on the applicant for a modification order to serve a notice on every owner or occupier of any land to which the application related.[1]

5.2.5   Countryside and Rights of Way Act 2000

The CROW Act 2000 has introduced three useful reforms in relation to definitive maps and statements. First, a surveying authority (normally the unitary authority, or the county council where there are two tiers of local government) has power to include in legal event orders, that is where a highway is stopped up, diverted, widened or extended, changed in status, or created, as the result of the coming into operation of any enactment, instrument or other event, provision to alter the definitive map at the same time.[2] The Secretary of State may make regulations specifying the type of order which will be covered and the procedures to be followed. This reform should reduce bureaucracy and delay. In the past, sometimes no modification order was made for several years after the legal event order.

An authority may at any time before an order comes into operation, and is under a duty to do so if the order becomes subject to special parliamentary procedure, withdraw an order and substitute for it an order without the modification of the definitive map provisions. Where modification provisions are included there is no need for confirmation of those provisions.

The second reform allows surveying authorities to produce consolidated definitive maps and statements comprising maps and statements which have been made for different parts of their areas, including partial maps and statements inherited from other surveying authorities.[3] This may have occurred as a consequence of government reorganisation. There is no power to create a single definitive map and statement if any parts of the area have no definitive map at all. Nor may maps be consolidated where any orders making changes to the definitive map are outstanding.

The relevant date for the purpose of the consolidated maps and statement will be the date determined by the authority, not being earlier than 6 months before their preparation.

Every surveying authority is under a duty to take steps to bring the preparation of consolidated maps and statements to the attention of the public. A copy of the maps which are superseded by the consolidated map must be kept available for public inspection.[4]

The third reform is that every surveying authority is under a duty to keep a register of applications to modify the definitive map.[5] Regulations will

---

1   WLCA 1981, Sch 14, para 2.
2   Section 51, Sch 5, para 2; WLCA 1981, s 53A.
3   CROW Act 2000, Sch 5, paras 7(5) and 8. This power may still be exercised, even if the local authority has not reclassified all RUPPs under WLCA 1981, s 54.
4   WLCA 1981, s 57(6).
5   CROW Act 2000, Sch 5, para 2.

prescribe what information must be shown on the register. The register must be available for inspection free of charge at all reasonable hours. This provision deals with a problem encountered by landowners, and especially potential purchasers. Having made a local authority search, they often subsequently discover that an order is made to add an additional path to the definitive map or upgrade an existing one. The register will give them information as to whether it is likely that an order may be made in the near future.

5.2.6 London

London has had special treatment under the legislation. NPACA 1949 did not impose a duty on the London County Council to prepare definitive maps. The London Government Act 1963 abolished the London County Council and established 32 London boroughs. These new boroughs became the surveying authorities. The outer London boroughs were required to continue with the procedures for definitive maps if NPACA 1949 applied to the predecessor authority. However, 'any area, which immediately before 1 April 1965, formed part of the administrative county of London' was excluded from the duty. London Borough Councils can, however, opt into the provisions.[1]

5.2.7 Definition

Because of the complex legislative history of the preparation of definitive maps, the definition of the definitive map and statement in relation to any area is:

'(a) the latest revised map and statement prepared in definitive form for that area under s 33 of the 1949 Act; or

(b) where no such map and statement have been so prepared, the original definitive map and statement prepared for that area under s 32 of that Act; or

(c) where no such map and statement have been so prepared, the map and statement prepared for that area under s 55(3).'[2]

5.2.8 Importance of history

An understanding of the procedures under NPACA 1949 and CA 1968 is important when claims are made under current legislation to correct the definitive map. It may be, for instance, that the landowner had no knowledge of rights being claimed over his land or the case-law at the time precluded greater rights being claimed by users.[3]

---

1 WLCA 1981, s 58.
2 Ibid, s 53(1).
3 For a discussion of the history see the Court of Appeal judgments in *R v Secretary of State for the Environment ex parte Sims and Burrows* [1991] 2 QB 354.

5.3   DUTIES OF THE SURVEYING AUTHORITY

5.3.1   To prepare a definitive map

WLCA 1981 provided that there should be no more surveys or reviews under NPACA 1949. Where on that date a surveying authority[1] had not completed a survey or review begun earlier, the Secretary of State could after consultation with the surveying authority direct that the survey or review be completed or abandoned either wholly or in part.[2]

Where a survey had not been begun or having been begun, was abandoned, the surveying authority was under a duty to prepare a map and statement for the relevant area. It had to modify the map and statement to give effect to any final decisions made under the earlier legislation.[3]

5.3.2   To keep the definitive map and statement under review

The surveying authority is under a duty to keep the map up to date and to take account of events before the coming into force of WLCA 1981 as well as subsequently.[4]

Alterations to the map are made by means of modification orders. There are powers for a surveying authority to prepare an updated version of the map incorporating the modification orders. The authority must keep a register of applications for modification orders.[5]

5.3.3   To reclassify RUPPs

RUPP (road used as a public path) was a term introduced by NPACA 1949 and was defined as 'highway, other than a public path, used by the public mainly for the purposes for which footpaths or bridleways are so used.'[6] Although the definition implied that such a right of way was subject to vehicular rights, NPACA 1949 provided that the showing of a way as a RUPP on the definitive map was conclusive evidence only of the public's rights to use it on foot or on horseback.[7] It was therefore uncertain whether there were rights for vehicles or not. It appears that in preparing the definitive map under NPACA 1949, local authorities were confused. Sometimes the term RUPP was used when a public footpath or public bridleway existed over a private road.

---

1   County Council, Welsh Council, Metropolitan District Councils, London Borough
     Council. WLCA 1981, s 66(1) as amended by the Local Government Act 1985, s 7,
     Sch 3. Local Government (Wales) Act 1994, Sch 16.
2   WLCA 1981, s 55.
3   Under NPACA 1949, s 29(3), (4), (6). CA 1968, Sch 3, Part II, para 4(4).
4   WLCA 1981, s 53(2)(a).
5   CROW Act 2000, s 51, Sch 5, para 2, introducing s 53B into the Highways Act 1980.
6   NPACA 1949, s 27(6).
7   Ibid, s 32(4)(b).

Because of the confusion, CA 1968[1] provided that RUPPs should be reclassified. In making a reclassification the highway authority had to consider whether:

(a) any vehicular rights of way had been shown to exist;
(b) it was suitable for vehicles having regard to its position and width, its condition and state of repair, and the nature of the soil; and
(c) if it had been used by vehicular traffic, whether the extinguishment of vehicular rights would cause undue hardship.

CA 1968, which was meant to clarify the position, in fact turned out to make the situation much more confusing. A circular from the Ministry of Housing and Local Government stated:

> 'The fact that a road may not be suitable for all traffic need not deter the authority from an initial classification as a byway open to all traffic.'[2]

However, this statement was disapproved by a Court of Appeal decision because CA 1968 specifically stated that (b) and (c) above had to be taken into account when deciding status.[3]

CA 1968 also failed to make clear whether the vehicular rights were extinguished for ever where a RUPP was reclassified as a bridleway on the ground that it was not suitable for vehicles. If the reclassification does not have this effect, there seems little point in reclassifying the route as a bridleway. On the other hand, there are dicta in two cases which suggest that vehicular rights cannot be taken away unless there is an express statutory provision to that effect.[4]

A further problem was highlighted in *R v Secretary of State for the Environment, ex parte Hood.*[5] A RUPP was reclassified as a footpath. This was challenged by the British Horse Society on the ground that there was no power to do this and it should have been reclassified as a bridleway. The Court of Appeal held that as NPACA 1949 provided that the entry of a RUPP was conclusive evidence of bridleway rights, in the absence of new evidence or of evidence not previously considered by the surveying authority, the RUPP should not be reclassified as a footpath.

A third attempt was therefore made to deal with the problem of RUPPs in WLCA 1981.

Section 54 of WLCA 1981 imposes a duty on the authority to reclassify RUPPs on the basis of rights which are shown to exist. The presumption is that a RUPP has bridleway status. If there are vehicular rights, then they must be proved or if there are footpath rights only, this too must be proved. To do this it has to be

---

1 Schedule 3, para 10.
2 Minister of Housing and Local Government Circular 44/68, para 6.
3 *Pearson v Secretary of State for the Environment* (1981) 42 P&CR 40.
4 *Fowler v Secretary of State for the Environment and Devon County Council* (1992) 64
    P&CR 16. In *R v Secretary of State for the Environment ex parte Riley* (1990) 59 P&CR 1,
    the matter was left undecided being unnecessary for the decision.
5 [1975] 1 QB 891.

shown that bridleway rights do not exist. This gives statutory effect to the decision in *R v Secretary of State for the Environment ex parte Hood*.

The purpose of the reclassification is to establish the existing position and to record the public rights accurately. It is not a process for creating or downgrading existing rights. The procedure for making a reclassification order is the same as making a modification order except that there is no formal application. The authority is under a duty to make an order. It is not an option.

The duty to reclassify will cease when s 47 of the CROW Act 2000 comes into force.

5.3.4　To inform the public of the redesignation of RUPPs as restricted byways

The CROW Act 2000 provides that, on the coming into force of s 47 of the Act, s 54 of WLCA 1981, which imposes the duty on surveying authorities to reclassify RUPPs, will be repealed. Instead, every way which immediately before the commencement of the section was shown on the definitive map as a RUPP is to be treated as if it were shown as a restricted byway. The term 'road used as a public path' must not be used as a description of a way on any definitive map or statement.

The Countryside Commission (now the Countryside Agency) had originally recommended that all RUPPs should be reclassified as Byways Open to All Traffic (BOATs). The Government in its consultation paper in July 1999 recommended that they should be reclassified as bridleways. The restricted byway is a compromise.

Every surveying authority is under a duty to take such steps as it considers expedient for bringing to the attention of the public the automatic conversion of RUPPs to restricted byways.

5.4　RESTRICTED BYWAYS

On a restricted byway the public have a right of way on foot, on horseback or leading a horse, and a right for vehicles other than mechanically propelled vehicles.[1] A mechanically propelled vehicle does not include an electrically assisted pedal cycle. The rights are referred to in the CROW Act 2000 as restricted byway rights. The public may also have a right to drive animals of any description along a restricted byway. Such rights would have to be proved.

A highway can be a restricted byway even if it is at the side of a river, canal or other inland navigation and the public have the right to use it in connection with navigation.

Although a RUPP becomes a restricted byway, this is without prejudice to any greater rights. Where there is evidence that rights existed immediately before

---

1　CROW Act 2000, s 48; WLCA 1981, s 53(4A), (4B).

the commencement of s 47 and continue to exist for mechanically propelled vehicles, an application should be made for a modification order upgrading the restricted byway to a BOAT. This procedure is also available to alter the status of footpaths and bridleways which have been reclassified under earlier legislation relating to RUPPs.

There will be no restricted byway rights where immediately before the commencement of s 47 there was no public right of way.[1] Although entry on the definitive map as a RUPP would confer a legal right of way by virtue of s 56 of WLCA 1981, it must be assumed that this subsection means this is to occur where it can be shown that no entry should have been made.

Restricted byway rights are subject to any enactment or instrument, whether coming into operation before or after the commencement of s 47 and to any legal event order whereby a highway is authorised to be stopped up, diverted, widened or extended or becomes a public path.

Under s 53(5) of WLCA 1981, any person may apply for a modification order if evidence is discovered which shows that the map is wrong. The right is triggered by the discovery of evidence. Evidence which has already been considered is not sufficient on its own for making an application. However, where there is a claim for vehicular rights over a restricted byway, the evidence is treated as not having been discovered before the section creating restricted byway rights came into force.

The effect of the statutory redesignation is that it will no longer be possible to apply for a modification order to downgrade a restricted byway to a bridleway or footpath. It will, however, be possible for modification orders to remove a restricted byway from the definitive map where there is evidence that there was no right of way. Transitional provisions protect reclassification and modification orders for downgradings, and applications for such orders, made before the section is brought into force. The public right of way will have the rights which are confirmed by those orders and will not have restricted byway rights.

Restricted byway rights are subject to any condition or limitation to which the RUPP was subject. Examples might be a dedication subject to a right to plough or erect a gate. There is also a specific provision for owners or lessees of adjoining or adjacent premises to have a right of way for vehicular and all other kinds of traffic over the relevant highway for the reasonable enjoyment and occupation of the premises. A relevant highway is one which becomes maintainable at public expense for the first time because of the automatic redesignation of RUPPs as restricted highways. Presumably the reason this section is considered necessary is that before the right of way became publicly maintainable, the surface was vested in the landowner. He could therefore use the land for his own purposes provided they did not amount to an interference with the public rights. However, once there is a statutory transfer of the surface to the highway authority, any unauthorised use of the surface would amount to a trespass.

---

1   CROW Act 2000, s 48(3).

The Secretary of State has power to make consequential amendments by statutory instrument approved by a resolution of each House of Parliament in any enactment contained in an Act passed before or in the same session as the CROW Act 2000 or in any subordinate legislation.[1] He also has power to make regulations to provide that existing legislation applying to highways, or highways of a particular kind, for example to footpaths or bridleways, should apply or not apply to restricted byways or ways shown on the definitive map as restricted byways. He could under this power enable restricted byways to be created, diverted or stopped up. The National Assembly for Wales may submit proposals to the Secretary of State relating to the exercise of these powers.

Before making regulations which have effect in Wales, the Secretary of State is required to consult the National Assembly for Wales and, where the regulations will amend or revoke secondary legislation made by the Assembly, obtain its consent.

The National Assembly for Wales may amend by regulation any local or private Act relating only to Wales passed before or in the same session as the CROW Act 2000 to take account of restricted byways. It may also amend for the same purpose any existing subordinate legislation which it has power to amend or revoke as respects Wales.

5.5   EFFECT OF DEFINITIVE MAP AND STATEMENT

5.5.1   The definitive map

The effect of the entry of a route on the definitive map is that it is conclusive evidence of the existence and status of the public right of way at the relevant date.[2]

If a way is shown as:

(1) *a footpath* – it is conclusive evidence that the public had a right of way on foot at the relevant date but without prejudice to the existence of any greater rights;[3]
(2) *a bridleway* – it is conclusive evidence that the public had a right of way on foot, on horseback and leading a horse at the relevant date but without prejudice to the existence of any greater rights. It does not provide conclusive evidence for any rights for bicycles, although use of bicycles is permitted by s 30 of the Countryside Act 1968;[4]

---

1   CROW Act 2000, s 52.
2   WLCA 1981, s 56; CROW Act 2000, s 48.
3   Under s 32(4)(a) of the NPACA 1949 there was no reference to the entry being without prejudice to any greater rights. In *Suffolk County Council v Mason* [1979] AC 705, the House of Lords therefore held that the entry of a footpath on the definitive map was conclusive evidence that only footpath rights existed. *R v Devon County Council, ex parte Fowler* [1991] JPL 520 held that showing a footpath under ss 32(4)(a) did not have the effect of extinguishing higher rights.
4   WLCA 1981, s 66(3).

(3) *a RUPP* – it is conclusive evidence that the public had a right of way on foot, on horseback and leading a horse at the relevant date but without prejudice to any greater rights;

(4) *a restricted byway* – it is conclusive evidence that the public had a right of way on foot, on horseback and leading a horse and for vehicles other than mechanically propelled vehicles at the relevant date but without prejudice to any greater rights;

(5) *a BOAT* – it is conclusive evidence that the public had a right of way on foot, on horseback and in or on vehicles including motor vehicles and pedal cycles at the relevant date.

'The relevant date' is the date of the survey on which the map was prepared or modified. It depends on whether the route was shown as a result of:

(a) the preparation or revision of the definitive map under NPACA 1949, or a consolidated or new map prepared under WLCA 1981, or

(b) as a result of a modification order under WLCA 1981.

Where a new, revised or consolidated map is prepared, the relevant date is the date specified in the statement which must not be earlier than 6 months before the date on which notice of the preparation of the draft map or review was published under NPACA 1949[1] or, where the map is prepared under WLCA 1981, not earlier than 6 months before the preparation of the map.[2] Modification orders will state the relevant date which must be more than 6 months before the making of the order.

A right of way recorded on the definitive map has legal existence even if it has no physical existence on the ground and even if the entry was made in error. It is, however, possible to apply to modify the definitive map to remove or downgrade a public right of way. Until the order is confirmed the right of way will continue to have legal existence.

On the other hand, the map is a statement of minimum rights only. It does not preclude the existence of perfectly valid greater rights, even before they are recorded. These rights may have existed before the relevant date or arisen subsequently.

A person therefore may be able to show that a bridleway or RUPP has in fact vehicular rights. If he could do this he would have had a legal right to drive on the route even though no BOAT was recorded on the definitive map. However, the position has now been altered by Sch 7 to the CROW Act 2000. The Act has amended s 34 of the Road Traffic Act 1988 to make it an offence to drive on a footpath, bridleway or restricted byway and has provided that limited categories of persons only are entitled to claim higher rights. See **9.8.2**.

Such additional rights must be proved. If evidence comes to light an application should be made for a modification order to the definitive map to record the correct rights.

---

1   NPACA 1949, ss 27(3) and 34.
2   WLCA 1981, s 57(4).

5.5.2   The statement

The statement is conclusive evidence of any particulars contained in the statement as to the position or width at the relevant date, provided that a public right of way is shown on the definitive map.[1] However, this is without prejudice to other limitations or conditions. A landowner could therefore claim that there are additional limitations or conditions.

5.6   OCCASIONS FOR MAKING THE ORDER

5.6.1   Legal event orders

A modification order should be made to record that the status of the highway has been changed through the coming into operation of any enactment or instrument or any other event, both before and after the commencement date of WLCA 1981. These events are divided into three.[2]

The first one is where the highway has been authorised to be stopped up, diverted, widened or extended.

A stopping-up or diversion order will usually be made under the Highways Act 1980. There are powers under the same Act to widen a public path, but in order to effect such a widening it may be necessary to get the agreement of the adjoining landowner or to have a compulsory purchase order or public path creation order. If the path were to be extended then a creation agreement or order would be necessary.

The second category of legal events is where a highway of a particular description has ceased to be a highway of that description. This would cover greater rights over a footpath or bridleway created by agreement or order or where the path has been downgraded as a result of an order.

The third category of rights is where the new right of way, being a public path (ie footpath or bridleway), has been created either by agreement or order.

The new s 53A of WLCA 1981[3] makes it possible for surveying authorities to include in legal event orders provisions to modify the definitive map and statement without the need for a separate modification order. Regulations will prescribe which orders will be covered by the section and the procedure to be followed.

5.6.2   Deemed dedication

Where a right of way has been used by the public without force, secrecy or permission for a period of at least 20 years and there is not sufficient evidence of lack of intention to dedicate, there is a statutory presumption that the way has

---

1   WLCA 1981, s 56(1)(e).
2   Ibid, s 53(3)(a)(i), (ii), (iii).
3   Inserted by the CROW Act 2000, s 51, Sch 5, para 2.

been dedicated as a highway.[1] If this use of a public path is established a modification order may be made. It is usual, however, for applications for modification orders to be made on a combination of use and documentary evidence.

Even if it is user alone, reliance can be placed on s 53(3)(c) as well as s 53(3)(b) of WLCA 1981.[2] There may be an advantage in relying on s 53(3)(c), where the test is that the path is reasonably alleged to subsist, rather than on s 53(3)(b), where user for the requisite period must be shown.

5.6.3 Discovery of evidence

If evidence is discovered by the authority showing that a right of way should be added to the map, that status should be altered or that there is no public right of way, a modification order may be made.[3]

In *Rubinstein v Secretary of State for the Environment*,[4] because s 56 of WLCA 1981 made definitive maps conclusive as to the rights of way recorded, there was no right to delete or downgrade a right of way. However, *R v Secretary of State for the Environment ex parte Sims and Burrows*[5] overruled *Rubinstein v Secretary of State for the Environment* and held that s 53(3)(c)(ii) and (iii) enabled the map to be revised to delete or downgrade paths which were wrongly recorded. The error did not have to have arisen after the map was prepared. It could have arisen previously but the evidence of error must have been discovered subsequently.

As a result of this case, the Department of the Environment in its Circular 18/90 issued guidance stating that compelling evidence would be required to remove a path from the map. In *Trevelyan v Secretary of State for the Environment, Transport and the Regions*,[6] the Court of Appeal approved this statement. Lord Phillips MR said:

'Where the Secretary of State or an inspector appointed by him has to consider whether a right of way that is marked on a definitive map in fact exists, he must start with an initial presumption that it does. If there were no evidence which made it reasonably arguable that such a right of way existed, it should not have been marked on the map. In the absence of evidence to the contrary, it should be assumed that the proper procedures were followed and thus that such evidence existed. At the end of the day, when all the evidence has been considered, the standard of proof required to justify a finding that no right of way exists is no more than the balance of probabilities. But evidence of some substance must be put in the balance, if it is to outweigh the initial presumption that the right of way exists. Proof of a negative is seldom easy, and the more time that elapses, the more difficult will be the task of adducing the positive evidence that is necessary to

---

1   WLCA 1981, s 53(3).
2   *O'Keefe v Secretary of State for the Environment and Isle of Wight County Council* [1996] JPL 42 at 48.
3   WLCA 1981, s 53(3)(a).
4   (1987) 57 P&CR 111.
5   [1991] 3 WLR 1070.
6   [2001] 1 WLR 1264.

establish that a right of way that has been marked on a definitive map has been marked there by mistake.'

The word used in the section is 'discovered' and so some fresh evidence must be produced which was not considered when the definitive map was prepared or revised. 'Discovered' has been interpreted by the courts to mean 'The finding of some information which was previously unknown'.[1] It does not matter if the evidence was available in the county council's archives if it was not actually considered.

The new evidence does not of itself have to be sufficient to alter the designation on the map. This is because the statute says that it is 'the discovery by the authority of evidence which (when considered with all other relevant evidence available to them)', that a particular entry was incorrect. Therefore evidence which was previously considered may be re-evaluated in the light of the new evidence.[2]

The wording in s 53(3)(c) of the WLCA 1981 for: (a) the entry of an additional right; or (b) the altering of the status of the right or the deletion of a highway, is slightly different. In the case of the discovery of evidence relating to an additional right of way the wording is:

'(1) That a right of way which is not shown on the map and statement subsists or is reasonably alleged to subsist over land in the area to which the map relates.'

Therefore, it is not necessary to show that the right of way subsists but merely that it is reasonably alleged to subsist.

The cases[3] which highlight this distinction were concerned with the order making stage not the confirmation of the order. In both cases a local authority had refused to make an order so the applicants applied to the Secretary of State under Sch 14 to the WLCA 1981 for him to direct the Councils to make the order. The Secretary of State refused to do so. The court held that, if there were conflicting evidence but a right of way was reasonably alleged to subsist, the Secretary of State should have given the direction. It was not for him to consider the merits of the case. This was a matter for a public inquiry when the evidence of both sides could be tested. The Secretary of State's decision was therefore quashed. The question remains whether at confirmation stage the test should be that on the balance of probabilities a right of way does subsist, rather than is reasonably alleged to subsist. No help is provided by the wording of the legislation itself, but the reasoning of the judges in the two cases suggests that the answer should be in the affirmative.[4]

---

1   *R v Secretary of State for the Environment ex parte Sims and Burrows* [1991] 3 WLR 1070; *R v Secretary of State for the Environment ex parte Riley* (1989) 59 P&CR 1. See also *Fowler v Secretary of State for the Environment and Devon County Council* (1991) 54 P&CR 16, 22.

2   *Mayhew v Secretary of State for the Environment* (1992) 65 P&CR 344.

3   *R v Secretary of State for the Environment ex parte Bagshaw*; sub nom *R v Secretary of State for the Environment ex parte Norton* (1994) 68 P&CR 402; *R v Secretary of State for Wales ex parte Emery* [1998] 4 All ER 367.

4   See George Laurence 'Definitive Map – Continuous Review' RWLR 8.2, p 63.

The test of assigning a different status to a highway, or removing it altogether, is more stringent than that in s 53(3)(c)(i). The wording is as follows:

> '(ii) that a highway shown in the map and statement that a highway of a particular description ought to be there shown as a highway of a different description; or
> (iii) that there is no public right of way over land shown in the map and statement as a highway of any description or any other particulars contained in the map and statement require modification.'

There are also provisions to make modifications to the statement accompanying the definitive map. These include the addition to the statement of particulars as to the position and width of any public path or BOAT and any limitations or conditions affecting the public right of way thereover.

It would, therefore, seem that it would be possible under s 53 to modify the map to show a different route for the public right of way. There is a very confusing case, *R v Secretary of State for the Environment ex parte Kent County Council*,[1] in which the judge upheld the inspector's refusal to make an order deleting a route under s 53 where part of the route of the path was uncertain. As a matter of principle, it would seem that, if part of the route is uncertain, then that part should not continue to have existence as a public right of way.

5.7   CUT-OFF DATES FOR DEFINITIVE MAP

5.7.1   Purpose

One of the problems about definitive maps is that they are conclusive as to what is recorded but not as to what is not. A purchaser may buy land, having made all the standard searches and inquiries and find shortly after he has completed his purchase that there are perfectly valid additional rights of way or rights of a higher status than those recorded. The claim to the rights may be based on documents in local records offices or on user which occurred many years ago. The CROW Act 2000[2] has dealt with the problem by setting a cut-off date for the recording of certain rights of way on the definitive map and also for downgrading of bridleways. This will make the definitive map a more accurate record of the rights of way which have legal validity.

5.7.2   BOATs

Where there is no highway shown on the definitive map, a new BOAT cannot be added after 1 January 2026.[3] However, any vehicular rights will not be extinguished. This means that claims for vehicular use could be claimed if, say, evidence was produced of a carriageway validly set out under an Inclosure Award.

---

1   (1995) 93 LGR 322.
2   Sections 53–56.
3   CROW Act 2000, Sch 5, inserting s 54A into the WLCA 1981.

Where rights for mechanically propelled vehicles were created before 1 January 1949 but the definitive map shows only a restricted byway, bridleway or a footpath, those vehicular rights over BOATs will be extinguished on the cut-off date.[1] Vehicular rights will not be extinguished over highways carrying vehicular rights where the highway would not qualify as a BOAT.

5.7.3 Footpaths and bridleways not shown on the definitive map

Provided the footpath or bridleway:

(1) was a footpath or bridleway before 1 January 1949;
(2) is a footpath or bridleway on the cut-off date;
(3) remained a footpath or bridleway between those dates; and
(4) is not an excepted highway,

all such rights of way will be immediately extinguished on the cut-off date.[2]

Where bridleway rights are extinguished, any right to cycle on bridleways conferred by s 30 of the Countryside Act 1968 is also extinguished.[3]

The excepted highways are:[4]

(a) as much of a footpath or bridleway as, after 1 January 1949, has been diverted, extended or had part of its width stopped up, provided it connects with another highway directly or indirectly. If it connects indirectly, then as much of the rest of the path as is necessary to connect with the other highway is also not extinguished;
(b) a bridleway which became a footpath after 1949 after the stopping up of bridleway rights, or a footpath which became a bridleway after 1949 by the creation of bridleway rights over it, provided in either case it connects with another highway either directly or indirectly;
(c) as much of a footpath or bridleway as passes over a bridge or through a tunnel and connects with another highway directly or indirectly;
(d) a footpath or bridleway any part of which is in inner London;
(e) a footpath or bridleway which runs at the side of a carriageway or between two carriageways;
(f) a footpath or bridleway of any other description specified in regulations made by the Secretary of State or the National Assembly for Wales;
(g) a particular footpath or bridleway specified in regulations.

5.7.4 Public rights shown on definitive map as a footpath, a bridleway or restricted byway

Where the definitive map records a footpath, bridleway or restricted byway, which are not excepted highways, on the cut-off date any higher rights created

---

1   CROW Act 2000, s 53.
2   Ibid.
3   Ibid, s 53(5).
4   Ibid, s 54.

before 1949 will be extinguished.[1] Where a footpath is shown on the definitive map, higher rights mean bridleway rights, restricted byway rights, vehicular rights for mechanically propelled vehicles over BOATs, and any right to drive animals. Where the definitive map shows a bridleway on the cut-off date higher rights mean vehicular rights and rights for mechanically propelled vehicles over BOATs. Where the definitive map shows a restricted byway on the cut-off date, higher rights means right for mechanically propelled vehicles over BOATs.

The excepted highways are:

(a) public rights of way subsisting on the cut-off date which were created after 1 January 1949 (apart from the statutory right to ride a pedal cycle on a bridleway conferred by s 30 of the CA 1968).

(b) rights of way over a highway any part of which is in inner London;

(c) rights of way specified or of such description as may be specified in regulations by the Secretary of State or National Assembly for Wales.

5.7.5 Footpaths recorded as bridleways

Where a highway was, immediately before 1949, a footpath or bridleway and is a footpath on the cut-off date, but is wrongly recorded on the definitive map as a bridleway, bridleway rights will be created over the path. It will not be possible after the cut-off date to apply for the bridleway to be downgraded to a footpath.[2]

5.7.6 The cut-off date

The cut-off date, for the purpose of extinguishing public rights of way, is 1 January 2026.[3] The Secretary of State and the National Assembly for Wales have power to make regulations to substitute a later cut-off date. Different dates may be specified for different areas, but in areas in which rights of way have been recorded on definitive maps since NPACA 1949 took effect, the date may not be later than 1 January 2031.

Some areas were not required by NPACA 1949 to record rights of way on definitive maps. NPACA 1949 did not apply to the Isles of Scilly. County councils were able by resolution to exclude built-up areas from the requirements of the Act. County boroughs were not required to produce definitive maps before WLCA 1981 came into effect. In these areas, a substituted cut-off date can be later than 2031. No final date is specified.

Where a highway crosses a boundary of two areas with different cut-off dates, the later date will apply.

---

1   CROW Act 2000, s 53.
2   Ibid, s 55.
3   Ibid, s 56.

5.7.7   Transitional provisions

Regulations may make transitional provisions where definitive map orders have been made but not confirmed, or applications for orders have been made before the cut-off date, or orders have been quashed because of a legal error.

5.8   PROCEDURE FOR MAKING AND CONFIRMING THE ORDER

5.8.1   Who can initiate the process

A surveying authority may, as part of its duty to keep the definitive map and statement under review, make modification orders of its own accord. The authorities are also under a duty to make an order where there has been a legal event order under s 53(3)(a). However, any person may apply to the authority for a modification order on the grounds set out in WLCA 1981, s 53(3)(b) and (c).

5.8.2   Application for orders

The application has to be made on a form prescribed by regulations and must be accompanied by a map and by evidence in support of the application.[1] Most surveying authorities provide their own forms for the use of applicants. The map must be on a scale of not less than 2½ inches to one mile or 1:25,000. The supporting evidence may be a combination of documentary evidence and user statements.

5.8.3   Notification to owners and occupiers

The applicant for an order must serve notice of the application on the owners and occupiers of any land to which the application relates. The notice has to be in the prescribed form or substantially in the prescribed form.

Where it is not practicable to ascertain the name and address of any owner or occupier, the authority may authorise notice to be served by addressing it to him as an owner or occupier and fixing it to some conspicuous object on the land.

If the title to the land is registered, it is possible to obtain from the Land Registry details of ownership under the provisions of the Land Registration Act 1988.

5.8.4   Certificate of notification

The applicant must give a certificate in the prescribed form to the local authority certifying that he has complied with the notice requirement. Until

---

1   WLCA 1981, Sch 14. Wildlife and Countryside Act 1981 (Definitive Maps and Statements) Regulations 1993, SI 1993/12.

the authority receives such a certificate it is not under an obligation to proceed with the application.

5.8.5 Determination by the authority

As soon as reasonably practical after receiving the certificate, the authority is under a duty to investigate the matters in the application. It must also consult with every local authority whose areas include the land to which the application relates. This means the district council or non-metropolitan councils, the parish council, if there is one, and, where there is not, the parish meeting. The authority will normally consult the owner and occupier of the land concerned and organisations representing users. Having done so, it must decide whether or not to make the order. In making its decision, the authority must weigh up the evidence and explain any legal principles. Failure to do so has, in the past, given rise to a successful challenge by judicial review.[1] However, recent case-law suggests that the courts will be reluctant to interfere until a final decision on whether to confirm the order or not has been made.[2] If any order is confirmed, the correct procedure is a statutory review. If the order is not made or confirmed, then the challenge should be by way of judicial review.

An inspector may decide to award costs at a public inquiry where he considers that a county council has acted unreasonably in making a definitive map modification order which is not confirmed.[3]

5.8.6 Failure to make a determination

If the authority has not determined the application within 12 months of receiving the certificate, the applicant may make representation to the Secretary of State.[4] The applicant should send a copy of the application form and set out reasons why an early determination is necessary. The Secretary of State may direct the authority to determine the application within a specified time. The Secretary of State is not under a duty to make such a direction. It must consult with the authority before deciding whether to set a deadline.

---

1   *Isle of Wight County Council v O'Keefe* (1990) 59 P&CR 283. On the lessons to be drawn from this case, see Michael Fisher 'Procedures for Modification Orders', RWLR 10.4, p 1.
2   *R v Cornwall County Council, ex parte Huntington; R v Devon County Council ex parte Isaac* [1994] 1 All ER 694. However, this may apply only when the order has been made by the highway authority. Judicial review may still be available for the procedure leading up to the order.
3   *R v Secretary of State for the Environment ex parte Smith and Deller* [1995] JPL 42 and Circular 8/93.
4   WLCA 1981, Sch 14, para 3(2).

5.8.7   Appeal against the decision not to make an order

When the authority has determined the application, it must give notice of its decision to the applicant and to every owner and occupier of land to which the application relates.

Where the authority has decided not to make an order, the applicant may, within 28 days after service on him of the notice of decision, appeal to the Secretary of State.[1]

The applicant should give the grounds for appeal, accompanied by copies of the application, a map showing the way, supporting documentation and the authority's decision. A copy of the notice of appeal should be served on the surveying authority.

When the appeal is received, the planning inspectorate will ask the authority for a statement explaining its decision not to make the order. This statement will be sent to the applicant for comments. In the light of the authority's statement and the appellant's comments, the Secretary of State will re-examine the evidence. If he considers that an order should be made, he will give such directions as appear to him to be necessary. They could include a direction as to the time in which the order should be made.[2] The Secretary of State cannot himself authorise the modification of the definitive map nor make the order.

It sometimes happens that the Secretary of State will consider the evidence at two stages. He may have heard or determined an appeal from the council's refusal to make an order and subsequently, when the order is made to which there are objections, he will have to decide whether to confirm the order under Sch 15. The practice is for the Secretary of State to tell the parties on a successful appeal under Sch 14 that his decision is without prejudice to any subsequent decision he might reach at a Sch 15 inquiry.

5.8.8   Notice of the order

The making of the order is only the first stage in the process. Once the order has been made, notice has to be served on various people and organisations who then have an opportunity to object to the order.[3] If there is an objection, the matter must go to public inquiry.

The notice must be given in the form prescribed by the regulations to:

(1) the owner and occupiers of the land affected;
(2) local authorities whose area includes the land;
(3) any person who has required the authority to give him notice of such orders;

---

1   WLCA 1981, Sch 14, para 4.
2   Ibid, Sch 14, para 4, as amended by the CROW Act 2000, s 51, Sch 5, para 10.
3   WLCA 1981, Sch 15, para 3; Wildlife and Countryside Act 1981 (Definitive Maps and Statements) Regulations 1993, SI 1993/12.

(4) the organisations specified in prescribed regulations (the Autocycle Union, the British Horse Society, Byways and Bridleways Trust, Commons Open Spaces and Footpaths Preservation Society and the Ramblers' Association; in addition, where the land is within Wales, the Welsh Trail Riders Association and, where it is within specified counties, the Chiltern Society and the Peak Northern Footpaths Society).

The notice must be advertised in local papers and must be displayed, together with a plan showing the effect of the order, at the ends of the route which are affected by the order. The order must be available for inspection in the council offices in the locality of the affected land and in such other places as the authority considers appropriate. The notice must indicate the general effect of the order, that it has been made and requires confirmation. Details must be given of where the order may be inspected, free of charge.

The landowners, occupiers, relevant local authorities and the prescribed bodies must be given copies the order and plan.

5.8.9   Objections

The notice must also give information on the time limits (being not less than 42 days from the publication of the notice) and manner in which representations in respect of the order must be made. Any person may inspect and take copies of the documents which the authority took into account when making the order. This does not prevent the authority from bringing forward further evidence at an inquiry or hearing which is subsequently held.

5.8.10   Confirmation of the order by the authority

If no objections are duly made or objections are withdrawn, the local authority may confirm the order. Objections have been held to be duly made even where they are made on irrelevant grounds or without stating any grounds.[1]

The CROW Act 2000[2] gives the Secretary of State (or National Assembly for Wales) discretion as to whether to hold an inquiry or hearing to confirm or not a definitive map order where the objections are irrelevant.

If there are objections to part of an order only, concerning several alleged rights of way, the authority may divide the order into two parts and confirm the unopposed part, whilst referring the other to the Secretary of State.[3]

5.8.11   Confirmation or otherwise by the Secretary of State

Where there are objections which are not withdrawn, the order must be referred to the Secretary of State. He may appoint an inspector to hold a public inquiry or settle the matter by written representations.[4]

---

1   *Lasham Parish Meeting v Hampshire CC* (1992) 65 P&CR 331.
2   Section 51, Sch 5, para 11.
3   WLCA 1981, Sch 15, para 5.
4   Ibid, Sch 15, para 7.

The inspector must give a statement of reasons for his decision.[1]

The Secretary of State, having considered the report of the inspector, may confirm the order, refuse to confirm the order or modify the order.

If the modifications involve land not affected by the order or where the modifications are to add or delete or alter the status of a public right of way, notice of at least 28 days must be given to allow for objections and representations.[2]

If objections are made and not withdrawn, a further inquiry or hearing must be held unless the Secretary of State decides not to hold an inquiry or hearing because he does not consider the objections duly made.[3] The inquiry or hearing is limited to dealing with objections to the modifications made by the inspector at the previous inquiry or hearing. It is not an opportunity to have a rerun of the evidence on parts of the order which are not affected by those modifications.[4]

If there is fresh evidence about other parts of the order such evidence can be considered only by reopening the original inquiry.[5]

5.8.12   Notice of confirmation

If an order is confirmed, the authority must give notice of the confirmation in the same way as it gave notice of the making of the order. If it is not confirmed, the authority must inform the people and organisations who were notified of the making of the order.[6] It does not have to publish notice of the decision not to confirm, nor put notices at the ends of the route.

Where an order is confirmed the definitive map and statement will be modified in accordance with the order and a sealed copy sent to the Ordnance Survey.

5.8.13   Challenging a confirmed order

After the publication of notice of the confirmed order, there can be a statutory review of the decision within 42 days.[7] This is limited to challenging the decision on the grounds that the proper procedures have not been followed and the applicant's interests have been substantially prejudiced by the failure to comply with those regulations or the Secretary of State has exceeded his powers.[8] Otherwise, the order cannot be challenged in any legal proceedings.

---

1   Tribunal and Inquiries Act 1971.
2   WLCA 1981, Sch 15, para 8; cf *Dyfed County Council v Secretary of State for Wales* (1990) 59 P&CR 275 – failure to advertise proposed modification to order did not justify quashing inspector's decision.
3   Ibid, Sch 5, para 11.
4   *Marriott v Secretary of State for the Environment,Transport and the Regions* (unreported, 10 October 2000).
5   See Ross Crail 'Marriott v SoS for DETR', RWLR 10.6, p 1.
6   WLCA 1981, Sch 5, para 11.
7   Ibid, para 12.
8   Courts have been prepared to examine inspectors' decisions where points of law involved: see *Jaques v Secretary of State for the Environment* [1995] JPL 1031.

The Court of Appeal has held that no challenge may be made in any other way once an order has been made. In the words of Brooke J (as he then was):[1]

> 'It is quite clear, in my judgment, that Parliament intended to prescribe a comprehensive programme of the events which should happen from the time the relevant authority sets in motion the consultation process mentioned in para 1 of Sch 15 and that once the order is made the prescribed procedure then follows, without any interruption for legal proceedings in which the validity of the order is questioned, until the stage is reached, if at all, when notice of a decision is given pursuant to the procedure prescribed in para 11. It is then, and then only, that Parliament intends that a person aggrieved by an order which has taken effect shall have the opportunity of questioning its validity in the High Court provided that he takes the opportunity provided for him by para 12(1) of Sch 15 ...'

If the legal challenge is successful, the court will direct the Secretary of State to reconsider the case. The High Court cannot change the decision, merely quash it.

5.8.14 Challenging the refusal to make or confirm an order

The statutory review is available only where an order is confirmed. If it is not confirmed or if an order is not made, the decision may be challenged by judicial review.

An application for leave for judicial review should be made without delay and in any event within 3 months of the decision.

5.8.15 Statutory review and judicial review

It may be necessary to bring two sets of proceedings at the same time. This has occurred where a landowner challenged:

(a) the refusal of the Secretary of State to downgrade a bridleway to a footpath (judicial review); and
(b) the Secretary of State's decision to confirm the highway authority's modification order to the definitive statement specifying that the width of the bridleway was 18 feet (statutory review).

5.8.16 Practical points

The statutory time for challenging a definitive map order is after the order has been made. However, it may be advisable for an objector to challenge the evidence before an order is made. The public's right to have information about meetings is discussed at **4.7.6**. A locally elected councillor can be asked to put the objector's arguments at the relevant committee meeting. In any event, it is important that the objector receives reports of any meetings so that he may discover on what basis the decision was taken on whether or not to make the order. Sometimes there will be more than one meeting at which the decision is discussed.

---

1   *R v Cornwall County Council ex parte Huntington* [1992] 3 All ER 566 at 576.

The statutory provisions relating to modifying definitive maps are extremely complex. The general rule is that notwithstanding any entries made on the definitive map or reclassifications of RUPPs, modification orders may be made on the 'discovery' of very slight new evidence. The cases set out below are important decisions on this area of law.

R v Secretary of State for the Environment ex parte Simms and Burrows[1] established that a right of way, recorded on a definitive map, could be downgraded or deleted by a modification order.

R v Secretary of State for the Environment ex parte Riley[2] held that a way reclassified as a bridleway under Part III of Sch3 to CA 1968 could subsequently be upgraded by modification order to a BOAT, even though the highway authority always had sufficient evidence of vehicular status of the route. The discovery of further evidence triggered the right to apply for a modification order.[3]

In *Fowler v Secretary of State for the Environment*,[4] the Court of Appeal held that a footpath recorded under the provisions of NPACA 1949 could be upgraded to a bridleway, even though the entry of a footpath under NPACA 1949 was conclusive and there was no provision that it was not without prejudice to greater rights.

Mayhew v Secretary of State for the Environment[5] makes it clear that the test for the discovery of new evidence to trigger a modification order is very lenient. Discovery includes evidence which was always available in the council's archives.

---

1   [1991] 3 WLR 1070.
2   (1989) 59 P&CR 1.
3   For the argument that the same result would apply if the reclassification had been to a footpath, see George Laurence 'Upgrading of Reclassified RUPPs', RWLR 8.2, p 21.
4   [1991] JPL 742.
5   (1993) 65 P&CR 344.

Chapter 6

CONFIRMATION OF ORDERS

6.1 INTRODUCTION

Once a local authority has made a public path order, or a definitive map order, to which objections are duly made, the order has to be referred to the Secretary of State for confirmation, modification or refusal of confirmation (unless in the case of a public path order the council decides to withdraw the order[1]). The Secretary of State may deal with the matters by written representations, public inquiry or a hearing. Objections are duly made if they are made within the time-limits, even though the objections may be irrelevant.[2] The Secretary of State (or National Assembly for Wales) has a discretion as to whether to hold a public inquiry or hearing into a definitive map modification order if the only objections are not relevant to the decision whether to confirm the order.[3]

If there are no objections to an order, the local authority may itself confirm the order. Where objections are received, it may decide to withdraw the order by formal resolution.[4] However, once the order has been passed to the Secretary of State for confirmation, this option is no longer available.

6.2 PUBLIC PATH ORDERS

The highway authority has power to make public path orders under ss 26, 118, 118A, 118B and 119, 119A, 119B, 119D of the Highways Act and ss 257, 258 and 261 of the Town and Country Planning Act 1990.

Where the order is referred to the Secretary of State because there are objections to the order, the Planning Inspectorate will check that the order complies with the Public Path Orders Regulations 1993 or the Town and Country Planning (Public Path Orders) Regulations 1993.

If the Planning Inspectorate considers that the order does not comply with the regulations, it will be returned to the authority. The authority may then make another order.

Besides checking that the order complies with the regulations, the Planning Inspectorate will ensure that all the correct documents accompany the order.

---

1   *R (Hargrave) v Stroud District Council* [2001] NPC 180.
2   *Lasham Parish Meeting v Hampshire County Council* (1992) 65 P&CR 331.
3   CROW Act 2000, s 51, Sch 5, para 11, inserting para 7(2A) into Sch 15 to WLCA 1981.
4   See Department of the Environment Circular 2/93.

These include the statement of reasons why the authority considers the order should be confirmed, the objections and the authority's comments on the objections.

If an order has been made under the Highways Act 1980, the authority must send the Inspectorate a certificate showing that the organisations specified under the regulations have been consulted.

6.3   DEFINITIVE MAP ORDERS

The highway authority is under a duty, if the criteria set out in WLCA 1981 are met, to make orders modifying the definitive map.[1]

If objections are made to the order, the order is sent to the Secretary of State for confirmation. The Planning Inspectorate will check that it conforms with the Wildlife and Countryside (Definitive Maps and Statements) Regulations 1993.

If the Planning Inspectorate considers that the order does not comply with the regulations it will be returned to the authority. The authority may then make another order.

As with public path orders, the Planning Inspectorate also checks that all the necessary documents, including statement of reasons, objections and the authority's comments on the objections have been sent with the order.

Sometimes, the authority which makes the order will not be supporting it. In such situations, the authority must state who will be supporting the order. This is likely to occur where an authority has refused to make an order and the applicant has made a successful appeal to the Secretary of State who then directs the authority to make the order.

It may also happen that, after the authority has made the order, more evidence is discovered which results in the authority considering that the order should not be confirmed.

6.4   THE PROCEDURES

The Secretary of State will decide whether to confirm the order on the basis of written representations, public inquiry or a hearing. He will write to the authority, or supporters of the order, where the local authority is not supporting a modification order, and the objectors stating the procedure to be followed. Generally, he will appoint an inspector, selected from the Lord Chancellor's panel of independent inspectors, to act on his behalf.

6.5   WRITTEN REPRESENTATIONS

This procedure may be followed where the orders have attracted only a few objections, with none from the county or district council. It is not suitable

---

1   WLCA 1981, s 53.

where there is complex or lengthy evidence. The local authority or objectors may insist that the matter should be heard by an inspector.

Provided there is agreement on written representations the Secretary of State will write to the objectors with the authority's statement of reasons and the comments on the objections. The objectors have 2 weeks to reply to the authority's statement and comments. The authority have a further 2 weeks to comment on the objector's replies. The exchange of comments will continue until the authority and objectors have no more comments to make.

It has been held that, where there was an opposed public path order, a supporter of the order who had written to the council had made a representation and was entitled to be treated as a party.[1]

The next stage is for the inspector to make a site visit. Objectors can ask to accompany the inspector. If they do so the local authority must also be present.

The purpose of the site visit is for the inspector to see the order route and surrounding paths and to note the physical features. During the site visit, the inspector cannot discuss the arguments of either side.

If further evidence is sent to the inspector after the site visit but before he makes his decision, and it is material to the decision, he will send the evidence to everyone who has made written representations and give them the opportunity to reply.

6.6 PUBLIC INQUIRY

6.6.1 Introduction

The Secretary of State for the Environment, Food and Rural Affairs has a general power to hold such inquiries as he considers necessary for the purpose of his functions under the Highways Act 1980,[2] the Town and Country Planning Act 1990[3] and the WLCA 1981.[4] Any inquiry so held will be governed by the provisions of the Local Government Act 1972.[5] There are at present no specific procedural rules for inquiries or public path and definitive map orders. This may change.

In practice, public inquiries follow the same format whether they are concerned with public path orders or modification orders. Anyone may attend and may be professionally represented or appear in person. Inquiries usually last 1 or 2 days but can last much longer. The length varies on the amount of evidence and the number of people who wish to speak.

---

1   *R v Secretary of State for the Environment ex parte Slot* [1998] JPL 692. For the natural justice aspect of the case, see James Stephens 'Ex parte Slot and Natural Justice', RWLR 10.2, p 55.

2   Highways Act 1980, s 302.

3   Sections 320 and 321.

4   Schedule 15, para 8.

5   Section 250.

6.6.2 Date and place

The Planning Inspectorate writes to all objectors telling them of its proposal to hold a public inquiry. The authority will usually fix a date and a place for the inquiry with the Planning Inspectorate. The place is likely to be a village hall reasonably near the order route.

Once the date and the place have been agreed, the Planning Inspectorate will write to the authority, all the objectors and certain national organisations. An inspector for the Secretary of State will be appointed.

The notice given for such an inquiry tends to be rather short. Often it will be no more than a month. This may prove inconvenient for the objectors or their advisers. It is very rare, however, for the Inspectorate to agree that the inquiry should be held on a different date.

Where it is known in advance that certain dates will be impossible, it is worth contacting the local authority before a date is fixed and requesting that a hearing should not be held at that time.

6.6.3 Advertising the inquiry

The inquiry must be advertised by the authority in a local newspaper and a notice put up at either end of each way affected by the order as well as at a place where public notices are usually displayed in the district. This must be done at least 14 days before the inquiry is due to start.

6.6.4 Proof of evidence

The Inspectorate recommends that the authority and the objectors prepare a proof of evidence: that is a written statement of the evidence intended to be given at the inquiry, together with any supporting documents.

The proof should be prepared 3 weeks before the inquiry. The authority should send a copy to the inspector and to the objectors, and the objectors should send copies to the inspector and the authority.

There is no obligation to do so and even if a proof is submitted it can be added to at the inquiry itself.

6.6.5 The inquiry

Although there are no procedural rules for a public inquiry relating to public rights of way, in practice most inquiries will be conducted in a similar manner.

The inspector will introduce himself and may explain when he intends to allow breaks in the proceedings. He will usually ask for the names of those who wish to speak. In practice, most inspectors allow those who do not give their names, or arrive late, to speak. Those who have to leave the inquiry early should inform the inspector so that he can arrange for them to be heard.

The inspector will pass round an attendance list for everyone to sign with their full address. He will also ask if there is any member of the press present.

He will usually start the proceedings by asking the authority to present its case for the order first, unless it no longer supports the order, when a supporter will present the case.

The authority may introduce witnesses who have proofs of evidence. Copies should be provided for the inspector and the objectors. The objectors may cross-examine the witnesses. However, the inspector may intervene if the questions are irrelevant or repetitive or if the process is being abused. The inspector too may question the witnesses. Normally, the supporters of the order will not be allowed to cross-examine their own side.

Other people who support the order will then be asked to speak. They must be prepared to be cross-examined.

The objectors will then present their case and call their witnesses. They, in turn, may be cross-examined by the supporters of the order.

Sometimes unexpected questions are raised and the other party may ask for an adjournment to consider them. The inspector will decide whether to allow an adjournment. Often it may be for a few minutes only. More rarely, it may be necessary to adjourn the inquiry to another date. The inspector will have to announce the date and place for the adjournment.

Where there is no adjournment, the main objector will usually be given an opportunity of summing up the evidence of the objectors and making the relevant legal submissions on the evidence. Although ideally the legal submissions should be in writing, this is sometimes not possible as they may have emerged during the course of the inquiry. Inspectors will often ask for hand-written submissions and provide for copies to be made for the authority.

Finally, the authority will make a closing statement which will probably deal with points raised by the objectors. The statement should not raise any new evidence. If, however, the authority suggests a modification to the order, the objectors will be given a chance to reply.

6.6.6 The site visit

Although the inspector will have visited the site before the inquiry, he will normally make another visit accompanied by at least one person supporting the order and one objecting. Anyone can accompany him, but he will not make the visit accompanied by one side alone. No new evidence can be given, but anyone may point out the physical features mentioned at the inquiry.

6.6.7 Evidence produced after the inquiry

Sometimes evidence is given to the Planning Inspectorate after the inquiry but before the inspector makes his decision. The evidence will be passed to him. If the inspector decides that new points have been raised which will affect his decision, he will send the evidence to anyone who presented their case or objected at the inquiry, giving them the chance to reply.

Where the Secretary of State is to make the decision, the evidence will be sent to him.

6.7   HEARING PROCEDURES

6.7.1   When will it be used?

The Planning Inspectorate has decided that in some cases it would be better to have a hearing rather than a public inquiry. This is because public inquiries may be too formal and intimidating for members of the public. Hearings are often used in planning appeals.

The procedure is not suitable if there are:

(1) too many people wanting to speak;
(2) complicated policy matters;
(3) important legal issues; or
(4) a need for cross-examination.

6.7.2   What is a hearing?

A hearing is a discussion led by the inspector who will decide the case. Everyone involved will sit round a table, usually in a small committee room.

The inspector will explain what the hearing is about. He will set out the issues as he understands them, having read the papers, visited the site and asked for clarification, if necessary, on points arising on the order or plans.

The authority will explain its case. Documents and written material should have been produced beforehand. If new material is produced, it may be necessary to postpone the hearing.

Everyone round the table may ask questions and discuss the issues.

There will then be a site visit. Some of the issues may be discussed at the site itself if all the parties are able to attend. Sometimes, however, the hearing will have closed before the site visit taking place. Where this happens there can be no further discussion.

6.7.3   Procedure before the hearing

Although a hearing is essentially informal, it will be held only if all the parties agree. The Planning Inspectorate will offer a hearing where it considers it appropriate and those involved have 10 working days to decide whether to accept the offer. The Inspectorate aims to hold the hearing within 12 weeks from the date of the agreement.

The Inspectorate will give everyone involved at least 28 days' notice of the date, time and place of the hearing. This includes the authority and the known objectors. It is the duty of the authority to inform the landowners and anyone who has written to it about the order and where they can inspect the pre-hearing statements and other relevant documents.

The authority must also advertise the hearing in the local area, for example by putting notices at the ends of the relevant paths.

The authority and objectors should send the inspectorate a written statement of their case with accompanying documents at least 3 weeks before the date of the hearing. Copies of the statements and documents will be sent to the other parties. This is so that everyone can study the issues beforehand.

It may be that it will become clear in the pre-hearing procedure that a hearing is not appropriate. On other occasions this may become apparent at the hearing itself. In either case, the inspector can decide that the hearing procedure be abandoned and a public inquiry held.

6.8   SUBSTANTIVE ISSUES

6.8.1   General principles

Public rights of way generate a great deal of controversy. Many irrelevant points are likely to be aired at inquiries and hearings and indeed in written representations. Although inspectors tend to be extremely patient and tolerant, these irrelevant matters will not affect the decision. They merely prolong the procedures and in extreme cases may affect the result in an order for costs.

6.8.2   Public path orders

Before confirming a public path order, the inspector has to ensure that the tests set out in the relevant section relating to the order are fulfilled. These have been discussed in detail in Chapters 3 and 4.

For a creation order, an inspector must be satisfied that there is a need for a new path and that it is expedient to create one, taking into account the extent to which the path would add to the convenience or enjoyment of a substantial section of the public or those living in the area and any effect it would have on those with an interest in the land, after considering their entitlement to compensation.[1]

To extinguish a path, the inspector must consider how often the path is or could be used and the effect on the adjoining land of closing the path, taking into account the compensation provisions.[2] Obstructions which block the route are ignored in answering these questions. In other words, the inspector considers how the path would be used if the obstructions were not there.

Questions of conservation, environment, privacy and serenity are irrelevant when deciding whether or not to extinguish a public right of way.

An inspector must not confirm a diversion order unless he is satisfied that the diverted path will not be substantially less convenient to the public and that it is expedient to confirm the order having regard to the public enjoyment of the

---

1   Highways Act 1980, s 26.
2   Ibid, s 118.

path as a whole, the effect it would have on other land served by the existing public right of way and on the land over which the path is to be diverted, taking into account the compensation provisions.[1]

When considering concurrent orders for a public path creation order or diversion order and an extinguishment order, the inspector may consider if the route is still needed after a new path is created or an existing path diverted. There is no provision, however, for creating or diverting a path on the basis that another path is extinguished. It therefore seems that the creation and diversion tests must be fulfilled independently before a decision can be made to extinguish a path.

Unless the orders are drafted to be inter-dependent, the inspector may confirm the creation or diversion order but not the extinguishment order.

In confirming a diversion or stopping-up order under the Town and Country Planning Acts, the inspector must be satisfied that the order is necessary for the development to be carried out.[2] He must also take into account in making his decision whether the advantages of a diversion or stopping up of the route outweigh the disadvantages.

Where the authority stops up a footpath or bridleway on its own land, the inspector must be sure that the authority has or will provide an alternative way or that such a way is not needed.[3]

6.8.3   Modification orders

Before confirming a definitive map order, the inspector has to consider whether or not the evidence supports the order. He is concerned only with ascertaining whether a public right of way exists and what is its status. He is not concerned with whether or not the path is wanted, nor with the effect it would have on amenity, security, privacy or the environment.

Unlike public path orders which change the status of public rights of way, modification orders are concerned only with ensuring that the definitive map and statement record accurately the existing position.

6.8.4   Reclassification orders

These orders are to make clear what public rights exist over the particular RUPP which is subject to the order. Like modification orders, reclassification orders do not create new rights. Their purpose is to record existing rights. Once s 47 of the CROW Act 2000 comes into force, there will be no more reclassification orders. All RUPPs will be automatically redesignated restricted byways.

---

1   Highways Act 1980, s 119.
2   Town and Country Planning Act 1990, s 259.
3   Ibid, s 258.

The presumption is that a RUPP has bridleway rights. If vehicular rights exist, they must be proved. If bridleway rights do not exist and the RUPP should be recorded merely as a footpath, that too must be proved.[1]

An inspector cannot decide on a reclassification order that no public right of way of any kind exists. If that is the position, the authority should make a modification order under s 53 of the WLCA 1981.

6.8.5   Evidence

In confirming or otherwise modification orders and re-classification orders, the inspector bases his decision on evidence. This may be documentary or user evidence or, as is usual, a combination of the two.

Documentary evidence includes maps, plans, highway orders and other documents and is discussed more fully in Chapter 7. It is seldom that the evidence is clear-cut. The highway authority and objectors are likely to interpret the documents in different ways.

User evidence is evidence of the use by the public of the routes covered by the order. It may include declarations, written statements or oral evidence. Obviously, if witnesses appear at the inquiry and give evidence which may be subject to cross-examination, their evidence will carry more weight.

Although the WLCA 1981[2] defines BOAT as 'a highway over which the public have a right of way for vehicular and all other kinds of traffic but which is used by the public mainly for the purpose for which footpaths and bridleways are so used', actual user has been held to be irrelevant in a case where there was an application to modify a RUPP.[3] User would also be irrelevant in reclassifying a RUPP under s 54 of the WLCA 1981. The question remains whether user evidence is relevant when adding a BOAT[4] to the definitive map for the first time or upgrading a footpath or bridleway to a BOAT.[5]

6.9   THE DECISION

Most orders are decided by an inspector on behalf of the Secretary of State. Where the decision is particularly important or sensitive, the Secretary of State may call in the decision and make it himself.

The inspector will send his decision in a letter to the authority. The letter will describe the physical features of the path, set out the main arguments of the authority and the objectors and give his conclusions and decision. Copies of

---

1   WLCA 1981, s 54.
2   Section 66(1).
3   *Masters v Secretary of State for the Environment* [2000] 4 All ER 458. The classification was determined by the character of the way being more suitable for horse or pedestrian use than for vehicles.
4   WLCA 1981, s 53(3)(c)(i).
5   Ibid, s 53(3)(c)(ii). See *Buckland v Secretary of State for the Environment* [2000] 3 All ER 205; *R v Wiltshire County Council ex parte Nettlecombe Ltd* [1998] JPL 707.

the letter will be sent to the objectors and to other people who have requested a copy.

If the Secretary of State has called in the decision, he will consider the inspector's report and recommendations but does not necessarily follow them. He will give his decision in a letter to the authority. Copies will be sent to the same people as would receive a copy had the decision been made by an inspector.

The decision, whether made by the inspector or Secretary of State, will be to confirm the order, refuse to confirm the order or confirm the order with modifications.

Certain modifications have to be re-advertised. Where a public path order or definitive map order is modified and the modification involves moving the line of the path or widening it, such changes must be advertised. In addition, a modified definitive map order which shows a new path, deletes all or part of a path, or changes the status of a path in an order must be advertised.[1]

Objections can be made to the advertised modified order and, if these are not withdrawn, there will have to be another inquiry unless the parties agree to proceed by written representations or a hearing. The inquiry is limited to dealing with objections to the modifications only. It is not an opportunity to object to those parts of the order which are not affected by the modifications.[2]

6.10   COSTS

There is no power to award that costs be paid by the other side where the written representations are followed. Where there is a public inquiry or a hearing[3] and an order is confirmed under the Town and Country Planning Act 1990 or the WLCA 1981 or under the Highways Act 1980, then, subject to the exceptions set out below, each side will normally pay its own costs.

There is an exception where one party has behaved unreasonably, vexatiously or frivolously. For instance, if the inspector holds that the order is fundamentally defective, the authority may have to pay the objector's costs. Another example is where the evidence shows that the local authority should not have made an order in the first place.[4] Objectors who persist in irrelevant objections may be held to have behaved unreasonably and be ordered to pay the authority's costs. An objector who requests an inquiry and fails to turn up or appoint someone to represent him may be liable for costs.

---

1   Highways Act 1980, Sch 6, para 2(3); WLCA 1981, Sch 15, para 8.
2   *Marriott v Secretary of State for the Environment, Transport and the Regions* (2000) unreported, 10 October.
3   CROW Act 2000, Sch 5 adds para 10A to Sch 15 to WLCA 1981 with the effect that s 250(2)–(5) applies to hearings as well as public inquiries.
4   *R v Secretary of State ex parte Smith and Deller* [1995] JPL 42 (inspector's decision not to award costs quashed on judicial review).

Creation orders under the Highways Act 1980 are similar to compulsory purchase orders. If they are confirmed they will take away some of the landowner's interests in his land. The landowner is entitled to compensation. He may also be entitled to compensation where there is a diversion or extinguishment order. Such orders are known as analogous orders (analogous to compulsory purchase orders). If a landowner makes a successful objection to an analogous order at a public inquiry, his costs will automatically be paid by the authority.[1]

Applications for costs should be made after the authority has made its closing statement, but before the public inquiry has been officially closed. The inspector will give the other side a chance to counter the claim. A report will be made to the Secretary of State on the application for costs. He will decide whether or not to award costs.

Normally, applications for costs cannot be made after the inquiry has closed. The inspector should make this clear at the start of the inquiry. Where there is a good reason for a late application, this should be made to the Planning Inspectorate. If the application is accepted, both sides will be asked to make written representations before the Secretary of State makes his decision.

6.11   CHALLENGING THE DECISION

6.11.1   Statutory review

Where the inspector has confirmed the order, an application may be made to the High Court challenging the decision on the ground that the decision is not within the powers of the inspector or that the proper procedures have not been followed and, as a consequence, the claimant's interests have been substantially prejudiced. The application must be made within 42 days of the decision being published in the newspaper. From the time an order is made, the decision may not be challenged in any other legal proceedings whatsoever.[2]

6.11.2   Judicial review

Where the inspector refuses to confirm an order, an application may be made for leave for judicial review. Judicial review proceedings must be brought without delay and in any event within 3 months of the decision.

In order to succeed on judicial review it will be necessary to show that the inspector has acted totally unreasonably or that there has been a mistake of law.

A judicial review is neither an appeal nor an opportunity for re-running the evidence.

---

1   Local Authorities (Recovery of Costs for Public Path Orders) Regulations 1993, SI 1993/407.
2   Highways Act 1980, Sch 2, para 1; WLCA 1981, Sch 15, para 12. *R v Cornwall County Council ex parte Huntington* [1994] 1 All ER 694.

6.12   COMPLAINTS

6.12.1   The Planning Inspectorate

A person who is dissatisfied with the inspector or the way the order is being handled by DEFRA may write to the Planning Inspectorate. However, the only way to challenge a decision of the inspector is by a statutory or judicial review.

6.12.2   The Parliamentary Commissioner for Administration (the Ombudsman)

Complaints about the Planning Inspectorate or the inspector may be made to the Ombudsman through an MP. He cannot, however, alter or question the decision. He is not concerned with the merits of the case but with the administration procedure.

6.12.3   The Council on Tribunals

Complaints about the basic procedure in processing an order can be made to the Council on Tribunals.

6.12.4   The Local Ombudsman

Complaints about the way the authority handled the order may be made to the Local Ombudsman. He cannot, however, question the merits of the order or change the decision.

Chapter 7

ASCERTAINING PUBLIC RIGHTS OF WAY

7.1   THE NEED

It is important that landowners, occupiers, purchasers, their professional advisers and local authorities should know the status and route of public rights of way. The definitive map is the starting point, but additional inquiries may be necessary, as there may be additional rights or rights of a higher status not recorded.

7.2   THE DEFINITIVE MAP AND STATEMENT

7.2.1   Inspection of definitive map

The definitive map and statement is a record maintained by the county council of the public right of way within its area. It should be available for inspection free of all charge at all reasonable hours.[1]

The district council should also have a copy of that part of the definitive map which covers that district and any orders which have been made amending the map and statement.

Parish councils will normally have a copy of that part of the map and statement which covers their parish.

Landowners should obtain copies of the relevant part of the definitive map and statement so that they and their tenants and employees are aware of the status and route of the public rights of way on their land and keep them unobstructed. Ignorance of the existence of the routes as shown on the definitive map will be no defence to any prosecution for obstruction.

7.2.2   Limitations of definitive map

The definitive map and statement is conclusive as to what is recorded.[2] However, there may be perfectly valid rights of way which are not recorded.[3]

There may, for instance, be:

---

1   WLCA 1981, s 57.
2   Ibid, s 56.
3   CROW Act 2000, ss 53–56 introduce provisions for extinguishing specified unrecorded rights of way in 2026. See **5.7** for a discussion of the sections.

(1) public path orders confirmed but not yet been recorded on the definitive map;
(2) definitive map orders and public path orders made, but not confirmed;
(3) applications for definitive map or public path orders;
(4) documentary evidence of the valid existence of public rights of way;
(5) user evidence which would support a claim although no application has yet been made.

7.3 THE BUYER'S SOLICITOR

7.3.1 Inquiries of a local authority

A buyer's solicitor should make sure that he asks the optional question relating to public rights of way when making inquiries of a local authority (Con 29 Pt II Question 5):

> **'Public Paths or Byways**
> Is any public path, bridleway or road used as a public path or byway which abuts on or crosses the property shown in a Definitive Map or revised Definitive Map prepared under Part IV of the National Parks and Access to the Countryside Act 1949 or Part III of the Wildlife and Countryside Act 1981? If so, please mark its approximate position on the attached plan.'

Failure to ask this question may be negligent, especially in a rural area.[1] Representations by landowners and users to have this question made compulsory have not found acceptance with the Association of County Councils or The Law Society.

In addition, the solicitor should raise a further inquiry:

> 'Has the Council any knowledge of any public footpath, bridleway, road used as a public path or byway, across or adjoining the property, which is being claimed but is not yet on the Definitive Map?'

The CROW Act 2000 has introduced a new duty on surveying authorities to keep a register with information to be prescribed on applications for modification orders to the definitive map.[2]

7.3.2 Inquiries of seller

When making preliminary inquiries before contracts are exchanged, the buyer's solicitor should ask whether the seller has any knowledge of public rights of way being claimed which do not appear on the definitive map.

7.3.3 Inspection of site

The buyer should be asked to inspect the site for any evidence that tracks on the land are being used by the public.

---

1   See *G & K Ladenbau Ltd v Crawley and de Reya* [1978] 1 WLR 266.
2   Section 51, Sch 5, para 2, introducing s 53A into WLCA 1981.

7.3.4 Title deeds

A landowner's title deeds may show the existence of public rights of way. The grant or reservation of private rights of way may indicate that at that time there was not considered to be a public right of way. However, in most cases title deeds will not reveal any evidence of public rights of way. The fact that the deeds are silent cannot be taken to mean that the rights do not exist.

Where the title is registered, a buyer will take the property subject to overriding interests, whether or not he knows of them. These include public rights of way, but not an adoption agreement under s 38 of the Highways Act 1980.[1]

Where the highway is publicly maintainable, the surface vests in the highway authority, even where the road or path is expressly included in the registered title.[2]

7.3.5 Inspection of other documentary evidence

In some purchases, the existence of a public right of way, or a right of way of a higher status may be so detrimental to a prospective buyer that he may employ a solicitor or other professional to investigate documentary records. This process would not normally be undertaken by a solicitor when instructed to act for a buyer.

7.4 DOCUMENTARY EVIDENCE

7.4.1 General principles

Documentary evidence is important in establishing:

(1) whether there are public rights of way which are not shown on the definitive map; or
(2) whether the rights of way which are shown should be of a different status;
(3) the correct status for RUPPs on a reclassification.

The weight to be given to the documentary evidence depends on the date of the document, who compiled it and for what purpose, and where it has been kept.

Section 32 of the Highways Act 1980 provides:

> 'A court or other tribunal, before determining whether a way has or has not been dedicated as a highway, or the date on which such dedication, if any, took place, shall take into consideration any map, plan or history of the locality or other relevant document which is tendered in evidence, and shall give such weight thereto as the Court or Tribunal considers justified by the circumstances,

---

1   *Overseas Investment Services Ltd v Simcobuild* (1995) 70 P&CR 322. On the limitations of registered title for evidence of public rights of way, see A Pain 'Rights of way and registered land', RWLR 2.3, p 11.

2   *Secretary of State for the Environment, Transport and the Regions v Baylis (Gloucester) Ltd* [2000] EGLR 92. Rule 278 of the Land Registration Rules 1925, SR&O 1925/1093 (the general boundaries rule) does not divest the highway authority of its interest in the surface.

including the antiquity of the tendered document, the status of the person by whom and the purpose for which it was made or compiled, and the custody in which it has been kept and from which it is produced.'

Often documents are ambiguous and will be interpreted by each side in the way best suited to their arguments.

Documents which are in the custody of a local authority may be inspected by local government electors in the area.[1] Documents which are required to be deposited with a local authority may be inspected free of charge.[2]

Set out below are some of the main kinds of documentary evidence which are useful in public inquiries.

7.4.2 Inclosure awards and plans

Many Inclosure Acts gave powers to the commissioners to stop up and divert existing roads and to create replacement roads. The plan and awards made under those Acts may be evidence of highways. It is important to check that the award is within the powers conferred by the enabling Act.

The interpretation of inclosure awards is no easy matter. Each award has to be construed in accordance with all the terms used in that particular award and in the light of the surrounding circumstances. In the words of Lord Blackburn in *River Wear Commissioners v Adamson*:[3]

'In all cases the object is to see what is the intention expressed by the words used. But from the imperfection of language, it is impossible to know what that intention was without enquiring further, and seeing what the circumstances were with reference to which the words were used, and what was the object, appearing from those circumstances, which the person using them had in view, for the meaning of words varies according to the circumstances with respect to which they were used.'

In construing an inclosure award, it is necessary first of all to consider the enabling Act. There is a fundamental difference between Acts which pre-dated the General Inclosure Act 1801 and those which were passed later and incorporated the provisions of that Act.

Acts passed before 1801 vary enormously but generally they gave wide powers to the Inclosure Commissioners to establish new highways and re-route and preserve existing ones. Most Acts extinguished existing highways which were not specifically dealt with in an award. The powers given to commissioners generally extended not only to carriageways, but also to bridleways and footpaths.

Unless the enabling Act made a contrary provision, a highway set out in an award would automatically become subject to public rights without the need for any further procedure.

---

1   Local Government Act 1972, s 118.
2   Ibid, s 225.
3   (1877) 2 App Case 743.

Because of the time and expense and possibly lack of local drafting skills, the General Inclosure Act 1801 provided a set of general clauses which could be incorporated into the local Acts. The local Acts could alter or add to the general Act.

The powers given in the General Inclosure Act 1801 have been restrictively interpreted by the court in *R v Secretary of State for the Environment ex parte Andrews*.[1] The power to set out highways of 30 feet in s 8 of the Act has been held to be a power to set out carriageways, but not footpaths. Therefore, s 11, which gives the Commissioners powers to extinguish all roads, ways and paths which shall not be 'set aforesaid' has also been interpreted as applying to carriageways only. This means that public footpaths and bridleways which existed across the land before inclosure will continue to exist as public rights of way.

The only power to deal with bridleways and footpaths under the 1801 Act is to stop or divert them where they would otherwise interfere with the proper use of a new public carriageway.

Section 9 of the General Inclosure Act 1801 sets out the procedure which must be followed once the award has set out the highway. Until that has been done, the award is not effective to create new public rights of way.[2] There may be, of course, an implied dedication and acceptance by subsequent use.

Many local Acts have extended the powers of the General Inclosure Act 1801, in particular with regard to public paths.

One of the difficulties in construing awards has been to decide whether the roads set out are private or public. In *Dunlop v Secretary of State for the Environment*,[3] the court held on the construction of that particular award private carriage road meant just that and not a public road open to private carriages.

If a road is publicly maintainable this may or may not indicate the public status. It depends on the particular wording in the context of the award. An added complication is that some roads were not private in the sense of easements to particular properties but, being available to the inhabitants of a village or hamlet rather than the public at large, were not highways. Such routes could be maintainable by the inhabitants but that would not make them public.[4]

7.4.3 Finance Act 1910 maps and records

The Finance Act 1910 provided an increment value duty tax on land. Owners were able to apply for a reduction in the duty if a public right of way existed across a particular plot of land.

---

1   (1996) 71 P&CR 1.
2   *Cubitt v Maxse* (1873) LR 8 CP 704.
3   (1995) 70 P&CR 307.
4   See *Dunlop v Secretary of State for the Environment* (1995) 70 P&CR 307 and J Sugden 'Inclosure commissioners at work', RWLR 9.2, p 39.

There are four sets of records. The working plans and valuation books may be available in county record offices. Record plans and field books are held at the Public Record Office at Kew. The valuation books identify the land and provide a key to find the information in the record plans and field books.[1]

The records may refer to a public right of way but do not identify the route as such. Therefore other evidence of the route will be needed. On the other hand, where the maps show public roads (which may be carriageways, bridleways or footpaths) this is very good evidence of their public status.[2]

7.4.4   Tithe awards and maps

Tithe maps are concerned with identifying titheable land. Barren land was not titheable. If a road is shown without a tithe number, it may be a public or private road. The importance of the map is to show the physical existence of the route at that date. On its own it is no evidence of a public right of way, let alone a public right of way of a particular status. However, it may lend support to other evidence.[3]

7.4.5   Highway orders

Highway orders diverting and extinguishing public roads and paths or removing the maintenance liability have existed since the 18th century. Before 1947, such orders could only be made by a justice of the peace. It is important to check the Highway Act under which the order was made to ensure that it was a valid order. The orders may contain evidence either in the text or plan of the status of paths and roads adjoining the order route. The orders may be in the county records office or in the surveyor's department.

7.4.6   Deposited plans of public undertakings

Undertakings such as railways, major roads, canals and drainage channels have to deposit with the appropriate public authority plans of their proposed works. Where the works were authorised by Act of Parliament, the Act, plans and books of reference can be inspected at the House of Lords Records Office. Such documents, when considered together, may provide evidence of public rights of way.

The status of a right of way over a railway may depend on the size of the bridge. The Railway Clauses Consolidation Act 1845 sets out standard bridge dimensions. For instance, bridges carrying a public carriageway had to be at least 20 feet in width.[4]

---

1   See Z Bowles 'Right of way and the 1910 Finance Act', RWLR 9.3, p 17.
2   *Robinson Webster Holdings v Agomber* [2002] 1 P&CR 20. Cf *Maltbridge Management Co v Secretary of State for the Environment and Hertfordshire County Council* [1998] EWHC Admin 830 (unreported). See also David Braham 'Uncoloured roads on 1910 Finance Act maps' RWLR 9.3, p 153.
3   See articles in RWLR 9.2: C Padley 'Tithe records', p 25; J Andrews 'Tithe map case studies', p 67; R Kain 'Interpreting tithe map evidence', p 97.
4   See B Riley 'Railway and canal deposited plans', RWLR 9.2, p 21.

7.4.7 Estate map

County record offices often include in their records maps of private estates. In order to inspect them, it will usually be necessary to get the consent of the owner who deposited them.

7.4.8 Local maps

Many county maps were prepared by private surveyors for publication, which will give physical evidence of a route at a particular time. However, the maps are not evidence of status and their reliability varies.[1] They are usually used in conjunction with other evidence to support a particular claim.

7.4.9 Ordnance Survey maps

Ordnance Survey maps are evidence not of the status of the road but only of the physical features on the ground. Like the county maps, they are useful in showing the existence of a road at a particular date or even the non-existence of a road.

Current Ordnance Survey maps show public rights of way on the basis of information supplied by the local authorities from the definitive map. Such information will only be recorded when there is a new edition of the Ordnance Survey, so the maps may often be out of date.

Where the information has not been so supplied, the representation on the Ordnance Survey map of a path or road is only a topographical feature and cannot be taken as evidence that it is or is not a public right of way.

In some areas, the first edition of the Ordnance Survey 25-inch map was supplemented by a published book of reference for each parish. This gives the land use of each separately numbered parcel of land and also indicates roads. The maps and books of reference are available in the map department of the British Library.

7.4.10 Section 31(6) map

In order to rebut a claim on deemed dedication, a landowner is able to deposit a statement and map under s 31(6) of the Highways Act 1980 stating what rights of way he admits to having dedicated as highways. This provision was first introduced under the Rights of Way Act 1932 and the statements and declarations made are strong evidence of the existence and status of rights of way. The council is under an obligation to keep a register of maps, statements and declarations.[2]

---

1   See Y Hodson 'The evaluation of older maps', RWLR 9.3, p 29.
2   Highways Act 1980, s 31A, inserted by CROW Act 2000, Sch 6.

7.4.11   List of streets

Every highway authority is under a duty to make and keep up to date, a list of streets within its area which are highways maintainable at public expense.[1] The list has to be deposited at the offices of the council by which it was made and may be inspected by any person, free of charge, at all reasonable hours.[2] The county council must supply to the district council within the county an up-to-date list of the streets within that district's area.

'Street' is widely defined so that it covers paths, bridleways, BOATs and RUPPs as well as urban highways.[3] The nature of the public's rights (ie whether on foot, horse or in vehicle) is unlikely to be recorded.

However, the list does not include highways which are not maintainable at public expense and may omit ones which are. The accuracy of the list varies from area to area. Sometimes the list may include routes which are not highways.

Further information may be obtained from the register compiled under s 53 of the New Roads and Streets Works Act 1991. This register must contain details of all streets that are highways regardless of who is responsible for their maintenance.

7.4.12   Maintenance records

The records, where they exist, may contain account books of the parish highway surveyors who were responsible for the upkeep of the road until late in the 19th century.[4]

In some parts of the country, highway districts were set up under the Highways Act 1862.

7.4.13   Other parish records

Besides the maintenance records, there may be evidence in the Minute Books and other miscellaneous papers about rights of way. These would be especially important when the first definitive map was under discussion and survey cards were being compiled.

7.4.14   Wartime records

Various powers were given to stop up or divert highways or to allow them to be ploughed during the Second World War.[5] After the war, orders may have been

---

1   Highways Act 1980, s 36(6).
2   Ibid, s 36(7).
3   Ibid, s 329(1).
4   For further information on **7.4.12**, **7.4.13** and **7.4.14** see Riddall and Trevelyan *Rights of Way – A Guide to Law and Practice*, 3rd edn, pp 137–147.
5   Defence (General) Regulations 1939.

made to stop up or divert permanently those paths which had been subject to temporary orders.[1]

The orders made under those Acts are kept at the Public Record Office at Kew and some may be available in local record offices.

7.4.15 User evidence

A highway authority may have collections of user forms which were submitted when the first definitive maps were being compiled or, subsequently, when reviews were undertaken.

7.4.16 Other records

The above list is not exhaustive. Many other documents may supply useful information. For instance, there may be indictments for non-repair of highways or for obstructions. Records of property sales, solicitors' files or old title deeds sometimes refer to public rights of way.

7.4.17 Aerial photographs

Aerial photographs are often helpful in establishing the line of previous tracks and paths. The Ordnance Survey has collections of aerial photographs.

7.4.18 Local history

There may be written or oral records of local history relating to use by the public of rights of way in the area.

7.5 USER EVIDENCE

7.5.1 Purpose

Use by the public of a defined route may be evidence:

(1) of acceptance of a dedicated route, which is a prerequisite for a highway unless it is created under statutory powers;
(2) of dedication itself, whether or not supported by documentary evidence; and
(3) of the correct classification of rights over an RUPP; and
(4) that the definition of a BOAT ('used by the public mainly for the purpose for which footpaths and bridleways are so used') for entry on the definitive map has been fulfilled.[2]

In other words, use by the public is important in ascertaining whether a public right of way exists and if so, the status of such a right.

---

1   Requisitioned Land and War Works Act 1945.
2   Cf *Masters v Secretary of State for the Environment* [2000] 2 All ER 788, where user was considered unnecessary on a modification order relating to an RUPP.

User evidence should be submitted with applications for modification orders and should also be produced at public inquiries. Many local authorities provide user forms, but there is no special format. Statements and declarations should give the name and address of the person, his or her date of birth and occupation and a description of the path with grid references. They should give details of the use of the path. If possible, those who make statements should appear as witnesses if there is a public inquiry. Greater weight will be given to evidence which has been subjected to cross-examination.

7.6   CUL-DE-SACS

Although highways generally lead from one public place to another, there is nothing to prevent a highway ending in a cul-de-sac. For instance, highways may lead to a beauty spot,[1] the sea[2] or a river.[3] When considering evidence as to the existence of a highway, a cul-de-sac without purpose may indicate that no public right of way exists.

In *Roberts v Webster*,[4] Widgery J said:

> 'The authorities clearly show that there is no rule of law which compels a conclusion that a country cul-de-sac can never be a highway. The principle stated in the authorities is not a rule of law but one of common sense based on the fact that the parties do not claim to use a path as of right unless there is some point in their doing so and to walk down a country cul-de-sac merely for the privilege of walking back again is a pointless activity. However, if there is some kind of attraction at the far end which might cause the public to wish to use the road, it is clear that may be sufficient to justify the conclusion that a public highway was created.'

A cul-de-sac may indicate in some circumstances that there was a through route, the centre part of which has disappeared.[5] On the other hand, if the route ends at a farm, it may be that it became a public right of way as a result of the farmer having taken a grant to make up the road under the Agricultural Improvements Act 1955. One condition of the grant was that the road, when made up, should become a highway.

Where vehicular use is claimed over a lane, part of which is a footpath or bridleway, the legal result may be a cul-de-sac. This is because user over the footpath part of the lane will be discounted, being illegal. Twenty years' use, from a point with vehicular access, may create a vehicular route over the lane up to the point of the lane which is a footpath or bridleway.

The position is the same where an existing highway has been stopped up at one end.[6]

---

1   *Moser v Ambleside UDC* (1925) 89 JP 118. For a recent case see *R v Secretary of State for the Environment ex parte Bagshaw and North* (1994) 68 P&CR 402.
2   *Williams-Ellis v Cobb* [1935] 1 QB 310.
3   *Campbell v Lang* (1853) 1 Eq Rep 98.
4   (1967) 66 LGR 298.
5   *Eyre v New Forest Highways Board* (1892) 56 JP 512.
6   *R v Downshire* (1836) 4 A&E 698.

7.7 THE WIDTH

7.7.1 The definitive map and statement

The definitive map will show the route of the public right of way. However, given the scale of most definitive maps, it may not show the route with sufficient accuracy on the ground. The statement accompanying the map may describe physical features which will identify the position more accurately. Sometimes the statement will give the legal width. However, care must be taken in interpreting the statement. A description of a path in the statement may be giving a legal width or may be just describing the surrounding features.

7.7.2 Other documents

The width may be specified in old maps, title deeds and other documents. Where rights of way are created by statute or orders or agreements under statute, the width may be set out. Justices' certificates on the setting out of roads or proceedings relating to non-repair of highways may provide evidence of width.

7.7.3 Historic use

In the absence of clear documentary evidence, historic evidence of width enjoyed on the ground by the public will need to be investigated. This may be on the basis of topographical features, maps, aerial photographs and statements by users. The legal presumptions set out at **2.2.2** may assist in ascertaining the width.

7.7.4 Open land

Where a right of way crosses open land, the width will be a reasonable strip in the absence of any evidence to the contrary.[1]

7.7.5 Rights of Way Act 1990

The Rights of Way Act 1990 introduced a new section into the Highways Act 1980 to deal with crops and overhanging vegetation.[2] For the purposes of restoring paths after ploughing and cultivation, the minimum and maximum widths are specified in the legislation. These widths, however, are not relevant for other purposes.

---

1   *Secretary of State for Defence v Percy* [1999] 1 All ER 732.
2   Section 137A. See also s 134 and Sch 12A. These provisions are discussed in Chapter 9.

7.8   PROCEDURES TO ESTABLISH PUBLIC RIGHTS OF WAY

7.8.1   Modification orders

The highway authority is under a duty to keep the definitive map up to date.[1] If there is evidence that there are omissions or the recorded rights are incorrect, the map and statement should be altered by modification orders. The making and confirming of modification orders is a democratic, if slow and cumbersome, method of testing all the available evidence.

7.8.2   Declarations

A declaration may be sought in the High Court or in the county court to establish whether or not a highway exists. This procedure is often used where a highway authority claims that a particular route is a highway and this is denied by the landowner.

7.8.3   Other court actions

The issue of whether or not a route is a highway may have to be decided in the context of other court actions. Examples include actions for trespass, public nuisance, negligence.

The legal existence or not of the highway may also be relevant in applications to the magistrates' court for stopping-up or diversion orders, or under s 56 of the Highways Act 1980 in connection with the repair of highways.

---

1   WLCA 1981, s 53.

Chapter 8

MAINTENANCE OF HIGHWAYS

8.1 HISTORY OF HIGHWAY MAINTENANCE

8.1.1 The common law

The general rule was that the inhabitants of the parish were liable to repair all the highways within that parish. Exceptionally, a smaller unit such as a tithing or hamlet might be liable to repair or the obligation might be imposed on an individual as discussed below.

8.1.2 Highways Act 1835

Section 23 of the Highways Act 1835 ended the automatic liability of the parish to repair all highways within the parish. There was a procedure whereby roads constructed or dedicated after the Act came into force would become maintainable at public expense. The Act did not affect the liability of the inhabitants for highways which existed before the Act.

Nor did the Act apply to footpaths or bridleways which continued to be maintainable by the inhabitants of the parish.

8.1.3 National Parks and Access to the Countryside Act 1949

As s 23 of the Highways Act 1835 did not apply to footpaths and bridleways, the inhabitants at large continued to be liable for their maintenance. However, s 49 of the NPACA 1949 provided that s 23 was to apply to all paths dedicated after commencement of the Act unless in pursuance of a public path agreement. This means that if footpaths and bridleways are to be publicly maintainable the proper procedure for adoption must be followed.

8.1.4 Highways Acts 1959 and 1980

The liability of the inhabitants at large to repair highways was abolished by the Highways Act 1959.[1] Thereafter, highways were said to be maintainable at public expense.

---

1   Section 38.

The 1980 Act and its predecessors make possible the creation of new paths by public path creation orders or agreements.[1] Such paths will be maintainable at public expense, as will highways which have been adopted under the procedures set out in the Highways Acts.

The Highways Act 1980 requires the landowner to give notice to the highway authority and to repair the way for at least 12 months before it can be publicly maintainable.[2] If the highway authority considers that it is not of sufficient utility to the public to justify it being maintainable at public expense, it may apply to the magistrates' court for an order to that effect.

8.2 LIABILITY TO REPAIR

8.2.1 No liability

If the procedural formalities stipulated originally in the Highways Act 1835, now s 37 of the Highways Act 1980, are not followed, the highway will not be repairable at public expense. Therefore, it is possible that a public right of way may have been dedicated without anyone being liable to maintain it.

Where this is likely to occur is where there has been a deemed dedication after 16 December 1949 and no formal public path creation order or agreement has been entered into.

As the surface of a public right, which is not publicly maintainable, remains vested in the landowner, he can repair the path should he wish to do so. He must be careful not to commit any of the statutory offences under the Highways Act 1980 in so doing.[3] Where he does repairs, it will be on a voluntary basis and will not impose on him a continuing liability.

The highway authority has neither a duty nor a right to do repairs. The same is true of the highway users, but they may do what is necessary to abate a nuisance.

8.2.2 Statutory liability

A local or private Act of Parliament may provide that some person or body is liable to maintain the highway. Examples occur under the Turnpike Acts and the Inclosure Acts. Unless the particular statute removes the liability from the parish, now the highway authority, there will be concurrent liability.[4]

8.2.3 Prescriptive liability

This form of liability must have existed from time immemorial. Evidence that the highway came into existence after 1189 would rebut the claim, but

---

1   Sections 25 and 26.
2   Section 37.
3   See Chapter 9.
4   *R v Netherthong (Inhabitants)* (1818) 2 B&A 179.

evidence need not be produced that the liability has existed since that time. Use for a long period raises the presumption.

To establish prescriptive liability, there must be some benefit (except possibly for corporations) to recompense a person for being subject to this burden. An example would be a right to levy a toll.[1]

8.2.4   *Ratione tenurae*

This liability appears to have been based upon a grant of land in return for an undertaking to keep it in repair.[2] The liability must pre-date the Statute *Quia Emptores* 1290.[3]

The occupier is primarily liable, although he can claim recompense from the owner.[4] Where plots are divided, any one occupier may be liable for the whole of the original area.

Liability will terminate if the highway is altered so that the original structure is not apparent.

8.2.5   Liability by enclosure

Highways often became impassable and common law therefore recognised that a traveller might divert onto adjoining land. However, this would not be possible if the highway did not cross open land, but was enclosed. It was therefore held that a landowner who had enclosed the land so that deviation was not possible, was under a duty to keep the highway in repair.[5] Like a prescriptive right, it could only arise where the highway had existed from time immemorial. It did not apply to a dedication which had taken place in living memory.[6]

8.2.6   Highway authority

The general rule is that carriageways will be maintainable at public expense by the highway authority. The exceptions are where the highway was created after 1835 and was not adopted in accordance with the statutory procedures laid down by that Act and subsequent Highway Acts.

8.2.7   Dual liability

Where a footpath or bridleway is maintainable at public expense, the relevant highway authority is under a duty to maintain it. However, if a private individual is also liable to maintain 'under a special enactment or by reasons of tenure, enclosure or presumption' he will be concurrently liable.[7] The

---

1   *R v St Giles, Cambridge (Inhabitants)* 1816 5 M&S 260.
2   *Anon* (1497) YB 12 Hen 7 Fol 15, PL1.
3   *R v Hatfield (Inhabitants)* (1820) 4 B&A 75.
4   *Daventry RDC v Parker* [1900] 1 QB 1.
5   *Henn's case* (1632) WJ 296.
6   *R v Flecknow (Inhabitants)* (1758) 1 Burr 461.
7   Highways Act 1980, s 50.

authority may do the work and recover the expense of so doing from that person after giving the relevant notice.

8.3   PUBLIC RIGHTS OF WAY

8.3.1   Dedication before 16 December 1949

Section 47 of the NPACA 1949 declared that all existing public paths were repairable by the inhabitants at large. This was generally thought to be the position as s 23 of the Highways Act 1835 did not apply to footpaths and bridleways. Therefore it was considered that the duty to maintain such paths would lie with the parish, even if there had been no formal adoption.

8.3.2   Paths created by public path creation orders or agreements

Section 38 of the Highways Act 1959 provided that footpaths and bridleways created after the passing of the Act, pursuant to public path creation orders and agreements, should be maintained at public expense.

8.3.3   Paths constructed under the Housing Acts 1957 and 1985

A highway constructed by a council within its own area under Part V of the Housing Act 1957 or Part II of the Housing act 1985 will be publicly maintainable.[1]

8.3.4   Formally adopted paths

A landowner may expressly dedicate a public right of way, but unless it is formally adopted following the statutory procedures it will not be maintainable at public expense. He must give notice to the highway authority and repair it for at least 12 months.[2]

8.3.5   Diverted paths

Paths diverted pursuant to diversion orders, including special and SSSI diversion orders, and agreements will be maintainable at public expense.[3] Informal diversions, on the other hand, will not be publicly maintainable.

8.3.6   RUPPs, restricted byways and BOATs

RUPPs, reclassified under the WLCA 1981 as footpaths, bridleways or BOATs are publicly maintainable.[4]

---

1   See *Gulliksen v Pembrokeshire County Council* [2002] 3 WLR 1072.
2   Highways Act 1980, s 37.
3   Ibid, s 36(2)(d)–(f).
4   WLCA 1981, s 54(4); CROW Act 2000, s 47.

If an RUPP was reclassified under the CA 1968, the path would become publicly maintainable 'as from the date of publication of the definitive map and statement in the special review'.[1] Therefore, if the map was published, the path would become publicly maintainable. The position is preserved by the CROW Act 2000.

Where an RUPP was shown on a draft map and statement on a review under the NPACA 1949 and was then shown on the definitive map and statement as a BOAT, bridleway or footpath under the provisions of s 55 of the WLCA 1981, the reclassified path will be publicly maintainable.[2]

Many of the special reviews were abandoned in accordance with s 55 of the WLCA 1981. If it can be proved that the reclassification was to have been to a footpath or bridleway and that the path existed in December 1949, then the paths will be publicly maintainable under that Act.

Restricted byways will, from the date of the commencement of s 48 of the CROW Act 2000 (being the section which confers restricted byway rights on the public), be highways maintainable at public expense.[3] Any other liability to maintain under a special enactment, or by reason of tenure, enclosure or prescription will be extinguished.

If a BOAT is added to the definitive map by a modification order rather than a reclassification order, maintenance liability will depend on when the BOAT is shown to have been created. If it was created before 1835, then it will be publicly maintainable. If after that date, it will have had to have been formally adopted.

It may be that the BOAT was created under statute or an inclosure award which sets out who is responsible for maintenance.

8.3.7 Deemed dedication

Where a public right of way comes into existence on the basis of user which occurs after 1949, there will be no one responsible for maintenance unless the path is formally adopted by the highway authority. If the path had legal existence before 16 December 1949, it will be publicly maintainable.

8.3.8 List of streets

Every highway authority must make and keep up to date, a list of streets within its area which are highways maintainable at public expense.[4] 'Street' is defined to include:

> 'any highway and any road, lane, footpath, square, court, alley or passage, whether a thoroughfare or not, and includes any part of a street.'[5]

---

1 Countryside Act 1968, Sch 3, para 9(2)(a).
2 WLCA 1981, s 55, as amended by the CROW Act 2000, Sch 5, para 5.
3 Section 49.
4 Highways Act 1980, s 36(6).
5 Ibid, s 329.

It should therefore be possible to ascertain whether or not public rights of way are publicly maintainable. The trouble is that the list is often inaccurate. Some publicly maintainable streets are not included.

The list may be inspected at the county council's offices free of charge. The county council is obliged to supply each district within the county with an up-to-date list of publicly maintainable streets within the area of the district. This too may be inspected free of charge at the relevant district office.[1]

8.3.9   Publicly maintainable assumption

In *Attorney General v Watford Rural District Council*,[2] it was held that it was for the inhabitants at large to prove that s 23 of the Highways Act 1835 applied and therefore that a vehicular highway was not maintainable by them. With regard to public rights of way, many highway authorities take the view that it is less expensive to assume that they are publicly maintainable than to do the necessary research. Whether or not it is in the interests of the landowner to accept such an assumption will depend on the particular circumstances.

8.4   PHYSICAL EXTENT OF DUTY TO MAINTAIN

8.4.1   Extent of the highway

The extent of the highway is a question of fact. It may or may not include the verges. Sometimes it is obvious how far the highway extends, but at other times it will be necessary to research the matter. Title deeds of the adjoining landowners and also highway records may clarify the position. How the land has been treated over the years is also relevant. Even where the highway includes the verges, the duty to maintain its vehicular standard is applied only to the part used by vehicles.[3]

8.4.2   Ditches

Sometimes the adjoining land will be separated by a hedge and a ditch, with a ditch on the side of the track. Although there is a presumption that, where properties are separated by a hedge and a ditch, the boundary is on the far side of the ditch from the hedge, this may not apply where there is a highway. Ditches were often put in to drain the highway.

8.4.3   Walls

Whether or not a wall is part of the highway is again a question of evidence. Walls may have been constructed to protect the highway or to support it. In such cases, the walls would be part of the highway.[4] Normally, however, walls

---

1   Highways Act 1980, s 36(7).
2   [1912] 1 Ch 417.
3   *Kind v Newcastle-upon-Tyne City Council* [2001] EWHC Admin 616, [2001] 36 EG 179.
4   *Sandgate UDC v Kent County Council* (1898) 79 LT 424. Cf *Attorney General v Staffordshire County Council* [1905] 1 Ch 336.

and fences will mark the boundaries of the land belonging to the adjoining landowner and will not form part of the highway.

It seems that even if a retaining wall is not considered to be part of the highway, perhaps because it pre-dated dedication, there may in some circumstances be a duty on the highway authority to repair.

8.4.4 Culverts and bridges

The law relating to the maintenance of bridges is extremely complex.[1] Generally, bridges which carry public rights of way will be regarded as part of the highway and maintainable by the highway authority if that authority is liable to maintain the surface of the path.[2] The same goes for culverts unless they were constructed for the purpose of draining the adjoining land.

The maintenance liability, if any, will be limited to maintenance for the public rights. So if there are bridleway rights only, the highway authority will not be liable to provide a bridge suitable for vehicles.

8.4.5 Stiles and gates

Stiles and gates will normally be erected for the convenience of the landowner and not as part of the highway. In order to erect a stile or gate, the landowner will need to obtain the consent of the highway authority.[3] Such consent will be given only if the land is used for agriculture and the stiles or gates are needed for preventing the 'ingress or egress of animals'. Although the maintenance will be the responsibility of the landowner, unless there is an agreement or condition to the contrary, he is entitled to recover at least 25 per cent of the cost from the highway authority.

8.4.6 The surface of the highway

Subject to the specific provisions relating to the above features, the duty of the highway authority is to maintain the surface of the highway. The surface of publicly maintainable highways is vested in the highway authority.[4] The depth of the surface depends on how much is needed to support the road. It has been described as the top two spits.[5]

The responsibility for dealing with any overhanging vegetation is that of the adjoining landowner, unless the vegetation is growing on land forming part of the highway, such as the highway verge. The ownership of trees growing in the highway has not been clearly settled. This is because in a publicly maintainable highway there are different strata of ownership. The roots of the trees will be in

---

1   See S Sauvain and R Crail 'Bridges: Responsibility to repair them (1), (2) and (3)', RWLR 5.1, pp 31, 37 and 45.
2   Highways Act 1980, s 328(2): 'Where a highway passes over a bridge or through a tunnel, that bridge or tunnel is to be taken for the purposes of this Act to be part of the highway'.
3   Ibid, s 147.
4   Ibid, s 263(1).
5   *Tithe Redemption Commissioners v Runcorn UDC* [1954] 2 WLR 518.

the subsoil belonging to the landowner. The tree will grow through the surface which is vested in the highway authority, and finally, it is likely to shoot up into the airspace which is in the ownership of the landowner. However, regardless of ownership the highway authority has sufficient control to remove the trees and because of its ownership of the surface the responsibility for doing so rests with the authority, rather than the landowner.[1]

8.4.7 Drainage

The highway authority, as well as having a duty to maintain the surface, is also given wide powers to effect improvements. One particular power, which may impinge on the land of the adjoining owner, is the right to drain the highway and prevent surface water from flowing onto it.[2] In the exercise of this power, the highway authority may construct and lay drains not only in the highway itself, but also in the adjoining land. It may also scour and cleanse any existing drains on adjoining land. No easement is required to discharge water into existing drains. Compensation is payable to the landowner if damage results from the exercise of these powers.

Where a highway authority constructed a drainage culvert in highway land which subsequently became inadequate and caused flooding on to the adjoining land, it was held liable in nuisance.[3]

8.5 STANDARD OF MAINTENANCE

8.5.1 Meaning of maintenance

'Maintenance' is defined to include repair.[4] Maintenance, or a duty to repair, does not include the removal of obstructions. The leading case is *Hereford and Worcester County Council v Newman*,[5] in which there were several problems relating to three footpaths. A distinction was made between want of repair and obstruction. A hawthorn fence and other vegetation growing on the surface of the path made the paths out of repair, but wire fences and overhanging fences did not; they were obstructions.

A highway is not out of repair when blocked by natural and man-made obstructions.

There is no duty on a highway authority to improve rather than maintain a highway.

8.5.2 Ordinary traffic

Where a highway authority is liable for maintenance, it must keep the highway in such a state as to be safe and fit for the ordinary traffic of the neighbourhood

---

1   See Stephen Sauvain *Highway Law* (Sweet & Maxwell, 1997, 2nd edn), pp 62–70.
2   Highways Act 1980, s 100.
3   *Bybrook Barn Garden Centre v Kent County Council* (2001) *The Times*, January 5.
4   Highways Act 1980, s 329.
5   [1975] 1 WLR 901.

at all seasons of the year.[1] Where the ordinary traffic changes over time, the duty of repair is increased. The converse, however, is not true.

Where, however, liability is imposed on, say, a railway undertaking or a canal company, whether or not the standard of repair will increase depends on the particular Act under which the railway or a canal was constructed. There have been several cases where there was no obligation on the canal company to strengthen a bridge to carry the heavier vehicles which were currently using the bridge.[2]

Where a byway open to all traffic has been added to the definitive map by a modification order, or an RUPP has been reclassified as a BOAT, there is no obligation on a highway authority to provide a metalled carriageway or a carriageway which is by any other means provided with a surface suitable for the passage of vehicles.[3] Nor is there any obligation for a highway authority to provide on a restricted byway a metalled carriageway or carriageway which is by other means provided with a surface suitable for cycles or other vehicles.[4]

Although a bicycle may be ridden on a bridleway, the highway authority is under no obligation to do anything to facilitate the use of the bridleway by cyclists.[5]

As to what is the required standard for the maintenance of footpaths or bridleways, there are no statutory guidelines. It depends on the amount of use, where the path is situated and by whom it is likely to be used. The surface of the path must not create a hazard but, as Cumming-Bruce LJ said in *Littler v Liverpool Corporation*,[6] 'A highway is not to be criticised by the standards of a bowling green'.

8.5.3   Extraordinary traffic

If a publicly maintainable highway is damaged by traffic of excessive weight or by other extraordinary traffic, the highway authority may recover the extra expense incurred from the person causing the damage.[7] Proceedings have to be started within 12 months of the damage occurring or where there is a contract for work extending over a period of time, within 6 months of the completion of that contract. However, before a claim may be made or expenses recovered, there must be a certificate from the highway authority's proper officer to the effect that extraordinary expenses have been or will be incurred by the authority in maintaining the highway.

---

1   *R v High Halden (Inhabitants)* (1859) 1 F&F 678.
2   Eg *Sharpness New Docks and Gloucester & Birmingham Navigation Company v Attorney General* [1915] AC 654.
3   WLCA 1981, s 54(7).
4   CROW Act 2000, s 49(4).
5   CA 1968, s 30(3).
6   [1968] 2 All ER 343.
7   Highways Act 1980, s 59.

It may be difficult to ascertain what amounts to extraordinary traffic. In *Hill v Thomas*,[1] Bowen LJ gave some guidelines. He stated:

> '... extraordinary traffic is really a carriage of articles over the road, at either one or more times, which is so exceptional in the quality or quantity or articles carried, or in the mode or time of user of the road, as substantially to alter and increase the burden imposed by ordinary traffic on the road and to cause damage and expenses thereby beyond what is common.'

A claim for extraordinary traffic is most likely to be made in the public rights of way context where four-wheel drive vehicles use BOATs in unsuitable conditions so that they destroy the surface of the road. However, it is difficult to see how this can be extraordinary traffic as byways carry rights for vehicles.

8.5.4　Public and private rights

The duty of the highway authority is to maintain a public right of way for the ordinary traffic. If there is, therefore, a public bridleway or footpath, the authority is not under a duty to repair it for the use of vehicles by the landowner or other person with a private right.

However, the landowner or person entitled to the benefit of a private right of way has no right to interfere with the surface of the right of way which is vested in the authority. He would therefore need the authority's consent and planning permission. The simpler course would be to persuade the authority to do the work in return for payment of the additional costs.

Even if the public right of way is not publicly maintainable, the person with the private vehicular right may have problems in upgrading the route. He may find that, in order to do so, he will be committing a number of criminal offences, as it is likely to involve the obstruction of the route. He could, therefore, be guilty of public nuisance or of committing offences under the Highways Act 1980 (eg removing soil or turf from any part of a highway,[2] wilfully obstructing the free passage along a highway,[3] depositing anything on a highway to the interruption of a user[4] or resulting in a user being injured or endangered[5]).

However, it has been suggested that, where a private right of way pre-dates the dedication of the public right, the dedication will be subject to rights already granted.[6]

A private right of way under an express grant carried an implied ancillary right to maintain and improve. (A prescriptive right entitles the grantee to maintain only. There is no right to improve.[7])

1　[1893] 2 QB 333.
2　Highways Act 1980, s 131.
3　Ibid, s 137.
4　Ibid, s 148.
5　Ibid, s 161.
6　CP Sydenham 'Greater rights over minor highways', RWLR 3.3, p 1.
7　*Mills v Silver* [1991] Ch 271.

Planning permission will not be necessary if the works do not extend beyond the boundaries of the existing route. The carrying out of works required for the maintenance or improvement of the street or way on land within the boundaries of an unadopted street or private way is permitted development within the General Development Order 1988.[1]

8.5.5 Erosion

A practical problem often arises where a riverside or cliff path is eroded. If the path is maintainable at public expense, the question is whether the highway authority is under an obligation to maintain the path or whether it can allege that the path has been extinguished by its physical disappearance.

The answer to these questions will depend to a large extent on the factual situation. However, it is suggested that, where a cliff path has disappeared, it will usually be impractical for the path to be repaired and, indeed, the right of way will cease to exist along with the maintenance liability.

The same is true where there is a riverbank path that is eroded.[2] However, this is likely to be a more gradual process and the highway authority is probably under a duty to shore up the path before it disappears. In deciding whether the highway has been destroyed, it seems that the court may have regard to whether it would be economic to do the repairs.[3]

8.6 WHO SHOULD DO THE WORK?

8.6.1 County councils

Highway authorities are currently the unitary authority, county, metropolitan district or outer London borough councils.

It is the highway authority which has the duty to maintain publicly maintainable highways.[4] However, agreements may be made with the district council which undertakes the work.

8.6.2 District councils

The county council may arrange for the district council to carry out its duties under an agency agreement.[5] Although the district council will exercise the powers, it is acting in the name of the highway authority, which will remain liable for the maintenance duties.

---

1   SI 1988/1813. Art 3, Sch 2, Pt 9.
2   *R v Secretary of State for the Environment, Transport and the Regions ex parte Gloucestershire County Council* [2000] EGCS 150.
3   *R v Greenhow Inhabitants* (1876) 1 QBD 703.
4   Highways Act 1980, s 41.
5   Local Government Act 1972, s 101.

The district council has maintenance powers in respect of certain kinds of publicly maintainable highways within its district.[1] These include footpaths and bridleways. Schedule 7 to the Highways Act 1980 sets out the procedures. The district council must give notice to the county council of its intention to exercise these powers in relation to specific highways. A district council, in exercising powers, must indemnify the county council against any liability arising out of work it has done or failed to do.

District councils may also undertake the maintenance of footpaths and bridleways which are maintainable by some other person or by no one at all.[2]

8.6.3   Parish councils

These councils may also undertake the maintenance of footpaths and bridleways, whether or not they are publicly maintainable. Where they do so, the highway authority or other person who is liable to maintain will not be relieved of liability. The parish council is not entitled to automatic reimbursement. However, there are powers for the highway authority or district council to pay all or part of the parish or community council's expenses in maintaining those paths which are publicly maintainable.[3]

8.6.4   Contracting out maintenance work

Some authorities enter into maintenance agreements with farmers and landowners. In return for payment, the farmer or owner agrees to mow or otherwise control vegetation on the surface of a path which is the highway authority's responsibility. The agreement may cover one or more farms, not necessarily in the same ownership.

The maintenance costs may be less than if the local authority had to do the job, as the equipment may be on site. It is also a means of obtaining the co-operation of farmers. In order to receive the payments they must keep all their paths unobstructed. Also, by doing the work, they often come to understand the point and importance of public rights of way.

8.6.5   Voluntary initiatives

There are various schemes whereby volunteer groups such as the Ramblers' Association, British Horse Society, Young Farmers' Clubs and British Trust for Conservation Volunteers help with path maintenance.

Local people may be involved with keeping paths in order through the Parish Paths Partnership, operated by some highway authorities.

---

1   Highways Act 1980, s 42.
2   Ibid, s 50.
3   Ibid, ss 43 and 50.

8.6.6 Landowner's responsibilities

Where the highway is publicly maintainable, it is still the landowner's responsibility to make sure that the route is not obstructed. Therefore, he must cut back overhanging trees and vegetation from the side of rights of way and not plant crops on headland paths. Cross-field paths may be cultivated only when it is not convenient to avoid them and the surface must then be made good so that it is reasonably convenient to use within 14 days of first being cultivated for that crop or within 24 hours of any subsequent cultivation (unless a longer period has been agreed in advance in writing by the highway authority). The paths must be apparent on the ground at all times and must not be obstructed by crops.[1]

8.7 ENFORCEMENT OF THE DUTY TO REPAIR

The duty to repair is enforced by following the procedures set out in s 56 of the Highways Act 1980.

(1) A notice must be served on the highway authority or other person who it is considered is liable to repair the highway. A notice requires the recipient to state whether he admits that the way or bridge is a highway and that he is liable to repair it.

(2) Within one month of receiving such a notice, the recipient must state whether he agrees that the highway is maintainable by him or, if the recipient is a highway authority, that it is repairable at public expense.

(3) When the complainant has received the notice of admission he has 6 months to apply to a magistrates' court for an order requiring the highway to be repaired. The magistrate will decide whether or not the highway is out of repair. If it is out of repair, the court will stipulate a time within which the repairs should be done.

(4) If the highway has not been put into repair at the end of that period, the magistrate may extend the period or authorise the complainant to do the work. The complainant can then recover the expenses of so doing as a civil debt from the highway authority or other person against whom the order was made.

If no notice of admission is given within one month of the original notice, the complainant may apply to the Crown Court to determine whether the highway is a highway and whether the respondent is liable to repair it.

If either the magistrates' court or the Crown Court orders the person responsible for maintenance to carry out the work by the end of a specified period and this is not done, the complainant may apply to the magistrates' court for an order authorising him to carry out the works himself.

---

1 Highways Act 1980, ss 134 and 137A.

The magistrates' court may either extend the period for doing the works or make a new order authorising the complainant to do the work. If he does the work, he can recover expenses as a civil debt.

8.8   LIABILITY FOR FAILURE TO MAINTAIN

8.8.1   Misfeasance and nonfeasance

There used to be a distinction between nonfeasance (ie failure to do something) and misfeasance (ie doing something badly). There was no liability on a highway authority for nonfeasance. However, the Highways (Miscellaneous Provisions) Act 1961, which came into force on 4 August 1964, made a highway authority liable for nonfeasance as well as misfeasance.

It seems that those who were liable to repair a highway by reason of tenure, prescription or inclosure may never have been able to rely on the defence of nonfeasance.

8.8.2   Highways Act 1980, s 41

This section imposes on a highway authority a duty to maintain highways which are maintainable at the public expense.

In order to make out a claim for damages under s 41, it is necessary to show that the highway is dangerous to traffic, ie likely to cause physical injury or damage. It does not enable an adjoining landowner to claim economic loss because his business suffers due to the want of repair of the road.[1]

In ascertaining whether a highway is dangerous to traffic, foreseeability is an important element. The danger must have been caused by the breach of the duty to maintain the highway.

The House of Lords has held in *Goodes v East Sussex County Council*[2] that a highway authority's duty under s 41(1) of the Highways Act 1980 is an absolute duty to maintain the fabric of the highway in such good repair as to render the physical condition safe for ordinary traffic to pass at all seasons of the year. However, the duty to maintain does not include a duty to prevent the formation of ice or remove the accumulation of snow on the road.

8.8.3   The statutory defence

A highway authority has a defence to an action against it in respect of its failure to maintain a highway maintainable at the public expense.[3] A highway authority must show that it has taken such care as in all the circumstances is

---

1   *Wentworth v Wiltshire County Council* [1993] 2 WLR 175.
2   [2000] 1 WLR 1356. See consequential amendments made to the Road Traffic Act 1998, s 21(2)(b) and the Highways Act 1980, s 300 introduced by the CROW Act 2000, s 70 as explained in DETR Circular 04/2001, paras 42–43.
3   Highways Act 1980, s 58.

reasonably required to secure that the part of the highway to which the action relates is not dangerous for traffic.

The court is directed to take into account:

(a) the character of the highway, and the traffic which was reasonably to be expected to use it;
(b) the standard of maintenance appropriate for a highway of that character and used by such traffic;
(c) the state of repair in which a reasonable person would have expected to find the highway;
(d) whether the highway authority knew, or could reasonably have been expected to know, that the condition of the part of the highway to which the action relates was likely to cause danger to users of the highway;[1]
(e) where the highway authority could not reasonably have been expected to repair that part of the highway before the cause of action arose, what warning notice of its condition had been displayed.

However, for the purposes of such a defence, it is not relevant to prove that the highway authority had arranged for a competent person to carry out or supervise the maintenance of the part of the highway to which the action relates, unless it is also proved that the authority had given him proper instructions with regard to the maintenance of the highway and that he had carried out the instructions.

Most of the cases concerned with the statutory defence relate to urban pavements. However, a case in which the council was successful in relation to a footpath was *Whiting v Hillingdon Borough Council*.[2] The plaintiff stepped into some undergrowth at the side of the path to allow someone to pass. She injured her leg on a tree stump which was obscured by vegetation. The path had been regularly inspected and had been repaired 2 months before the accident. The court held that the council had exercised reasonable care and was not obliged to beat the foliage for hidden traps or dangers.

Councils should therefore ensure they have a regular inspection regime in force and that they keep records of such inspections. They should be able to show that they have cleared the actual surface of the path and have repaired any serious defects such as potholes. Drainage and other remedial actions may be called for in specific situations, or notices warning of hazards.

Lack of resources is not likely to provide a defence. In *R v Gloucestershire County Council ex parte Barry*,[3] the House of Lords decided that financial resources could only be taken into account in assessing services for the disabled under the Chronically Sick and Disabled Persons Act 1970 when measured against a set of criteria for assessing need. Once that need was

---

1   Regular inspections are obviously important. See *Pridham v Hemel Hempstead Corporation* (1971) 69 LGR 523.
2   (1970) 68 LGR 437.
3   [1997] 2 All ER 1, followed in *R v Sefton Metropolitan Borough Council ex parte Help the Aged* [1997] 1 WLR 57.

established, the authority had to provide the statutory services. In *R v East Sussex County Council ex parte T*,[1] the House of Lords held that it was unlawful for the Local Education Authority to reduce a child's tuition from 5 to 3 hours in order to save money. The council was not entitled to consider the resources when performing its statutory duty to provide suitable education for children at home. Although these cases are not concerned with public rights of way, the reasoning underlying the decisions would apply equally to a council who had failed to maintain through lack of funds.

8.9 EXTINGUISHMENT OF LIABILITY

Liability to maintain will cease when the highway is extinguished or when the liability to maintain is extinguished by court order.

A highway authority may apply to the magistrates' court to extinguish the maintenance liability.[2] However, an application may not be made in respect of footpaths or bridleways.

Extinguishment of the highway itself may occur where it physically ceases to exist (eg due to coastal erosion) or where there has been a successful application to the magistrates' court under s 116 of the Highways Act 1980 to extinguish the highway. Bridleways and footpaths may also be extinguished under s 118 of the 1980 Act if an order is confirmed by the local authority or Secretary of State.

An individual's liability to repair may be extinguished by an agreement with the highway authority. On the date specified in the agreement, the highway becomes maintainable at public expense.[3]

An individual's liability may also be extinguished by an order of the magistrates' court or where there is a diversion under s 116.[4]

In both cases, the route or diverted route will become maintainable at public expense, if it is not so already, and the individual will have to pay compensation for being relieved of his responsibility.

---

1   [1998] 2 WLR 884.
2   Highways Act 1980, s 47(1).
3   Ibid, s 38.
4   Ibid, s 54.

Chapter 9

INTERFERENCE WITH PUBLIC RIGHTS OF WAY

9.1 INTRODUCTION

Highway authorities are under a statutory duty to protect and assert the rights of the public to the use and enjoyment of highways for which they are the highway authority and to prevent the stopping up and obstruction of such highways.[1] They, together with other local authorities, have enforcement powers to remove obstructions and prevent interference. A member of the public may prosecute for obstruction, or persuade the Attorney-General to take civil proceedings on behalf of the public[2] and, if he has suffered special damage, may be able to bring civil proceedings himself for obstruction.[3]

Besides physical obstructions, a public nuisance in relation to a highway is 'any wrongful act or omission upon or near a highway, whereby the public are prevented from freely, safely and conveniently passing along the highway'.[4]

Frontagers (ie the owners of property adjoining the highway) have been accorded special treatment by the courts. They can allow vehicles to stop for the purpose of unloading passengers or goods without committing a public nuisance. They have also been allowed to obstruct the highway by scaffolding and hoardings while working on their adjoining property, provided the obstruction is no greater in degree, nor longer in duration, than necessary.[5]

This reflects the nature of the law of public nuisance. A balance has to be struck between the interests of the landowners and the highway users.

As Romer LJ said in *Harper v Haden & Sons Ltd*:[6]

'The law relating to the user of highways is in truth the law of give and take. Those who use them must in doing so have reasonable regard to the convenience and comfort of others and must not themselves expect a degree of convenience and comfort only obtainable by disregarding that of other people. They must expect to be obstructed occasionally. It is the price they pay for the privilege of obstructing others.'

---

1 Highways Act 1980, s 130.
2 Ibid, s 137.
3 See B Hough 'Entitlement to enforce right of way', RWLR 10.5, p 1.
4 *Jacobs v London County Council* [1950] AC 361 at 375; see also *R v Mathias* (1861) 2 F&F 570 at 574.
5 *Harper v Haden & Sons* [1933] 1 Ch 298.
6 [1933] 1 Ch 298 at 320.

Although the disputes in public rights of way cases usually concern landowners, obstructions and interferences may also be committed by other users of the highway. Whether or not one user obstructs another's use warrants a legal action depends on what is reasonable in all the circumstances. It is accepted that travellers may stop and rest on a highway. However, parking a vehicle on a BOAT for a number of days would amount to an obstruction. The problems associated with misuse of the highway are discussed in Chapter 10.

9.2   OBSTRUCTION

9.2.1   General principles

An obstruction is 'anything which substantially prevents the public from having free access over the whole of the highway which is not purely temporary in nature'.[1]

For a person to have a claim where a private right of way is obstructed he must show that there has been a substantial interference. This is not so where there is a public right of way. Any obstruction of the route will be a public nuisance, even if it covers only part of the width of a route, provided it is not de minimis.[2]

The removal of the obstructions is not included in the highway authority's maintenance duties. It is, however, covered by the authority's duty to assert and protect the rights of the public to the use and enjoyment of any highway for which it is the highway authority. As part of this duty, the authority must prevent, as far as possible, the stopping up or obstruction of highways. In *R v Surrey County Council ex parte Send Parish Council*, the court held that although, where there was an obstruction, the county council had a discretion on the form of the proceedings and the way in which, and the extent to which, they ought to be prosecuted, the discretion did not extend to stopping up an obstructed path and replacing it with another.[3] Such a policy would not promote the policy or object of the Highways Act 1980.

The highway authority is not under a duty to assert and protect the rights of the public where there is a genuine dispute as to the existence of the highway.[4] However, if it does so, and subsequently the right of way is found not to exist, the proceedings will not be unauthorised.[5] Where a parish council represents to a local authority that a highway has been unlawfully stopped up or obstructed, the highway authority is under a duty to take proceedings unless satisfied that the representations are incorrect.[6]

---

1   *Seekings v Clarke* (1961) 59 LGR 268 at 269.
2   *Trevett v Lee* [1955] 1 WLR 113.
3   (1979) 40 P&CR 390.
4   *R v Lancashire County Council ex parte Guyer* [1980] 1 WLR 1024.
5   Highways Act 1980, s 130(7).
6   Ibid, s 130(6).

9.2.2 Enforcement of duty to prevent obstructions

The CROW Act 2000 has introduced into the Highways Act 1980 new powers for enforcing the highway authority's duty to remove obstructions.[1] Previously, the only way of doing this was by judicial review.

The new s 130A enables any person to serve a notice (the request notice) on a highway authority for the relevant area requiring it to secure the removal of certain types of obstruction from a footpath, bridleway, restricted byway, or a way shown on the definitive map and statement as a restricted byway or BOAT. Other vehicular highways are not included. The section does not apply to inner London.

The obstructions covered are structures, things deposited on the highway which are causing a nuisance, overhanging vegetation and other obstructions which may be specified by regulations. Specifically excluded are buildings, whether temporary or permanent, or works for the construction of a building, structures, including a tent, caravan, or vehicle, which are used as a dwelling, and people. The section does not apply to obstructions caused by want of repair.

The person who serves the notice must include, if he has the information, the name and address of the person responsible for the obstruction.

The highway authority on whom the request notice is served must, within one month, serve notice on the person who is, or appears to it to be, responsible for the obstruction, informing him that a request notice has been served and what, if any, action the authority proposes to take. The authority must also serve a notice on the person who gave the request notice giving the names and addresses of each person to whom the authority has served notice and stating what action, if any, the authority proposes to take. A person who is responsible for the obstruction includes the owner, any person who has possession or control of the obstruction, or who may be required to remove it.

The form of these notices will be prescribed by regulations.

If the obstruction is not removed within 2 months from the service of the request notice on the highway authority, the person who served the notice may apply to the magistrates' court for an order.[2] Five days' notice in the prescribed form of the intention to apply to the court for an order must be given to the highway authority.[3] The application must be made within 6 months of the serving of request notice on the highway authority.

The applicant must give the court details of the names and addresses of those whom, they have been informed by the highway authority, were served with notices[4] on the ground that they were or appeared to be responsible for the obstruction. The court must give notice of the hearing to such persons and of

---

1   Section 63, which inserts ss 130A, 130B, 130C and 130D into the Highways Act 1980.
2   Section 130B.
3   Highways Act 1980, s 130C.
4   Notices given under s 130A(6)(b).

the right of those responsible for the obstruction to be heard and the right of appeal to the Crown Court against any decision.[1]

Before making the order, the court must be satisfied that the obstruction is:

(a) one to which s 130A applies, or that it did at the time of the notice but that subsequently the structure was used for human habitation;
(b) that the way exists as a footpath, bridleway, or restricted byway or is shown on the definitive map as a restricted byway or byway open to all traffic; and
(c) that the obstruction significantly interferes with the public's right of way.[2]

No order may be made if the highway authority satisfies the court that the existence of the highway is seriously disputed, or that it is not the highway authority for the highway in question and the obstruction is not prejudicial to the interest of its area. It is also a defence if the highway authority can satisfy the court that arrangements have been made by the authority for the removal of the obstruction within a reasonable time, having regard to the number and seriousness of obstructions in its area. If the authority is going to raise any of these defences, it should inform the applicant beforehand. Otherwise, it might find itself liable for costs.[3]

The order, if granted, must specify the steps to be taken by the authority to remove the obstruction. The order will not take effect before 21 days after it has been made or, where there is an appeal, either to the Crown Court or by case stated to the High Court, until the appeal is determined or withdrawn. The highway authority against whom the order is made must, as soon as practicable, display notice of the order and the right to appeal against it on the relevant highway. Regulations will stipulate the form and content of the notice and where on the highway it must be displayed.

A highway authority on which an order has been made may apply for its variation.

9.2.3   Penalties for wilful obstruction

Under s 137, a person who, without lawful authority or excuse, wilfully obstructs a highway is guilty of an offence and is liable to pay a fine. The CROW Act 2000 has introduced an additional remedy.[4]

A magistrates' court may, on the conviction of a person for wilful obstruction of the highway, order that person to remove the obstruction, provided it is in that person's power to do so. This may be additional to, or instead of, a fine. The order must stipulate what steps are required to remove the obstruction and the timescale within which it must be done. The time allowed by the order may be extended on an application made before the time runs out.

---

1   Highways Act 1980, ss 130B(2), (6), 317, as amended by the CROW Act 2000, s 63(2).
    The right to be heard is only on matters set out in s 130B(4).
2   Ibid, s 130B(4).
3   Ibid, s 130D. Magistrates' Courts Act 1980, s 64(1).
4   Section 64, inserting s 137ZA into the Highways Act 1980.

Failure to comply without reasonable excuse with an order to remove an obstruction is an offence punishable by a fine up to level 5 on the standard scale.[1] If the offence is continued, the convicted person is guilty of a further offence and is liable to a fine not exceeding one-twentieth of that level for each day on which the offence is continued. No offence, or further offence, is committed during any time given by the court to the person against whom the order has been made to effect the removal.

Where a person has been convicted for failure to remove an obstruction and the highway authority remove the obstruction, the authority can claim from that person their expenses in doing so.

9.2.4 Stiles, gates, fences, wires

Such structures across a public right of way amount to an obstruction unless the path was originally dedicated subject to them. The statement accompanying the definitive map should record any limitation on the dedication. On looking at the statement, care should be taken to distinguish between a mere description of the route with obstructions and a dedication which is specifically limited by the obstructions.

If a way has not been dedicated subject to gates or stiles, a statutory notice may be served on the occupier requiring him to remove the structure.[2] If he fails to do so, the authority may remove it and recover its reasonable expenses. In addition, the highway authority may prosecute for obstruction.[3]

Gates in carriageways and bridleways are required to be of a minimum width. For a bridleway, the minimum width is 5 feet, for a carriageway, including a BOAT, the minimum width is 10 feet, measured between the posts. Where the gate is less than the minimum width, the highway authority may, by notice to the owner of the gate, require him to enlarge it to that width or remove it. Failure to do so within 21 days of service of the notice is an offence.[4]

In limited circumstances the highway authority may give permission to an owner, lessee or occupier for the erection on footpaths or bridleways of a gate or stile to prevent the ingress or egress of animals on land which is used, or is being brought into use, for agriculture or forestry or for the breeding and keeping of horses.[5] The authority has no power to authorise gates or stiles for other purposes such as security. Conditions may be imposed on the size and type of barrier.

In exercising its powers, the authority must have regard to the needs of those with mobility problems. The Secretary of State has the power to issue guidance on the matters which must be taken into account when the authority exercises its power to authorise stiles, gates and other works.

---

1 Currently £5,000.
2 Highways Act 1980, s 143.
3 Ibid, s 137.
4 Ibid, s 145.
5 Ibid, s 147, as amended by the CROW Act 2000, s 69.

The maintenance of a stile, gate or other structure is the responsibility of the landowner, subject to a contribution of not less than one-quarter of any expenses from the highway authority.[1]

If a landowner does not maintain a stile in a safe condition and to the standard of repair required to prevent unreasonable interference with the rights of the persons using the footpath or bridleway, the highway authority or district council, after giving 14 days' notice, may enter and do the work and recover the whole of the cost.[2]

The maintenance liability may be imposed on either the highway authority or the district council under an agreement made with the landowner.

Where a gate or stile has been erected under s 147 or s 147ZA, the maintenance responsibilities will be in accordance with the conditions imposed by the authorisation.

The CROW Act 2000 has introduced a new section into the Highways Act 1980[3] covering agreements made between the owner, lessee or occupier and the highway authority or district council relating to improvements for the benefit of those with mobility problems. There is provision for the owner, lessee or occupier to do the work in return for payment or part payment of the costs by the competent authority. Alternatively, the agreement could be for the authority to do the work and the owner, lessee or occupier to make the payments. The agreement may contain such conditions as the competent authority thinks fit. These could include conditions as to the maintenance of the structure and for ensuring that the right of way could be exercised without undue inconvenience to the public. Any conditions imposed will replace any previous conditions which existed when the path was created or which were entered into when an authorisation for a structure was granted under s 147 of the Highways Act 1980. The previous conditions or authorisations will cease to have effect 12 months from the date of the agreement or on such earlier date as is specified in the agreement. If there is non-compliance with any condition the structure will cease to be authorised and the competent authority may, by notice, require its removal.

Fences across a path, unless authorised, will be an obstruction. Electric or barbed wire fences along the side of the path may amount to a public nuisance. If members of the public using the path are likely to wander into the fence, bearing in mind that the path may be used at night, the fence will amount to a nuisance.[4]

As well as being a nuisance at common law, a barbed wire fence can be the subject of a statutory notice under the Highways Act 1980.[5] The occupier of the land may be required to remove the fence within a specified time and, if he

---

1   Highways Act 1980, s 146.
2   Ibid, s 146(2).
3   Ibid, s 147ZA introduced by the CROW Act 2000, s 69. See also the Highways Act 1980, s 175A.
4   *Stewart v Wright* (1893) 9 TLR 480.
5   Highways Act 1980, s 164.

fails to do so, a complaint may be made to a magistrates' court for the making of an abatement order. If the order is not complied with, the authority may do the work in default and recover the expenses.

It is an offence under the Highways Act 1980[1] to place a rope or wire across a highway in such a way as to cause danger to a user of the highway. This is sometimes done on public paths temporarily to control stock, but it can be dangerous to horse riders, pedestrians and farm traffic which may have a private right of way along the track.

9.2.5   Overhanging vegetation

Vegetation which overhangs the sides of a path may obstruct the passage of vehicles or pedestrians or endanger or obstruct the passage of horse riders. Where it does so, the highway authority may serve a notice on the owner of the tree, shrub or hedge or on the occupier of the land on which it is growing, to cut back or lop the vegetation so as to remove the cause of danger, obstruction or interference.[2] Any person aggrieved by the notice may appeal to the magistrates' court. If the works are not carried out in accordance with the notice, the authority can do the work itself and recover the expenses. This power is available whether the vegetation has grown naturally or was deliberately planted.

Where the vegetation grows naturally, it seems no offence of wilful obstruction will have been committed.

9.2.6   Crop spraying

The over-spraying of crops can interfere with the use of a right of way. It can also endanger people and animals and give rise to an offence under the Health and Safety at Work etc Act 1974.

If the product label states that people and animals should stay out of a treated crop, warning signs should be placed where the paths enter the sprayed area. The signs should state something to the effect of 'Sprayed: Please Keep to the Path'. They should be left in place until it is safe.

Spraying should be stopped if anyone is using a path which crosses or adjoins the field which is being sprayed.

Any herbicides used to deal with vegetation should be applied in accordance with Health and Safety Regulations and any current DEFRA Codes of Practice.

9.3   RIGHTS OF WAY ACT 1990

9.3.1   Purpose

The purpose of the Rights of Way Act 1990 (RWA 1990) was to clarify the rights and responsibilities of farmers and local authorities where paths were

---

1   Highways Act 1980, s 162.
2   Ibid, s 154, as amended by the CROW Act 2000, s 65.

disturbed by agricultural activity. Its aim was to strike a balance between the need to farm without undue hindrance and the right of path users to enjoy the countryside, while at the same time giving local authorities a clearer framework within which to operate.

The previous provisions giving a statutory right to plough, together with the ploughing code, had not proved satisfactory in achieving these objectives.

9.3.2   Ploughing and other disturbances

Ploughing a public right of way is an interference amounting to a public nuisance at common law.

It is possible that a right of way may have been dedicated subject to the right to plough.[1] If this right is recorded in a statement accompanying the definitive map, it is conclusive evidence of its existence. Otherwise, the onus is on the farmer to show that he has a common law right to plough. In most circumstances, the farmer would be better advised to rely on his statutory right to plough.

The statutory right to plough or otherwise to disturb the surface of a footpath or bridleway is contained in the Highways Act 1980, as amended by the RWA 1990.[2] The statutory right applies only to cross-field footpaths and bridleways over agricultural land. There is no right to plough field-edge paths. These are defined as footpaths or bridleways that follow the sides or headlands of fields or enclosures.

BOATs may not be ploughed. Whether or not a RUPP may be ploughed depends on whether it has vehicular rights. Until the RUPP is reclassified under the WLCA 1981 it may not be clear what rights do exist on the RUPP. The presumption is that it is a bridleway. If it is alleged that there is no right to plough across a field RUPP it must be proved that vehicular rights exist.

When s 47 of the CROW Act 2000 comes into force, RUPPs will automatically become restricted byways. As a restricted byway has vehicular rights, albeit for non-mechanically propelled vehicles, there will be no right to plough under s 134 of the Highways Act 1980.

The right to plough or otherwise disturb in accordance with the rules of good husbandry the surface of cross-field bridleways and footpaths is permitted only where it is not reasonably convenient to avoid ploughing or disturbing the surface when sowing or cultivating a crop.

After ploughing or other disturbance, the surface must be made good to at least the minimum width, so that it is reasonably convenient to use and the line is apparent on the ground to at least the minimum width. This must be done within 14 days of the first disturbance for the sowing of the crop or of any subsequent disturbance in connection with that crop within 24 hours, unless a

---

1   *Mercer v Woodgate* (1869) LR 5 QB 26.
2   Highways Act 1980, s 134.

longer period has first been agreed in writing by the highway authority. Where an extension is required, an application must be made to the highway authority before the disturbance occurs or within the relevant time. The extension is subject to a maximum of 28 days.

9.3.3   Crops

Crops, other than grass, will be an obstruction if they grow on or overhang the minimum width of any footpath, bridleway or unmade carriageway so as to inconvenience the public or prevent the line being apparent on the ground.[1] Unmade carriageways include BOATs and RUPPs with vehicular rights and restricted byways. A crop will be treated as grass only if 'it is of a variety or mixture commonly used for pasture, silage or haymaking, whether or not it is intended for such a use in that case and is not a cereal crop'.

9.3.4   Excavations and other operations

There is no automatic right to carry out excavations or engineering operations on a public right of way. Where, however, such works are reasonably necessary for the purposes of agriculture, the occupier may apply to the highway authority for an order allowing him to disturb the surface of a footpath or bridleway for the period specified in the order.[2] The period is limited to a maximum of 3 months.

The highway authority must make the order if it is satisfied that it is practicable temporarily to divert the path in a manner reasonably convenient to users or that the existing path will be or can be made sufficiently convenient while the works are undertaken. When a diversion is made onto land not occupied by the applicant the written consent of the occupier of that land, and any other person whose consent is needed to obtain access to it, must be obtained.

The order may be made subject to conditions for the benefit of users of the path and where there is a diversion, conditions relating to the provision of signposts and other notices, stiles, bridges and gates.

The authority may recover from the applicant expenses in connection with the order.

9.3.5   Minimum width

The minimum widths referred to in **9.3.2** (Ploughing and other disturbances), **9.3.3** (Crops) and **9.3.4** (Excavations and other operations) are as follows:

(a)   the width recorded in the statement attached to the definitive map, if there is such a width recorded (and there seldom is); or

(b)   (i)   a footpath: 1 metre for a cross-field path, 1.5 metres for a field-edge path;

---

1   Highways Act 1980, s 137A.
2   Ibid, s 135.

(ii) a bridleway: 2 metres for a cross-field path, 3 metres for a field-edge path;

(iii) for any other right of way: 3 metres whether a cross-field or field-edge.[1]

9.3.6 Enforcement and default powers

If the occupier does not restore within the statutory time-limits a path to the minimum width the highway authority has powers of entry to do the necessary work and recover the cost.[2] The authority must give not less than 24 hours' notice before entering to do the work. No notice is needed if the entry is just for the purpose of obtaining information. The default powers may be exercised up to a maximum width. This is to provide some tolerance for different types of machinery and equipment and is intended to limit disputes about the exact width that has been restored or cleared. The maximum widths are as follows:

(a) the width (if any) recorded in the statement attached to the definitive map, but if there is no such width recorded;

(b) (i) a footpath: 1.8 metres for a cross-field path and field-edge path;
(ii) a bridleway: 3 metres for a cross-field path and field-edge path;
(iii) other unsurfaced highways: 5 metres.

Only the highway authority or the council of the district, parish or community in which the offence is committed may bring a prosecution against the occupier for not complying with the ploughing or disturbance[3] provisions of the RWA 1990, as incorporated into the Highways Act 1980. This limitation was removed on 1 April 2001 for offences committed after that date[4] when s 70 of the CROW Act 2000 came into force. There is no such limitation where an occupier fails to keep a public right of way clear of crops.[5] Any person can bring a prosecution.

9.4 MISLEADING NOTICES

It is an offence for any person to place or maintain on or near any footpath, bridleway or RUPP shown on a definitive map a notice containing any false or misleading statement likely to deter the public from using the way.[6] The offence does not cover misleading signs on or near BOATs. An example of a misleading sign is 'Trespassers Will be Prosecuted'. As trespass, with limited exceptions, is a civil offence and not a crime, this is a false statement. A notice stating 'Beware of the Bull' would be misleading if there was no bull in the field. The highway authority or district council of the area in which the notice is placed, are the authorities which can bring prosecutions under this section. The magistrates' court may impose a fine and order the notice to be removed.

---

1 Highways Act 1980, Sch 12A.
2 Ibid.
3 Ibid, ss 134, 135.
4 CROW Act 2000 (Commencement No 1) Order 2001, SI 2001/114 (C4).
5 Section 137.
6 NPACA 1949, s 57.

9.5 DANGERS

9.5.1 Occupiers' liability

Neither the highway authority nor the landowner is liable under the provisions of the Occupiers' Liability Acts 1957 and 1984 to users of the highway. This is because the public have a legal right to use the public right of way and neither the authority nor the landowner can exclude them.[1]

Where, however, a landowner or occupier offers the public an alternative route, which is not an official division, the public are given a licence to use that route. The public are not using the route as of right. As they enter that part of the land by express or implied permission, they become invitees. Therefore, there is potential liability under the Occupiers' Liability Act 1957.

The position may be the same where, because of an obstruction caused by the landowner, the user deviates onto land in the ownership of the same landowner.[2] This is on the basis that the landowner has given an implied permission for the deviation.

The landowner owes to the invitee a duty of care. The duty is 'to take such care as in all the circumstances of the case is reasonable to see that the visitor will be reasonably safe in using the premises for those purposes for which he is invited or permitted by the occupier to be there'.[3]

The Occupiers' Liability Act 1957 provides that the occupier must be prepared for children to be less careful than adults.[4] Therefore, although warning notices may be sufficient to discharge the duty as far as adults are concerned, they may not do so if young children are involved. Any warning must enable the visitor to be reasonably safe.

The duty does not extend to risks willingly accepted by a visitor.[5] Any damages may be reduced by the contributory negligence of the person who is injured.

It is possible to exclude the duty of care, provided the exclusion is brought to the attention of the visitor. This is subject to the Unfair Contracts Act 1977, which provides that liability for death or personal injury cannot be excluded where a person enters premises for the business purposes of the occupier.

Where a user trespasses onto adjoining land, the landowner could be liable under the Occupiers' Liability Act 1984. Liability will only be established if:

(1) the occupier is aware of the damage or has reasonable grounds to believe that it exists;
(2) he knows that a person other than a visitor is near, or may come near, the danger; and

---

1   *Gautret v Egerton* (1867) LR 2 CP 371; *Greenhalgh v British Railways Board* [1969] 2 QB 286. Occupiers Liability Act 1984, s 1(7).
2   *Stacey v Sherrin* (1913) 29 TLR 555.
3   Occupiers' Liability Act 1957, s 2(2).
4   Ibid, s 2(3).
5   Ibid, s 2(5).

(3) the risk posed by the danger is one against which, in all the circumstances he owes a duty to take such care as is reasonable to see that the person does not suffer injury.[1]

The duty may be discharged by appropriate warnings[2] and no duty is owed to those who willingly accept the risks.[3] The liability is in respect of injury to persons, not property.[4]

Where a private road or path becomes a public right of way by long use, there will be no duty of care owed by the landowner to the public.[5] Nor, it seems, will there be any liability towards those who use the path as invitees of the landowner.

9.5.2   Occupier's negligence or nuisance

Where an occupier acts in such a way either on the public right of way or on the adjoining land that a person using the route is injured, the occupier may be liable in negligence. The essentials of the tort of negligence are:

(1) a breach of a duty of care owed by the defendant to the claimant;
(2) a causal connection which is not too remote between the breach and the damage suffered by the claimant; and
(3) the foreseeability that such conduct would have inflicted on that claimant the particular kind of damage which he suffered.

In ascertaining the amount of damages for any injury, any contributory negligence of the claimant will be taken into account.

An occupier may be liable in nuisance if he does something which interferes with a member of the public's enjoyment of a right of way. An example would be depositing something on the path, or erecting a wire fence too close to a footpath.

9.5.3   Highway authority's negligence

Where the highway authority acts negligently in exercising any of its functions, it will be liable for any injury caused to persons or property.[6]

If a danger arises from the failure of a highway authority to repair the surface of a highway under its statutory duties, there will be potential liability under the Highways Act 1980. This is discussed at **8.8**.

In some circumstances, a highway authority may be liable for the negligent failure to exercise a power (as distinct from a duty). This is an extremely

---

1   Occupiers' Liability Act 1984, s 1(3).
2   Ibid, s 1(5).
3   Ibid, s 1(6).
4   Ibid, s 1(8).
5   *McGeown v NI Housing Executive* [1994] 3 All ER 53.
6   In *Kane v New Forest District Council* [2002] 1 WLR 312, a planning authority required a developer to construct a footpath. It was held liable when a walker was struck by a car

complex area of the law and the courts are reluctant to impose liability. In *Stovin v Wise*,[1] Lord Hoffman held that, in order to impose liability, certain preconditions had to be fulfilled. He stated:

> 'First, that it would in the circumstances have been irrational not to have exercised the power, so there was in effect a public law duty to act, and secondly, that there are exceptional grounds for holding the policy of the statute requires compensation to be paid to persons who suffer loss because the power is not exercised.'

In *Stovin v Wise*, the council knew that, because of the poor visibility caused by a bank on adjoining land, accidents were likely to happen. Although the landowner was asked to remove the obstruction, nothing further was done for over 2 years and an accident did happen. Nevertheless, the council was held not to be liable.

9.5.4 Dangerous trees

A highway authority has the power to serve a notice on the owner or occupier of land in which a hedge, tree or shrub is growing to cut or fell it if it is dead, diseased, damaged or insecurely rooted and is likely to cause danger by falling onto the highway.[2] There is a right of appeal against the notice to the magistrates' court. If there is no appeal and the work is not done, the highway authority can do the work and recover the costs from the owner. The owner of a tree falling onto a public right of way which causes injury to a user is not liable for the damage unless negligence can be proved against him.[3] Liability depends on whether the owner knew, or should have known, that the tree was likely to fall and cause injury. Owners of trees adjoining the highway should therefore have periodic inspections and fell trees where necessary. It is wise to insure against the risk of damage by trees falling onto the highway.

Highway authorities have powers to remove trees which are blown down across highways. The authority has powers to recover its reasonable costs for removal of fallen trees except where the owner can show that he took reasonable care to secure that the tree did not cause or contribute to the obstruction.[4] So, the owner of trees who has them regularly inspected and finds them healthy and safe would not be liable to pay the highway authority's expenses of removal should the tree fall over in a gale.[5]

9.5.5 Shooting and firearms

It is an offence under the Highways Act 1980 to discharge any firearm or firework within 50 feet of the centre of a carriageway without lawful authority or excuse if, as a result, a user of the highway is injured, interrupted or

---

because it allowed the footpath to be opened before the highway authority had improved the visibility.

1   [1996] 3 WLR 388.
2   Highways Act 1980, s 154(2).
3   *Quinn v Scott* [1965] 1 WLR 1004; *Caminer v Northern and London Investment Trust Ltd* [1951] AC 88.
4   Highways Act 1980, s 150.
5   *Williams v Devon County Council* (1966) 65 LGR 119.

endangered.[1] This offence relates only to BOATs and RUPPs which have vehicular rights, but not to footpaths, bridleways or restricted byways.

Although there is no specific offence of shooting across a footpath or bridleway, it may amount to a public nuisance or to wilful obstruction of the highway. There may also be liability in negligence where it is known that people are on the path.

The Firearms Act 1968 makes it an offence if a person, without lawful authority or reasonable excuse, has in a public place a loaded shotgun or loaded air weapon or any other firearm, whether or not loaded, together with ammunition.[2] A 'public place' is defined to include any highway and any other premises to which at the material time the public have or are permitted to have access.

The Town Police Clauses Act 1847 prohibits the discharge of firearms in any street, so as to obstruct annoy or endanger residents or passers by.[3] Although originally this provision applied only to those towns which adopted it, the provision was subsequently extended to all urban areas. Due to local government reorganisation, the Act now applies to all of England and Wales. 'Street' is defined as 'any road, square, court, alley and thoroughfare or public passage'.[4]

9.5.6 Fires

If a person, without lawful authority or excuse, lights a fire on a carriageway or on land adjoining the carriageway and, as a result, a user is injured, interrupted or endangered by the fire or the smoke, he will be guilty of an offence.[5]

9.5.7 Unfenced dangers

Where there is an unfenced or inadequately fenced source of danger near a public right of way, the local authority may, by notice on the owner or occupier of the land, require him to do such works as will obviate the danger.[6] The person who is aggrieved by such a notice may appeal to the magistrates' court. If he does not appeal and fails to comply with the notices within the specified time, the authority may execute the works and recover the expenses.

9.5.8 Mines and Quarries Act 1954

Abandoned and disused mines must be fenced so as to prevent any person from accidentally falling down a shaft or entering an outlet.[7] Failure to do so where,

---

1   Highways Act 1980, s 161(2).
2   Section 19.
3   Section 28.
4   Section 3.
5   Highways Act 1980, ss 161A, 161(2). NB defences under s 161A(2).
6   Ibid, s 165.
7   Mines and Quarries Act 1954, s 151, as amended by the Environmental Protection Act 1990, Sch 15, para 5.

by reason of its accessibility from the highway or a place of public resort, the mine constitutes a danger amounts to a statutory nuisance.

The same is true for quarries, whether or not being worked, where they are not provided with an efficient and properly maintained barrier, or so designed and constructed as to prevent any person from falling into them.

9.6 OTHER OFFENCES UNDER THE HIGHWAYS ACT 1980

9.6.1 General principles

Part IX of the Highways Act 1980 deals with unlawful interference and obstruction with highways and streets. The provisions are without prejudice to any liability under other enactments or at common law. Many of these provisions have been discussed above and some are not relevant to public rights of way as distinct from the ordinary highway network. The offences which are likely to affect public rights of way are discussed below.

9.6.2 Removal or defacement of signs

It is an offence without lawful authority or excuse to pull down or obliterate a traffic sign, milestone or direction sign.[1] It is a defence if the direction sign or milestone was in the wrong place.

9.6.3 Unauthorised signs

It is an offence without the consent of the highway authority to paint, inscribe or fix any picture, letter, sign or other mark on the surface of the highway or on any tree, structure or works, in or on the highway.[2] The highway authority has power to remove the sign or other object.

There is also power under the Road Traffic Regulation Act 1984 to order an owner or occupier of land to remove any object or device for the guidance or direction of persons and, on failure to do so, the highway authority may effect the removal and recover the costs.[3]

9.6.4 Deposits on the highway

It is an offence if someone without lawful authority or excuse deposits on a made-up carriage any dung, compost or other materials for dressing land or any rubbish or, on any other highway, anything which interrupts the use of the highway.[4] The deposit must be intentional. If cattle are driven along a made-up road and deposit dung, there would be no liability because the deposit is made by the animals rather than a person.

---

1   Highways Act 1980, s 131(2).
2   Ibid, s 132.
3   Section 69.
4   Highways Act 1980, s 148.

Where something has been deposited on a highway so as to constitute a nuisance, the authority may serve a notice on the person who deposited it, requiring its removal.[1] Where the highway authority considers that there is some immediate danger, the authority may remove the thing forthwith and recover the expenditure for doing so from the person who deposited the object.

9.6.5   Structures

Where a structure has been put up on a highway, the highway authority or the district council may require the person having control or possession of the structure to remove it within such time as may be specified in the notice.[2] If it is not removed, the authority may remove the structure and charge the person for so doing. 'Structure' is defined to include any machine, pump, post or other object capable of causing obstruction, even if it is on wheels.

9.6.6   Landslip

The highway authority or district council may serve a notice on the owner or occupier of land adjoining a public right of way, provided that it is maintainable at public expense, requiring him, within 28 days from the service of the notice, to do what is necessary to prevent soil from the adjoining land from falling or being washed or carried onto the street in such quantities as to obstruct the street.[3] The 'street' is defined so as to include a public right of way.

There may also be liability in nuisance, even though the landslide happens through natural causes or has not been caused by the landowner. He must either have known, or have had reasonable cause to have known of the risk.[4]

There is a duty on the highway authority to remove any obstruction caused by the accumulation of snow or from the falling down of banks on the side of the highway or from any other cause.[5] If the highway authority fails to move such an obstruction, complaint may be made to the magistrates' court who can order the removal of the obstruction within such time as it considers reasonable, having regard to all the circumstances. There are guidelines which the court must follow in deciding whether or not to make an order and the time for complying with any order which is made. These are the character of the highway and the nature and amount of the traffic by which it is ordinarily used, the nature and extent of the obstruction and the resources of manpower, vehicles and equipment available for the work.

A highway authority which removes an obstruction may recover its reasonable expenses from the person who causes the obstruction, unless such person can

---

1   Highways Act 1980, s 149.
2   Ibid, s 143.
3   Ibid, s 151.
4   *Leakey v National Trust for Places of Historic Interest or Natural Beauty* [1980] QB 485.
5   Highways Act 1980, s 150. See *Worcestershire County Council v Newman* [1974] 1 WLR 938.

show he took reasonable care, or the event which led to the obstruction was not reasonably foreseeable.[1]

Where the highway is maintainable by someone other than the highway authority, the same duty is imposed on him.

9.6.7 Damage to the surface

It is an offence if a person without lawful authority or excuse makes a ditch or excavation in the highway which consists of or comprises a carriageway. It is also an offence to remove soil or turf from any part of the highway (except to improve the highway with the consent of the highway authority) and to deposit anything on the highway so as to damage it.[2]

A highway authority, non-metropolitan district or local council can (and, where it is desirable in the public interest, must) prosecute anyone who, without lawful authority or excuse, disturbs the surface of a footpath, bridleway or unmade-up carriageway, so as to render it inconvenient for the exercise of a public right of way.[3]

9.7 ANIMALS

9.7.1 General principles

The keeping of animals on or near a public right of way may amount to an obstruction or highway nuisance if it prevents the free, safe and uninterrupted passage of the public.

9.7.2 Bulls

There are special provisions in the WLCA 1981 relating to bulls.[4] The general rule is that it is an offence for the occupier of a field crossed by a right of way to keep a bull in the field. No offence will be committed if the bull is either less than 10 months old or not a recognised dairy breed and is at large with cows or heifers. Dairy breeds are Ayrshire, British Friesian, British Holstein, Dairy Shorthorn, Guernsey, Jersey and Kerry.

This provision is not wholly satisfactory, as many people are unable to make the distinction between dairy and beef cattle. However, it is a compromise between the farming community and the users.

Even if the bull comes within the exception, there may be liability under the Health and Safety at Work etc Act 1974. Section 3 places an obligation on employers and self-employed persons not to put at risk the health and safety of persons not in their employment.

---

1   *Devon County Council v Webber* [2002] 18 EG 153 (wash-off from fields caused by heavy rainstorms).
2   Highways Act 1980, s 131.
3   Ibid, s 131A.
4   Ibid, s 59.

Where a bull is to be kept in a field, the Health & Safety Executive insist on a notice warning that a bull is present. It is advisable to state 'Bull in Field' rather than 'Beware of the Bull' as this might be taken as evidence that the owner knew the bull had vicious tendencies, see **9.7.4**. It is important that the notice is removed when the bull is not in the field as the notice would then be misleading, see **9.4**.

9.7.3 Dogs

A dog which prevents the use of a path by behaving in a threatening manner may constitute a public nuisance at common law. However, it has been held that there was no obstruction where a user was frightened by Rottweiler dogs in an adjoining garden putting their paws and muzzles on a fence adjoining a public footpath.[1]

It is an offence under the Town Police Clauses Act 1847[2] in any street (defined to include any road, square, court, alley, thoroughfare or public passage) for a person to allow an unmuzzled ferocious dog to be at large or to set on or urge any other dog or other animal to attack, worry or put in fear any person or animal.

The Dogs Act 1871,[3] as extended by the Dangerous Dogs Act 1989, empowers a magistrates' court to order a dangerous dog to be kept under proper control or destroyed.

Under the Guard Dogs Act 1975, it is an offence to use a guard dog at any premises, other than a dwelling or agricultural land, unless it is tied up or in the control of a handler and a notice warning of the dog's presence is exhibited at the entrance of the premises.[4]

The Dangerous Dogs Act 1991[5] makes it an offence if a dog is dangerously out of control in the public place and an aggravated offence if the dog, while so out of control, injures any person. 'Public place' means any street, road or other place to which the public have, or are permitted to have, access. A dog is dangerously out of control on any occasion on which there are grounds for reasonable apprehension that it will injure any person, whether or not it actually does so.

9.7.4 Other animals

The Animals Act 1971[6] imposes liability on the keeper of an animal belonging to a dangerous species or of an animal which, although not of a dangerous species, is known to have vicious tendencies. It is unlikely that animals of a dangerous species will be set free on public rights of way, but animals such as

---

1   *Kent County Council v Holland* [1996] EGCS 135.
2   Section 28.
3   Section 2.
4   Sections 1 and 5.
5   Section 3.
6   Section 2(1), (2).

horses and bulls, even though not prohibited, may be known to cause injury to passers-by. There will be no liability, however, if damage was wholly the fault of the injured person.[1]

In the unreported county court case of *Birch v Mills*,[2] a solicitor was exercising his dogs on short leads on a public right of way. He was injured when a herd of Charolais cows charged at the dogs. A similar incident had occurred a few weeks earlier and had been reported to the farm manager. The defendant was therefore held liable.

9.7.5   Straying animals

Straying animals may amount to an obstruction of the highway. It is the duty of the owner of livestock to keep his animals fenced in.

If the highway runs across land which is traditionally unfenced there is a special statutory provision. The Animals Act 1971[3] provides:

> 'Where damage is caused by animals straying from unfenced land to a highway a person who placed them on the land shall not be regarded as having committed a breach of duty to take care by reason only of placing them there if –
>
> (a)   the land is common land, or is land situated in an area where fencing is not customary, or is a town or village green, and
> (b)   he had a right to place the animals on that land.'

Under the Highways Act 1980 the keeper of any horses, cattle, sheep, goats or swine found straying on or lying on or at the side of a highway will be guilty of an offence.[4] The offence will not be committed where the highway crosses common, waste or unenclosed land.

9.8   MOTOR VEHICLE OFFENCES

9.8.1   Road Traffic Act 1988, s 34

The Road Traffic Act 1988, s 34 makes it an offence to drive without lawful authority a mechanically propelled vehicle on any footpath, bridleway or restricted byway.[5] It is also an offence to drive a mechanically propelled vehicle on any common land, moorland or other land not forming part of a road. It is not an offence to drive a mechanically propelled vehicle on any land within 15 yards of a public carriage road for the purpose of parking. However, this does not give a right to drive on private land. Although no offence is committed under the Road Traffic Act 1988, it is still a trespass against the landowner and, if damage is done, there may be an offence under the Criminal Damage Act 1971.[6]

---

1   Highways Act 1980, s 5.
2   [1995] CLY 3683.
3   Section 8.
4   Section 155.
5   Section 34.
6   Section 1.

'Mechanically propelled vehicle' has been substituted by the CROW Act 2000 for the original reference to motor vehicle. This was because a motor vehicle was defined as 'a mechanically propelled vehicle intended or adapted for use on a road' and it was there considered that the definition did not cover scrambler or quad bikes. The term 'mechanically propelled vehicles' covers these bikes, but excluded from the definition are invalid carriages, lawnmowers controlled by pedestrians and electrically assisted pedal cycles.

It is not an offence to drive a car on a BOAT, but the driver must not drive recklessly, carelessly or inconsiderately.[1]

The owner of the land over which a bridleway or footpath runs will generally have an implied reservation from the dedication to use the land for his own purposes. This would include driving a mechanically propelled vehicle and authorising others to do so. Such drivers would have lawful authority and so would not be committing an offence. Where an RUPP has been redesignated as a byway, owners and lessees of adjoining premises are given specific vehicular rights.[2] However, an owner who does drive on a footpath, bridleway or restricted byway must do so with due care and the vehicle must be properly taxed and insured. It is an offence to drive a motor vehicle which is not taxed or insured on any road. 'Road' is defined to include any highway and any other road to which the public has access.

9.8.2   Prosecutions for driving mechanically propelled vehicles on public rights of way

Entry on a definitive map of a footpath, bridleway, or RUPP is without prejudice to the existence of any higher rights.[3] It has, therefore, been difficult to convict a person of driving illegally on a public right of way because the burden of proof is on the prosecution to show that the particular right of way did not carry vehicular rights. The burden of proof is not the civil burden that, on the balance of probabilities, the right did not exist, but the more stringent criminal test that there is no reasonable doubt about their non-existence.

The CROW Act 2000 has amended s 34 to deal with this problem.[4] If the definitive map records a footpath, bridleway or restricted byway, it is presumed for the purposes of s 34 that the public right of way is of that status and does not carry higher rights, unless the contrary is shown.

The new s 34A, according to the side heading, sets out the exceptions to the presumption. This, however, is not an accurate statement of what the section does. The section is not very happily drafted but it appears that anyone who wants to rebut the presumption must first satisfy the court that he belongs to a particular category of person. It is only if he can do this that he is allowed to produce evidence to show that the right of way has vehicular status.[5]

---

1   Road Traffic Act 1988, ss 2 and 3.
2   CROW Act 2000, s 50(2).
3   WLCA 1981, s 56.
4   Schedule 7, para 5.
5   See House of Lords Third Reading, 23 November 2000, Vol 619, col 1040.

The categories are:

(1) that he was a person interested in any land and that the driving of the vehicle by him was reasonably necessary to obtain access to the land; or

(2) that the driving of the vehicle by him was reasonably necessary to obtain access to any land, and was for the purpose of obtaining access to the land as a lawful visitor; or

(3) that the driving of the vehicle by him was reasonably necessary for the purposes of any business, trade or profession.

'Lawful visitor' is defined to include 'any person who enters the land for any purpose in the exercise of a right conferred by law'.

The Secretary of State may prescribe by regulations other circumstances when the presumption can be rebutted.

9.8.3   Other motor vehicle offences on public rights of way

It is an offence to promote or participate in a race or trial of speed between motor vehicles on a public right of way.[1] A person who promotes or takes part in a competition or trial, other than a race or trial of speed, involving the use of motor vehicles on a public right of way will also be guilty of an offence unless the competition or trial is authorised under regulations.[2] A person must not promote or take part in a trial of any description between motor vehicles on a footpath or bridleway unless the holding of the trial has been authorised by the local authority and the owner or occupier of the land over which the path runs has given his consent in writing.[3]

The Road Vehicles (Construction and Use) Regulations 1986[4] state that:

> 'no person in charge of a motor vehicle or trailer shall cause or permit the vehicle to stand on a road so as to cause an unnecessary obstruction of the road.'

A road is defined to include footpaths and bridleways as well as other roads to which the public have access but over which there is not a public right of way.

Specific powers are given to local authorities to use mechanically propelled vehicles for cleansing, maintaining or improving footpaths, footways or bridleways or their verges, for preventing or removing obstructions to them or otherwise preventing nuisances or other interferences with them, or for maintaining structures or other works situated therein.[5]

---

1   Road Traffic Act 1988, s 12.
2   Ibid, s 13.
3   Ibid, s 33.
4   SI 1986/1078, reg 103.
5   Highways Act 1980, s 300.

9.9 PROBLEMS WITH VEHICULAR RIGHTS OF WAY ACROSS COMMONS AND VILLAGE GREENS AND OTHER LAND

9.9.1 Legislation

The courts are anxious to uphold long-established rights and find legal authority for doing so. Private and public rights of way may arise through long user (by prescription and deemed dedication respectively) but not where it is contrary to statute. There are several statutes which make it an offence to drive on land. Two of these are of particular importance for rights of way: namely, s 193 of the Law of Property Act 1925 and s 34 of the Road Traffic Act 1988.

Section 193 of the Law of Property Act 1925 makes it an offence for any person to draw or drive without lawful authority on land to which the section applies, any carriage, cart, caravan truck, or other vehicle. The section applies to Metropolitan commons within the meaning of the Metropolitan Commons Act 1866–1898 or commons which immediately before 1 April 1974 were wholly or partly in a borough or urban district. It also applies to land where the owner of the soil has declared by deed that the section will apply.

Section 34 of the Road Traffic Act 1988[1] provides:

'(1) Subject to the provisions of this section, if without lawful authority a person drives a mechanically propelled vehicle –
(a) on or upon any common land, moorland, or land of any other description, not being land forming part of a road, or
(b) on any road being a footpath, a bridleway or restricted byway,
he is guilty of an offence.
(2) It is not an offence under this section to drive a mechanically propelled vehicle on any land within fifteen yards of a road, being a road on which a motor vehicle may lawfully be driven, for the purpose only of parking the vehicle on that land.'

'Road' is defined in the Road Traffic Act 1988 as 'any highway and any other road to which the public has access'.[2] Section 34 therefore is a very wide section and covers most types of land. It is not limited to common land as the heading to s 68 of the CROW Act 2000 might suggest.[3]

9.9.2 Without lawful authority

Under both statutes the offence is committed only where the driving takes place without lawful authority. Therefore it would not be an offence if the landowner himself, or someone authorised by him, drove across the land. As an express grant confers lawful authority a presumed grant should do the same. Long user does not create a right, but is evidence that a grant was made even though it cannot now be produced. In other words a prescriptive right is based

---

1   As amended by the CROW Act 2000, s 67, Sch 7.
2   Section 192.
3   See *Massey v Boulden* [2002] EWCA Civ 1634, [2002] TLR 496, where the *eiusdem generis* rule was held not to apply to the wording in s 34.

on a presumed grant. However, the argument that a presumed grant constituted lawful authority was not accepted by the Court of Appeal.[1] It is hoped that the point will be decided by the House of Lords. If so, the regulations discussed below would no longer be necessary.

9.9.3   The CROW Act 2000 and the regulations

The case of *Hanning v Top Deck Travel Group*[2] highlighted the legal rule that no right could arise from committing an offence. As a result of the case, owners of commons have asked for large sums from owners of property adjoining the common for formal easements, even though the adjoining property owners have been driving unhindered over the common for years.

The CROW Act 2000 dealt with the problem of vehicular access over commons and other land by making provision for regulations to be made by statutory instrument which would enable claims to be made for a statutory easement.

Section 68:

> 'applies to a way which the owner or occupier (from time to time) of any premises has used as a means of access for vehicles to the premises, if the use of the way –
>
> (a)   was an offence under an enactment applying to the land crossed by the way, but
> (b)   would otherwise have been sufficient to create on after the prescribed date, and keep in existence, an easement giving a right of way for vehicles.'

The regulations[3] under s 68 were made on 3 July 2002 and came into force a day later.

An application for an easement must be made by the applicant serving a notice on the landowner. The application must be made by 4 July 2003 or, if later, within 12 months of the use of the right of way ceasing. The policy is that an application may be made only where there is recent user. However, it is accepted that landowners may have prevented use after the decision in *Hanning v Top Deck Travel Group*. It is for that reason that there is a 12-month period after the regulations came into effect for people to make claims. The prescribed date referred to in s 68 is 5 May 1993, the date of the decision in *Hanning v Top Deck Travel Group*. If user had ceased before that date no claim may be made for a statutory easement.

Where the landowner of the land crossed by the right of way does not object to the application he must, within 3 months of the receipt of the application, serve a notice of agreement on the applicant.

---

1   *Hanning v Top Deck Travel Group* (1993) 68 P&CR 14.
2   Ibid.
3   Vehicular Access Across Common and Other Land (England) Regulations 2002, SI 2002/1711.

A landowner may serve a counter-notice objecting to the application on the grounds that:

(a) the application was served out of time;
(b) the application did not contain the information required by the Schedule to the regulations;
(c) the information provided by the applicant is incorrect;
(d) the easement should be subject to limitations;
(e) the incidental rights described in the appliction are not agreed; or
(f) the value of the premises are not agreed.

The applicant has the right to serve an amended application within 2 months dealing with the objections and any alternatives set out in the counter-notice. The landowner may serve a notice agreeing to, or a counter-notice objecting to, the amended application. The applicant may, within 2 months, serve a notice on the landowner agreeing to the amended counter-notice.

Once a counter-notice has been served, either party may refer any dispute, other than one relating to value, to the Lands Tribunal.

One of the most controversial points has been the amount of compensation which should be paid to the landowner. The regulations provide as follows:

> '11(1) Subject to paragraph (2), the compensation sum shall be 2% of the value of the premises.
> (2)   Where the premises were in existence on –
>   (a)   31 December 1905; or
>   (b)   30 November 1930,
>   the compensation sum shall be 0.25 per cent or 0.5 per cent of the value of the premises respectively.
> (3)   Where the premises are in residential use and replaced other premises on the same site which were also in residential use ("the former premises"), the compensation sum shall be calculated in accordance with paragraph (2) by reference to the date on which the former premises were in existence.
> (4)   For the purposes of these Regulations, the value of the premises shall be calculated as at the valuation date on the basis of the open market value of the premises with the benefit of the easement.
> (5)   In paragraph (4), the valuation date means the date as at which the premises are valued for the purposes of the application, being a date no more than 3 months before the date on which the application is served.'

Where no agreement can be reached on value, either party may serve a valuation notice on the other requiring the amount to be determined by a chartered surveyor.

9.9.4 Premises

Premises are defined as 'the premises served by the way in respect of which an application is made'. Premises are not therefore limited to buildings. In the context of s 68 the premises would appear to be the entire dominant tenement, ie all the land and buildings which obtained a benefit from the right of way at the time and were included in the application for a statutory easement. If subsequently there were further houses built on the dominant tenement, they would have the benefit of the easement which is attached to each and every part of the dominant tenement. Case-law has established that intensification of use is permitted, provided there is not a radical change in use of the dominant tenement.[1] Thus, a right of way used for one house could be used for two or more houses.[2] However, it could not be used for business purposes if it had not been so used during the prescriptive period.[3]

Therefore the general law relating to a presumed grant, or prescription, will apply subject to any specific statutory modification to overcome the problems caused by the user being contrary to statute. Section 68(3) provides:

> 'An easement created in accordance with the regulations is subject to any enactment or rule of law which would apply to such an easement granted by the owner of the land.'

DEFRA in its non-statutory guidance notes states with regard to regulation 11(3) quoted above, 'Where an original [residential] property has been replaced by two or more properties on the same site, regulation 11(3) will not apply and compensation will be payable by each property according to the date on which it was built'. It is difficult to see how this proposition is derived from regulation 11(3).

9.9.5 Bridleways

In the Analysis of Response and Conclusions on the draft regulations on vehicular access over common land, under s 68 of the CROW Act 2000, DEFRA stated at paragraph 12:

> 'Concern was expressed that applications will be received in respect of access over footpaths and bridleways not on common land, on the grounds that such land meets the criteria in [the regulations]. Section 68 states that it must be an offence to drive *on the land crossed by the way*. This would exclude an easement arising on a footpath or bridleway crossing land on which it is not an offence to drive.'

Section 34 of the Road Traffic Act 1988, however, makes it an offence to drive on any land not being a road. Therefore, in most situations s 68 would apply. Moreover, it is not clear what is the meaning of 'crossed' in this context. The DEFRA Guidance Notes suggest it means the land bordering the way claimed as an easement. Again, in most cases it will be an offence to drive on the land bordering a bridleway. However, the word 'crossed' could also refer to the land over which the way runs.[4] If the land is, say, common land it is an offence to drive on the strip of land over which a prescriptive easement could otherwise be claimed. Similarly, it is an offence to drive over the route of a bridleway. It is for these reasons that it is considereed that s 68 and the regulations will apply to footpaths and bridleways.

1　*British Railways Board v Glass* [1965] Ch 358.
2　*Giles v County Building Constructors (Hertford) Ltd* (1971) 22 P&CR 978.
3　Meggary and Wade, 6th edn, at para 18–200.
4　In *Massey v Boulden* [2002] EWCA Civ 1634, [2002] TLR 496, driving across a path was held to include driving on it. See Sedley LJ at para 67 and Simon Brown LJ at para 27.

Section 34(3) of the Road Traffic Act provides that:

> 'It is not an offence under [section 34] to drive a mechanically propelled vehicle on any land within fifteen yards of a road, being a road on which a motor vehicle may lawfully be driven, for the purposes only of parking on that land.'

This means that if someone drives no more than 15 yards onto a bridleway or footpath and parks there he will not be committing an offence under the section. However, this does not give him the right to park and the owner of the land could sue him for trespass. After 20 years of parking it might be possible for a claim to be made for an easement to park, provided it did not amount to exclusive possession of that area of land. On the other hand, if the path was narrow, the parking might amount to an obstruction and so be a statutory offence under the Highways Act 1980, which would prevent an easement being claimed.

9.9.6   Town and village greens

Although the section covers village greens as well as commons, there may still be problems concerning village greens. This is because even if a private right of way for vehicles is granted expressly, anyone who constructs or uses a right of way is likely to be committing an offence for which a fine is payable. Section 68(3) of the CROW Act 2000 specifically provides that the easement created in accordance with the regulations under the Act will be subject to any enactment or rule of law which would apply to an easement granted by the owner of the land.

Section 12 of the Inclosure Act 1857[1] makes it an offence to cause injury to, or to commit a nuisance on, a town or village green. Moreover, under s 29 of the Commons Act 1876,[2] any encroachment on, or inclosure of, a town or village green and any disturbance to the green otherwise than with a view to its better enjoyment is deemed to be a public nuisance. There is no defence of lawful authority as there is under s 193 of the Law of Property Act 1925 or s 34 of the Road Traffic Act 1988.

In its Common Land Policy Statement, issued in July 2002, DEFRA proposed future legislation which would provide that where an easement was granted pursuant to an application under s 68, driving across a village green would not be an offence. This would appear to leave those with express easements in a worse position than those with prescriptive easements. Although a grantee under an express grant would have a perfectly valid easement, if he exercised the easement he might be committing an offence under the existing legislation relating to village greens. Indeed, those owning a village green might be committing an offence if they drove on the green.[3]

---

1   It seems, however, that this Act and the Commons Act 1876 apply only to traditional greens and not to those greens which achieve their status merely through registration.
2   This section applies only where the green has a known and defined boundary.
3   These problems were aired but not resolved in *Massey v Boulden* [2002] EWCA Civ 1634, [2002] TLR 496.

9.9.7   Roadside waste

Some Lords of the Manor have been claiming sums from landowners whose property is separated from the highway by a verge or roadside waste. However, it is for the claimant to show that he has title. The presumption is that the adjoining owner owns the land up to the middle of the highway where it is contiguous with his boundary; this includes any intervening verges or roadside waste.[1]

9.10   BICYCLES

A person who rides a cycle recklessly or carelessly on a road, which includes a bridleway, commits an offence, as does a person who rides without due care and attention or without reasonable consideration for other persons using a road.[2]

A 'cycle' is defined to include a bicycle, a tricycle or a cycle having four or more wheels, not being a motor vehicle.[3]

It is an offence to promote or take part in an unauthorised race or trial of speed between cycles on a public right of way. A 'public right of way' for the purpose of the section includes a bridleway, but not a footpath. Races or trials of speed may be authorised on roads other than footpaths or bridleways.[4]

9.11   PROCESSIONS AND PICKETING

A procession will not normally amount to an obstruction unless it unreasonably restricts the rights of other highway users. A static meeting is more likely to amount to an obstruction. The law is somewhat conflicting in this area, but the general principle is that the procession or meeting must not amount to a nuisance and must be a reasonable use of the highway.[5]

Where a proposed public procession is to demonstrate support for, or opposition to, the views or actions of any body or persons, to publicise a cause or campaign or to mark or commemorate an event, prior written notice must be given to the police.[6]

9.12   REMEDIES

9.12.1   Who may bring an action?

The Attorney-General may bring proceedings on behalf of the public for a declaration or an injunction relating to highway nuisances. Local authorities

---

1   *Doe d' Pring and Another v Pearsey* [1824–34] All ER Rep 164.
2   Road Traffic Act 1988, ss 28 and 29.
3   Ibid, s 192.
4   Road Traffic Act 1988, s 31.
5   See Michael Doherty 'Public's rights of access to the highway', RWLR 4.3, p 39.
6   Public Order Act 1986, s 11.

may also bring proceedings in their own name under the Local Government Act 1972.[1] This power is given to them in order to promote or protect the interests of the inhabitants in their area. Councils of counties, non-metropolitan districts, metropolitan districts, unitary authorities and the London boroughs have powers to bring proceedings to protect and assert the rights of the public to the use and enjoyment of the highway.[2]

A private individual may only bring proceedings for damages or for an injunction to restrain, or require the removal of, a highway nuisance where he has suffered special damage.[3] That is, he must suffer loss above that which is suffered by the public at large. Examples include physical injury, pecuniary loss and prevention of access to property. The purpose of the rule was to prevent multiplicity of suits: 'If one man may have an action, for the same reason a hundred thousand may'.[4]

9.12.2   Information as to ownership

A local authority may serve on any person with an interest in the land either as freeholder, mortgagee or lessee, or a manager of the land a notice requiring him to give the authority details of the nature of his interest in the land and the name and address of any other person with an interest.[5] A similar power is given to highway authorities for the purpose of enabling them to discharge or exercise any of their functions under the Highways Act 1980.[6]

9.12.3   Abatement of nuisance

A highway authority may also abate a nuisance but, in practice, it is likely to rely on the statutory provisions as explained in **9.2** above.

Individuals using the highway may also abate a nuisance, although this remedy should be exercised with care. A path user should do no more than is necessary to enable him to use the path. In *James v Hayward*,[7] a 17th-century case, the removal of an unlawfully erected gate was justified on the ground that 'women and old men are more troubled with opening of gates than they should be if there were none'. In *Bateman v Bluck*,[8] however, it was held that, in order to be justified in removing an obstruction, the defendant had to show that there was no way in which he could exercise the right of way without its removal.

It has been suggested that it would not be unreasonable 'for a walker to take with him a pair of pocket secateurs, and he will not be acting unlawfully if he uses these to clear vegetation that impedes his progress along a path, provided

---

1   Section 222. See *London Borough of Wandsworth v Railtrack* [2001] 1 WLR 368.
2   Highways Act 1980, s 130.
3   *Winterbottom v Derby (Lord)* (1867) LR 2 Ex 316.
4   *Iveson v Moore* (1699) 1 Ld Raym 486, 492. For criticism of the rule see B Hough 'Entitlement to enforce rights of way', RWLR 10.5, p 1.
5   Local Government (Miscellaneous Provisions) Act 1976, s 16.
6   Section 297.
7   (1630) Cro Car 184.
8   (1852) 18 QB 870.

always that he does no more than is necessary to enable him to make his way conveniently along the route'.[1]

However, the authors go on to point out that he runs the risk of various criminal offences. For instance, he could be guilty of damaging property without lawful authority under the Criminal Damage Act 1971, or of having an article that has a blade or is sharply pointed in a place to which the public have access, contrary to s 139 of the Criminal Justice Act 1988.

9.12.4 Trespass and public nuisance

Actions may be brought for trespass or public nuisance for interference with a highway. However, in practice, more reliance is placed on the statutory provisions of the Highways Act 1980.

9.12.5 Remedies under the Highways Act 1980

Specific statutory powers are given in the Highways Act 1980 to serve notices on persons causing an obstruction and on failure to comply with the notice to do the necessary works and recover the expenses.

Powers are also given to highway authorities to bring prosecutions. In some instances individuals, as well as the highway authority, may bring a prosecution.

9.12.6 Lawful authority or excuse

Many provisions under the Highways Act 1980 and other statutes provide that a person shall be guilty of an offence if he does something without lawful authority or excuse.

The meaning of lawful authority depends on the particular offence. Sometimes it will mean the authority of the landowner. An example is where a landowner gives permission for someone to drive on a footpath or bridleway. Other examples of lawful authority occur where a highway is dedicated subject to existing obstructions. Such obstructions will be lawful.

There may also be statutory provisions which give lawful authority, such as the statutory power to break open the surface of a highway in order to install utilities.

Lawful excuse is not a defence if there is a mistake of law. However, it may provide a defence if there is an honest belief in the existence of the facts which, if they had been true, would have justified the person in doing what he did.[2]

It seems that the burden of proving whether or not he had lawful authority or excuse lies with the accused.

---

1   Riddall and Trevelyan *Rights of Way* 3rd edn, p 243.
2   *Cambridgeshire and Isle of Ely County Council v Rust* [1972] 2 QB 426.

In *Nagy v Weston*,[1] Parker LJ, having found that there was a wilful obstruction, said:

> 'two further elements must be proved, first that the defendant had no lawful authority or excuse, and, secondly, that the use to which he was putting the highway was an unreasonable one ... excuse and reasonableness are really the same ground.'

He then went on to state:

> 'Whether or not the user amounting to an obstruction is or is not an unreasonable use of the highway is a question of fact. It depends on all the circumstances, including the length of time the obstruction continues, the place where it occurs, the purpose for which it is done, and, of course, whether it does in fact cause an actual obstruction as opposed to a potential obstruction.'

In *Durham v Scott*,[2] the erection of gates across a bridleway to prevent livestock straying onto a nearby A-classified road and thereby protecting them and motorists from danger was held not to amount to lawful excuse. A similar decision was reached in *Campodonic v Evans*[3] where a farmer put up and padlocked gates across a public footpath to prevent his cattle straying.

9.12.7 Judicial review

Where a highway authority does not exercise its duties and powers to deal with interferences with the highway, it may be possible to challenge its decisions on the grounds of illegality, irrationality or procedural impropriety by way of judicial review. The applicant will have to show that he has a sufficient interest in the matter to which the application relates.

The technical rules relating to judicial review are outside the scope of this book.

9.12.8 Criminal Damage Act 1971

Under the Criminal Damage Act 1971 it is an offence to destroy or damage any property belonging to another, intending to destroy or damage any such property, or being reckless as to whether any such property would be damaged or destroyed. This would include damaging the surface of a public right of way.[4] Where it is publicly maintainable, the owner, for the purposes of the section, would be the highway authority.

9.12.9 Environmental Protection Act 1990

It has been suggested that the provisions relating to statutory nuisance under the above Act could be utilised for dealing with obstructions and nuisances relating to public rights of way.[5] However, the recent case of *Westley v*

---

1   [1965] 1 WLR 280.
2   [1990] Crim LR 726.
3   (1966) 200 EG 857.
4   Section 1.
5   Riddall and Trevelyan *Rights of Way* 2nd edn, pp 186–188 but see 3rd edn, p 322.

Hertfordshire County Council[1] has held that the obstruction of a highway, although a nuisance at common law, is not included in the offence of a statutory nuisance under the Act.

---

1   [1998] JPL 947.

Chapter 10

MANAGEMENT, COMMON PROBLEMS AND CONSERVATION

10.1 INTRODUCTION

The previous chapter discussed obstructions and other interferences with highways, which hindered the right of the public to pass and repass. This chapter looks at the powers the highway authority has to make it easier for users to travel on the route and regulate such user. It also considers some of the common problems experienced by landowners in relation to rights of way. Finally, it considers the potential conflict between public rights of way and conservation.

10.2 SIGNS

10.2.1 Highway authority duty

The highway authority is under a duty to erect and maintain a signpost where a footpath, bridleway or byway leaves a metalled road.[1] The statutory wording is somewhat convoluted, but it is considered that the duty must be exercised after consultation with the owner or occupier of the land over which the path runs. The owner does not have to consent, but he should be consulted. This makes practical sense. If the consultation has not taken place, difficulties can arise. Signs which have been put up without the landowner's knowledge cause ill-will. Users have also been frustrated by finding that signs lead to paths which are completely obstructed by impenetrable growth. Had the landowner been consulted, there would have been the opportunity to get him to clear the obstructions before the sign was erected.

The counter-argument is that although subs 27(2) of the CA 1968 refers back to subs 27(1), 'consultation with the owner or occupier of the land concerned' means the owner or occupier of the land in which the signpost is erected, rather than the owner of the land which the path crosses. As this will be the highway verge, the owner will be the highway authority. This argument is not convincing. First, it may be that the sign is erected not just in the surface of the verge, but in the subsoil which belongs to the adjoining landowner. Secondly, signs along a path may actually be erected on the path itself, ie in highway land,

---

1   Countryside Act 1968, s 27(2).

but it is not suggested that the landowner or occupier of the land which is crossed by the route should not be consulted.

The highway authority does not need to erect a sign if it considers it unnecessary and the parish council or the chairman of the parish meeting agrees.[1]

Any sign erected in pursuance of the duty should indicate whether it is a public footpath, bridleway or byway and, where the authority considers it appropriate or convenient, the place to which the path leads and its distance.[2]

10.2.2   Highway authority's powers

The highway authority, after consultation with the owner or occupier of the land concerned, may erect waymarks along any public right of way. It should do this where, in its opinion, it will assist people unfamiliar with the area. Other people may erect signs with the consent of the highway authority.[3] A highway authority has power to enter land for the purpose of erecting or removing signs.[4]

10.3   BARRIERS ON FOOTPATHS

A highway authority may provide and maintain in a publicly maintainable footpath or bridleway such barriers, posts, rails and fences as it thinks necessary for safeguarding people using the highway.[5] Barriers could be put in at the ends of the path to prevent access. This power could prove useful where footpaths or bridleways are being used illegally by motor vehicles. The power did not originally apply to bridleways, but this has been altered by the CROW Act 2000.[6]

10.4   OTHER POWERS OF IMPROVEMENT

There are numerous specific powers in the Highways Act 1980 for improving a highway. These include the widening and levelling of highways, constructing and reconstructing bridges, planting trees and shrubs, metalling, draining and provision of ditches, provision of cattle grids and the construction of road humps.[7] In executing any works, the authority must have regard to the needs of the disabled and blind.[8]

---

1   Countryside Act 1968, s 27(3).
2   Ibid, s 27(2).
3   Ibid, s 27(1).
4   Road Traffic Regulation Act 1984, s 71.
5   Highways Act 1980, s 66(3), as amended by the CROW Act 2000, s 70(1).
6   Section 70(1).
7   Highways Act 1980, ss 62–102.
8   Ibid, s 175A.

There is also a duty to provide for horse riders an adequate grass or other margin by the side of a made-up carriageway where the highway authority considers it necessary or desirable in the interests of safety or convenience.[1]

The Parish Councils Act 1957 gives parish councils, with the consent of the owner or occupier, power to provide seats, shelters and lighting on public paths.[2]

There is also power under the Local Government Act 1972[3] to incur expenditure on anything which, in its opinion, is in the interests of its area, or any part of it, or all or some of its inhabitants. For improvements to public paths, the consent of the landowner will generally be necessary.

10.5 TRAFFIC REGULATION ORDERS

10.5.1 Scope

Traffic regulation orders can be made by county and metropolitan councils to secure the expeditious, convenient and safe movement of vehicular and other traffic (including pedestrians) and the provision of suitable and adequate parking facilities on and off the highway. They may be made:

(a) for avoiding danger to persons or other traffic using the road or any other road or for preventing the likelihood of any such danger arising; or

(b) for preventing damage to the road or to any building on or near the road; or

(c) for facilitating the passage on any road or any other road of any class of traffic (including pedestrians); or

(d) for preventing the use of the road by vehicular traffic of a kind which, or issue by vehicular traffic in a manner which, is unsuitable having regard to the existing character of the road or adjoining property; or

(e) (without prejudice to the generality of paragraph (d) above) for preserving the character of the road in a case where it is specially suitable for use by persons on horseback or on foot; or

(f) for preserving or improving the amenities of the area through which the road runs.[4]

In addition, traffic regulation orders may be made in special areas in the countryside 'for the purpose of conserving or enhancing the natural beauty of the area, or of affording better opportunities for the public to enjoy the amenities of the area, or recreation or the study of nature in the area'.[5] Conserving the natural beauty means conserving its flora, fauna and geological and physiographical features. The list of special areas includes National Parks,

---

1   Highways Act 1980, s 71.
2   Sections 1, 3 and 5.
3   Section 137.
4   Road Traffic Regulation Act 1984, s 1.
5   Ibid, s 22, as amended by the CROW Act 2000, s 66.

country parks which fulfil certain criteria, nature reserves, AONBs, SSSIs, long distance routes and land held by The National Trust on an inalienable basis.

Where the highway is not in a special area, a traffic regulation order may be made controlling vehicular traffic on unclassified roads for the purpose of conserving or enhancing natural beauty.[1] No order under this provision may be made for a special road, trunk road, classified road, GLA road, cycle track, bridleway, or footpath. Public vehicular traffic would not in any event be allowed on footpaths or bridleways.

If the route has vehicular rights, even though shown on the definitive map as a footpath or bridleway, an order restricting vehicles could be made. This is because entry on the definitive map of a footpath or bridleway is without prejudice to the existence of any higher rights. If there were strong evidence of vehicular rights, the authority could make a traffic regulation order before the map was modified.

The purpose of the new provision is to exclude or restrict vehicular traffic on green lanes. However, the power given to the authorities is discretionary only. They are not required to exercise or consider exercising their power. Under s 22(4) of the Road Traffic Regulation Act 1984, the Secretary of State (or National Assembly for Wales) has power to make a traffic regulation order in the special areas where the authority does not propose to do so, provided that the Countryside Agency (or Countryside Council for Wales) has made a submission as to the desirability of making an order. There is no equivalent provision in the new section dealing with orders outside the special areas.

A traffic regulation order may prohibit, restrict or regulate the use of a road, or of any part of a width by vehicular traffic and pedestrians. If the road is a footpath, bridleway or BOAT, the traffic regulation order may prohibit restrict or regulate the use of any person 'driving, riding or leading a horse or other animal of draught or burden'.[2]

10.5.2   Procedure

The procedure is set out in regulations.[3] The order-making authority must consult with road user organisations before making the order unless it appears to the authority that there are no such organisations. Notice of the proposal to make the order has to be published in a local paper and in the *London Gazette*. In some circumstances, the notice should also be placed on site. The order and the map and the authority's reasons for making the order must be made available for public inspection during the objection period. This must be at least 21 days. The authority must consider all objections and may decide to hold a public inquiry. Once the order is made, the authority must notify objectors and publish notices of the order. Any relevant documents must be available for inspection for 6 weeks from the making of the order.

---

1   Road Traffic Regulation Act 1984, s 22A.
2   Ibid, s 127.
3   Local Authorities' Traffic Orders (Procedure) (England and Wales) Regulations 1989,
     SI 1989/1120.

The only way to challenge an order, once made, is by judicial review.[1]

10.5.3   Temporary orders

Temporary orders may be made for works undertaken on or near the road or where there is a likelihood of danger to the public or serious damage to the highway, or for the purposes of litter clearing and cleaning.[2] 'Danger to the public' does not include danger from air pollution.[3]

Temporary orders for footpaths, bridleways, cycle tracks or BOATs must not last for more than 6 months.[4] Temporary orders for other highways may last for not more than 18 months. The time-limits may be extended by the Secretary of State in certain circumstances.

The traffic authority for a road may, by notice rather than order, restrict or prohibit the use of a road where it appears to it that it is necessary to do so without delay. A notice served for road works or for litter must not continue in force for more than 5 days and those for danger to the public or serious damage to the road, for not more than 21 days.

10.5.4   Access to premises

Neither a permanent nor temporary road traffic order must at any time prevent access for pedestrians to any premises situated on or adjacent to the road, or any other premises accessible for pedestrians from, and only from, the road.[5] A traffic regulation order shall not, subject to exceptions, prevent, for more than 8 hours in any period of 24 hours, access for vehicles of any class to any premises situated on or adjacent to the road or to any other premises accessible for vehicles of that class from, and only from, the road.

This restriction will not apply where the authority is satisfied that an unrestricted order is necessary (and if it is stated in the order that it is so satisfied) to avoid or prevent danger to persons or other traffic using the road, to prevent damage to the road or nearby buildings, for facilitating the passage of vehicular traffic and for preserving or improving the amenity of the area by banning or restricting heavy commercial vehicles.

10.5.5   Traffic regulation orders and BOATs

Because highway authorities, as part of their duty to keep definitive maps under review, have no choice as to whether to add a BOAT, or upgrade a footpath, bridleway or restricted byway to a BOAT or reclassify a RUPP to a BOAT where the evidence supports vehicular rights, there is often a demand that, once the definitive map has been altered, vehicles should be prohibited from using the

---

1   *Great House at Sonning Ltd v Berks County Council* [1996] RTR 407.
2   Road Traffic Regulation Act 1984, s 14.
3   *R v Greenwich LBC ex parte Williams* [1997] JPL 62, QBD.
4   Road Traffic (Temporary Restrictions) Act 1991.
5   Road Traffic Regulation Act 1984, s 3.

track by order. Such an order is likely to provoke opposition from user groups (including those who might only want to use the track as walkers or horse riders) on the basis that their rights are being eroded. Suggestions that public inquiries should deal at the same time with assessing whether vehicular rights exist and making a decision on traffic regulation orders have been rejected.

The practicalities appear to be that, generally speaking, a highway authority will not make an order unless damage has been done to the track or is almost certain to occur. The advice to those who want vehicular rights restricted must be to keep a diary recording use of the route and to take photographs of its condition.

When traffic regulation orders are made, there is a power for the traffic authority to place bollards or other physical obstructions to prevent the passage of vehicles.[1] There is a duty to erect signs stating the effect of the order.[2]

10.5.6   Effect of the order

The effect of the order is to prevent use in accordance with the terms of the order. It does not extinguish the highway or any particular rights over it.

A person who contravenes a traffic regulation order, or who uses or permits a vehicle to be used in contravention of an order, is guilty of an offence.[3]

A plaintiff will have no private law action for damages where his business suffers from a traffic regulation order. His only remedy would be the public law remedy of challenging the order by judicial review.[4]

10.6   EXTINGUISHMENT OF VEHICULAR RIGHTS

Traffic regulation orders can restrict either wholly or partially the use of public rights of way by vehicles. They cannot extinguish those rights; in order for them to be extinguished, an application would have to be made to the magistrates' court under the Highways Act 1980.[5]

10.7   MANAGEMENT OF VEHICULAR USE

Some problems which occur through legitimate use of public rights of way with vehicles may be solved by liaison with national vehicle user organisations. The organisations have codes of conduct and are keen to promote responsible use. Vehicles clubs will often police their own members, help to reduce incidents of misuse by non-members and voluntarily agree to restrain use when weather conditions mean that the surface of the track is likely to be damaged.

---

1   Road Traffic Regulation Act 1984, s 392.
2   Ibid, ss 64 and 65. The Local Authority Traffic Orders (Procedure) (England and Wales) Regulations 1989, Part III, reg 17(1)(a).
3   Road Traffic Regulation Act 1984, s 5(1).
4   *Great House at Sonning Ltd v Berks County Council* [1996] RTR 407.
5   Section 116.

10.8   CAR PARKING

Car parking can cause problems. It is generally accepted that, as part of the public's right to pass and repass, they may park for incidental purposes on public rights of way. Motorists must not obstruct the route of any access to or exit from it.

There is no right to park on private land adjoining the highway.

10.9   PROMOTED ROUTES

Sometimes, routes are promoted by the local authority or user organisations or other persons. This can cause problems, especially where the routes are not on the definitive map. If there are discrepancies, the landowner or occupier should consult the public rights of way department of the local authority.

If a local or national guide book has misrepresented the public rights of way, the matter should be drawn to the attention of the author, the publishers and the Outdoor Writers Guild.

10.10   SPONSORED EVENTS AND COMPETITIONS

Organisers of sponsored events and competitions would be wise to consult the highway authority in advance. This will ensure that any problems can be addressed before the event takes place.

Where possible, the owners should also be informed and the events published in the local farming press and newsletters.

The Ramblers' Association, the Long Distance Walkers Association and the NFU have produced Codes of Practice for sponsored walks and events.

10.11   LITTER

Local authorities can require litter and rubbish which constitutes a nuisance to be removed from public rights of way under s 149 of the Highways Act 1980.

Under the Environmental Protection Act 1990,[1] it is an offence to dump rubbish or leave litter on a publicly maintainable highway.

Landowners are responsible for clearing litter from their own property, whoever put it there. Fly tipping should be reported to the Environment Agency.

Local authorities are responsible for keeping publicly maintainable rights of way in their area free of litter.[2]

---

1   Section 87(5).
2   Environmental Protection Act 1990, ss 86(9), 89(1) and (2).

10.12   DOGS

10.12.1   General principles

Dogs are a major cause of problems on rights of way. It is generally accepted, though untested by the courts, that they are a natural accompaniment to a walker.[1] Any legislation aimed at banning dogs from public rights of way, or even ruling that they should be kept on a lead at all times, would cause a public outcry.

If dogs do not keep to the line of the path, but run onto adjoining land, there will be no liability in trespass unless the person in control of the dog either deliberately sent the dog onto the adjoining land or was negligent in allowing it to stray.[2]

10.12.2   Dangerous dogs

Dangerous dogs have been discussed under **9.7.3** in the context of interfering with the right of the public to pass and repass along a public right of way. They may also cause problems for the landowner. If so, he should report the matter to the police with a view to proceedings being brought under the Dangerous Dogs Act 1991.

10.12.3   Dogs (Protection of Livestock) Act 1953

It is an offence under the Dogs (Protection of Livestock) Act 1953 to allow a dog to attack or chase livestock. It is also an offence to allow a dog to be at large in a field or enclosure in which there are sheep. If a dog is on enclosed land where there are sheep, it must be kept on a lead or otherwise under close control.

Close control has not been defined. A dog attacking a farm animal would be out of control and could be shot by the farmer. The shooting must be reported to the police within 48 hours. The offence does not apply to a dog owned or controlled by the occupier of the field, the owner of the sheep or a person authorised by either of them. Police dogs, guide dogs, trained sheepdogs, working gundogs and packs of hounds are excluded from the provisions.

10.12.4   Road Traffic Act 1988, s 27

A local authority can make an order under the above section requiring dogs on a specified right of way to be kept on a lead. Failure to do so amounts to an offence.

Before making the order, the authority must consult the police and representative organisations. It must publish a notice in the local press on or near the paths affected by the order. In some cases, it may be necessary to hold a public inquiry.

---

1   *R v Mathias* (1861) 2 F&F 570. See P Carty 'Dogs with walkers', RWLR 3.2, p 11.
2   *League Against Cruel Sports v Scott* [1985] 2 All ER 489.

If the authority makes the order, any objectors must be informed. Notice of the order must be published in the local press and signs erected on the path indicating the effect of the order.[1]

10.12.5 Bylaws

The Local Government Act 1972[2] enables district or borough councils to make bylaws for the whole or part of their district or borough 'for good rule and government and the prevention and suppression of nuisances'.

Bylaws must be reasonable, certain in their terms, consistent with the general law and within the powers of the enabling statute.

They have been used to control dogs on beaches and could be used to control dogs on public rights of way, provided they fulfil the criteria set out above.

10.12.6 Dog fouling

Dog fouling may be a problem on public rights of way. The Environmental Health Officer of the local district council may be able to offer advice.

'Poop Scoop' bylaws can be made by a local authority under s 86 of the Environmental Protection Act 1990 and the Litter (Animal Droppings) Order 1991, SI 1991/961, to require owners to clear up after their dogs. However, they cannot be made where the routes cross open countryside.

In some areas, a 'fido field' is set aside by the local landowner where, in return for an annual payment, dog owners may exercise their dogs.

10.13 LIVESTOCK STRAYING FROM THE HIGHWAY

Under s 4 of the Animals Act 1971, a person in possession of livestock on a highway may be liable for any damage done or expense incurred if livestock stray from the highway onto adjoining land. However, it is a defence under s 5 if the presence of the livestock was a lawful use of the highway and they were not being driven negligently or if the claimant was under a duty to maintain fences and failed to do so.

10.14 CRIME

10.14.1 Perceptions

Some landowners consider that the presence of public rights of way leads to more crime. It is unlikely, however, that those bent on criminal activity will be much concerned whether or not a track or path features on the definitive map.

---

1   Control of Dogs on Roads Order (Procedure) (England and Wales) Regulations 1962, SI 1962/2340.
2   Section 235.

Crimes will be committed whether or not there are public rights of way. However, it is true that a public right of way gives a person an excuse for being present near buildings and farm equipment. There is no right for a landowner to ask anyone to leave, even if he suspects they may be burglars.

10.14.2   Theft

Theft occurs in towns as well as in the country. It is not a reason for the diversion or closure of a right of way. Indeed, thieves may be detected where there are well-used public rights of way. Walkers, riders and motor vehicle users can play an important role in reporting suspicious behaviour.

Improved security measures are likely to be more effective than diverting a public right of way from farm or estate buildings. Machinery and implements should be locked away, where possible.

The local police crime prevention officer will give advice on securing premises and discouraging crime. Many police forces organise schemes to tackle particular forms of crime: Neighbourhood Watch, Country Watch, Farm Watch, Horse Watch, Poacher Watch and so on.

10.14.3   Poaching and disturbance of wildlife and flora

If poaching is taking place, the police should be contacted. Poaching incidents relating to fishing can be reported to the Environment Agency, which has a freephone emergency hotline.

It is illegal to dig for badgers,[1] steal eggs or disturb wild birds, other than recognised pests, during the nesting season.[2]

A person who picks, uproots or destroys wild plants without the permission of the landowners may be guilty of an offence under the WLCA 1981.[3]

No criminal offence is committed by picking wild mushrooms or fruit such as blackberries from wild plants as long as it is not being done for commercial purposes. However, a person who strays from a public right of way in order to do so will be trespassing.

Suspected incidents of illegal poisoning of wildlife and animals, both wild and domestic, should be reported to DEFRA.

English Nature and the Royal Society for the Protection of Birds may provide advice where wildlife is disturbed. Local police headquarters may have a wildlife or environmental liaison officer.

---

1   Badgers Act 1973, s 2(1)(c), as amended by the WLCA 1981, Sch 2, para 9(2) and the Wildlife and Countryside (Amendments) Act 1985, s 1(2).
2   WLCA 1981, s 1.
3   Ibid, s 13.

10.15 TRESPASS

10.15.1 Nature of trespass

Trespass is a civil wrong. Except where statute has made it so, for instance trespass onto railway land, it is not a crime.[1] The remedy for trespass is damages. Where no physical damage has occurred, the damages are likely to be nominal only. Persistent trespassers may be restrained by an injunction.

If a trespasser declines to leave land on request, the occupier may physically eject him provided no more force is used than is reasonably necessary. This course of action is not, however, recommended. Use of excessive force can result in criminal or civil proceedings being brought against the ejector or his agents.

10.15.2 Trespass onto adjoining land

A properly maintained path, well waymarked, should cut down the incidents of trespass. It is not always easy to follow maps when the position is not clear on the ground. Many users will not have maps with them. Entry by a walker onto adjoining land will generally amount to trespass. However, if a right of way is obstructed by the owner of the land, the path user may deviate onto other land in the same ownership adjoining the path in order to get round the obstruction.[2]

The position is less clear if the path is obstructed by natural causes, such as a landslip or flood. Nor has it been decided if there is any right to deviate onto land of an adjoining owner. Obiter dicta by Lord Mansfield in *Taylor v Whitehead* may support an argument for a general right to deviate where there are obstructions. He said:

> '... highways are for the public service, and if the usual tract is impossible, it is for the general good that people should be able to pass in another line.'[3]

It would also be a trespass to use a public right of way for metal detecting.

Where the surface is vested in the highway authority, the trespass will be against the authority. In *Wiltshire County Council v Frazer*,[4] the county council was held able to bring summary proceedings against squatters who had put their caravans on the highway.

There may also be a trespass where greater rights than those established on a public right of way are exercised. Thus, it would be a trespass to ride a horse or bicycle on a footpath or to drive on a public right of way without vehicular rights if the activity were carried on without the consent of the landowner.

---

1   Railway Regulations Act 1840, s 16.
2   *Stacey v Sherrin* (1913) 29 TLR 555.
3   *Taylor v Whitehead* (1781) 2 Doug KB 745.
4   (1984) 47 P&CR 69.

10.15.3   Criminal Justice Act 1994 and Public Order Act 1986

The Criminal Justice Act 1994 and the Public Order Act 1986 were passed to deal with the problems caused by new age travellers and raves, but amongst other things they gave the police wide powers to deal with certain kinds of trespass on public rights of way.

A senior police officer has power to request a person to leave land where he believes certain conditions exist.[1] These are that:

(1) there are present on the land two or more persons who have the common purpose of residing on the land;
(2) they are trespassers on the land;
(3) reasonable steps have been taken by or on behalf of the occupier to ask them to leave; and
(4) either (a) any of those persons has caused damage to the land or to property on the land or has used threatening, abusive or insulting words or behaviour towards the occupier, or (b) those persons have between them six or more vehicles on the land.

Any person who fails to comply with the police officer's directions to leave as soon as practicable or having left re-enters within 3 months as a trespasser, commits a criminal offence.

'Land' is defined to exclude land forming part of the highway unless that highway is a footpath, bridleway, RUPP, restricted byway, BOAT or cycle track. 'Trespass' is trespass against the occupier of the land. 'Occupier' is defined as 'the person entitled to possession of the land by virtue of an estate or interest held by him'.

If the right of way is publicly maintainable, it seems that the highway authority having an interest in the nature of a determinable fee simple would be the occupier. The landowner, as owner of the subsoil, would also come within the definition.

An offence of aggravated trespass is committed where a trespasser does anything to obstruct or disrupt the lawful activities of persons on that or adjoining land or which is intended to intimidate them into not engaging in that activity. This is aimed at hunt saboteurs. The offender may be arrested without a warrant or directed to leave the land.

A highway authority may also give a direction to persons it believes to be residing in a vehicle or vehicles on any land, including land forming part of a highway, to leave the land and remove their vehicles and any other property they have with them.[2] Although notice of a direction must be served on the persons concerned, they do not have to be named. Failure to leave the land with their vehicles or returning within 3 months is an offence. The magistrates' court, on the application of the local authority, may make an order for the removal of the vehicles.

---

1   Criminal Justice Act 1994, s 61, as amended by the CROW Act 2000, Sch 5, para 16.
2   Ibid, s 77.

The Public Order Act 1986 contains various provisions for prohibiting and regulating public processions. This Act has been amended by the 1994 Act[1] to enable the police to obtain orders prohibiting trespassory assemblies which may result in serious disruption to the life of the community or where the land or a building or monument on it is of historical, architectural, archaeological or scientific importance, in significant damage to the land, building or monument. These orders will be made by the district council on application of the chief officer of police where he believes that 20 people or more are likely to be present on land to which the public have no right of access or only a limited right. It could therefore apply to public rights of way which are being used for purposes other than passing and re-passing.

There are similar powers to make directions prohibiting raves. 'Raves' are defined as gatherings of 100 or more persons in, or partly in, the open air playing loud amplified music in the night such as by reason of its loudness and duration and the time at which it is played is likely to cause serious distress to the inhabitants of the locality.[2]

A rave on a public right of way would be a trespass without recourse to the Act. However, there are provisions whereby a constable in uniform has power to turn back a person whom he reasonably believes is proceeding to a prohibited assembly or rave within an area of up to a 5-mile radius to which the order prohibiting the assembly or rave applies.

10.15.4   Civil remedies for regaining occupation

A landowner or occupier may bring summary proceedings for recovery of possession of land occupied by unauthorised persons. Such proceedings are brought by a claim form under Part 8 of the Civil Procedure Rules 1998. The claim form should be supported by a witness statement setting out:

(1) the claimant's interest in the land;
(2) the circumstances in which the land has been occupied and which has given rise to the claim;
(3) that, other than the persons named in the claim form, the persons occupying the land are unknown to the claimant.

The claim form and any supporting documents must be served on any person in occupation named therein. Where the occupying persons are unknown, service is effected by fixing the relevant documents, in a sealed envelope, to stakes placed in conspicuous parts of the occupied land.

Except in matters of urgency, or where the court has given permission, the hearing will take place not less than 2 days after the date of service of the claim form.

---

1   Public Order Act 1986, s 14A, inserted by the Criminal Justice and Public Order Act 1994, s 70.
2   Criminal Justice and Public Order Act 1994, s 63(1), (10).

At the hearing, the court will decide whether the claimant can recover possession of the land and make an order accordingly. A warrant of enforcement may be issued up to 3 months after the date of the order.

10.16 CONSERVATION

10.16.1 General principles

A glance at the index of most standard textbooks on public rights of way or highways reveals that conservation does not feature.[1] This is hardly surprising, as highway law is of ancient origin whilst conservation and environmental concerns are a comparatively recent development. Nevertheless, many public rights of way are part of our heritage and their routes often follow old historic tracks. They give the public access to the countryside and have a conservation and environmental importance in their own right.

Parts III and IV of the CROW Act 2000 deal specifically with nature conservation, wildlife protection and the management of areas of outstanding natural beauty. However, Part I (Access to the Countryside) and Part II (Public Rights of Way and Road Traffic) also provide for environmental protection. This is a significant departure in highway law.

10.16.2 The definitive map

The duty imposed on the surveying authority is to keep the definitive map up to date.[2] Public rights of way are added, deleted or their status changed on the basis of evidence. Conservation and environmental considerations are irrelevant for the purpose. Nor were they relevant when reclassifying RUPPs.[3]

10.16.3 Traffic regulation orders

Traffic regulation orders may be made in special areas of the countryside for conserving and enhancing the natural beauty of the area.[4] A new section has been introduced into the Road Traffic Regulation Act 1984 to enable orders to be made regulating vehicular traffic for certain highways outside special areas.[5]

10.16.4 Public path orders and agreements under the Highways Act 1980

In order for an order to be made and confirmed, the tests set out in the sections of the relevant Act must be satisfied. The tests used not to include environmental considerations. The CROW Act 2000 has now imposed a duty on local authorities and the Secretary of State in making and confirming public

1 See, however, J Harte 'Conservation and Rights of Way Conflicts', RWLR 3.1, p 1.
2 WLCA 1981, s 53.
3 Ibid, s 54. This section is to be repealed when s 47 of the CROW Act 2000 comes into force.
4 Road Traffic Regulation Act 1984, s 22.
5 Ibid, s 22A. See **10.5.1** above.

path orders and creation agreements to have regard to the desirability of conserving flora, fauna and geological and physiographical features.[1] Public rights of way may be diverted for the protection of SSSIs.[2]

10.16.5 General duties to exercise functions in furtherance of conservation

Section 74 of the CROW Act 2000 imposes a duty on any Minister of the Crown, any Government Department and the National Assembly for Wales in carrying out their functions to have regard to the purpose of conserving biological diversity in accordance with the United Nations Environmental Programme on Biological Diversity 1997.

Section 85 of the CROW Act 2000 imposes an obligation on a relevant authority in exercising its functions to have regard to the purpose of conserving and enhancing the natural beauty of the area within an AONB.

---

1   CROW Act 2000, Sch 6, para 2.
2   Ibid, para 12.

Chapter 11

BACKGROUND TO THE COUNTRYSIDE AND RIGHTS OF WAY ACT 2000

11.1 BACKGROUND

Ever since the middle of the 19th century there has been a call for a right to roam over common land and open country. The Law of Property Act 1925 gave the public the right of access for air and exercise to metropolitan and urban district commons, which included large areas in the Lake District and South Wales. In 1949, the NPACA 1949 enabled agreements and orders to be made for public access to open country. It is estimated that 50,000 hectares were made available for access under this Act, but that there are some 5,000,000 hectares of open countryside in England and Wales where access is not permitted and a further 600,000 hectares where public access occurs on an informal basis.[1]

The Royal Commission on Common Land[2] recommended that common land should be open to the public as of right, subject to the restrictions in Sch 2 to the NPACA 1949. The Common Land Reform Report[3] recommended a right of access to common land on foot for the purpose of quiet enjoyment.

Due to representations from the Moorland Association, these proposals were not enacted by the Conservative Government. The Labour Party, in its manifesto in 1997, committed itself to granting public access not only to commons but to open country.

The Labour Government produced its Consultation Paper on Access on 24 February 1998. It estimated that the total extent of mountain, moor, heath, down and registered common land was between 1.2 and 1.8 million hectares or about 10 per cent of the land area in England and Wales. In this Paper, a voluntary approach was put forward as a possible alternative to a new statutory right of access. The Government stated:

> 'We have not ruled out the voluntary approach to achieving this [greater access] but would have to have firm assurances that, broadly, the degree of access outlined in this consultation document under a statutory approach would be achieved through such means.'

---

1   Explanatory Notes to the Countryside and Rights of Way Act 2000, para 7, prepared by DETR.
2   Report of the Royal Commission on Common Land 1955–1958 (Cmnd 462).
3   Common Land: The Report of the Common Land Forum, CCP215 (1986).

The Government acknowledged the Country Landowners Association's action under Access 2000 to improve the quality, diversity and quantity of managed public access and recreation in the countryside:

> 'We welcome this initiative but would need to be convinced that such voluntary initiatives could be made to deliver substantially greater access in future if we were to adopt this approach in preference to new legislation.'

The Consultation Paper stressed that proposals for new voluntary access put forward by organisations or individuals would have to be assessed against six criteria:

(1) extent of access;
(2) quality of access;
(3) permanency;
(4) clarity and certainty;
(5) cost;
(6) monitoring and enforcement.

In the event, the Government decided on the compulsory access. The justification for this approach was given by Michael Meacher (DETR) in the following words:

> 'Over the past 50 years, a voluntary approach has delivered relatively little, and despite some commendable initiatives, there is little prospect of much new access being provided voluntarily in future. Even if a great deal more access could be secured through voluntary arrangements, the access would not be permanent and the cost would be high. Only a new statutory right will deliver cost effectively the extent and permanence of access we are seeking.'[1]

The Government asked the countryside bodies and the Forestry Commission to report on access to woods, coastal land and rivers. The Countryside Agency recommended that the statutory right should be extended to coastal land, but further research was necessary.

11.2 ACCESS AS OF RIGHT OTHER THAN UNDER THE COUNTRYSIDE AND RIGHTS OF WAY ACT 2000

11.2.1 General principles

There is no general right to roam, although in uncultivated areas there is often *de facto* access. Members of the public do not have a general right of access to land in England and Wales except on highways. Access has been provided to areas of land, rather than on defined routes, only as a result of specific Acts of Parliament, by the granting of rights by landowners, or by agreement with landowners. The courts also accept that local inhabitants of an area, but not the

---

1   Government Announcement, 8 March 1999. For background papers published by DETR, see Access to the Open Countryside in England and Wales (February 1998); Improving Rights of Way in England and Wales (July 1999); The Government's Framework for Access to the Countryside in England and Wales (March 1999).

general public, can acquire the right to use village greens for 'lawful sports and pastimes', where there has been a tradition of such use.

11.2.2   Common land

There is considerable confusion about public rights over 'common land'. Many people wrongly believe that common land implies public ownership and they have a right to wander over it at will. In fact, most common land is private land over which commoners have specific rights of use (eg to graze sheep or cattle, to collect firewood or to fish). These rights are in addition to those of the owner of the common. Some common land is land which is, or was, 'waste land of the manor, not subject to rights of common'.[1]

The public have access on public rights of way over common land just as they do on rights of way over any other land. Otherwise, there is no general right of public access unless granted by statute or by the landowner.

Section 193 of the Law of Property Act 1925 gives the public a right of access for air and exercise over metropolitan and urban commons (ie those commons which were within the areas covered by the former urban district councils). Case-law[2] has established that this includes horse riding. Section 193(2) provides that the landowners can declare by revocable or irrevocable deed that the provisions shall apply to any of their land which is subject to rights of common. The CROW Act 2000 will repeal this subsection as it will no longer be required. Wider powers of dedication of open land for public access are given by s 16 of the new Act.

The public may also enjoy a right of access over certain rural commons by orders made under the Commons Act 1876, or over commons subject to a management scheme under the Commons Act 1899, or over commons subject to special local Acts. For example, the Dartmoor Commons Act 1985 provides a right of access for the purpose of open-air recreation to commons registered under the Commons Registration Act 1965 which are situated within specified districts. This right includes access on horseback as well as on foot.

The Public Health and Open Spaces Act 1906 enables local authorities to purchase any land as an open space. The National Trust is obliged by the National Trust Act 1907 to keep its commons unenclosed and unbuilt upon as open spaces for the recreation and enjoyment of the public.

11.2.3   Town and village greens

Town and village greens are areas of land, registered under the Commons Registration Act 1965, which come within the following definition:

(a) land which has been allotted by or under any Act for the exercise or recreation of the inhabitants of the locality;

---

1   *Hampshire County Council v Milburn* [1990] 2 WLR 1240.
2   *R v Secretary of State for the Environment, Transport and the Regions ex parte Billson* [1998] 2 All ER 587.

(b) land on which the inhabitants of any locality have a customary right to indulge in local sports and pastimes;

(c) land on which the inhabitants of any locality have indulged in such sports and pastimes as of right for not less than 20 years.[1]

The phrase 'lawful sports and pastimes' includes such activities as the village cricket match, maypole dancing and practising archery.

The recent case of *R v Oxfordshire County Council ex parte Sunningwell PC*[2] has made it much easier to register new town and village greens under (c) above. First, 'sports and pastimes' was held to include more informal activities such as blackberry picking, flying kites and tobogganing. Secondly, the case establishes that 'as of right' merely means without force, secrecy or permission and does not require any subjective belief by the inhabitants of the existence of the right. Nor is toleration by the landowner inconsistent with user as of right. Thirdly, it was held to be sufficient if the land was used predominantly, rather than exclusively, by the inhabitants of the village.

In *R (Beresford) v Sunderland City Council*,[3] an application to register a village green failed because the user was held to be pursuant to an implied licence and therefore was not user as of right. The fact that the land was owned by a local authority was relevant in inferring permission for recreational use. Other relevant factors would be any overt acts by the landowner or circumstances from which inference of a licence could be drawn, even though possibly unknown to the users.

The predominant test has been altered by the CROW Act 2000.[4] Land will now qualify under (c) above if 'a significant number of the inhabitants of any locality, or of any neighbourhood within a locality' have used it for at least 20 years for lawful sports and pastimes. This removes the need to demonstrate that use is predominantly by people from the locality and means that use by people from outside that locality will no longer have to be taken into account by registration authorities. The amendment also deals with the problem of showing that users come from a particular village or parish. This is difficult in large built-up areas and so the concept of neighbourhood has been introduced.

With regard to the words 'a significant number of the inhabitants', Sullivan J said in *R (Alfred McAlpine Homes Ltd) v Staffordshire County Council*:[5]

> 'I do not accept the proposition that significant in the context of section 22(1) as amended means a considerable or a substantial number. A neighbourhood may have a very limited population and a significant number of the inhabitants of such a neighbourhood might not be so great as to be properly described as a considerable or substantial number . . . what matters is that the number of people using the land signifies that it is in general use by the local community for informal recreation, rather than occasional use by individuals as trespassers.'

---

1   Commons Registration Act 1965, s 22.
2   [1999] 3 WLR 160.
3   [2001] 1 WLR 1327.
4   Section 98, amending Commons Registration Act 1965, s 22.
5   [2002] EWHC Admin 76, [2002] ACD 63.

Another difficulty has also been dealt with by the amendment. The application for the registration of a town or village green had to show 20-year use up to the date of the application.[1] Often when the use is prevented by the landowner it takes a considerable time to collect the necessary evidence to make the application. By the time this is done, there may be a gap in the user which would defeat the claim. Provision has therefore been made for the application to be made where user has ceased for not more than a period which is to be prescribed. The Government's intentions are that it should be 2 years. If no application has been made within the prescribed period of the land ceasing to be used for lawful sports and pastimes, the owner or developer will be able to take whatever steps are necessary to develop the land in the certainty that an application for the registration of a green will be rejected. Until the regulations are made, the effect of s 22(1A) of the Commons Registration Act 1965 is that the user must continue until the date of the application.

Two Acts were passed in the 19th century which provide protection for village greens. Section 12 of the Inclosure Act 1857 makes it an offence to damage or encroach upon a village green. The section covers any act which injures the green or interrupts its use as a place for exercise and recreation. Section 29 of the Commons Act 1876 makes 'encroachment on or inclosure of a town or village green, also any erection thereon or disturbance or interference with or occupation of the soil thereof which is made otherwise than with a view to the better enjoyment of such town or village greens' an offence.

11.3 ACCESS BY AGREEMENT

11.3.1 General principles

There have been various schemes under which landowners and farmers can provide public access to areas of land in return for payments. These are operated by government departments (eg the Countryside Access Scheme for set-aside land, The Access Tier in Environmentally Sensitive Areas, operated by DEFRA), statutory agencies (eg the Countryside Stewardship Scheme, operated originally by the Countryside Commission and now by DEFRA) and local authorities (eg access agreements under s 64 of the NPACA 1949 or management agreements (which may incorporate access) under s 30 of the WLCA 1981). The conditions of the DEFRA schemes vary from year to year. It is likely that they will continue on land which does not qualify as access land.

Public access may also have been granted in exchange for conditional exemption from inheritance tax. Informal arrangements could also be made without payment.

11.3.2 Local authority agreements

The largest areas with negotiated access arrangements were those areas of 'open country' covered by agreements under s 64 of the NPACA 1949. Such

---

1   *Ministry of Defence v Wiltshire County Council* [1995] 4 All ER 931, but obiter dicta only.

agreements provided for payments and the application of bylaws and ranger services to the land involved. It was also possible to make access orders under s 65 of the NPACA 1949, although very few orders were made.

'Open Country' was defined originally for the purposes of such agreements as land consisting wholly or predominantly of mountain, moor, heath and down. The definition was widened by the Countryside Act 1968 to include cliff and foreshore, woodland, rivers, canals, expanses of water through which such rivers flow and land adjacent to them. When s 46 of the CROW Act 2000 comes into force, it will no longer be possible to make access agreements or orders relating to open country, as defined in that Act, or to registered common land. Agreements and orders under Part V of the NPACA 1949 may still be made in relation to water including rivers.

Local authorities also have powers under s 39 of the WLCA 1981 to enter into management agreements 'for the purposes of conserving or enhancing the natural beauty or amenity of the countryside or promoting its enjoyment by the public'. Such agreements apply to any type of rural land, not simply open country. The CROW Act 2000[1] has amended the section to enable the Countryside Agency and the Countryside Council for Wales and conservation boards in AONBs to enter into such agreements, and for agreements to be made by such bodies, and local authorities, whether or not the land is in the country. Agreements can be made with landowners for the dedication of land under s 16 of the CROW Act 2000 and for its long-term preservation, including preventing the land from becoming excepted land under Sch 1. Millennium greens in towns and villages can be preserved under s 39 as amended.

11.4   COUNTRYSIDE AND RIGHTS OF WAY ACT 2000

11.4.1   General principles

The CROW Act 2000 received Royal Assent on 30 November 2000. It was presented as a Bill to the House of Commons on 3 March 2000 and was subject to much criticism as it was debated in both Houses of Parliament. Many of the amendments were made at third reading in the House of Lords.

The CROW Act 2000 is divided into five parts.

– Part I gives the public a new right of access to mountain, moor, heath, down and registered common land.

– Part II amends the rights of way legislation. The various amendments are discussed under the relevant chapters of the first part of this book.

– Part III amends the law relating to nature conservation by strengthening protection for SSSIs through tougher penalties and providing extra powers for the prosecution of wildlife offences.

---

1   Section 96.

– Part IV is concerned with Areas of Outstanding Natural Beauty (AONBs). Nature conservation, wildlife protection and AONBs are outside the ambit of this book.

– Part V contains miscellaneous and supplementary provisions.

11.4.2   Commencement

On the date of Royal Assent, namely 30 November 2000, s 103, which contains the provisions relating to the commencement of the different sections, and s 104, the interpretation, short title and extent section, came into force. The only other section which came into force on that day was s 81. The section, which is in Part III of the CROW Act 2000, provides that, in future, Regulations to implement the European Union Habitats Directive (Council Directive 92/43 EEC), the EU Wildlife Trade Regulation (Council Regulation 338/97) and Commission Regulation 939/97/EC will be able to create offences, which, on a summary conviction, will carry a custodial sentence of up to 6 months.

The main provisions in Part I giving the right of access will come into force on such day as the Secretary of State (as respects England) or the National Assembly for Wales (as respects Wales) may order by statutory instrument. Part II of the Act, which deals with public rights of way, will come into force on the day appointed by the Secretary of State in a statutory instrument. Different days may be appointed for different purposes or areas for both Parts I and II of the CROW Act 2000.

Before the access provisions can be implemented, certain preliminary work needs to be done. The CROW Act 2000 therefore provides that s 1 and Sch 1, ss 3–11 and Sch 3, ss 15–17, s 19, Chapters II and III of Part I, ss 40–45, s 52, ss 58–59, ss 64–67 and Sch 7 (apart from paras 6 and 7 of that Schedule) should come into force 2 months after the Royal Assent. These sections cover the matters listed below.

Part I   Access to the Countryside

(1)   Access Land
Section 1 gives the principle definitions in Part I of the CROW Act 2000. In particular, it sets out the categories of access land over which the public will have a right of access. Schedule 1 lists the excepted land which will not be subject to the right of access. Section 3 enables the Secretary of State to amend the definition of open land to include coastal land. Section 16 provides that landowners may dedicate land as access land for the purposes of Part I of the CROW Act 2000. Section 15 sets out the existing legislation under which the public have a right of access to open land, but which does not count as access land for the purposes of the CROW Act 2000.

(2)   Bylaws
Section 17 enables the National Park or local highway authority to make bylaws.

(3)   Mapping

Sections 4–11 relate to the preparation, publication and review of maps of registered common land and open country. Schedule 3 deals with the delegation of functions where there are appeals against the showing of land as open land or registered common land on provisional maps.

(4)   Notices indicating boundaries or restrictions

Section 19 gives access authorities power to erect and maintain notices indicating the boundaries of access or excepted land. They may also display notices informing the public of the general restrictions relating to access land or of any particular restrictions or exclusions.

(5)   Exclusions or restrictions

Chapter II (ss 21–33) sets out the exclusions or restrictions which may be imposed on access land.

(6)   Physical means of access

Chapter III (ss 34–39) contains provisions to ensure that the public are not prevented by barriers or other obstructions from entering access land.

(7)   Powers of entry

Section 40 gives the countryside bodies, the highway authorities and the National Park authorities powers of entry onto land in order to carry out their statutory functions. Section 41 provides for compensation relating to those powers.

(8)   Public places

Where there is a provision in any Act passed before or in the same session as the CROW Act 2000 relating to things done or omitted to be done in public places, regulations under s 42 may provide that the term will not cover the right of access conferred by s 2(1) either generally or in specific cases. For instance, regulations could provide that access land would not be treated as a public place for the purposes of the Firearms Act 1968. This would mean that the landowner would not need to show lawful authority or reasonable excuse for using or carrying a firearm when on the land.

(9)   The Crown

Section 43 provides that Part I of the CROW Act 2000 shall bind the Crown. No contravention by the Crown makes it criminally liable, but the High Court may declare any act or omission unlawful if it amounts to a contravention. Part I applies to persons in the public service of the Crown as it applies to other persons.

(10)   Orders and regulations

Section 44 gives powers to the Secretary of State or the National Assembly for Wales to make orders and regulations by statutory instrument.

(11)   Interpretation of Part I

Section 45 is the interpretation section for Part I of the Act.

Part II Public Rights of Way and Road Traffic

(1) Regulations relating to restricted byways

Section 52 enables the Secretary of State to make special provisions in existing legislation, or legislation inserted or amended by the CROW Act 2000 that such legislation shall not apply or shall apply, with or without modifications, to restricted byways.

(2) Creation orders

Section 58 gives the Countryside Agency and the Countryside Council for Wales power to apply for a creation order for the purpose of enabling the public to obtain access to any access land.

(3) Stopping up and diversions

Section 59 provides that the existence of access land is to be disregarded in deciding whether or not to make or confirm extinguishment and diversion orders.

(4) Obstructions

Section 64 introduces a new section, s 137ZA, into the Highways Act 1980, giving the court power to order an offender to remove an obstruction from a public right of way. Section 65 amends s 154 of the Highways Act 1980 to provide that overhanging vegetation must not endanger or obstruct the passage of horse-riders.

(5) Traffic regulation orders

Section 66 extends the existing power to make road traffic orders for environmental reasons.

(6) Prohibition of driving mechanically propelled vehicles elsewhere than on roads

Section 67 and Sch 7 substitute the term 'mechanically propelled vehicles' for motor car in various statutes and makes other minor amendments. Section 34 of the Road Traffic Act 1988 is amended to make it easier to prosecute persons driving on public rights of way which are recorded as footpaths, bridleways, RUPPs or restricted byways.

Part V Miscellaneous and Supplementary Provisions

(1) Local access forums

Sections 94 and 95 provide for the establishment of local access forums.

(2) Registration of town and village greens

Section 98 makes it easy to claim village greens on the basis of long use.

11.4.3 Extent

The CROW Act 2000 applies to England and Wales. Part I (Access to the Countryside) does not apply to the Isles of Scilly, nor do the provisions in Part II relating to improvement plans. However, the Secretary of State may, after consultation with the Council of Scilly, provide by statutory instrument that Part I and the improvement plan provisions should apply with such modifications as may be specified in the order.[1]

Section 67, which prevents the driving of mechanically propelled vehicles elsewhere than on roads, and the supplementary provisions in paras 3 and 5–7 contained in Sch 7 apply to Scotland.[2]

11.4.4 Wales

Ministerial functions under the Highways Act 1980 and the WLCA 1981 relating to Wales were transferred to the National Assembly for Wales by the National Assembly for Wales (Transfer of Functions) Order 1999.[3] The references to those Acts in Sch 1 to the order are to be taken as if to those Acts as amended by the CROW Act 2000.[4] The effect is that the new functions conferred on the Secretary of State by the CROW Act 2000 will be exercisable in Wales by the National Assembly.

11.4.5 Compensation

There is no provision in the CROW Act 2000 for landowners to be given compensation, should their land be devalued as a result of public access. According to the Government's Framework Paper:

> 'The Government has taken into account the limited nature of the new right of access; its application only to land which is undeveloped and not used for intensive agricultural purposes; the continued ability of landowners to develop and use their land after the introduction of the right; and the extensive provision made for closure of land for land management and other reasons. The cost/benefit research by independent consultants supports the view that landowners will not suffer significant losses or costs as a result of a new right of access to open countryside, such as would warrant the provision of compensation. Local Authorities will, however, be able to assist, where necessary, with the management of the new right of access, for example, by the provision of points of entry and signs.'

When presenting the Bill to the House of Commons the Secretary of State, the Rt Hon John Prescott MP, made the following statement under s 19(1)(a) of the Human Rights Act 1998:

> 'In my view the provisions of the Countryside and Rights of Way Bill are compatible with the Convention rights.'

However, there are arguments that introducing a statutory right of access without compensation would be a breach of the Convention of Human Rights.[5] The answer is not clear cut. Article 1 of Protocol 1 provides as follows:

---

1   Section 100.
2   CROW Act 2000, s 104(5).
3   SI 1999/672.
4   CROW Act 2000, s 99.
5   See *Hansard*, Third Reading, 23 November 2000, vol 619, cols 1008–1022, and *Chassagnou and Others v France* (2000) 29 EHRR 615.

'Every natural or legal person is entitled to the peaceful enjoyment of his possessions. No one shall be deprived of his possessions except in the public interest and subject to the conditions provided for by law and by the general provisions of international law.

The proceeding provision shall not, however, in any way impair the right of the State to enforce such laws as it deems necessary to control the use of property in accordance with the general interest ...'

A statutory right of access does not deprive a landowner of his possessions. Even if it did, it could be argued that the statutory right was in the public interest and therefore was perfectly permissible. The explanatory notes published by the DETR state:

'The Act contains measures to improve public access while recognising the legitimate interests of those who own and manage the land concerned.'

An analogy may be drawn with the Town and Country Planning Acts. As pointed out by Sir Robert Megarry:

'Planning control affects the use and enjoyment of land, but not the estates or interests in it ... The right to use property in a particular way is not itself property, and the fee simple in land remains the fee simple as before. All that has happened is that the fruits of ownership have become less sweet; but that is nothing new in land law.'[1]

11.5   ENGLISH COMMENCEMENT ORDERS (as at 31 December 2002)

11.5.1   Countryside and Rights of Way Act 2000 (Commencement No 1) Order 2001[2]

This Order brought in force on 30 January 2001 includes certain provisions not covered by s 103 of the CROW Act 2000.

These are:

- s 57 in relation to the amendments of para 18(a) and 19 of Sch 6, which amend the Highways Act 1980, but only to the extent that they make changes relating to rail crossing, extinguishment and diversion orders;
- s 72, the interpretation section of Part II;
- s 100 (relating to the application of the Act to the Isles of Scilly) except for subs (3) and (5)(a); and
- s 102 (which introduces the repeals in Sch 16).

The Order provided that the following sections should come into force on 1 April 2001:

- s 68, which provides for statutory easements over Commons;
- Part IV of Schs 13 and 14, which amends the law relating to AONBs;

---

1   Megarry and Wade *The Law of Real Property* 5th edn, p 1084.
2   SI 2001/114 (C4).

- s 100(3), which applies the provision to the Scilly Isles and s 97, which places a duty on public bodies in relation to the Norfolk and Suffolk Broads;
- s 134(5), which restricts who may bring a prosecution for ploughing of footpaths and bridleways is repealed but only for offences committed after 1 April 2001.

11.5.2   Countryside and Rights of Way Act 2000 (Commencement No 2) Order 2002[1]

This order came into force on 19 November 2002 and brought into force ss 60–62 of the Countryside and Rights of Way Act 2000 relating to improvement plans.

11.6   WELSH COMMENCEMENT ORDERS (as at December 2002)

11.6.1   Countryside and Rights of Way Act 2000 (Commencement No 1) (Wales) Order 2001[2]

This order brought into force, on 30 January 2001, s 99 of the CROW Act 2000. The effect is that references in the National Assembly for Wales (Transfer of Functions) Order 1991 to the Highways Act 1980 and the WLCA 1981 are to be read as referring to those Acts as amended by the CROW Act 2000. It also enables the National Assembly to exercise the functions of the Secretary of State specified in Sch 11 (Transitional Provisions and Savings Relating to Sites of Special Scientific Interest).

11.6.2   Countryside and Rights of Way Act 2000 (Commencement No 2) (Wales) Order 2001[3]

This order brought into effect on 1 May 2001:

- s 57 in relation to paras 18 and 19 of Sch 6 (which amend the Highways Act 1980);
- paras 18(a) and 19 of Sch 6 to the extent that they make changes relating to rail crossing extinguishment and diversion orders;
- s 68 (which relates to vehicular access over common land);
- s 72, the interpretation section of Part 11;
- Part IV and Schs 13 and 14 amending the law relating to AONBs;
- s 102, which introduces the repeals schedule;

---

1   SI 2002/2833 (C.89).
2   SI 2001/203 (W.9) (C.10).
3   SI 2001/1410 (W.96) (C.50).

–   s 134(5), which restricts who may bring a prosecution for ploughing footpaths and bridleways, is repealed – but only for offences committed after 1 May 2001;
–   certain other minor and consequential provisions.

11.6.3   Countryside and Rights of Way Act 2000 (Commencement No 3) (Wales) Order 2002[1]

This order brought into force, on 1 November 2002, s 60 of the CROW Act 2000, which imposes a duty on highway authorities to prepare and publish a rights of way improvement plan.

---

1   SI 2001/2615 (W.253) (C.82).

Chapter 12

ACCESS LAND

12.1 INTRODUCTION

If the public are to be given a right to wander over open country, and are not to be confined to defined linear routes, it is important that it should be absolutely clear where they are allowed to go. The understandable concern of landowners has been that, although access land might be defined in the CROW Act 2000, it would not necessarily be easy to determine on the ground whether or not the land was open country.

The legislation has dealt with the problem by providing that access land will either be readily identifiable or be such open country as is shown on specially drawn maps. The different forms of access land are discussed below. Access land does not include excepted land and land accessible to the public under other statutory provisions.[1]

12.2 DEFINITION OF ACCESS LAND

12.2.1 Mapped open country

The CROW Act 2000 defines 'open country' as land which 'appears to the appropriate countryside body to consist wholly or predominately of mountain, moor, heath or down, and is not registered common land'. 'Mountain' includes any land situated more than 600 metres above sea level. However, 'mountain, moor, heath or down' does not include land which appears to the countryside body to consist of improved or semi-improved grassland. In England, the appropriate countryside body is the Countryside Agency; in Wales, the Countryside Council for Wales.

Once the countryside body has decided that land comes within the definition of open land and has been shown as such in conclusive form on the map, such land has the status of access land unless it is excepted land or land accessible to the public under other specified legislation.[2]

---

1   CROW Act 2000, s 1(1)(e).
2   Ibid, ss 1(1), (2), 15. See **12.3** and **12.4**.

12.2.2   Registered common land

Registered common land may or may not come within the definition of open country. However, it is easily ascertained as maps and registers of such land are kept by the county councils. If the land is shown on a map as registered common land it will be access land, unless it is excepted land or accessible to the public under other specified legislation.[1] It will also be access land if it is registered common land in any area outside Inner London for which no map has been issued.[2]

'Registered common land' means land which is registered under the Commons Registration Act 1965, where the registration has become final. Land which was not registered as common land under the Commons Registration Act 1965 lost its status as common land, although some land, such as the New Forest, Epping Forest, the Forest of Dean and land specially exempted by an order of the Secretary of State, was not subject to the 1965 Act. Such land may be mapped as open land if it meets the relevant criteria.

Land which was registered common land on 30 November 2000, the day on which the legislation was passed, or becomes registered common land after that date, will continue to be access land even if it subsequently becomes deregistered. It will not, however, remain access land if the land was deregistered pursuant to an application made before 30 November 2000. Nor will the land continue to be access land where the land ceases to be common land as a result of a compulsory purchase, appropriation, sale or exchange under powers conferred by statute.

Village greens will not be mapped as common land. They may be mapped as open country if they come within the definition.

12.2.3   Land above 600 metres

Land situated more than 600 metres above sea level will qualify immediately as access land even before it is put on the map.[3] This is because it will be easily recognised as coming within the definition of open country. Although it is intended that eventually all mountains will be put on the map, it was not originally considered necessary to delay public access to land over 600 metres until this has been done. The policy has now changed. Public access will be brought in on a regional basis once the conclusive maps have been produced for that area. There will not be accelerated access for land over 600 metres.

'Mountain' is defined to include any land over 600 metres.[4] Mountains of a lesser height will have to be shown on the maps prepared under the Act before they will qualify as access land.

---

1   CROW Act 2000, ss 1(1)(b), (15).
2   Ibid, s 1(1)(c).
3   Ibid, s 1(1)(d).
4   Ibid, s 1(2).

12.2.4 Dedicated land

A fee simple owner, and a leaseholder with a lease which has at least 90 years left to run, may dedicate any of his land to the public as access land.[1] If the dedication is made by the leaseholder, it will be effective only for the remainder of his term.[2] Where anyone (other than the person making the dedication or a person with a superior leasehold interest[3]) has a leasehold or other prescribed interest in the land to be dedicated, that person must join in the dedication or give his consent.[4]

Dedication is likely to be of advantage to a landowner where there is existing *de facto* access. His duty of care under the Occupiers' Liability Act 1984 will be limited in accordance with s 13 of the CROW Act 2000 and he will benefit from any bylaws or wardening services.

The land dedicated may also be open country or registered common land. The purpose of dedicating land, which would in any event be access land, might be to ensure that the land remains available for public access even if it ceases to be open land or registered common land. Another reason might be to lift any of the restrictions which are imposed by Sch 2.

A dedication is irrevocable, and will bind successive owners and occupiers of the land.[5] However, the dedication will not prevent the land subsequently becoming excepted land. A dedication is a local land charge and should be registered.[6]

Regulations may allow the person dedicating the land to do so without all or some of the general restrictions to which other access land is subject.[7] He might, for instance, allow horse riding. Although restrictions originally imposed can subsequently be released, the converse is not true. In other words, the regulations will not enable him later to impose or re-impose restrictions.

Regulations may govern the form of any document required for the dedication[8] and may provide for notice of dedication to be given to the appropriate countryside body and access authority.[9]

12.2.5 Power to extend to coastal land

The Secretary of State or the National Assembly for Wales may, by order (approved by a resolution of each House of Parliament), extend the definition of open country so as to include coastal land or coastal land of any

---

1   CROW Act 2000, s 16(1).
2   Ibid, s 16(4).
3   Ibid, s 16(3).
4   Ibid, s 16(2).
5   Ibid, s 16(7).
6   Ibid, s 16(8).
7   Ibid, s 16(6)(b), (c).
8   Ibid, s 16(6)(a).
9   Ibid, s 16(6)(d).

description.[1] 'Coastal land' means the foreshore or land adjacent to it, including in particular any cliff, bank, barrier, dune, beach or flat.[2]

12.3   EXCEPTED LAND

12.3.1   General principles

Access land does not include excepted land, even though it might be registered common land or mapped open country. Moreover, access land may be converted into excepted land by a landowner, provided that, where development takes place, he has obtained any necessary planning consents. Alternatively, excepted land may cease to be so and become access land. The difficulty will be for the public to know what open country is excepted land. There is no provision for excepted land to be shown separately on maps of open country. This is because some areas, for instance an isolated barn, will be too small to show on a map. Also, many of the categories of excepted land will be obvious on the ground. Further, land may come in and out of the category of excepted land depending on its use from time to time. It will be up to the landowner to put up notices indicating the existence and extent of any excepted land where there could be doubt about the matter.

12.3.2   Types of land

It is not intended that the right of access should interfere unduly with the landowner's privacy or business. The excepted land set out in Sch 1 to the Act reflects this policy. The list (using the paragraph numbers of the Schedule) is as follows.

(1)   Cultivated land. That is:

'land on which the soil is being, or has at any time within the previous 12 months been, disturbed by any ploughing or drilling undertaken for the purposes of planting or sowing crops or trees.'

'Ploughing and drilling' include agricultural or forestry operations similar to ploughing and drilling.[3]

(2)   Land covered by buildings or the curtilage of such land. 'Buildings' include structures (which include any tent, caravan, or other temporary or moveable structure), erections, parts of buildings but not fences or walls or a means of access to open land.[4]

(3)   Land within 20 metres of a dwelling.

(4)   Land used as a park or garden.

---

1   CROW Act 2000, s 44(3).
2   Ibid, s 3.
3   Ibid, Sch 1, para 14.
4   Ibid.

(5)   Land used for the getting of minerals by surface working including quarrying. 'Minerals' have the same meaning as in the Town and Country Planning Act 1990.[1]

(6)   Land used for the purposes of a railway (including a light railway) or tramway.

(7)   Land used for the purposes of a golf course, racecourse or aerodrome.

(8)   Land which does not fall within any of the above and is covered by works used for the purposes of a statutory undertaking or a telecommunication code system, or the curtilage of any such land. 'Statutory undertaking' means the undertaking of any statutory undertaker or an airport to which Part V of the Airports Act 1986 applies. Statutory undertaker means:

'(a)   a person authorised by any enactment to carry on any railway, light railway, tramway, road transport, water transport, canal, inland navigation, dock, harbour, pier or lighthouse undertaking or any undertaking for the supply of hydraulic power,

(b)   any public transporter, within the meaning of Part 1 of the Gas Act 1986,

(c)   any water or sewerage undertaker,

(d)   any holder of a licence under section 6(1) of the Electricity Act 1989, or

(e)   the Environment Agency, the Post Office or the Civil Aviation Authority.'[2]

(9)   Land as respects which development which will result in the land falling within (2) to (8) above is in the course of being carried out. Planning permission for the development must have been granted or the development must be treated as lawful under s 191(2) of the Town and Country Planning Act 1990.[3]

(10)   Land within 20 metres of a livestock building, not being a temporary or moveable structure. However, this will not exclude access where it is a means of access to access land or any way leading to such a means of access and this is necessary for giving the public reasonable access to access land.[4]

(11)   Land covered by pens in use for the temporary reception or detention of livestock.

(12)   Land habitually used for the training of racehorses is excepted between dawn and midday and at any other time when it is in use for that purpose.[5]

---

1   CROW Act 2000, Sch 1, para 14.
2   Ibid.
3   Ibid, para 15.
4   Ibid, para 16.
5   Ibid, para 17.

(13) Land the use of which is regulated by bylaws under s 14 of the Military
      Lands Act 1892 or s 2 of the Military Lands Act 1900.

12.4   ACCESS UNDER OTHER ENACTMENTS

12.4.1   General principles

Land which is accessible to the public under s 193 of the Law of Property Act
1925, or the Commons Act 1899, or Part V of the NPACA 1949 does not count
as access land for the purposes of the CROW Act 2000. The existing right of
access will endure.

12.4.2   Law of Property Act 1925, s 193

This section gives the public a right for air and exercise on foot and on horse[1]
over metropolitan and urban commons (ie those commons which were within
an area which immediately before 1 April 1974 was a borough or urban
district). A landowner could also apply the section to any of his land by a
revocable or irrevocable deed.[2] This power will be repealed on a date to be
specified by statutory instrument. Similar, although wider, powers are given to
landowners by s 16 of the CROW Act 2000.

Where land has been dedicated by a revocable deed under s 193, a landowner
might be advised to revoke the deed in favour of access under the CROW Act
2000. Depending on the terms of the s 193 deed there may be advantages to the
landowner in managing the land under the CROW Act 2000 (eg exclusions and
restrictions, occupiers' liability, possibly bylaws and wardens).

12.4.3   Commons Act 1899

Public access for open air recreation may have been granted by a local or private
Act or a scheme under the Commons Act 1899. Where the right of access was
limited to the inhabitants of a particular district or neighbourhood the CROW
Act 2000[3] extends the right to the public generally.

12.4.4   Part V of the National Parks and Access to the
Countryside Act 1949

Existing access agreements and orders under NPACA 1949 will continue, but
the land over which that access is obtained will not count as access land for the
purpose of the CROW Act 2000. It will not be possible to make future
agreements or orders for registered common land or mapped open country.

---

1   *R v Secretary of State for the Environment ex parte Billson* [1998] 2 All ER 587.
2   Law of Property Act 1925, s 193(2).
3   Section 15(2).

12.4.5 Ancient Monuments and Archaeological Areas Act 1979

The public have access to any monument under the ownership or guardianship of the Secretary of State or the Commission for Ancient Monuments or a local authority.[1] There is power to restrict access in certain circumstances. Where the public have access under the Ancient Monuments and Archaeological Areas Act 1979, or would have if access were not excluded or restricted, such land does not count as access land for the purposes of the CROW Act 2000.

12.5 MAPPING

12.5.1 General principles

With the exception of registered common land and land over 600 metres,[2] there will be no new public access until open country is recorded on maps. Inner London is also excluded from the mapping requirement as the areas are too small to show in any helpful manner on maps.

12.5.2 Duty to prepare maps

The Countryside Agency (in England[3]) and the Countryside Council for Wales (in Wales[4]) are under a duty to prepare maps showing all registered common land and all open country. The maps must distinguish between registered common land and open country, but not between the different types of open country.[5]

The Countryside Agency has produced a booklet, *Mapping Methodology for England*, which sets out the strategy and methodology for producing draft maps of open country and registered common land, the stages in creating, modifying, editing and issuing the maps, and aspects of the data standards and data formula to be applied.

For the purposes of the mapping programme, England has been divided into eight areas which are being mapped in turn. These are:

(1) Southeast
(2) Lower Northwest
(3) Central southern England
(4) Upper Northwest
(5) Northeast
(6) Southwest
(7) West
(8) East.

---

1 Ancient Monuments and Archaeological Areas Act 1979, s 19.
2 Although there is statutory provision for access to be given before these areas are mapped (CROW Act 2000, s (1)(c)(d)), the Government has now decided that access will be granted on a regional basis when all the land for the area has been mapped.
3 CROW Act 2000, s 4(1).
4 Ibid, s 4(2).
5 Ibid, s 4(4).

Although the original timetable has slipped, it is still expected that conclusive maps for all the areas will be in place by 2005.

Maps of open country are based on an ordnance survey map known as the Master Map (formerly called the Digital National Framework (DNF)). The map defines geographical areas, called polygons, based on land parcel boundaries such as walls, hedges and fences. Each parcel has a Topographic Identifier, referred to as a TOID.

Where a parcel of land contains a mixture of open country and other land the Countryside Agency will make the following presumptions:

– parcels of land of which one half or less comprise mountain, moor, heath or down will not be treated as open country;
– parcels of which more than three-quarters comprise mountain, moor, heath or down will be treated as open country;
– parcels of land of which over one half but less than three-quarters are mountain, moor, heath or down will be considered against specified criteria, namely the quality of the qualifying land type, the character of the parcel as a whole, whether the parcel makes the open country boundary easier to follow on the ground and the character of the adjacent parcels.

The Mapping Methodology sets out the criteria for identifying open country. It does so by reference to geology and vegetation. The Methodology also sets out how the Countryside Agency determine whether the land is improved or semi-improved grassland. In applying the criteria the Countryside Agency will use existing databases and aerial photography.

The Countryside Agency's definitions are as follows:

> '**Mountain** – by which we mean all land over 600 metres above sea level and other upland areas comprising rugged and steep land, crag, scree, fell, or other bare rock and associated rough vegetation. It does not include coastal cliffs. It includes semi-natural upland vegetation, but does not include improved or semi-improved grassland. It may include areas of bracken, scattered trees, open water, rivers, streams, bogs, mires, bare peat, or a mosaic of these.
>
> **Moor** – by which we mean land usually of an open character with semi-natural vegetation such as: mires (including blanket bog), heaths, rough unimproved acid grassland, and upland calcareous grassland. It does not include agriculturally improved or semi-improved grassland, but may include areas of unimproved bent-fescue grassland, scattered trees, scrub, bracken, open water, rivers, streams, bare peat, rock outcrops or other bare ground, or a mosaic of these. Moor usually occurs in upland areas but may also be found in lowland areas.
>
> **Heath** – by which we mean land of a generally open character, usually characterised by natural ericaceous dwarf shrubs. Heath usually occurs in lowland areas on nutrient poor soils. The typical vegetation types are heathers, gorse, bilberry, mires, scrub, unimproved grassland, and bracken. It does not include agriculturally improved or semi-improved grassland, but may include areas of scattered or dense regenerating trees, open water, rivers, streams, carr, sand or other bare ground, or a mosaic of these.

Down – by which we mean land comprising semi-natural grassland in areas of chalk or limestone geology generally within an open landscape. The typical vegetation type is unimproved grassland often with scattered scrub. It does not include agriculturally improved or semi-improved grassland, but may include areas of scattered trees, dwarf shrubs, streams, springs, or a mosaic of these.

Improved grasslands are typically the result of re-seeding, drainage, artificial fertilisation, and herbicide application either singly or in combination. Despite being bright green and often lush they may be dominated by a limited range of species (such as rye grass, *Lolium perenne*) often derived from commercially available seed, and very few herb species, but often including white clover *Trifolium repens*. Many improved fields may start to revert to less improved forms if intensive treatment is not maintained.

Semi-improved grassland is a transition category which has a range of species which is often less diverse than unimproved grassland, as a consequence of either having been partially modified by artificial fertilisers, liming, slurry, herbicides, or reseeding, or having reverted towards a more natural composition following a reduction in intensive treatment.'

12.5.3 Small areas

The appropriate countryside body may decide not to show small areas of open country on the map where it considers it would serve no useful purpose.[1] There is no such discretion in the mapping of registered common land.

The Countryside Agency will show all parcels of 5 hectares or more on the draft map. Parcels of less than 5 hectares will be considered on an individual basis, taking into account:

– the proximity of the land to a settlement, visitor attraction, road or public right of way;
– the amount of access land available in the vicinity;
– whether the land contains a feature likely to be of interest to the public;
– whether the land could provide a means to reach other access land;
– whether there are nearby land parcels which have the potential to be linked with the one in question to form a larger unit of open country or access land.

12.5.4 Boundaries

The countryside bodies also have a discretion to take a physical feature as the boundary of an area of open country even if the result is that some other land is included or some open land is excluded.[2]

The Countryside Agency's priority tiers for selecting appropriate boundaries will be:

(1) walls, hedges, fences, roads (metalled public highways), rivers, lakes shores;
(2) other watercourses, unfenced vehicular tracks, raised banks;

---

1   CROW Act 2000, s 4(5)(a).
2   Ibid, s 4(5)(b).

(3) cliffs, woodland edges, dry ditches, breaks of slope; and
(4) other paths or tracks.

12.5.5 Draft maps

The procedures for preparing maps are similar to those for the definitive maps relating to public rights of way. The appropriate countryside body (Countryside Agency for England and Countryside Council for Wales) will prepare the draft maps showing the registered common land and open country.[1] Representations may then be made by anyone within a prescribed period if land has been shown as registered common or open country which should not have been so shown or that such land has been wrongly omitted.

Regulations have been made separately for England[2] and Wales.[3]

The English regulations provide for the preparation and scale of draft maps (not less than 1:10,000) and the form in which they are to be prepared by the Countryside Agency.[4] The agency must issue the map and send it to specified persons for consultation including any local access forums.[5] It must inform the public of the issue of the map in draft form and where it can be inspected.[6] Maps must be prepared, issued, published and made available for inspection in electronic form.[7]

The regulations provide for the deposit of reduced scale maps on the internet and with county and district councils, London borough councils, National Park authorities, library authorities and commons registration authorities.[8]

Representations with respect to the showing of, or failure to show, any area of land as registered common land or open country on the draft map may be made within 3 months of the date of issue.[9]

The Welsh regulations set out the procedures and requirements for the preparation of draft maps by the Countryside Council for Wales. Maps are to be prepared at a scale of not less than 1:10,000, or if not possible at that scale using the base technology reasonably available to the Council, the largest scale practicable using that technology.[10] The regulations set out how the draft map is to be published and made available to the public.[11]

---

1   CROW Act 2000, s 5(a), (b).
2   Access to the Countryside (Maps in Draft Form) (England) Regulations 2001, SI 2001/
    3301.
3   Countryside Access (Draft Maps) (Wales) Regulations 2001, SI 2001/4001 (W329).
4   Access to the Countryside (Maps in Draft Form) (England) Regulations 2001, SI 2001/
    3301, reg 3.
5   Ibid, reg 4.
6   Ibid, regs 5 and 6.
7   Ibid, reg 3.
8   Ibid, regs 8–11.
9   Ibid, reg 12.
10 Countryside Access (Draft Maps) (Wales) Regulations 2001, SI 2001/4001 (W329),
    reg 3.
11 Ibid, regs 4 and 5.

Representations as to the showing of, or failure to show any area of land on the draft map as open country or registered common land, may be made within the period specified as the consultation period, being not less than 3 months from the publication of the draft map.[1]

12.5.6 Provisional maps

Having considered any representations made to the draft map, the appropriate body will then confirm the draft map, with or without modifications, and issue a provisional map. If the map has been confirmed with modifications the provisional map will incorporate those modifications.[2]

As with draft maps, there are separate regulations for England[3] and Wales[4] relating to provisional and conclusive maps.

The English regulations provide that provisional maps issued by the Countryside Agency must be to a scale of not less than 1:10,000.[5] The regulations stipulate how the public are to be informed of the issue of the provisional maps[6] and where they can be inspected.[7] Reduced scale maps are to be supplied to certain prescribed bodies, members of the public,[8] local authorities, National Park authorities,[9] libraries,[10] common registration authorities[11] and are to be made available on the internet.[12]

The Welsh regulations provide for the Countryside Council of Wales to prepare provisional maps at a scale of less than 1:10,000 but not less than 1:25,000 and to produce copies.[13] The regulations stipulate how the provisional maps are to be issued[14] and published.[15]

12.5.7 Appeals

Any person with an interest in any land may appeal to the Secretary of State, if the land is in England, and to the National Assembly in Wales, if the land is in Wales, against the inclusion of land as registered common land or open

---

1 Countryside Access (Draft Maps) (Wales) Regulations 2001, SI 2001/4001 (W329), reg 6.
2 Ibid, s 5(c), (d), (e).
3 Access to the Countryside (Provisional and Conclusive Maps) (England) Regulations 2002, SI 2002/1710.
4 Countryside Access (Provisional and Conclusive Maps) (Wales) Regulations 2002, SI 2002/1796 (W171).
5 Access to the Countryside (Provisional and Conclusive Maps) (England) Regulations 2002, SI 2002/1710, reg 3.
6 Ibid, reg 4.
7 Ibid, reg 6.
8 Ibid, reg 8.
9 Ibid, reg 10.
10 Ibid, reg 11.
11 Ibid, reg 12.
12 Ibid, reg 9.
13 Countryside Access (Provisional and Conclusive Maps) (Wales) Regulations 2002, SI 2002/1797 (W171), reg 3.
14 Ibid, reg 4.
15 Ibid, reg 5.

country on the provisional map.[1] Interest is defined to include any right exercisable by virtue of ownership, licence or agreement and includes rights of commoners and sporting rights.[2] The only ground of appeal in the case of common land is that it is not registered common land.[3] The only grounds of appeal relating to open country are that the land does not consist wholly or predominantly of mountain, moor, heath or down or that the appropriate body should not have exercised its discretion to map the boundary of the land to coincide with a nearby physical feature so as to include land which was not open country.[4] There is no appeal if the appropriate body has included small areas of land which serve no useful purpose. Where such areas are added after the draft map stage the effect is that the landowner has no opportunity to make representation against such inclusion.

On an appeal, the Secretary of State or the National Assembly for Wales may approve the whole or part of the map, with or without modifications. Alternatively, they may require the appropriate body to prepare a completely new map relating to all or part of the area covered by the map which is subject to the appeal.[5] If a new map is prepared, further consultation will take place on the draft.

The appeal may take the form of a private or public hearing or a local inquiry, if either the appellant or the appropriate countryside body so requests or if the Secretary of State or the National Assembly for Wales thinks fit.[6] Otherwise, the appeal will be dealt with by correspondence.

Where a hearing or inquiry is held, witnesses may be required to attend and give evidence and costs may be awarded. Costs may also be awarded where a hearing or inquiry has been arranged at the request of a party, but does not take place.[7]

The Secretary of State or the National Assembly for Wales may appoint any person to determine an appeal or any matter involved in an appeal or may refer any matter to such a person as they may appoint for that purpose.[8] An appointment must be in writing and may be revoked by notice in writing at any time before the appeal or matter has been determined. The appointment may relate to any particular appeal or matter or to appeals or matters of a specified description. It may provide for the person appointed to exercise his functions unconditionally or subject to the fulfilment of such conditions as may be specified in the appointment.[9] Schedule 3 to the Act sets out the details of the powers relating to delegated functions on appeals.

---

1   CROW Act 2000, s 6(1).
2   Ibid, s 45.
3   Ibid, s 6(2).
4   Ibid, s 6(3).
5   Ibid, s 6(4).
6   Ibid, s 7(1).
7   Ibid, s 7(2), (3). Local Government Act 1972, s 250(2)–(9).
8   CROW Act 2000, s 8 and Sch 3.
9   Ibid, Sch 3, para 2.

The procedures to be followed are set out in regulations. These are different for England and Wales.

In England, an appeal has to be made within 3 months from the date on which the provisional map for the relevant area was published.[1] The appeal must be made to the Secretary of State on a standard form. The appellant can choose whether the appeal is to be by written representations, or a hearing or public inquiry. However, the Secretary of State has power to decide on the method of appeal irrespective of the choice made by the appellant. For all procedures there are strict time-limits which must be adhered to. If an appeal is to be made, it is therefore important to study the regulations and any guidance produced by DEFRA or the Countryside Agency.

Any member of the public may make representations and may speak at a hearing or inquiry.

The Inspector will make his decision in writing. This will be sent to the appellant. All the Inspector's decisions will be published on the internet.[2]

Costs will usually be paid by the appellant unless where there is a hearing or inquiry the Countryside Agency has behaved unreasonably. Costs may be awarded against the appellant where he or she has behaved unreasonably.

In Wales, an appeal form must be sent to the National Assembly within the appeal period.[3] This is the period specified in the notice given by the Countryside Council for Wales to a person with an interest in the land shown on the provisional map as open country or registered common. The period must not expire earlier than 3 months after the publication of the provisional map in a daily newspaper circulating in the relevant part of Wales.

Details of the procedures to be followed are given in regulations.[4] The appeal may be decided on the basis of written representations, a local inquiry or a hearing. Time-limits and notice requirements are specified in the regulations. The National Assembly must notify the decision on the appeal in writing to the appellant and other interested parties.[5]

12.5.8 Maps in conclusive form

Once the time has elapsed for bringing appeals and either there are no appeals or all the appeals have been withdrawn or determined, the appropriate countryside body must issue the map in conclusive form.[6] If the map or any part of it has, on appeal, been approved with modifications, those modifi-

---

1 Access to the Countryside (Provisional and Conclusive Maps) (England) Regulations 2002, SI 2002/1710, reg 16.
2 Ibid, regs 27, 39, *http://www.planning-inspectorate.gov.uk/access*.
3 Countryside Access (Provisional and Conclusive Maps) (Wales) Regulations 2002, SI 2002/1796 (W171), reg 6.
4 Countryside Access (Appeals Procedures) (Wales) Regulations 2002, SI 2002/1794 (W169).
5 Ibid, regs 9, 16, 28.
6 CROW Act 2000, s 9(1).

cations will be shown on the map in conclusive form.[1] The Secretary of State or the National Assembly for Wales may at any time direct the countryside body to issue any part of the provisional map, rather than the whole, in conclusive form, provided there are no appeals outstanding in respect of that part.[2]

A document purporting to be certified by the appropriate countryside body as a copy of a map in conclusive form shall be accepted as evidence in court.[3]

There are separate regulations in England[4] and Wales[5] relating to conclusive maps.

The English regulations provide that the conclusive maps shall be at a scale of not less than 1:10,000.[6] The Countryside Agency must inform the public of the issue of conclusive maps[7] and where the maps may be inspected.[8] Reduced scale conclusive maps must be deposited with local authorities and National Park authorities[9] and made available for inspection on the internet.[10]

The Welsh regulations provide for the preparation and issue of conclusive maps by the Countryside Council for Wales.[11] The council has a duty to inform the public of the contents of conclusive maps.[12]

12.5.9 Errors

The Access to the Countryside (Provisional and Conclusive Maps) (England) Regulations 2002[13] make no provision for the correction of errors or omissions in maps of open country and registered common land.[14] However, when the Countryside Agency issued the first provisional map, covering part of south-east England, on 29 July 2002, 20 errors were identified. These had occurred because the provisional map did not show the decisions made by the Countryside Agency to modify the draft map. The provisional map was therefore withdrawn and reissued on 7 October 2002 with a further 3 months being allowed for appeals against the reissued provisional map.

---

1   CROW Act 2000, s 9(2).
2   Ibid, s 9(3), (4).
3   Ibid, s 9(6).
4   Access to the Countryside (Provisional and Conclusive Maps) (England) Regulations 2002, SI 2002/1710.
5   Countryside Access (Provisional and Conclusive Maps) (Wales) Regulations 2002, SI 2002/1796 (W171).
6   Access to the Countryside (Provisional and Conclusive Maps) (England) Regulations 2002, SI 2002/1710, reg 3.
7   Ibid, reg 4.
8   Ibid, reg 7.
9   Ibid, reg 10.
10 Ibid, reg 9.
11 Countryside Access (Provisional and Conclusive Maps) (Wales) Regulations 2002, SI 2002/1796 (W171), regs 7 and 8.
12 Ibid, reg 9.
13 SI 2002/1710.
14 For reasoning see DEFRA Consultation Paper (November 2001) on proposals for regulations on Provisional and Conclusive Maps under s 11 of the Countryside and Rights of Way Act 2000.

In the light of this experience, DEFRA produced on 10 October 2002 a Consultation Paper on Correcting Errors in Maps. The proposals in the paper are as follows:

(1) The agency should be able to correct oversights in:

    (a) a provisional map, where the map does not reflect a decision made by the Agency to modify following a consultation on the draft map; and

    (b) a conclusive map, where the map does not reflect a modification on appeal.

(2) The Agency should be able to correct minor errors in provisional (but not conclusive) maps so as to remove land shown in error as open country or registered common land where it can be shown that the error has arisen solely as a result of technical problems in the underlying OS Mastermap mapping data.

(3) Where the Agency exercises the power under Proposal 1(a) so as to *add* land to a provisional map, the period for bringing an appeal (against the showing of that land on the map as open country or registered common land) should run from 3 months from the date on which the modification is made.

(4) Where the Agency exercises the power under proposal 1(a) or 2 to modify a provisional map (whether to add or remove land), the Agency must as soon as reasonably practicable, notify any person with an interest in the land affected. The Agency will only need to do this where it is reasonably practicable to identify such persons.

(5) Where the Agency exercises the power under Proposal 1(b) to modify a conclusive map, the Agency must, as soon as reasonably practicable, notify any person who took part in the appeal to which the modification relates.

(6) The powers in Proposals 1 and 2 should be exercisable for 3 months after the date of the issue of the map.

(7) Any modification to a map made under Proposals 1 and 2 should be described in a notice published in one or more local or regional newspapers and available for inspection on the Agency's website. The Agency should be under a duty to ensure that, so far as is reasonably practicable, any reduced scale map derived from the map affected by the modification is itself updated.

12.5.10   Review of maps

The countryside bodies are under an obligation to review the maps published in conclusive form within 10 years and at not more than 10-yearly intervals thereafter. Regulations may alter these periods.[1]

On a review, the countryside bodies must consider whether land shown on the map as open country or as registered common land remains of that description and whether other land should be shown as open country or as registered common land.

---

1   CROW Act 2000, s 10.

12.5.11   Powers of entry

A person authorised by the appropriate countryside body may enter any land for the purpose of surveying in connection with the preparation or review of any maps.[1] The rules governing this power are discussed at **16.7.2**.

12.6   PRACTICAL QUESTIONS

Questions have been asked whether land such as set-aside or bird reserves will be subject to a right of access. The answers depend on whether:

(a) the land is mapped open country, registered common land or land above 600 metres; and, if so
(b) is excepted land; and, if not
(c) is subject to particular exclusions or restrictions under Chapter II of the CROW Act 2000.

The flowchart below illustrates these principles.

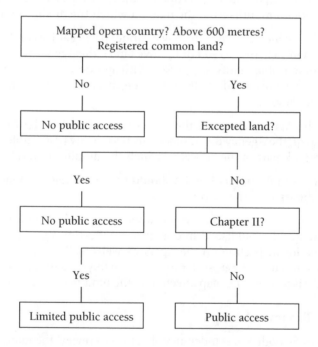

---

1   CROW Act 2000, s 40(1)(a).

12.7 SUMMARY OF TERMINOLOGY

12.7.1 Names and duties of the CROW Act 2000 bodies

Various terms are used to describe the bodies who are given specified duties and powers under the CROW Act 2000. Their main duties and powers in relation to public rights of access are given below.

12.7.2 The appropriate countryside body

This is the Countryside Agency in England the Countryside Council in Wales. Their duties include: preparing and reviewing definitive maps;[1] issuing codes of conduct;[2] acting as a relevant authority in respect of exclusions and restrictions under Chapter II; and giving guidance to the National Parks and Forestry Commission where they are the relevant authority.[3]

12.7.3 The relevant authority

The relevant authority is the appropriate countryside body, the National Park where the land is within a National Park, or the Forestry Commission where land dedicated under s 16 consists wholly or predominantly of woodland and the Forestry Commissioners have given the appropriate countryside body or the National Park notice that the Forestry Commissioners are to be the relevant authority.[4] Its duties and power relate to exclusions and restrictions under Chapter II of the Act.

12.7.4 The relevant advisory body

These are English Heritage in England and the Countryside Agency for Wales and the National Assembly in Wales.[5] Their duty is to give advice to the relevant authority where a direction is under consideration for excluding public access for nature conservation or heritage preservation reasons.

12.7.5 Access authority

An access authority is the National Park or the local highway authority.[6] These authorities have powers to make bylaws,[7] appoint wardens[8] and erect notices[9] giving information about access. They also have power to enter into agreements with landowners relating to works enabling physical access to the land and to take measures to enforce such agreements.[10]

---

1   CROW Act 2000, ss 4, 5, 9, 10.
2   Ibid, s 20.
3   Ibid, ss 21–33.
4   Ibid, s 21(5)(6).
5   Ibid, s 26(6).
6   Ibid, s 1(2).
7   Ibid, s 17.
8   Ibid, s 18.
9   Ibid, s 19.
10   Ibid, ss 34–39.

12.7.6   Appointing authority

The appointing authority is the local highway authority or where the land is in the National Park, the National Park. The appointing authority has functions in relation to local access forums.[1]

12.8   GUIDANCE NOTES

12.8.1   DEFRA

DEFRA has published the following guidance notes.

Mapping open country and registered common land – conclusive maps and excepted land.[2]

Mapping of open country and registered common land subject to existing statutory rights of access.[3]

De facto and de jure access to the countryside.[4]

Copying of maps of open country and registered common land.[5]

12.8.2   Countryside Agency

The Countryside Agency has published the following guidance notes which relate to England only.

Countryside and Rights of Way Act 2000 Mapping Methodology for England.[6]

Appeals under section 6 of the Countryside and Rights of Way Act 2000: A Guide for Appellants.[7]

---

1   CROW Act 2000, s 94. Countryside Access (Local Access Forums) (Wales) Regulations 2001, SI 2001/4002 (W330); Local Access Forums (England) Regulations 2002, SI 2002/1836.
2   Published 21 December 2001: updated 24 July 2002.
3   Published 21 December 2001: updated 27 September 2002.
4   Published 21 December 2001: updated 18 April 2002.
5   Revised November 2002.
6   Published 31 August 2001: Second version 31 October 2002.
7   Published.

Chapter 13

RIGHTS AND OBLIGATIONS OF THE PUBLIC

13.1 INTRODUCTION

13.1.1 Nature of the right

A member of the public is entitled to enter and remain on access land for the purpose of open-air recreation as long as he does so without breaking or damaging any wall, fence, hedge, stile or gate, and provided that he observes the general restrictions and any special restrictions relating to that area of access land.[1] The right does not exist where:

(a) entry is prohibited under any other public legislation;
(b) the land, although access land, qualifies as excepted land; or
(c) the right of access has been excluded or restricted under Chapter 11 of the CROW Act 2000.

The nature of the general restrictions is such that, unless they are waived, the right of the public is limited to access on foot for leisure purposes only. The reason for not simply specifying 'on foot' is so as not to exclude those in wheelchairs or pushchairs.

13.2 SCHEDULE 2 RESTRICTIONS

13.2.1 General principles

The general restrictions in Sch 2 to the CROW Act 2000 are an expanded version of those contained in Sch 2 to the NPACA 1949. The Schedule restricts activities and behaviour which are not compatible with the quiet exercise of the right. The restrictions, other than those relating to dogs, may be altered by regulations, provided they are approved by an affirmative resolution of both Houses of Parliament.[2]

13.2.2 The restrictions

A person is not entitled to be on any land if, in or on that land, he (using the lettering in para 1 of the Schedule):

---

1   CROW Act 2000, s 2(1).
2   Ibid, s 44(3).

(a) drives or rides any vehicle other than an invalid carriage as defined by s 20(2) of the Chronically Sick and Disabled Persons Act 1970;

(b) uses a vessel or sailboard on any non-tidal water;

(c) has with him any animal other than a dog;

(d) commits any criminal offence;

(e) lights or tends a fire or does any act which is likely to cause a fire;

(f) intentionally or recklessly takes, kills, injures or disturbs any animal, bird or fish;

(g) intentionally or recklessly takes, damages or destroys any eggs or nests;

(h) feeds any livestock;

(i) bathes in any non-tidal water;

(j) engages in any operations of or connected with hunting, shooting, fishing, trapping, snaring, taking or destroying of animals, birds or fish or has with him any engine, instrument or apparatus used for hunting, shooting, fishing, trapping, snaring, taking or destroying of animals, birds or fish;

(k) uses or has with him any metal detector ('metal detector' means any device designed or adapted for detecting or locating any metal or mineral in the ground);

(l) intentionally removes, damages or destroys any plant, shrub, tree or root or any part of a plant, shrub, tree or root;

(m) obstructs the flow of any drain or watercourse, or opens, shuts or otherwise interferes with any sluice-gate or other apparatus;

(n) without reasonable excuse, interferes with any fence, barrier or other device designed to prevent accidents to people or to enclose livestock;

(o) neglects to shut any gate or fasten it where any means of doing so is provided, except where it is reasonable to assume that a gate is intended to be left open;

(p) affixes or writes any advertisement, bill, placard or notice;

(q) in relation to any lawful activity which persons are engaging in or are about to engage in on that or adjoining land, does anything which is intended by him to have the effect:

   (i)   of intimidating those persons so as to deter them or any of them from engaging in that activity; or

   (ii) of obstructing that activity; or

   (iii) of disrupting that activity.

These provisions are directed against hunt saboteurs. An activity is lawful if a person may do it without committing an offence or trespassing on the land;

(r) without reasonable excuse, does anything which (whether or not intended by him to have effect mentioned in (q) above) disturbs, annoys or obstructs any persons engaged in a lawful activity on the land;

(s) engages in any organised games, or in camping, hang-gliding or para-gliding; or

(t) engages in any activity which is organised or undertaken (whether by him or another) for any commercial purpose.

13.2.3 Dogs

There are special restrictions dealing with dogs. These restrictions cannot be altered by regulations. Between 1 March and 31 July in every year, dogs must be kept on a short lead.[1] Where a dog is in the vicinity of livestock, it must also be kept on a short lead.[2] 'Livestock' is defined as cattle, sheep, goats, swine, horses and poultry. 'Cattle' means bulls, oxen, heifers, or calves; 'horses' includes asses and mules; and 'poultry' means domestic fowls, turkeys, geese or ducks.[3] A 'short lead' means a lead of fixed length not exceeding 2 metres.[4] Dogs may be excluded altogether under Chapter II for specified periods, for grouse moor management[5] and during the lambing season.[6]

13.2.4 Exclusion of general restrictions

The National Park or the appropriate countryside body may, by direction, with the consent of the owner of any land, exclude any of the general restrictions either indefinitely or for a specified period in every calendar year or for a period determined by the owner, in accordance with the direction and notified by him to the countryside body or National Park (where the land is situated in a National Park).[7]

Regulations may provide for the giving, revocation, and variation of directions, the giving or revocation of the owner's consent and for the giving of information to the public about any direction or its revocation.

'Owner' means the freeholder or, where there is a tenancy under the Agricultural Tenancies Act 1995 or Agricultural Holdings Act 1986, the tenant.

Where the land has been dedicated by a landowner as access land, the terms of the dedication may exclude some or all of the restrictions.[8]

13.3 OBLIGATIONS

13.3.1 Nature of the obligations

The public's right of access is conditional on not breaking or damaging any wall, fence, hedge, stile or gate, the observance of the restrictions in Sch 2 and any other restrictions imposed in relation to the land under Chapter II.[9]

---

1   CROW Act 2000, Sch 1, para 4.
2   Ibid, Sch 1, para 5.
3   Ibid, s 45(1).
4   Ibid, Sch 1, para 6.
5   Ibid, s 23(1).
6   Ibid, s 23(2).
7   Ibid, Sch 1, para 7.
8   Ibid, Sch 1, para 8.
9   Ibid, s 2(1).

13.3.2   Failure to comply

If a member of the public does not observe the restrictions, he becomes a trespasser. The penalty is that, for the next 72 hours after leaving that land, he will not have a right of access to that land or to any other land in the same ownership. Where the land is let under the Agricultural Tenancies Act 1995 or the Agricultural Holdings Act 1986, it is the tenant who is defined as the owner.

13.3.3   Criminal liability

No criminal liability is imposed by the CROW Act 2000 for failure to comply with the obligations. However, there may be liability under other regulations. For instance, a member of the public could be liable under the Criminal Damage Act 1971 or the Public Order Act 1986. The right to enter and remain on access land does not entitle a person to do anything on land which is prohibited under any public legislation.[1]

---

1   CROW Act 2000, s 2(3).

Chapter 14

RIGHTS AND OBLIGATIONS OF OWNERS AND OCCUPIERS

14.1 RIGHT TO IMPOSE EXCLUSIONS AND RESTRICTIONS

14.1.1 General principles

In certain circumstances, the public's right of entry to access land, which is not excepted land, may be excluded or restricted.

Where the countryside body or the National Park authority (or the Secretary of State for Defence) makes a direction for a restriction or exclusion, the restriction or exclusion must be the minimum which is consistent with the purpose for which it is sought.

14.1.2 Definitions

An exclusion is where the right of access granted by s 2(1) of the CROW Act 2000 is excluded.[1] A restriction is where a person stipulates that a right of access given by s 2 of the CROW Act 2000 is exercisable only:

(a) along specified routes or ways; or
(b) after entering the land at a specified place or places; or
(c) by persons who do not take dogs on the land; or
(d) by persons who satisfy any other specified conditions.[2]

The 'owner of land' which is subject to a tenancy governed by the Agricultural Holdings Act 1986 or the Agricultural Tenancies Act 1995 means the tenant, except under the provisions for the exclusion of dogs for the management of grouse moors.[3]

The 'relevant authority' means a National Park authority where the land is in the National Park, or otherwise the Countryside Agency or the Countryside Council for Wales.[4] Where land, which appears to the Forestry Commission to be wholly or predominantly woodland, has been dedicated as access land, the Forestry Commission may give the relevant authority notice that the Forestry

---

1   CROW Act 2000, s 21(2).
2   Ibid, s 21(3).
3   Ibid, s 21(4).
4   Ibid, s 21(5).

Commission will be the relevant authority for that land.[1] Should the land cease to be wholly or predominantly woodland, the Forestry Commission can revoke the notice by giving a further notice to the erstwhile relevant body.[2]

14.1.3   28-day exclusions or restrictions

Owners and other persons with an interest in land who fall within a description to be prescribed by regulations may exclude or restrict access to any access land for up to 28 days in any calendar year.[3] If the regulations provide that two or more persons have an interest in land for this purpose, they must also provide for how the days are to be divided between them, so that the total does not exceed 28.[4]

The exclusion or restriction can apply to any area of land within a particular land holding. It does not have to apply to the whole of the holding. This enables the owner to exclude access to different areas for up to 28 days each. However, there is provision for regulations to be made to determine the boundaries of areas of land to which the exclusions or restrictions will relate.[5]

Access must not be excluded or restricted on Christmas Day, Good Friday or any bank holiday.[6] No more than 4 days in any calendar year may be either a Saturday or a Sunday. No Saturday, in the period beginning with 1 June and ending with 11 August in any year, may be excluded. No Sunday, in the period beginning with 1 June and ending with 30 September in any year, may be excluded.[7] The purpose of these rules is to ensure that access is not precluded during the periods when the public are most likely to want to exercise the statutory right. The less strict rule for summer Saturdays after 11 August is in response to representations made by the shooting lobby.

Notice of the intended exclusion or restriction must be given to the relevant authority.[8]

14.1.4   Exclusion of dogs

The owner of a grouse moor may exclude, for a specified period not exceeding 5 years, people with dogs, if it appears necessary for the management of the land.[9] The owner of land used for lambing may exclude, for one period of not more than 6 weeks in any calendar year, people with dogs from any field or enclosure of not more than 15 hectares.[10]

---

1   CROW Act 2000, s 21(6).
2   Ibid, s 21(7).
3   Ibid, s 22(2), (3), (4).
4   Ibid, s 22(5).
5   Ibid, s 22(8).
6   Ibid, s 22(6).
7   Ibid, s 22(7).
8   Ibid, s 22(1).
9   Ibid, s 23(1), (4)(a).
10   Ibid, s 23(2), (3), (4)(b).

The exclusions do not prevent a blind person taking a trained guide dog, or a deaf person a trained hearing dog, with him.[1]

The steps which an owner must take before the exclusions operate will be specified in regulations.[2]

14.1.5 Land management

A person with an interest in access land may apply to the relevant authority to exclude or restrict access for land management reasons.[3] The relevant authority has power to make a direction excluding or restricting access for a specified period. The period may be a specified period in every calendar year or may be determined by the applicant in accordance with the direction and notified to the relevant authority in accordance with regulations made under the CROW Act 2000.[4]

In determining whether a direction is necessary for purposes of land management, the relevant authority must have regard to the extent to which, and the purposes for which, the applicant has exercised, or proposes to exercise, his right to exclude or restrict access under the 28-day rules.[5]

An application may be made where the land is not access land but will be granted only if the relevant authority is satisfied that it is likely that the land will be access land during all or part of the period to which the application relates.[6]

14.1.6 Avoidance of fire risk or danger to the public

A person with an interest in land may apply to the relevant authority for a direction to exclude or restrict public access where, because of exceptional weather conditions, or any exceptional change in the condition of the land, it is necessary to prevent fire. He may also do so where it is necessary to protect the public from danger due to anything done or intended to be done on the land or on adjacent land.[7] The relevant authority has power to make a direction for a specified period. This may be a specified period in every calendar year or a period determined by a specified person in accordance with the direction and notified to the relevant authority in accordance with regulations made under the CROW Act 2000.[8]

In determining whether the conditions for making the order are satisfied, the relevant authority must take into account the extent to which, and the

---

1   CROW Act 2000, s 23(5).
2   Ibid, s 32(1)(b).
3   Ibid, s 24(1).
4   Ibid, s 24(2).
5   Ibid, s 24(3).
6   Ibid, s 24(4).
7   Ibid, s 25(1).
8   Ibid, s 25(2).

purposes for which, the applicant has exercised, or proposes to exercise, his rights under the 28-day rules.[1]

The relevant authority may make a direction where the exclusion or restriction is for the avoidance of fire risk or of danger to the public on its own initiative without any application having been made.[2]

An application may be made where the land is not access land but will be granted only if the relevant authority is satisfied that it is likely that the land will be access land during all or part of the period to which the application relates.[3]

14.1.7   Nature conservation and heritage preservation

No direct right is given to a person with an interest in land to make an application for a direction excluding or restricting access for conservation or heritage reasons. However, the relevant authority has power to make a direction for the purpose of conserving flora, fauna or geological or physio-graphical features of the land. It may also do so to preserve any monument scheduled under the Ancient Monuments and Archaeological Areas Act 1979 or any other structure, work, site, garden, or area which is of historic, architectural, traditional, artistic or archaeological interest.[4]

In England, the relevant authority must have regard to any advice given by English Nature or the Historic Buildings and Monuments Commission (English Heritage). In Wales, a National Park authority must have regard to any advice given by the Countryside Council for Wales, for proposals relating to wildlife and conservation, and by the National Assembly for Wales (Cadw) for proposals relating to sites of heritage or archaeological importance. The Countryside Council for Wales must have regard to any advice given by Cadw on exclusions or restrictions to protect sites of historical or archaeological interest.[5]

Private landowners who want to obtain exclusions or restrictions for nature conservation or heritage preservation should, therefore, discuss their concerns with the relevant advisory body.

Any direction made may be for the period specified in the direction or during a specified period in every calendar year, or during a period determined by a specified person in accordance with the direction and notified to the relevant authority in accordance with regulations made under the CROW Act 2000. A direction may also be expressed to have effect indefinitely.[6]

---

1   CROW Act 2000, s 25(4).
2   Ibid, s 25(3).
3   Ibid, s 25(5).
4   Ibid, s 26(1), (3).
5   Ibid, s 26(4), (5), (6).
6   Ibid, s 26(2).

14.1.8   Consultation, variations, revocations and reviews

Before excluding or restricting access indefinitely or for a period which exceeds or may exceed 6 months, for the purposes of land management, or for the prevention of fire or other danger to the public, or for nature conservation or heritage preservation, the relevant authority should consult any local access forum which exists for the area.[1]

Directions which exclude or restrict access for land management, fire risk or danger to the public nature conservation and heritage preservation may be varied or revoked by a subsequent direction of the relevant authority.[2] Where reasonably practicable, the relevant authority must consult the person who made the original application or his successor in title or, for directions made on nature, conservation or preservation of heritage grounds, the relevant advisory body.[3]

Long-term exclusions and restrictions (ie indefinite, or for a specified period of more than 5 years, or for part of every year, or of each of 6 or more calendar years) must be reviewed at least every 5 years with the same obligations to consult.[4]

14.1.9   Defence or national security

The Secretary of State may exclude or restrict access for purposes of defence or national security.[5] The exclusion or restriction may be for the period specified in the direction, during a specified period in every calendar year, determined in accordance with the direction by a person authorised by the Secretary of State and notified by that person to the relevant authority in accordance with regulations made under the CROW Act 2000, or the period may be indefinite.[6] Any direction may be revoked or varied by a subsequent direction.[7]

Where a direction excludes or restricts access indefinitely, or for a period of more than 5 years, or for part of every year or for each of 6 or more consecutive years, the Secretary of State must review the direction at least every 5 years.[8]

If, in any calendar year, the Secretary of State reviews a defence direction, he must prepare a report on all reviews of defence directions taken during the year and lay a copy of the report before each House of Parliament.[9]

---

1   CROW Act 2000, s 27(1).
2   Ibid, s 27(2).
3   Ibid, s 27(5), (6).
4   Ibid, s 27(3).
5   Ibid, s 28(1).
6   Ibid, s 28(2).
7   Ibid, s 28(3).
8   Ibid, s 28(4).
9   Ibid, s 28(6).

14.1.10 Appeals

Where, in spite of the advice given by the advisory body, the relevant authority decides not to authorise the exclusion or restriction or decides to vary or revoke an existing direction or otherwise fails to act in accordance with the advice, the advisory body may make a reference to the Secretary of State (or, where the Forestry Commission are the relevant authority, DEFRA), or, for land in Wales, the National Assembly for Wales.[1] The Secretary of State or the Assembly may require the authority to make or cancel such directions relating to restrictions or exclusions as they think fit.[2] This provision does not apply to exclusions or restrictions relating to sites of historical or archaeological importance in Wales, as Cadw is an executive agency of the National Assembly for Wales.

Where a person with an interest in any access land has applied for a direction for an exclusion or restriction for land management reasons or for the avoidance of fire risk or danger to the public, or has made representations on a proposed revocation or variation of a direction, but the relevant authority decides not to act in accordance with the application or revocation, it must give the applicant its reasons for the decision.[3] The applicant may appeal against the decision to the Secretary of State or the National Assembly for Wales.[4] The Secretary of State or the Assembly may, if he or it thinks fit, cancel any direction given by the relevant authority or require the relevant authority to make directions under the relevant sections.[5]

The appeal procedures and the powers of the Secretary of State and National Assembly to delegate their appeal functions are the same for references by relevant advisory bodies and applicants with an interest in land as they are for appeals relating to provisional maps.[6]

14.1.11 Emergencies

Regulations may enable a relevant authority to exclude or restrict access for up to 3 months in an emergency for land management, avoidance of fire risk or other danger to the public, or for nature conservation or heritage preservation reasons.[7]

Regulations may apply with modifications any of the provisions in Chapter II, discussed above, relating to the making of directions.[8]

---

1   CROW Act 2000, s 29(1), (2).
2   Ibid, s 29(3).
3   Ibid, s 30(1), (2).
4   Ibid, s 30(3).
5   Ibid, s 30(4).
6   Ibid, s 29(4), s 30(5). See **12.5.7**.
7   Ibid, s 31(1).
8   Ibid, s 31(2).

14.1.12   Regulations

Regulations may be made on procedures, and the content of any notices and applications, relating to directions including the giving of notices for the 28-day exclusion, the exclusion of dogs on grouse moors and in fields and enclosures used for lambing, the giving of notices relating to the duration of the exclusions, the application rights of commoners, consultation, the giving of directions, notification of decisions, provision of information to the public, reviews and appeals.[1]

14.1.13   Guidance by countryside bodies

The Countryside Agency and the Countryside Council for Wales are responsible for administering the provisions on exclusions and restrictions outside National Parks. For land within the National Parks, they are given power to issue guidance to the National Park authorities. Where the land is dedicated woodland and the Forestry Commission has become the relevant authority, the countryside bodies are given power to give guidance to the Forestry Commission.[2] The guidance given by the Countryside Agency must first be approved by the Secretary of State; that of the Countryside Council for Wales by the National Assembly for Wales.[3]

Any guidance must be published[4] and the National Park authority and the Forestry Commissioners are under a duty to pay regard to the guidance.[5]

14.2   EFFECT OF ACCESS

14.2.1   No increase in liability under other enactments

The right of access does not increase the liability, under any enactment not contained in the CROW Act 2000 or under any rule of law, of a person interested in access land or adjoining land for the state of the land or things done or omitted to be done on it.[6]

14.2.2   Covenants

The right of access conferred by the CROW Act 2000 will override any restrictive covenant.[7] To that extent, any person interested in access land will not be liable for breach of covenant.

---

1   CROW Act 2000, s 32.
2   Ibid, s 33(1), (2).
3   Ibid, s 33(3).
4   Ibid, s 33(4).
5   Ibid, s 33(5).
6   Ibid, s 12(1).
7   Ibid, s 12(2).

14.2.3   Easements

Under the law of prescription, a person may claim a right of way across the land of another for the benefit of his own land. However, where he enters another's land by virtue of s 2(1) of the CROW Act 2000, this will not give rise to an easement based on long use.[1]

14.2.4   Highways

Long use may give rise to a claim that there has been a presumed dedication at common law or a statutory deemed dedication. Any exercise of the right conferred by s 2(1) of the CROW Act 2000 is to be disregarded for the purpose of such a claim.[2]

14.2.5   Village greens

It is possible for new village greens to be claimed on the basis of 20 years' use of the land by the inhabitants of the locality for lawful sports and pastimes. Any use of the land by the inhabitants for the purpose of open-air recreation pursuant to s 2(1) of the CROW Act 2000 is to be disregarded.[3]

14.3   OCCUPIERS' LIABILITY

A person who enters access land under the CROW Act 2000 does not count as a visitor for the purposes of the Occupiers' Liability Act 1957.[4] The occupier does, however, owe a duty of care, similar to that owed to trespassers, under the Occupiers' Liability Act 1984. However, any duty, in respect of a risk resulting from a natural feature of the landscape or of any river, stream, ditch or pond, whether or not it is a natural feature, is specifically excluded. Plants, shrubs or trees, of whatever origin, are regarded as a natural feature of the landscape. Also excluded are risks of a person suffering injury when passing over, under, or through any wall, fence or gate, except by proper use of the stile or gate.[5] However, the occupier will owe a duty where the danger is due to anything done by the occupier with the intention of creating the risk or being reckless as to whether that risk was created.

The duty arises if an occupier:

(1) is aware of a danger or has reasonable grounds to believe that it exists; and
(2) knows that a person is near a danger or may come near it; and

if the risk is one against which, in all the circumstances of the case, he might reasonably be expected to offer some protection.

---

1   CROW Act 2000, s 33(3).
2   Ibid.
3   Ibid, s 33(4).
4   Ibid, s 13(1).
5   Ibid, s 13(2).

The duty is to take such care as is reasonable in all the circumstances to see that the person does not suffer injury.[1] The occupier may discharge his duty by giving warnings of the danger or discouraging people from taking the risk.

In determining whether a duty and, if so, what duty is owed by an occupier of land where there is a right of access under the CROW Act 2000, regard is to be had to:

(a) the fact that the existence of that right ought not to place an undue financial or other burden on the occupier;

(b) the importance of maintaining the character of the countryside, including features of historic, traditional or archaeological interest; and

(c) any relevant guidance given in codes of conduct or otherwise by the Countryside Agency or the Countryside Council for Wales.[2]

Where a person is owed a duty under the Occupiers' Liability Act 1984, the occupier does not incur any liability for loss or damage to property. No duty is owed to any persons for risks willingly accepted.

14.4 MISLEADING NOTICES

It is an offence to display a notice containing false or misleading information on or near access land, or on or near a way leading to it, likely to deter the exercise of the statutory right.[3] This is similar to the offence of displaying misleading notices on public rights of way.

An example of a misleading notice might be a sign indicating that the access land was closed, when it was not, or that a dangerous bull was at large, when no bull was on the land.

The penalty for displaying an offending sign is a fine of up to Level 1 on the standard scale. The courts may order the offender to remove the sign within a specified period, not being less than 4 days.[4] A person who does not comply with the order commits a further offence, which carries a fine not exceeding Level 3 on the standard scale.[5]

---

1   Occupiers' Liability Act 1984, s 1.
2   CROW Act 2000, s 13(3).
3   Ibid, s 14(1).
4   Ibid, s 14(2).
5   Ibid, s 14(3).

Chapter 15

ENTRY TO ACCESS LAND

15.1 INTRODUCTION

Access land is not necessarily accessible. The land may be surrounded by other land to which there is no public right of access or there may be physical impediments to access.

15.2 LEGAL ACCESS

There is an existing power under the Highways Act 1980[1] for a local authority to make an order creating a new footpath or bridleway, if it is satisfied that it is expedient to do so, having regard to:

(a) the extent to which the path would add to the convenience or enjoyment of a substantial section of the public, or to the convenience of persons resident in the area; and

(b) the effect which the creation of the path would have on the rights of persons interested in the land taking into account the provisions on compensation.

The CROW Act 2000[2] enables the Countryside Agency or the Countryside Council for Wales to apply to the Secretary of State or the National Assembly for Wales respectively, for a public path creation order for the purpose of enabling the public to obtain access to any access land or of facilitating such access. Before applying for the order, the countryside bodies must have regard to any rights of way improvement plan prepared by the local highway authority for the area in which the proposed public path would be situated.

15.3 PHYSICAL ACCESS

15.3.1 General principles

A highway authority or, in the National Park, the National Park authority (the access authorities) is given powers to seek agreement with landowners to create or safeguard physical means of entry onto access land. If the authorities are unable to secure agreement, they can carry out the work themselves.

---

1   Section 26.
2   Section 58.

A means of access is defined as:

(a) any opening in a wall, fence or hedge bounding the land (or part of the land), with or without a gate, stile or other works for regulating the passage through the opening;
(b) any stairs or steps for enabling persons to enter on the land (or part of the land); or
(c) any bridge, stepping stone or other works for crossing a watercourse, ditch or bog on land or adjoining the boundary of land.[1]

15.3.2   Agreements on means of access

An access authority may enter into an agreement with a landowner for the carrying out of specified works which appear to the authority to be necessary for giving the public reasonable entry to access land.[2] The works are:

(a) the opening up, improvement or repair of any means of access to the land;
(b) the construction of any new means of access to the land;
(c) the maintenance of any means of access to the land.

The agreement may provide that the works shall be carried out by the owner or the occupier or by the access authority itself. Where the owner or occupier carries out the works, the agreement may provide for the access authority to pay or make a contribution towards the costs incurred by the owner or occupier in carrying out the agreed works.

The authority may also impose, by agreement with the landowner, restrictions on the destruction, removal, alteration or stopping-up of any means of access to the land, or on the doing of anything whereby the use of any such means of access to the land by the public would be impeded. The agreement may provide for a payment to be made by the access authority for the imposition of any restriction.[3]

15.3.3   Failure to comply with agreement

The required works must be carried out within the time specified in, or determined in accordance with, the agreement. If there is no such time-limit imposed the works must be carried out within a reasonable time. On the failure of the landowner or occupier to comply with the time-limits, the access authority, after giving not less than 21 days' notice, may take all necessary steps for carrying out the works. The authority may recover any expenses reasonably incurred by it in carrying out the works, reduced by the authority's contribution under the agreement.[4]

If the owner or occupier fails to observe any restriction under the agreement, the authority may serve a notice requiring him, within a specified period of not

---

1   CROW Act 2000, s 34.
2   Ibid, s 35(1).
3   Ibid, s 35(2)(b)(ii).
4   Ibid, s 36(1)(2).

less than 21 days, to remedy the failure by carrying out the works specified in the notice.[1] The notice must contain particulars of the right of appeal to the Secretary of State or the National Assembly for Wales.[2]

Where a landowner or occupier does not comply with the notice, the authority may carry out the works and recover the costs from the defaulting landowner or occupier.[3]

15.3.4 Failure to obtain an agreement

Where the access authority considers that it is necessary for giving the public reasonable access to access land to open up, improve or repair, construct, or maintain any means of access to the land, but is unable to enter into an agreement with the landowner or occupier, it may serve on him a notice stating its intention, after a period of at least 21 days, of doing the required work.[4] The notice must contain particulars of the right of appeal.[5] The authority must serve a copy of the notice on any other owner or occupier of the land.[6] It must also, in exercising its powers in relation to the provision of access, have regard to the requirements of efficient management of the land in deciding where the means of access should be provided.[7]

If, at the end of the time specified in the notice, the work has not been carried out, the access authority may do the work.[8]

15.3.5 Appeals

Where a notice has been served on a landowner or occupier, he, or any other landowner or occupier of the land, may appeal against the notice to the Secretary of State or, where the land is in Wales, to the National Assembly for Wales.[9]

An appeal against a notice to carry out work because of a failure to observe a restriction may be brought on the grounds that:

(a) the works are not necessary to remedy a breach of the agreement;
(b) the works have already been carried out; or
(c) the time specified in the notice for carrying out the works is too short.[10]

An appeal against a notice stating what work the access authority intends to undertake may be brought on the grounds that:

(a) the works are unnecessary for giving the public reasonable access;

---

1 CROW Act 2000, s 36(3).
2 Ibid, s 36(4).
3 Ibid, s 36(5), (6).
4 Ibid, s 37(1).
5 Ibid, ss 37(2), 38.
6 Ibid, s 37(3).
7 Ibid, s 37(4).
8 Ibid, s 37(5).
9 Ibid, s 38(1).
10 Ibid, s 38(2).

(b) the means of access should be provided elsewhere or a different means of
     access should be provided; or
(c) the works have already been carried out.[1]

Where an appeal is made, the Secretary of State or the National Assembly may
confirm the notice with or without modifications or cancel it.[2] The appeal
procedure and the right of the Secretary of State or the National Assembly for
Wales to delegate their appeal functions is the same as it is for appeals against
provisional maps.[3]

Regulations may be made on the timing and method of appeals, the advertising
of appeals and the manner in which they are to be considered.[4]

Where an appeal has been brought against a notice to do work to remedy a
breach of a restriction in an agreement, or, in the absence of an agreement, a
notice relating to works for the provision or improvement of a means of access,
the access authority may not do the works before the appeal is determined or
withdrawn.[5]

15.4   OBSTRUCTIONS

An access authority may apply to a magistrates' court for an order that a person,
who has been given two or more access notices within the preceding 3 years,
should, within such time as may be specified in the order, take such steps as
may be specified to remove any obstructions of the means of access and not
obstruct it at any time when the right of access under s 2(1) is exercisable.[6] An
access notice is a notice, which is not subject to an appeal, served on an owner
or occupier:

(a) requiring him to carry out works to remedy a failure to observe a
     restriction in an agreement he has entered into with an access authority; or
(b) where the authority has not been able to make an agreement, informing
     him of the authority's intention to carry out works specified in the notice
     for the opening up, improvement, repair, construction or maintenance of
     the means of access.[7]

If a person fails to comply with a magistrates' order, he is liable to a fine up to
Level 3 on the standard scale. In addition, the access authority may remove the
obstruction and recover the costs of doing so.[8]

---

1   CROW Act 2000, s 38(3).
2   Ibid, s 38(4).
3   Ibid, s 38(5).
4   Ibid, s 38(6).
5   Ibid, s 38(7).
6   Ibid, s 39(1).
7   Ibid, s 39(3).
8   Ibid, s 39(2).

Chapter 16

MANAGEMENT

16.1 GENERAL PRINCIPLES

Management is obviously a key issue if the right of access conferred by the CROW Act 2000 is to work satisfactorily. This was acknowledged by the Labour Party in its manifesto of 1997:

> 'our policies include greater freedom to explore open countryside. We will not however, permit any abuse of the right to greater access.'

It was also recognised by Michael Meacher MP, when announcing the intention to legislate:

> 'We have also been conscious of the need to respect the countryside. Greater freedom would become self-defeating if the landscape itself were harmed, its tranquillity eroded and its wildlife put at risk. Nor do we want to see any damage to the economic base of rural areas.'

16.2 BYLAWS

Access authorities, defined as highway authorities and, in the National Parks, the National Park authority,[1] are given power to make bylaws for:

(a) the preservation of order;
(b) the prevention of damage to the land or anything on or in it; and
(c) securing that those exercising the right of access so behave themselves as to avoid undue interference with the enjoyment of land by other persons.[2]

The bylaws may relate to all the access land in the area of the access authority or only to particular land.[3] They must not interfere with:

(a) the exercise of any public right of way;
(b) any authority having under any other enactment functions relating to the land to which the bylaws apply;
(c) the running of a telecommunications code system or the exercise of any right conferred by or in accordance with the telecommunications code on the running of any such system.[4]

---

1   CROW Act 2000, s 1(2).
2   Ibid, s 17(1).
3   Ibid, s 17(3).
4   Ibid, s 17(4).

Before making any bylaws, the access authority must consult the appropriate countryside body and any local access forum for the area to which the bylaws relate.[1] Otherwise, the procedures for making bylaws are those laid down in the Local Government Act 1972.[2] Bylaws under the CROW Act 2000 must be confirmed, as respects England, by the Secretary of State, and for Wales, by the National Assembly for Wales.[3]

Bylaws may not be made unless the land is access land, or is likely to become access land, and may not be confirmed unless the land is access land.[4]

Bylaws may be enforced by the access authorities which have power to make them. A county council or district or parish council may enforce bylaws for land in their area made by another authority.[5] Fines not exceeding Level 2 on the standard scale may be imposed by the bylaws for a breach of their provisions.[6]

16.3   WARDENS

An access authority or district council may appoint wardens to:

(a) secure compliance with bylaws and the general restrictions in Sch 2 and any other restrictions imposed under Chapter II;

(b) enforce any exclusions imposed under Chapter II;

(c) advise and assist the public and landowners, occupiers and others with an interest in access land on the right of access;

(d) perform any other duties in relation to access land as the authority shall determine.[7]

A warden is entitled to enter upon access land for the performance of his duties.[8] He has no authority to do anything else which would be actionable by a person with an interest in the land.[9] He must produce evidence of his appointment if it is required.[10]

16.4   INFORMATION

An access authority may erect and maintain notices:

(a) indicating the boundaries of access land and excepted land;

---

1   CROW Act 2000, s 17(3).
2   Sections 236–238.
3   CROW Act 2000, s 17(6).
4   Ibid, s 17(7).
5   Ibid, s 17(8).
6   Ibid, s 17(5).
7   Ibid, s 18(3).
8   Ibid, s 18(4).
9   Ibid, s 18(6).
10   Ibid, s 18(5).

(b) informing the public of the effect of the general restrictions in Sch 2 and any restrictions or exclusions under Chapter II of the CROW Act 2000 and any other matter relating to access land which the authority considers appropriate.[1]

Before erecting such a notice, the access authority must, if reasonably practicable, consult the landowner or occupier.[2]

An access authority may also pay or make a contribution towards the costs of any person (eg the landowner or user groups) who displays the notices mentioned in the previous paragraph.[3]

16.5   CODES OF CONDUCT

The Countryside Agency and the Countryside Council for Wales are under a duty to issue, and revise from time to time, codes of conduct for the guidance of those exercising the right of access and for owners and others with an interest in the access land.[4] The countryside bodies may use the code of conduct as a means of fulfilling their existing duties under s 86(1) of the NPACA 1949 to prepare a country code relating to National Parks, AONBs and long-distance routes.[5]

They must also take such steps as seem to them expedient:

(a) to keep the public informed of the situation, extent of, and means of access to access land; and
(b) to keep the public and those with an interest in the land informed of their rights and obligations with regard to access, public rights of way, and nature conservation on access land.

The countryside bodies have a power to contribute to the expenses incurred by other persons in providing information.[6]

16.6   ACCESS FORUMS

16.6.1   National access forums

The remit of the national access forum is to consider how to improve opportunities for various types of informal recreation in the countryside. The forum will also have to consider the implementation of the new statutory right of access, including management issues.

---

1   CROW Act 2000, s 19(1).
2   Ibid, s 19(3).
3   Ibid, s 19(4).
4   Ibid, s 20(1), (2).
5   Ibid, s 20(3).
6   Ibid, s 20(4).

16.6.2   Local access forums

The local highway authority or, where the land is in a National Park,[1] the National Park authority (the appointing authority) is under a duty to establish a local access forum, which will consist of members appointed by the appointing authority in accordance with regulations.[2]

The function of the local access forum is to advise the appointing authority, any body exercising functions in relation to access land in the area, the local highway authority (where the appointing authority is the National Park) and such other bodies as may be prescribed.[3] The bodies must, in carrying out their functions, have regard to any relevant advice given by the local access forum.[4] The advice will relate to the improvement of public access to land in that area for the purpose of open-air recreation and the enjoyment of the area and to other matters which may be prescribed.

The views of local access forums are to be taken into account in the preparation of draft maps of open country,[5] making bylaws,[6] appointing wardens[7] and, before making a direction for an exclusion or restriction, which may exceed 6 months, for reasons of land management, avoidance of fire risk or other danger to the public, or for nature conservation or heritage preservation.[8] Local access forums must also be contacted on rights of way improvement plans.[9]

The local access forum in carrying out its functions must have regard to:

(a)   the needs of land management;
(b)   conservation of the natural beauty of the area including the flora, fauna, and geological and physiographical features; and
(c)   guidance given from time to time by the Secretary of State or the National Assembly for Wales.[10]

Access forums do not have to be established by councils of London boroughs for any part of their area, unless the councils so resolve.[11]

The Secretary of State or the National Assembly for Wales, if satisfied that no local access forum is required for any area or part of an area, may direct that the duty to establish a forum shall not apply.[12] Before making such a direction, he

---

1   The Broads, as defined in the Norfolk and Suffolk Broads Act 1988, are treated as a National Park. CROW Act 2000, s 95(6), (7).
2   CROW Act 2000, s 94(1), (2), (3).
3   Ibid, s 94(4).
4   Ibid, s 94(5).
5   Ibid, s 11(2)(c); Access to the Countryside (Maps in Draft Form) (England) Regulations 2001, SI 2001/3301, reg 4.
6   Ibid, s 17(3)(b).
7   Ibid, s 18(2).
8   Ibid, s 27(1).
9   Ibid, s 61.
10   Ibid, s 94(6); Guidance was given by the Secretary of State for the Environment, Food and Rural Affairs on 14 November 2002.
11   Ibid, s 94(7).
12   Ibid, s 94(8).

or it must consult the appointing authority for the area and the Countryside Agency or the Countryside Council for Wales.[1]

Regulations have now been made in England and Wales for the establishment and conduct of local access forums.[2]

In England, local access forums have to be established before 8 August 2003 by the appointing authority.[3] This is the local highway authority or, where the area is in a National Park, the National Park.[4] The local forum must consist of between 10 and 22 members. The members must be representatives of users of rights of way or access land, owners or occupiers of access land or land over which rights of way subsist and any other interests relevant to the particular area. There has to be a reasonable balance between owners and occupiers. Where the forum consists of only 16 members not more than two may be members of a district or county council or National Park authority for any part of the area covered by the forum. Where the forum is only 17 the restriction is 3 such members.[5]

Members must be appointed for not less than one and not more than 3 years. A member may resign by notice in writing. The appointing authority must terminate the appointment if a member becomes a district or county council member or member of the National Park authority and the quota for the council or authority members has already been filled. The appointing authority may terminate the appointment where a member is absent from all the forum meetings in a year without the consent of the appointing authority or fails to declare an interest in any matter brought up for consideration at a meeting.[6]

The forum must have at least two meetings per year. At the first meeting of the forum a chairman and vice chairman must be appointed.[7] A secretary must also be appointed to administer the forum. He must either be a member of the forum or the appointing authority.[8] Every local access forum should produce an annual report.[9]

The public are entitled to attend meetings and inspect the agenda and copies of any reports before the meeting. Copies of the minutes of the meeting and other relevant documents must also be open to inspection by the public after the meeting.[10]

---

1   CROW Act 2000, s 94(9).
2   Local Access Forums (England) Regulations 2002, SI 2002/1836 which came into force on 7 August 2002. Countryside Access (Local Access Forums) (Wales) Regulations 2001, SI 2001/4002 (W330) which came into force on 1 January 2002.
3   Local Access Forums (England) Regulations 2002, SI 2002/1836, reg 3.
4   CROW Act 2000, s 94(2).
5   Local Access Forums (England) Regulations 2002, SI 2002/1836, reg 4.
6   Ibid, reg 5.
7   Ibid, reg 6.
8   Ibid, reg 10.
9   Ibid, reg 12.
10   Ibid, regs 7 and 8.

Two or more appointing authorities may establish a joint local access forum for their areas or any part of their areas.[1]

DEFRA has given guidance to local highway authorities, National Park authorities and the Broads Authority on their duties under s 94 of the CROW Act 2000 to establish local access forums in their area.[2] It has also given initial statutory guidance to local access forums in England on how the forums should carry out their functions.[3]

In Wales local access forums had to be established by 1 January 2003 unless there was a direction by the National Assembly that no local access forum was required for any area or part of an area. Two or more appointing authorities may establish a joint access forum.[4]

A forum must consist of a Chair and Deputy Chair and a Secretary and between 10 and 20 members.[5] The appointing authority must ensure that membership of the forum achieves a reasonable balance between the users of local rights of way or access land and the owners and occupier of access land or land over which the rights of way subsist.[6] Members hold office for 3 years unless terminated earlier.[7]

The regulations set out the duties of the Secretary,[8] the procedure for appointing the Chair and Deputy Chair,[9] the conduct of meetings,[10] and the circumstances when a person's membership of the forum will terminate.[11] The appointing authority must prepare and approve annual reports as soon as practicable after 31 March in each year.[12] This must be sent to the Countryside Council for Wales. The authority must also notify the Council of any changes in membership and provide the Council with such other information as it may request.[13]

16.7 POWERS OF ENTRY

16.7.1 General principles

In order that the access provisions of the CROW Act 2000 may work properly, powers of entry for specific purposes are given to persons authorised by the

---

1   Local Access Forums (England) Regulations 2002, SI 2002/1836, reg 13.
2   DEFRA circular letter 26 July 2002 available at *www.defra.gov.uk/wildlife-countryside/cl/ index.htm.*
3   Published 14 November 2002.
4   Countryside Access (Local Access Forums) (Wales) Regulations 2001, SI 2001/4002 (W330), reg 3.
5   Ibid, reg 4.
6   Ibid, reg 7.
7   Ibid, reg 4.
8   Ibid, reg 10.
9   Ibid, reg 12.
10   Ibid, reg 15.
11   Ibid, reg 14.
12   Ibid, reg 16.
13   Ibid, reg 17.

appropriate countryside body, the local highway authority and a National Park authority. The authorised person must produce evidence of his authority before entering the land and at any time while he remains on the land, if required to do so.[1] The power of entry does not extend to a dwelling house.[2] If a person enters land which is unoccupied or from which the occupier is temporarily absent, he must leave it as effectively secured against unauthorised entry when he departs as when he found it.[3]

Before entering the land, the authorised person must give to the occupier at least 24 hours' notice unless it is not reasonably practicable to do so. No notice of entry is required where a person enters for the purpose of ascertaining whether a person has either displayed a notice deterring the public from exercising their right of access or obstructed the means of access.[4]

The authorised person may use a vehicle to enter the land. He may take a constable if he reasonably believes he is likely to be obstructed. He may also take any necessary equipment and materials. His powers extend to taking samples of the land and anything on it.[5]

Any person who intentionally obstructs a person with a power of entry is guilty of an offence and is liable on a summary conviction to a fine not exceeding Level 2 on the standard scale.[6]

If any person suffers damage as a result of the authorised entry, or by the failure to ensure the security of unoccupied premises, the authorising body must pay compensation to that person, unless he himself caused the damage.[7] Any dispute as to the entitlement or amount of compensation is to be referred to an arbitrator appointed, in default of agreement, by the Secretary of State or National Assembly for Wales.[8]

16.7.2   Authorisation by countryside body

The appropriate countryside body (Countryside Agency or Countryside Council for Wales) may authorise a person to enter the land for the following purposes:

(a)   to survey the land in the connection with the preparation or review of a statutory access map;

(b)   to determine whether any restrictions or exclusions should be granted under Chapter II;

(c)   to ascertain whether the public are being permitted to exercise their right of access;

---

1   CROW Act 2000, s 40(7).
2   Ibid, s 40(9).
3   Ibid, s 40(6).
4   Ibid, s 40(8).
5   Ibid, s 40(5).
6   Ibid, s 40(10).
7   Ibid, s 41(1).
8   Ibid, s 41(2).

(d) to obtain information in connection with appeals;

(e) to determine whether to apply to the Secretary of State or the National Assembly for Wales for a public path creation order.[1]

16.7.3   Authorisation by a local highway authority

A local highway authority may authorise a person to enter land for the following purposes.

(a) To determine whether the local highway authority should:
   (i)   enter into an agreement with a landowner or occupier concerning works needed for a means of access;
   (ii) give notice where a landowner or occupier has failed to carry out works within the specified time-limits, or has failed to observe the restrictions, in an agreement;
   (iii) where no agreement has been reached, give notice of the authority's intention to do the work itself;
   (iv) carry out works on the landowner's or occupier's failure to do so or failure to observe restrictions under the terms of their agreement, or where there is no agreement; or
   (v)   remove an obstruction.

(b) To ascertain whether a person has displayed a notice deterring the public from exercising their right of access or has obstructed the means of access.

(c) To erect or maintain notices indicating the boundaries of access and excepted land and giving information to the public on the general restrictions and any particular exclusions or restrictions relating to the land.[2]

16.7.4   Authorisation by the National Park authority

The National Park authority may authorise a person to enter land for the following purposes.

(a) To enable the authority to determine whether to exercise any powers relating to exclusions and restrictions under Chapter II.

(b) To determine whether the public are being permitted to exercise their right of access.

(c) To obtain information in connection with appeals.

(d) To determine whether the local highway authority should:
   (i)   enter into an agreement with a landowner or occupier concerning works needed for a means of access;
   (ii) give notice where a landowner or occupier has failed to carry out works within the specified time-limits, or has failed to observe the restrictions, in an agreement;

---

1   CROW Act 2000, s 40(1).
2   Ibid, s 40(2).

(iii) where no agreement has been reached, give notice of the authority's intention to do the work itself;

(iv) carry out works on the landowner's or occupier's failure to do so or failure to observe restrictions under the terms of their agreement, or where there is no agreement; or

(v) remove an obstruction.

(e) To ascertain whether a person has displayed a notice deterring the public from exercising their right of access or has obstructed the means of access.

(f) To erect or maintain notices indicating the boundaries of access and excepted land and giving information to the public on the general restrictions and any particular exclusions or restrictions relating to the land.[1]

16.7.5 Authorisation by Forestry Commissioners

The Forestry Commissioners may authorise a person to enter land for the following purposes.

(a) To determine whether the Forestry Commissioners should impose any restrictions or exclusions on access land.

(b) To obtain information in connection with appeals.[2]

---

1   CROW Act 2000, s 40(3).
2   Ibid, s 40(4).

APPENDICES

Appendix 1

COUNTRYSIDE AND RIGHTS OF WAY ACT 2000

(2000 c 37)

Part I and II, Part V, Schedules 1–7 and Schedule 16, Parts I and II

ARRANGEMENT OF SECTIONS

PART I

ACCESS TO THE COUNTRYSIDE

CHAPTER I

RIGHT OF ACCESS

General

An Act to make new provision for public access to the countryside; to amend the law relating to public rights of way; to enable traffic regulation orders to be made for the purpose of conserving an area's natural beauty; to make provision with respect to the driving of mechanically propelled vehicles elsewhere than on roads; to amend the law relating to nature conservation and the protection of wildlife; to make further provision with respect to areas of outstanding natural beauty; and for connected purposes.

[30th November 2000]

PART I

ACCESS TO THE COUNTRYSIDE

CHAPTER I

RIGHT OF ACCESS

General

1   Principal definitions for Part I

(1) In this Part 'access land' means any land which –

  (a) is shown as open country on a map in conclusive form issued by the appropriate countryside body for the purposes of this Part,
  (b) is shown on such a map as registered common land,

    (c) is registered common land in any area outside Inner London for which no such map relating to registered common land has been issued,

    (d) is situated more than 600 metres above sea level in any area for which no such map relating to open country has been issued, or

    (e) is dedicated for the purposes of this Part under section 16,

but does not (in any of those cases) include excepted land or land which is treated by section 15(1) as being accessible to the public apart from this Act.

(2) In this Part –

'access authority' –

    (a) in relation to land in a National Park, means the National Park authority, and

    (b) in relation to any other land, means the local highway authority in whose area the land is situated;

'the appropriate countryside body' means –

    (a) in relation to England, the Countryside Agency, and

    (b) in relation to Wales, the Countryside Council for Wales;

'excepted land' means land which is for the time being of any of the descriptions specified in Part I of Schedule 1, those descriptions having effect subject to Part II of that Schedule;

'mountain' includes, subject to the following definition, any land situated more than 600 metres above sea level;

'mountain, moor, heath or down' does not include land which appears to the appropriate countryside body to consist of improved or semi-improved grassland;

'open country' means land which –

    (a) appears to the appropriate countryside body to consist wholly or predominantly of mountain, moor, heath or down, and

    (b) is not registered common land.

(3) In this Part 'registered common land' means –

    (a) land which is registered as common land under the Commons Registration Act 1965 (in this section referred to as 'the 1965 Act') and whose registration under that Act has become final, or

    (b) subject to subsection (4), land which fell within paragraph (a) on the day on which this Act is passed or at any time after that day but has subsequently ceased to be registered as common land under the 1965 Act on the register of common land in which it was included being amended by reason of the land having ceased to be common land within the meaning of that Act.

(4) Subsection (3)(b) does not apply where –

    (a) the amendment of the register of common land was made in pursuance of an application made before the day on which this Act is passed, or

    (b) the land ceased to be common land by reason of the exercise of –

        (i) any power of compulsory purchase, of appropriation or of sale which is conferred by an enactment,

        (ii) any power so conferred under which land may be made common land within the meaning of the 1965 Act in substitution for other land.

Explanatory text — see **12.1**, **12.2**, **12.3**.

2   Rights of public in relation to access land

(1) Any person is entitled by virtue of this subsection to enter and remain on any access land for the purposes of open-air recreation, if and so long as –

- (a) he does so without breaking or damaging any wall, fence, hedge, stile or gate, and
- (b) he observes the general restrictions in Schedule 2 and any other restrictions imposed in relation to the land under Chapter II.

(2) Subsection (1) has effect subject to subsections (3) and (4) and to the provisions of Chapter II.

(3) Subsection (1) does not entitle a person to enter or be on any land, or do anything on any land, in contravention of any prohibition contained in or having effect under any enactment, other than an enactment contained in a local or private Act.

(4) If a person becomes a trespasser on any access land by failing to comply with –

- (a) subsection (1)(a),
- (b) the general restrictions in Schedule 2, or
- (c) any other restrictions imposed in relation to the land under Chapter II,

he may not, within 72 hours after leaving that land, exercise his right under subsection (1) to enter that land again or to enter other land in the same ownership.

(5) In this section 'owner', in relation to any land which is subject to a farm business tenancy within the meaning of the Agricultural Tenancies Act 1995 or a tenancy to which the Agricultural Holdings Act 1986 applies, means the tenant under that tenancy, and 'ownership' shall be construed accordingly.

Explanatory text — see **13.1**, **13.2**, **13.3**.

3   Power to extend to coastal land

(1) The Secretary of State (as respects England) or the National Assembly for Wales (as respects Wales) may by order amend the definition of 'open country' in section 1(2) so as to include a reference to coastal land or to coastal land of any description.

(2) An order under this section may –

- (a) make consequential amendments of other provisions of this Part, and
- (b) modify the provisions of this Part in their application to land which is open country merely because it is coastal land.

(3) In this section 'coastal land' means –

- (a) the foreshore, and
- (b) land adjacent to the foreshore (including in particular any cliff, bank, barrier, dune, beach or flat which is adjacent to the foreshore).

Explanatory text — see **12.2.5**.

Maps

4   Duty to prepare maps

(1) It shall be the duty of the Countryside Agency to prepare, in respect of England outside Inner London, maps which together show –

  (a) all registered common land, and
  (b) all open country.

(2) It shall be the duty of the Countryside Council for Wales to prepare, in respect of Wales, maps which together show –

  (a) all registered common land, and
  (b) all open country.

(3) Subsections (1) and (2) have effect subject to the following provisions of this section and to the provisions of sections 5 to 9.

(4) A map prepared under this section must distinguish between open country and registered common land, but need not distinguish between different categories of open country.

(5) In preparing a map under this section, the appropriate countryside body –

  (a) may determine not to show as open country areas of open country which are so small that the body consider that their inclusion would serve no useful purpose, and
  (b) may determine that any boundary of an area of open country is to be treated as coinciding with a particular physical feature (whether the effect is to include other land as open country or to exclude part of an area of open country).

Explanatory text — see **12.5.2**, **12.5.3**, **12.5.4**.

5   Publication of draft maps

The appropriate countryside body shall –

  (a) issue in draft form any map prepared by them under section 4,
  (b) consider any representations received by them within the prescribed period with respect to the showing of, or the failure to show, any area of land on the map as registered common land or as open country,
  (c) confirm the map with or without modifications,
  (d) if the map has been confirmed without modifications, issue it in provisional form, and
  (e) if the map has been confirmed with modifications, prepare a map incorporating the modifications, and issue that map in provisional form.

Explanatory text — see **12.5.5**, **12.5.6**.

---

6   Appeal against map after confirmation

(1) Any person having an interest in any land may appeal –

    (a) in the case of land in England, to the Secretary of State, or
    (b) in the case of land in Wales, to the National Assembly for Wales,

against the showing of that land on a map in provisional form as registered common land or as open country.

(2) An appeal relating to the showing of any land as registered common land may be brought only on the ground that the land is not registered common land.

(3) An appeal relating to the showing of any land as open country may be brought only on the ground that –

    (a) the land does not consist wholly or predominantly of mountain, moor, heath or down, and
    (b) to the extent that the appropriate countryside body have exercised their discretion under section 4(5)(b) to treat land which is not open country as forming part of an area of open country, the body ought not to have done so.

(4) On an appeal under this section, the Secretary of State or the National Assembly for Wales may –

    (a) approve the whole or part of the map which is the subject of the appeal, with or without modifications, or
    (b) require the appropriate countryside body to prepare under section 4 a new map relating to all or part of the area covered by the map which is the subject of the appeal.

Explanatory text — see **12.5.7**.

---

7   Appeal procedure

(1) Before determining an appeal under section 6, the Secretary of State or the National Assembly for Wales may, if he or it thinks fit –

    (a) cause the appeal to take, or continue in, the form of a hearing, or
    (b) cause a local inquiry to be held;

and the appeal authority shall act as mentioned in paragraph (a) or (b) if a request is made by either party to the appeal to be heard with respect to the appeal.

(2) Subsections (2) to (5) of section 250 of the Local Government Act 1972 (local inquiries: evidence and costs) apply to a hearing or local inquiry held under this section as they apply to a local inquiry held under that section, but as if –

    (a) references in that section to the person appointed to hold the inquiry were references to the Secretary of State or the National Assembly for Wales, and
    (b) references in that section to the Minister causing an inquiry to be held were references to the Secretary of State or the Assembly.

(3) Where –

(a) for the purposes of an appeal under section 6, the Secretary of State or the National Assembly for Wales is required by subsection (1) –
    (i) to cause the appeal to take, or continue in, the form of a hearing, or
    (ii) to cause a local inquiry to be held, and
(b) the inquiry or hearing does not take place, and
(c) if it had taken place, the Secretary of State or the Assembly or a person appointed by the Secretary of State or the Assembly would have had power to make an order under section 250(5) of the Local Government Act 1972 requiring any party to pay the costs of the other party,

the power to make such an order may be exercised, in relation to costs incurred for the purposes of the inquiry or hearing, as if it had taken place.

(4) This section has effect subject to section 8.

Explanatory text — see 12.5.7.

---

8 Power of Secretary of State or Assembly to delegate functions relating to appeals

(1) The Secretary of State or the National Assembly for Wales may –

(a) appoint any person to exercise on his or its behalf, with or without payment, the function of determining –
    (i) an appeal under section 6, or
    (ii) any matter involved in such an appeal, or
(b) refer any matter involved in such an appeal to such person as the Secretary of State or the Assembly may appoint for the purpose, with or without payment.

(2) Schedule 3 has effect with respect to appointments under subsection (1)(a).

Explanatory text — see 12.5.7.

---

9 Maps in conclusive form

(1) Where –

(a) the time within which any appeal under section 6 may be brought in relation to a map in provisional form has expired and no appeal has been brought, or
(b) every appeal brought under that section in relation to a map has –
    (i) been determined by the map or part of it being approved without modifications, or
    (ii) been withdrawn,

the appropriate countryside body shall issue the map (or the part or parts of it that have been approved without modifications) as a map in conclusive form.

(2) Where –

(a) every appeal brought under section 6 in relation to a map in provisional form has been determined or withdrawn, and

(b) on one or more appeals, the map or any part of it has been approved with modifications,

the appropriate countryside body shall prepare a map which covers the area covered by the map in provisional form (or the part or parts of the map in provisional form that have been approved with or without modifications) and incorporates the modifications, and shall issue it as a map in conclusive form.

(3) Where either of the conditions in subsection (1)(a) and (b) is satisfied in relation to any part of a map in provisional form, the Secretary of State (as respects England) or the National Assembly for Wales (as respects Wales) may direct the relevant countryside body to issue that part of the map as a map in conclusive form.

(4) Where on an appeal under section 6 part of a map in provisional form has been approved with modifications but the condition in subsection (2)(a) is not yet satisfied, the Secretary of State (as respects England) or the National Assembly for Wales (as respects Wales) may direct the relevant countryside body to issue a map which covers the area covered by that part of the map in provisional form and incorporates the modifications, and to issue it as a map in conclusive form.

(5) Where a map in conclusive form has been issued in compliance with a direction under subsection (3) or (4), subsections (1) and (2) shall have effect as if any reference to the map in provisional form were a reference to the part not affected by the direction.

(6) A document purporting to be certified on behalf of the appropriate countryside body to be a copy of or of any part of a map in conclusive form issued by that body for the purposes of this Part shall be receivable in evidence and shall be deemed, unless the contrary is shown, to be such a copy.

Explanatory text — see **12.5.8**.

---

10   Review of maps

(1) Where the appropriate countryside body have issued a map in conclusive form in respect of any area, it shall be the duty of the body from time to time, on a review under this section, to consider –

    (a) whether any land shown on that map as open country or registered common land is open country or registered common land at the time of the review, and

    (b) whether any land in that area which is not so shown ought to be so shown.

(2) A review under this section must be undertaken –

    (a) in the case of the first review, not more than ten years after the issue of the map in conclusive form, and

    (b) in the case of subsequent reviews, not more than ten years after the previous review.

(3) Regulations may amend paragraphs (a) and (b) of subsection (2) by substituting for the period for the time being specified in either of those paragraphs such other period as may be specified in the regulations.

Explanatory text — see **12.5.10**.

11   Regulations relating to maps

(1) Regulations may make provision supplementing the provisions of sections 4 to 10.

(2) Regulations under this section may in particular make provision with respect to –

(a) the scale on which maps are to be prepared,

(b) the manner and form in which they are to be prepared and issued,

(c) consultation with access authorities, local access forums and other persons on maps in draft form,

(d) the steps to be taken for informing the public of the issue of maps in draft form, provisional form or conclusive form,

(e) the manner in which maps in draft form, provisional form or conclusive form are to be published or to be made available for inspection,

(f) the period within which and the manner in which representations on a map in draft form may be made to the appropriate countryside body,

(g) the confirmation of a map under section 5(c),

(h) the period within which and manner in which appeals under section 6 are to be brought,

(i) the advertising of such an appeal,

(j) the manner in which such appeals are to be considered,

(k) the procedure to be followed on a review under section 10, including the issue of maps in draft form, provisional form and conclusive form on a review, and

(l) the correction by the appropriate countryside body of minor errors or omissions in maps.

(3) Regulations made by virtue of subsection (2)(b) or (e) may authorise or require a map to be prepared, issued, published or made available for inspection in electronic form, but must require any map in electronic form to be capable of being reproduced in printed form.

(4) Regulations made by virtue of subsection (2)(k) may provide for any of the provisions of this Chapter relating to appeals to apply (with or without modifications) in relation to an appeal against a map issued in provisional form on a review.

Explanatory text — see **12.5.5**, **12.5.6**, **12.5.7**, **12.5.8**.

Rights and liabilities of owners and occupiers

12   Effect of right of access on rights and liabilities of owners

(1) The operation of section 2(1) in relation to any access land does not increase the liability, under any enactment not contained in this Act or under any rule of law, of a person interested in the access land or any adjoining land in respect of the state of the land or of things done or omitted to be done on the land.

(2) Any restriction arising under a covenant or otherwise as to the use of any access land shall have effect subject to the provisions of this Part, and any liability of a person interested in any access land in respect of such a restriction is limited accordingly.

(3) For the purposes of any enactment or rule of law as to the circumstances in which the dedication of a highway or the grant of an easement may be presumed, or may be established by prescription, the use by the public or by any person of a way across land in the exercise of the right conferred by section 2(1) is to be disregarded.

(4) The use of any land by the inhabitants of any locality for the purposes of open-air recreation in the exercise of the right conferred by section 2(1) is to be disregarded in determining whether the land has become a town or village green.

Explanatory text — see 14.2.

---

13   Occupiers' liability

(1) In section 1 of the Occupiers' Liability Act 1957 (liability in tort: preliminary), for subsection (4) there is substituted –

'(4) A person entering any premises in exercise of rights conferred by virtue of –

(a) section 2(1) of the Countryside and Rights of Way Act 2000, or
(b) an access agreement or order under the National Parks and Access to the 1949 Countryside Act 1949,

is not, for the purposes of this Act, a visitor of the occupier of the premises.'

(2) In section 1 of the Occupiers' Liability Act 1984 (duty of occupier to persons other than his visitors), after subsection (6) there is inserted –

'(6A) At any time when the right conferred by section 2(1) of the Countryside and Rights of Way Act 2000 is exercisable in relation to land which is access land for the purposes of Part I of that Act, an occupier of the land owes (subject to subsection (6C) below) no duty by virtue of this section to any person in respect of –

(a) a risk resulting from the existence of any natural feature of the landscape, or any river, stream, ditch or pond whether or not a natural feature, or
(b) a risk of that person suffering injury when passing over, under or through any wall, fence or gate, except by proper use of the gate or of a stile.

(6B) For the purposes of subsection (6A) above, any plant, shrub or tree, of whatever origin, is to be regarded as a natural feature of the landscape.

(6C) Subsection (6A) does not prevent an occupier from owing a duty by virtue of this section in respect of any risk where the danger concerned is due to anything done by the occupier –

(a) with the intention of creating that risk, or
(b) being reckless as to whether that risk is created.'

(3) After section 1 of that Act there is inserted –

'1A   Special considerations relating to access land

In determining whether any, and if so what, duty is owed by virtue of section 1 by an occupier of land at any time when the right conferred by section 2(1) of the

Countryside and Rights of Way Act 2000 is exercisable in relation to the land, regard is to be had, in particular, to –

(a) the fact that the existence of that right ought not to place an undue burden (whether financial or otherwise) on the occupier,

(b) the importance of maintaining the character of the countryside, including features of historic, traditional or archaeological interest, and

(c) any relevant guidance given under section 20 of that Act.'

Explanatory text — see 14.3.

---

14   Offence of displaying on access land notices deterring public use

(1) If any person places or maintains –

(a) on or near any access land, or

(b) on or near a way leading to any access land,

a notice containing any false or misleading information likely to deter the public from exercising the right conferred by section 2(1), he is liable on summary conviction to a fine not exceeding level 1 on the standard scale.

(2) The court before whom a person is convicted of an offence under subsection (1) may, in addition to or in substitution for the imposition of a fine, order him to remove the notice in respect of which he is convicted within such period, not being less than four days, as may be specified in the order.

(3) A person who fails to comply with an order under subsection (2) is guilty of a further offence and liable on summary conviction to a fine not exceeding level 3 on the standard scale.

Explanatory text — see 14.4.

Access under other enactments or by dedication

15   Rights of access under other enactments

(1) For the purposes of section 1(1), land is to be treated as being accessible to the public apart from this Act at any time if, but only if, at that time –

(a) section 193 of the Law of Property Act 1925 (rights of the public over commons and waste lands) applies to it,

(b) by virtue of a local or private Act or a scheme made under Part I of the Commons Act 1899 (as read with subsection (2)), members of the public have a right of access to it at all times for the purposes of open-air recreation (however described),

(c) an access agreement or access order under Part V of the National Parks and Access to the Countryside Act 1949 is in force with respect to it, or

(d) the public have access to it under subsection (1) of section 19 of the Ancient Monuments and Archaeological Areas Act 1979 (public access to monuments under public control) or would have access to it under that subsection but for any provision of subsections (2) to (9) of that section.

(2) Where a local or private Act or a scheme made under Part I of the Commons Act 1899 confers on the inhabitants of a particular district or neighbourhood (however described) a right of access to any land for the purposes of open-air recreation (however described), the right of access exercisable by those inhabitants in relation to that land is by virtue of this subsection exercisable by members of the public generally.

Explanatory text — see 12.4.

---

16   Dedication of land as access land

(1) Subject to the provisions of this section, a person who, in respect of any land, holds –

(a) the fee simple absolute in possession, or
(b) a legal term of years absolute of which not less than 90 years remain unexpired,

may, by taking such steps as may be prescribed, dedicate the land for the purposes of this Part, whether or not it would be access land apart from this section.

(2) Where any person other than the person making the dedication holds –

(a) any leasehold interest in any of the land to be dedicated, or
(b) such other interest in any of that land as may be prescribed,

the dedication must be made jointly with that other person, in such manner as may be prescribed, or with his consent, given in such manner as may be prescribed.

(3) In relation to a dedication under this section by virtue of subsection (1)(b), the reference in subsection (2)(a) to a leasehold interest does not include a reference to a leasehold interest superior to that of the person making the dedication.

(4) A dedication made under this section by virtue of subsection (1)(b) shall have effect only for the remainder of the term held by the person making the dedication.

(5) Schedule 2 to the Forestry Act 1967 (power for tenant for life and others to enter into forestry dedication covenants) applies to dedications under this section as it applies to forestry dedication covenants.

(6) Regulations may –

(a) prescribe the form of any instrument to be used for the purposes of this section,
(b) enable a dedication under this section to include provision removing or relaxing any of the general restrictions in Schedule 2 in relation to any of the land to which the dedication relates,
(c) enable a dedication previously made under this section to be amended by the persons by whom a dedication could be made, so as to remove or relax any of those restrictions in relation to any of the land to which the dedication relates, and
(d) require any dedication under this section, or any amendment of such a dedication by virtue of paragraph (c), to be notified to the appropriate countryside body and to the access authority.

(7) A dedication under this section is irrevocable and, subject to subsection (4), binds successive owners and occupiers of, and other persons interested in, the land to which it relates, but nothing in this section prevents any land from becoming excepted land.

(8) A dedication under this section is a local land charge.

Explanatory text — see **12.2.4**.

Miscellaneous provisions relating to right of access

17   Byelaws

(1) An access authority may, as respects access land in their area, make byelaws –

(a) for the preservation of order,

(b) for the prevention of damage to the land or anything on or in it, and

(c) for securing that persons exercising the right conferred by section 2(1) so behave themselves as to avoid undue interference with the enjoyment of the land by other persons.

(2) Byelaws under this section may relate to all the access land in the area of the access authority or only to particular land.

(3) Before making byelaws under this section, the access authority shall consult –

(a) the appropriate countryside body, and

(b) any local access forum established for an area to which the byelaws relate.

(4) Byelaws under this section shall not interfere –

(a) with the exercise of any public right of way,

(b) with any authority having under any enactment functions relating to the land to which the byelaws apply, or

(c) with the running of a telecommunications code system or the exercise of any right conferred by or in accordance with the telecommunications code on the running of any such system.

(5) Sections 236 to 238 of the Local Government Act 1972 (which relate to the procedure for making byelaws, authorise byelaws to impose fines not exceeding level 2 on the standard scale, and provide for the proof of byelaws in legal proceedings) apply to all byelaws under this section whether or not the authority making them is a local authority within the meaning of that Act.

(6) The confirming authority in relation to byelaws made under this section is –

(a) as respects England, the Secretary of State, and

(b) as respects Wales, the National Assembly for Wales.

(7) Byelaws under this section relating to any land –

(a) may not be made unless the land is access land or the access authority are satisfied that it is likely to become access land, and

(b) may not be confirmed unless the land is access land.

(8) Any access authority having power under this section to make byelaws also have power to enforce byelaws made by them; and any county council or district or parish council may enforce byelaws made under this section by another authority as respects land in the area of the council.

Explanatory text — see **16.2**.

18　Wardens

(1) An access authority or a district council may appoint such number of persons as may appear to the authority making the appointment to be necessary or expedient, to act as wardens as respects access land in their area.

(2) As respects access land in an area for which there is a local access forum, an access authority shall, before they first exercise the power under subsection (1) and thereafter from time to time, consult the local access forum about the exercise of that power.

(3) Wardens may be appointed under subsection (1) for the following purposes –

(a) to secure compliance with byelaws under section 17 and with the general restrictions in Schedule 2 and any other restrictions imposed under Chapter II,
(b) to enforce any exclusion imposed under Chapter II,
(c) in relation to the right conferred by section 2(1), to advise and assist the public and persons interested in access land,
(d) to perform such other duties (if any) in relation to access land as the authority appointing them may determine.

(4) For the purpose of exercising any function conferred on him by or under this section, a warden appointed under subsection (1) may enter upon any access land.

(5) A warden appointed under subsection (1) shall, if so required, produce evidence of his authority before entering any access land in the exercise of the power conferred by subsection (4), and shall also produce evidence of his authority while he remains on the access land, if so required by any person.

(6) Except as provided by subsection (4), this section does not authorise a warden appointed under subsection (1), on land in which any person other than the authority who appointed him has an interest, to do anything which apart from this section would be actionable at that person's suit by virtue of that interest.

Explanatory text — see **16.3**.

19　Notices indicating boundaries, etc

(1) An access authority may erect and maintain –

(a) notices indicating the boundaries of access land and excepted land, and
(b) notices informing the public of –
　(i)　the effect of the general restrictions in Schedule 2,
　(ii)　the exclusion or restriction under Chapter II of access by virtue of section 2(1) to any land, and
　(iii)　any other matters relating to access land or to access by virtue of section 2(1) which the access authority consider appropriate.

(2) In subsection (1)(b)(ii), the reference to the exclusion or restriction of access by virtue of section 2(1) is to be interpreted in accordance with section 21(2) and (3).

(3) Before erecting a notice on any land under subsection (1) the access authority shall, if reasonably practicable, consult the owner or occupier of the land.

(4) An access authority may also, as respects any access land in their area, defray or contribute towards, or undertake to defray or contribute towards, expenditure incurred or to be incurred in relation to the land by any person in displaying such notices as are mentioned in subsection (1)(a) and (b).

Explanatory text — see 16.4.

---

20 Codes of conduct and other information

(1) In relation to England, it shall be the duty of the Countryside Agency to issue, and from time to time revise, a code of conduct for the guidance of persons exercising the right conferred by section 2(1) and of persons interested in access land, and to take such other steps as appear to them expedient for securing –

  (a) that the public are informed of the situation and extent of, and means of access to, access land, and
  (b) that the public and persons interested in access land are informed of their respective rights and obligations –
    (i)   under this Part, and
    (ii) with regard to public rights of way on, and nature conservation in relation to, access land.

(2) In relation to Wales, it shall be the duty of the Countryside Council for Wales to issue, and from time to time revise, a code of conduct for the guidance of persons exercising the right conferred by section 2(1) and of persons interested in access land, and to take such other steps as appear to them expedient for securing the results mentioned in paragraphs (a) and (b) of subsection (1).

(3) A code of conduct issued by the Countryside Agency or the Countryside Council for Wales may include provisions in pursuance of subsection (1) or (2) and in pursuance of section 86(1) of the National Parks and Access to the Countryside Act 1949.

(4) The powers conferred by subsections (1) and (2) include power to contribute towards expenses incurred by other persons.

Explanatory text — see 16.5.

CHAPTER II

EXCLUSION OR RESTRICTION OF ACCESS

21 Interpretation of Chapter II

(1) References in this Chapter to the exclusion or restriction of access to any land by virtue of section 2(1) are to be interpreted in accordance with subsections (2) and (3).

(2) A person excludes access by virtue of subsection (1) of section 2 to any land where he excludes the application of that subsection in relation to that land.

(3) A person restricts access by virtue of subsection (1) of section 2 to any land where he provides that the right conferred by that subsection –

  (a) is exercisable only along specified routes or ways,

(b) is exercisable only after entering the land at a specified place or places,

(c) is exercisable only by persons who do not take dogs on the land, or

(d) is exercisable only by persons who satisfy any other specified conditions.

(4) In this Chapter, except section 23(1), 'owner', in relation to land which is subject to a farm business tenancy within the meaning of the Agricultural Tenancies Act 1995 or a tenancy to which the Agricultural Holdings Act 1986 applies, means the tenant under that tenancy.

(5) Subject to subsection (6), in this Chapter 'the relevant authority' –

(a) in relation to any land in a National Park, means the National Park authority, and

(b) in relation to any other land, means the appropriate countryside body.

(6) Where –

(a) it appears to the Forestry Commissioners that any land which is dedicated for the purposes of this Part under section 16 consists wholly or predominantly of woodland, and

(b) the Forestry Commissioners give to the body who are apart from this subsection the relevant authority for the purposes of this Chapter in relation to the land a notice stating that the Forestry Commissioners are to be the relevant authority for those purposes as from a date specified in the notice,

the Forestry Commissioners shall as from that date become the relevant authority in relation to that land for those purposes, but subject to subsection (7).

(7) Where it appears to the Forestry Commissioners that any land in relation to which they are by virtue of subsection (6) the relevant authority for the purposes of this Chapter has ceased to consist wholly or predominantly of woodland, the Forestry Commissioners may, by giving notice to the body who would apart from subsection (6) be the relevant authority, revoke the notice under subsection (6) as from a date specified in the notice under this subsection.

Explanatory text — see **14.1.2**.

---

22   Exclusion or restriction at discretion of owner and others

(1) Subject to subsections (2) and (6), an entitled person may, by giving notice to the relevant authority in accordance with regulations under section 32(1)(a), exclude or restrict access by virtue of section 2(1) to any land on one or more days specified in the notice.

(2) The number of days on which any entitled person excludes or restricts under this section access by virtue of section 2(1) to any land must not in any calendar year exceed the relevant maximum.

(3) In this section 'entitled person', in relation to any land, means –

(a) the owner of the land, and

(b) any other person having an interest in the land and falling within a prescribed description.

(4) Subject to subsection (5), in this section 'the relevant maximum' means twenty-eight.

(5) If regulations are made under subsection (3)(b), the regulations must provide that, in cases where there are two or more entitled persons having different interests in the land, the relevant maximum in relation to each of them is to be determined in accordance with the regulations, but so that the number of days on which access by virtue of section 2(1) to any land may be excluded or restricted under this section in any calendar year does not exceed twenty-eight.

(6) An entitled person may not under this section exclude or restrict access by virtue of section 2(1) to any land on –

(a) Christmas Day or Good Friday, or
(b) any day which is a bank holiday under the Banking and Financial Dealings Act 1971 in England and Wales.

(7) An entitled person may not under this section exclude or restrict access by virtue of section 2(1) to any land –

(a) on more than four days in any calendar year which are either Saturday or Sunday,
(b) on any Saturday in the period beginning with 1st June and ending with 11th August in any year,
(c) on any Sunday in the period beginning with 1st June and ending with 30th September in any year.

(8) Regulations may provide that any exclusion or restriction under subsection (1) of access by virtue of section 2(1) to any land must relate to an area of land the boundaries of which are determined in accordance with the regulations.

Explanatory text — see **14.1.3**.

---

23   Restrictions on dogs at discretion of owner

(1) The owner of any land consisting of moor managed for the breeding and shooting of grouse may, so far as appears to him to be necessary in connection with the management of the land for that purpose, by taking such steps as may be prescribed, provide that, during a specified period, the right conferred by section 2(1) is exercisable only by persons who do not take dogs on the land.

(2) The owner of any land may, so far as appears to him to be necessary in connection with lambing, by taking such steps as may be prescribed, provide that during a specified period the right conferred by section 2(1) is exercisable only by persons who do not take dogs into any field or enclosure on the land in which there are sheep.

(3) In subsection (2) 'field or enclosure' means a field or enclosure of not more than 15 hectares.

(4) As respects any land –

(a) any period specified under subsection (1) may not be more than five years,
(b) not more than one period may be specified under subsection (2) in any calendar year, and that period may not be more than six weeks.

(5) A restriction imposed under subsection (1) or (2) does not prevent a blind person from taking with him a trained guide dog, or a deaf person from taking with him a trained hearing dog.

Explanatory text — see **14.1.4**.

24   Land management

(1) The relevant authority may by direction, on an application made by a person interested in any land, exclude or restrict access to that land by virtue of section 2(1) during a specified period, if the authority are satisfied that the exclusion or restriction under this section of access by virtue of section 2(1) to the extent provided by the direction is necessary for the purposes of the management of the land by the applicant.

(2) The reference in subsection (1) to a specified period includes a reference to –

    (a) a specified period in every calendar year, or
    (b) a period which is to be –
        (i)   determined by the applicant in accordance with the direction, and
        (ii) notified by him to the relevant authority in accordance with regulations under section 32(1)(d).

(3) In determining whether to any extent the exclusion or restriction under this section of access by virtue of section 2(1) during any period is necessary for the purposes of land management, the relevant authority shall have regard to –

    (a) the existence of the right conferred by section 22,
    (b) the extent to which the applicant has exercised or proposes to exercise that right, and
    (c) the purposes for which he has exercised or proposes to exercise it.

(4) Where an application under this section relates to land which is not access land at the time when the application is made, the relevant authority shall not give a direction under this section unless they are satisfied that it is likely that the land will be access land during all or part of the period to which the application relates.

Explanatory text — see **14.1.5**.

25   Avoidance of risk of fire or of danger to the public

(1) The relevant authority may by direction exclude or restrict access by virtue of section 2(1) in relation to any land during a specified period if the authority are satisfied –

    (a) that, by reason of any exceptional conditions of weather or any exceptional change in the condition of the land, the exclusion or restriction under this section of access to the land by virtue of section 2(1) to the extent provided by the direction is necessary for the purpose of fire prevention, or
    (b) that, by reason of anything done, or proposed to be done, on the land or on adjacent land, the exclusion or restriction under this section of access to the land by virtue of section 2(1) to the extent provided by the direction is necessary for the purpose of avoiding danger to the public.

(2) The reference in subsection (1) to a specified period includes a reference to –

    (a) a specified period in every calendar year, and
    (b) a period which is to be –
        (i)   determined by a specified person in accordance with the direction, and

(ii)   notified by him to the relevant authority in accordance with regulations under section 32(1)(d).

(3) The relevant authority may exercise their powers under subsection (1) on the application of any person interested in the land, or without any such application having been made.

(4) In determining on an application made by a person interested in the land whether the condition in subsection (1)(a) or (b) is satisfied, the relevant authority shall have regard to –

(a)   the existence of the right conferred by section 22,
(b)   the extent to which the applicant has exercised or proposes to exercise that right, and
(c)   the purposes for which he has exercised or proposes to exercise it.

(5) Where an application under this section relates to land which is not access land at the time when the application is made, the relevant authority shall not give a direction under this section unless they are satisfied that it is likely that the land will be access land during all or part of the period to which the application relates.

Explanatory text — see 14.1.6.

---

26   Nature conservation and heritage preservation

(1) The relevant authority may by direction exclude or restrict access by virtue of section 2(1) to any land during any period if they are satisfied that the exclusion or restriction of access by virtue of section 2(1) to the extent provided by the direction is necessary for either of the purposes specified in subsection (3).

(2) A direction under subsection (1) may be expressed to have effect –

(a)   during a period specified in the direction,
(b)   during a specified period in every calendar year, or
(c)   during a period which is to be –
   (i)   determined by a specified person in accordance with the direction, and
   (ii)   notified by him to the relevant authority in accordance with regulations under section 32(1)(d), or
(d)   indefinitely.

(3) The purposes referred to in subsection (1) are –

(a)   the purpose of conserving flora, fauna or geological or physiographical features of the land in question;
(b)   the purpose of preserving –
   (i)   any scheduled monument as defined by section 1(11) of the Ancient Monuments and Archaeological Areas Act 1979, or
   (ii)   any other structure, work, site, garden or area which is of historic, architectural, traditional, artistic or archaeological interest.

(4) In considering whether to give a direction under this section, the relevant authority shall have regard to any advice given to them by the relevant advisory body.

(5) Subsection (4) does not apply where the direction is given by the Countryside Council for Wales for the purpose specified in subsection (3)(a) or revokes a direction given by them for that purpose.

(6) In this section 'the relevant advisory body' –

  (a) in relation to a direction which is to be given for the purpose specified in subsection (3)(a) or which revokes a direction given for that purpose, means –
    (i) in the case of land in England, English Nature, and
    (ii) in the case of land in Wales in respect of which the Countryside Council for Wales are not the relevant authority, the Countryside Council for Wales, and

  (b) in relation to a direction which is to be given for the purpose specified in subsection (3)(b) or which revokes a direction given for that purpose, means –
    (i) in the case of land in England, the Historic Buildings and Monuments Commission for England, and
    (ii) in the case of land in Wales, the National Assembly for Wales.

Explanatory text — see 14.1.7.

---

27   Directions by relevant authority: general

(1) Before giving a direction under section 24, 25 or 26 in relation to land in an area for which there is a local access forum so as to exclude or restrict access to the land –

  (a) indefinitely, or
  (b) during a period which exceeds, or may exceed, six months,

the relevant authority shall consult the local access forum.

(2) Any direction under section 24, 25 or 26 may be revoked or varied by a subsequent direction under that provision.

(3) Where a direction given under section 24, 25 or 26 in relation to any land by the relevant authority excludes or restricts access to the land –

  (a) indefinitely,
  (b) for part of every year or of each of six or more consecutive calendar years, or
  (c) for a specified period of more than five years,

the authority shall review the direction not later than the fifth anniversary of the relevant date.

(4) In subsection (3) 'the relevant date', in relation to a direction, means –

  (a) the day on which the direction was given, or
  (b) where it has already been reviewed, the day on which it was last reviewed.

(5) Before revoking or varying a direction under section 24 or 25 which was given on the application of a person interested in the land to which the direction relates ('the original applicant'), the relevant authority shall –

  (a) where the original applicant still holds the interest in the land which he held when he applied for the direction and it is reasonably practicable to consult him, consult the original applicant, and
  (b) where the original applicant does not hold that interest, consult any person who holds that interest and with whom consultation is reasonably practicable.

(6) Before revoking or varying a direction under section 26, the relevant authority shall consult the relevant advisory body as defined by section 26(6), unless the direction falls within section 26(5).

Explanatory text — see **14.1.8**.

28 Defence or national security

(1) The Secretary of State may by direction exclude or restrict access by virtue of section 2(1) to any land during any period if he is satisfied that the exclusion or restriction of such access to the extent provided by the direction is necessary for the purposes of defence or national security.

(2) A direction under subsection (1) may be expressed to have effect –

   (a) during a period specified in the direction,
   (b) during a specified period in every calendar year,
   (c) during a period which is to be –
      (i)   determined in accordance with the direction by a person authorised by the Secretary of State, and
      (ii) notified by that person to the relevant authority in accordance with regulations under section 32(1)(c), or
   (d) indefinitely.

(3) Any direction given by the Secretary of State under this section may be revoked or varied by a subsequent direction.

(4) Where a direction given under this section in relation to any land excludes or restricts access to the land –

   (a) indefinitely,
   (b) for part of every year or of each of six or more consecutive calendar years, or
   (c) for a specified period of more than five years,

the Secretary of State shall review the direction not later than the fifth anniversary of the relevant date.

(5) In subsection (4) 'the relevant date', in relation to a direction, means –

   (a) the day on which the direction was given, or
   (b) where it has previously been reviewed, the day on which it was last reviewed.

(6) If in any calendar year the Secretary of State reviews a defence direction, he shall –

   (a) prepare a report on all reviews of defence directions which he has undertaken during that year, and
   (b) lay a copy of the report before each House of Parliament.

(7) In subsection (6) 'defence direction' means a direction given under this section for the purposes of defence.

Explanatory text — see **14.1.9**.

29 Reference by relevant advisory body

(1) Subsections (2) and (3) apply where –

   (a) the relevant advisory body has given advice under section 26(4) or on being consulted under section 27(6), but

(b) in any respect, the relevant authority decide not to act in accordance with that advice.

(2) The relevant advisory body may refer the decision –

(a) in the case of land in England, to the [Secretary of State], or
(b) in the case of land in Wales, to the National Assembly for Wales.

(3) On a reference under this section the [Secretary of State] or the National Assembly for Wales may, if he or it thinks fit –

(a) cancel any direction given by the relevant authority, or
(b) require the relevant authority to give such direction under section 26 as the [Secretary of State] or, as the case may be, the Assembly, think fit.

(4) Sections 7 and 8 (and Schedule 3) have effect in relation to a reference under this section as they have effect in relation to an appeal under section 6 . . . .

(5) In this section –

. . .

'the relevant advisory body' has the same meaning as in section 26, except that it does not include the National Assembly for Wales.

Amendments — Ministry of Agriculture, Fisheries and Food (Dissolution) Order 2002, SI 2002/794. **Explanatory text** — see **14.1.10**.

---

30   Appeal by person interested in land

(1) Subsections (2) and (3) apply where –

(a) a person interested in any land (in this section referred to as 'the applicant') –
   (i)   has applied for a direction under section 24 or 25, or
   (ii)   has made representations on being consulted under section 27(5), but
(b) in any respect, the relevant authority decide not to act in accordance with the application or the representations.

(2) The relevant authority shall inform the applicant of their reasons for not acting in accordance with the application or representations.

(3) The applicant may appeal against the decision –

(a) in the case of land in England, to the [Secretary of State], or
(b) in the case of land in Wales, to the National Assembly for Wales.

(4) On appeal under this section the [Secretary of State] or the National Assembly for Wales may, if he or it thinks fit –

(a) cancel any direction given by the relevant authority, or
(b) require the relevant authority to give such direction under section 24 or 25 as the [Secretary of State] or, as the case may be, the Assembly, think fit.

(5) Sections 7 and 8 (and Schedule 3) have effect in relation to an appeal under this section as they have effect in relation to an appeal under section 6 . . . .

(6) . . .

Amendments — Ministry of Agriculture, Fisheries and Food (Dissolution) Order 2002, SI 2002/794.
Explanatory text — see **14.1.10**.

31 Exclusion or restriction of access in case of emergency

(1) Regulations may make provision enabling the relevant authority, where the authority are satisfied that an emergency has arisen which makes the exclusion or restriction of access by virtue of section 2(1) necessary for any of the purposes specified in section 24(1), 25(1) or 26(3), by direction to exclude or restrict such access in respect of any land for a period not exceeding three months.

(2) Regulations under this section may provide for any of the preceding provisions of this Chapter to apply in relation to a direction given under the regulations with such modifications as may be prescribed.

Explanatory text — see **14.1.11**.

32 Regulations relating to exclusion or restriction of access

(1) Regulations may make provision –

  (a) as to the giving of notice under section 22(1),
  (b) as to the steps to be taken under section 23(1) and (2),
  (c) as to the procedure on any application to the relevant authority under section 24 or 25, including the period within which any such application must be made,
  (d) as to the giving of notice for the purposes of section 24(2)(b)(ii), 25(2)(b)(ii), 26(2)(c)(ii) or 28(2)(c)(ii),
  (e) prescribing the form of any notice or application referred to in paragraphs (a) to (d),
  (f) restricting the cases in which a person who is interested in any land only as the holder of rights of common may make an application under section 24 or 25 in respect of the land,
  (g) as to requirements to be met by relevant authorities or the Secretary of State in relation to consultation (whether or not required by the preceding provisions of this Chapter),
  (h) as to the giving of directions by relevant authorities or the Secretary of State,
  (i) as to notification by relevant authorities or the Secretary of State of decisions under this Chapter,
  (j) as to steps to be taken by persons interested in land, by relevant authorities, by the bodies specified in section 26(6) or by the Secretary of State for informing the public about the exclusion or restriction under this Chapter of access by virtue of section 2(1), including the display of notices on or near the land to which the exclusion or restriction relates,
  (k) as to the carrying out of reviews by relevant authorities under section 27(3) or by the Secretary of State under section 28(4),
  (l) as to the period within which and manner in which appeals under section 30 are to be brought,
  (m) as to the advertising of such an appeal, and
  (n) as to the manner in which such appeals are to be considered.

(2) Regulations made under subsection (1)(k) may provide for any of the provisions of this Chapter relating to appeals to apply (with or without modifications) on a review under section 27.

Explanatory text — see 14.1.12.

---

33   Guidance by countryside bodies to National Park authorities

(1) Subject to subsection (3), the Countryside Agency may issue guidance –

   (a) to National Park authorities in England with respect to the discharge by National Park authorities of their functions under this Chapter, and

   (b) to the Forestry Commissioners with respect to the discharge by the Forestry Commissioners of any functions conferred on them by virtue of section 21(6) in relation to land in England.

(2) Subject to subsection (3), the Countryside Council for Wales may issue guidance –

   (a) to National Park authorities in Wales with respect to the discharge by National Park authorities of their functions under this Chapter, and

   (b) to the Forestry Commissioners with respect to the discharge by the Forestry Commissioners of any functions conferred on them by virtue of section 21(6) in relation to land in Wales.

(3) The Countryside Agency or the Countryside Council for Wales may not issue any guidance under this section unless the guidance has been approved –

   (a) in the case of the Countryside Agency, by the Secretary of State, and

   (b) in the case of the Countryside Council for Wales, by the National Assembly for Wales.

(4) Where the Countryside Agency or the Countryside Council for Wales issue any guidance under this section, they shall arrange for the guidance to be published in such manner as they consider appropriate.

(5) A National Park authority or the Forestry Commissioners shall have regard to any guidance issued to them under this section.

Explanatory text — see 14.1.13.

CHAPTER III

MEANS OF ACCESS

34   Interpretation of Chapter III

In this Chapter –

'access land' does not include any land in relation to which the application of section 2(1) has been excluded under any provision of Chapter II either indefinitely or for a specified period of which at least six months remain unexpired;

'means of access', in relation to land, means –

(a) any opening in a wall, fence or hedge bounding the land (or part of the land), with or without a gate, stile or other works for regulating passage through the opening,

(b) any stairs or steps for enabling persons to enter on the land (or part of the land), or

(c) any bridge, stepping stone or other works for crossing a watercourse, ditch or bog on the land or adjoining the boundary of the land.

Explanatory text — see **15.3.1**.

---

35 Agreements with respect to means of access

(1) Where, in respect of any access land, it appears to the access authority that –

(a) the opening-up, improvement or repair of any means of access to the land,

(b) the construction of any new means of access to the land,

(c) the maintenance of any means of access to the land, or

(d) the imposition of restrictions –

    (i) on the destruction, removal, alteration or stopping-up of any means of access to the land, or

    (ii) on the doing of any thing whereby the use of any such means of access to the land by the public would be impeded,

is necessary for giving the public reasonable access to that land in exercise of the right conferred by section 2(1), the access authority may enter into an agreement with the owner or occupier of the land as to the carrying out of the works or the imposition of the restrictions.

(2) An agreement under this section may provide –

(a) for the carrying out of works by the owner or occupier or by the access authority, and

(b) for the making of payments by the access authority –

    (i) as a contribution towards, or for the purpose of defraying, costs incurred by the owner or occupier in carrying out any works for which the agreement provides, or

    (ii) in consideration of the imposition of any restriction.

Explanatory text — see **15.3.2**.

---

36 Failure to comply with agreement

(1) If the owner or occupier of any access land fails to carry out within the required time any works which he is required by an agreement under section 35 to carry out, the access authority, after giving not less than twenty-one days' notice of their intention to do so, may take all necessary steps for carrying out those works.

(2) In subsection (1) 'the required time' means the time specified in, or determined in accordance with, the agreement as that within which the works must be carried out or, if there is no such time, means a reasonable time.

(3) If the owner or occupier of any access land fails to observe any restriction which he is required by an agreement under section 35 to observe, the access authority may give

him a notice requiring him within a specified period of not less than twenty-one days to carry out such works as may be specified in the notice, for the purpose of remedying the failure to observe the restriction.

(4) A notice under subsection (3) must contain particulars of the right of appeal conferred by section 38.

(5) If the person to whom a notice under subsection (3) is given fails to comply with the notice, the access authority may take all necessary steps for carrying out any works specified in the notice.

(6) Where the access authority carry out any works by virtue of subsection (1), the authority may recover the amount of any expenses reasonably incurred by them in carrying out the works, reduced by their contribution under the agreement, from the person by whom under the agreement the cost (apart from the authority's contribution) of carrying out the works would fall to be borne.

(7) Where the access authority carry out any works by virtue of subsection (5), the authority may recover the amount of any expenses reasonably incurred by them in carrying out the works from the person to whom the notice under subsection (3) was given.

Explanatory text — see 15.3.3.

---

37   Provision of access by access authority in absence of agreement

(1) Where, in respect of any access land –

   (a) it appears to the access authority that –
      (i)   the opening-up, improvement or repair of any means of access to the land,
      (ii) the construction of any new means of access to the land, or
      (iii) the maintenance of any means of access to the land,
     is necessary for giving the public reasonable access to that land, or to other access land, in pursuance of the right conferred by section 2(1), and
   (b) the access authority are satisfied that they are unable to conclude on reasonable terms an agreement under section 35 with the owner or occupier of the land for the carrying out of the works,

the access authority may, subject to subsection (3), give the owner or occupier a notice stating that, after the end of a specified period of not less than twenty-one days, the authority intend to take all necessary steps for carrying out the works specified in the notice for the opening-up, improvement, repair, construction or maintenance of the means of access.

(2) A notice under subsection (1) must contain particulars of the right of appeal conferred by section 38.

(3) Where a notice under subsection (1) is given to any person as the owner or occupier of any land, the access authority shall give a copy of the notice to every other owner or occupier of the land.

(4) An access authority exercising the power conferred by subsection (1) in relation to the provision of a means of access shall have regard to the requirements of efficient management of the land in deciding where the means of access is to be provided.

(5) If, at the end of the period specified in a notice under subsection (1), any of the works specified in the notice have not been carried out, the access authority may take all necessary steps for carrying out those works.

Explanatory text — see **15.3.4**.

---

38   Appeals relating to notices

(1) Where a notice under section 36(3) or 37(1) has been given to a person in respect of any land, he or any other owner or occupier of the land may appeal against the notice –

(a) in the case of land in England, to the Secretary of State, and
(b) in the case of land in Wales, to the National Assembly for Wales.

(2) An appeal against a notice under section 36(3) may be brought on any of the following grounds –

(a) that the notice requires the carrying out of any works which are not necessary for remedying a breach of the agreement,
(b) that any of the works have already been carried out, and
(c) that the period specified in the notice as that before the end of which the works must be carried out is too short.

(3) An appeal against a notice under section 37(1) may be brought on any of the following grounds –

(a) that the notice requires the carrying out of any works which are not necessary for giving the public reasonable access to the access land in question,
(b) in the case of works to provide a means of access, that the means of access should be provided elsewhere, or that a different means of access should be provided, and
(c) that any of the works have already been carried out.

(4) On an appeal under this section, the Secretary of State or the National Assembly for Wales may –

(a) confirm the notice with or without modifications, or
(b) cancel the notice.

(5) Sections 7 and 8 (and Schedule 3) have effect in relation to an appeal under this section as they have effect in relation to an appeal under section 6.

(6) Regulations may make provision as to –

(a) the period within which and manner in which appeals under this section are to be brought,
(b) the advertising of such an appeal, and
(c) the manner in which such appeals are to be considered.

(7) Where an appeal has been brought under this section against a notice under section 36(3) or 37(1), the access authority may not exercise their powers under section 36(5) or section 37(5) (as the case may be) pending the determination or withdrawal of the appeal.

Explanatory text — see **15.3.5**.

39   Order to remove obstruction

(1) Where at any time two or more access notices relating to a means of access have been given to any person within the preceding thirty-six months, a magistrates' court may, on the application of the access authority, order that person –

  (a) within such time as may be specified in the order, to take such steps as may be so specified to remove any obstruction of that means of access, and
  (b) not to obstruct that means of access at any time when the right conferred by section 2(1) is exercisable.

(2) If a person ('the person in default') fails to comply with an order under this section –

  (a) he is liable on summary conviction to a fine not exceeding level 3 on the standard scale, and
  (b) the access authority may remove any obstruction of the means of access and recover from the person in default the costs reasonably incurred by them in doing so.

(3) In this section 'access notice' means a notice under section 36(3) or 37(1) in respect of which the period specified in the notice has expired, other than a notice in respect of which an appeal is pending or which has been cancelled on appeal.

Explanatory text — see **15.4**.

CHAPTER IV

GENERAL

40   Powers of entry for purposes of Part I

(1) A person who is authorised by the appropriate countryside body to do so may enter any land –

  (a) for the purpose of surveying it in connection with the preparation of any map under this Part or the review of any map issued under this Part,
  (b) for the purpose of determining whether any power conferred on the appropriate countryside body by Chapter II should be exercised in relation to the land,
  (c) for the purpose of ascertaining whether members of the public are being permitted to exercise the right conferred by section 2(1),
  (d) in connection with an appeal under any provision of this Part, or
  (e) for the purpose of determining whether to apply to the Secretary of State or the National Assembly for Wales under section 58.

(2) A person who is authorised by a local highway authority to do so may enter any land –

  (a) for the purpose of determining whether the local highway authority should enter into an agreement under section 35, give a notice under section 36(1) or (3) or section 37(1) or carry out works under section 36(1) or (5), section 37(5) or section 39(2)(b),

(b) for the purpose of ascertaining whether an offence under section 14 or 39 has been or is being committed, or
(c) for the purposes of erecting or maintaining notices under section 19(1).

(3) A person who is authorised by a National Park authority to do so may enter any land –

(a) for the purpose of enabling the authority to determine whether to exercise any power under Chapter II of this Act in relation to the land,
(b) for the purpose of determining whether members of the public are being permitted to exercise the right conferred by section 2(1),
(c) in connection with an appeal under any provision of this Part,
(d) for the purpose of determining whether the authority should enter into an agreement under section 35, give a notice under section 36(1) or (3) or section 37(1) or carry out works under section 36(1) or (5), section 37(5) or section 39(2)(b),
(e) for the purpose of ascertaining whether an offence under section 14 or 39 has been or is being committed, or
(f) for the purposes of erecting or maintaining notices under section 19(1).

(4) A person who is authorised by the Forestry Commissioners to do so may enter any land –

(a) for the purpose of determining whether any power conferred on the Forestry Commissioners by Chapter II should be exercised in relation to the land, or
(b) in connection with an appeal under any provision of this Part.

(5) A person acting in the exercise of a power conferred by this section may –

(a) use a vehicle to enter the land;
(b) take a constable with him if he reasonably believes he is likely to be obstructed;
(c) take with him equipment and materials needed for the purpose for which he is exercising the power of entry;
(d) take samples of the land and of anything on it.

(6) If in the exercise of a power conferred by this section a person enters land which is unoccupied or from which the occupier is temporarily absent, he must on his departure leave it as effectively secured against unauthorised entry as he found it.

(7) A person authorised under this section to enter upon any land –

(a) shall, if so required, produce evidence of his authority before entering, and
(b) shall produce such evidence if required to do so at any time while he remains on the land.

(8) A person shall not under this section demand admission as of right to any occupied land, other than access land, unless –

(a) at least twenty-four hours' notice of the intended entry has been given to the occupier, or
(b) it is not reasonably practicable to give such notice, or
(c) the entry is for the purpose specified in subsection (2)(b) and (3)(e).

(9) The rights conferred by this section are not exercisable in relation to a dwelling.

(10) A person who intentionally obstructs a person acting in the exercise of his powers under this section is guilty of an offence and liable on summary conviction to a fine not exceeding level 2 on the standard scale.

Explanatory text — see **16.7**.

41   Compensation relating to powers under s 40

(1) It is the duty of a body by which an authorisation may be given under section 40 to compensate any person who has sustained damage as a result of –

(a) the exercise of a power conferred by that section by a person authorised by that body to do so, or

(b) the failure of a person so authorised to perform the duty imposed on him by subsection (6) of that section,

except where the damage is attributable to the fault of the person who sustained it.

(2) Any dispute as to a person's entitlement to compensation under this section or as to its amount shall be referred to an arbitrator to be appointed, in default of agreement –

(a) as respects entry on land in England, by the Secretary of State, and

(b) as respects entry on land in Wales, by the National Assembly for Wales.

Explanatory text — see **16.7**.

42   References to public places in existing enactments

(1) This section applies to any enactment which –

(a) is contained in an Act passed before or in the same Session as this Act, and

(b) relates to things done, or omitted to be done, in public places or places to which the public have access.

(2) Regulations may provide that, in determining for the purposes of any specified enactment to which this section applies whether a place is a public place or a place to which the public have access, the right conferred by section 2(1), or access by virtue of that right, is to be disregarded, either generally or in prescribed cases.

Explanatory text — see **11.4.2(8)**.

43   Crown application of Part I

(1) This Part binds the Crown.

(2) No contravention by the Crown of any provision of this Part shall make the Crown criminally liable; but the High Court may declare unlawful any act or omission of the Crown which constitutes such a contravention.

(3) The provisions of this Part apply to persons in the public service of the Crown as they apply to other persons.

Explanatory text — see **11.4.2(9)**.

44 Orders and regulations under Part I

(1) Any power to make an order or regulations which is conferred by this Part on the Secretary of State or the National Assembly for Wales is exercisable by statutory instrument.

(2) Any power to make an order or regulations which is conferred by this Part on the Secretary of State or the National Assembly for Wales includes power –

(a) to make different provision for different cases, and
(b) to make such incidental, supplementary, consequential or transitional provision as the person making the order or regulations considers necessary or expedient.

(3) No order under section 3 or regulations under paragraph 3 of Schedule 2 shall be made by the Secretary of State unless a draft has been laid before, and approved by a resolution of, each House of Parliament.

(4) Any statutory instrument containing regulations made by the Secretary of State under any other provision of this Part shall be subject to annulment in pursuance of a resolution of either House of Parliament.

Explanatory text — see **11.4.2(10)**, **12.2.5**, **13.2.2**.

45 Interpretation of Part I

(1) In this Part, unless a contrary intention appears –

'access authority' has the meaning given by section 1(2);

'access land' has the meaning given by section 1(1);

'the appropriate countryside body' has the meaning given by section 1(2);

'excepted land' has the meaning given by section 1(2);

'Inner London' means the area comprising the inner London boroughs, the City of London, the Inner Temple and the Middle Temple;

'interest', in relation to land, includes any estate in land and any right over land, whether the right is exercisable by virtue of the ownership of an estate or interest in land or by virtue of a licence or agreement, and in particular includes rights of common and sporting rights, and references to a person interested in land shall be construed accordingly;

'livestock' means cattle, sheep, goats, swine, horses or poultry, and for the purposes of this definition 'cattle' means bulls, cows, oxen, heifers or calves, 'horses' include asses and mules, and 'poultry' means domestic fowls, turkeys, geese or ducks;

'local highway authority' has the same meaning as in the Highways Act 1980;

'local or private Act' includes an Act confirming a provisional order;

'mountain' has the meaning given by section 1(2);

'open country' has the meaning given by section 1(2);

'owner', in relation to any land, means, subject to subsection (2), any person, other than a mortgagee not in possession, who, whether in his own right or as trustee for another person, is entitled to receive the rack rent of the land, or, where the land is not let at a rack rent, would be so entitled if it were so let;

'prescribed' means prescribed by regulations;

'registered common land' has the meaning given by section 1(3);

'regulations' means regulations made by the Secretary of State (as respects England) or by the National Assembly for Wales (as respects Wales);

'rights of common' has the same meaning as in the Commons Registration Act 1965;

'telecommunications code' and 'telecommunications code system' have the same meaning as in Schedule 4 to the Telecommunications Act 1984.

(2) In relation to any land which is subject to a farm business tenancy within the meaning of the Agricultural Tenancies Act 1995 or a tenancy to which the Agricultural Holdings Act 1986 applies, the definition of 'owner' in subsection (1) does not apply where it is excluded by section 2(5) or 21(4) or by paragraph 7(4) of Schedule 2.

(3) For the purposes of this Part, the Broads are to be treated as a National Park and the Broads Authority as a National Park authority.

(4) In subsection (3) 'the Broads' has the same meaning as in the Norfolk and Suffolk Broads Act 1988.

Explanatory text — see **11.4.2(11)**, **12.7**.

46　Repeal of previous legislation, and amendments relating to Part I

(1) The following provisions (which are superseded by the provisions of this Part) shall cease to have effect –

   (a)　in section 193 of the Law of Property Act 1925, subsection (2) (power by deed to declare land subject to that section), and
   (b)　sections 61 to 63 of the National Parks and Access to the Countryside Act 1949 (which relate to reviews of access requirements and the preparation of maps).

(2) No access agreement or access order under Part V of the National Parks and Access to the Countryside Act 1949 (access to open country) may be made after the commencement of this section in relation to land which is open country or registered common land for the purposes of this Part.

(3) Schedule 4 (which contains minor and consequential amendments relating to access to the countryside) has effect.

Explanatory text — see **11.2.2**, **11.3.2**.

PART II

PUBLIC RIGHTS OF WAY AND ROAD TRAFFIC

Public rights of way and definitive maps and statements

47   Redesignation of roads used as public paths

(1) In the Wildlife and Countryside Act 1981 (in this Act referred to as 'the 1981 Act'), section 54 (duty to reclassify roads used as public paths) shall cease to have effect.

(2) Every way which, immediately before the commencement of this section, is shown in any definitive map and statement as a road used as a public path shall be treated instead as shown as a restricted byway; and the expression 'road used as a public path' shall not be used in any definitive map and statement to describe any way.

Explanatory text — see **5.3.4**.

48   Restricted byway rights

(1) Subject to subsections (2) and (3), the public shall have restricted byway rights over any way which, immediately before the commencement of section 47, is shown in a definitive map and statement as a road used as a public path.

(2) Subsection (1) has effect subject to the operation of any enactment or instrument (whether coming into operation before or after the commencement of section 47), and to the effect of any event otherwise within section 53(3)(a) of the 1981 Act, whereby a highway –

(a) is authorised to be stopped up, diverted, widened or extended, or
(b) becomes a public path;

and subsection (1) applies accordingly to any way as so diverted, widened or extended.

(3) Subsection (1) does not apply to any way, or part of a way, over which immediately before the commencement of section 47 there was no public right of way.

(4) In this Part –

'restricted byway rights' means –

(a) a right of way on foot,
(b) a right of way on horseback or leading a horse, and
(c) a right of way for vehicles other than mechanically propelled vehicles; and

'restricted byway' means a highway over which the public have restricted byway rights, with or without a right to drive animals of any description along the highway, but no other rights of way.

(5) A highway at the side of a river, canal or other inland navigation is not excluded from the definition of 'restricted byway' in subsection (4) merely because the public

have a right to use the highway for purposes of navigation, if the highway would fall within that definition if the public had no such right over it.

(6) Subsection (1) is without prejudice to any question whether the public have over any way, in addition to restricted byway rights, a right of way for mechanically propelled vehicles or any other right.

(7) In subsections (4) and (6) 'mechanically propelled vehicle' does not include a vehicle falling within paragraph (c) of section 189(1) of the Road Traffic Act 1988.

(8) Every surveying authority shall take such steps as they consider expedient for bringing to the attention of the public the effect of section 47(2) and this section.

(9) The powers conferred by section 103(5) must be so exercised as to secure that nothing in section 47 or this section affects the operation of section 53 or 54 of, or Schedule 14 or 15 to, the 1981 Act in relation to –

  (a) a relevant order made before the commencement of section 47, or

  (b) an application made before that commencement for a relevant order.

(10) In subsection (9) 'relevant order' means an order which relates to a way shown in a definitive map and statement as a road used as a public path and which –

  (a) is made under section 53 of the 1981 Act and contains modifications relating to that way by virtue of subsection (3)(c)(ii) of that section, or
  (b) is made under section 54 of the 1981 Act.

(11) Where –

  (a) by virtue of an order under subsection (3) of section 103 ('the commencement order') containing such provision as is mentioned in subsection (5) of that section, an order under Part III of the 1981 Act ('the Part III order') takes effect, after the commencement of section 47, in relation to any way which, immediately before that commencement, was shown in a definitive map and statement as a road used as a public path,
  (b) the commencement order does not prevent subsection (1) from having effect on that commencement in relation to that way, and
  (c) if the Part III order had taken effect before that commencement, that way would not have fallen within subsection (1),

all rights over that way which exist only by virtue of subsection (1) shall be extinguished when the Part III order takes effect.

Explanatory text — see **5.3.4**, **5.4**.

---

49   Provisions supplementary to ss 47 and 48

(1) Every way over which the public have restricted byway rights by virtue of subsection (1) of section 48 (whether or not they also have a right of way for mechanically propelled vehicles or any other right) shall, as from the commencement of that section, be a highway maintainable at the public expense.

(2) As from the commencement of that section, any liability, under a special enactment (within the meaning of the Highways Act 1980) or by reason of tenure, enclosure or prescription, to maintain, otherwise than as a highway maintainable at the public expense, a restricted byway to which subsection (1) applies is extinguished.

(3) Every way which, in pursuance of –

(a) paragraph 9 of Part III of Schedule 3 to the Countryside Act 1968, or
(b) any order made under section 54(1) of the 1981 Act before the coming into force of section 47,

is shown in any definitive map and statement as a byway open to all traffic, a bridleway or a footpath, shall continue to be maintainable at the public expense.

(4) Nothing in subsections (1) and (3) or in section 48(1) obliges a highway authority to provide on any way a metalled carriageway or a carriageway which is by any other means provided with a surface suitable for cycles or other vehicles.

(5) Nothing in section 48, or in section 53 of the 1981 Act, limits the operation of orders under the Road Traffic Regulation Act 1984 or the operation of any byelaws.

(6) Section 67 of the 1981 Act (application to the Crown) has effect as if this section and sections 47, 48 and 50 were contained in Part III of that Act.

Explanatory text — see **8.3.5**.

---

50 Private rights over restricted byways

(1) Restricted byway rights over any way by virtue of subsection (1) of section 48 are subject to any condition or limitation to which public rights of way over that way were subject immediately before the commencement of that section.

(2) Any owner or lessee of premises adjoining or adjacent to a relevant highway shall, so far as is necessary for the reasonable enjoyment and occupation of the premises, have a right of way for vehicular and all other kinds of traffic over the relevant highway.

(3) In subsection (2), in its application to the owner of any premises, 'relevant highway' means so much of any highway maintainable at the public expense by virtue of section 49(1) as was, immediately before it became so maintainable, owned by the person who then owned the premises.

(4) In subsection (2), in its application to the lessee of any premises, 'relevant highway' means so much of any highway maintainable at the public expense by virtue of section 49(1) as was, immediately before it became so maintainable, included in the lease on which the premises are held.

(5) In this section –

'lease' and 'lessee' have the same meaning as in the 1980 Act;

'owner', in relation to any premises, means a person, other than a mortgagee not in possession, who is for the time being entitled to dispose of the fee simple of the premises, whether in possession or in reversion, and 'owned' shall be construed accordingly; and

'premises' has the same meaning as in the 1980 Act.

Explanatory text — see **5.4**.

---

51 Amendments relating to definitive maps and statements and restricted byways

Schedule 5 to this Act (which contains amendments relating to definitive maps and statements and restricted byways) has effect.

Explanatory text — see **5.2.5**, **5.5**, **5.6**, **5.7.4**.

---

52 Restricted byways: power to amend existing legislation

(1) The Secretary of State may by regulations –

   (a) provide for any relevant provision which relates –
      (i) to highways or highways of a particular description,
      (ii) to things done on or in connection with highways or highways of a particular description, or
      (iii) to the creation, stopping up or diversion of highways or highways of a particular description,

     not to apply, or to apply with or without modification, in relation to restricted byways or to ways shown in a definitive map and statement as restricted byways, and
   (b) make in any relevant provision such amendments, repeals or revocations as appear to him appropriate in consequence of the coming into force of sections 47 to 50 or provision made by virtue of paragraph (a) or subsection (6)(a).

(2) In this section –

'relevant provision' means a provision contained –

   (a) in an Act passed before or in the same Session as this Act, or
   (b) in any subordinate legislation made before the passing of this Act;

'relevant Welsh provision' means a provision contained –

   (a) in a local or private Act passed before or in the same Session as this Act and relating only to areas in Wales, or
   (b) in any subordinate legislation which was made before the passing of this Act and which the National Assembly for Wales has power to amend or revoke as respects Wales.

(3) In exercising the power to make regulations under subsection (1), the Secretary of State –

   (a) may not make provision which has effect in relation to Wales unless he has consulted the National Assembly for Wales, and
   (b) may not without the consent of the National Assembly for Wales make any provision which (otherwise than merely by virtue of the amendment or repeal of a provision contained in an Act) amends or revokes subordinate legislation made by the Assembly.

(4) The National Assembly for Wales may submit to the Secretary of State proposals for the exercise by the Secretary of State of the power conferred by subsection (1).

(5) The powers conferred by subsection (1) may be exercised in relation to a relevant provision even though the provision is amended or inserted by this Act.

(6) As respects Wales, the National Assembly for Wales may by regulations –

   (a) provide for any relevant Welsh provision which relates –
     (i) to highways or highways of a particular description,
     (ii) to things done on or in connection with highways or highways of a particular description, or
     (iii) to the creation, stopping up or diversion of highways or highways of a particular description,

   not to apply, or to apply with or without modification, in relation to restricted byways or to ways shown in a definitive map and statement as restricted byways, and
   (b) make in any relevant Welsh provision such amendments, repeals or revocations as appear to the Assembly appropriate in consequence of the coming into force of sections 47 to 50 or provision made by virtue of subsection (1)(a) or paragraph (a).

(7) Regulations under this section shall be made by statutory instrument, but no such regulations shall be made by the Secretary of State unless a draft of the instrument containing them has been laid before, and approved by a resolution of, each House of Parliament.

(8) Where the Secretary of State lays before Parliament the draft of an instrument containing regulations under subsection (1) in respect of which consultation with the National Assembly for Wales is required by subsection (3)(a), he shall also lay before each House of Parliament a document giving details of the consultation and setting out any representations received from the Assembly.

Explanatory text — see **5.4**.

---

53   Extinguishment of unrecorded rights of way

(1) Subsection (2) applies to a highway if –

   (a) it was on 1st January 1949 a footpath or a bridleway, is on the cut-off date (in either case) a footpath or a bridleway, and between those dates has not been a highway of any other description,
   (b) it is not on the cut-off date shown in a definitive map and statement as a highway of any description, and
   (c) it is not on the cut-off date an excepted highway, as defined by section 54(1).

(2) All public rights of way over a highway to which this subsection applies shall be extinguished immediately after the cut-off date.

(3) Where a public right of way created before 1949 –

   (a) falls within subsection (4) on the cut-off date, and
   (b) is not on that date an excepted right of way, as defined by section 54(5),

that right of way shall be extinguished immediately after the cut-off date.

(4) A public right of way falls within this subsection if it is –

(a) a public right of way on horseback, leading a horse or for vehicles over a bridleway, restricted byway or byway open to all traffic which is shown in a definitive map and statement as a footpath;

(b) a right for the public to drive animals of any description along a bridleway, restricted byway or byway open to all traffic which is shown in a definitive map and statement as a footpath;

(c) a public right of way for vehicles over a restricted byway or byway open to all traffic which is shown in a definitive map and statement as a bridleway; or

(d) a public right of way for mechanically propelled vehicles over a byway open to all traffic which is shown in a definitive map and statement as a restricted byway.

(5) Where by virtue of subsection (3) a highway ceases to be a bridleway, the right of way created over it by section 30 of the Countryside Act 1968 (riding of pedal cycles on bridleways) is also extinguished.

(6) In determining –

(a) for the purposes of subsection (1) whether any part of a highway was on 1st January 1949 a footpath or bridleway, or

(b) for the purposes of subsection (3) whether a public right of way over any part of a highway was created before 1st January 1949,

any diversion, widening or extension of the highway on or after that date (and not later than the cut-off date) is to be treated as having occurred before 1st January 1949.

(7) Where a way shown on the cut-off date in a definitive map and statement has at any time been diverted, widened or extended, it is to be treated for the purposes of subsections (1) to (5) as shown as so diverted, widened or extended, whether or not it is so shown.

(8) In this section –

'cut-off date' has the meaning given in section 56, and

'mechanically propelled vehicle' does not include a vehicle falling within paragraph (c) of section 189(1) of the Road Traffic Act 1988.

Explanatory text — see 5.7.

---

54 Excepted highways and rights of way

(1) A footpath or bridleway is an excepted highway for the purposes of section 53(1) if –

(a) it is a footpath or bridleway which satisfies either of the conditions in subsections (2) and (3),

(b) it is, or is part of, a footpath or bridleway any part of which is in an area which, immediately before 1st April 1965, formed part of the administrative county of London,

(c) it is a footpath or bridleway –

(i)   at the side of (whether or not contiguous with) a carriageway constituting or comprised in another highway, or

    (ii) between two carriageways comprised in the same highway (whether or not the footpath or bridleway is contiguous with either carriageway),

  (d) it is a footpath or bridleway of such other description as may be specified in regulations made (as respects England) by the Secretary of State or (as respects Wales) by the National Assembly for Wales, or

  (e) it is a footpath or bridleway so specified.

(2) A footpath or bridleway ('the relevant highway') satisfies the first condition if –

  (a) it became a footpath or bridleway on or after 1st January 1949 by the diversion, widening or extension of a footpath or, as the case may be, of a bridleway by virtue of an event within section 53(3)(a) of the 1981 Act,

  (b) it became a footpath on or after 1st January 1949 by the stopping up of a bridleway,

  (c) it was on 1st January 1949 a footpath and is on the cut-off date a bridleway,

  (d) it is so much of a footpath or bridleway as on or after 1st January 1949 has been stopped up as respects part only of its width, or

  (e) it is so much of a footpath or bridleway as passes over a bridge or through a tunnel,

and it communicates with a retained highway, either directly or by means of one or more footpaths or bridleways each of which forms part of the same highway as the relevant highway and each of which either falls within any of paragraphs (a) to (e) or satisfies the condition in subsection (3).

(3) A footpath or bridleway satisfies the second condition if –

  (a) it extends from a footpath or bridleway ('the relevant highway') which –
    (i)   falls within any of paragraphs (a) to (e) of subsection (2), or
    (ii) is an excepted highway by virtue of subsection (1)(c),
    to, but not beyond, a retained highway, and

  (b) it forms part of the same highway as the relevant highway.

(4) A retained highway for the purposes of subsections (2) and (3) is any highway over which, otherwise than by virtue of subsection (1)(a), section 53(2) does not extinguish rights of way.

(5) A public right of way is an excepted right of way for the purposes of section 53(3) if –

  (a) it subsists over land over which there subsists on the cut-off date any public right of way created on or after 1st January 1949 otherwise than by virtue of section 30 of the Countryside Act 1968 (riding of pedal cycles on bridleways),

  (b) it subsists over the whole or part of a way any part of which is in an area which, immediately before 1st April 1965, formed part of the administrative county of London,

  (c) it is a public right of way of such other description as may be specified in regulations made (as respects England) by the Secretary of State or (as respects Wales) by the National Assembly for Wales, or

  (d) it subsists over land so specified.

(6) Regulations under subsection (1)(d) or (e) or (5)(c) or (d) shall be made by statutory instrument, and a statutory instrument containing such regulations made by the Secretary of State shall be subject to annulment in pursuance of a resolution of either House of Parliament.

Explanatory text — see **5.7.3**, **5.7.4**.

55 Bridleway rights over ways shown as bridleways

(1) Subject to subsections (2) and (3), the public shall, as from the day after the cut-off date, have a right of way on horseback or leading a horse over any way which –

- (a) was immediately before 1st January 1949 either a footpath or a bridleway, and
- (b) is, throughout the period beginning with the commencement of this section and ending with the cut-off date,

a footpath which is shown in a definitive map and statement as a bridleway.

(2) Subsection (1) has effect subject to the operation of any enactment or instrument (whether coming into operation before or after the cut-off date), and to the effect of any event otherwise within section 53(3)(a) of the 1981 Act, whereby a highway is authorised to be stopped up, diverted, widened or extended; and subsection (1) applies accordingly to any way as so diverted, widened or extended.

(3) Subsection (1) does not apply in relation to any way which is, or is part of, a footpath any part of which is in an area which, immediately before 1st April 1965, formed part of the administrative county of London.

(4) Any right of way over a way by virtue of subsection (1) is subject to any condition or limitation to which the public right of way on foot over that way was subject on the cut-off date.

(5) Where –

- (a) by virtue of regulations under section 56(2) an order under Part III of the 1981 Act takes effect after the cut-off date in relation to any footpath which, at the cut-off date was shown in a definitive map and statement as a bridleway,
- (b) the regulations do not prevent subsection (1) from having effect after the cut-off date in relation to that footpath, and
- (c) if the order had taken effect before that date, that footpath would not have fallen within subsection (1),

all rights over that way which exist only by virtue of subsection (1) shall be extinguished when the order takes effect.

(6) In this section 'cut-off date' has the meaning given in section 56.

Explanatory text — see **5.7.5**.

56 Cut-off date for extinguishment etc

(1) The cut-off date for the purposes of sections 53 and 55 is, subject to regulations under subsection (2), 1st January 2026.

(2) The Secretary of State (as respects England) or the National Assembly for Wales (as respects Wales) may make regulations –

- (a) substituting as the cut-off date for the purposes of those sections a date later than the date specified in subsection (1) or for the time being substituted under this paragraph;

(b) containing such transitional provisions or savings as appear to the Secretary of State or the National Assembly for Wales (as the case may be) to be necessary or expedient in connection with the operation of those sections, including in particular their operation in relation to any way as respects which –
  (i) on the cut-off date an application for an order under section 53(2) of the 1981 Act is pending,
  (ii) on that date an order under Part III of that Act has been made but not confirmed, or
  (iii) after that date such an order or any provision of such an order is to any extent quashed.

(3) Regulations under subsection (2)(a) –

  (a) may specify different dates for different areas; but
  (b) may not specify a date later than 1st January 2031, except as respects an area within subsection (4).

(4) An area is within this subsection if it is in –

  (a) the Isles of Scilly, or
  (b) an area which, at any time before the repeal by section 73 of the 1981 Act of sections 27 to 34 of the National Parks and Access to the Countryside Act 1949 –
    (i) was excluded from the operation of those sections by virtue of any provision of the 1949 Act, or
    (ii) would have been so excluded but for a resolution having effect under section 35(2) of that Act.

(5) Where by virtue of regulations under subsection (2) there are different cut-off dates for areas into which different parts of any highway extend, the cut-off date in relation to that highway is the later or latest of those dates.

(6) Regulations under this section shall be made by statutory instrument, and a statutory instrument containing such regulations made by the Secretary of State shall be subject to annulment in pursuance of a resolution of either House of Parliament.

Explanatory text — see **5.7.6**.

Creation, stopping up and diversion of highways

57 Creation, stopping up and diversion of highways

The Highways Act 1980 (in this Act referred to as 'the 1980 Act') has effect subject to the amendments in Part I of Schedule 6 (which relate to the creation, stopping up and diversion of highways); and Part II of that Schedule (which contains consequential amendments of other Acts) has effect.

Explanatory text — see Chapters 3 and 4.

---

58 Application for path creation order for purposes of Part I

(1) An application for the making of a public path creation order under section 26(2) of the 1980 Act for the purpose of enabling the public to obtain access to any access land (within the meaning of Part I) or of facilitating such access, may be made –

(a) by the Countryside Agency to the Secretary of State, or

(b) by the Countryside Council for Wales to the National Assembly for Wales.

(2) Before making a request under subsection (1), the body making the request shall have regard to any rights of way improvement plan prepared by any local highway authority whose area includes land over which the proposed footpath or bridleway would be created.

Explanatory text — see **15.2**.

---

59 Effect of Part I on powers to stop up or divert highways

(1) This section applies to any power to stop up or divert a highway of any description or to make or confirm an order authorising the stopping up or diversion of a highway of any description; and in the following provisions of this section –

(a) 'the relevant authority' means the person exercising the power, and

(b) 'the existing highway' means the highway to be stopped up or diverted.

(2) Where the relevant authority is required (expressly or by implication) to consider –

(a) whether the existing highway is unnecessary, or is needed for public use,

(b) whether an alternative highway should be provided, or

(c) whether any public right of way should be reserved,

the relevant authority, in considering that question, is not to regard the fact that any land is access land in respect of which the right conferred by section 2(1) is exercisable as reducing the need for the existing highway, for the provision of an alternative highway or for the reservation of a public right of way.

(3) Where –

(a) the existing highway is situated on, or in the vicinity of, any access land, and

(b) the relevant authority is required (expressly or by implication) to consider the extent (if any) to which the existing highway would, apart from the exercise of the power, be likely to be used by the public,

the relevant authority, in considering that question, is to have regard, in particular, to the extent to which the highway would be likely to be used by the public at any time when the right conferred by section 2(1) is not exercisable in relation to the access land.

(4) In this section 'access land' has the same meaning as in Part I.

Explanatory text — see **4.4.2**, **4.5.1**.

Rights of way improvement plans

60 Rights of way improvement plans

(1) Every local highway authority other than an inner London authority shall, within five years after the commencement of this section, prepare and publish a plan, to be known as a rights of way improvement plan, containing –

(a) the authority's assessment of the matters specified in subsection (2),

(b) a statement of the action they propose to take for the management of local rights of way, and for securing an improved network of local rights of way, with particular regard to the matters dealt with in the assessment, and

(c) such other material as the Secretary of State (as respects England) or the National Assembly for Wales (as respects Wales) may direct.

(2) The matters referred to in subsection (1)(a) are –

(a) the extent to which local rights of way meet the present and likely future needs of the public,

(b) the opportunities provided by local rights of way (and in particular by those within paragraph (a) of the definition in subsection (5)) for exercise and other forms of open-air recreation and the enjoyment of the authority's area,

(c) the accessibility of local rights of way to blind or partially sighted persons and others with mobility problems, and

(d) such other matters relating to local rights of way as the Secretary of State (as respects England) or the National Assembly for Wales (as respects Wales) may direct.

(3) An authority by whom a rights of way improvement plan is published shall, not more than ten years after first publishing it and subsequently at intervals of not more than ten years –

(a) make a new assessment of the matters specified in subsection (2), and

(b) review the plan and decide whether to amend it.

(4) On such a review the authority shall –

(a) if they decide to amend the plan, publish it as amended, and

(b) if they decide to make no amendments to it, publish a report of their decision and of their reasons for it.

(5) In this section –

'cycle track' –

(a) means a way over which the public have the following, but no other, rights of way, that is to say, a right of way on pedal cycles (other than pedal cycles which are motor vehicles within the meaning of the Road Traffic Act 1988) with or without a right of way on foot; but

(b) does not include a way in or by the side of a highway consisting of or comprising a made-up carriageway (within the meaning of the 1980 Act);

'inner London authority' means Transport for London, the council of an inner London borough or the Common Council of the City of London;

'local highway authority' has the same meaning as in the 1980 Act;

'local rights of way' in relation to a local highway authority, means –

(a) the footpaths, cycle tracks, bridleways and restricted byways within the authority's area, and

(b) the ways within the authority's area which are shown in a definitive map and statement as restricted byways or byways open to all traffic.

(6) In subsection (5) the definition of 'local rights of way' has effect until the commencement of section 47 with the substitution for the references to restricted byways and to ways shown in a definitive map and statement as restricted byways of a

reference to ways shown in a definitive map and statement as roads used as public paths.

Explanatory text — see **3.2**.

61   Rights of way improvement plans: supplemental

(1) Before preparing or reviewing a rights of way improvement plan, and in particular in making any assessment under section 60(1)(a) or (3)(a), a local highway authority shall consult –

(a) each local highway authority whose area adjoins their area;
(b) each district council, and each parish or community council, whose area is within their area;
(c) the National Park authority for a National Park any part of which is within their area;
(d) where any part of the Broads is within their area, the Broads Authority;
(e) any local access forum established for their area or any part of it;
(f) the Countryside Agency or the Countryside Council for Wales (as appropriate);
(g) such persons as the Secretary of State (as respects England) or the National Assembly for Wales (as respects Wales) may by regulations prescribe in relation to the local highway authority's area; and
(h) such other persons as the local highway authority may consider appropriate.

(2) In preparing or amending a rights of way improvement plan, a local highway authority shall –

(a) publish a draft of the plan or of the plan as amended,
(b) publish, in two or more local newspapers circulating in their area, notice of how a copy of the draft can be inspected or obtained and how representations on it can be made to them, and
(c) consider any representations made in accordance with the notice.

(3) As regards their rights of way improvement plan, any draft plan on which representations may be made and any report under section 60(4)(b), a local highway authority shall –

(a) keep a copy available for inspection free of charge at all reasonable times at their principal offices, and
(b) supply a copy to any person who requests one, either free of charge or on payment of a reasonable charge determined by the authority.

(4) Local highway authorities shall, in carrying out their functions under section 60 and this section, have regard to such guidance as may from time to time be given to them by the Secretary of State (as respects England) or the National Assembly for Wales (as respects Wales).

(5) A local highway authority may make arrangements with –

(a) any district council whose area is within their area, or
(b) the National Park authority for a National Park any part of which is within their area,

for the functions of the local highway authority under section 60 and this section so far as relating to the area of that council or to the part of the Park within the local highway authority's area, to be discharged jointly by the local highway authority and by that council or National Park authority.

(6) Regulations under subsection (1)(g) shall be made by statutory instrument, and a statutory instrument containing such regulations made by the Secretary of State shall be subject to annulment in pursuance of a resolution of either House of Parliament.

(7) In this section –

'local highway authority' has the same meaning as in the 1980 Act;

'the Broads' has the same meaning as in the Norfolk and Suffolk Broads Act 1988.

Explanatory text — see 3.2.

62   Application of ss 60 and 61 to Inner London

(1) The council of an Inner London borough or the Common Council of the City of London may by resolution adopt sections 60 and 61 as respects their area or any part of it which is specified in the resolution.

(2) On the passing by any authority of a resolution under subsection (1), sections 60 and 61 shall, as respects their area or the part of it specified in the resolution, apply in relation to that authority –

  (a) as they apply in relation to a local highway authority other than an Inner London authority, but
  (b) with the substitution for the reference in subsection (1) of section 60 to the commencement of that section of a reference to the date on which the resolution comes into operation.

Explanatory text — see 3.2.6.

Removal of obstructions from highways

63   Enforcement of duty to prevent obstructions

(1) After section 130 of the 1980 Act there is inserted –

'130A   Notices to enforce duty regarding public paths

(1) Any person who alleges, as respects any highway for which a local highway authority other than an Inner London authority are the highway authority –

  (a) that the highway falls within subsection (2) below, and
  (b) that it is obstructed by an obstruction to which this section applies,

may serve on the highway authority notice requesting them to secure the removal of the obstruction from the highway.

(2) A highway is within this subsection if it is –

  (a) a footpath, bridleway, or restricted byway, or
  (b) a way shown in a definitive map and statement as a restricted byway or a byway open to all traffic.

(3) Subject to subsection (4) below, this section applies to an obstruction of the highway if the obstruction is without lawful authority and either –

- (a) the powers conferred by section 143, 149 or 154 below are exercisable in respect of it, or
- (b) it is of a description prescribed by regulations made by the Secretary of State and the authority have power (otherwise than under any of those sections) to secure its removal.

(4) This section does not apply to an obstruction if –

- (a) it is or forms part of –
  - (i) a building (whether temporary or permanent) or works for the construction of a building, or
  - (ii) any other structure (including a tent, caravan, vehicle or other temporary or movable structure) which is designed, adapted or used for human habitation,
- (b) an order may be made in respect of it under section 56 above, or
- (c) the presence of any person constitutes the obstruction.

(5) A person serving a notice under subsection (1) above must include in the notice the name and address, if known to him, of any person who it appears to him may be for the time being responsible for the obstruction.

(6) A highway authority on whom a notice under subsection (1) above is served shall, within one month from the date of service of the notice, serve –

- (a) on every person whose name and address is, pursuant to subsection (5) above, included in the notice and, so far as reasonably practicable, on every other person who it appears to them may be for the time being responsible for the obstruction, a notice informing that person that a notice under subsection (1) above has been served in relation to the obstruction and stating what, if any, action the authority propose to take, and
- (b) on the person who served the notice under subsection (1) above, a notice containing the name and address of each person on whom notice is served under paragraph (a) above and stating what, if any, action the authority propose to take in relation to the obstruction.

(7) For the purposes of this section the persons for the time being responsible for an obstruction include the owner and any other person who for the time being –

- (a) has possession or control of it, or
- (b) may be required to remove it.

(8) A notice under subsection (1) or (6) above shall be in such form and contain such information as may be prescribed by regulations made by the Secretary of State.

(9) In this section "Inner London authority" means Transport for London, the council of an inner London borough or the Common Council of the City of London.

(10) Subsection (2) above has effect until the commencement of section 47 of the Countryside and Rights of Way Act 2000 with the substitution for the references to a restricted byway and to a way shown in a definitive map and statement as a

restricted byway of a reference to a way shown in a definitive map and statement as a road used as a public path.

130B Orders following notice under section 130A

(1) Where a notice under section 130A(1) above has been served on a highway authority in relation to any obstruction, the person who served it, if not satisfied that the obstruction has been removed, may apply to a magistrates' court in accordance with section 130C below for an order under this section.

(2) An order under this section is an order requiring the highway authority to take, within such reasonable period as may be fixed by the order, such steps as may be specified in the order for securing the removal of the obstruction.

(3) An order under this section shall not take effect –

  (a) until the end of the period of twenty-one days from the day on which the order is made; or
  (b) if an appeal is brought in respect of the order within that period (whether by way of appeal to the Crown Court or by way of case stated for the opinion of the High Court), until the final determination or withdrawal of the appeal.

(4) Subject to subsection (5) below, the court may make an order under this section if it is satisfied –

  (a) that the obstruction is one to which section 130A above applies or, in a case falling within subsection (4)(a)(ii) of that section, is one to which that section would apply but for the obstruction having become used for human habitation since service of the notice relating to it under subsection (1) of that section,
  (b) that the way obstructed is a highway within subsection (2) of that section, and
  (c) that the obstruction significantly interferes with the exercise of public rights of way over that way.

(5) No order shall be made under this section if the highway authority satisfy the court –

  (a) that the fact that the way obstructed is a highway within section 130A(2) above is seriously disputed,
  (b) on any other grounds, that they have no duty under section 130(3) above to secure the removal of the obstruction, or
  (c) that, under arrangements which have been made by the authority, its removal will be secured within a reasonable time, having regard to the number and seriousness of obstructions in respect of which they have such a duty.

(6) A highway authority against whom an order is made under this section shall, as soon as practicable after the making of the order, cause notice of the order and of the right to appeal against it to be displayed in such manner and at such places on the highway concerned as may be prescribed by regulations made by the Secretary of State, and the notice shall be in such form and contain such information as may be so prescribed.

(7) An order under this section may be varied on the application of the highway authority to whom it relates.

130C   Section 130B: procedure

(1) A person proposing to make an application under section 130B above shall before making the application serve notice of his intention to do so on the highway authority concerned.

(2) A notice under subsection (1) above shall be in such form and contain such information as may be prescribed by regulations made by the Secretary of State.

(3) The notice may not be served before the end of two months beginning with the date of service on the highway authority of the notice under section 130A(1) above ("the request notice").

(4) An application in respect of which notice has been served under subsection (1) above may be made at any time –

  (a) after the end of five days beginning with the date of service of that notice, and
  (b) before the end of six months beginning with the date of service on the highway authority of the request notice.

(5) On making the application the applicant must give notice to the court of the names and addresses of which notice was given to the applicant under section 130A(6)(b) above.

(6) On the hearing of the application any person who is, within the meaning of section 130A above, a person for the time being responsible for the obstruction to which the application relates has a right to be heard as respects the matters mentioned in section 130B(4) above.

(7) Notice of the hearing, of the right to be heard under subsection (6) above and of the right to appeal against a decision on the application shall be given by the court to each person whose name and address is notified to the court under subsection (5) above.

130D   Section 130B: costs

Where an application under section 130B above is dismissed by virtue of paragraph (a), (b) or (c) of subsection (5) of that section, the court, in determining whether and if so how to exercise its power under section 64(1) of the 1980 Magistrates' Courts Act 1980 (costs), shall have particular regard to any failure by the highway authority to give the applicant appropriate notice of, and information about, the grounds relied on by the authority under that paragraph.'.

(2) In section 317 of the 1980 Act (appeals to the Crown Court from decisions of magistrates' courts) after subsection (2) there is inserted –

'(3) Any person who, in relation to the decision of a magistrates' court on an application under section 130B above, does not fall within subsection (1) above but –

  (a) is, within the meaning of section 130A above, a person for the time being responsible for the obstruction to which the application related, or
  (b) when the application was heard, was such a person and was, or claimed to be, heard on the application,

may appeal to the Crown Court against the decision on any ground relating to the matters mentioned in section 130B(4) above.'.

Explanatory text — see 9.2.2.

---

64 Power to order offender to remove obstruction

(1) After section 137 of the 1980 Act (penalty for wilful obstruction) there is inserted –

'137ZA Power to order offender to remove obstruction

(1) Where a person is convicted of an offence under section 137 above in respect of the obstruction of a highway and it appears to the court that –

(a) the obstruction is continuing, and
(b) it is in that person's power to remove the cause of the obstruction,

the court may, in addition to or instead of imposing any punishment, order him to take, within such reasonable period as may be fixed by the order, such steps as may be specified in the order for removing the cause of the obstruction.

(2) The time fixed by an order under subsection (1) above may be extended or further extended by order of the court on an application made before the end of the time as originally fixed or as extended under this subsection, as the case may be.

(3) If a person fails without reasonable excuse to comply with an order under subsection (1) above, he is guilty of an offence and liable to a fine not exceeding level 5 on the standard scale; and if the offence is continued after conviction he is guilty of a further offence and liable to a fine not exceeding one-twentieth of that level for each day on which the offence is so continued.

(4) Where, after a person is convicted of an offence under subsection (3) above, the highway authority for the highway concerned exercise any power to remove the cause of the obstruction, they may recover from that person the amount of any expenses reasonably incurred by them in, or in connection with, doing so.

(5) A person against whom an order is made under subsection (1) above is not liable under section 137 above in respect of the obstruction concerned –

(a) during the period fixed under that subsection or any extension under subsection (2) above, or
(b) during any period fixed under section 311(1) below by a court before whom he is convicted of an offence under subsection (3) above in respect of the order.'.

(2) Subsection (1) does not have effect in relation to any offence under section 137 of the 1980 Act committed before the commencement of this section.

Explanatory text — see 9.2.3.

---

65 Overhanging vegetation obstructing horse-riders

In section 154 of the 1980 Act (cutting or felling etc trees etc that overhang or are a danger to roads or footpaths) in subsection (1) after 'public lamp,' there is inserted 'or overhangs a highway so as to endanger or obstruct the passage of horse-riders,'.

Explanatory text — see **9.2.5**.

Miscellaneous

66   Making of traffic regulation orders for purposes of conserving natural beauty, etc

(1) In section 22 of the Road Traffic Regulation Act 1984 (traffic regulation for special areas in the countryside), in subsection (1)(a) –

- (a) the words '(other than Greater London)' are omitted,
- (b) at the end of paragraph (vi), the word 'or' is omitted, and
- (c) before the word 'and' at the end of paragraph (vii) there is inserted –
  'or
  (viii) a site of special scientific interest (within the meaning of the Wildlife and Countryside Act 1981);'.

(2) In subsection (2) of that section, for 'the paragraphs of subsection (1) of that section' there is substituted 'paragraphs (a) to (g) of subsection (1) of that section and referred to in section 6(1)(b) of this Act'.

(3) After subsection (4) of that section there is inserted –

'(5) In subsection (2) above the reference to conserving the natural beauty of an area shall be construed as including a reference to conserving its flora, fauna and geological and physiographical features.'.

(4) After that section there is inserted –

'22A   Traffic regulation on certain roads for purpose of conserving natural beauty

(1) This section applies to roads other than –

- (a) roads to which section 22 of this Act applies,
- (b) special roads, or
- (c) any road which is a trunk road, a classified road, a GLA road, a cycle track, a bridleway or a footpath, as those expressions are defined by section 329 of the Highways Act 1980.

(2) This Act shall have effect as respects roads to which this section applies as if, in relation to the making of provision with respect to vehicular traffic, the list of purposes for which a traffic regulation order under section 1 of this Act may be made, as set out in paragraphs (a) to (g) of subsection (1) of that section and referred to in section 6(1)(b) of this Act, included the purpose of conserving or enhancing the natural beauty of the area.

(3) In subsection (2) above the reference to conserving the natural beauty of an area shall be construed as including a reference to conserving its flora, fauna and geological and physiographical features.'.

Explanatory text — see **10.5.1**, **10.5.5**, **10.16.3**.

67 Prohibition on driving mechanically propelled vehicles elsewhere than on roads

Schedule 7 (which makes amendments relating to the driving of mechanically propelled vehicles elsewhere than on roads) has effect.

Explanatory text — see **9.8.2**.

68 Vehicular access across common land etc

(1) This section applies to a way which the owner or occupier (from time to time) of any premises has used as a means of access for vehicles to the premises, if that use of the way –

(a) was an offence under an enactment applying to the land crossed by the way, but
(b) would otherwise have been sufficient to create on or after the prescribed date, and to keep in existence, an easement giving a right of way for vehicles.

(2) Regulations may provide, as respects a way to which this section applies, for the creation in accordance with the regulations, on the application of the owner of the premises concerned and on compliance by him with prescribed requirements, of an easement subsisting at law for the benefit of the premises and giving a right of way for vehicles over that way.

(3) An easement created in accordance with the regulations is subject to any enactment or rule of law which would apply to such an easement granted by the owner of the land.

(4) The regulations may in particular –

(a) require that, where an application is made after the relevant use of the way has ceased, it is to be made within a specified time,
(b) specify grounds on which objections may be made and the procedure to apply to the making of objections,
(c) require any matter to be referred to and determined by the Lands Tribunal, and make provision as to procedure and costs,
(d) make provision as to the payment of any amount by the owner of the premises concerned to any person or into court and as to the time when any payment is to be made,
(e) provide for the determination of any such amount,
(f) make provision as to the date on which any easement is created,
(g) specify any limitation to which the easement is subject,
(h) provide for the easement to include any specified right incidental to the right of way,
(i) make different provision for different circumstances.

(5) In this section –

'enactment' includes an enactment in a local or private Act and a byelaw, regulation or other provision having effect under an enactment;

'owner', in relation to any premises, means –

(a) a person, other than a mortgagee not in possession, who is for the time being entitled to dispose of the fee simple of the premises, whether in possession or in reversion, or

(b) a tenant under a long lease, within the meaning of the Landlord and Tenant Act 1987;

'prescribed' means prescribed by regulations;

'regulations' means regulations made, as respects England, by the Secretary of State and, as respects Wales, by the National Assembly for Wales.

(6) Regulations under this section shall be made by statutory instrument, and no such regulations shall be made by the Secretary of State unless a draft has been laid before, and approved by a resolution of, each House of Parliament.

Explanatory text — see 9.9.

---

69   Erection or improvement of stiles, etc

(1) In section 147 of the 1980 Act (power to authorise erection of stiles etc on footpath or bridleway) after subsection (2) there is inserted –

'(2A) In exercising their powers under subsection (2) above a competent authority shall have regard to the needs of persons with mobility problems.

(2B) The Secretary of State may issue guidance to competent authorities as to matters to be taken into account for the purposes of subsection (2) above; and in exercising their powers under subsection (2) above competent authorities shall have regard to any such guidance issued to them.'

(2) In subsection (5) of that section, at the end there is inserted 'or for the breeding or keeping of horses.'

(3) After that section there is inserted –

'147ZA   Agreements relating to improvements for benefit of persons with mobility problems

(1) With respect to any relevant structure, a competent authority may enter into an agreement with the owner, lessee or occupier of the land on which the structure is situated which provides –

(a) for the carrying out by the owner, lessee or occupier of any qualifying works and the payment by the competent authority of the whole or any part of the costs incurred by him in carrying out those works, or

(b) for the carrying out by the competent authority of any qualifying works at their own expense or subject to the payment by the owner, lessee or occupier of the whole or any part of the costs incurred in carrying out those works.

(2) In this section –

(a) "competent authority" has the same meaning as in section 147 above,

(b) "relevant structure" means a stile, gate or other structure which –

(i) is authorised by a condition or limitation subject to which the public right of way over the footpath or bridleway was created, or

(ii) is authorised under section 147 above, but does not include a structure to which an agreement falling within section 146(5)(b) above relates, and

(c) "qualifying works", in relation to a relevant structure, means works for replacing or improving the structure which will result in a structure that is safer or more convenient for persons with mobility problems.

(3) An agreement under this section may include such conditions as the competent authority think fit.

(4) Those conditions may in particular include conditions expressed to have enduring effect –

(a) for the maintenance of the structure as replaced or improved, and

(b) for enabling the public right of way to be exercised without undue inconvenience to the public.

(5) Where an agreement under this section has been entered into in relation to any structure –

(a) the public right of way is to be deemed to be subject to a condition that the structure as replaced or improved may be erected and maintained in accordance with the agreement so long as any conditions included by virtue of subsection (4) above are complied with,

(b) in a case falling within subsection (2)(b)(i) above, as from the effective date the previous condition or limitation relating to the relevant structure shall cease to have effect, and

(c) in a case falling within subsection (2)(b)(ii) above, as from the effective date the previous authorisation under section 147 above shall cease to have effect in relation to the relevant structure.

(6) In subsection (5) above "the effective date" means –

(a) the first anniversary of the day on which the agreement was entered into, or

(b) such earlier date as may be specified for the purposes of this subsection in the agreement.

(7) For the purposes of section 143 above, any stile, gate or other structure replaced or improved in pursuance of an agreement under this section is to be deemed to be erected under this section only if any conditions included by virtue of subsection (4) above are complied with.

(8) A competent authority may not enter into an agreement under this section except with the consent of every owner, lessee or occupier of the land on which the relevant structure is situated who is not a party to the agreement.

(9) The Secretary of State may issue guidance to competent authorities as to matters to be taken into account for the purposes of this section; and in exercising their powers under this section competent authorities shall have regard to any such guidance issued to them.'.

(4) In section 146 of the 1980 Act (duty to maintain stiles etc on footpaths and bridleways) in subsection (5), before the word 'or' at the end of paragraph (a) there is inserted –

'(aa) if any conditions for the maintenance of the structure imposed by virtue of subsection (4) of section 147ZA below are for the time being in force under that section,'.

(5) In section 344 of the 1980 Act (application to Isles of Scilly) in subsection (2)(a) after '147,' there is inserted '147ZA,'.

Explanatory text — see 9.2.4.

---

70   Minor amendments to Highways Act 1980

(1) In section 66(3) of the 1980 Act (works for safeguarding persons using footpaths) –

(a) after 'footpath' there is inserted 'or bridleway', and
(b) after 'barriers,' there is inserted 'posts,'.

(2) In section 134 of that Act, subsection (5) (which limits the persons who may bring proceedings for failure to restore a public path disturbed by ploughing etc) is omitted.

(3) In section 300 of that Act (right of local authorities to use vehicles and appliances on footways and bridleways), in subsection (1) after 'verges,' there is inserted 'for preventing or removing obstructions to them or otherwise preventing or abating nuisances or other interferences with them,'.

(4) In section 21(2)(b) of the Road Traffic Act 1988 (defence to charge of driving or parking on cycle track for highway authority vehicles), after 'verges' there is inserted ', or the preventing or removing of obstructions to the cycle track or the preventing or abating in any other way of nuisances or other interferences with the cycle track,'.

Explanatory text — see 2.2.4, 8.8.2, 9.3.6, 10.3.

---

71   Reports on functions relating to rights of way

(1) The Secretary of State (as respects England) or the National Assembly for Wales (as respects Wales) may make regulations requiring local highway authorities of a description specified in the regulations to publish reports on the performance of any of their functions so far as relating to local rights of way (whether or not those functions are conferred on them as highway authorities).

(2) Subsection (1) is without prejudice to section 230 of the Local Government Act 1972 (reports and returns).

(3) Regulations under subsection (1) may prescribe the information to be given in such reports and how and when reports are to be published.

(4) Regulations under subsection (1) shall be made by statutory instrument, and a statutory instrument containing such regulations made by the Secretary of State shall be subject to annulment in pursuance of a resolution of either House of Parliament.

(5) In this section –

'local highway authority' has the same meaning as in the 1980 Act, except that it does not include Transport for London; and

'local rights of way' has the same meaning as in section 60.

Explanatory text — see **2.2.5**.

---

72 Interpretation of Part II

(1) In this Part, unless a contrary intention appears –

  (a) 'restricted byway' and 'restricted byway rights' have the meaning given by section 48(4);
  (b) expressions which are defined for the purposes of Part III of the 1981 Act by section 66(1) of that Act have the same meaning as in that Part.

(2) In this Part any reference to a highway includes a reference to part of a highway.

Explanatory text — see **5.4**.

. . .

PART V

MISCELLANEOUS AND SUPPLEMENTARY

Local access forums

94 Local access forums

(1) The appointing authority for any area shall in accordance with regulations establish for that area, or for each part of it, an advisory body to be known as a local access forum.

(2) For the purposes of this section –

  (a) the local highway authority is the appointing authority for their area, except any part of it in a National Park, and
  (b) the National Park authority for a National Park is the appointing authority for the National Park.

(3) A local access forum consists of members appointed by the appointing authority in accordance with regulations.

(4) It is the function of a local access forum, as respects the area for which it is established, to advise –

  (a) the appointing authority,
  (b) any body exercising functions under Part I in relation to land in that area,
  (c) if the appointing authority is a National Park authority, the local highway authority for any part of that area, and
  (d) such other bodies as may be prescribed,

as to the improvement of public access to land in that area for the purposes of open-air recreation and the enjoyment of the area, and as to such other matters as may be prescribed.

(5) The bodies mentioned in paragraphs (a) to (d) of subsection (4) shall have regard, in carrying out their functions, to any relevant advice given to them by a local access forum under that subsection or any other provision of this Act.

(6) In carrying out its functions, a local access forum shall have regard to –

    (a) the needs of land management,

    (b) the desirability of conserving the natural beauty of the area for which it is established, including the flora, fauna and geological and physiographical features of the area, and

    (c) guidance given from time to time by the Secretary of State (as respects England) or the National Assembly for Wales (as respects Wales).

(7) Subsection (1) does not apply to the council of a London borough or to any part of their area unless the council so resolve.

(8) The Secretary of State, as respects England, or the National Assembly for Wales, as respects Wales, if satisfied that no local access forum is required for any area or part of any area, may direct that subsection (1) is not to apply in relation to that area or part.

(9) Before giving a direction under subsection (8) as respects an area or part of an area, the Secretary of State or the National Assembly for Wales must consult the appointing authority for the area and the appropriate countryside body.

(10) In this section –

'appropriate countryside body' has the same meaning as in Part I;

'local highway authority' has the same meaning as in the 1980 Act;

'prescribed' means prescribed by regulations;

'regulations' means regulations made, as respects England, by the Secretary of State, and, as respects Wales, by the National Assembly for Wales.

Explanatory text — see **14.1.8**, **16.6.2**.

---

95   Local access forums: supplementary

(1) Regulations under section 94 may in particular include provision –

    (a) as to the appointment as members of a local access forum of persons appearing to the appointing authority to be representative of persons of any specified description or of any specified body;

    (b) as to the establishment by appointing authorities of joint local access forums.

(2) The regulations must provide for the appointment of persons appearing to the appointing authority to be representative of –

    (a) users of local rights of way or the right conferred by section 2(1);

    (b) owners and occupiers of access land or land over which local rights of way subsist;

    (c) any other interests especially relevant to the authority's area.

(3) In subsection (2) –

'access land' has the same meaning as in Part I;

'local rights of way' has the meaning given by section 60(5), but as if the references there to a local highway authority and their area were references to an appointing authority and their area.

(4) The Secretary of State and the National Assembly for Wales, in making regulations under section 94 containing such provision as is mentioned in subsection (2), must have regard to the desirability of maintaining a reasonable balance between the number of members of any local access forum appointed in accordance with paragraph (a) and in accordance with paragraph (b) of subsection (2).

(5) Regulations under section 94 may include such supplementary or incidental provision as appears to the Secretary of State or National Assembly for Wales (as the case may be) to be necessary or expedient.

(6) For the purposes of section 94, the Broads are to be treated as a National Park and the Broads Authority as a National Park authority.

(7) In subsection (6) 'the Broads' has the same meaning as in the Norfolk and Suffolk Broads Act 1988.

(8) Regulations under section 94 shall be made by statutory instrument, and a statutory instrument containing such regulations made by the Secretary of State shall be subject to annulment in pursuance of a resolution of either House of Parliament.

Explanatory text — see **16.6.2**.

Management agreements

96 Management agreements

In section 39 of the 1981 Act (management agreements with owners and occupiers of land) –

(a) in subsection (1) the words 'both in the countryside and' are omitted, and
(b) at the end of subsection (5) (authorities which may enter into management agreements) there is inserted –

'(d) as respects any land in England, the Countryside Agency;
(e) as respects any land in Wales, the Countryside Council for Wales;
(f) as respects land in any area of outstanding natural beauty designated under section 82 of the Countryside and Rights of Way Act 2000 for which a conservation board has been established under section 86 of that Act, that board.'

Explanatory text — see **11.3.2**.

Norfolk and Suffolk Broads

97 Duty of public bodies etc. regarding the Broads

In Part IV of the Norfolk and Suffolk Broads Act 1988, before section 18 there is inserted –

'17A General duty of public bodies etc

(1) In exercising or performing any functions in relation to, or so as to affect, land in the Broads, a relevant authority shall have regard to the purposes of –

(a) conserving and enhancing the natural beauty of the Broads;

(b) promoting the enjoyment of the Broads by the public; and

(c) protecting the interests of navigation.

(2) The following are relevant authorities for the purposes of this section –

(a) any Minister of the Crown,

(b) any public body,

(c) any statutory undertaker,

(d) any person holding public office.

(3) In subsection (2) –

"public body" includes –

(a) a county council, district council or parish council;

(b) a joint planning board within the meaning of section 2 of the Town and Country Planning Act 1990;

(c) a joint committee appointed under section 102(1)(b) of the Local Government Act 1972;

"public office" means –

(a) an office under Her Majesty;

(b) an office created or continued in existence by a public general Act; or

(c) an office the remuneraiton in respect of which is paid out of money provided by Parliament.'

Explanatory text — see 10.16.1.

Town and village greens

98   Registration of town and village greens

(1) Section 22 of the Commons Registration Act 1965 (interpretation) is amended as follows.

(2) In subsection (1), in the definition of 'town or village green' for the words after 'lawful sports and pastimes' there is substituted 'or which falls within subsection (1A) of this section.'

(3) After that subsection there is inserted —

'(1A) Land falls within this subsection if it is land on which for not less than twenty years a significant number of the inhabitants of any locality, or of any neighbourhood within a locality, have indulged in lawful sports and pastimes as of right, and either —

(a) continue to do so, or

(b) have ceased to do so for not more than such period as may be prescribed, or determined in accordance with prescribed provisions.

(1B) If regulations made for the purposes of paragraph (b) of subsection (1A) of this section provide for the period mentioned in that paragraph to come to an end unless prescribed steps are taken, the regulations may also require registration authorities to make available in accordance with the regulations, on payment of any prescribed fee, information relating to the taking of any such steps.'

Explanatory text — see **11.2.3**.

Supplementary

99   Wales

(1) In Schedule 1 to the National Assembly for Wales (Transfer of Functions) Order 1999 –

  (a) the reference to the 1980 Act is to be treated as referring to that Act as amended by this Act, and
  (b) the reference to the 1981 Act is to be treated as referring to that Act as amended by this Act.

(2) In that Schedule, at the end of the list of Public General Acts there is inserted –

  '**Countryside and Right of Way Act 2000 (c. 37)** Schedule 11.'

(3) Subsection (1), and the amendment made by subsection (2), do not affect the power to make further Orders varying or omitting the references mentioned in subsection (1) or the provision inserted by subsection (2).

100   Isles of Scilly

(1) Subject to the provisions of any order under this section, the following provisions of this Act do not apply in relation to the Isles of Scilly –

  (a) Part I; and
  (b) sections 58 to 61 and 71.

(2) The Secretary of State may by order made by statutory instrument provide for the application of any of the provisions mentioned in subsection (1) in relation to the Isles of Scilly, subject to such modifications as may be specified in the order.

(3) Part IV applies in relation to the Isles of Scilly subject to such modifications as may be specified in an order made by the Secretary of State by statutory instrument.

(4) Before making an order under subsection (2) or (3), the Secretary of State shall consult the Council of the Isles of Scilly.

(5) In section 344 of the 1980 Act (application to the Isles of Scilly) –

  (a) in subsection (2)(a) for '121' there is substituted '121E, 130A to 130D', and
  (b) before '146' there is inserted '137ZA(4)'.

Explanatory text — see **11.4.3**.

---

101   Expenses

There shall be paid out of money provided by Parliament –

  (a) any increase attributable to this Act in the sums required by the Secretary of State for making grants to the Countryside Agency or English Nature,

   (b) any administrative expenses of a Minister of the Crown which are attributable to this Act,

   (c) any other expenditure of a Minister of the Crown or Government department which is attributable to this Act,

   (d) any increase attributable to this Act in the sums which under any other enactment are payable out of money so provided.

102 Repeals

The enactments mentioned in Schedule 16 are repealed to the extent specified.

103 Commencement

(1) The following provisions of this Act come into force on the day on which this Act is passed –

. . .

this section, and

. . .

(2) The following provisions of this Act come into force at the end of the period of two months beginning with the day on which this Act is passed –

section 1 and Schedule 1,

sections 3 to 11 and Schedule 3,

sections 15 to 17,

section 19,

Chapters II and III of Part I,

sections 40 to 45,

section 52,

sections 58 and 59,

sections 64 to 67 and . . .

(3) The remaining provisions of this Act come into force on such day as the Secretary of State (as respects England) or the National Assembly for Wales (as respects Wales) may by order made by statutory instrument appoint.

(4) Different days may be appointed under subsection (3) for different purposes or different areas.

(5) An order under subsection (3) may contain such transitional provisions or savings (including provisions modifying the effect of any enactment) as appear to the Secretary of State or the National Assembly for Wales (as the case may be) to be necessary or expedient in connection with any provision brought into force by the order.

Explanatory text — see **11.4.2.**

---

104   Interpretation, short title and extent

(1) In this Act –

'the 1980 Act' means the Highways Act 1980;

'the 1981 Act' means the Wildlife and Countryside Act 1981;

'local access forum' means a local access forum established under section 94.

(2) Any reference in this Act, or in any enactment amended by this Act, to the commencement of any provision of this Act is, in relation to any area, a reference to the commencement of that provision in relation to that area.

(3) This Act may be cited as the Countryside and Rights of Way Act 2000.

(4) Subject to the following provisions of this section, this Act extends to England and Wales only.

(5) The following provisions extend also to Scotland –

sections 67 and 76;

in Schedule 7, paragraphs 3 and 5 to 7;

in Schedule 10, paragraph 2.

(6) Paragraph 1 of Schedule 10 extends to Scotland only.

(7) The provisions of Schedule 8 and of so much of Part III of Schedule 16 as relates to the enactments referred to in paragraphs 2 and 3 of Schedule 8 have the same extent as the enactments which they amend or repeal.

Explanatory text — see **11.4.3**, **11.4.4.**

SCHEDULES

SCHEDULE 1

EXCEPTED LAND FOR PURPOSES OF PART I

PART I

EXCEPTED LAND

1. Land on which the soil is being, or has at any time within the previous twelve months been, disturbed by any ploughing or drilling undertaken for the purposes of planting or sowing crops or trees.

2. Land covered by buildings or the curtilage of such land.

3. Land within 20 metres of a dwelling.

4. Land used as a park or garden.

5. Land used for the getting of minerals by surface working (including quarrying).

6. Land used for the purposes of a railway (including a light railway) or tramway.

7. Land used for the purposes of a golf course, racecourse or aerodrome.

8. Land which does not fall within any of the preceding paragraphs and is covered by works used for the purposes of a statutory undertaking or a telecommunications code system, or the curtilage of any such land.

9. Land as respects which development which will result in the land becoming land falling within any of paragraphs 2 to 8 is in the course of being carried out.

10. Land within 20 metres of a building which is used for housing livestock, not being a temporary or moveable structure.

11. Land covered by pens in use for the temporary reception or detention of livestock.

12. Land habitually used for the training of racehorses.

13. Land the use of which is regulated by byelaws under section 14 of the Military Lands Act 1892 or section 2 of the Military Lands Act 1900.

Explanatory text — see **12.3.2**.

PART II

SUPPLEMENTARY PROVISIONS

14. In this Schedule –

'building' includes any structure or erection and any part of a building as so defined, but does not include any fence or wall, or anything which is a means of access as defined by section 34; and for this purpose 'structure' includes any tent, caravan or other temporary or moveable structure;

'development' and 'minerals' have the same meaning as in the Town and Country Planning Act 1990;

'ploughing' and 'drilling' include respectively agricultural or forestry operations similar to ploughing and agricultural or forestry operations similar to drilling;

'statutory undertaker' means –

  (a) a person authorised by any enactment to carry on any railway, light railway, tramway, road transport, water transport, canal, inland navigation, dock, harbour, pier or lighthouse undertaking or any undertaking for the supply of hydraulic power,

  (b) any public gas transporter, within the meaning of Part I of the Gas Act 1986,

  (c) any water or sewerage undertaker,

  (d) any holder of a licence under section 6(1) of the Electricity Act 1989, or

  (e) the Environment Agency, [a universal service provider (within the meaning of the Postal Services Act 2000) in connection with the provision of a universal postal service (within the meaning of that Act)] [, the Civil Aviation Authority or a person who holds a licence under Chapter I of Part I of the Transport Act 2000 (to the extent that the person is carrying out activities authorised by the licence)];

'statutory undertaking' means –

  (a) the undertaking of a statutory undertaker [(which, in the case of a universal service provider (within the meaning of the Postal Services Act 2000), means his undertaking so far as relating to the provision of a universal postal service (within the meaning of that Act) [and, in the case of a person who holds a licence under Chapter I of Part I of the Transport Act 2000, means that person's undertaking as licence holder])], or

  (b) an airport to which Part V of the Airports Act 1986 applies.

15.—(1) Land is not to be treated as excepted land by reason of any development carried out on the land, if the carrying out of the development requires planning permission under Part III of the Town and Country Planning Act 1990 and that permission has not been granted.

(2) Sub-paragraph (1) does not apply where the development is treated by section 191(2) of the Town and Country Planning Act 1990 as being lawful for the purposes of that Act.

16. The land which is excepted land by virtue of paragraph 10 does not include –

  (a) any means of access, as defined by section 34, or

  (b) any way leading to such a means of access,

if the means of access is necessary for giving the public reasonable access to access land.

17. Land which is habitually used for the training of racehorses is not to be treated by virtue of paragraph 11 as excepted land except –

  (a) between dawn and midday on any day, and

  (b) at any other time when it is in use for that purpose.

Amendments — Postal Services Act 2000 (Consequential Modifications No 1) Order 2001, SI 2001/1149; Transport Act 2000 (Consequential Amendments) Order 2001, SI 2001/4050.
Explanatory text — see **12.3.2**.

Section 2   SCHEDULE 2

RESTRICTIONS TO BE OBSERVED BY PERSONS EXERCISING RIGHT OF
ACCESS

General restrictions

1. Section 2(1) does not entitle a person to be on any land if, in or on that land, he –

   (a) drives or rides any vehicle other than an invalid carriage as defined by section
        20(2) of the Chronically Sick and Disabled Persons Act 1970,
   (b) uses a vessel or sailboard on any non-tidal water,
   (c) has with him any animal other than a dog,
   (d) commits any criminal offence,
   (e) lights or tends a fire or does any act which is likely to cause a fire,
   (f) intentionally or recklessly takes, kills, injures or disturbs any animal, bird or
        fish,
   (g) intentionally or recklessly takes, damages or destroys any eggs or nests,
   (h) feeds any livestock,
   (i) bathes in any non-tidal water,
   (j) engages in any operations of or connected with hunting, shooting, fishing,
        trapping, snaring, taking or destroying of animals, birds or fish or has with him
        any engine, instrument or apparatus used for hunting, shooting, fishing,
        trapping, snaring, taking or destroying animals, birds or fish,
   (k) uses or has with him any metal detector,
   (l) intentionally removes, damages or destroys any plant, shrub, tree or root or any
        part of a plant, shrub, tree or root,
   (m) obstructs the flow of any drain or watercourse, or opens, shuts or otherwise
        interferes with any sluice-gate or other apparatus,
   (n) without reasonable excuse, interferes with any fence, barrier or other device
        designed to prevent accidents to people or to enclose livestock,
   (o) neglects to shut any gate or to fasten it where any means of doing so is provided,
        except where it is reasonable to assume that a gate is intended to be left open,
   (p) affixes or writes any advertisement, bill, placard or notice,
   (q) in relation to any lawful activity which persons are engaging in or are about to
        engage in on that or adjoining land, does anything which is intended by him to
        have the effect –
        (i)   of intimidating those persons so as to deter them or any of them from
              engaging in that activity,
        (ii) of obstructing that activity, or
        (iii) of disrupting that activity,
   (r) without reasonable excuse, does anything which (whether or not intended by
        him to have the effect mentioned in paragraph (q)) disturbs, annoys or
        obstructs any persons engaged in a lawful activity on the land,
   (s) engages in any organised games, or in camping, hang-gliding or para-gliding, or
   (t) engages in any activity which is organised or undertaken (whether by him or
        another) for any commercial purpose.

2.—(1) In paragraph 1(k), 'metal detector' means any device designed or adapted for
detecting or locating any metal or mineral in the ground.

(2) For the purposes of paragraph 1(q) and (r), activity on any occasion on the part of a
person or persons on land is 'lawful' if he or they may engage in the activity on the land
on that occasion without committing an offence or trespassing on the land.

3. Regulations may amend paragraphs 1 and 2.

4. During the period beginning with 1st March and ending with 31st July in each year, section 2(1) does not entitle a person to be on any land if he takes, or allows to enter or remain, any dog which is not on a short lead.

5. Whatever the time of year, section 2(1) does not entitle a person to be on any land if he takes, or allows to enter or remain, any dog which is not on a short lead and which is in the vicinity of livestock.

6. In paragraphs 4 and 5, 'short lead' means a lead of fixed length and of not more than two metres.

Explanatory text — see **13.2.1**, **13.2.2**.

Removal or relaxation of restrictions

7.—(1) The relevant authority may by direction, with the consent of the owner of any land, remove or relax any of the restrictions imposed by paragraphs 1, 4 and 5 in relation to that land, either indefinitely or during a specified period.

(2) In sub-paragraph (1), the reference to a specified period includes references –

(a) to a specified period in every calendar year, or
(b) to a period which is to be determined by the owner of the land in accordance with the direction and notified by him to the relevant authority in accordance with regulations.

(3) Regulations may make provision as to –

(a) the giving or revocation of directions under this paragraph,
(b) the variation of any direction given under this paragraph by a subsequent direction so given,
(c) the giving or revocation of consent for the purposes of sub-paragraph (1), and
(d) the steps to be taken by the relevant authority or the owner for informing the public about any direction under this paragraph or its revocation.

(4) In this paragraph –

'the relevant authority' has the meaning given by section 21;

'owner', in relation to any land which is subject to a farm business tenancy within the meaning of the Agricultural Tenancies Act 1995 or a tenancy to which the Agricultural Holdings Act 1986 applies, means the tenant under that tenancy.

Explanatory text — see **13.2.4**.

Dedicated land

8. In relation to land to which a dedication under section 16 relates (whether or not it would be access land apart from the dedication), the provisions of this Schedule have effect subject to the terms of the dedication.

Explanatory text — see **12.2.4**.

SCHEDULE 3

DELEGATION OF APPELLATE FUNCTIONS

Interpretation

1. In this Schedule –

'appointed person' means a person appointed under section 8(1)(a);

'the appointing authority' means –

    (a) the Secretary of State, in relation to an appointment made by him, or
    (b) the National Assembly for Wales, in relation to an appointment made by it;

'appointment', in the case of any appointed person, means appointment under section 8(1)(a).

Appointments

2. An appointment under section 8(1)(a) must be in writing and –

    (a) may relate to any particular appeal or matter specified in the appointment or to appeals or matters of a description so specified,
    (b) may provide for any function to which it relates to be exercisable by the appointed person either unconditionally or subject to the fulfilment of such conditions as may be specified in the appointment, and
    (c) may, by notice in writing given to the appointed person, be revoked at any time by the appointing authority in respect of any appeal or matter which has not been determined by the appointed person before that time.

Powers of appointed person

3. Subject to the provisions of this Schedule, an appointed person shall, in relation to any appeal or matter to which his appointment relates, have the same powers and duties as the appointing authority, other than –

    (a) any function of making regulations;
    (b) any function of holding an inquiry or other hearing or of causing an inquiry or other hearing to be held; or
    (c) any function of appointing a person for the purpose –
        (i) of enabling persons to appear before and be heard by the person so appointed; or
       (ii) of referring any question or matter to that person.

Holding of local inquiries and other hearings by appointed persons

4.—(1) If either of the parties to an appeal or matter expresses a wish to appear before and be heard by the appointed person, the appointed person shall give both of them an opportunity of appearing and being heard.

(2) Whether or not a party to an appeal or matter has asked for an opportunity to appear and be heard, the appointed person –

(a) may hold a local inquiry or other hearing in connection with the appeal or matter, and

(b) shall, if the appointing authority so directs, hold a local inquiry in connection with the appeal or matter.

(3) Where an appointed person holds a local inquiry or other hearing by virtue of this Schedule, an assessor may be appointed by the appointing authority to sit with the appointed person at the inquiry or hearing and advise him on any matters arising, notwithstanding that the appointed person is to determine the appeal or matter.

(4) Subject to paragraph 5, the costs of a local inquiry held under this Schedule shall be defrayed by the appointing authority.

Local inquiries under this Schedule: evidence and costs

5. Subsections (2) to (5) of section 250 of the Local Government Act 1972 (local inquiries: evidence and costs) shall apply to local inquiries or other hearings held under this Schedule by an appointed person as they apply to inquiries caused to be held under that section by a Minister, but as if –

(a) in subsection (2) (evidence) the reference to the person appointed to hold the inquiry were a reference to the appointed person,

(b) in subsection (4) (recovery of costs of holding the inquiry) –

  (i) references to the Minister causing the inquiry to be held were references to the appointing authority, and

  (ii) references to a local authority included references to the appropriate countryside body, and

(c) in subsection (5) (orders as to the costs of the parties) the reference to the Minister causing the inquiry to be held were a reference to the appointed person or the appointing authority.

Revocation of appointments and making of new appointments

6.—(1) Where under paragraph 2(c) the appointment of the appointed person is revoked in respect of any appeal or matter, the appointing authority shall, unless he proposes to determine the appeal or matter himself, appoint another person under section 8(1)(a) to determine the appeal or matter instead.

(2) Where such a new appointment is made, the consideration of the appeal or matter, or any hearing in connection with it, shall be begun afresh.

(3) Nothing in sub-paragraph (2) shall require any person to be given an opportunity of making fresh representations or modifying or withdrawing any representations already made.

Certain acts and omissions of appointed person to be treated as those of appointing authority

7.—(1) Anything done or omitted to be done by an appointed person in, or in connection with, the exercise or purported exercise of any function to which the appointment relates shall be treated for all purposes as done or omitted to be done by the appointing authority.

(2) Sub-paragraph (1) does not apply –

(a) for the purposes of so much of any contract made between the appointing authority and the appointed person as relates to the exercise of the function, or

(b) for the purposes of any criminal proceedings brought in respect of anything done or omitted to be done as mentioned in that sub-paragraph.

Explanatory text — see 12.5.7.

Section 46(3)   SCHEDULE 4

MINOR AND CONSEQUENTIAL AMENDMENTS RELATING TO PART I

Law of Property Act 1925 (c.20)

1. In section 193(1) of the Law of Property Act 1925 (rights of public over commons and waste lands), in paragraph (b) of the proviso, after 'injuriously affected,' there is inserted 'for conserving flora, fauna or geological or physiographical features of the land,'.

Forestry Act 1967 (c.10)

2. In section 9 of the Forestry Act 1967 (requirement of licence for felling), in the definition of 'public open space' in subsection (6), after '1949' there is inserted 'or Part I of the Countryside and Rights of Way Act 2000)'.

Agriculture Act 1967 (c.52)

3. In section 52 of the Agriculture Act 1967 (control of afforestation), in the definition of 'public open space' in subsection (15), after '1949' there is inserted 'or Part I of the Countryside and Rights of Way Act 2000)'.

Countryside Act 1968 (c.41)

4. In section 2(6) of the Countryside Act 1968 (Countryside Agency and Countryside Council for Wales to make recommendations to public bodies in relation to byelaws) for 'and the Act of 1949' there is substituted ', the Act of 1949 and Part I of the Countryside and Rights of Way Act 2000'.

Local Government Act 1974 (c.7)

5. In section 9 of the Local Government Act 1974 (grants and loans by Countryside Agency and Countryside Council for Wales), for 'or the National Parks and Access to the Countryside Act 1949' there is substituted ', the National Parks and Access to the Countryside Act 1949 or the Countryside and Rights of Way Act 2000'.

Wildlife and Countryside Act 1981 (c.69)

6. In paragraph 13(1) of Schedule 13 to the Wildlife and Countryside Act 1981 (Countryside Agency's annual report on the discharge of their functions) after '1968 Act' there is inserted ', the Countryside and Rights of Way Act 2000'.

Section 51   SCHEDULE 5
DEFINITIVE MAPS AND STATEMENTS AND RESTRICTED BYWAYS

PART I

AMENDMENTS OF PART III OF WILDLIFE AND COUNTRYSIDE ACT 1981

1.—(1) Section 53 of the 1981 Act is amended as follows.

(2) In subsection (1) (meaning of 'definitive map and statement') after 'subject to section 57(3)' there is inserted 'and 57A(1)'.

(3) In subsection (3)(a)(iii), after 'public path' there is inserted 'or a restricted byway'.

(4) In subsection (3)(c)(i) for 'a right of way to which this Part applies' there is substituted 'a right of way such that the land over which the right subsists is a public path or, subject to section 54A, a byway open to all traffic'.

(5) In subsection (4), after 'public path' there is inserted ', restricted byway'.

(6) After subsection (4) there is inserted –

'(4A) Subsection (4B) applies to evidence which, when considered with all other relevant evidence available to the surveying authority, shows as respects a way shown in a definitive map and statement as a restricted byway that the public have, and had immediately before the commencement of section 47 of the Countryside and Rights of Way Act 2000, a right of way for vehicular and all other kinds of traffic over that way.

(4B) For the purposes of subsection (3)(c)(ii), such evidence is evidence which, when so considered, shows that the way concerned ought, subject to section 54A, to be shown in the definitive map and statement as a byway open to all traffic.'.

(7) After subsection (5) there is inserted –

'(5A) Evidence to which subsection (4B) applies on the commencement of section 47 of the Countryside and Rights of Way Act 2000 shall for the purposes of subsection (5) and any application made under it be treated as not having been discovered by the surveying authority before the commencement of that section.'.

2. After section 53 of that Act there is inserted –

'53A   Power to include modifications in other orders

(1) This section applies to any order –

    (a) which is of a description prescribed by regulations made by the Secretary of State,
    (b) whose coming into operation would, as regards any definitive map and statement, be an event within section 53(3)(a),
    (c) which is made by the surveying authority, and
    (d) which does not affect land outside the authority's area.

(2) The authority may include in the order such provision as it would be required to make under section 53(2)(b) in consequence of the coming into operation of the other provisions of the order.

(3) An authority which has included any provision in an order by virtue of subsection (2)—

(a) may at any time before the order comes into operation, and

(b) shall, if the order becomes subject to special parliamentary procedure,

withdraw the order and substitute for it an order otherwise identical but omitting any provision so included.

(4) Anything done for the purposes of any enactment in relation to an order withdrawn under subsection (3) shall be treated for those purposes as done in relation to the substituted order.

(5) No requirement for the confirmation of an order applies to provisions included in the order by virtue of subsection (2), but any power to modify an order includes power to make consequential modifications to any provision so included.

(6) Provisions included in an order by virtue of subsection (2) shall take effect on the date specified under section 56(3A) as the relevant date.

(7) Where any enactment provides for questioning the validity of an order on any grounds, the validity of any provision included by virtue of subsection (2) may be questioned in the same way on the grounds –

(a) that it is not within the powers of this Part, or

(b) that any requirement of this Part or of regulations made under it has not been complied with.

(8) Subject to subsections (5) to (7), the Secretary of State may by regulations provide that any procedural requirement as to the making or coming into operation of an order to which this section applies shall not apply, or shall apply with modifications prescribed by the regulations, to so much of the order as contains provision included by virtue of subsection (2).

(9) Regulations under this section shall be made by statutory instrument which shall be subject to annulment in pursuance of a resolution of either House of Parliament.

53B   Register of applications under section 53

(1) Every surveying authority shall keep, in such manner as may be prescribed, a register containing such information as may be prescribed with respect to applications under section 53(5).

(2) The register shall contain such information as may be prescribed with respect to the manner in which such applications have been dealt with.

(3) Regulations may make provision for the register to be kept in two or more parts, each part containing such information relating to applications under section 53(5) as may be prescribed.

(4) Regulations may make provision –

(a) for a specified part of the register to contain copies of applications and of the maps submitted with them, and

(b) for the entry relating to any application, and everything relating to it, to be removed from any part of the register when –

(i)   the application (including any appeal to the Secretary of State) has been finally disposed of, and

(ii) if an order is made, a decision has been made to confirm or not to confirm the order, (without prejudice to the inclusion of any different entry relating to it in another part of the register).

(5) Every register kept under this section shall be available for inspection free of charge at all reasonable hours.

(6) In this section –

"prescribed" means prescribed by regulations;

"regulations" means regulations made by the Secretary of State by statutory instrument;

and a statutory instrument containing regulations under this section shall be subject to annulment in pursuance of a resolution of either House of Parliament.'.

3.—(1) Until the coming into force of section 47(1) of this Act, section 54 of the 1981 Act (duty to reclassify roads used as public paths) has effect as follows.

(2) In subsection (2)—

    (a) for the words from the beginning to 'by' there is substituted 'Where the particulars relating to any road used as a public path have been reviewed under subsection (1)(a), the definitive map and statement shall be modified so as to show that way by', and
    (b) the words from 'and shall not' to the end are omitted.

(3) In subsection (3), for the words 'A road used as a public path' there is substituted 'Such a way'.

(4) After subsection (5) there is inserted –

    '(5A) No order under this Part modifying a definitive map and statement, and no provision included by virtue of section 53A(2) in any order, shall use the expression "road used as a public path" to describe any way not already shown as such in the map and statement.'.

4. After section 54 of that Act there is inserted –

'54A BOATs not to be added to definitive maps

(1) No order under this Part shall, after the cut-off date, modify a definitive map and statement so as to show as a byway open to all traffic any way not shown in the map and statement as a highway of any description.

(2) In this section "the cut-off date" means, subject to regulations under subsection (3), 1st January 2026.

(3) The Secretary of State may make regulations –

    (a) substituting as the cut-off date a date later than the date specified in subsection (2) or for the time being substituted under this paragraph;
    (b) containing such transitional provisions or savings as appear to the Secretary of State to be necessary or expedient in connection with the operation of subsection (1), including in particular its operation in relation to –
        (i) an order under section 53(2) for which on the cut-off date an application is pending,
        (ii) an order under this Part which on that date has been made but not confirmed,

(iii) an order under section 55 made after that date, or

(iv) an order under this Part relating to any way as respects which such an order, or any provision of such an order, has after that date been to any extent quashed.

(4) Regulations under subsection (3)(a)—

(a) may specify different dates for different areas; but

(b) may not specify a date later than 1st January 2031, except as respects an area within subsection (5).

(5) An area is within this subsection if it is in –

(a) the Isles of Scilly, or

(b) an area which, at any time before the repeal by section 73 of this Act of sections 27 to 34 of the 1949 Act –

(i) was excluded from the operation of those sections by virtue of any provision of the 1949 Act, or

(ii) would have been so excluded but for a resolution having effect under section 35(2) of that Act.

(6) Where by virtue of regulations under subsection (3) there are different cut-off dates for areas into which different parts of any way extend, the cut-off date in relation to that way is the later or latest of those dates.

(7) Where it appears to the Secretary of State that any provision of this Part can by virtue of subsection (1) have no further application he may by order make such amendments or repeals in this Part as appear to him to be, in consequence, necessary or expedient.

(8) An order or regulations under this section shall be made by statutory instrument which shall be subject to annulment in pursuance of a resolution of either House of Parliament.'.

5. In section 55 of that Act (no further surveys or reviews under the National Parks and Access to the Countryside Act 1949), after subsection (6) there is inserted –

'(7) Every way which –

(a) in pursuance of an order under subsection (5) is shown in a definitive map and statement as a byway open to all traffic, a bridleway or a footpath, and

(b) before the making of the order, was shown in the map and statement under review as a road used as a public path,

shall be a highway maintainable at the public expense.

(8) Subsection (7) does not oblige a highway authority to provide, on a way shown in a definitive map and statement as a byway open to all traffic, a metalled carriageway or a carriageway which is by any other means provided with a surface suitable for the passage of vehicles.'.

6.—(1) Section 56 of that Act (effect of definitive map and statement) is amended as follows.

(2) In subsection (1)(d) –

(a) for 'road used as a public path' there is substituted 'restricted byway',

(b) after 'the map shall' there is inserted ', subject to subsection (2A),', and

(c) after 'leading a horse' there is inserted 'together with a right of way for vehicles other than mechanically propelled vehicles'.

(3) After subsection (1) there is inserted –

'(1A) In subsection (1)(d) "mechanically propelled vehicle" does not include an electrically assisted pedal cycle of a class prescribed for the purposes of section 189(1)(c) of the Road Traffic Act 1988.'.

(4) In subsection (2) –

(a) in paragraph (a) –
  (i) after 'this Part' there is inserted 'or an order to which section 53A applies which includes provision made by virtue of subsection (2) of that section', and
  (ii) after 'means' there is inserted ', subject to subsection (2A),' and
(b) in paragraph (b), after '(3)' there is inserted 'or (3A)'.

(5) After that subsection there is inserted –

'(2A) In the case of a map prepared before the date of the coming into force of section 47 of the Countryside and Rights of Way Act 2000 –

(a) subsection (1)(d) and (e) have effect subject to the operation of any enactment or instrument, and to any other event, whereby a way shown on the map as a restricted byway has, on or before that date –
  (i) been authorised to be stopped up, diverted or widened, or
  (ii) become a public path, and
(b) subsection (2)(a) has effect in relation to any way so shown with the substitution of that date for the date mentioned there.'.

(6) After subsection (3) there is inserted –

'(3A) Every order to which section 53A applies which includes provision made by virtue of subsection (2) of that section shall specify, as the relevant date for the purposes of the order, such date as the authority may in accordance with regulations made by the Secretary of State determine.'.

(7) After subsection (4) there is inserted –

'(4A) Regulations under this section shall be made by statutory instrument which shall be subject to annulment in pursuance of a resolution of either House of Parliament.'.

(8) Subsection (5) is omitted.

7.—(1) Section 57 of that Act (supplementary provisions as to definitive maps and statements) is amended as follows.

(2) In subsection (1), the words 'on such scale as may be so prescribed,' are omitted.

(3) In subsection (2), for 'section 55(3)' there is substituted 'subsection (1) or any other provision of this Part'.

(4) In subsection (3) after 'for the purposes of the foregoing provisions of this Part' there is inserted ', and for the purposes of section 57A(1),'.

(5) After that subsection there is inserted –

'(3A) Where as respects any definitive map and statement the requirements of section 53(2), and of section 55 so far as it applies, have been complied with, the map and statement are to be regarded for the purposes of subsection (3) as having been modified in accordance with the foregoing provisions of this Part whether or not, as respects the map and statement, the requirements of section 54 have been complied with.'.

(6) After subsection (6) there is inserted –

'(6A) In subsection (1), the reference to an order under the foregoing provisions of this Part includes a reference to so much of an order to which section 53A applies as contains provision made by virtue of subsection (2) of that section; and subsections (5) and (6) apply to –

(a) orders to which section 53A applies modifying the map and statement, and
(b) such documents relating to them as may be prescribed by regulations made by the Secretary of State,

as those subsections apply to orders under this Part modifying the map and statement.

(6B) Regulations under paragraph (b) of subsection (6A) may require any document to be prepared by a surveying authority for the purposes of that paragraph, and any such document shall be in such form as may be prescribed by the regulations.

(6C) Regulations made by the Secretary of State may require any surveying authority –

(a) to keep such other documents as may be prescribed by the regulations available for inspection at such times and places and in such manner as may be so prescribed, or
(b) to provide to any other surveying authority any document so prescribed which that authority is, by regulations under paragraph (a), required to keep available for inspection.'.

8. After section 57 of that Act there is inserted –

'57A   Consolidation of definitive maps and statements

(1) Where –

(a) different definitive maps and statements relate to different parts of a surveying authority's area,
(b) as respects so much of each definitive map and statement as relates to that area the requirements of section 53(2), and of section 55 so far as it applies, have been complied with, and
(c) there is no part of that area to which no definitive map and statement relate,

the authority may, if it appears to them expedient to do so, prepare a map and statement comprising copies of so much of each definitive map and statement as relates to the authority's area; and where they do so the map and statement so prepared and not, so far as copied, the earlier maps and statements shall be regarded for the purposes of sections 53 to 56 and 57(2) and (3) as the definitive map and statement for the area to which they relate.

(2) The power conferred by subsection (1) is not exercisable by a surveying authority if the definitive map and statement relating to any part of the authority's area is a map and statement in respect of which a review under section 33 of the 1949 Act was begun before the commencement date but has been neither abandoned in pursuance of a direction under section 55(1) nor completed.

(3) References in subsection (1) to a definitive map and statement are, in the case of a map and statement modified in accordance with any of the foregoing provisions of this Part, references to the map and statement as modified.

(4) The statement prepared under subsection (1) shall specify, as the relevant date for the purposes of the map, such date, not being earlier than six months before the preparation of the map and statement, as the authority may determine.

(5) Every surveying authority shall take such steps as they consider expedient for bringing to the attention of the public the preparation by them of any map and statement under subsection (1).'.

9. In section 66(1) of that Act (interpretation of Part III) after the definition of 'public path' there is inserted –

'"restricted byway" has the same meaning as in Part II of the Countryside and Rights of Way Act 2000;'.

10. In Schedule 14 to that Act (applications for certain orders under Part III), in paragraph 4(2) at the end there is inserted '(which may include a direction as to the time within which an order is to be made)'

11.—(1) Schedule 15 to that Act (procedure in connection with certain orders) is amended as follows.

(2) In paragraph 3, in sub-paragraph (1)(c) after 'order' there is inserted ', which must include particulars of the grounds relied on,'.

(3) In sub-paragraph (9) of that paragraph –

  (a) after 'sub-paragraph' there is inserted '(1)(c) or', and
  (b) after 'limiting' there is inserted 'the grounds which may be relied on or'.

(4) In paragraph 7, in sub-paragraph (2) after 'shall' there is inserted ', subject to sub-paragraph (2A),'.

(5) After sub-paragraph (2) of that paragraph there is inserted –

'(2A) The Secretary of State may, but need not, act as mentioned in sub-paragraph (2)(a) or (b) if, in his opinion, no representation or objection which has been duly made and not withdrawn relates to an issue which would be relevant in determining whether or not to confirm the order, either with or without modifications.'.

(6) In sub-paragraph (3) of that paragraph, for 'the person appointed to hold the inquiry' there is substituted 'any person appointed to hold an inquiry'.

(7) In paragraph 8 –

  (a) in sub-paragraph (2)(a) after 'the proposal' there is inserted ', which must include particulars of the grounds relied on,',
  (b) for sub-paragraph (2)(b) and (c) there is substituted –

'(b) if any representation or objection duly made is not withdrawn (but subject to sub-paragraph (3)), hold a local inquiry or afford any person by whom any such representation or objection has been made an opportunity of being heard by a person appointed by the Secretary of State for the purpose; and

(c) consider the report of any person appointed to hold an inquiry or to hear representations or objections.

(3) The Secretary of State may, but need not, act as mentioned in sub-paragraph (2)(b) if, in his opinion, no representation or objection which has been duly made and not withdrawn relates to an issue which would be relevant in determining whether or not to confirm the order in accordance with his proposal.

(4) Sub-paragraph (2)(a) shall not be construed as limiting the grounds which may be relied on at any local inquiry or hearing held under this paragraph.'.

(8) Paragraph 9 is omitted and after paragraph 10 there is inserted –

'Hearings and local inquiries

10A.—(1) Subject to sub-paragraph (2), subsections (2) to (5) of section 250 of the Local Government Act 1972 (giving of evidence at, and defraying of costs of, inquiries) shall apply in relation to any hearing or local inquiry held under paragraph 7 or 8 as they apply in relation to a local inquiry which a Minister causes to be held under subsection (1) of that section.

(2) In its application to a hearing or inquiry held under paragraph 7 or 8 by a person appointed under paragraph 10(1), subsection (5) of that section shall have effect as if the reference to the Minister causing the inquiry to be held were a reference to the person so appointed or the Secretary of State.

(3) Section 322A of the Town and Country Planning Act 1990 (orders as to costs where no hearing or inquiry takes place) shall apply in relation to a hearing or local inquiry under paragraph 7 or 8 as it applies in relation to a hearing or local inquiry for the purposes referred to in that section.'.

Explanatory text — see Chapter 5.

PART II

AMENDMENTS OF OTHER ACTS

National Parks and Access to the Countryside Act 1949 (c.97)

12.—(1) Section 51 of the National Parks and Access to the Countryside Act 1949 (general provisions as to long-distance routes) is amended as follows.

(2) In subsection (2)(a), for the words from 'any public path' to the end there is substituted 'any highway along which the route passes and which is a public path, a restricted byway or a way shown in a definitive map and statement as a restricted byway or byway open to all traffic;'.

(3) In subsection (5), for the words from 'existing public paths' to 'route passes' there is substituted 'existing highways falling within paragraph (a) of that subsection'.

(4) After that subsection there is inserted –

'(6) In this section –

"definitive map and statement" has the same meaning as in Part III of the Wildlife and Countryside Act 1981; and

"restricted byway" has the same meaning as in Part II of the Countryside and Rights of Way Act 2000.'.

13.—(1) Section 57 of that Act (penalty for displaying on footpaths notices deterring public use) is amended as follows.

(2) In subsection (1), for 'road used as a public path' there is substituted 'restricted byway'.

(3) In subsection (3), for 'or road used as a public path' there is substituted 'restricted byway or byway open to all traffic'.

(4) After that subsection there is inserted –

'(4) In this section –

"byway open to all traffic" has the same meaning as in Part III of the Wildlife and Countryside Act 1981;

"restricted byway" has the same meaning as in Part II of the Countryside and Rights of Way Act 2000.'.

Countryside Act 1968 (c.41)

14. In section 41(11) of the Countryside Act 1968 (power to make byelaws and related provision about wardens) –

(a) for 'road used as a public path' there is substituted 'restricted byway', and
(b) after '27(6) of the Act of 1949' there is inserted 'and section 48(4) of the Countryside and Rights of Way Act 2000'.

Highways Act 1980 (c.66)

15. In section 116 of the 1980 Act (power of magistrates' court to authorise stopping up or diversion of highway) in subsection (4), for 'or bridleway' there is substituted ', bridleway or restricted byway'.

16. In section 329 of the 1980 Act (interpretation) –

(a) in subsection (1) after the definition of 'reconstruction' there is inserted –

'"restricted byway" has the same meaning as in Part II of the Countryside and Rights of Way Act 2000;',

(b) in subsection (2) for 'either "bridleway" or "footpath"' there is substituted '"bridleway", "footpath" or "restricted byway"'.

Criminal Justice and Public Order Act 1994 (c.33)

17. In section 61 of the Criminal Justice and Public Order Act 1994 (power to remove trespassers on land), in paragraph (b)(i) of the definition of 'land' in subsection (9) for the words from 'it falls' to 'public path)' there is substituted 'it is a footpath, bridleway or byway open to all traffic within the meaning of Part III of the Wildlife and Countryside

Act 1981, is a restricted byway within the meaning of Part II of the Countryside and Rights of Way Act 2000'.

AMENDMENTS RELATING TO CREATION, STOPPING UP AND DIVERSION OF HIGHWAYS

PART I

AMENDMENTS OF HIGHWAYS ACT 1980

1. In section 26 of the 1980 Act (compulsory powers for creation of footpaths and bridleways) after subsection (3) there is inserted –

'(3A) The considerations to which –

   (a) the Secretary of State is to have regard in determining whether or not to confirm or make a public path creation order, and
   (b) a local authority are to have regard in determining whether or not to confirm such an order as an unopposed order,

include any material provision of a rights of way improvement plan prepared by any local highway authority whose area includes land over which the proposed footpath or bridleway would be created.'.

2. For section 29 of the 1980 Act there is substituted –

'29   Duty to have regard to agriculture, forestry and nature conservation

(1) In the exercise of their functions under this Part of this Act relating to the making of public path creation agreements and public path creation orders it shall be the duty of councils to have due regard to –

   (a) the needs of agriculture and forestry, and
   (b) the desirability of conserving flora, fauna and geological and physio-graphical features.

(2) In this section, "agriculture" includes the breeding or keeping of horses.'.

3. In section 31 of the 1980 Act (dedication of way as highway presumed after public use for 20 years), in subsection (6), in each of paragraphs (i) and (ii) for 'six' there is substituted 'ten'.

4. After section 31 of the 1980 Act there is inserted –

'31A   Register of maps, statements and declarations

(1) The appropriate council shall keep, in such manner as may be prescribed, a register containing such information as may be prescribed with respect to maps and statements deposited and declarations lodged with that council under section 31(6) above.

(2) Regulations may make provision for the register to be kept in two or more parts, each part containing such information as may be prescribed with respect to such maps, statements and declarations.

(3) Regulations may make provision as to circumstances in which an entry relating to a map, statement or declaration, or anything relating to it, is to be removed from the register or from any part of it.

(4) Every register kept under this section shall be available for inspection free of charge at all reasonable hours.

(5) In this section –

"appropriate council" has the same meaning as in section 31(6) above;

"prescribed" means prescribed by regulations;

"regulations" means regulations made by the Secretary of State.'.

5. In section 36 of the 1980 Act (highways maintainable at public expense) in subsection (2), after paragraph (e) there is inserted –

'(f) a highway, being a footpath, a bridleway, a restricted byway or a way over which the public have a right of way for vehicular and all other kinds of traffic, created in consequence of a special diversion order or an SSSI diversion order.'.

6. In section 118 of the 1980 Act (stopping up of footpaths and bridleways) after subsection (6) there is inserted –

'(6A) The considerations to which –

(a) the Secretary of State is to have regard in determining whether or not to confirm a public path extinguishment order, and

(b) a council are to have regard in determining whether or not to confirm such an order as an unopposed order,

include any material provision of a rights of way improvement plan prepared by any local highway authority whose area includes land over which the order would extinguish a public right of way.'.

7. After section 118 of the 1980 Act there is inserted –

'118ZA   Application for a public path extinguishment order

(1) The owner, lessee or occupier of any land used for agriculture, forestry or the breeding or keeping of horses may apply to a council for the area in which the land is situated for the making of a public path extinguishment order in relation to any footpath or bridleway which crosses the land.

(2) An application under this section shall be in such form as may be prescribed and shall be accompanied by a map, on such scale as may be prescribed, showing the land over which it is proposed that the public right of way should be extinguished, and by such other information as may be prescribed.

(3) Regulations may provide –

(a) that a prescribed charge is payable on the making of an application under this section, and

(b) that further prescribed charges are payable by the applicant if the council make a public path extinguishment order on the application.

(4) An application under this section is not to be taken to be received by the council until the requirements of regulations under section 121A below have been satisfied in relation to it.

(5) A council which receives an application under this section shall determine the application as soon as reasonably practicable.

(6) Before determining to make a public path extinguishment order on an application under this section, the council may require the applicant to enter into an agreement with them to defray, or to make such contribution as may be specified in the agreement towards, any compensation which may become payable under section 28 above as applied by section 121(2) below.

(7) Where –

(a) an application under this section has been made to a council, and
(b) the council have not determined the application within four months of receiving it,

the Secretary of State may, at the request of the applicant and after consulting the council, by direction require the council to determine the application before the end of such period as may be specified in the direction.

(8) As soon as practicable after determining an application under this section, the council shall –

(a) give to the applicant notice in writing of their decision and the reasons for it, and
(b) give a copy of the notice to such other persons as may be prescribed.

(9) The council to whom an application under this section has been made may make a public path extinguishment order on the application only if the land over which the public right of way is to be extinguished by the order is that shown for the purposes of subsection (2) above on the map accompanying the application.

(10) Any reference in this Act to the map accompanying an application under this section includes a reference to any revised map submitted by the applicant in prescribed circumstances in substitution for that map.

(11) This section has effect subject to the provisions of sections 121A and 121C below.

(12) In this section –

"prescribed" means prescribed by regulations;

"regulations" means regulations made by the Secretary of State.'.

8. After section 118A of the 1980 Act there is inserted –

'118B   Stopping up of certain highways for purposes of crime prevention, etc

(1) This section applies where it appears to a council –

(a) that, as respects any relevant highway for which they are the highway authority and which is in an area designated by the Secretary of State by order for the purposes of this section, the conditions in subsection (3) below are satisfied and it is expedient, for the purpose of preventing or reducing crime which would otherwise disrupt the life of the community, that the highway should be stopped up, or
(b) that, as respects any relevant highway for which they are the highway authority and which crosses land occupied for the purposes of a school, it is expedient, for the purpose of protecting the pupils or staff from –
    (i)   violence or the threat of violence,
    (ii) harassment,

   (iii) alarm or distress arising from unlawful activity, or
   (iv) any other risk to their health or safety arising from such activity,

that the highway should be stopped up.

(2) In subsection (1) above "relevant highway" means –

   (a) any footpath, bridleway or restricted byway,
   (b) any highway which is shown in a definitive map and statement as a footpath, a bridleway, or a restricted byway, but over which the public have a right of way for vehicular and all other kinds of traffic, or
   (c) any highway which is shown in a definitive map and statement as a byway open to all traffic,

but does not include a highway that is a trunk road or a special road.

(3) The conditions referred to in subsection (1)(a) above are –

   (a) that premises adjoining or adjacent to the highway are affected by high levels of crime, and
   (b) that the existence of the highway is facilitating the persistent commission of criminal offences.

(4) Where this section applies, the council may by order made by them and submitted to and confirmed by the Secretary of State, or confirmed as an unopposed order, extinguish the public right of way over the highway.

(5) An order under subsection (4) above is in this Act referred to as a "special extinguishment order".

(6) Before making a special extinguishment order, the council shall consult the police authority for the area in which the highway lies.

(7) The Secretary of State shall not confirm a special extinguishment order made by virtue of subsection (1)(a) above, and a council shall not confirm such an order as an unopposed order, unless he or, as the case may be, they are satisfied that the conditions in subsection (3) above are satisfied, that the stopping up of the highway is expedient as mentioned in subsection (1)(a) above and that it is expedient to confirm the order having regard to all the circumstances, and in particular to –

   (a) whether and, if so, to what extent the order is consistent with any strategy for the reduction of crime and disorder prepared under section 6 of the Crime and Disorder Act 1998,
   (b) the availability of a reasonably convenient alternative route or, if no reasonably convenient alternative route is available, whether it would be reasonably practicable to divert the highway under section 119B below rather than stopping it up, and
   (c) the effect which the extinguishment of the right of way would have as respects land served by the highway, account being taken of the provisions as to compensation contained in section 28 above as applied by section 121(2) below.

(8) The Secretary of State shall not confirm a special extinguishment order made by virtue of subsection (1)(b) above, and a council shall not confirm such an order as an unopposed order unless he or, as the case may be, they are satisfied that the stopping up of the highway is expedient as mentioned in subsection (1)(b) above

and that it is expedient to confirm the order having regard to all the circumstances, and in particular to –

(a) any other measures that have been or could be taken for improving or maintaining the security of the school,

(b) whether it is likely that the coming into operation of the order will result in a substantial improvement in that security,

(c) the availability of a reasonably convenient alternative route or, if no reasonably convenient alternative route is available, whether it would be reasonably practicable to divert the highway under section 119B below rather than stopping it up, and

(d) the effect which the extinguishment of the right of way would have as respects land served by the highway, account being taken of the provisions as to compensation contained in section 28 above as applied by section 121(2) below.

(9) A special extinguishment order shall be in such form as may be prescribed by regulations made by the Secretary of State and shall contain a map, on such scale as may be prescribed, defining the land over which the public right of way is thereby extinguished.

(10) Schedule 6 to this Act has effect as to the making, confirmation, validity and date of operation of special extinguishment orders.

118C   Application by proprietor of school for special extinguishment order

(1) The proprietor of a school may apply to a council for the making by virtue of section 118B(1)(b) above of a special extinguishment order in relation to any highway for which the council are the highway authority and which –

(a) crosses land occupied for the purposes of the school, and

(b) is a relevant highway as defined by section 118B(2) above.

(2) Subsections (2) to (11) of section 118ZA above shall apply to applications under this section as they apply to applications under that section, with the substitution for references to a public path extinguishment order of references to a special extinguishment order; and regulations made under that section by virtue of this subsection may make different provision for the purposes of this section and for the purposes of that section.'.

9.—(1) Section 119 of the 1980 Act (diversion of footpaths and bridleways) is amended as follows.

(2) In subsection (1)(b), for 'so specified' there is substituted 'specified in the order or determined'.

(3) For subsection (3), there is substituted –

'(3) Where it appears to the council that work requires to be done to bring the new site of the footpath or bridleway into a fit condition for use by the public, the council shall –

(a) specify a date under subsection (1)(a) above, and

(b) provide that so much of the order as extinguishes (in accordance with subsection (1)(b) above) a public right of way is not to come into force until the local highway authority for the new path or way certify that the work has been carried out.'.

(4) In subsection (5) –

(a) after 'diversion order' there is inserted 'on an application under section 119ZA below or', and
(b) for 'him' there is substituted 'the person who made the application or representations'.

(5) After subsection (6) there is inserted –

'(6A) The considerations to which –

(a) the Secretary of State is to have regard in determining whether or not to confirm a public path diversion order, and
(b) a council are to have regard in determining whether or not to confirm such an order as an unopposed order,

include any material provision of a rights of way improvement plan prepared by any local highway authority whose area includes land over which the order would create or extinguish a public right of way.'.

10. After section 119 of the 1980 Act there is inserted –

'119ZA Application for a public path diversion order

(1) Subject to subsection (2) below, the owner, lessee or occupier of any land used for agriculture, forestry or the breeding or keeping of horses may apply to a council for the area in which the land is situated for the making of a public path diversion order in relation to any footpath or bridleway which crosses the land, on the ground that in his interests it is expedient that the order should be made.

(2) No application may be made under this section for an order which would create a new footpath or bridleway communicating with –

(a) a classified road,
(b) a special road,
(c) a GLA road, or
(d) any highway not falling within paragraph (a) or (b) above for which the Minister is the highway authority,

unless the application is made with the consent of the highway authority for the way falling within paragraph (a), (b), (c) or (d) above.

(3) No application under this section may propose the creation of a new right of way over land covered by works used by any statutory undertakers for the purposes of their undertaking or the curtilage of such land, unless the application is made with the consent of the statutory undertakers; and in this subsection "statutory undertaker" and "statutory undertaking" have the same meaning as in Schedule 6 to this Act.

(4) An application under this section shall be in such form as may be prescribed and shall be accompanied by a map, on such scale as may be prescribed –

(a) showing the existing site of so much of the line of the path or way as it is proposed to divert and the new site to which it is proposed to be diverted,
(b) indicating whether it is proposed to create a new right of way over the whole of the new site or whether some of it is already comprised in a footpath or bridleway, and
(c) where some part of the new site is already so comprised, defining that part,

and by such other information as may be prescribed.

(5) Regulations may provide –

  (a) that a prescribed charge is payable on the making of an application under
       this section, and
  (b) that further prescribed charges are payable by the applicant if the council
       make a public path diversion order on the application.

(6) An application under this section is not to be taken to be received by the
council until the requirements of regulations under section 121A below have been
satisfied in relation to it.

(7) A council which receives an application under this section shall determine the
application as soon as reasonably practicable.

(8) Where –

  (a) an application under this section has been made to a council, and
  (b) the council have not determined the application within four months of
       receiving it,

the Secretary of State may, at the request of the applicant and after consulting the
council, by direction require the council to determine the application before the
end of such period as may be specified in the direction.

(9) As soon as practicable after determining an application under this section, the
council shall –

  (a) give to the applicant notice in writing of their decision and the reasons for
       it, and
  (b) give a copy of the notice to such other persons as may be prescribed.

(10) The council to whom an application under this section has been made may
make a public path diversion order on the application only if –

  (a) the land over which the public right of way is to be extinguished by the
       order, and
  (b) the new site to which the path or way is to be diverted,

are those shown for the purposes of subsection (4) above on the map
accompanying the application.

(11) Any reference in this Act to the map accompanying an application under this
section includes a reference to any revised map submitted by the applicant in
prescribed circumstances in substitution for that map.

(12) This section has effect subject to the provisions of sections 121A and 121C
below.

(13) In this section –

"prescribed" means prescribed by regulations;

"regulations" means regulations made by the Secretary of State.'.

11.—(1) Section 119A (diversion of footpaths and bridleways crossing railways) is
amended as follows.

(2) In subsection (2)(b), for 'so specified' there is substituted 'specified in the order or
determined under subsection (7) below'.

(3) For subsection (7) there is substituted –

'(7) Where it appears to the council that work requires to be done to bring the new site of the footpath or bridleway into a fit condition for use by the public, the council shall –

(a) specify a date under subsection (2)(a) above, and
(b) provide that so much of the order as extinguishes (in accordance with subsection (2)(b) above) a public right of way is not to come into force until the local highway authority for the new path or way certify that the work has been carried out.'.

12. After section 119A of the 1980 Act there is inserted –

'119B   Diversion of certain highways for purposes of crime prevention, etc

(1) This section applies where it appears to a council –

(a) that, as respects any relevant highway for which they are the highway authority and which is in an area designated by the Secretary of State by order under section 118B(1)(a) above, the conditions in subsection (3) below are satisfied and it is expedient, for the purpose of preventing or reducing crime which would otherwise disrupt the life of the community, that the line of the highway, or part of that line should be diverted (whether on to land of the same or another owner, lessee or occupier), or
(b) that, as respects any relevant highway for which they are the highway authority and which crosses land occupied for the purposes of a school, it is expedient, for the purpose of protecting the pupils or staff from –
(i)   violence or the threat of violence,
(ii) harassment,
(iii) alarm or distress arising from unlawful activity, or
(iv) any other risk to their health or safety arising from such activity,
that the line of the highway, or part of that line, should be diverted (whether on to land of the same or another owner, lessee or occupier).

(2) In subsection (1) above "relevant highway" means –

(a) any footpath, bridleway or restricted byway,
(b) any highway which is shown in a definitive map and statement as a footpath, a bridleway, or a restricted byway, but over which the public have a right of way for vehicular and all other kinds of traffic, or
(c) any highway which is shown in a definitive map and statement as a byway open to all traffic,

but does not include a highway that is a trunk road or a special road.

(3) The conditions referred to in subsection (1)(a) above are –

(a) that premises adjoining or adjacent to the highway are affected by high levels of crime, and
(b) that the existence of the highway is facilitating the persistent commission of criminal offences.

(4) Where this section applies, the council may by order made by them and submitted to and confirmed by the Secretary of State, or confirmed as an unopposed order –

(a) create, as from such date as may be specified in the order, any such –

    (i)   new footpath, bridleway or restricted byway, or
    (ii) in a case falling within subsection (2)(b) or (c) above, new highway over which the public have a right of way for vehicular and all other kinds of traffic,

    as appears to the council requisite for effecting the diversion, and

  (b) extinguish, as from such date as may be specified in the order or determined in accordance with the provisions of subsection (8) below, the public right of way over so much of the highway as appears to the council to be requisite for the purpose mentioned in paragraph (a) or (b) of subsection (1) above.

(5) An order under subsection (4) above is in this Act referred to as a "special diversion order".

(6) Before making a special diversion order, the council shall consult the police authority for the area in which the highway is situated.

(7) A special diversion order shall not alter a point of termination of the highway –

  (a) if that point is not on a highway, or
  (b) (where it is on a highway) otherwise than to another point which is on the same highway, or a highway connected with it.

(8) Where it appears to the council that work requires to be done to bring the new site of the highway into a fit condition for use by the public, the council shall –

  (a) specify a date under subsection (4)(a) above, and
  (b) provide that so much of the order as extinguishes (in accordance with subsection (4)(b) above) a public right of way is not to come into force until the local highway authority for the new highway certify that the work has been carried out.

(9) A right of way created by a special diversion order may be either unconditional or (whether or not the right of way extinguished by the order was subject to limitations or conditions of any description) subject to such limitations or conditions as may be specified in the order.

(10) The Secretary of State shall not confirm a special diversion order made by virtue of subsection (1)(a) above, and a council shall not confirm such an order as an unopposed order unless he or, as the case may be, they are satisfied that the conditions in subsection (3) above are satisfied, that the diversion of the highway is expedient as mentioned in subsection (1)(a) above and that it is expedient to confirm the order having regard to all the circumstances, and in particular to –

  (a) whether and, if so, to what extent the order is consistent with any strategy for the reduction of crime and disorder prepared under section 6 of the Crime and Disorder Act 1998,
  (b) the effect which the coming into operation of the order would have as respects land served by the existing public right of way, and
  (c) the effect which any new public right of way created by the order would have as respects the land over which the right is so created and any land held with it,

so, however, that for the purposes of paragraphs (b) and (c) above the Secretary of State or, as the case may be, the council shall take into account the provisions as to compensation contained in section 28 above as applied by section 121(2) below.

(11) The Secretary of State shall not confirm a special diversion order made by virtue of subsection (1)(b) above, and a council shall not confirm such an order as an unopposed order unless he or, as the case may be, they are satisfied that the diversion of the highway is expedient as mentioned in subsection (1)(b) above and that it is expedient to confirm the order having regard to all the circumstances, and in particular to –

    (a) any other measures that have been or could be taken for improving or maintaining the security of the school,

    (b) whether it is likely that the coming into operation of the order will result in a substantial improvement in that security,

    (c) the effect which the coming into operation of the order would have as respects land served by the existing public right of way, and

    (d) the effect which any new public right of way created by the order would have as respects the land over which the right is so created and any land held with it,

so, however, that for the purposes of paragraphs (c) and (d) above the Secretary of State or, as the case may be, the council shall take into account the provisions as to compensation contained in section 28 above as applied by section 121(2) below.

(12) A special diversion order shall be in such form as may be prescribed by regulations made by the Secretary of State and shall contain a map, on such scale as may be so prescribed –

    (a) showing the existing site of so much of the line of the highway as is to be diverted by the order and the new site to which it is to be diverted,

    (b) indicating whether a new right of way is created by the order over the whole of the new site or whether some part of it is already comprised in a highway, and

    (c) where some part of the new site is already so comprised, defining that part.

(13) Schedule 6 to this Act has effect as to the making, confirmation, validity and date of operation of special diversion orders.

(14) Section 27 above (making up of new footpaths and bridleways) applies to a highway created by a special diversion order with the substitution –

    (a) for references to a footpath or bridleway of references to a footpath, a bridleway, a restricted byway or a highway over which the public have a right of way for vehicular and all other kinds of traffic,

    (b) for references to a public path creation order of references to a special diversion order, and

    (c) for references to section 26(2) above of references to section 120(3) below.

(15) Neither section 27 nor section 36 above is to be regarded as obliging a highway authority to provide on any highway created by a special diversion order a metalled carriageway.

119C   Application by proprietor of school for special diversion order

(1) The proprietor of a school may apply to a council for the making by virtue of section 119B(1)(b) above of a special diversion order in relation to any highway for which the council are the highway authority and which –

    (a) crosses land occupied for the purposes of the school, and

(b) is a relevant highway as defined by section 119B(2) above.

(2) No application may be made under this section for an order which would create a new highway communicating with –

    (a) a classified road,
    (b) a special road,
    (c) a GLA road, or
    (d) any highway not falling within paragraph (a) or (b) above for which the Minister is the highway authority,

unless the application is made with the consent of the highway authority for the way falling within paragraph (a), (b), (c) or (d) above.

(3) Before determining to make a special diversion order on an application under this section, the council may require the applicant to enter into an agreement with them to defray, or to make such contribution as may be specified in the agreement towards –

    (a) any compensation which may become payable under section 28 above as applied by section 121(2) below, or
    (b) to the extent that the council are the highway authority for the highway in question, any expenses which they may incur in bringing the new site of the highway into fit condition for use by the public, or
    (c) to the extent that the council are not the highway authority, any expenses which may become recoverable from them by the highway authority under the provisions of section 27(2) above as applied by section 119B(14) above.

(4) Subsections (3) to (12) of section 119ZA above shall apply to applications under this section as they apply to applications under that section, with the substitution –

    (a) for references to a public path diversion order of references to a special diversion order, and
    (b) for references to a footpath or bridleway of references to a highway,

and regulations made under that section by virtue of this subsection may make different provision for the purposes of this section and for the purposes of that section.

119D   Diversion of certain highways for protection of sites of special scientific interest

(1) Subsection (3) below applies where, on an application made in accordance with this section by the appropriate conservation body, it appears to a council, as respects any relevant highway for which they are the highway authority and which is in, forms part of, or is adjacent to or contiguous with, a site of special scientific interest –

    (a) that public use of the highway is causing, or that continued public use of the highway is likely to cause, significant damage to the flora, fauna or geological or physiographical features by reason of which the site of special scientific interest is of special interest, and
    (b) that it is expedient that the line of the highway, or part of that line should be diverted (whether on to land of the same or another owner, lessee or occupier) for the purpose of preventing such damage.

(2) In subsection (1) "relevant highway" means –

(a) a footpath, bridleway or restricted byway,

(b) a highway which is shown in a definitive map and statement as a footpath, a bridleway or a restricted byway but over which the public have a right of way for vehicular and all other kinds of traffic, or

(c) any highway which is shown in a definitive map and statement as a byway open to all traffic,

but does not include any highway that is a trunk road or special road.

(3) Where this subsection applies, the council may, by order made by them and submitted to and confirmed by the Secretary of State, or confirmed as an unopposed order –

(a) create, as from such date as may be specified in the order, any such –
   (i) new footpath, bridleway or restricted byway, or
   (ii) in a case falling within subsection (2)(b) or (c) above, new highway over which the public have a right of way for vehicular and all other kinds of traffic,
   as appears to the council requisite for effecting the diversion, and

(b) extinguish, as from such date as may be specified in the order or determined in accordance with the provisions of subsection (6) below, the public right of way over so much of the way as appears to the council to be requisite for the purpose mentioned in subsection (1)(b) above.

(4) An order under this section is referred to in this Act as an "SSSI diversion order".

(5) An SSSI diversion order shall not alter a point of termination of the highway –

(a) if that point is not on a highway, or

(b) (where it is on a highway) otherwise than to another point which is on the same highway, or a highway connected with it.

(6) Where it appears to the council that work requires to be done to bring the new site of the highway into a fit condition for use by the public, the council shall –

(a) specify a date under subsection (3)(a) above, and

(b) provide that so much of the order as extinguishes (in accordance with subsection (3)(b) above) a public right of way is not to come into force until the local highway authority for the new highway certify that the work has been carried out.

(7) A right of way created by an SSSI diversion order may be either unconditional or (whether or not the right of way extinguished by the order was subject to limitations or conditions of any description) subject to such limitations or conditions as may be specified in the order.

(8) Before determining to make an SSSI diversion order, the council may require the appropriate conservation body to enter into an agreement with them to defray, or to make such contribution as may be specified in the agreement towards –

(a) any compensation which may become payable under section 28 above as applied by section 121(2) below,

(b) to the extent that the council are the highway authority for the highway, any expenses which they may incur in bringing the new site of the highway into fit condition for use for the public, or

(c) to the extent that the council are not the highway authority, any expenses which may become recoverable from them by the highway authority under the provisions of section 27(2) above as applied by section 119E(6) below.

(9) The Secretary of State shall not confirm an SSSI diversion order, and a council shall not confirm such an order as an unopposed order, unless he, or as the case may be, they are satisfied that the conditions in subsection (1)(a) and (b) are satisfied, and that it is expedient to confirm the order having regard to the effect which –

(a) the diversion would have on public enjoyment of the right of way as a whole;
(b) the coming into operation of the order would have as respects other land served by the existing public right of way; and
(c) any new public right of way created by the order would have as respects the land over which the right is so created and any land held with it,

so, however, that for the purposes of paragraphs (b) and (c) above the Secretary of State or, as the case may be, the council shall take into account the provisions as to compensation referred to in subsection (8)(a) above.

(10) Schedule 6 to this Act has effect as to the making, confirmation, validity and date of operation of SSSI diversion orders.

(11) This section has effect subject to section 119E below.

(12) In this section –

"the appropriate conservation body" means –

(a) as respects England, English Nature, and
(b) as respects Wales, the Countryside Council for Wales;

"site of special scientific interest" has the same meaning as in the Wildlife and Countryside Act 1981.

119E   Provisions supplementary to section 119D

(1) An application under section 119D above shall be in such form as may be prescribed and shall be accompanied by –

(a) a map, on such scale as may be prescribed –
    (i)   showing the existing site of so much of the line of the highway as would be diverted if the order were made and the new site to which it would be diverted,
    (ii)   indicating whether a new right of way would be created by the order over the whole of the new site or whether some of it is already comprised in a highway, and
    (iii) where some part of the new site is already so comprised, defining that part,
(b) by an assessment in the prescribed form of the effects of public use of the right of way on the site of special scientific interest, and
(c) by such other information as may be prescribed.

(2) At least fourteen days before making an application under section 119D above, the appropriate conservation body shall give a notice in the prescribed form of their intention to do so –

(a) to any owner, lessee or occupier of land over which the proposed order would create or extinguish a public right of way;

(b) to such other persons as may be prescribed; and

(c) in the case of English Nature, to the Countryside Agency.

(3) A council, in determining whether it is expedient to make or confirm an SSSI diversion order, and the Secretary of State, in determining whether to confirm such an order, shall, in particular, have regard to the following questions –

(a) whether the council would be able to prevent damage of the kind referred to in section 119D(1) above by making a traffic regulation order, and

(b) if so, whether the making of a traffic regulation order would cause less inconvenience to the public than that which would be caused by the diversion of the highway.

(4) The Secretary of State, in determining whether it is expedient to make an SSSI diversion order under section 120(3) below in a case where by virtue of section 22(4) of the Road Traffic Regulation Act 1984 he has power to make a traffic regulation order shall, in particular, have regard to the following questions –

(a) whether he would be able to prevent damage of the kind referred to in section 119D(1) above by making a traffic regulation order, and

(b) if so, whether the making of a traffic regulation order would cause less inconvenience to the public than that which would be caused by the diversion of the highway.

(5) An SSSI diversion order shall be in such form as may be prescribed and shall contain a map, on such scale as may be prescribed –

(a) showing the existing site of so much of the line of the highway as is to be diverted by the order and the new site to which it is to be diverted,

(b) indicating whether a new right of way is created by the order over the whole of the new site or whether some part of it is already comprised in a highway, and

(c) where some part of the new site is already so comprised, defining that part.

(6) Section 27 above (making up of new footpaths and bridleways) applies to a highway created by an SSSI diversion order with the substitution –

(a) for references to a footpath or bridleway of references to a footpath, a bridleway, a restricted byway or a highway over which the public have a right of way for vehicular and all other kinds of traffic,

(b) for references to a public path creation order, of references to an SSSI diversion order, and

(c) for references to section 26(2) above, of references to section 120(3) below.

(7) Neither section 27 nor section 36 above is to be regarded as obliging a highway authority to provide on any highway created by an SSSI diversion order a metalled carriageway.

(8) In this section –

"the appropriate conservation body" has the same meaning as in section 119D above;

"prescribed" means prescribed by regulations made by the Secretary of State;

"site of special scientific interest" has the same meaning as in the Wildlife and Countryside Act 1981;

"traffic regulation order" means an order under section 1 or 6 of the Road Traffic Regulation Act 1984.'.

13.—(1) Section 120 of the 1980 Act (exercise of powers of making public path extinguishment and diversion orders) is amended as follows.

(2) In subsection (1), for 'to 119A' there is substituted ', 118A, 119 and 119A'.

(3) After that subsection there is inserted –

'(1A) Where a council are the highway authority for only part of a highway, the powers conferred on the council by sections 118B, 119B and 119D above are exercisable with respect to the whole of the highway, but subject to subsection (2) and only with the consent of every other council which is a highway authority for any other part with respect to which the powers are exercised.'.

(4) In subsection (2) –

   (a) for 'to 119A' there is substituted 'to 119D', and
   (b) for 'footpath or bridleway', wherever occurring, there is substituted 'highway'.

(5) In subsection (3) –

   (a) after 'or diverted' there is inserted 'or where it appears to the Secretary of State as respects a relevant highway as defined by section 118B(2), 119B(2) or 119D(2) that it is expedient as mentioned in section 118B(1)(a) or (b), 119B(1)(a) or (b) or 119D(1)(b) that the highway should be stopped up or diverted',
   (b) in paragraph (a), for 'a rail crossing diversion order or a public path diversion order' there is substituted 'a special extinguishment order, a public path diversion order, a rail crossing diversion order, a special diversion order or an SSSI diversion order',
   (c) in paragraph (b), for 'to 119A' there is substituted 'to 119D',
   (d) for '(subject to subsection (3A) below)' there is substituted '(subject to the following provisions of this section)', and
   (e) at the end there is inserted 'and, in the case of an SSSI diversion order, with the appropriate conservation body'.

(6) After subsection (3) there is inserted –

'(3ZA) Where an appeal to the Secretary of State is brought under section 121D(1) below, paragraph (a) of subsection (3) above does not apply, and the power conferred on him by that subsection may be exercised without consultation with the appropriate authority.'.

(7) After subsection (3A) there is inserted –

'(3B) Unless an appeal to the Secretary of State is brought under section 121D(1) below, the power conferred on the Secretary of State by subsection (3) above to make a special extinguishment order or a special diversion order is exercisable only after consultation with the police authority in whose area the highway lies.

(3C) The power conferred on the Secretary of State by subsection (3) above to make an SSSI diversion order may be exercised even though the appropriate conservation body has not made an application under section 119D above to the council who are the highway authority for the highway.

(3D) Where –

(a) the appropriate conservation body has made an application under section 119D above to a council in respect of a highway for which the council are the highway authority, and

(b) the council have neither confirmed the order nor submitted it to the Secretary of State for confirmation within 6 months of receiving the application,

the power conferred on the Secretary of State by subsection (3) above to make an SSSI diversion order may be exercised without consultation with the council.'.

(8) In subsection (4) –

(a) for 'or a rail crossing diversion order' there is substituted ', a rail crossing diversion order, a special diversion order or an SSSI diversion order', and

(b) for 'path or way' there is substituted 'highway'.

(9) For subsection (5) there is substituted –

'(5) The Secretary of State may, before determining –

(a) under subsection (3) above, to make a public path diversion order,

(b) under subsection (3) above, to make a public path extinguishment order, special extinguishment order, public path diversion order or special diversion order on an appeal under section 121D(1)(a) below,

(c) to confirm a public path extinguishment order, special extinguishment order, public path diversion order or special diversion order in respect of which an appeal under section 121D(1)(b) or (c) below has been brought, or

(d) under subsection (3) above, to make a rail crossing diversion order on the representations of the operator of the railway concerned,

require the appropriate person to enter into such agreement as he may specify with such council has he may specify for that person to defray, or to make such contribution as may be specified in the agreement towards, any such compensation or expenses as are specified in paragraphs (a), (b) and (c) of section 119(5), or as the case may be, section 118ZA(6), 119A(8) or 119C(3) above.

(6) In subsection (5) above 'the appropriate person' means –

(a) in a case falling within paragraph (a) of that subsection –
(i) where an appeal under section 121D(1)(a) below has been brought, the appellant, or
(ii) in any other case, the person on whose representations the Secretary of State is acting,

(b) in a case falling within paragraph (b) or (c) of that subsection, the appellant, and

(c) in a case falling within paragraph (d) of that subsection, the operator of the railway concerned.'.

(10) After subsection (6) there is inserted –

'(7) Where under subsection (3) above the Secretary of State decides to make an SSSI diversion order he may require the appropriate conservation body to enter into an agreement with such council as he may specify for the body to defray, or to make such contribution as may be specified in the agreement towards, any such compensation or expenses as are specified in paragraphs (a), (b) and (c) of section 119D(8) above.

(8) In this section "the appropriate conservation body" has the same meaning as in section 119D above.'.

14.—(1) Section 121 of the 1980 Act (supplementary provisions as to public path extinguishment and diversion orders) is amended as follows.

(2) In subsection (1) –

(a) after 'rail crossing extinguishment order,' there is inserted 'a special extinguishment order',

(b) for 'or a rail crossing diversion order', wherever occurring, there is substituted ', a rail crossing diversion order, a special diversion order or an SSSI diversion order', and

(c) for 'path or way', wherever occurring, there is substituted 'highway'.

(3) In subsection (2) –

(a) after 'rail crossing extinguishment orders,' there is inserted 'special extinguishment orders',

(b) for 'and rail crossing diversion orders' there is substituted ', rail crossing diversion orders, special diversion orders and SSSI diversion orders', and

(c) for the words from 'but' onwards there is substituted –

'but as if –

(a) the references in it to section 26(2) above were references to section 120(3) above, and

(b) in relation to special extinguishment orders, special diversion orders and SSSI diversion orders, the reference in section 28(4) to a footpath or bridleway included a reference to a restricted byway or a highway over which the public have a right of way for vehicular and all other kinds of traffic.'.

(4) In subsection (3) –

(a) for '(protection for agriculture and forestry)' there is substituted '(duty to have regard to agriculture, forestry and nature conservation)',

(b) after 'rail crossing extinguishment orders,' there is inserted 'special extinguishment orders', and

(c) for 'and rail crossing diversion orders' there is substituted ', rail crossing diversion orders, special diversion orders and SSSI diversion orders'.

(5) In subsection (4) –

(a) after 'rail crossing extinguishment order,' there is inserted 'a special extinguishment order', and

(b) for 'or a rail crossing diversion order' there is substituted ', a rail crossing diversion order, a special diversion order or an SSSI diversion order'.

(6) After subsection (5) there is inserted –

'(5A) Before making a determination under subsection (5) above the appropriate Minister may, if he thinks fit, give any person an opportunity to be heard on the question, and he must either give such an opportunity or cause a local inquiry to be held if a request to be heard with respect to the question to be determined is made –

(a) by the statutory undertakers,
(b) in the case of an order made on an application under section 118ZA, 118C, 119ZA or 119C above, by the person who made the application, and
(c) in the case of an order to be made on an appeal under section 121D(1)(a) below, by the appellant.

(5B) The appropriate Minister may appoint any person to exercise on his behalf, with or without payment, the function of determining a question falling to be determined under subsection (5) above.

(5C) Schedule 12ZA to this Act shall have effect with respect to appointments under subsection (5B) above; and subsection (5A) above has effect subject to the provisions of that Schedule.

(5D) Subsections (2) to (5) of section 250 of the Local Government Act 1972 (giving of evidence at, and defraying of costs of, inquiries) shall apply in relation to hearings or local inquiries which the appropriate Minister causes to be held under subsection (5A) above as they apply (by virtue of section 302(1) of this Act) to local inquiries which the Secretary of State causes to be held under this Act.

(5E) Section 322A of the Town and Country Planning Act 1990 (orders as to costs where no hearing or inquiry takes place) applies in relation to a hearing or inquiry under subsection (5A) above as it applies in relation to a hearing or local inquiry for the purposes referred to in that section, but as if references to the Secretary of State were references to the appropriate Minister.'.

(7) In subsection (6), for 'subsection (5)' there is substituted 'subsections (5) to (5E)'.

15. After section 121 of the 1980 Act there is inserted –

'121A Regulations with respect to applications for orders

(1) The Secretary of State may by regulations make provision as respects applications under section 118ZA, 118C, 119ZA or 119C above –

(a) requiring the applicant to issue a certificate as to the interests in, or rights in or over, the land to which the application relates and the purpose for which the land is used,
(b) requiring the applicant to give notice of the application to such persons as may be prescribed,
(c) requiring the applicant to certify that any requirement of regulations under this section has been complied with or to provide evidence that any such requirement has been complied with,
(d) as to the publicising of any application,
(e) as to the form, content and service of such notices and certificates, and
(f) as to the remission or refunding in prescribed circumstances of the whole or part of any prescribed charge.

(2) If any person –

(a) issues a certificate which purports to comply with any requirement imposed by virtue of subsection (1) above and contains a statement which he knows to be false or misleading in a material particular; or
(b) recklessly issues a certificate which purports to comply with any such requirement and contains a statement which is false or misleading in a material particular,

he shall be guilty of an offence.

(3) A person guilty of an offence under this section shall be liable on summary conviction to a fine not exceeding level 5 on the standard scale.

(4) Notwithstanding section 127 of the Magistrates' Courts Act 1980 (limitation of time for taking proceedings) summary proceedings for an offence under this section may be instituted at any time within three years after the commission of the offence.

121B   Register of applications

(1) Every council shall keep, in such manner as may be prescribed, a register containing such information as may be prescribed with respect to applications under section 118ZA, 118C, 119ZA or 119C above.

(2) The register shall contain such information as may be prescribed with respect to the manner in which such applications have been dealt with.

(3) Regulations may make provision for the register to be kept in two or more parts, each part containing such information relating to applications under section 118ZA, 118C, 119ZA or 119C above as may be prescribed.

(4) Regulations may make provision –

- (a) for a specified part of the register to contain copies of applications and of the maps submitted with them, and
- (b) for the entry relating to any application, and everything relating to it, to be removed from any part of the register when the application (including any appeal to the Secretary of State) has been finally disposed of (without prejudice to the inclusion of any different entry relating to it in another part of the register).

(5) Every register kept under this section shall be available for inspection by the public free of charge at all reasonable hours.

(6) In this section –

"prescribed" means prescribed by regulations;

"regulations" means regulations made by the Secretary of State.

121C   Cases where council may decline to determine applications

(1) A council may decline to determine an application under section 118ZA, 118C, 119ZA or 119C above if, within the period of three years ending with the date on which the application is received, the Secretary of State –

- (a) has refused to make an order on an appeal under section 121D(1)(a) below in respect of a similar application, or
- (b) has refused to confirm an order which is similar to the order requested.

(2) Before declining under subsection (1) above to determine an application under section 118C or 119C above, the council shall consider whether since the previous decision of the Secretary of State was made the risks referred to in subsection (1)(b)(i) to (iv) of section 118B or of section 119B have substantially increased.

(3) A council may decline to determine an application under section 118ZA, 118C, 119ZA or 119C above if –

(a) in respect of an application previously made to them under that section which is similar to the current application or relates to any of the land to which the current application relates, the council have not yet determined whether to make a public path extinguishment order, special extinguishment order, public path diversion order or special diversion order, or

(b) the council have made a similar order or an order which relates to any of the land to which the current application relates but no final decision as to the confirmation of the order has been taken.

(4) For the purposes of this section an application or order is similar to a later application or order only if they are, in the opinion of the council determining the later application, the same or substantially the same, but an application or order may be the same or substantially the same as a later application or order even though it is made to or by a different council.

121D   Right of appeal to Secretary of State in respect of applications for orders

(1) Subject to the provisions of this section, where, in relation to an application made under section 118ZA, 118C, 119ZA or 119C above, the council to which the application was made –

(a) refuse to make an order on the application,

(b) refuse to confirm as an unopposed order an order made on the application, or

(c) refuse to submit to the Secretary of State an order which is made on the application and against which any representation or objection has been duly made and not withdrawn,

the applicant may, by giving notice to the Secretary of State, appeal to the Secretary of State.

(2) Subsection (1)(a) above does not confer any right to appeal to the Secretary of State where –

(a) the council have no power to make the order requested without the consent of another person and that consent has not been given, or

(b) the reason, or one of the reasons, for the refusal to make the order is that the applicant has refused to enter into an agreement required by the council –
   (i) in the case of a public path extinguishment order, under subsection (6) of section 118ZA above,
   (ii) in the case of a special extinguishment order, under that subsection as applied by section 118C(2) above,
   (iii) in the case of a public path diversion order, under section 119(5) above,
   (iv) in the case of a special diversion order, under section 119C(3) above.

(3) Paragraph (b) of subsection (1) above does not confer any right to appeal to the Secretary of State in a case where the council has no power to confirm the order without the consent of another person and that consent has not been given; and paragraph (c) of that subsection does not confer any right to appeal to the Secretary of State in a case where, if the order had been unopposed, the council would have had no power to confirm it without the consent of another person and that consent has not been given.

121E   Determination of appeals

(1) Where an appeal to the Secretary of State is brought under section 121D(1)(a) above, the Secretary of State shall –

    (a) prepare a draft of a public path extinguishment order, special extinguishment order, public path diversion order or special diversion order under section 120(3) above giving effect to the application and containing such other provisions as, after consultation with such persons as he thinks fit, the Secretary of State may determine,

    (b) give notice of the draft order in accordance with paragraph 1(2) of Schedule 6 to this Act, and

    (c) subject to subsection (6) below and to paragraph 2 of that Schedule, determine whether to make the order (with or without modifications) under section 120(3) above.

(2) Where an appeal to the Secretary of State is brought under section 121D(1)(b) or (c) above, the order made on the application shall be treated as having been submitted to him for confirmation (with or without modifications).

(3) Where an appeal to the Secretary of State is brought under section 121D(1) above, the Secretary of State may not make or confirm a public path diversion order or special diversion order if it appears to him that –

    (a) work is necessary to bring the new highway created by the order into a fit condition for use by the public,

    (b) if the order were made, the work could not be carried out by the highway authority without –

        (i) the consent of another person, or

        (ii) any authorisation (however described) which is required by or under any enactment, and

    (c) the consent or authorisation has not been obtained.

(4) Where an appeal to the Secretary of State is brought under section 121D(1) above, the Secretary of State may not –

    (a) make a public path diversion order or special diversion order so as to create a public right of way over land covered by works used for the purposes of a statutory undertaking or the curtilage of such land, or

    (b) modify such an order so as to create such a public right of way,

unless the statutory undertaker has consented to the making or modification of the order.

(5) In subsection (4) above "statutory undertaker" and "statutory undertaking" have the same meaning as in Schedule 6 to this Act.

(6) Subsection (1)(c) above does not apply where any consent required by section 121(4) above has not been obtained.

(7) The Secretary of State may by regulations make further provision with respect to appeals under section 121D(1) above.

(8) Regulations under subsection (7) above may, in particular, make provision –

    (a) as to the manner in which, and time within which, notice of an appeal is to be given,

(b) as to the provision of information to the Secretary of State by the council to which the application to which the appeal relates was made,

(c) for the payment by the applicant of any expenses incurred by the Secretary of State –

(i) in preparing a draft order,

(ii) in giving any notice required by subsection (1)(b) above or Schedule 6 to this Act,

(d) requiring the production by the council to whom the application was made of any certificates required by regulations under section 121A(1)(a) above,

(e) requiring the applicant to give notice of the appeal to such persons as may be prescribed,

(f) requiring the applicant to certify that any requirement of regulations under this section has been complied with or to provide evidence that any such requirement has been complied with,

(g) as to the publicising of any appeal,

(h) as to the form, content and service of such notices and certificates,

(i) modifying the provisions of Schedule 6 to this Act in their application to the procedure on appeals under section 121D(1) above, and

(j) as to the remission or refunding in prescribed circumstances of any prescribed charge.

(9) The Secretary of State may by regulations provide that section 28 above, as applied by section 121(2) above, is to have effect in cases where a public path extinguishment order, special extinguishment order, public path diversion order or special diversion order is made under section 120(3) above on an appeal under section 121D(1)(a) above, as if the reference to such one of the authorities referred to as may be nominated by the Secretary of State were a reference to such one of those authorities as may be specified in or determined in accordance with, the regulations.

(10) Subsections (2) to (4) of section 121A above shall apply in relation to any certificate purporting to comply with a requirement imposed by virtue of this section as they apply to a certificate purporting to comply with a requirement imposed by virtue of subsection (1) of that section.

(11) For the purposes of this section –

(a) a draft public path extinguishment order or special extinguishment order gives effect to an application under section 118ZA or 118C above only if the land over which the public right of way is to be extinguished by the order is that shown for the purposes of subsection (2) of section 118ZA above (or that subsection as applied by section 118C(2) above) on the map accompanying the application, and

(b) a draft public path diversion order or draft special diversion order gives effect to an application made to a council under section 119ZA or 119C above only if –

(i) the land over which the public right of way is to be extinguished by the order, and

(ii) the new site to which the highway is to be diverted,

are those shown for the purposes of subsection (4) of section 119ZA above (or that subsection as applied by section 119C(4) above) on the map accompanying the application.

(12) In this section "prescribed" means prescribed by regulations made by the Secretary of State.'.

16. After section 135 of the 1980 Act there is inserted –

'135A   Temporary diversion for dangerous works

(1) Where works of a prescribed description are likely to cause danger to users of a footpath or bridleway which passes over any land, the occupier of the land may, subject to the provisions of this section, temporarily divert –

(a) so much of the footpath or bridleway as passes over that land, and
(b) so far as is requisite for effecting that diversion, so much of the footpath or bridleway as passes over other land occupied by him.

(2) A person may not under this section divert any part of a footpath or bridleway if –

(a) the period or periods for which that part has been diverted under this section, and
(b) the period or periods for which any other part of the same footpath or bridleway passing over land occupied by him has been diverted under this section,

amount in aggregate to more than fourteen days in any one calendar year.

(3) Where a person diverts a footpath or bridleway under this section –

(a) he shall do so in a manner which is reasonably convenient for the exercise of the public right of way, and
(b) where the diversion is by means of a temporary footpath or bridleway, he shall so indicate the line of the temporary footpath or bridleway on the ground to not less than the minimum width that it is apparent to members of the public wishing to use it.

(4) This section does not authorise a person –

(a) to divert a footpath or bridleway on to land not occupied by him without the consent of the occupier of that land and of any other person whose consent is needed to obtain access to it,
(b) to divert a footpath onto a highway other than a footpath or bridleway, or
(c) to divert a bridleway onto a highway other than a bridleway.

(5) The person by whom a footpath or bridleway is diverted under this section shall –

(a) at least fourteen days before the commencement of the diversion, give notice of the diversion in accordance with subsection (6) below,
(b) at least seven days before the commencement of the diversion, publish notice of the diversion in a local newspaper circulating in the area in which the footpath or bridleway is situated, and
(c) display such notices as may be prescribed at such places, in such manner and at such times before or during the diversion as may be prescribed.

(6) Notice under subsection (5)(a) above shall be given –

(a) to the highway authority for the footpath or bridleway,
(b) if the footpath or bridleway is on or contiguous with access land in England, to the Countryside Agency, and

(c) if the footpath or bridleway is on or contiguous with access land in Wales, to the Countryside Council for Wales.

(7) A notice under subsection (5)(a), (b) or (c) above shall be in such form and contain such information as may be prescribed.

(8) If a person –

(a) in a notice which purports to comply with the requirements of subsection (5)(a) or (b) above, makes a statement which he knows to be false in a material particular,

(b) by a notice displayed on or near a footpath or bridleway, falsely purports to be authorised under this section to divert the footpath or bridleway, or

(c) in diverting a footpath or bridleway under this section, fails to comply with subsection (3) above,

he shall be guilty of an offence and liable to a fine not exceeding level 3 on the standard scale.

(9) In this section –

"access land" has the same meaning as in Part I of the Countryside and Rights of Way Act 2000;

"minimum width" in relation to a temporary footpath or bridleway, means the minimum width, within the meaning of Schedule 12A to this Act, of the footpath or bridleway diverted;

"prescribed" means prescribed by regulations made by the Secretary of State.

135B   Temporary diversion for dangerous works: supplementary

(1) The person by whom a footpath or bridleway is diverted under section 135A above shall, before the diversion ceases to be authorised by that section, make good any damage to the footpath or bridleway resulting from the works mentioned in subsection (1) of that section, and remove from the footpath or bridleway any obstruction resulting from those works.

(2) Any person who fails to comply with the duty imposed on him by subsection (1) above is guilty of an offence and liable to a fine not exceeding level 3 on the standard scale.

(3) The highway authority may make good any damage, or remove any obstruction, in respect of which any person has failed to comply with that duty and recover from that person the amount of any expenses reasonably incurred by them in or in connection with doing so.

(4) Paragraph 3(1) of Schedule 12A to this Act does not apply in relation to any disturbance of the surface of a footpath or bridleway which subsection (1) above requires any person to make good; but paragraphs 7 and 8 of that Schedule apply for the purposes of subsection (3) above as if –

(a) references to the authority were references to the highway authority,

(b) references to the work were references to work carried out under subsection (3) above in relation to a footpath or bridleway, and

(c) references to the relevant land were references to the land over which the footpath or bridleway passes.

(5) The diversion of a footpath or bridleway under section 135A above does not –

(a) affect the liability of any person for anything done in relation to the path or way otherwise than for the purposes of or in consequence of the works mentioned in subsection (1) of that section, or

(b) authorise any interference with the apparatus or works of any statutory undertakers.

(6) Without prejudice to section 130 (protection of public rights of way) above, it is the duty of the highway authority to enforce the provisions of section 135A and this section.'.

17. In section 293 of the 1980 Act (powers of entry for purposes connected with certain orders relating to footpaths and bridleways), in subsection (1) –

(a) after 'rail crossing extinguishment order,' there is inserted 'a special extinguishment order', and

(b) for 'or a rail crossing diversion order' there is substituted ', a rail crossing diversion order, a special diversion order or an SSSI diversion order'.

18. In section 325 of the 1980 Act (regulations, schemes and orders) –

(a) in subsection (1)(d), for '118, 119,' there is substituted '118, 118A, 118B(4), 119, 119A, 119B(4), 119D', and

(b) in subsection (2)(b), after '17' there is inserted 'or 118B(1)(a)'.

19. In section 326 of the 1980 Act (revocation and variation of schemes and orders) in subsection (5), for 'a public path diversion order' there is substituted 'a rail crossing extinguishment order, a special extinguishment order, a public path diversion order, a rail crossing diversion order, a special diversion order or an SSSI diversion order'.

20. In section 329(1) of the 1980 Act (interpretation) –

(a) after the definition of 'cycle track' there is inserted –
'"definitive map and statement" has the same meaning as in Part III of the Wildlife and Countryside Act 1981;'

(b) after the definition of 'proposed highway' there is inserted –
'"proprietor", in relation to a school, has the same meaning as in the Education Act 1996;'

(c) after the definition of 'road-ferry' there is inserted –
'"school" has the same meaning as in the Education Act 1996;'

(d) after the definition of 'service area' there is inserted –
'"special diversion order" means an order under section 119B(4) above;'

(e) after the definition of 'special enactment' there is inserted –
'"special extinguishment order" means an order under section 118B(4) above;' and

(f) after the definition of 'special road authority' there is inserted –
'"SSSI diversion order" means an order under section 119D above;'.

21. In section 334 of the 1980 Act (savings relating to telecommunications apparatus) in subsection (2), for 'and a public path diversion order' there is substituted ', a special extinguishment order, a public path diversion order, a special diversion order and an SSSI diversion order'.

22. In section 344 of the 1980 Act (application to Isles of Scilly) in subsection (2)(a) after '135,' there is inserted '135A, 135B,'.

23.—(1) Schedule 6 to the 1980 Act (provisions as to making, confirmation, validity and date of operation of certain orders relating to footpaths and bridleways), including that Schedule as applied by section 32(2) of the Acquisition of Land Act 1981, is amended as follows.

(2) In paragraph 1(1) and (2) –

(a) after 'rail crossing extinguishment order,' there is inserted 'a special extinguishment order', and

(b) for 'or a rail crossing diversion order' there is substituted ', a rail crossing diversion order, a special diversion order or an SSSI diversion order'.

(3) In paragraph 1(3A) –

(a) after 'rail crossing extinguishment orders,' there is inserted 'special extinguishment orders', and

(b) for 'and rail crossing diversion orders' there is substituted ', rail crossing diversion orders, special diversion orders and SSSI diversion orders'.

(4) In paragraph 1(3B) –

(a) after 'draft rail crossing extinguishment orders,' there is inserted 'draft special extinguishment orders', and

(b) for 'and draft rail crossing diversion orders' there is substituted ', draft rail crossing diversion orders, draft special diversion orders and draft SSSI diversion orders'.

(5) In paragraph 2 –

(a) in sub-paragraph (1), at the beginning of paragraph (a) there is inserted 'subject to sub-paragraph (2A)',

(b) in sub-paragraphs (2) and (3), for 'or a public path diversion order,' there is substituted ', a public path diversion order, a special diversion order or an SSSI diversion order', and

(c) after sub-paragraph (2) there is inserted –

'(2A) Before making or confirming an order on an appeal under section 121D(1) of this Act, the Secretary of State shall –

(a) if requested by the authority who made an order to which the appeal relates to cause a local inquiry to be held, cause such an inquiry to be held, and

(b) if a request to be heard with respect to the question to be determined is made by the appellant, either afford to the appellant an opportunity of being heard by a person appointed by the Secretary of State for the purpose or cause a local inquiry to be held,

whether or not he would be required to do so apart from this sub-paragraph.'.

(6) After paragraph 2 there is inserted –

'**2ZA.**—(1) Where a public path extinguishment order, a special extinguishment order, a public path diversion order or a special diversion order is made by an authority other than the Secretary of State on an application under section 118ZA, 118C, 119ZA or 119C of this Act, that authority shall, as soon as reasonably practicable after the expiry of the time for representations, determine –

(a) whether, in the case of an unopposed order, to confirm it under paragraph 2(1)(b) above, or

(b) whether to submit the order to the Secretary of State.

(2) The authority making a determination required by sub-paragraph (1) above shall, as soon as practicable after making it, give to the applicant notice in writing of their determination and the reasons for it and give a copy of the notice to such other persons as may be prescribed.

(3) Where –

> (a) an authority other than the Secretary of State have made a public path extinguishment order, a special extinguishment order, a public path diversion order or a special diversion order on an application under section 118ZA, 118C, 119ZA or 119C of this Act, and
> (b) at the end of the period of two months beginning with the expiry of the time for representations, that authority have not determined –
>> (i) whether, in the case of an unopposed order, to confirm it under paragraph 2(1)(b) above, or
>> (ii) whether to submit the order to the Secretary of State,

the Secretary of State may, at the request of the person on whose application the order was made, by direction require the authority to determine that question before the end of such period as may be specified in the direction.

(4) In this paragraph "the time for representations" means the time specified by the authority in accordance with paragraph 1(1)(c) above.

2ZB. Where, in relation to any public path extinguishment order, special extinguishment order, public path diversion order or special diversion order which was made by an authority other than the Secretary of State on an application under section 118ZA, 118C, 119ZA or 119C of this Act, no representations or objections are duly made or any representations or objections so made are withdrawn, that authority may not submit the order to the Secretary of State for confirmation with any modification of the map contained in the order.'

(7) In paragraph 2A(1), for the words from the beginning to 'shall' there is substituted –

'The following decisions –

> (a) a decision of the Secretary of State under paragraph 2 above as respects an order made by an authority other than the Secretary of State including any related decision under section 120(5) of this Act, and
> (b) a decision of the Secretary of State under section 121E(1)(c) of this Act, including any related decision under section 120(5) of this Act,

shall'.

(8) After paragraph 2A there is inserted –

'**2B.**—(1) Subject to sub-paragraph (2), subsections (2) to (5) of section 250 of the Local Government Act 1972 (giving of evidence at, and defraying of costs of, inquiries) apply to a hearing which the Secretary of State causes to be held under paragraph 2 above as they apply (by virtue of section 302(1) of this Act) to a local inquiry which he causes to be held under this Act.

(2) In its application to a hearing or local inquiry held under paragraph 2 above by a person appointed under paragraph 2A(1) above, subsection (5) of section 250 of that Act shall have effect as if the reference to the Minister causing the inquiry to be held were a reference to the person so appointed or the Secretary of State.

(3) Section 322A of the Town and Country Planning Act 1990 (orders as to costs where no hearing or inquiry takes place) applies in relation to a hearing or inquiry under paragraph 2 above as it applies in relation to a hearing or local inquiry for the purposes referred to in that section.'.

(9) In paragraph 3(2) –

(a) for 'or a rail crossing extinguishment order' there is substituted ', a rail crossing extinguishment order or a special extinguishment order', and

(b) for 'or a rail crossing diversion order' there is substituted ', a rail crossing diversion order, a special diversion order or an SSSI diversion order'.

(10) At the end of paragraph 4(3) there is inserted 'other than any person on whom notice of the decision is required to be served under paragraph 2ZA(2) above'.

24. After Schedule 12 to the 1980 Act there is inserted –

'SCHEDULE 12ZA

DELEGATION OF FUNCTION OF MAKING DETERMINATION

Interpretation

1. In this Schedule –

"appointed person" means a person appointed under section 121(5B) of this Act;

"appropriate Minister" has the same meaning as in section 121(5) of this Act;

"appointment", in the case of any appointed person, means appointment under section 121(5B) of this Act.

Appointments

2. An appointment under section 121(5B) of this Act must be in writing and –

(a) may relate to a particular question specified in the appointment or to questions of a description so specified,

(b) may provide for any function to which it relates to be exercisable by the appointed person either unconditionally or subject to the fulfilment of such conditions as may be specified in the appointment, and

(c) may, by notice in writing given to the appointed person, be revoked at any time by the appropriate Minister in respect of any question which has not been determined by the appointed person before that time.

Powers of appointed person

3. Subject to the provisions of this Schedule, an appointed person shall, in relation to the determination of any question to which his appointment relates, have the same powers and duties as the appropriate Minister, other than –

(a) any function of holding an inquiry or other hearing or of causing an inquiry or other hearing to be held; or

(b) any function of appointing a person for the purpose –

(i) of enabling persons to appear before and be heard by the person so appointed; or

(ii)   of referring any question or matter to that person.

Holding of inquiries and other hearings by appointed persons

4.—(1) If either of the following persons –

(a) the statutory undertakers to which the question relates, and
(b) in the case of an order to be made on an application under section 118ZA, 118C, 119ZA or 119C of this Act, the person who made the application,

express a wish to appear before and be heard by the appointed person, the appointed person shall give them an opportunity of appearing and being heard.

(2) Whether or not sub-paragraph (1) above applies, the appointed person –

(a) may hold an inquiry or other hearing in connection with the determination of the question, and
(b) shall, if the appropriate Minister so directs, hold an inquiry in connection with that determination.

(3) Where an appointed person holds an inquiry or other hearing by virtue of this Schedule, an assessor may be appointed by the appropriate Minister to sit with the appointed person at the inquiry or hearing and advise him on any matters arising, notwithstanding that the appointed person is to determine the question.

(4) Subject to paragraph 7 below, the costs of an inquiry or other hearing held under this Schedule shall be defrayed by the appropriate Minister.

Revocation of appointments and making of new appointments

5.—(1) Where under paragraph 2(c) above the appointment of the appointed person is revoked in respect of any question, the appropriate Minister shall, unless he proposes to determine the question himself, appoint another person under section 121(5B) of this Act to determine the question instead.

(2) Where such a new appointment is made, the consideration of the question, or any hearing in connection with it, shall be begun afresh.

(3) Nothing in sub-paragraph (2) above shall require any person to be given an opportunity of making fresh representations or modifying or withdrawing any representations already made.

Certain acts and omissions of appointed person to be treated as those of appropriate Minister

6.—(1) Anything done or omitted to be done by an appointed person in, or in connection with, the exercise or purported exercise of any function to which the appointment relates shall be treated for all purposes as done or omitted to be done by the appropriate Minister.

(2) Sub-paragraph (1) above does not apply –

(a) for the purposes of so much of any contract made between the appropriate Minister and the appointed person as relates to the exercise of the function, or
(b) for the purposes of any criminal proceedings brought in respect of anything done or omitted to be done as mentioned in that sub-paragraph.

Local inquiries and hearings: evidence and costs

7. Subsections (2) to (5) of section 250 of the Local Government Act 1972 (local inquiries: evidence and costs) shall apply to local inquiries or other hearings held under this Schedule by an appointed person as they apply to inquiries caused to be held under that section by a Minister, but as if –

(a) in subsection (2) (evidence) the reference to the person appointed to hold the inquiry were a reference to the appointed person,

(b) in subsection (4) (recovery of costs of holding inquiry) references to the Minister causing the inquiry to be held were references to the appropriate Minister, and

(c) in subsection (5) (orders as to the costs of the parties) the reference to the Minister causing the inquiry to be held were a reference to the appointed person or the appropriate Minister.'.

Explanatory text — see Chapters 3 and 4.

PART II

CONSEQUENTIAL AMENDMENTS OF OTHER ACTS

Norfolk and Suffolk Broads Act (c.4)

25. In Schedule 3 to the Norfolk and Suffolk Broads Act 1988 (functions of Broads Authority), in paragraph 47 (footpaths and bridleways) –

(a) for '118 to 121' there is substituted '118 to 121E', and

(b) after 'footpaths etc)' there is inserted ', except sections 118B and 119B of that Act (stopping up and diversion for purposes of crime prevention, etc),'.

Environment Act 1995 (c.25)

26. In Schedule 9 to the Environment Act 1995 (miscellaneous functions of National Park authorities), in paragraph 11 (footpaths and bridleways) for paragraph (c) there is substituted –

'(c) sections 118 to 121E (stopping up and diversion of public paths, etc), except sections 118B and 119B (stopping up and diversion for purposes of crime prevention, etc), and'.

SCHEDULE 7

DRIVING OF MECHANICALLY PROPELLED VEHICLES ELSEWHERE THAN ON ROADS

National Parks and Access to the Countryside Act 1949 (c.97)

1. In section 51(1) of the National Parks and Access to the Countryside Act 1949 (general provisions as to long-distance routes), for 'not being a motor vehicle' there is substituted 'not being a mechanically propelled vehicle'.

Countryside Act 1968 (c.41)

2.—(1) Section 30 of the Countryside Act 1968 (riding of pedal cycles on bridleways) is amended as follows.

(2) In subsection (1), for 'not being a motor vehicle' there is substituted 'not being a mechanically propelled vehicle'.

(3) For subsection (5) there is substituted –

'(5) In this section "mechanically propelled vehicle" does not include a vehicle falling within paragraph (c) of section 189(1) of the Road Traffic Act 1988.'.

Chronically Sick and Disabled Persons Act 1970 (c.44)

3. In section 20 of the Chronically Sick and Disabled Persons Act 1970 (use of invalid carriages on highways), in subsection (1)(b) after 'sections 1 to 4,' there is inserted '21, 34,'.

Road Traffic Act (c.52)

4.—(1) Section 21 of the Road Traffic Act 1988 (prohibition of driving or parking on cycle tracks) is amended as follows.

(2) In subsection (1), for 'motor' there is substituted 'mechanically propelled'.

(3) In subsection (3), after paragraph (a) there is inserted –

'(aa) in subsection (1) "mechanically propelled vehicle" does not include a vehicle falling within paragraph (a), (b) or (c) of section 189(1) of this Act,'.

5. For section 34 of that Act there is substituted –

'34 Prohibition of driving mechanically propelled vehicles elsewhere than on roads

(1) Subject to the provisions of this section, if without lawful authority a person drives a mechanically propelled vehicle –

(a) on to or upon any common land, moorland or land of any other description, not being land forming part of a road, or
(b) on any road being a footpath, bridleway or restricted byway,

he is guilty of an offence.

(2) For the purposes of subsection (1)(b) above, a way shown in a definitive map and statement as a footpath, bridleway or restricted byway is, without prejudice to section 56(1) of the Wildlife and Countryside Act 1981, to be taken to be a way of the kind shown, unless (subject to section 34A of this Act) the contrary is proved.

(3) It is not an offence under this section to drive a mechanically propelled vehicle on any land within fifteen yards of a road, being a road on which a motor vehicle may lawfully be driven, for the purpose only of parking the vehicle on that land.

(4) A person shall not be convicted of an offence under this section with respect to a vehicle if he proves to the satisfaction of the court that it was driven in contravention of this section for the purpose of saving life or extinguishing fire or meeting any other like emergency.

(5) It is hereby declared that nothing in this section prejudices the operation of –

(a) section 193 of the Law of Property Act 1925 (rights of the public over commons and waste lands), or

(b) any byelaws applying to any land,

or affects the law of trespass to land or any right or remedy to which a person may by law be entitled in respect of any such trespass or in particular confers a right to park a vehicle on any land.

(6) Subsection (2) above and section 34A of this Act do not extend to Scotland.

(7) In this section –

"definitive map and statement" has the same meaning as in Part III of the Wildlife and Countryside Act 1981;

"mechanically propelled vehicle" does not include a vehicle falling within paragraph (a), (b) or (c) of section 189(1) of this Act; and

"restricted byway" means a way over which the public have restricted byway rights within the meaning of Part II of the Countryside and Rights of Way Act 2000, with or without a right to drive animals of any description along the way, but no other rights of way.'.

6. After that section there is inserted –

'34A   Exceptions to presumption in section 34(2)

(1) Where a person is charged with an offence under section 34 of this Act in respect of the driving of any vehicle, it is open to that person to prove under subsection (2) of that section that a way shown in a definitive map and statement as a footpath, bridleway or restricted byway is not a way of the kind shown only –

    (a) if he proves to the satisfaction of the court –
        (i)   that he was a person interested in any land and that the driving of the vehicle by him was reasonably necessary to obtain access to the land,
        (ii) that the driving of the vehicle by him was reasonably necessary to obtain access to any land, and was for the purpose of obtaining access to the land as a lawful visitor, or
        (iii) that the driving of the vehicle by him was reasonably necessary for the purposes of any business, trade or profession; or
    (b) in such circumstances as may be prescribed by regulations made by the Secretary of State (and paragraph (a) above is without prejudice to this paragraph).

(2) In subsection (1) above –

"interest", in relation to land, includes any estate in land and any right over land, whether the right is exercisable by virtue of the ownership of an estate or interest in land or by virtue of a licence or agreement, and in particular includes rights of common and sporting rights, and the reference to a person interested in land shall be construed accordingly;

"lawful visitor", in relation to land, includes any person who enters the land for any purpose in the exercise of a right conferred by law.'.

7. In section 195 of that Act –

    (a) in subsection (3), after 'that section)' there is inserted '34A', and
    (b) in subsection (4), after '14' there is inserted ', 34A'.

Road Traffic Offenders Act 1988 (c.53)

8. In Schedule 2 to the Road Traffic Offenders Act 1988 (prosecution and punishment of offences), in the second column of the entry in Part I relating to section 34 of the Road Traffic Act 1988, for 'motor' there is substituted 'mechanically propelled'.

9. In Schedule 3 to that Act (fixed penalty offences), in the second column of the entry relating to section 34 of the Road Traffic Act 1988, for 'motor' there is substituted 'mechanically propelled'.

Explanatory text — see **9.8**.

Section 102   SCHEDULE 16

REPEALS

PART I

ACCESS TO THE COUNTRYSIDE

Chapter	Short title	Extent of repeal
1925 c. 20.	The Law of Property Act 1925.	Section 193(2).
1949 c. 97.	The National Parks and Access to the Countryside Act 1949.	Sections 61 to 63. In section 111A(3)(a), the words '61 to 63,'.
1972 c. 70.	The Local Government Act 1972.	In Schedule 17, paragraphs 35 and 35A.
1980 c. 65.	The Local Government, Planning and Land Act 1980.	In Schedule 3, paragraph 6.
1985 c. 51.	The Local Government Act 1985.	In Schedule 3, paragraph 5(9).
1990 c. 43.	The Environmental Protection Act 1990.	In Schedule 8, in paragraph 1(8), the words '62(1) and'.
1994 c. 19.	The Local Government (Wales) Act 1994.	In Schedule 6, paragraph 13.

PART II

PUBLIC RIGHTS OF WAY AND ROAD TRAFFIC

Chapter	Short title	Extent of repeal
1980 c. 66.	The Highways Act 1980.	Section 134(5).
1981 c. 69.	The Wildlife and Countryside Act 1981.	Section 54. Section 56(5). In section 57(1), the words 'on such scale as may be so prescribed,'. In Schedule 15, paragraph 9.
1984 c. 27.	The Road Traffic Regulation Act 1984.	In section 22(1)(a), the words '(other than Greater London)' and, at the end of paragraph (vi), the word 'or'.
1992 c. 42.	The Transport and Works Act 1992.	In Schedule 2, paragraphs 5(2), (4)(a), (d) and (e), (6) and (7), 6(2)(b) and 10(4)(a).

Appendix 2

PASSAGE OF THE CROW ACT 2000 THROUGH PARLIAMENT

Stage	Date	Hansard Ref
House of Commons		
Introduction	3 Mar	Vol 345 Col 664
Second Reading	20 Mar	Vol 346 Col 720–820
Committee	28 Mar 30 Mar 4 Apr 6 Apr 11 Apr 13 Apr 18 Apr 2 May 9 May 11 May 16 May 18 May 23 May	Hansard Standing Committee B
Report	13–14 June	Vol 351 Col 794–1061
Third Reading	14 Jun	Vol 351 Col 1061–1075
House of Lords		
Introduction	16 Jun	Vol 613 Col 1910
Second Reading	26 Jun	Vol 614 Col 629–756
Committee	27 Sep 3 Oct 5 Oct 9 Oct 11 Oct 16 Oct	Vol 616 Col 791–847 + 865–934 Vol 616 Col 1271–1404 + 1405–1508 Vol 616 Col 1691–1755 + 1772–1814 Vol 617 Col 10–86 + 101–148 Vol 617 Col 337–405 + 422–496 Vol 617 Col 673–744 + 760–872
Report	1 Nov 2 Nov 7 Nov 16 Nov	Vol 618 Col 949–1017 Vol 618 Col 1085–1108 Vol 619 Col 1399–1435 + 1440–1524 Vol 619 Col 367–516
Third Reading	23 Nov	Vol 619 Col 951–1066
Commons Consideration of Lords Amendments	28 Nov	Vol 357 Col 837–911
Royal Assent	30 Nov	Vol 357 Col 1232

Appendix 3

STATUTORY INSTRUMENTS UNDER THE CROW ACT 2000

COUNTRYSIDE AND RIGHTS OF WAY ACT 2000 (COMMENCEMENT NO 1) ORDER 2001, SI 2001/14

1 Citation, interpretation and extent

(1) This Order may be cited as the Countryside and Rights of Way Act 2000 (Commencement No 1) Order 2001.

(2) In this Order references to sections, Parts and Schedules are references to sections and Parts of, and Schedules to, the Act.

(3) This Order applies in relation to England only.

2 Appointed days

(1) 30th January 2001 is the day appointed for the coming into force of the following provisions of the Act –

    (a) section 57 (amendments to the 1980 Act and other Acts) in so far as it gives effect to the substitutions referred to in sub-paragraphs (e) and (f) below;

    (b) section 72 (interpretation provisions of Part II);

    (c) section 100 (application of the Act to the Isles of Scilly) except subsections (3) and (5)(a);

    (d) section 102 (which introduces Schedule 16) in so far as it relates to –

        (i) the provision in Schedule 16 referred to in sub-paragraph (g) below; and

        (ii) Parts III and IV of Schedule 16 (repeals relating to sites of special scientific interest and wildlife);

    (e) paragraph 18(a) of Schedule 6 (amendments to the 1980 Act) to the extent that in section 325(1)(d) of the 1980 Act it substitutes for '118, 119,' references to sections 118, 118A, 119 and 119A;

    (f) paragraph 19 of Schedule 6 to the extent that in section 326(5) of the 1980 Act it substitutes for 'a public path diversion order' references to a rail crossing extinguishment order, a public path diversion order and a rail crossing diversion order; and

    (g) Part II of Schedule 16 (repeals relating to public rights of way and road traffic) in so far as it repeals part of section 22(1)(a) of the Road Traffic Regulation Act 1984.

(2) 1st April 2001 is the day appointed for the coming into force of the following provisions of the Act –

    (a) section 46(1)(b) (repeals of sections 61 to 63 of the National Parks and Access to the Countryside Act 1949);

    (b) section 46(3) (which introduces Schedule 4) in so far as it relates to the provisions of Schedule 4 referred to in sub-paragraph (j) below;

    (c) section 68 (vehicular access across common land);

    (d) section 70(2) and (4) (minor amendments);

    (e) Part IV (designation and management of areas of outstanding natural beauty) (and accordingly Schedules 13, 14 and 15);

    (f) section 96 (amendments to section 39 of the 1981 Act);

    (g) section 97 (duties of public bodies regarding the Norfolk and Suffolk Broads);

(h) section 100(3) (application of provisions relating to areas of outstanding natural beauty to the Isles of Scilly);

(i) section 102 in so far as it relates to the provisions in Schedule 16 referred to in sub-paragraphs (k) to (m) below;

(j) paragraphs 1, 4, 5 and 6 of Schedule 4;

(k) Part 1 of Schedule 16 (repeals relating to access to the countryside) except in so far as it repeals –

(i) section 193(2) of the Law of Property Act 1925;

(ii) paragraph 35A of Schedule 17 to the Local Government Act 1972; and

(iii) paragraph 13 of Schedule 6 to the Local Government (Wales) Act 1994;

(l) Part II of Schedule 16 in so far as it repeals section 134(5) of the 1980 Act; and

(m) Parts V and VI of Schedule 16 (repeals relating to areas of outstanding natural beauty and the 1981 Act).

3   Transitional provision

The repeal of section 134(5) of the 1980 Act commenced by article 2(2)(d) and (1) shall not have effect in relation to any offence under section 134 of that Act committed before 1st April 2001.

COUNTRYSIDE AND RIGHTS OF WAY ACT 2000 (COMMENCEMENT NO 1) (WALES) ORDER 2001, SI 2001/203

1   Citation, interpretation and application

(1) This Order may be cited as the Countryside and Rights of Way Act 2000 (Commencement No 1) (Wales) Order 2001.

(2) In this Order 'the Act' means the Countryside and Rights of Way Act 2000.

(3) This Order applies to Wales.

2   Appointed day

30 January 2001 is the appointed day on which section 99 of the Act shall come into force.

COUNTRYSIDE AND RIGHTS OF WAY ACT 2000 (COMMENCEMENT NO 2) (WALES) ORDER 2001, SI 2001/1410

1   Citation, interpretation and application

(1) This Order may be cited as the Countryside and Rights of Way Act 2000 (Commencement No 2) (Wales) Order 2001.

(2) In this Order –

'the Act' ('y Ddeddf') means the Countryside and Rights of Way Act 2000 and unless otherwise stated references to sections, Parts and Schedules are references to sections and Parts of, and Schedules to, the Act;

'the 1980 Act' ('Deddf 1980') means the Highways Act 1980;

'the 1981 Act' ('Deddf 1981') means the Wildlife and Countryside Act 1981;

(3) This Order applies to Wales.

2   Appointed day

1st May 2001 is the day appointed on which the following provisions of the Act come into force –

(a) section 46(1)(b) (repeals of sections 61 to 63 of the National Parks and Access to the Countryside Act 1949);

(b) section 46(3) (which introduces Schedule 4) in so far as it relates to the provisions of Schedule 4 referred to in sub-paragraph (j) below;

(c) section 57 (amendments to the 1980 Act and other Acts) in so far as it gives effect to the substitutions referred to in sub-paragraphs (k) and (l) below;

(d) section 68 (vehicular access across common land);

(e) section 70(2) and (4) (minor amendments);

(f) section 72 (interpretation provisions of Part II);

(g) Part IV (designation and management of areas of outstanding natural beauty) (and accordingly Schedules 13, 14 and 15);

(h) Section 96 (amendments to section 39 of the 1981 Act);

(i) Section 102 in so far as it relates to the provisions in Schedule 16 referred to in sub-paragraphs (m) to (q) below;

(j) paragraphs 1, 4, 5 and 6 of Schedule 4;

(k) paragraph 18(a) of Schedule 6 (amendments to the 1980 Act) to the extent that in section 325(1)(d) of the 1980 Act it substitutes for '118, 119,' references to sections 118, 118A, 119 and 119A;

(l) paragraph 19 of Schedule 6 to the extent that in section 326(5) of the 1980 Act it substitutes for 'a public path diversion order' references to a rail crossing extinguishment order, a public path diversion order and a rail crossing diversion order;

(m) Part I of Schedule 16 (repeals relating to access to the countryside) except in so far as it repeals –

(i)   section 193(2) of the Law of Property Act 1925;

  (ii)   paragraph 35A of Schedule 17 to the Local Government Act 1972; and
  (iii) paragraph 13 of Schedule 6 to the Local Government (Wales) Act 1994;
(n) Part II of Schedule 16 (repeals relating to public rights of way and road traffic) in so far as it repeals part of section 22(1)(a) of the Road Traffic Regulation Act 1984;
(o) Part II of Schedule 16 in so far as it repeals section 134(5) of the 1980 Act;
(p) Parts III and IV of Schedule 16 (repeals relating to sites of special scientific interest and wildlife); and
(q) Parts V and VI of Schedule 16 (repeals relating to areas of outstanding natural beauty and the 1981 Act).

3   Transitional provision

The repeal of section 134(5) of the 1980 Act commenced by article 2(e) and (o) shall not have effect in relation to any offence under section 134 of that Act committed before 1st May 2001.

ACCESS TO THE COUNTRYSIDE (MAPS IN DRAFT FORM) (ENGLAND) REGULATIONS 2001, SI 2001/3301

1   Citation, commencement and extent

(1) These Regulations may be cited as the Access to the Countryside (Maps in Draft Form) (England) Regulations 2001 and shall come into force on 1st November 2001.

(2) These Regulations extend to England only.

2   Interpretation

(1) In these Regulations –

'the Agency' means the Countryside Agency;

'parish council' has the same meaning as in Part I of the Local Government Act 1972;

'proper officer' shall be construed in accordance with section 270(3) of the Local Government Act 1972; and

'reduced scale map' means, in relation to a map issued by the Agency in draft form, a copy in printed or electronic form of the map which may be on a smaller scale than the scale of the map (or of any part of the map) issued in draft form but –
- (a) for the purposes of regulation 11, must be on a scale of not less than 1/10,000, and
- (b) for all other purposes, must be on a scale of not less than 1/25,000.

(2) In these Regulations references to sections are references to sections of the Countryside and Rights of Way Act 2000.

3   Preparation and scale of maps in draft form

(1) Any map prepared by the Agency under section 4 and issued in draft form shall –
- (a) be on a scale of not less than 1/10,000,
- (b) be in electronic form,
- (c) use the same notation to show all registered common land, and
- (d) use the same notation to show all open country.

(2) The scale of any part of any such map may vary, provided each part is on a scale of not less than 1/10,000.

4   Consultation on maps in draft form

(1) Subject to paragraph (3), where the Agency have issued a map in draft form they shall, as soon as reasonably practicable on or after the date of issue, send to the persons specified in the Schedule to these Regulations –
- (a) in the case of those persons specified in Part I of the Schedule, the Countryside Council for Wales and the Historic Buildings and Monuments Commission for England, one reduced scale map, and
- (b) in the case of all other persons specified in the Schedule, two reduced scale maps.

(2) The Agency shall at the same time send to the persons specified in the Schedule –

(a) an invitation to make representations with respect to the showing of, or the failure to show, any area of land on the map in draft form as registered common land or as open country, and

(b) the information required by paragraph (1)(a) and (d) to (j) of regulation 5 to be contained in the notice published in accordance with that regulation in relation to that map.

(3) Where the functions of a person specified in Part I of the Schedule relate to only part of the area of land covered by the map in draft form, the Agency may send to that person a reduced scale map relating to only that part.

5   Informing the public of the issue of maps in draft form

(1) Where the Agency have issued a map in draft form, they shall, as soon as reasonably practicable on or after the date of issue, publish a notice which –

(a) states the date of issue,

(b) describes the area of land to which the map in draft form relates,

(c) invites representations with respect to the showing of, or the failure to show, any area of land on the map in draft form as registered common land or as open country,

(d) states where (in accordance with regulation 6) the map in draft form is to be made available for inspection,

(e) states how (in accordance with regulation 7) reduced scale maps may be obtained including whether a fee is payable,

(f) states where (in accordance with regulation 8) a reduced scale map may be inspected on the internet,

(g) states in general terms where (by virtue of regulations 9, 10 and 11) reduced scale maps are to be made available for inspection,

(h) states that representations on the map in draft form must be made so as to be received by the Agency within a period of three months beginning with the date of issue,

(i) states the manner in which representations must be made to the Agency including the effect of regulation 12(2) and (3), and

(j) states the general effect of the right conferred on the public by section 2(1).

(2) The notice referred to in paragraph (1) shall be published in such local or regional newspapers circulating in the area of land to which the map in draft form relates as the Agency consider necessary for informing the public of the issue of the map.

6   Where maps in draft form are to be available for inspection

(1) Subject to paragraph (2), where the Agency have issued a map in draft form, they shall, as soon as reasonably practicable on or after the date of issue, make the map available for inspection by members of the public at all reasonable hours in such regional office of the Agency as they consider appropriate.

(2) The map shall be available for inspection for a period which ends three months after the date on which the Agency have issued a map in conclusive form covering the area of land to which the map issued in draft form relates or, where more than one map is issued in conclusive form covering that area of land, for a period which ends three months after the date on which the Agency have issued the last map in conclusive form relating to that area.

7   Supply of reduced scale maps to members of the public

(1) Subject to paragraph (2), where the Agency have issued a map in draft form they shall supply a reduced scale map in printed form to any person who, within a period of three months beginning with the date of issue, requests such a map and who pays to the Agency such reasonable fee as the Agency may determine.

(2) Where a person requests a reduced scale map relating to only part of the area of land to which the map in draft form relates, he shall provide the Agency with such information as the Agency reasonably require to enable that part to be identified, and the Agency shall supply a reduced scale map relating, so far as reasonably practicable, to only that part.

8   Reduced scale maps on the internet

Where the Agency have issued a map in draft form, they shall make a reduced scale map available for inspection on a website they maintain on the internet for a period of three months beginning with the date of issue.

9   Deposit of reduced scale maps with county councils, district councils, London borough councils and National Park authorities

(1) Subject to paragraph (2), where the Agency have issued a map in draft form, they shall, as soon as reasonably practicable on or after the date of issue, deposit a reduced scale map with the proper officer of any county council, district council, London borough council or National Park authority exercising functions for any area of land to which the map in draft form relates.

(2) Where the functions of a council or authority relate to only part of the area of land covered by the map in draft form, a reduced scale map relating to only that part may be deposited.

(3) The proper officer shall, in accordance with section 225(1) of the Local Government Act 1972, receive and retain the reduced scale map for a period which ends three months after the date of issue for the purpose of it being available for inspection and making copies in accordance with section 228 of that Act.

10   Deposit of reduced scale maps with library authorities

(1) Subject to paragraphs (2) and (3), where the Agency have issued a map in draft form, they shall, as soon as reasonably practicable on or after the date of issue, deposit reduced scale maps with the proper officer of any library authority exercising functions for any area of land to which the map in draft form relates.

(2) Where the functions of an authority relate to only part of the area of land covered by the map in draft form, reduced scale maps relating to only that part may be deposited.

(3) The number of reduced scale maps deposited shall be such number as the Agency consider appropriate, after consultation with the proper officer of the library authority.

(4) The proper officer shall, in accordance with section 225(1) of the Local Government Act 1972, receive and retain the reduced scale maps for the purpose of their being available for inspection and making copies in accordance with section 228 of that Act –

(a) for a period which ends three months after the date of issue, and

(b) in such public libraries in the area of the library authority as the proper officer considers appropriate.

(5) In this regulation 'library authority' means a library authority under the Public Libraries and Museums Act 1964.

11 Deposit of reduced scale maps with commons registration authorities

(1) Subject to paragraph (2), where the Agency have issued a map in draft form, they shall, as soon as reasonably practicable on or after the date of issue, deposit relevant extracts of a reduced scale map with the proper officer of any registration authority exercising functions for any area of land to which the map in draft form relates.

(2) Where the functions of an authority relate to only part of the area of land covered by the map in draft form, relevant extracts of a reduced scale map relating to only that part may be deposited.

(3) The proper officer shall, in accordance with section 225(1) of the Local Government Act 1972, receive and retain the relevant extracts of the reduced scale map for the purpose of their being available for inspection and making copies in accordance with section 228 of that Act –

(a) for a period which ends three months after the date of issue, and
(b) in such place as will enable the public to compare the relevant extracts with the register of common land which the registration authority is required to maintain under section 3 of the Commons Registration Act 1965.

(4) In this regulation –

(a) 'registration authority' has the same meaning as in the Commons Registration Act 1965, and
(b) 'relevant extracts' means extracts of the reduced scale map which show registered common land.

12 Representations on maps in draft form

(1) Where the Agency have issued a map in draft form they shall consider any representations, with respect to the showing of, or the failure to show, any area of land on the map as registered common land or as open country, received by them within a period of three months beginning with the date of issue.

(2) The representations must provide the following information –

(a) the name and postal address of the person making the representation,
(b) the location and extent of the land to which the representation relates, sufficient to enable it to be identified, whether by marking it on a map or otherwise, and
(c) where the person making the representation has an interest in the whole or a part of the area of land to which the representation relates, the nature of his interest.

(3) The representations must be made in writing and may be made in electronic form.

13 Certification of copies of maps issued in draft form

A document purporting to be certified on behalf of the Agency to be a copy of or of any part of a map issued by the Agency in draft form shall be receivable in evidence and shall be deemed, unless the contrary is shown, to be such a copy.

14 Maps in electronic form

Any map authorised or required by these Regulations to be prepared, issued or made available for inspection in electronic form must be capable of being reproduced in printed form.

SCHEDULE

PERSONS TO BE CONSULTED ON MAPS ISSUED IN DRAFT FORM

Regulation 4

PART 1

PERSONS EXERCISING FUNCTIONS FOR A PARTICULAR AREA

The following persons exercising functions for the area of land to which the map relates –

conservation boards established under Part IV of the Countryside and Rights of Way Act 2000 (areas of outstanding natural beauty),

county councils,

district councils,

local access forums,

London borough councils,

National Park authorities,

parish councils.

PART 2

OTHER PERSONS

British Association for Shooting and Conservation,

British Mountaineering Council,

Countryside Council for Wales, in respect of any map which relates to land adjoining land in Wales,

Country Land and Business Association,

English Nature,

Historic Buildings and Monuments Commission for England,

Moorland Association,

National Farmers' Union,

Open Spaces Society,

Ramblers' Association,

Royal Institution of Chartered Surveyors,

Tenant Farmers Association.

COUNTRYSIDE ACCESS (DRAFT MAPS) (WALES) REGULATIONS 2001, SI 2001/4001

1 Citation, commencement and application

(1) These Regulations may be cited as the Countryside Access (Draft Maps) (Wales) Regulations 2001 and shall come into force on 1 January 2002.

(2) These Regulations apply to Wales.

2 Interpretation

(1) In these Regulations –

'the Act' ('y Ddeddf') means the Countryside and Rights of Way Act 2000;

references to the 'confirmation' ('cadarnhau') of a draft map are references to its confirmation in accordance with section 5(c) of the Act;

'consultation period' ('cyfnod ymgynghori') means the period referred to in Regulation 4(2)(h);

'the Council' ('y Cyngor') means the Countryside Council for Wales;

'draft map' ('map drafft') means a map issued by the Council in accordance with section 5(a) of the Act;

'electronic form' ('ffurf electronig') means a form capable of being stored on, transmitted to and from, and read by means of a computer;

'inset map' ('map mewnosod') means a map showing part only of the area to which a draft map relates and to a larger scale than that draft map and whether appearing on or annexed to the draft map;

'interest' ('buddiant') has the meaning given by section 45(1) of the Act;

'issued' ('wedi'i ddyroddi' or 'wedi'u dyroddi') means issued by the Council in accordance with section 5(a) of the Act;

'local access forum' ('fforwm mynediad lleol') means an advisory body established under section 94 of the Act;

'open country' ('tir agored') has the meaning given by section 1(2) of the Act;

'person' ('person') and 'persons' ('personau') include individuals, corporations and unincorporated bodies;

'registered common land' ('tir comin cofrestredig') has the meaning given by section 1(3) of the Act;

'relevant local access forum' ('fforwm mynediad lleol perthnasol') means, in relation to a draft map, a local access forum in respect of which the area for which it is established includes an area contained in that draft map;

'relevant local authority' ('awdurdod lleol perthnasol') means, in relation to a draft map, a county or county borough council whose area includes an area contained in that draft map;

'relevant National Park authority' ('awdurdod Parc Cenedlaethol perthnasol') means, in relation to a draft map, a National Park authority for a National Park whose area includes an area contained in that draft map;

'section 4(2) land' ('tir adran 4(2)') means the registered common land and open country in respect of which the Council is required to prepare maps in accordance with section 4(2) of the Act.

(2) In these Regulations, unless the context otherwise requires, any reference to a numbered regulation is a reference to the regulation bearing that number in these Regulations, and any reference in a regulation to a numbered paragraph is a reference to the paragraph bearing that number in that regulation.

(3) In reckoning any period which is expressed in these Regulations to be a period from a given date, that date is to be excluded and, where the day or the last day on which anything is required by, or in pursuance with, these Regulations to be done is a Sunday, Christmas Day, Good Friday, bank holiday or a day appointed for public thanksgiving or mourning, the requirement shall be deemed to relate to the first day thereafter which is not one of the days before-mentioned.

3   Preparation of draft map

(1) A draft map prepared by the Council may relate to such area as the Council may determine, having regard to local authority boundaries, the areas for which local access forums have been established, the boundaries of National Parks and of areas of outstanding natural beauty and the location of natural and other geographical features including mountains, rivers and highways.

(2) The map base on which a draft map is drawn may include areas in respect of which section 4(2) land is intended to be shown as such on another draft map but in such case the map base must clearly identify the boundaries of the area in respect of which it is the draft map.

(3) A draft map must be prepared to a scale of not less than 1:10,000 or, if it is not possible to achieve that scale using the base map technology reasonably available to the Council, the largest scale practicable using that base map technology, but where it is necessary or desirable for the purpose of accurately showing a part of the boundary of any section 4(2) land that the draft map, or an inset map, be prepared to a larger scale, the Council must do so either by preparing a draft map to such larger scale or by including on or annexed to a draft map of the general area an inset map to such larger scale and, where an inset map is not included on the draft map itself, by noting on the relevant area of the draft map the fact that an inset map of that area has been prepared and how access to that inset map is to be obtained.

(4) Where the boundary of an area of section 4(2) land is shown both on the draft map of the general area and on a inset map of larger scale prepared in accordance with paragraph (3) the representation of that boundary on the inset map is to be taken to be its representation on the draft map.

(5) A draft map, and any inset map, must, unless it is not reasonably practicable to do so, be prepared in electronic form but must be capable of being reproduced in printed

form and the Council must ensure that the draft map and any inset map relating to it is at all times readily identifiable as such.

(6) A draft map must separately identify those areas of section 4(2) land which consist of open country, and those which consist of registered common land, and may identify any other relevant features, by the use of such different colours, shading, lines and symbols as the Council may think fit but all draft maps and any copies of draft maps produced under paragraph (7) must show each such class of section 4(2) land and all such other features by use of the corresponding colours, shading, lines or other symbols as the case may be.

(7) The Council may for the purpose of discharging its duty to issue a draft map under section 5(a) of the Act, or for any purpose incidental thereto, produce and publish copies of the draft map in such form, including electronic form, as it may determine and any such copy published by or with the authority of the Council shall be deemed to be identical to the draft map unless the contrary is shown.

(8) The Council shall, for the purpose of illustrating the existence and extent of the section 4(2) land shown on one or more draft maps, and for the purpose of making available for inspection copies of the draft map in accordance with regulation 4(1)(a) and 4(1)(b), or for complying with a request of a kind referred to in regulation 4(2)(f), produce and publish copies of draft maps showing such section 4(2) land, which may be at a scale of less than 1:10,000 but not less than 1:25,000.

(9) Copies of draft maps produced under paragraph (8) –

  (a) must clearly identify the classes of section 4(2) land and other features referred
       to in paragraph (6) which appear on the draft map of which they are copies, but
       the colours (if any), shading, lines or other symbols used to do so need not be
       identical to those used for that purpose on that draft map;
  (b) are not to be regarded as evidence of the contents of those draft maps.

(10) The Council must, for the purpose of ensuring that all draft maps which it prepares are as accurate as possible, use such relevant data as is reasonably available to it.

4   Issue of draft maps

(1) The Council is to be taken to have discharged its duty to issue a draft map in accordance with section 5(a) of the Act when it has –

  (a) made such arrangements as are within its power for a copy of the draft map
       produced under regulation 3(8) in printed form and, where possible in
       electronic form, to be available for inspection by members of the public at all
       reasonable times (subject, in the case of inspection at offices other than its own,
       to such requirement for the making of appointments to do so as the relevant
       authority may require) throughout the consultation period at the –
       (i)   head office of the Council and the local office of the Council, which is
             nearest to the area to which the draft map relates, not including any office
             which is not open during normal office hours; and
       (ii) head office of each relevant local authority and relevant National Park
             authority, if any;
  (b) despatched a copy of the draft map produced under regulation 3(8) to a scale of
       not less than 1:25,000 either in printed form or, if the Council and the recipient
       agree, in electronic form, together with a notice containing the same information
       as that required to be contained in the notice to be published under
       sub-paragraph (c) of this paragraph, to each of the organisations specified in

Schedule 1 to these Regulations and to such other persons as it considers appropriate;

(c) published a notice complying with the requirements of paragraph (2) in at least one daily newspaper circulating throughout that part of Wales which includes the area to which the draft map relates and such other newspapers or publications circulating in that part of Wales as the Council thinks fit;

(d) sent a notice in writing or in electronic form, complying with the requirements of paragraph (2), to each of the public libraries listed in Schedule 2 and accompanied by a request that a copy of the notice be displayed to the public at that library.

(2) A notice complying with the requirements of this paragraph must –

(a) identify the area to which the draft map relates;

(b) state that the effect of the draft map, if confirmed, will be to fix provisionally the extent of the land to which the public will, subject to such exceptions and restrictions as the Act provides, be entitled to exercise access under section 2 of the Act when that section comes into force;

(c) state that confirmation of the draft map will be without prejudice to the right of any person having an interest in land included in the land shown on the draft map as section 4(2) land to appeal to the National Assembly for Wales following such confirmation against its inclusion;

(d) give particulars of the means by which members of the public may inspect a copy of the draft map;

(e) give particulars of the means by which members of the public may make representations to the Council as to the showing of, or the failure to show, any area of land on the draft map as open country as defined in the Act or as registered common land and explain that the Council will be obliged to consider such representations only if they are received by the Council within the consultation period and that any person making such representations should bear in mind that the terms of those representations may be made public;

(f) state that any person who has an interest in any land shown on the draft map as section 4(2) land may, by a request in writing received before the end of the consultation period, and identifying the nature of that interest and the land to which it relates, require the Council to provide that person free of charge with one copy produced under regulation 3(8) of the draft map or of an extract from the draft map relating to that land, which copy must be in printed form or, if the Council and that person agree, in electronic form;

(g) state the address to which any request under sub-paragraph (f) should be sent;

(h) specify the consultation period, being a period of not less than three months from the date when notice complying with this paragraph is first published; and

(i) be first published no earlier than the date on which the Council has complied, with respect to the draft map to which the notice relates, with all the requirements of paragraphs (1)(a) and (1)(b).

(3) Any notice published in accordance with paragraph (1)(c) or sent in accordance with paragraph (1)(d) may, in addition to such information as is required to be included under paragraph (2), include such further information as the Council shall think fit.

5   General duty to inform the public of the provisions of draft maps

(1) The Council must consider and give effect to such steps as are reasonable in order to inform the public of the provisions of draft maps and must in particular consider the desirability of –

(a) making available, so far as is practicable, information equivalent to that shown on draft maps by means of smaller scale maps published on any website it maintains on the internet; and

(b) bringing to the attention of those appearing to have an interest in land shown as section 4(2) land on a draft map, by whatever means are appropriate, the fact that such map has been issued and where it can be inspected.

(2) The duty imposed by paragraph (1) is to be without prejudice to the duties of the Council under regulation 4 but any failure on the part of the Council to discharge the duty imposed by paragraph (1) in relation to a draft map is not to invalidate the issue of that draft map by the Council or any other action required to be taken by the Council under these Regulations.

6   Consideration of representations relating to draft maps

(1) The Council must consider any representation received by it within the consultation period with respect to the showing of, or the failure to show, any area of land as open country or registered common land on a draft map if such representation complies with the requirements of paragraph (2).

(2) A representation complies with the requirements of this paragraph if it –

(a) is made in writing or in electronic form;

(b) bears the name, address and postcode of the person making the representation;

(c) contains sufficient particulars of the land to which it relates as to enable that land to be identified;

(d) contains such particulars as enable the Council to understand any modification which the person making the representation proposes should be made to the draft map; and

(e) if made by a person claiming to have an interest in the land to which it relates, identifies the nature of that interest.

(3) Without prejudice to paragraph (4), the Council may, if it receives any representation which, by reason of the fact that it omits certain information, does not comply with the requirements of paragraph (2), request that the person making the representation provide any information omitted within such further period as the Council may allow and the Council must, if such information is provided within such period, consider such representation.

(4) If a representation fails to include sufficient particulars of the land to which it relates to enable that land to be identified the information which the Council may request under paragraph (3) includes a map or plan on which the boundaries of the land in question are marked.

(5) The Council may, in its discretion, consider any representation which does not comply with the requirements of paragraph (2) or any request for information made under paragraph (3), and may consult with such other persons as it may think fit.

7   Confirmation of draft map

(1) The Council, having considered such representations as it is required to consider under the provisions of regulation 6(1) or (2) together with such further representations as it decides, in its discretion, to consider under regulation 6(4), may confirm the draft map with or without modifications.

(2) If the Council confirms the draft map without modifications it shall note that fact on the draft map and on any copy of the draft map made after that confirmation.

(3) If the Council confirms the draft map with modifications it must –

    (a) prepare a map which shall be in identical form to the draft map except to the extent that it incorporates those modifications;

    (b) prepare a written statement identifying those modifications and incorporating a concise statement of its reasons for making them; and

    (c) note on the map prepared in accordance with sub-paragraph (a) of this paragraph and on any copy of that map the fact that it represents the draft map as confirmed with modifications.

(4) References in this regulation to the confirmation of a draft map are references to its conformation pursuant to section 5(c) of the Act.

SCHEDULE 1

ORGANISATIONS TO BE CONSULTED PURSUANT TO REGULATION 4(1)(B)

Regulation 4(1)(b)

British Association for Shooting and Conservation

British Mountaineering Council

Country Land and Business Association

The Countryside Agency (where land included in a draft map has a border with England)

Farmers' Union of Wales

Forestry Commission

Relevant local access forums

The Ministry of Defence

National Farmers' Union, Wales

. . .

National Trust Wales

Open Spaces Society

Ramblers' Association

[Relevant National Park authorities]

Town and Community Councils in Wales whose area of responsibility covers land included in a draft map

Relevant local authorities

Clwyd-Powys Archaeological Trust, or

Dyfed Archaeological Trust, or

Glamorgan-Gwent Archaeological Trust, or

Gwynedd Archaeological Trust, or

(if the area of responsibility of that Archaeological Trust covers land included in a draft map)

Amendments – Entry 'National Park authorities in Wales' revoked and entry 'Relevant National Park authorities' inserted by Countryside Access (Provisional and Conclusive Maps) (Wales) Regulations 2002, SI 2002/1796, reg 12(1), (2), with effect from 1 August 2002.

SCHEDULE 2

PUBLIC LIBRARIES TO WHICH NOTICE IS TO BE SENT PURSUANT TO REGULATION 4(1)(D)

Regulation 4(1)(d)

Aberdare

Aberystwyth

Bangor

Barry

Blackwood

Brecon

Bridgend

Brynmawr

Caernarfon

Cardiff Central

Cardigan

Carmarthen

Chepstow

Colwyn Bay

Cwmbran

Dolgellau

Flintshire

Grangetown

Haverfordwest

Llandrindod Wells

Llandudno

Llanelli

Llangefni

Llanrwst

Maesteg

Merthyr Tydfil

Neath

Newport Central

Newtown

Pembroke Dock

Penarth

Pontypridd

Port Talbot

Pwllheli

Rhuthin

Rhymney

Rhyl

Swansea East

Treorchy

Wrexham

COUNTRYSIDE ACCESS (LOCAL ACCESS FORUMS) (WALES) REGULATIONS 2001, SI 2001/ 4002

1 Citation, commencement and application

(1) These Regulations may be cited as The Countryside Access (Local Access Forums) (Wales) Regulations 2001 and shall come into force on 1st January 2002.

(2) These Regulations apply to Wales.

2 Interpretation

(1) Unless otherwise stated, in these Regulations –

'access land' ('tir mynediad') has the meaning given in section 1(1) of the Act;

'the Act' ('y Ddeddf') means the Countryside and Rights of Way Act 2000;

'annual report' ('adroddiad blynyddol') means the report prepared by the relevant authority under regulation 16(1);

'appointing authority' ('awdurdod penodi') has the meaning given in section 94(2) of the Act but includes, where the context so requires, one or more appointing authorities acting jointly with respect to a forum established under regulation 3(5) in accordance with such arrangements as are agreed between the relevant appointing authorities for that purpose;

'forum' ('fforwm') means a local access forum established under section 94(1) of the Act and includes a joint access forum similarly established;

'local rights of way' ('hawliau tramwy lleol') has the meaning given in section 95(3) of the Act;

'the National Assembly' ('y Cynulliad Cenedlaethol') means the National Assembly for Wales;

'person presiding' ('y person sy'n llywyddu') has the meaning given in regulation 15(3).

(2) Unless the context otherwise requires, in these Regulations any reference to a numbered regulation is a reference to the regulation bearing that number in these Regulations and any reference in a regulation to a numbered paragraph is a reference to the paragraph bearing that number in that regulation.

3 Establishment of a forum

(1) Subject to paragraph (3), an appointing authority must establish a forum or forums for the whole of the area for which it is the appointing authority.

(2) An appointing authority may either establish a single forum for the whole of the area for which it is the appointing authority or, alternatively, a number of forums, each for such part of the area for which it is the appointing authority as it thinks fit.

(3) The duty imposed on an appointing authority by paragraph (1) does not apply to the area for which it is the appointing authority or to a part of that area if there is in force

in relation to that area or that part of that area a direction given by the National Assembly under section 94(8) of the Act.

(4) The appointing authority must discharge the duty imposed by paragraph (1) within one calendar year of the date on which these Regulations come into force.

(5) An appointing authority may, with respect to any area for which it is the appointing authority or part of that area, discharge the duty imposed by paragraph (1) by appointing a forum jointly with one or more other appointing authorities, in accordance with such arrangements as it may make with such other appointing authority or authorities, in respect of an area which includes that area or part of that area.

(6) Where the appointing authority considers it appropriate to establish a forum for part of its area, it must, in considering the area which that forum is to cover, consult with such local authorities and other bodies as it thinks fit.

4   Membership of a forum

(1) A forum must consist of a Chair and Deputy Chair, appointed in accordance with regulation 12, and a Secretary, together with not less than 10 and not more than 20 other members (or such other number of members outside that range as the National Assembly may authorise in writing).

(2) A forum is to be regarded as having been established on the date specified by the appointing authority in the letters of appointment it sends to persons who are to be appointed as members of that forum, that date being the date of the first meeting of the forum.

(3) A person's membership of a forum continues until the expiry of the period of 3 years from the date of the first meeting of the forum, or such shorter period as is specified by the appointing authority in the letters of appointment referred to in paragraph (2), unless that person's membership terminates in accordance with regulation 14.

(4) A person who ceases to be a member of a forum is eligible for re-appointment.

5

(1) An appointing authority may, in addition to appointing members in order to fill casual vacancies in the membership of a forum, at any time appoint further members to a forum provided the total number of members, excluding the Chair and Deputy Chair, does not as a result exceed 20 (or such other number as may be authorised by the National Assembly pursuant to regulation 4(1)).

(2) When a casual vacancy arises in the membership of a forum, the appointing authority may refrain from appointing a member to fill that vacancy provided the membership of the forum, excluding the Chair and Deputy Chair, does not as a result fall below 10 (or such other number as may be authorised by the National Assembly pursuant to regulation 4(1)).

(3) Before an appointing authority exercises its power under paragraph (1) to appoint a further member or members of a forum in addition to any required to fill a casual vacancy, or its power under paragraph (2) to refrain from appointing a member to fill a casual vacancy in the membership of a forum, it must consult the forum and such other bodies as it thinks fit.

6

(1) Where the area of a forum falls entirely within the area of the appointing authority, that authority must appoint one (but may not appoint more than one) member to a forum who is either an officer or member of the appointing authority.

(2) Where the area of a forum falls within the area of more than one appointing authority and there are –

(a) two appointing authorities, each appointing authority in respect of that forum must appoint one (but may not appoint more than one) member of the forum who is either an officer or member of that appointing authority;

(b) more than two appointing authorities, the appointing authorities in respect of that forum must appoint, in accordance with arrangements as shall have been agreed by those appointing authorities at the time the forum is established, no more than a total of two members of the forum who are either officers or members of appointing authorities.

7

When considering what persons to appoint as members of a forum, an appointing authority –

(a) must consult such individuals and organisations having an interest in the functions of the forum as it thinks fit;

(b) must place an advertisement in a newspaper circulating in the locality of the forum giving persons an opportunity of expressing an interest in becoming a member of a forum;

(c) may invite any organisation having an interest in the functions of the forum to nominate a person for consideration by the appointing authority for membership of the forum;

(d) must have regard to the desirability of appointing persons who reside in, or are otherwise particularly familiar with, or who have any other interests especially relevant to, the area of the forum;

(e) must ensure that the membership of the forum achieves a reasonable balance between the interests of users of local rights of way or the rights of access conferred by section 2(1) of the Act and of owners and occupiers of access land or land over which local rights of way subsist;

(f) must have regard to the need to ensure, so far as is reasonably practicable, a fair balance between persons of different genders, races, ages, disabilities and other characteristics.

8

An appointing authority must not appoint as a member of a forum any person who appears to the authority to have or to be likely to have such pecuniary or other interest in the matters on which the forum is required to advise as is likely to have a substantially adverse effect on the ability of that person properly and effectively to discharge the function of a member of the forum.

9

Before appointing a person as a member of a forum the appointing authority must require that person to provide it with such information as it may reasonably require for the purpose of assessing that person's suitability to be a member of that forum.

10 Administration of a forum

(1) The appointing authority must in relation to each forum appoint a person (who shall not be a member of the forum) to act as its Secretary and to be responsible for the administration of a forum.

(2) Notwithstanding the generality of paragraph (1), the duties of the Secretary include –

   (a) arranging meetings and the drawing-up, keeping, production and submission to the next meeting, of minutes;

   (b) managing any financial resources provided to the forum for its use in the exercise of its functions;

   (c) ensuring that –

      (i) notice of a proposed meeting;

      (ii) a copy of the agenda drawn up by the Secretary in consultation with the Chair and Deputy Chair and specifying the principal business proposed to be transacted at a meeting; and

      (iii) any other papers relevant to a meeting;

      are delivered, either in person or by post to such address as a member may specify for the purpose, to each member of the forum so as to be received (or in the case of delivery by post so as to be delivered in the normal course of posting) at least seven clear days before the date of a meeting;

   (d) drawing to the attention of the forum the provisions of any national codes of practice, guidance issued by the Countryside Council for Wales or the National Assembly for Wales and statutory requirements to which the forum is to have regard when exercising its functions;

(3) The Secretary must be present at all meetings of a forum and may attend meetings of any committee established under regulation 13.

(4) In the event of the temporary incapacity of the Secretary the appointing authority must appoint an Acting Secretary to discharge the duties of the Secretary during the period of that incapacity.

11

The appointing authority must defray all reasonable expenses incurred by a forum in discharging its functions including such expenses (other than loss of earnings and other costs directly related to a person's employment) reasonably and necessarily incurred by the Chair, Deputy Chair and members of the forum in attending meetings.

12 Appointment of Chair and Deputy Chair

(1) The Secretary must –

   (a) at the first meeting of the forum held after the meeting at which the appointment of all members of the forum takes effect (whether upon establishment of the forum or upon the appointment of members after the membership of all members ceases under regulation 4(3)), ensure that the first item of business to be conducted is the election of the Chair and Deputy Chair; and

   (b) on a subsequent vacancy in the post of Chair or Deputy Chair, ensure that the first item of business to be conducted at the next meeting of the forum is the election of a Chair and/or Deputy Chair, as required.

(2) The Chair and Deputy Chair shall be members of the forum to which they are to be elected Chair and Deputy Chair and shall be elected by the other members of the forum by secret ballot.

(3) The Secretary must preside at any meeting of the forum until the Chair and Deputy Chair have been elected and must conduct the election of the Chair and Deputy Chair.

(4) If the result of the first or any subsequent ballot is that a candidate receives the votes of more than one-half of the members voting the Secretary must declare that person elected.

(5) If the result of the first or any subsequent ballot is that no candidate receives the votes of more than one-half of the members voting the Secretary must conduct a further ballot excluding the candidate who received the lowest number of votes at the previous ballot.

(6) In the event that on any ballot there is an equality of votes between two candidates and the number of votes which they each receive is less than that received by any other candidate the Secretary must determine by lot which of them is to be excluded from any further ballot.

13   Establishment of a committee by a forum

(1) The members of a forum may, with the agreement of the Chair, establish such committee or committees of members as they think fit.

(2) Subject to anything contained in these Regulations to the contrary, where a committee is established, the manner in which it is chaired, the appointment of its members, and its terms of reference are to be decided by the members of the forum which established it.

14   Termination of membership

(1) A person's membership of a forum, including that of the Chair and Deputy Chair, terminates on the happening of any of the following events –

(a) the expiration of the term of membership;
(b) the death of the member;
(c) the receipt by the Secretary of written notice of resignation of a member;
(d) the giving by the appointing authority of written notice to a member that, in the opinion of the authority, the circumstances are such that had the authority been considering whether to appoint that person as a member of the forum it would have been prevented from doing so by the provisions of regulation 8;
(e) the giving by the appointing authority, after having consulted the forum as to the proposed action, of written notice to a member of specified circumstances which, in the opinion of the authority, make it desirable in the interests of the effective conduct of the functions of the forum that the person in question should cease to be a member;
(f) the election of the member as a member of the appointing authority or the appointment of the member as an officer of the appointing authority or, where a forum has been established by more than one appointing authority, of any of those authorities;
(g) the failure of a member to attend any meeting of a forum, or meeting of any committee of the forum, over a continuous period of 12 months unless the member has, following a written request to the appointing authority made within that period and specifying the reasons for the request, been granted leave

of absence by the appointing authority for such period as the appointing authority may think fit in which case the period of 12 months specified in this paragraph is not to include any period to which such leave of absence relates.

(2) The Secretary must notify the appointing authority of any vacancy in the membership of the forum of which the appointing authority are not or may not otherwise be aware and an appointing authority which becomes aware of any such vacancy must, subject to regulation 5, appoint a person to fill that vacancy.

(3) If a member of a forum is elected Chair or Deputy Chair of that forum the appointing authority must, subject to regulation 5, appoint a person as a member of the forum as if the person elected Chair or Deputy Chair had ceased to be a member of the forum.

15   Conduct of meetings of a forum

(1) The first meeting of a forum after the meeting at which the appointment of all members of the forum takes effect (whether upon establishment of the forum or upon the appointment of members after the membership of all members ceases under regulation 4(3)), is to take place at such time and place as may be decided by the appointing authority, its agenda is to be decided by the appointing authority, and the Secretary is to preside over it, but thereafter the forum may meet at such intervals as it considers appropriate, but must meet at least twice in each twelve-month period calculated by reference to the date on which it was established.

(2) Meetings of the forum may be held on such days and at such places as may be agreed by the members and shall be open to the public unless the person presiding rules that a particular item of business to be considered at a meeting makes it appropriate for the public to be excluded during consideration of that item of business.

(3) At any meeting of the forum, the person who is to preside (the 'person presiding') is, subject to regulation 12(3), –

   (a) if present, the Chair;
   (b) if the Chair is absent, the Deputy Chair; or
   (c) if the Chair and Deputy Chair are absent, such member as the members present choose.

(4) No business may be conducted by a forum unless the number of members present, excluding the person presiding, exceeds one-third of the total membership.

(5) Subject to anything contained in these Regulations to the contrary, or to any guidance given by the National Assembly under section 94(6)(c) of the Act, a forum may regulate its own procedure.

(6) The proceedings of any meeting shall not be invalidated if any person so entitled fails to receive any notice or other documents relevant to the meeting concerned which are otherwise required to be delivered or sent under these Regulations.

(7) The minutes of the proceedings of a meeting (which shall include the names of those members present and absent) shall be drawn-up, submitted for agreement at the next meeting and be signed by the person presiding at that next meeting.

(8) The Chair may invite observers and/or advisers to a meeting, and those invited may, if the person presiding considers it appropriate, contribute to the proceedings of the forum.

(9) A representative of the National Assembly and/or the Countryside Council for Wales, and any officer of an authority which (in respect of the forum concerned) is an appointing authority, may attend any meeting of the forum, or of a committee established by that forum, as an observer.

(10) When the person presiding considers it appropriate to put any question to a vote, the person presiding must formulate that question, in writing if requested, and any vote is to be by show of hands of those members present (except that the person presiding shall not be entitled to vote unless there is an equality of votes, in which case the person presiding is to have a casting vote).

16 Annual reports

(1) An appointing authority must, in relation to each forum for which it is the appointing authority, prepare and approve, as soon as reasonably practicable after 31 March in each year, an annual report.

(2) An annual report prepared under paragraph (1) must include –

  (a) information relating to the performance of the forum's functions during the twelve-month period ending on the date referred to in paragraph (1); and
  (b) a programme of works which has been agreed between the forum and the appointing authority which the forum plans to undertake during the twelve months commencing immediately after that date.

(3) A copy of the annual report must, when it has been approved, be made available for inspection by members of the public at the offices of the appointing authority during normal office hours free of charge.

(4) An appointing authority must, on application by any member of the public, provide that person with a copy of any annual report prepared and approved under this Regulation, or of any part thereof, on payment of the cost of postage and such further sum not exceeding 10 pence per page as the appointing authority may require.

17 Notification of appointments etc

The appointing authority must –

  (a) notify the Countryside Council for Wales (the Council) of the names and addresses of all persons appointed to be members (including Chairs and Deputy Chairs) of forums and of any changes in the membership of those forums;
  (b) send to the Council a copy of each annual report when approved; and
  (c) provide the Council on request with such other information as to the activities of any forum as the Council may reasonably require.

ACCESS TO THE COUNTRYSIDE (PROVISIONAL AND CONCLUSIVE MAPS) (ENGLAND) REGULATIONS 2002, SI 2002/1710

PART I

PRELIMINARY

1   Title, commencement and extent

(1) These Regulations may be cited as the Access to the Countryside (Provisional and Conclusive Maps) (England) Regulations 2002 and shall come into force on 29th July 2002.

(2) These Regulations extend to England only.

2   General interpretation

(1) In these Regulations, ... –

'the Act' means the Countryside and Rights of Way Act 2000;

'the Agency' means the Countryside Agency;

'conclusive map' means a map issued by the Agency in conclusive form under section 9;

'draft map' means a map prepared by the Agency under section 4 and issued by the Agency in draft form under section 5;

'parish council' has the same meaning as in Part I of the Local Government Act 1972;

'proper officer' shall be construed in accordance with section 270(3) of the Local Government Act 1972;

'provisional map' means a map issued by the Agency in provisional form under section 5(d) or (e);

'reduced scale map' means, in relation to a provisional or conclusive map, a copy of that map in printed or electronic form which may be on a smaller scale than the scale of the provisional or conclusive map (or any part of it) but –

   (a) for the purposes of regulation 12, must be on a scale of not less than 1/10,000, and
   (b) for all other purposes, must be on a scale of not less than 1/25,000; and

'review conclusive map' means a conclusive map issued by the Agency on a review under section 10.

(2) In these Regulations –

   (a) references to a period during which a provisional map remains current are references to the period which ends on the date on which the Agency have issued –

(i)   a conclusive map covering the area of land to which the provisional map relates, or

(ii)   a draft map covering that area, which the Agency have prepared in accordance with a requirement imposed on them under section 6(4)(b),

or, where maps are issued covering particular parts of that area, to the period which ends on the date on which the Agency have issued the last in a succession of such maps issued by them which together (in any combination of conclusive or draft maps) cover the whole of that area;

(b)   references to a period during which a conclusive map remains current are references to the period which ends on the date on which the Agency have issued a review conclusive map covering the area of land to which the conclusive map relates or, where review conclusive maps are issued covering particular parts of that area, to the period which ends on the date on which the Agency have issued the last in a succession of such maps issued by them which together cover the whole of that area;

(c)   references to a period during which a reduced scale map remains current are references to the period during which the provisional or conclusive map from which it is derived remains current; and

(d)   references to sections are references to sections of the Act and references to a Part are to the relevant Part of these Regulations.

Amendments – In para (1), words omitted by Access to the Countryside (Provisional and Conclusive Maps) (England) (Amendment) Regulations 2003, SI 2003/32, with effect from 3 February 2003.

PART II

PROVISIONAL OR CONCLUSIVE MAPS

3   Scale of provisional or conclusive maps

(1) Any provisional or conclusive map issued by the Agency shall be in electronic form and on a scale of not less than 1/10,000.

(2) The scale of any part of any such map may vary, provided each part is on a scale of not less than 1/10,000.

4   Informing the public of the issue of provisional maps

(1) Where the Agency have issued a provisional map, they shall, as soon as reasonably practicable on or after the date of issue, publish a notice which –

(a)   states the date of issue;

(b)   describes the area of land to which the map relates;

(c)   states where (in accordance with regulation 6) the map is to be made available for inspection;

(d)   states how (in accordance with regulation 8) reduced scale maps may be obtained, including whether a fee is payable and, if so, what fee;

(e)   states where (in accordance with regulation 9) a reduced scale map may be inspected on the internet;

(f)   states, in general terms, where (by virtue of regulations 10, 11 and 12) reduced scale maps are to be made available for inspection;

(g) describes the opportunity afforded to a person under section 6 to appeal against the showing of that land on the map as registered common land or open country within the period specified in regulation 16(1), the ground on which such an appeal may be brought and how such an appeal must be brought; and

(h) states the general effect of the right conferred on the public in relation to access land by section 2(1).

(2) The notice referred to in paragraph (1) shall be published –

(a) in such local or regional newspapers circulating in the area of land to which the map relates as the Agency consider necessary for informing the public of the issue of the map; and

(b) by being made available for inspection on a website maintained by the Agency for the period during which the map remains current.

5   Informing the public of the issue of conclusive maps

(1) Where the Agency have issued a conclusive map, they shall, as soon as reasonably practicable on or after the date of issue, publish a notice which –

(a) states the date of issue;

(b) describes the area of land to which the map relates;

(c) states where (in accordance with regulation 7) the map is to be made available for inspection;

(d) states how (in accordance with regulation 8) reduced scale maps may be obtained, including whether a fee is payable and, if so, what fee;

(e) states where (in accordance with regulation 9) a reduced scale map may be inspected on the internet;

(f) states in general terms where (by virtue of regulation 10) reduced scale maps are to be made available for inspection; and

(g) states the general effect of the right conferred on the public in relation to access land by section 2(1).

(2) The notice referred to in paragraph (1) shall be published –

(a) in such local or regional newspapers circulating in the area of land to which the map relates as the Agency consider necessary for informing the public of the issue of the map; and

(b) by being made available for inspection on a website maintained by the Agency for the period during which the map remains current.

6   Where provisional maps are to be available for inspection

(1) Subject to paragraph (2), where the Agency have issued a provisional map, they shall, as soon as reasonably practicable on or after the date of issue, make the map available for inspection by members of the public at all reasonable hours in such regional office of the Agency as they consider appropriate.

(2) The map shall be available for inspection for the period during which it remains current.

7   Where conclusive maps are to be available for inspection

(1) Subject to paragraph (2), where the Agency have issued a conclusive map, they shall, as soon as reasonably practicable on or after the date of issue, make the map

available for inspection by members of the public at all reasonable hours in such regional office of the Agency as they consider appropriate.

(2) The map shall be available for inspection for the period during which it remains current.

8 Supply of reduced scale maps to certain bodies and to members of the public

(1) Where the Agency have issued a provisional map, they shall, as soon as reasonably practicable on or after the date of issue –

- (a) [(subject to paragraph (2A))] send a reduced scale map in printed form to those persons specified in Part I of the Schedule to these Regulations; and
- (b) subject to paragraph (3), supply a reduced scale map in printed form to any person who requests such a map, and who pays to the Agency such reasonable fee as the Agency may determine, at any time in the period during which the map remains current.

(2) Where the Agency have issued a conclusive map, they shall, as soon as reasonably practicable on or after the date of issue –

- (a) [(subject to paragraph (2A))] send a reduced scale map in printed form to those persons specified in Part II of the Schedule to these Regulations; and
- (b) subject to paragraph (3), supply a reduced scale map in printed form to any person who requests such a map, and who pays to the Agency such reasonable fee as the Agency may determine, at any time in the period during which the map remains current.

[(2A) Where the functions of a person specified in Part I or II of the Schedule to these Regulations relate to only part of the area of land covered by the provisional or conclusive map, the Agency may send a reduced scale map relating to only that part.]

(3) Where a person requests a reduced scale map under paragraph (1)(b) or (2)(b) above relating to only part of the area of land to which the provisional or conclusive map relates, he shall provide the Agency with such information as the Agency reasonably require to enable that part to be identified, and the Agency shall supply a reduced scale map relating, so far as practicable, to only that part.

Amendments – Words inserted in paras (1)(a), (2)(a), and para (2A) inserted by Access to the Countryside (Provisional and Conclusive Maps) (England) (Amendment) Regulations 2003, SI 2003/32, with effect from 3 February 2003.

---

9 Reduced scale maps on the internet

Where the Agency have issued a provisional or conclusive map, they shall, as soon as reasonably practicable on or after the date of issue, make a reduced scale map available for inspection on a website maintained by the Agency on the internet for the period during which the reduced scale map remains current.

10 Deposit of reduced scale maps with local authorities and National Park authorities

(1) Subject to paragraph (2), where the Agency have issued a provisional or conclusive map they shall, as soon as reasonably practicable on or after the date of issue, deposit a

reduced scale map with the proper officer of any local authority or National Park authority exercising functions for any area of land to which the provisional or conclusive map (as the case may be) relates.

(2) Where the functions of a local authority or National Park authority relate to only part of the area of land covered by the provisional or conclusive map, a reduced scale map relating to only that part may be deposited.

(3) In the case of a provisional map, the proper officer shall, in accordance with section 225(1) of the Local Government Act 1972, retain the reduced scale map for the period during which the map remains current for the purpose of its being available for inspection and making copies in accordance with section 228(5) of that Act.

(4) In the case of a conclusive map –

   (a) the proper officer of a county council, a council exercising the functions of a county council or a London borough shall, in accordance with section 225(1) of the Local Government Act 1972, retain the reduced scale map permanently for the purpose referred to in paragraph (3) above; and

   (b) the proper officer of a district council (other than a district council exercising the functions of a county council) or National Park authority shall, in accordance with section 225(1) of that Act, retain the reduced scale map for the period during which the map remains current for that purpose.

(5) In this regulation, 'local authority' means a county council, district council or London borough council.

11   Deposit of reduced scale maps derived from provisional maps with library authorities

(1) Subject to paragraphs (2) and (3), where the Agency have issued a provisional map, they shall, as soon as reasonably practicable on or after the date of issue, deposit reduced scale maps with the proper officer of any library authority exercising functions for any area of land to which that map relates.

(2) Where the functions of an authority relate to only part of the area of land covered by the provisional map, reduced scale maps relating to only that part may be deposited.

(3) The number of reduced scale maps deposited shall be such number as the Agency consider appropriate, after consultation with the proper officer of the library authority.

(4) The proper officer shall, in accordance with section 225(1) of the Local Government Act 1972, retain the reduced scale maps for the purpose of their being available for inspection and making copies in accordance with section 228(5) of that Act –

   (a) for the period during which the maps remain current; and

   (b) in such public libraries in the area of the library authority as the proper officer considers appropriate.

(5) In this regulation, 'library authority' means a library authority under the Public Libraries and Museums Act 1964.

12   Deposit of reduced scale maps derived from provisional maps with commons registration authorities

(1) Subject to paragraph (2), where the Agency have issued a provisional map, they shall, as soon as reasonably practicable on or after the date of issue, deposit relevant

extracts of a reduced scale map with the proper officer of any registration authority exercising functions for any area of land to which that map relates.

(2) Where the functions of an authority relate to only part of the area of land covered by the provisional map, relevant extracts of a reduced scale map relating to only that part may be deposited.

(3) The proper officer shall, in accordance with section 225(1) of the Local Government Act 1972, retain the relevant extracts of the reduced scale map for the purpose of their being available for inspection and making copies in accordance with section 228(5) of that Act –

(a) for the period during which the map remains current; and
(b) in such place as will enable the public to compare the relevant extracts with the register of common land which the registration authority is required to maintain under section 3 of the Commons Registration Act 1965.

(4) In this regulation –

(a) 'registration authority' has the same meaning as in the Commons Registration Act 1965; and
(b) 'relevant extracts' means extracts of the reduced scale map which show registered common land.

13 Certification of copies of provisional maps

A document purporting to be certified on behalf of the Agency to be a copy of, or of any part, of a provisional map issued by the Agency shall be receivable in evidence and shall be deemed, unless the contrary is shown, to be such a copy.

14 Maps in electronic form

Any map authorised or required by this Part of these Regulations to be prepared, issued or made available for inspection in electronic form must be capable of being reproduced in printed form.

PART III

APPEALS AGAINST PROVISIONAL MAPS

CHAPTER I

INITIAL STAGES OF APPEALS

15 Interpretation

In this Part –

'appeal land' means the land which is the subject of an appeal;

'appeal period' means, in relation to a provisional map, the period referred to in regulation 16(1);

'appeal procedure' means the procedure for determining the issues arising on an appeal or for determining any consequential issue, by means of a hearing or inquiry or on the basis of written representations, as determined by the Secretary of State under regulation 19(1)(b);

'appointed person' means a person appointed by the Secretary of State under section 8 to determine an appeal or any matter involved in such an appeal and having the powers conferred by paragraphs 3 and 4 of Schedule 3 to the Act;

'assessor' means a person appointed by the Secretary of State under paragraph 4(3) of Schedule 3 to the Act to sit with an inspector at a hearing or inquiry and advise the inspector on any matters arising;

'consequential issue' means any issue, consequential on the determination of an appeal, as to the manner in which the discretion conferred on the Secretary of State by section 6(4) should be exercised;

'document' includes a photograph, map or plan;

'hearing' means a hearing in relation to which this Part applies;

'inquiry' means a local inquiry in relation to which this Part applies;

'inspector' means –

   (a) an appointed person; or
   (b) a person holding a hearing or inquiry and making a report to the Secretary of State in order for her to determine an appeal;

'questionnaire' means a document, in the form supplied by the Secretary of State, seeking information relating to the appeal or any consequential issue;

'pre-inquiry meeting' means a meeting held before an inquiry to consider what may be done with a view to securing that the inquiry is conducted efficiently and expeditiously, and, where two or more such meetings are held, references to the conclusion of a pre-inquiry meeting are references to the conclusion of the final meeting;

['prescribed period' means a period prescribed by these Regulations as one within which certain requirements so prescribed are to be met;]

'proof of evidence' means a proof of evidence sent to the Secretary of State in accordance with regulation 48;

['start date' means the date on which certain prescribed periods are to begin, and, in relation to any given appeal, means the date specified by the Secretary of State under paragraph (a) of regulation 19 in her written notice to the appellant and the Agency under that regulation;]

'statement of case' means a written statement which contains full particulars of the case which a person proposes to put forward, at a hearing or inquiry or by way of written representations, in relation to the appeal or any consequential issue, and includes copies of any supporting documents which that person intends to refer to or put in evidence;

'statement of common ground' means a written statement prepared jointly by the appellant and the Agency pursuant to regulation 49 which contains agreed factual information about the appeal;

'transferred appeal' means an appeal or any matter involved in an appeal, in respect of which the Secretary of State has exercised her power in section 8 to appoint a person to determine the appeal or the matter, as the case may be, on her behalf, and, in relation to any such appeal, references in these Regulations to a decision on an appeal shall be construed as references to a decision on the appeal or the matter involved in an appeal (as the case may be) which that person has been appointed to determine; and

'written representations' includes supporting documents.

Amendments – Definition 'prescribed period' inserted and definition 'start date' substituted by Access to the Countryside (Provisional and Conclusive Maps) (England) (Amendment) Regulations 2003, SI 2003/32, with effect from 3 February 2003.

---

16 Notice of appeal against provisional map

(1) Any appeal to the Secretary of State under section 6(1) against the showing of any land on a provisional map as registered common land or open country shall be made by notice given to the Secretary of State, on a form obtained from her, within three months of the date of the issue of the map.

(2) If the appellant wishes to withdraw an appeal before it is determined, he shall do so by giving notice to the Secretary of State before the appeal is determined, and the Secretary of State shall send a copy of that notice as soon as practicable to the Agency.

17 Notification of receipt of documents

The Secretary of State shall, as soon as practicable after she has received all the information required to enable her to entertain the appeal, notify the appellant and the Agency of this in writing and send a copy of the notice of the appeal to the Agency.

18 Preliminary information to be supplied by the Agency

The Agency shall ensure that, within two weeks of the receipt by them of notification in accordance with regulation 17, the following have been received by the Secretary of State and a copy has been received by the appellant –

    (a) a completed questionnaire (which shall also state the date on which it is sent to the Secretary of State) together with a copy of each document referred to in it;

    (b) the names and addresses of any persons who made representations to the Agency in respect of the showing of, or failure to show, the appeal land on a draft map; and

    (c) details of the time and place at which the Agency intends to make documents available for the purposes of regulation 57.

19 Notification of start of appeal etc

(1) The Secretary of State shall, as soon as practicable after receipt of the information required to be supplied by the Agency in accordance with regulation 18, notify in writing the appellant, the Agency and any other person who made representations to the Agency in respect of the showing of, or failure to show, the appeal land as registered common land or open country on a draft map of –

    (a) the start date;

    (b) whether the appeal procedure will take the form of a hearing or inquiry or will be disposed of on the basis of written representations;

    (c) whether the appeal will be determined by the Secretary of State or by the inspector;

    (d) the reference number allocated to the appeal;

(e) the addresses (including an e-mail address) to which written communications to the Secretary of State about the appeal are to be sent; and

(f) the time and place where documents relating to the appeal are to be made available for the purposes of regulation 57.

(2) A notice under paragraph (1) shall –

(a) state the name of the appellant and, sufficiently to enable it to be identified, the location and extent of the appeal land –

(b) state that the appeal is brought under section 6(2) in relation to the showing of the land as registered common land on a provisional map or under section 6(3) in relation to the showing of the land as open country on that map, as appropriate;

(c) state that the Agency –
  (i) has sent to the Secretary of State and the appellant the name and address of any person other than the appellant who made representations to the Agency in respect of the showing of, or the failure to show, the appeal land as registered common land or open country on a draft map; and
  (ii) is required to send a copy of such representations to the Secretary of State and the appellant;

(d) state that, if any such persons wish their representations to be disregarded by the Secretary of State for the purposes of the appeal, they should notify the Secretary of State of this in writing within six weeks of the start date;

(e) state that a person who has made any such representations may make further representations in writing to the Secretary of State in respect of the appeal by ensuring that they are received by the Secretary of State, at an address specified in the notice, within six weeks of the start date;

(f) state that any other person may also make representations in writing to the Secretary of State in respect of the appeal by ensuring that they are received by the Secretary of State at that address and within such time; and

(g) if there is to be a hearing or inquiry, state that any person, other than the appellant or the Agency, may be heard with the permission of the inspector and that such permission shall not be unreasonably withheld.

(3) The Secretary of State shall ensure that a copy of the notice of appeal is available for inspection on a website maintained by the Planning Inspectorate Executive Agency until the appeal is determined.

20 Supply of further information by the Agency

The Agency shall ensure that, within two weeks of the start date, the Secretary of State and the appellant have received copies of –

(a) any correspondence between the appellant and the Agency relating to the appeal land; and

(b) any representations made to the Agency in respect of the showing of, or failure to show, the appeal land as registered common land or open country on a draft map.

21 Submission of statements of case etc

Within six weeks of the start date –

(a) the Agency shall ensure that the Secretary of State has received two copies of their statement of case;

(b) the appellant shall ensure that the Secretary of State has received two copies of his statement of case; and

(c) any other person who wishes to make representations to the Secretary of State in respect of the appeal shall ensure that the Secretary of State has received three copies of such representations.

[22   Copies of documents etc

(1) The Secretary of State shall, as soon as practicable after the expiry of six weeks from the start date –

(a) send to the appellant a copy of any statement of case submitted by the Agency under regulation 21(a);

(b) send to the Agency a copy of any statement of case submitted by the appellant under regulation 21(b); and

(c) send to the appellant and the Agency a copy of any representations submitted by any person under regulation 21(c).

(2) The Secretary of State shall, as soon as practicable after the receipt of any further information which she or the inspector has required under regulation 24, send a copy of the document received –

(a) in the case of information received from the appellant or the Agency, to the other party; and

(b) in the case of information received from any other person, to the appellant and the Agency.]

Amendments – Regulation substituted by Access to the Countryside (Provisional and Conclusive Maps) (England) (Amendment) Regulations 2003, SI 2003/32, with effect from 3 February 2003.

23   Comments on statement of case etc

Within nine weeks of the start date –

(a) the appellant shall ensure that the Secretary of State has received any comments which he may wish to make on –
(i)   the Agency's statement of case, or
(ii) any representations made by any other person in respect of the appeal; and

(b) the Agency shall ensure that the Secretary of State has received any comments which they wish to make on the appellant's statement of case or any such representations.

24   Provision of further information

The Secretary of State, or the inspector, may require such further information as she or he may specify from –

(a) the appellant or the Agency in respect of their statement of case;

(b) any person who has made representations to the Secretary of State under regulation 21(c) in respect of such representations;

and all such information shall be provided in writing within such period as the Secretary of State, or the inspector, may reasonably require.

CHAPTER II
APPEALS DETERMINED ON THE BASIS OF WRITTEN REPRESENTATIONS

25 Site inspections

(1) Where it appears to the Secretary of State necessary or expedient to do so, she may arrange for an inspection of the appeal land to be made by an inspector; and the Secretary of State shall arrange for such an inspection to be made if so requested by the appellant or the Agency in relation to an appeal against the showing of any land as open country on a provisional map.

(2) Where the inspector intends to make an inspection under paragraph (1), the Secretary of State shall ask the appellant and the Agency whether they wish to be present or be represented.

(3) Where the appellant or the Agency has indicated that they wish to be present or be represented, the inspector shall give the appellant and the Agency reasonable notice of the date and time of the inspection and shall afford the appellant and the Agency, or their representatives, the opportunity of being present during the inspection.

(4) The inspector shall not be bound to defer an inspection if the appellant or the Agency, or their representative, is not present at the appointed time.

26 Decision on appeal

The Secretary of State or, as the case may be, the inspector may proceed to a decision on an appeal taking into account only such statements of case, representations and comments as have been provided within the time limits prescribed by or under these Regulations.

27 Notification of decision

The Secretary of State, or as the case may be, the inspector shall notify their decision on an appeal, and their reasons for it, in writing to –

  (a) the appellant;
  (b) the Agency; and
  (c) any person who has made representations to the Secretary of State in respect of the appeal under regulation 21(c);

and the Secretary of State shall also arrange for a copy of the decision to be made available for inspection on a website maintained by the Planning Inspectorate Executive Agency for the period during which the provisional map covering the appeal land remains current.

CHAPTER III
APPEALS DETERMINED BY WAY OF A HEARING

28 Date and notification of hearing

(1) The date fixed by the Secretary of State for a hearing shall be the earliest date after the expiry of the appeal period which she considers to be practicable having regard to the desirability of arranging consecutive hearings to be held in connection with appeals relating to land in the area to which the provisional map relates.

(2) Unless the Secretary of State agrees a lesser period of notice with the appellant and the Agency, she shall give the appellant, the Agency and any person who, under regulation 21(c), has made representations to the Secretary of State in respect of the appeal not less than four weeks' written notice of the date, time and place fixed by her for the holding of a hearing.

(3) The Secretary of State may at any time change the date fixed for the holding of a hearing (whether or not the new date is within the period mentioned in paragraph (1)) and paragraph (2) shall apply to the new date.

(4) The Secretary of State may at any time change the time or place for the holding of a hearing and shall give such notice of any change to the persons mentioned in paragraph (2).

(5) The Secretary of State may require the Agency, not less than two weeks before the date fixed for the hearing, or, in the case of a number of consecutive appeals relating to land in the area to which the provisional map relates, the date fixed for the hearing of the first of such appeals, to publish a notice of the hearing, or (as the case may be) of the hearing of the first of such appeals, in one or more newspapers circulating in the locality in which the appeal land is situated; and the Secretary of State shall ensure that the Planning Inspectorate Executive Agency makes a copy of such notice available for inspection on a website which it maintains until the appeal is determined.

(6) Every notice of hearing published pursuant to paragraph (5) shall contain –

- (a) a statement of the date and place of the hearing, or in the case of a number of consecutive appeals, of the hearing of the first of such appeals, and of the powers enabling the Secretary of State or inspector to determine the appeal in question; and
- (b) a brief description of the appeal land and of the grounds of appeal.

29　Consecutive hearings

The Secretary of State may arrange for two or more appeals to be heard consecutively where they relate to the same area of land or to areas of land which she considers to be clustered in such proximity as to make it expedient for the hearings to be held consecutively.

30　Appearances at hearing

(1) The persons entitled to appear at the hearing are –

- (a) the appellant; and
- (b) the Agency;

but the inspector may permit any other person to appear at a hearing, and such permission shall not be unreasonably withheld.

(2) Any person entitled or permitted to appear may appear in person or be represented by any other person.

31　Inspector acting in place of Secretary of State in respect of transferred appeals

(1) This regulation applies where a hearing is to be or has been held in respect of a transferred appeal.

(2) An inspector may in place of the Secretary of State take such steps as the Secretary of State is required or enabled to take under or by virtue of regulation 56(2) in respect of an appeal to be determined by way of a hearing; and, where an inspector requires further information or copies pursuant to regulation 56(2), such information or copies shall be sent to him.

32   Notification of name of inspector

The inspector shall, at the commencement of the hearing, announce his name and the fact of his appointment.

33   Notification of the appointment of an assessor

Where the Secretary of State has appointed an assessor in respect of a hearing, the inspector shall, at the commencement of the hearing, announce the name of the assessor and the fact of his appointment.

34   Procedure at hearing

(1) Except as otherwise provided in this Part, the inspector shall determine the procedure at a hearing.

(2) A hearing shall take the form of a discussion led by an inspector, and cross-examination shall not be permitted unless the inspector considers that cross-examination is required to ensure a thorough examination of the main issues.

(3) Where the inspector considers that cross-examination is required under paragraph (2), he shall consider, after consulting the appellant and the Agency, whether the hearing should be closed and an inquiry held instead.

(4) At the start of the hearing the inspector shall identify what are, in his opinion, the main issues to be considered at the hearing and any matters on which he requires further explanation from any person appearing at the hearing; but this shall not preclude the addition in the course of the hearing of other issues for consideration or any person appearing at the hearing from referring to issues which they consider relevant to the consideration of the appeal but which were not issues so identified by the inspector.

(5) The appellant and the Agency shall be entitled to give, or to call another person to give, oral evidence, and any other person may give, or call another person to give, oral evidence if so permitted by an inspector at his discretion, but notwithstanding any such entitlement or permission, the inspector may, at any stage in the procedings refuse to permit the giving of evidence or presentation of any other matter which he considers to be irrelevant or repetitious.

(6) Where the inspector refuses to permit the giving of oral evidence, the person wishing to give, or to call any other person to give, evidence may submit to him any evidence or other matter in writing before the close of the hearing.

(7) The inspector may require any person appearing or present at a hearing who, in his opinion, is behaving in a disruptive manner to leave the hearing; and the inspector may then refuse to permit that person to return or permit him to return only on such conditions as he may specify, but any such person may submit to the inspector any evidence or other matter in writing before the close of the hearing.

(8) The inspector may allow the appellant or the Agency to alter or make any addition to a statement of case submitted under regulation 21(a) or (b) so far as may be necessary for the purposes of the hearing.

(9) The inspector may –

(a) proceed with a hearing in the absence of any person entitled to appear at it;
(b) take into account any written representations or evidence or any other document received by him from any person before a hearing opens or during the hearing provided he discloses it at the hearing, and
(c) from time to time adjourn a hearing, and, if the date, time and place of the adjourned hearing are announced at the hearing before the adjournment, no further notice shall be required.

35 Site inspections

(1) Where it appears to an inspector that one or more matters would be more satisfactorily resolved by adjourning the hearing to the appeal site, he may adjourn the hearing to that site and conclude the hearing there provided he is satisfied that –

(a) the hearing would proceed satisfactorily and that no party would be placed at a disadvantage;
(b) all parties present at the hearing would have the opportunity to attend the adjourned hearing; and
(c) neither the appellant nor the Agency have raised any reasonable objections to its being continued at the appeal site.

(2) Unless the hearing is to be adjourned to the appeal site pursuant to paragraph (1), the inspector may, where it appears to him necessary or expedient to do so, arrange to make an inspection of the appeal land in the company of the appellant and the Agency, or their representatives; and the inspector shall arrange to make such an inspection if requested to do so by the appellant or the Agency before or during the hearing in relation to an appeal against the showing of any land as open country on a provisional map.

(3) In all cases where the inspector intends to make a site inspection he shall announce during the hearing the date and time at which he proposes to make it.

(4) The inspector shall not be bound to defer an inspection if the appellant or the Agency, or their representative, is not present at the appointed time.

36 Procedure after hearing – appeals determined by the Secretary of State

(1) This regulation applies where a hearing has been held for the purposes of any appeal determined by the Secretary of State.

(2) After the close of the hearing, the inspector shall make a report in writing to the Secretary of State which shall include his conclusions and his recommendations or his reasons for not making any recommendations.

(3) When making her determination the Secretary of State may disregard any written representations, evidence or other document received after the hearing has closed.

(4) If, after the close of the hearing, the Secretary of State –

(a) differs from the inspector on any matter of fact mentioned in, or appearing to her to be material to, a conclusion reached by the inspector, or

(b) takes into consideration any new evidence or new matter of fact,

and is, for that reason, disposed to disagree with a recommendation made by the inspector, she shall not come to a decision which is at variance with that recommendation without first notifying the appellant, the Agency and any other person who appeared at the hearing of her disagreement and the reasons for it, and affording them an opportunity of making written representations to her or, if the Secretary of State has taken into consideration any new evidence or new matter of fact, of asking for the re-opening of the hearing.

(5) Those persons making written representations or requesting the re-opening of the hearing pursuant to paragraph (4) shall ensure that such representations or requests are received by the Secretary of State within three weeks of the date of the Secretary of State's notification under that paragraph.

(6) The Secretary of State may, if she thinks fit, cause a hearing to be re-opened, and she shall do so if asked by the appellant or the Agency in the circumstances mentioned in paragraph (4) and within the period mentioned in paragraph (5); and where a hearing is re-opened (whether by the same or a different inspector) –

(a) the Secretary of State shall send to the persons mentioned in paragraph (4) a written statement of the matters with respect to which further evidence is invited; and
(b) paragraphs (2), (5) and (6) of regulation 28 shall apply as if the references to a hearing were references to a re-opened hearing.

37   Procedure after hearing – transferred appeals

(1) This regulation applies where a hearing has been held for the purposes of a transferred appeal.

(2) When making his decision, the inspector may disregard any written representations or evidence or any other document received after the hearing has closed.

(3) If, after the close of the hearing, an inspector proposes to take into account any new matter of fact which was not raised at the hearing and which he considers to be material to his decision, he shall not come to a decision without first –

(a) notifying the appellant and the Agency and any other person who appeared at the hearing; and
(b) affording them an opportunity of making written representations to him or of asking for the re-opening of the hearing;

and they shall ensure that such written representations or request to re-open the hearing are received by the Secretary of State within three weeks of the date of notification.

(4) An inspector may, if he thinks fit, cause a hearing to be re-opened, and he shall do so if asked by the appellant or the Agency in the circumstances and within the period mentioned in paragraph (3); and where a hearing is re-opened –

(a) the inspector shall send to the appellant, the Agency and any other person who appeared at the hearing a written statement of the matters with respect to which further evidence is invited; and
(b) paragraphs (2), (5) and (6) of regulation 28 shall apply as if the references to a hearing were references to a re-opened hearing.

38 Notification of decision – appeals determined by the Secretary of State

(1) This regulation applies where a hearing has been held for the purposes of any appeal determined by the Secretary of State.

(2) The Secretary of State shall notify her decision on the appeal, and her reasons for reaching it, in writing to –

   (a) the appellant and the Agency; and
   (b) any other person who –
      (i) appeared at the hearing, or
      (ii) has made representations to the Secretary of State under regulation 21(c).

(3) Where a copy of the inspector's report is not sent with the notification of the decision, the notification shall be accompanied by a statement of his conclusions and of any recommendations made by him; and if a person entitled to be notified of the decision has not received a copy of that report, he shall be supplied with a copy of it on written application to the Secretary of State.

(4) In this regulation, 'report' does not include any documents appended to the inspector's report; but any person who has received a copy of the report may apply to the Secretary of State in writing for an opportunity to inspect any such documents, and the Secretary of State shall afford him that opportunity.

(5) A person applying to the Secretary of State under paragraph (3) or (4) shall ensure that his application is received by the Secretary of State within four weeks and six weeks, respectively, of the date of the decision of the Secretary of State.

(6) The Secretary of State shall ensure that a copy of the notification given under paragraph (2) is available for inspection on the website maintained by the Planning Inspectorate Executive Agency for the period during which the provisional map covering the land to which the appeal relates remains current.

39 Notification of decision – transferred appeals

(1) This regulation applies where a hearing has been held for the purposes of a transferred appeal.

(2) An inspector shall notify his decision on the appeal, and his reasons for it, in writing to –

   (a) the appellant and the Agency; and
   (b) any other person who –
      (i) appeared at the hearing, or
      (ii) has made representations to the Secretary of State under regulation 21(c).

(3) Any person entitled to be notified of the inspector's decision under paragraph (2) may apply to the Secretary of State in writing for an opportunity of inspecting any documents listed in the notification, and the Secretary of State shall afford him that opportunity.

(4) Any person making an application under paragraph (3) shall ensure that it is received by the Secretary of State within six weeks of the date of the inspector's decision.

(5) The Secretary of State shall ensure that a copy of the notification given under paragraph (2) is available for inspection on a website maintained by the Planning

Inspectorate Executive Agency for the period during which the provisional map covering the appeal land remains current.

CHAPTER IV

APPEALS TO BE DETERMINED BY WAY OF AN INQUIRY

40   Statements of case

The appellant and the Agency may each in writing require the other to provide a copy of any document referred to in the list of documents comprised in their statement of case, and any such document (or relevant part of it) shall be sent, as soon as practicable, to the party who required it.

41   Procedure where the Secretary of State or inspector causes pre-inquiry meeting to be held

(1) The Secretary of State or the inspector shall hold a pre-inquiry meeting if it appears to them to be necessary, and any such meeting (or, where there is more than one, the first such meeting) shall be held within sixteen weeks of the start date or at the earliest practicable time thereafter.

(2) Where the Secretary of State or the inspector decides to hold such a meeting, she or he (as the case may be) shall notify in writing the appellant and the Agency of her (or his) intention to hold such a meeting.

(3) The Secretary of State or the inspector shall give not less than two weeks' written notice of the pre-inquiry meeting to –

- (a) the appellant and the Agency; and
- (b) any other person whose presence at the pre-inquiry meeting she (or he) considers desirable.

(4) The inspector –

- (a) shall preside at the pre-inquiry meeting;
- (b) shall determine the matters to be discussed and the procedure to be followed;
- (c) may require any person present at the pre-inquiry meeting who he considers is behaving in a disruptive manner to leave; and
- (d) may refuse to permit that person to return or to attend any further pre-inquiry meeting or may permit him to return or attend only on such conditions as he may specify.

(5) Where a pre-inquiry meeting is held pursuant to paragraph (1), the inspector may hold a further pre-inquiry meeting and he shall arrange for such notice to be given of a further pre-inquiry meeting as appears to him necessary; and paragraph (4) shall apply to such a pre-inquiry meeting.

(6) If the Secretary of State or the inspector requests any further information at the pre-inquiry meeting from the appellant, the Agency or any other person present at that meeting, the person required to provide the information shall ensure that two copies of it have been received by the Secretary of State, or the inspector, as the case may be, within four weeks of the conclusion of the pre-inquiry meeting; and the Secretary of State shall, as soon as practicable after receipt of any such information send a copy of it to the other parties entitled to appear at the inquiry.

42 Inquiry timetable

(1) Where a pre-inquiry meeting is held pursuant to regulation 41, the inspector shall arrange a timetable for the proceedings at, or at part of, the inquiry.

(2) The inspector shall specify in a timetable arranged pursuant to this regulation a date by which any proof of evidence sent in accordance with regulation 48 shall be received by the Secretary of State.

43 Date and notification of inquiry

(1) The date fixed by the Secretary of State for the holding of an inquiry shall, unless she considers such a date to be impracticable, be not later than –

(a) subject to sub-paragraph (b), twenty two weeks after the start date; or
(b) where a pre-inquiry meeting is held pursuant to regulation 41, eight weeks after the conclusion of that meeting.

(2) Where the Secretary of State considers it impracticable to fix a date in accordance with paragraph (1), the date fixed shall be the earliest date after the expiry of the relevant period mentioned in that paragraph which she considers to be practicable.

(3) Unless the Secretary of State agrees a lesser period of notice with the appellant and the Agency, she shall give to the appellant, the Agency and any persons who have made representations to the Secretary of State in respect of the appeal under regulation 21(c) not less than four weeks' written notice of the date, time and place fixed by her for the holding of an inquiry.

(4) The Secretary of State may –

(a) change the date fixed for the holding of an inquiry (whether or not the new date is within the relevant period mentioned in paragraph (1)); or
(b) change the time or place for the holding of an inquiry.

(5) Where, under paragraph (4)(a), the Secretary of State changes the date for the holding of an inquiry, paragraph (3) shall apply to the new date as it applied to the date originally fixed, and where, under paragraph (4)(b), she changes the time or place for the holding of an inquiry, she shall give such notice of the change as appears to her to be reasonable.

(6) The Secretary of State may require the Agency to publish, not less than two weeks before the date fixed for the holding of an inquiry, a notice of the inquiry in one or more newspapers circulating in the locality in which the appeal land is situated; and the Secretary of State shall ensure that the Planning Inspectorate Executive Agency makes a copy of such notice available for inspection on a website which it maintains until the appeal is determined.

(7) Every notice of an inquiry published pursuant to paragraph (6) shall contain –

(a) a statement of the date, time and place of the inquiry and of the powers enabling the Secretary of State to determine the appeal in question; and
(b) a brief description of the appeal land and of the grounds of appeal.

44 Notification of name of inspector

The inspector shall, at the commencement of the inquiry, announce his name and the fact of his appointment.

45 Notification of appointment of assessor

Where the Secretary of State has appointed an assessor in respect of an inquiry, the inspector shall, at the commencement of the inquiry, announce the name of the assessor and the fact of his appointment.

46 Appearances at inquiry

(1) The persons entitled to appear at an inquiry are –

  (a) the appellant; and
  (b) the Agency.

(2) The inspector may permit any other person to appear at any inquiry, which permission shall not be unreasonably withheld.

(3) Any person entitled or permitted to appear may appear in person or be represented by another person.

47 Inspector may act in place of Secretary of State

An inspector may, in place of the Secretary of State, take such steps as the Secretary of State is required or enabled to take under or by virtue of regulations . . . 54 and 56(2); and where an inspector requires further information or copies pursuant to regulation 56(2), that information or those copies shall be sent to him.

Amendments – Reference omitted by Access to the Countryside (Provisional and Conclusive Maps) (England) (Amendment) Regulations 2003, SI 2003/32, with effect from 3 February 2003.

---

48 Proofs of evidence

(1) Subject to paragraph (2), where the appellant or the Agency propose to give, or to call another person to give, evidence at the inquiry by reading a proof of evidence, he or they shall send two copies of the proof of evidence, together with any written summary accompanying it, to the Secretary of State; and the Secretary of State shall, as soon as practicable after receiving it, send a copy of the proof of evidence provided by the appellant or the Agency, as the case may be, together with any written summary accompanying it, to the other party.

(2) A written summary shall be required where the proof of evidence in question exceeds one thousand five hundred words.

(3) The appellant and the Agency shall ensure that the proof of evidence and any summary is received by the Secretary of State no later than –

  (a) four weeks before the date fixed for the holding of the inquiry; or
  (b) where a timetable has been arranged pursuant to regulation 42 which specifies a date by which the proof of evidence and any summary shall be received by the Secretary of State, that date.

(4) Where a written summary is provided in accordance with paragraph (1), only that summary shall be read at the inquiry, unless the inspector permits or requires otherwise.

(5) Any person required by this regulation to send copies of a proof of evidence to the Secretary of State shall send with them the same number of copies of the whole (or the

relevant part) of any document referred to in the proof of evidence, unless a copy of the document (or part of the document) in question is already available for inspection pursuant to this regulation.

49   Statement of common ground

The appellant and the Agency shall together prepare a statement of common ground, and the Agency shall ensure that the Secretary of State receives it not less than four weeks before the date fixed for the holding of the inquiry.

50   Procedure at inquiry

(1) Except as otherwise provided in these Regulations, the inspector shall determine the procedure at an inquiry.

(2) At the start of the inquiry the inspector shall identify what are, in his opinion, the main issues to be considered at the inquiry and any matters on which he requires further explanation from any person appearing at the inquiry.

(3) Nothing in paragraph (2) shall preclude the addition in the course of the inquiry of other issues for consideration or preclude any person entitled or permitted to appear from referring to issues which that person considers relevant to the consideration of the appeal but which were not issues identified by the inspector pursuant to that paragraph.

(4) Unless in a particular case the inspector otherwise determines, the Agency shall begin and the appellant shall have the right of final reply; and any other persons appearing at the hearing shall be heard in such order as the inspector shall determine.

(5) Subject to paragraph (6), a person appearing at an inquiry shall be entitled to give, or call any other person to give, oral evidence, and the appellant and the Agency shall be entitled to cross-examine persons giving evidence, and any other person, if so permitted by the the inspector at his discretion, may give or call another person to give evidence, and may cross-examine any person giving evidence.

(6) The inspector may at any stage in the proceedings refuse to permit –

   (a) the giving or production of evidence,
   (b) the cross-examination of persons giving evidence, or
   (c) the presentation of any matter,

which he considers to be irrelevant or repetitious.

(7) Where under paragraph (5) or (6) the inspector refuses to permit the giving of oral evidence, the person wishing to give the evidence may submit to him any evidence or other matter in writing before the close of the inquiry.

(8) Where a person gives evidence at an inquiry by reading a summary of his proof of evidence –

   (a) the proof of evidence referred to in regulation 48(1) shall be treated as tendered in evidence, unless the person required to provide the summary notifies the inspector that he now wishes to rely on the contents of that summary alone; and
   (b) the person whose evidence the proof of evidence contains shall then be subject to cross-examination on it to the same extent as if it were evidence he had given orally.

(9) The inspector may –

(a) require any person appearing at an inquiry who, in his opinion, is behaving in a disruptive manner to leave; and

(b) refuse to permit that person to return or permit him to return only on such conditions as he may specify;

but any such person may submit to the inspector any evidence or other matter in writing before the close of the inquiry.

(10) The inspector may allow any person to alter or add to a statement of case received by the Secretary of State under regulation 21 or a proof of evidence or summary sent to the Secretary of State under regulation 48(1) so far as may be necessary for the purposes of the inquiry; but he shall (if necessary by adjourning the inquiry) give every other person appearing at the inquiry an adequate opportunity of considering any fresh matter or document.

(11) The inspector may proceed with an inquiry in the absence of any person entitled to appear at it.

(12) The inspector may take into account any written representations, or evidence or any other document received by him from any person before an inquiry opens or during the inquiry, provided he discloses it at the inquiry.

(13) The inspector may from time to time adjourn an inquiry, and if the date, time and place of the adjourned inquiry are announced at the inquiry before the adjournment, no further notice shall be required.

51   Site inspections

(1) During an inquiry or after its close, the inspector may, where it appears to him necessary or expedient to do so, arrange to make an inspection of the appeal land; and the inspector shall arrange to make such an inspection if so requested by the appellant or the Agency before or during the inquiry in relation to an appeal against the showing of any land as open country on a provisional map.

(2) Where the inspector intends to make an inspection under paragraph (1), he shall ask the appellant and the Agency whether they wish to be present or be represented.

(3) Where the appellant or the Agency have indicated that they wish to be present or be represented, the inspector shall give the appellant and the Agency reasonable notice of the date and time of the inspection and shall afford the appellant and the Agency, or their representatives, the opportunity of being present during the inspection.

(4) The inspector shall not be bound to defer an inspection if the appellant or the Agency or their representative is not present at the appointed time.

52   Procedure after inquiry – appeals to be determined by the Secretary of State

(1) This regulation applies where an inquiry has been held for the purposes of any appeal determined by the Secretary of State.

(2) After the close of an inquiry the inspector shall make a report in writing to the Secretary of State which shall include his conclusions and his recommendations or his reasons for not making any recommendations.

(3) Where an assessor has been appointed, he shall, after the close of the inquiry, make a report in writing to the inspector in respect of the matters on which he was appointed to advise.

(4) Where an assessor makes such a report, the inspector shall append it to his own report and shall state in his own report how far he agrees or disagrees with the assessor's report and, where he disagrees with the assessor, his reasons for that disagreement.

(5) When making her decision the Secretary of State may disregard any written representations, evidence or other document received after the close of the inquiry.

(6) If, after the close of the inquiry, the Secretary of State –

(a) differs from the inspector on any matter of fact mentioned in, or appearing to her to be material to, a conclusion reached by the inspector, or
(b) takes into consideration any new evidence or new matter of fact,

and is for that reason disposed to disagree with a recommendation made by the inspector, she shall not come to a decision which is at variance with that recommendation without first notifying the appellant and the Agency, and any other person who appeared at the inquiry, of her disagreement and the reasons for it, and affording them an opportunity of making written representations to her or of asking for the re-opening of the inquiry.

(7) Those persons making written representations or requesting the inquiry to be re-opened under paragraph (6) shall ensure that such representations or requests are received by the Secretary of State within three weeks of the date of the Secretary of State's notification under that paragraph.

(8) The Secretary of State may, if she thinks fit, cause an inquiry to be re-opened, and she shall do so if asked by the appellant or the Agency in the circumstances mentioned in paragraph (6) and within the period mentioned in paragraph (7); and where an inquiry is re-opened (whether by the same or a different inspector) –

(a) the Secretary of State shall send to the persons who appeared at the inquiry a written statement of the matters with respect to which further evidence is invited; and
(b) paragraphs (3), (6) and (7) of regulation 43 shall apply as if the references to an inquiry were to a re-opened inquiry.

53 Procedure after inquiry – transferred appeals

(1) This regulation applies for the purposes of an inquiry held for the purposes of a transferred appeal.

(2) Where an assessor has been appointed, he shall, after the close of the inquiry, make a report in writing to the inspector in respect of the matters on which he was appointed to advise, and the inspector shall state in the notification of his decision pursuant to regulation 55 that such a report was made.

(3) When making his decision the inspector may disregard any written representations or evidence or other document received after the close of the inquiry.

(4) If, after the close of the inquiry, an inspector proposes to take into consideration any new evidence or any new matter of fact which was not raised at the inquiry, and which he considers to be material to his decision, he shall not come to a decision without first –

(a) notifying the persons entitled to appear at the inquiry who appeared at it of the matter in question; and
(b) affording them an opportunity of making written representations to him or of asking for the inquiry to be re-opened;

and they shall ensure that such written representations are received by the Secretary of State within three weeks of the date of the notification.

(5) An inspector may, if he thinks fit, cause an inquiry to be re-opened, and he shall do so if asked by the appellant or the Agency in the circumstances and within the period mentioned in paragraph (4); and where an inquiry is re-opened –

- (a) the inspector shall send to the persons entitled to appear at the inquiry who appeared at it a written statement of the matters with respect to which further evidence is invited; and
- (b) paragraphs (3), (6) and (7) of regulation 43 shall apply as if the references to an inquiry were references to a re-opened inquiry.

54   Notification of decision – appeals determined by the Secretary of State

(1) This regulation applies where an inquiry has been held for the purposes of any appeal to be determined by the Secretary of State.

(2) The Secretary of State shall, as soon as practicable, notify her decision on an appeal, and her reasons for it, in writing to –

- (a) the appellant and the Agency; and
- (b) any other person who –
  - (i) appeared at the inquiry, or
  - (ii) has made representations to the Secretary of State under regulation 21(c).

(3) Where a copy of the inspector's report is not sent with the notification of the decision, the notification shall be accompanied by a statement of his conclusions and of any recommendations made by him, and if a person entitled to be notified of the decision has not received a copy of that report, he shall be supplied with a copy of it on written application to the Secretary of State.

(4) In this regulation, 'report' includes any assessor's report appended to the inspector's report but not any other documents so appended; but any person who has received a copy of the report may apply to the Secretary of State, in writing, within six weeks of the date of the Secretary of State's decision, for an opportunity of inspecting such documents, and the Secretary of State shall afford him such an opportunity.

(5) Any person applying to the Secretary of State under paragraph (3) or (4) shall ensure that his application is received by the Secretary of State within four weeks of the Secretary of State's determination.

55   Notification of decision – transferred appeals

(1) This regulation applies where an inquiry has been held for the purposes of a transferred appeal.

(2) The inspector shall, as soon as practicable, notify his decision on the appeal, and his reasons for it, in writing to –

- (a) the appellant and the Agency;
- (b) any other person who –
  - (i) appeared at the inquiry, or
  - (ii) has made representations to the Secretary of State under regulation 21(c).

(3) Any person entitled to be notified of the inspector's decision under paragraph (2) may apply to the Secretary of State in writing for an opportunity to inspect any

documents listed in the notification and any report made by an assessor, and the Secretary of State shall afford him that opportunity.

(4) Any person making an application pursuant to paragraph (3) shall ensure that it is received by the Secretary of State within six weeks of the date of the decision.

CHAPTER V

GENERAL

56   Further time and additional copies

(1) The Secretary of State may, at any time and in any particular case, give directions setting later time limits than those prescribed by these Regulations for the taking of any step or the doing of any thing which is required or enabled to be taken or done by virtue of these Regulations; and references in these Regulations to a period within which any step or thing is required or enabled to be taken or done shall be construed accordingly.

(2) The Secretary of State may, at any time before the notification of her decision (in the case of an appeal to be determined by way of written representations), or (in the case of a hearing or inquiry) before the close of the hearing or inquiry, request from any person making written representations or appearing at the hearing or inquiry (as the case may be) –

(a) further written representations or evidence, or (in the case of a hearing or inquiry) oral evidence with regard to any matter on which she requires further information; and
(b) copies of (as appropriate) –
    (i)   a statement of case or comments sent in accordance with regulation 21 or 23, respectively;
    (ii) a proof of evidence sent in accordance with regulation 48; or
    (iii) any other document or information sent to the Secretary of State before or during a hearing or inquiry;

and may specify a reasonable time within which such representations or copies must be received by her; and any person so requested shall ensure that the representations or copies are received within the period specified.

57   Inspection and copying of documents

The Agency shall afford any person who so requests, an opportunity, at such time and place as the Agency may reasonably determine, to inspect and, where practicable, take copies of –

(a) the notice of appeal submitted by the appellant pursuant to regulation 16(1);
(b) the Agency's completed questionnaire (together with any documents referred to in it);
(c) the notice given by the Secretary of State pursuant to regulation 19;
(d) all documents submitted by the Agency pursuant to regulation 20, 21(a), 23(b) or 24;
(e) the statement of case submitted by the appellant pursuant to regulation 21(b);
(f) any representations made to the Agency in respect of the showing of, or the failure to show, the appeal land as registered common land or open country on a map in draft form;

(g) any representations made to the Secretary of State in respect of the appeal under regulation 21(c);

(h) any proof of evidence (together with any written summary) sent by or to the Agency pursuant to regulation 48(1); or

(i) any statement of common ground prepared by the appellant and the Agency pursuant to regulation 49.

58   Changes of procedure

(1) If, at any time before the Secretary of State or the inspector, in either case under regulation 27, notifies her or (as the case may be) his decision on an appeal, the appellant, the Agency or the Secretary of State wishes the appeal to be determined no longer by way of written representations but instead by way of a hearing or inquiry, the Secretary of State shall arrange for the appeal to proceed by way of a hearing or inquiry.

(2) Paragraphs (3) and (4) apply at any time before the Secretary of State, under regulation 38 or 54, or an inspector, under regulation 39 or 55, notifies her or (as the case may be) his decision on an appeal.

(3) If the appellant or the Agency wishes an appeal to be determined no longer by way of a hearing or inquiry but instead by way of written representations, the Secretary of State shall consult the other party, and, if both that party and the Secretary of State agree to such a change in procedure, the Secretary of State shall arrange for the appeal to be determined by way of written representations.

(4) If the appellant, the Agency or the Secretary of State wishes an appeal to be determined –

(i)   no longer by way of a hearing but instead by way of an inquiry, or

(ii) no longer by way of an inquiry but instead by way of a hearing,

the Secretary of State shall, after consulting the other party or, where the Secretary of State wishes the appeal procedure to be changed, both the parties, decide whether the hearing or inquiry (as the case may be) should proceed no further and an inquiry or hearing (as appropriate) be held instead.

(5) Where the appeal procedure is changed by the Secretary of State under this regulation –

(a) the Secretary of State shall –

(i)   notify the appellant, the Agency and any other person who has made representations in respect of the appeal of such change; and

(ii) ensure that a copy of such notice is available for inspection on a website maintained by the Planning Inspectorate Executive Agency until the appeal is determined; and

(b) in relation to the conduct of the appeal thereafter –

(i)   any step taken or thing done under these Regulations in relation to the former appeal procedure which could have been done under any corresponding provision of these Regulations relating to the new appeal procedure shall have effect as if taken or done under that corresponding provision; and

(ii) the Secretary of State may give any consequential directions as to the procedure to be applied as she may consider necessary.

59 Recovery of jurisdiction

Where the appointment of an appointed person is revoked under paragraph 2(c) of Schedule 3 to the Act and no new appointment is made at the time of such revocation, the appeal shall proceed as an appeal which falls to be determined by the Secretary of State instead of as a transferred appeal, and any step taken or thing done under these Regulations in relation to the transferred appeal which could have been taken or done in relation to an appeal which falls to be determined by the Secretary of State shall have effect as if it had been taken or done in relation to such an appeal.

60 Procedure following quashing of a decision

(1) Where the decision of the Secretary of State or an inspector in respect of an appeal is quashed in proceedings before any court, the Secretary of State –

(a) shall send to the appellant, the Agency and any other persons who appeared at the hearing or inquiry or who has made representations to the Secretary of State in respect of the appeal under regulation 21(c), a written statement of the matters with respect to which further representations are invited for the purposes of her further consideration of the appeal;

(b) shall afford to those persons the opportunity of making written representations to her in respect of those matters or of asking for the re-opening of the hearing or the inquiry; and

(c) may, as she thinks fit, cause the hearing or inquiry to be re-opened;

and, where she re-opens the hearing or inquiry, paragraphs (2), (5) and (6) of regulation 28 and paragraphs (3), (6) and (7) of regulation 43 shall apply as if the references to a hearing or inquiry were to a re-opened hearing or inquiry, respectively.

(2) Those persons making representations or asking for the inquiry to be re-opened under paragraph (1)(b) shall ensure that such representations or requests are received by the Secretary of State within three weeks of the date of the written statement sent under paragraph (1)(a).

61 Use of electronic communications

(1) Any requirement imposed by or under these Regulations as to the giving or sending by one person to another of a notice or other document may be met by means of an electronic communication if –

(a) the use of such a communication results in the information contained in that notice or document being available to the other person in all material respects as it would appear in a notice or document given or sent in printed form; and

(b) the other person has consented to the information being made available to him by such means.

(2) Where under paragraph (1) an electronic communication is used for the purposes of giving or sending a notice or document –

(a) any requirement for the notice or document to be given or sent by a particular time shall be met in respect of the electronic communication only if the conditions mentioned in paragraph (1) are met by that time; and

(b) any requirement for more than one copy of the notice or document to be sent on any single occasion may be complied with by a single such communication.

(3) For the purposes of paragraph (1)(a), 'in all material respects' means in all respects material to an exact reproduction of the content of the information as it would appear in a notice or document given or sent in printed form.

(4) In this regulation –

(a) 'electronic communication' has the meaning given in section 15(1) of the Electronic Communications Act 2000; and

(b) 'requirement' includes any condition of an authorisation.

SCHEDULE

PERSONS TO BE SENT REDUCED SCALE MAPS

Regulation 8

PART I

PERSONS TO BE SENT REDUCED SCALE MAPS DERIVED FROM PROVISIONAL MAPS

1

The following persons exercising functions for the area of land to which the map relates –

access authorities,

local access forums,

parish councils.

2

Other persons –

British Association for Shooting and Conservation,

British Mountaineering Council,

Countryside Council for Wales (in respect of any map which relates to land adjoining land in Wales),

Country Land and Business Association,

English Nature,

Historic Buildings and Monuments Commission for England,

Moorland Association,

National Farmers' Union,

Open Spaces Society,

Ramblers' Association,

Royal Institution of Chartered Surveyors,

Secretary of State for Defence,

Tenant Farmers Association.

PART II

PERSONS TO BE SENT REDUCED SCALE MAPS DERIVED FROM CONCLUSIVE MAPS

1

The following persons exercising functions for the area of land to which the map relates –

access authorities,

local access forums,

parish councils.

2

Other persons –

Countryside Council for Wales (in respect of any map which relates to land adjoining land in Wales),

English Nature,

Historic Buildings and Monuments Commission for England,

Ordnance Survey,

Secretary of State for Defence.

VEHICULAR ACCESS ACROSS COMMON AND OTHER LAND (ENGLAND) REGULATIONS 2002, SI 2002/1711

1 Title, commencement and extent

(1) These Regulations may be cited as the Vehicular Access Across Common and Other Land (England) Regulations 2002 and shall come into force on the day after the date on which they are made.

(2) These Regulations shall apply to land in England only.

(3) For the purposes of paragraph (2), 'land' means any land which is crossed by a way used as a means of access for vehicles to premises.

2 Interpretation

(1) In these Regulations –

'the Act' means the Countryside and Rights of Way Act 2000;

'the applicant', 'the land' and 'the land owner' have the meanings given in regulation 3(2);

'compensation sum' means the amount of compensation payable by the applicant;

'easement' means an easement subsisting at law for the benefit of the premises and giving a right of way for vehicles;

'the parties' means the applicant and the land owner and 'party' shall be construed accordingly;

'the premises' means the premises served by the way in respect of which an application for an easement is made;

'the value of the premises' has the meaning given in regulation 11(4).

(2) Any reference in these Regulations to a numbered regulation shall be construed as a reference to the regulation so numbered in these Regulations.

3 Entitlement to make an application

(1) An owner of any premises may, as respects a way to which section 68 of the Act applies, apply for the creation of an easement in accordance with these Regulations.

(2) For the purposes of these Regulations, the owner who makes an application shall be referred to as 'the applicant', the land crossed by the way shall be referred to as 'the land' and the person who, for the time being, has the freehold title to the land, shall be referred to as 'the land owner'.

4 Prescribed date

The prescribed date for the purpose of section 68(1)(b) of the Act is 5th May 1993.

5 Nature of easement

An easement created in accordance with these Regulations shall –

(a) be subject to any limitation agreed by the parties or determined by the Lands Tribunal;

(b) include any right incidental to the right of way agreed by the parties or determined by the Lands Tribunal; and

(c) be subject to any rule of law which would apply to the easement had it been acquired by prescription.

6 Procedure for making an application

(1) An application for the easement shall be made by the applicant serving a notice on the land owner.

(2) The application must be served within 12 months of the date on which these Regulations come into force or, if later, the date on which the relevant use of the way has ceased.

(3) The application shall contain the information specified in paragraph 1, and be accompanied by the information specified in paragraph 2, of the Schedule to these Regulations.

7 Unopposed applications

(1) Where the land owner does not object to the application he shall, within three months of receipt of the application, serve a notice on the applicant, agreeing to the application.

(2) The notice shall contain the following information –

(a) the name and address of the land owner and a description of his interest in the land; and

(b) a statement confirming that upon payment of the compensation sum he will provide a written receipt.

(3) The notice shall be accompanied by evidence of the land owner's title to the land.

8 Opposed applications

(1) Where the land owner has objections to the application, he shall, within three months of receipt of the application, serve a notice (a 'counter notice') on the applicant, objecting to the application.

(2) Objections to the application may be made on the following grounds –

(a) the applicant has served the application after the expiry of the period for service;

(b) the applicant has not provided the information required by regulation 6(3);

(c) information provided by the applicant is not correct;

(d) the easement should be subject to limitations other than those (if any) described in the application;

(e) any rights incidental to the right of way, which are described in the application as being rights which should be included in the easement, are not agreed;

(f) the value of the premises is not agreed.

(3) The counter notice shall contain the following information –

(a) the name and address of the land owner and a description of his interest in the land;

(b) the objections to the application; and

(c) any alternative proposals.

(4) The counter notice shall be accompanied by –

(a) any evidence relevant to the objections and alternative proposals; and

(b) evidence of the land owner's title to the land.

9   Amended application and amended counter notice

(1) Within two months of receipt of a counter notice, the applicant may serve on the land owner an amended application addressing the objections and any alternative proposals set out in the counter notice.

(2) An amended application shall contain the information specified in paragraph 1 of the Schedule to these Regulations and shall be accompanied by any evidence relevant to the applicant's response to the objections and any alternative proposals set out in the counter notice.

(3) Where the applicant has served an amended application on the land owner, the land owner shall, within two months of receipt of the amended application –

(a) serve a notice on the applicant agreeing to the amended application and confirming that upon payment of the compensation sum he will provide a written receipt, or

(b) serve an amended counter notice on the applicant objecting to the amended application.

(4) An amended counter notice shall comply with regulation 8(2), (3) and (4)(a) and, for this purpose, –

(a) references in regulation 8(2) and (3) to the application, except for the reference in sub-paragraph (a) of regulation 8(2), shall be treated as references to the amended application; and

(b) an objection may also be made on the ground that the applicant has served the amended application after the expiry of the period for service or has not provided the information required by paragraph (2) of this regulation.

(5) Where the land owner has served an amended counter notice on the applicant, the applicant may, within two months of receipt of the amended counter notice, serve a notice on the land owner agreeing to the amended counter notice.

10   Lands Tribunal

(1) Where a counter notice has been served, either party may, where there is a dispute relating to any matter other than the value of the premises, request the Lands Tribunal to determine the matter in dispute by sending a notice of reference to the Lands Tribunal in accordance with the Lands Tribunal Rules 1996.

(2) The notice of reference shall have annexed to it –

(a) the application;

(b) the counter notice; and

(c) if applicable, the amended application and amended counter notice.

11   Calculation of the compensation sum

(1) Subject to paragraph (2), the compensation sum shall be 2% of the value of the premises.

(2) Where the premises were in existence on –

(a) 31st December 1905; or
(b) 30th November 1930,

the compensation sum shall be 0.25% or 0.5% of the value of the premises respectively.

(3) Where the premises are in residential use and replaced other premises on the same site which were also in residential use ('the former premises'), the compensation sum shall be calculated in accordance with paragraph (2) by reference to the date on which the former premises were in existence.

(4) For the purposes of these Regulations, the value of the premises shall be calculated as at the valuation date on the basis of the open market value of the premises with the benefit of the easement.

(5) In paragraph (4), the 'valuation date' means the date as at which the premises are valued for the purposes of the application, being a date no more than 3 months before the date on which the application is served.

12   Determination of the compensation sum in default of agreement

(1) Where no agreement can be reached on the value of the premises, either party may serve on the other a notice (the 'valuation notice') requiring the amount to be determined by a chartered surveyor.

(2) Where a valuation notice has been served, the appointment of a chartered surveyor shall be agreed by the parties within one month of the service of the valuation notice and, where agreement on such appointment cannot be reached, either party may request the President of the Royal Institution of Chartered Surveyors to appoint a chartered surveyor.

(3) Where a chartered surveyor has been appointed in accordance with paragraph (2), the following provisions shall apply as appropriate –

(a) where the appointment has been made by the President of the Royal Institution of Chartered Surveyors, the parties shall be equally liable for the costs of that appointment;
(b) unless the parties agree that the chartered surveyor shall act as an independent expert, he shall act as an arbitrator and the provisions of the Arbitration Act 1996 shall apply; and
(c) where the chartered surveyor acts as an independent expert, the parties shall –
  (i) be bound by his final decision; and
  (ii) each party shall bear their own costs and shall be equally liable for the fees and costs of the chartered surveyor.

13   Payment of the compensation sum

(1) Where –

(a) the land owner has notified the applicant in accordance with regulation 7 or 9(3)(a);

(b) the applicant has notified the land owner in accordance with regulation 9(5); or

(c) any matters in dispute have been determined in accordance with regulation 10 or 12,

the applicant shall pay the compensation sum to the land owner.

(2) The compensation sum shall be paid within two months of –

(a) the date of notification under regulation 7 or paragraph (3)(a) or (5) of regulation 9, as the case may be; or

(b) where a determination is made under regulation 10 or 12, the date of the determination or, if more than one such determination is made, the date of the last determination.

(3) The land owner shall, within one month from the date of receipt of the compensation sum, provide the applicant with a written receipt for that sum.

14   Payment into court

Where –

(a) the land owner does not serve a notice in accordance with either regulation 7 or 8; or

(b) the applicant has served an amended application on the land owner and the land owner fails to act in accordance with regulation 9(3),

the applicant may, within two months of the expiry of the period for service of a notice under regulation 7, 8 or 9(3), as the case may be, pay the compensation sum into a county court in accordance with the Court Funds Rules 1987.

15   Creation of the easement

Upon payment of the compensation sum either –

(a) to the land owner in accordance with regulation 13; or

(b) into court in accordance with regulation 14,

the easement shall be created.

16   Notices

(1) A notice under these Regulations shall be in writing and may be served by sending it by post.

(2) Where any notice is required by these Regulations to be served within a specified period, the parties may, except in the case of an application, agree in writing to extend or further extend that period.

17   Abandonment etc by applicant

Where the applicant withdraws or otherwise fails to continue with the application at any stage, he shall be liable for the reasonable costs incurred by the land owner.

SCHEDULE

INFORMATION TO BE PROVIDED BY THE APPLICANT

Regulation 6(3)

1

The application shall contain the following information –

(a) the name and address of the applicant;
(b) a description of the premises;
(c) a description of the applicant's interest in the premises;
(d) details of the current use of the premises and the use during the period giving rise to the entitlement to apply for the easement;
(e) where the relevant use of the way has ceased, the date of the cessation;
(f) where the premises, or, where regulation 11(3) applies, the former premises, were in existence on 31st December 1905 or 30th November 1930, a statement confirming those facts;
(g) the nature of the use of the access, including any limitation or incidental right to which the easement should be subject or which should be included in the easement;
(h) the dimensions of the width of the way; and
(i) the proposed compensation sum to be paid to the land owner in respect of the easement, together with the basis on which it is calculated.

2

The application shall be accompanied by –

(a) a map of an appropriate scale (1:1250 or 1:2500) showing the premises (marked in blue), the way (marked in red) and sufficient other land to establish the exact location of the premises and the way in relation to the surrounding area;
(b) evidence (which may include a statutory declaration) that –
  (i) the way is a way to which section 68 of the Act applies; and
  (ii) where the application is served after 12 months of the date on which these Regulations come into force, either that the relevant use of the way has not ceased or that such use ceased no more than 12 months before the date on which the application is served; and
(c) an estimate prepared by a chartered surveyor of the value of the premises as at the valuation date, and 'valuation date' has the same meaning for this purpose as in regulation 11(4).

COUNTRYSIDE ACCESS (APPEALS PROCEDURES) (WALES) REGULATIONS 2002, SI 2002/1794

PART I

GENERAL

1   Citation, commencement and application

(1) These Regulations may be cited as the Countryside Access (Appeals Procedures) (Wales) Regulations 2002 and shall come into force on 1st August 2002.

(2) These Regulations apply to Wales.

2   Interpretation

(1) In these Regulations, words or phrases shall have the meaning given to them by the Act and –

'the Act' ('y Ddeddf') means the Countryside and Rights of Way Act 2000;

'appeal' ('apêl) means an appeal to the National Assembly under sections 6(1), 30(3) or 38(3) of the Act;

'appeal form' ('ffurflen apêl') means the document through which an appeal is brought;

'appellant' ('apelydd') means a person who brings an appeal and, where two or more persons join in bringing an appeal, refers to all those persons jointly;

'appointed person' ('person penodedig') means a person appointed by the National Assembly under section 8 of the Act;

'assessor' ('asesydd') means a person appointed by the National Assembly under paragraph 4(3) of Schedule 3 to the Act;

'conclusive map' ('map terfynol') means a map issued by the Council in conclusive form under section 9 of the Act;

'the Council' ('y Cyngor') means the Countryside Council for Wales;

'electronic form' ('ffurf electronig') means a form capable of being stored on, transmitted to and from, and read by means of a computer;

'inquiry' ('ymchwiliad') means a public local inquiry;

references to an 'interest' ('buddiant') in land are to be interpreted in accordance with section 45(1) of the Act;

'interested person' ('personau â diddordeb') means a person (other than an appellant or a respondent) who has made representations to the National Assembly in relation to an appeal, unless it appears to the National Assembly that the representation in question was made frivolously or vexatiously;

'legible form' ('ffurf ddarllenadwy') means, in relation to a document sent by means of an electronic communication, a form in which it is capable of being read on a computer screen;

'open country' ('tir agored') has the meaning given by section 1(2) of the Act;

'outline statement' ('datganiad amlinellol') means a statement outlining the case which a person wishes to put forward in relation to an appeal;

'person' ('person') and 'persons' ('personau') include individuals, corporations and unincorporated bodies;

'persons entitled to take part' ('personau â hawl i gymryd rhan') means those persons specified as such in regulations 13 and 23, as appropriate;

'pre-inquiry meeting' ('cyfarfod cyn-ymchwiliad') means a meeting held before an inquiry to consider what may be done with a view to securing that the inquiry is conducted efficiently and expeditiously and, where two or more such meetings are held, reference to the conclusion of a pre-inquiry meeting is a reference to the conclusion of the final meeting;

'provisional map' ('map dros dro') means a map issued by the Council in provisional form under section 5(d) or 5(e) of the Act;

'the Provisional Maps Regulations' ('Rheoliadau Mapiau Dros Dro') means the Countryside Access (Provisional and Conclusive Maps) (Wales) Regulations 2002;

'registered common land' ('tir comin cofrestredig') has the meaning given by section 1(3) of the Act;

'relevant time limits' ('terfynau amser perthnasol') means the time limits set by these Regulations or, where the National Assembly has exercised its power under regulation 31 to extend the time prescribed by these Regulation, those limits as so extended;

'the respondent' ('yr atebydd') means the person whose decision is the subject of the appeal;

'section 4(2) land' ('tir adran 4(2)') means the registered common land and open country in respect of which the Council is required to prepare maps in accordance with section 4(2) of the Act;

'starting date' ('dyddiad cychwyn') has the meaning given in regulation 5(4); and

'statement of case' ('datganiad o achos') means a written statement containing full particulars of the case which a person proposes to put forward in relation to an appeal, a list of documents which that party intends to rely on and any documents and/or maps which the National Assembly considers it necessary to request that person to provide.

(2) In these Regulations, unless otherwise specified, any reference to a numbered regulation is a reference to the regulation bearing that number in these Regulations and any reference in a regulation to a numbered paragraph is a reference to the paragraph bearing that number in that regulation.

(3) In reckoning any period which is expressed in these Regulations to be a period from a given date, that date is to be excluded and, where the day or the last day on which anything is required by, or in pursuance with, these Regulations to be done is a Sunday, Christmas Day, Good Friday, bank holiday or a day appointed for public thanksgiving or mourning, the requirement shall be deemed to relate to the first day thereafter which is not one of the days before-mentioned.

PART II

INITIAL STAGES OF APPEALS

3   Action by the National Assembly on receipt of an appeal form

The National Assembly must, as soon as reasonably practicable after it receives a completed appeal form, send a copy of it to the respondent.

4   Response by a respondent to an appeal

(1) The respondent must, within 14 days of receiving from the National Assembly a copy of an appeal form, send to the National Assembly and to the appellant –

  (a) a statement containing an indication as to whether it will oppose the appeal and, if so, its grounds for doing so;
  (b) copies of any relevant correspondence between the appellant and the respondent;
  (c) in the case of an appeal under section 6 of the Act, a copy of an extract showing that part of the provisional map to which it relates;
  (d) copies of any representations made to the respondent by any person other than the appellant in respect of the decision on the part of the respondent to which the appeal relates; and
  (e) any further information required by the National Assembly to be provided.

(2) Where the respondent has complied with the requirements of paragraph (1), the respondent must, before the expiry of the relevant period specified in regulation 5(2), send to the National Assembly and to the appellant –

  (a) a statement confirming whether they will oppose the appeal;
  (b) a statement as to whether they wish to be heard by a person appointed by the National Assembly in connection with the appeal (rather than the appeal be determined on the basis of written representations) and, if so, whether they wish to be heard at a local inquiry or, alternatively, at a hearing; and
  (c) any further information required by the National Assembly to be provided.

5   Notifying the parties of the appeal procedure

(1) The National Assembly must, no earlier than the end of the period specified in paragraph (2), give notice to the appellant and to the respondent of the form which the appeal is to take.

(2) Notice under paragraph (1) must not be given before –

  (a) the expiry of 21 days from the date specified in the notice or notices given or published under regulation 6(1)(a) or (b) as being the date by which representations to the National Assembly could be made; or
  (b) in the case of an appeal under section 6 of the Act, the expiry of three months from the date of issue of the provisional map to which the appeal relates,

whichever is the later.

(3) The notice given under paragraph (1) must be dated and must state whether the appeal is to take the form of –

  (a) a local inquiry;
  (b) a hearing; or

(c) neither (a) nor (b), and will therefore be determined on the basis of written representations.

(4) The date of the notice given under paragraph (1) is the 'starting date' for the purposes of these Regulations in relation to the appeal to which it refers and the notice must contain a statement to that effect.

(5) If the appeal is to take the form of a local inquiry, and the National Assembly intends to hold a pre-inquiry meeting, the notice given under paragraph (1) must also comply with the requirements of regulation 18(2)(a).

6 Notice to the public

(1) The National Assembly must, at the same time as it gives notice to the appellant and to the respondent under regulation 5(1), or as soon as practicable thereafter –

(a) publish notice of the appeal in at least one daily newspaper circulating throughout that part of Wales which includes the land to which the appeal relates and in such other newspapers or publications circulating in that part of Wales as the National Assembly thinks fit; and
(b) where practicable, publish notice of the appeal on a web-site maintained by or on behalf of the National Assembly; and
(c) in the case of an appeal under section 6 of the Act, send notice of the appeal to the organisations listed in Schedule 1 to the Provisional Maps Regulations.

(2) A notice published under paragraph (1)(a) or (b) or sent under paragraph (1)(c) must be dated and must state –

(a) the name of the appellant;
(b) sufficient information to identify the land in respect of which the appeal has been brought;
(c) if the appeal is brought under section 6 of the Act, on which of the grounds specified in section 6(3) it has been brought;
(d) the reference number allocated to the appeal;
(e) the starting date;
(f) the means by which members of the public may inspect, and take a copy of, documents relating to the appeal;
(g) that representations, which may be made either in the English language or the Welsh language, relating to the appeal may be made in writing or in electronic form to the National Assembly by such date as is specified in the notice, which must not be earlier than 6 weeks after the date on which the notice is published in accordance with paragraph (1)(a) or (b), and that copies of such representations will be provided to the appellant and to the respondent;
(h) the address to which written communications to the National Assembly are to be sent;
(i) whether the appeal is to take the form of a local inquiry or a hearing or is to be determined on the basis of written representations;
(j) if the appeal is to take the form of a local inquiry, that a person who makes representations in accordance with paragraph (2)(g) will be notified of the date and place of the inquiry and may attend, but will only be permitted to take part in, the inquiry with the permission of the person appointed to conduct it; and
(k) if the appeal is to take the form of a hearing, that a person who makes representations in accordance with paragraph (2)(g) will be notified of the date and place of the hearing but will only be permitted to attend and take part in the hearing with the permission of the person appointed to conduct it.

(3) If the appeal is to take the form of a local inquiry, and the National Assembly intends to hold a pre-inquiry meeting, the notice published under paragraph (1)(a) or (b) or sent under paragraph (1)(c) must also comply with the requirements of regulation 18(2)(b).

(4) Any notice published or sent in accordance with paragraph (1)(a), (b) or (c) may, in addition to such information as is required to be included in such a notice by this regulation, include such further information as the National Assembly shall think fit.

PART III
APPEALS DETERMINED ON THE BASIS OF WRITTEN REPRESENTATIONS

7 Application

Regulations 8 and 9 apply to appeals which are to be determined on the basis of written representations.

8 Exchange of evidence

(1) In addition to any documents already sent to the National Assembly by the appellant in accordance with regulation 6 of the Provisional Maps Regulations (in the case of an appeal under section 6 of the Act), and by the respondent in accordance with regulation 4 of these Regulations, the appellant and the respondent must, within 6 weeks of the starting date, send to the National Assembly two copies of any further written representations or other documents on which they wish to rely or, if they do not wish to rely on any such further representations or other documents, a notice to that effect.

(2) The National Assembly must, as soon as practicable after receiving any further representations, other documents or notices pursuant to paragraph (1), send a copy of those representations, documents or notices to the appellant or the respondent, as appropriate.

(3) The appellant and the respondent must, within 9 weeks of the starting date, send to the National Assembly two copies of any further representations, other documents or notices on which they wish to rely or, if they do not wish to rely on any such further representations or other documents, a notice to that effect.

(4) Where representations have been made to the National Assembly by anyone other than the appellant and the respondent, the National Assembly must, as soon as practicable after receiving those representations, send a copy of them to the appellant, and to the respondent, who must, if they wish to submit any comments on those representations to the National Assembly, send two copies of their comments to the National Assembly within 9 weeks of the starting date.

(5) The National Assembly may, in a particular case, invite the appellant and the respondent to send to the National Assembly and to each other, within such reasonable time as it may specify, such further representations or other documents as it believes are necessary in order to enable the appeal to be determined.

9 Decision on an appeal determined by an exchange of written representations

(1) The appointed person may, after the expiration of any time limits within which the appellant or the respondent are required or permitted to take any step in accordance

with these Regulations, and after giving to the appellant and the respondent written notice of the intention to do so, proceed to a decision on the appeal by taking into account only such representations and other documents as have been submitted to the National Assembly within the relevant time limits.

(2) The National Assembly must notify the decision on an appeal, and its reasons for reaching that decision, in writing to –

  (a) the appellant;
  (b) the respondent;
  (c) any interested person; and
  (d) any other person who has asked to be notified of the decision whom the National Assembly considers it reasonable to notify.

PART IV

APPEALS DETERMINED FOLLOWING A HEARING

10   Application

Regulations 11 to 16 apply to appeals which are to be determined following a hearing.

11   Exchange of evidence

Regulation 8 is to apply to an appeal to be determined following a hearing as it does to an appeal to be determined on the basis of written representations.

12   Date and notification of a hearing

(1) The National Assembly must –

  (a) as soon as practicable, notify the appellant, the respondent, any person who has made representations in relation to the appeal and any other person as it thinks fit, of the name of the appointed person who will conduct the hearing;
  (b) as soon as practicable after any change in the identity of the appointed person, give notification of that change to those persons entitled to be notified in accordance with sub-paragraph (a), unless it is not reasonably practicable to do so before the hearing is held, in which case the name of the appointed person and the fact of that person's appointment must be announced at the commencement of the hearing;
  (c) unless the National Assembly agrees a lesser period of notice with the appellant and the respondent, give not less than 4 weeks' written notice to the appellant, the respondent, any interested person and such other persons as it thinks fit of the date, time and place fixed for the hearing; and
  (d) not less than 2 weeks before the date fixed for the holding of a hearing, publish a notice of the hearing in one or more newspapers circulating in the locality in which the land is situated.

(2) Every notice of a hearing given in accordance with paragraph (1)(c) or published in accordance with paragraph (1)(d) must contain –

  (a) a statement of the date, time and place of the hearing and of the powers enabling the National Assembly to determine the appeal in question;
  (b) a written description of the land sufficient to identify its location and extent;
  (c) a brief description of the subject matter of the appeal; and

(d) details of where and when copies of documents relevant to the appeal may be inspected.

(3) Notwithstanding paragraph (1), the National Assembly may vary the date fixed for the holding of the hearing, whether or not the date as varied is within the period otherwise required by that paragraph and paragraph (1)(c) and (d) apply to a variation of a date as they applied to the date originally fixed.

(4) The National Assembly may vary the time or place fixed for the holding of the hearing and must give such notice of any variation as appears to it to be reasonable.

13 Rights of attendance at and participation in a hearing

The appellant and the respondent are entitled to attend and take part in a hearing, and the appointed person may permit any other persons to do so (whether on their own behalf or on behalf of any other person).

14 Procedure at a hearing

(1) Except as otherwise provided in these Regulations, the appointed person may determine the procedure at a hearing.

(2) A hearing is to take the form of a discussion led by the appointed person and cross-examination is not to be permitted unless the appointed person considers that it is required to ensure proper examination of the issues relevant to the appeal.

(3) An appointed person who considers that cross-examination is required under paragraph (2) must consider, after consulting the appellant and the respondent, whether the hearing should be closed and an inquiry held instead.

(4) At the start of the hearing, the appointed person must identify the issues which appear to the appointed person to be the main issues to be considered at the hearing and any matters on which the appointed person requires further explanation from any person entitled or permitted to take part.

(5) Nothing in paragraph (4) is to preclude any person entitled or permitted to take part in the hearing from referring to issues which they consider relevant to the consideration of the appeal but which were not issues identified by the appointed person pursuant to that paragraph.

(6) A person entitled to take part in a hearing may, subject to the foregoing and paragraphs (7) and (8), call evidence but, the calling of evidence is otherwise to be at the appointed person's discretion.

(7) The appointed person may refuse to permit the giving of oral evidence or the presentation of any other matter which the appointed person considers to be irrelevant or repetitious but, where the appointed person refuses to permit the giving of oral evidence, the person wishing to give the evidence may submit any evidence or other matter in writing to the appointed person before the close of the hearing.

(8) The appointed person may –

(a) require any person attending or taking part in a hearing who, in the opinion of the appointed person, is behaving in a disruptive manner to leave; and
(b) refuse to permit that person to return or permit that person to return only on such conditions as the appointed person may specify,

but any such person may submit any evidence or other matter in writing to the appointed person before the close of the hearing.

(9) The appointed person may allow any person to alter or add to a statement so far as may be necessary for the purposes of the hearing, but the appointed person must (if necessary by adjourning the hearing) give every other person entitled to take part in and who is actually taking part in the hearing an adequate opportunity of considering any fresh matter or document.

(10) The appointed person may proceed with a hearing in the absence of any person entitled to take part in it.

(11) The appointed person may take into account any written representation or evidence or any other document which the appointed person has received from any person before a hearing opens or during the hearing provided that the appointed person discloses it at the hearing.

(12) The appointed person may from time to time adjourn a hearing and, if the date, time and place of the adjourned hearing are announced at the hearing before the adjournment, no further notice is to be required.

15 Decision after a hearing

(1) The appointed person may disregard any written representations, evidence or other documents received after the hearing has closed.

(2) If, after the close of the hearing, the appointed person proposes to take into consideration any new evidence or any new matter of fact (not being a matter of government policy) which was not raised at the hearing and which the appointed person considers to be material to the decision, the appointed person must not do so without first –

(a) notifying persons entitled to take part in the hearing (whether or not they attended the hearing) of the matter in question; and
(b) affording them an opportunity of making written representations or of asking for the re-opening of the hearing,

provided such written representations or request to re-open the hearing are received by the National Assembly within 3 weeks of the date of the notification.

(3) An appointed person may cause a hearing to be re-opened and the appointed person must do so if asked by the appellant or the respondent in the circumstances and within the period mentioned in paragraph (2) and where a hearing is re-opened –

(a) the appointed person must send to the persons entitled to take part in the hearing and who took part in it a written statement of the matters with respect to which further evidence is invited; and
(b) regulation 12(1)(c) and (d) are to apply as if the references to a hearing were references to a re-opened hearing.

16 Notification of decision

(1) The decision of the appointed person, and the reasons for it, must be notified in writing to –

(a) the appellant;

(b) the respondent;

(c) any other person who, having taken part in the hearing, has asked to be notified of the decision.

(2) Any person entitled to be notified of the decision under paragraph (1) may apply to the National Assembly, in writing, for an opportunity to inspect any documents listed in the notification and the National Assembly must afford that person that opportunity.

(3) Any person making an application under paragraph (2) must ensure that it is received by the National Assembly within 6 weeks of the date of the decision on the appeal.

PART V

APPEALS DETERMINED FOLLOWING A PUBLIC LOCAL INQUIRY

17   Application

Regulations 18 to 28 apply to appeals which are to be determined following a public local inquiry.

18   Procedure where the National Assembly causes a pre-inquiry meeting to be held

(1) The National Assembly must hold a pre-inquiry meeting –

(a) if it expects an inquiry to last for 8 days or more, unless it considers such a meeting to be unnecessary;

(b) in respect of shorter inquiries, if it appears to it to be necessary.

(2) Where the National Assembly decides to hold a pre-inquiry meeting –

(a) the National Assembly must send with or include in the notice it gives in accordance with regulation 5(1) –

(i)   notice of its intention to hold a pre-inquiry meeting; and

(ii) a statement of the matters about which it particularly wishes to be informed for the purposes of its consideration of the appeal in question;

(b) the National Assembly must include in the notice it publishes in accordance with regulation 6(1)(a) or (b) or sends in accordance with regulation 6(1)(c), notice of its intention to hold a pre-inquiry meeting and a statement of the matters referred to in paragraph (2)(a)(ii); and

(c) the appellant and the respondent must each send two copies of their outline statement to the National Assembly within 8 weeks of the starting date.

(3) The National Assembly must, as soon as practicable after receipt, send a copy of the outline statement of the respondent to the appellant and that of the appellant to the respondent.

(4) The National Assembly may, in writing, require any interested persons who have notified it of an intention or a wish to take part in the inquiry to send an outline statement to it, to the appellant and to the respondent, and those interested persons must ensure that such statement is received by the National Assembly, the appellant and the respondent within 4 weeks of the date of the National Assembly's written requirement.

(5) The pre-inquiry meeting (or, where there is more than one, the first pre-inquiry meeting) must be held within 16 weeks of the starting date.

(6) The National Assembly must give not less than 3 weeks' written notice of the pre-inquiry meeting to the appellant, the respondent, any interested person known at the date of the notice to wish to take part in the inquiry and any other person whose presence at the pre-inquiry meeting appears to the National Assembly to be desirable, and it must, in relation to notification of the pre-inquiry meeting, take one or more of the steps specified, in relation to the inquiry, in regulation 22(6).

(7) The appointed person –

    (a) is to preside at the pre-inquiry meeting;
    (b) is to determine the matters to be discussed and the procedure to be followed;
    (c) may require any person present at the pre-inquiry meeting who, in the opinion of the appointed person, is behaving in a disruptive manner to leave; and
    (d) may refuse to permit that person to return or to attend any further pre-inquiry meeting, or may permit that person to return or attend only on such conditions as the appointed person may specify.

(8) Where a pre-inquiry meeting has been held pursuant to paragraph (1), the appointed person may hold a further pre-inquiry meeting and must arrange for such notice to be given of a further pre-inquiry meeting as appears to the appointed person to be necessary; and paragraph (7) is to apply to such a further pre-inquiry meeting.

(9) If the National Assembly requests any further information from the appellant or the respondent at the pre-inquiry meeting, the person from whom the further information has been requested must ensure that two copies of that information have been received by the National Assembly and a copy has been received by any interested person to whom the appointed person may require a copy to be supplied, within 4 weeks of the conclusion of the pre-inquiry meeting and the National Assembly must, as soon as practicable after receipt, send a copy of the further information received from the appellant to the respondent and a copy of the further information received from the respondent to the appellant.

19   Receipt of statements of case etc

(1) The respondent must ensure that within –

    (a) 6 weeks of the starting date; or
    (b) where a pre-inquiry meeting is held pursuant to regulation 18, 4 weeks of the conclusion of that pre-inquiry meeting,

two copies of the respondent's statement of case have been received by the National Assembly and a copy of that statement of case has been received by any interested person to whom the National Assembly may require a copy of that statement of case to be supplied.

(2) The respondent must include, in its statement of case, details of the place where, and times at which, the opportunity to inspect and take copies of the documents referred to in paragraph (12) below is to be afforded.

(3) The appellant must ensure that within –

    (a) 6 weeks of the starting date; or

(b) where a pre-inquiry meeting is held pursuant to regulation 18, 4 weeks of the conclusion of that pre-inquiry meeting,

two copies of the appellant's statement of case have been received by the National Assembly and a copy of that statement of case has been received by any interested person to whom the National Assembly may require a copy of that statement of case to be supplied.

(4) The National Assembly must, as soon as practicable after receipt, send a copy of the respondent's statement of case to the appellant and a copy of the appellant's statement of case to the respondent.

(5) The appellant and the respondent may, in writing, each require the other to send them a copy of any document, or the relevant part of any document, referred to in the list of documents comprised in the other's statement of case; and any such document, or relevant part, must be sent, as soon as practicable, to the party who required it.

(6) The National Assembly may, in writing, require any other person, who has notified it of a wish to seek the appointed person's permission to take part in the inquiry, to send –

(a) three copies of their statement of case to it within 4 weeks of being so required; and
(b) a copy of their statement of case to any specified interested person,

and the National Assembly must, as soon as practicable after receipt, send a copy of each such statement of case to the appellant and the respondent.

(7) The National Assembly must, as soon as practicable;

(a) send to a person from whom it requires a statement of case in accordance with paragraph (6) a copy of the statements of case of the appellant and the respondent; and
(b) inform that person of the name and address of every person to whom that person's statement of case is required to be sent.

(8) The National Assembly may in writing require any person, who has sent to it a statement of case in accordance with this regulation, to provide such further information about the matters contained in the statement of case as it may specify and may specify the time within which the information shall be received by it.

(9) Where the respondent or appellant is required to provide further information, they shall ensure that –

(a) two copies of that information in writing have been received by the National Assembly, within such time as is specified; and
(b) a copy has been received by any interested person to whom the National Assembly may require it to be supplied within such time as is specified,

and the National Assembly must, as soon as practicable after receipt, send to the appellant a copy of the further information received from the respondent and send to the respondent a copy of the further information received from the appellant.

(10) Any other person required to provide further information must ensure that –

(a) three copies of that information in writing have been received by the National Assembly, within the specified time; and
(b) a copy has been received by any interested person to whom the National Assembly may require it to be supplied within the specified time,

and the National Assembly must, as soon as practicable after receipt, send a copy of the further information to the respondent and the appellant.

(11) Any person other than the appellant who sends a statement of case to the National Assembly must send with it a copy of –

(a) any document; or
(b) the relevant part of any document,

referred to in the list comprised in that statement, unless a copy of the document or part of the document in question is already available for inspection pursuant to paragraph (12).

(12) The respondent must afford to any person who so requests a reasonable opportunity to inspect and, where practicable, take copies of –

(a) any statement of case, written comments, information or other document a copy of which has been sent to the respondent in accordance with this regulation; and
(b) the respondent's statement of case together with a copy of any document, or the relevant part of any document, referred to in the list comprised in that statement, and any written comments, information or other documents sent by the respondent pursuant to this regulation.

(13) If the respondent or the appellant wish to comment on the other's statement of case they must ensure that within 9 weeks of the starting date –

(a) two copies of their written comments have been received by the National Assembly; and
(b) a copy of their written comments has been received by any interested person to whom the National Assembly may require them to be supplied,

and the National Assembly must, as soon as practicable after receipt, send a copy of the written comments received from the appellant to the respondent and a copy of the written comments received from the respondent to the appellant.

(14) Any person, who sends a statement of case to the National Assembly under this regulation and who wishes to comment on another person's statement of case, must ensure that not less than 4 weeks before the date fixed for the holding of the inquiry –

(a) three copies of that person's written comments have been received by the National Assembly; and
(b) a copy of those written comments has been received by any interested person to whom the National Assembly may require them to be supplied,

and the National Assembly must, as soon as practicable after receipt, send a copy of the written comments to the appellant and the respondent.

(15) The National Assembly must, as soon as practicable after receipt, send to the appointed person any statement of case, document or further information or written comments sent to it in accordance with this regulation and received by it within the relevant period, if any, specified in this regulation.

20   Further power of appointed person to hold pre-inquiry meetings

(1) Where no pre-inquiry meeting is held pursuant to regulation 18, an appointed person may hold one if the appointed person thinks it necessary.

(2) An appointed person must give not less than 2 weeks' written notice of a pre-inquiry meeting to be held under paragraph (1) to –

(a) the appellant;

(b) the respondent;

(c) any person known at the date of the notice to be entitled to take part in the inquiry; and

(d) any other person whose presence at the pre-inquiry meeting appears to him to be desirable.

(3) Regulation 18(7) applies to a pre-inquiry meeting held under this regulation.

21 Inquiry timetable

(1) The appointed person must arrange a timetable for the proceedings at, or at part of, an inquiry where –

(a) a pre-inquiry meeting is held pursuant to regulation 18; or

(b) it appears to the National Assembly likely that an inquiry will last for 8 days or more.

(2) The appointed person may arrange a timetable for the proceedings at, or at part of, any other inquiry and may, at any time, vary the timetable arranged under this, or the preceding, paragraph.

(3) The appointed person may specify in a timetable arranged pursuant to this regulation a date by which any proof of evidence and summary sent in accordance with regulation 24(1) must be received by the National Assembly.

22 Date and notification of inquiry

(1) The date fixed by the National Assembly for the holding of an inquiry must, unless it considers such a date impracticable, be not later than –

(a) 22 weeks after the starting date; or

(b) in a case where a pre-inquiry meeting is held pursuant to regulation 18, 8 weeks after the conclusion of that meeting.

(2) Where the National Assembly considers it impracticable to fix a date in accordance with paragraph (1), the date fixed must be the earliest date after the end of the relevant period mentioned in that paragraph which it considers to be practicable.

(3) Unless the National Assembly agrees a lesser period of notice with the appellant and the respondent, it must give not less than 4 weeks' written notice of the date, time and place fixed by it for the holding of an inquiry to every person entitled to take part in the inquiry.

(4) The National Assembly may vary the date fixed for the holding of an inquiry, whether or not the date as varied is within the relevant period mentioned in paragraph (1); and paragraph (3) shall apply to a variation of a date as it applied to the date originally fixed.

(5) The National Assembly may vary the time or place for the holding of an inquiry and must give such notice of any variation as appears to it to be reasonable.

(6) The National Assembly must take one or more of the following steps –

(a) not less than 2 weeks before the date fixed for the holding of an inquiry, to publish a notice of the inquiry in one or more newspapers circulating in the locality in which the land is situated;

   (b) to send a notice of the inquiry to such persons or classes of persons as it may specify, within such period as it may specify.

(7) Every notice of inquiry published or sent pursuant to paragraph (6), must –

   (a) contain a clear statement of the date, time and place of the inquiry and of the powers enabling the National Assembly to determine the application or appeal in question;

   (b) contain a written description of the land sufficient to enable the approximate location and extent of the land to be identified;

   (c) briefly describe the subject matter of the appeal; and

   (d) provide details of where and when copies of the respondent's statement of case and any documents sent by and copied to the respondent pursuant to regulation 19 may be inspected.

23 Rights of attendance at and participation in an inquiry

(1) The persons entitled to take part in an inquiry are –

   (a) the appellant;

   (b) the respondent; and

   (c) any officer of any local authority or National Park authority whose area includes land to which the appeal relates.

(2) The appointed person may permit any other person to take part in an inquiry.

(3) Any person entitled or permitted to take part in an inquiry may do so on his own behalf or be represented by any other person.

24 Proofs of evidence

(1) Any person entitled to take part in an inquiry who proposes to give, or to call another person to give, evidence at the inquiry by reading a proof of evidence, must –

   (a) send two copies, in the case of the respondent and the appellant, or three copies in the case of any other person, of the proof of evidence together with any written summary, to the National Assembly; and

   (b) simultaneously send copies of these to any interested person to whom the National Assembly may require them to be supplied,

and the National Assembly must, as soon as practicable after receipt, send a copy of each proof of evidence together with any summary to the respondent and the appellant.

(2) No written summary is required where the proof of evidence proposed to be read contains no more than 1,500 words.

(3) The proof of evidence and any summary must be received by the National Assembly no later than –

   (a) 4 weeks before the date fixed for the holding of the inquiry; or

   (b) where a timetable has been arranged pursuant to regulation 21 which specifies a date by which the proof of evidence and any summary must be received by the National Assembly, that date.

(4) The National Assembly must send to the appointed person, as soon as practicable after receipt, any proof of evidence together with any summary sent to it in accordance with this regulation and received by it within the relevant period specified in this Regulation.

(5) Where a written summary is provided in accordance with paragraph (1), only that summary shall be read at the inquiry, unless the appointed person permits or requires otherwise.

(6) Any person required by this regulation to send copies of a proof of evidence to the National Assembly must send with them the same number of copies of the whole, or the relevant part, of any document referred to in the proof of evidence, unless a copy of the document or part of the document in question is already available for inspection pursuant to regulation 19(12).

(7) The respondent must afford to any person who so requests a reasonable opportunity to inspect and, where practicable, take copies of any document sent to or by the respondent in accordance with this regulation.

25   Statement of common ground

(1) The respondent and the appellant must –

- (a) together prepare an agreed statement of common ground; and
- (b) ensure that the National Assembly and any interested person to whom the National Assembly may require a copy to be supplied receive a copy of it not less than 4 weeks before the date fixed for the holding of the inquiry.

(2) The respondent must afford to any person who so requests, a reasonable opportunity to inspect, and where practicable, take copies of the statement of common ground sent to the National Assembly.

26   Procedure at inquiry

(1) Except as otherwise provided in these Regulations, the appointed person is to determine the procedure at an inquiry.

(2) At the start of the inquiry the appointed person must identify the issues which are, in the opinion of the appointed person, the main issues to be considered at the inquiry and any matters on which the appointed person requires further explanation from the persons entitled or permitted to take part.

(3) Nothing in paragraph (2) is to preclude any person entitled or permitted to take part from referring to issues which they consider relevant to the consideration of the application or appeal but which were not issues identified by the appointed person pursuant to that paragraph.

(4) Unless in any particular case the appointed person otherwise determines, the respondent is to begin and the appellant is to have the right of final reply; and the other persons entitled or permitted to take part are to be heard in such order as the appointed person may determine.

(5) A person entitled to take part in an inquiry is to be entitled to call evidence and the appellant, the respondent and any interested person is to be entitled to cross-examine persons giving evidence, but, subject to the foregoing and paragraphs (6) and (7), the calling of evidence and the cross-examination of persons giving evidence is otherwise to be at the discretion of the appointed person.

(6) The appointed person may refuse to permit the –

- (a) giving or production of evidence;

(b) cross-examination of persons giving evidence; or

(c) presentation of any other matter,

which the appointed person considers to be irrelevant or repetitious; but where the appointed person refuses to permit the giving of oral evidence, the person wishing to give the evidence may submit to the appointed person any evidence or other matter in writing before the close of the inquiry.

(7) Where a person gives evidence at an inquiry by reading a summary of a proof of evidence in accordance with regulation 24(5) –

(a) the proof of evidence referred to in regulation 24(1) must be treated as tendered in evidence, unless the person required to provide the summary wishes to rely on the contents of that summary alone and notifies the appointed person of that fact; and

(b) the person whose evidence the proof of evidence contains is then to be subject to cross-examination on it to the same extent as if it were evidence that person had given orally.

(8) The appointed person may direct that facilities are to be afforded to any person taking part in an inquiry to take or obtain copies of documentary evidence open to public inspection.

(9) The appointed person may –

(a) require any person taking part in or attending an inquiry who, in the opinion of the appointed person, is behaving in a disruptive manner to leave; and

(b) refuse to permit that person to return; or

(c) permit that person to return only on such conditions as the appointed person may specify,

but any such person may submit to the appointed person any evidence or other matter in writing before the close of the inquiry.

(10) The appointed person may allow any person to alter or add to a statement of case received by the National Assembly or by the appointed person under regulation 19 so far as may be necessary for the purposes of the inquiry, but the appointed person must (if necessary by adjourning the inquiry) give every other person entitled to take part and who is actually taking part in the inquiry an adequate opportunity of considering any fresh matter or document.

(11) The appointed person may proceed with an inquiry in the absence of any person entitled to take part in it.

(12) The appointed person may take into account any written representation or evidence or any other document received from any person before an inquiry opens or during the inquiry provided that the appointed person discloses it at the inquiry.

(13) The appointed person may from time to time adjourn an inquiry and, if the date, time and place of the adjourned inquiry are announced at the inquiry before the adjournment, no further notice is to be required.

(14) In respect of any inquiry that the National Assembly expects to last for 8 or more days, any person who takes part in the inquiry and makes closing submissions, must by the close of the inquiry provide the appointed person with a copy of those closing submissions in writing.

## 27	Decision after an inquiry

(1) Where an assessor has been appointed, the assessor may make a report in writing to the appointed person in respect of the matters on which the assessor was appointed to advise.

(2) When making a decision in relation to the appeal, the appointed person may disregard any written representations, or evidence or any other document received after the inquiry has closed.

(3) If, after the close of the inquiry, an appointed person proposes to take into consideration any new evidence or any new matter of fact (not being a matter of government policy) which was not raised at the inquiry and which the appointed person considers to be material to the decision, the appointed person must not come to a decision without first –

  (a) notifying persons entitled to take part in the inquiry who took part in it of the matter in question; and
  (b) affording them an opportunity of making written representations to the appointed person or of asking for the re-opening of the inquiry,

and they shall ensure that such written representations or request to re-open the inquiry are received by the appointed person within 3 weeks of the date of the notification.

(4) An appointed person may cause an inquiry to be re-opened and must do so if asked by the appellant or the respondent in the circumstances and within the period mentioned in paragraph (3); and where an inquiry is re-opened –

  (a) the appointed person must send to the persons entitled to take part in the inquiry and who actually took part in it a written statement of the matters with respect to which further evidence is invited; and
  (b) regulation 22(3) to (7) applies as if the references to an inquiry were references to a re-opened inquiry.

## 28	Notification of decision

(1) The decision of the appointed person and the reasons for it, must be notified in writing to –

  (a) the appellant;
  (b) the respondent;
  (c) any other persons entitled to take part in the inquiry who did take part; and
  (d) any other person who, having taken part in the inquiry, has asked to be notified of the decision.

(2) Any person entitled to be notified of the decision under paragraph (1) may apply to the National Assembly, in writing, for an opportunity to inspect any documents listed in the notification and the National Assembly must afford that person that opportunity.

(3) Any person making an application under paragraph (2) must ensure that it is received by the National Assembly within 6 weeks of the date of the decision.

PART VI

MISCELLANEOUS

29   Withdrawal of an appeal

(1) The appellant may withdraw an appeal by giving notice in writing to the National Assembly of a wish to do so.

(2) The National Assembly must, as soon as reasonably practicable after receiving notice of withdrawal of an appeal, give notice of that fact to all those persons to whom a notice was given under regulation 5(1).

30   Change to the form of an appeal

If at any time it appears to the National Assembly that it is more appropriate that the appeal should be determined in a way which is different from the form which was notified under regulation 5, it may determine that the appeal is to continue in a form other than that notified and may give any consequential guidance as to the procedure to be applied in relation to the appeal, including identifying any steps which are required to be taken by the parties under these Regulations which are to be deemed to have already been taken and varying as necessary the time within which any such step which has not already been taken.

31   Further or different procedures

The National Assembly may, if the circumstances relating to a particular appeal make it necessary, require any specified steps to be taken, either in addition to, or in substitution for, those prescribed by these Regulations and may extend the time prescribed by these Regulations, or otherwise required under these Regulations, for the taking of any step but must, before doing so, unless the effect is limited to an extension of time, consult the appellant and the respondent and may consult any interested person and must consider the representations made by any person consulted as to the desirability of such a requirement.

32   Notification of appointment of an assessor

Where the National Assembly exercises its power under paragraph 4(3) of Schedule 3 to the Act to appoint an assessor to assist an appointed person in the determination of an appeal, it must notify the appellant, the respondent and any interested person of the name of the assessor and the matters on which the assessor has been appointed to advise the appointed person.

33   Site inspections

(1) The appointed person may at any time make an unaccompanied inspection of the land without giving notice of an intention to do so to the appellant or the respondent.

(2) During an inquiry or hearing or after the close of an inquiry or hearing, the appointed person –

   (a) may, after announcing during the inquiry or hearing the date and time at which the inspection is proposed to be made, inspect the land in the company of the appellant, the respondent and any interested person; and

(b) must make such an inspection if so requested by the appellant or the respondent before or during an inquiry or hearing.

(3) If an appeal is being determined on the basis of written representations, the appointed person –

(a) may, after giving the appellant and the respondent reasonable notice in writing of an intention to do so, inspect the land in the company of the appellant, the respondent and any interested person; and

(b) must make such an inspection if so requested by the appellant or the respondent before the appointed person makes a decision.

(4) An appellant must take such steps as are reasonably within the appellant's power to enable the appointed person to obtain access to the land to be inspected.

(5) The appointed person is not to be bound to defer an inspection of the kind referred to in paragraphs (2) or (3) where any person mentioned in those paragraphs is not present at the time appointed.

34 Joint hearings or inquiries

Where two or more appeals give rise to a common issue or issues or, in the case of appeals under section 6 of the Act, relate to the same provisional map, the National Assembly may hold a joint hearing or inquiry relating to those appeals if in its opinion it is desirable to do so and, in such a case, the National Assembly must exercise its powers under regulation 31 with a view to modifying the provisions of these Regulations to such extent as is necessary in consequence of the decision to hold a joint hearing or inquiry.

35 Use of electronic communication

(1) Any document required or authorised to be sent by one person to another under the provisions of these Regulations may, as an alternative to any other method, be sent by means of an electronic communication, provided the person who sends the document has reasonable grounds for believing that the document will come to the attention of the person to whom it is sent, in legible form, within a reasonable time.

(2) Where, under these Regulations, there is a requirement that a copy of a statement, representation, notice or other document should be sent to the National Assembly then, if that copy is sent in electronic form, any further requirement that more than one copy should be sent is to be disregarded.

36 Publication of decisions on appeals under section 6 of the Act

The National Assembly must, unless it is not reasonably practicable to do so, publish on an internet web-site which it maintains notice of every decision made under these Regulations in relation to an appeal under section 6 of the Act and continue to do so until the conclusive map to which the appeal relates is issued.

COUNTRYSIDE ACCESS (PROVISIONAL AND CONCLUSIVE MAPS) (WALES) REGULATIONS 2002, SI 2002/1796

1 Citation, commencement and application

(1) These Regulations may be cited as the Countryside Access (Provisional and Conclusive Maps) (Wales) Regulations 2002 and shall come into force on 1st August 2002.

(2) These Regulations apply to Wales.

2 Interpretation

(1) In these Regulations –

'the Act' ('y Ddeddf') means the Countryside and Rights of Way Act 2000;

'appeal' ('apêl') means an appeal to the National Assembly under section 6 of the Act by a person having an interest in land against the showing of that land on a provisional map as registered common land or as open country;

'appeal form' ('ffurflen apêl') means a document which, when completed, contains the information specified in regulation 6(4);

'appeal period' ('cyfnod apêl') means, in relation to a provisional map, the period referred to in regulation 4(3)(d);

'appellant' ('apelydd') means a person who brings an appeal and, where two or more persons join in bringing an appeal, refers to all those persons jointly;

'appointed person' ('person penodedig') means a person appointed by the National Assembly under section 8 of the Act;

'Archaeological Trust' ('Ymddiriedolaeth Archeolegol') means the Clwyd-Powys Archaeological Trust, the Dyfed Archaeological Trust, the Glamorgan-Gwent Archae-ological Trust or the Gwynedd Archaeological Trust;

'conclusive map' ('map terfynol') means a map prepared by the Council for the purpose of being issued in accordance with section 9(1), (2), (3) or (4) of the Act;

references to the 'confirmation' ('cadarnhau') of a draft map are references to its confirmation in accordance with section 5(c) of the Act;

'the Council' ('y Cyngor') means the Countryside Council for Wales;

'draft map' ('map drafft') means a map issued by the Council under section 5(a) of the Act;

'draft map modification statement' ('datganiad addasiad o fap drafft') means a written statement prepared by the Council in accordance with regulation 7(3)(b) of the Draft Maps Regulations identifying modifications made to a draft map and the reasons for making them;

'the Draft Maps Regulations' ('y Rheoliadau Mapian drafft') means the Countryside Access (Draft Maps) (Wales) Regulations 2001;

'electronic communication' ('cyfathrebu electronig') means a communication transmitted (whether from one person to another, from one device to another or from a person to a device or vice versa) by means of a telecommunications system (within the meaning of the Telecommunications Act 1984) or by other means but while in electronic form;

'electronic form' ('ffurf electronig') means a form capable of being stored on, transmitted to and from, and read by means of a computer;

'interest' ('fuddiant') has the meaning given by section 45(1) of the Act;

references to the 'issue' ('dyroddi') of a provisional map or of a conclusive map (as the case may be) are references to its issue by the Council under section 5(d) or (e) of the Act or under section 9(1), (2), (3) or (4) of the Act, respectively;

'the National Assembly' ('y Cynulliad Cenedlaethol') means the National Assembly for Wales or, where a function of the National Assembly is being exercised by an appointed person, that person;

a 'notice of issue' ('hysbysiad dyroddi') of a provisional map or of a conclusive map (as the case may be) means a notice published pursuant to regulation 4(2)(c) or regulation 8(2)(d), respectively;

'open country' ('tir agored') has the meaning given by section 1(2) of the Act;

'person' ('person') and 'persons' ('personau') include individuals, corporations and unincorporated bodies;

'provisional map' ('map dros dro') means a draft map which has been confirmed by the Council in accordance with section 5(c) of the Act;

the 'provisional period' ('cyfnod dros dro') means the period beginning when a provisional map is issued and ending when the conclusive map which relates to it is issued or, if more than one conclusive map relates to that provisional map, when the last of those conclusive maps is issued;

'registered common land' ('tir comin cofrestredig') has the meaning given by section 1(3) of the Act;

'relevant Archaeological Trust' ('Ymddiriedolaeth Archeolegol perthnasol') means, in relation to a provisional map or to a conclusive map (as the case may be), an Archaeological Trust whose area of responsibility includes an area contained in that map;

'relevant draft map' ('map drafft perthnasol') means, in relation to a provisional map, a draft map which, on being confirmed, included land now included in that provisional map;

'relevant local authority' ('awdurdod lleol perthnasol') means, in relation to a provisional map or to a conclusive map (as the case may be), a county or county borough council whose area includes an area contained in that map;

'relevant National Park authority' ('awdurdod Parc Cenedlaethol') means, in relation to a provisional map or to a conclusive map (as the case may be), a National Park authority for a National Park whose area includes an area contained in that map; and 'section 4(2) land' ('tir adran 4(2)') means the registered common land and open country in respect of which the Council is required to prepare maps in accordance with section 4(2) of the Act.

(2) In these Regulations, unless the context otherwise requires, any reference to a numbered regulation is a reference to the regulation bearing that number in these Regulations, and any reference in a regulation to a numbered paragraph is a reference to the paragraph bearing that number in that regulation.

(3) In reckoning any period which is expressed in these Regulations to be a period from a given date, that date is to be excluded and, where, apart from this paragraph, the day or the last day on which anything may be done or is required to be done under, or pursuant to, these Regulations is a Sunday, Christmas Day, Good Friday, bank holiday or a day appointed for public thanksgiving or mourning, the requirement may be satisfied by doing it on the first day thereafter which is not one of the days before-mentioned.

3   Form of provisional maps

(1) The Council may, for the purpose of discharging its duty to issue a provisional map under section 5(d) or (e) of the Act, or for any purpose incidental thereto, produce and publish copies of that provisional map in such form, including electronic form, as it may determine and any such copy published by or with the authority of the Council is to be deemed to be identical to the provisional map unless the contrary is shown.

(2) The Council may, for the purpose of illustrating the existence and extent of the section 4(2) land shown on one or more provisional maps, and for the purpose of making available for inspection copies of the provisional map in accordance with regulation 4(2)(a) and (b), or for complying with a request of a kind referred to in regulation 4(3)(h), produce and publish copies of provisional maps showing such section 4(2) land at a scale of less than 1:10,000 but not less than 1:25,000.

(3) Copies of provisional maps produced under paragraph (1) –

   (a) must clearly identify the classes of section 4(2) land and other features which are identified, in accordance with regulations 3(6) and 7(3) of the Draft Maps Regulations, on the provisional map of which they are copies, by the use of different colours, shading, lines and symbols, but the colours (if any), shading, lines or other symbols used to do so need not be identical to those used for that purpose on that provisional map; and
   (b) are not to be regarded as evidence of the contents of those provisional maps.

4   Issue of provisional maps

(1) The Council is to be taken to have discharged its duty under section 5(d) or (e) of the Act (as the case may be) to issue a provisional map when it first publishes a notice of issue of that provisional map in accordance with paragraph (2)(c) of this regulation.

(2) The Council must not publish a notice of issue of a provisional map until it has –

   (a) made such arrangements as are within its power for a copy of that provisional map and, if the draft map on which it is based was confirmed with modifications, a copy of the draft map modification statement, in printed form and, where possible in electronic form, to be available for inspection by members of the public at all reasonable times (subject, in the case of inspection at offices other than its own, to such requirements for the making of appointments to do so as the relevant authority may require) throughout the appeal period at –

(i) the head office of the Council and the local office of the Council, not including any office which is not open during normal office hours, which is nearest to the area to which the provisional map relates; and

(ii) the head office of each relevant local authority and relevant National Park authority, if any;

(b) despatched a copy of that provisional map, together with any draft map modification statement which relates to it, either in printed form to a scale of not less than 1:25,000 or, if the Council and the recipient agree, in electronic form, together with a notice containing the same information as that required to be contained in the notice of issue of that provisional map, to each of the organisations specified in Schedule 1 to these Regulations and to such other persons as it considers appropriate;

(c) published the notice of issue of that provisional map in at least one daily newspaper circulating throughout that part of Wales which includes the area to which that map relates and such other newspapers or publications circulating in that part of Wales as the Council thinks fit;

(d) sent a copy of the notice of issue of that provisional map to each of the public libraries listed in Schedule 2, accompanied by a request that it be displayed to the public at that library;

(e) sent the National Assembly a copy of the notice of issue of that provisional map and notified the National Assembly when and in what newspaper it intends to publish that notice.

(3) A notice of issue of a provisional map must –

(a) identify the area to which the provisional map relates;

(b) state whether or not the draft map to which the provisional map relates was confirmed with modifications;

(c) state that the effect of the provisional map is, subject to any modifications made as a result of appeals relating to it, to show the areas of section 4(2) land over which the public will, subject to such exceptions and restrictions as the Act provides, be entitled to exercise a right of access under section 2 of the Act when that section comes into force;

(d) state that any person with an interest in any land shown on that map as registered common land or as open country may, no later than the end of a period specified in the notice, which must be a period expiring no earlier than three months after the date on which a notice of issue of that provisional map was first published in accordance with paragraph 2(c), appeal to the National Assembly against the showing of that land on the map as registered common land or open country, by sending or delivering an appeal form to the National Assembly so as to be received by the National Assembly within that period;

(e) give particulars of means by which a person who wishes to bring such an appeal may obtain an appeal form;

(f) state the address of the National Assembly to which an appeal form is to be sent or delivered;

(g) give particulars of the means by which members of the public may inspect the provisional map and, if the draft map to which the provisional map relates was confirmed with modifications, the draft map modifications statement;

(h) state that any person who has an interest in any land shown on that provisional map as section 4(2) land may, by a request in writing to the Council which identifies the nature of that interest and the land to which it relates, and which is received by the Council before the end of the appeal period, require the Council to provide that person, free of charge, with one copy of the provisional map or of an extract from the provisional map showing the land to which the request relates and, if that part of the draft map showing the land to which the request relates was confirmed with modifications, a copy of the draft map modifications statement or of that part which refers to the land to which the request relates, which copy or copies must be in printed form or, if the Council and that person agree, in electronic form;

(i) state the address to which any request under sub-paragraph (h) should be sent.

(4) Any notice published in accordance with paragraph (2)(c) or sent in accordance with paragraph (2)(d) may, in addition to such information as is required to be included under paragraph (3), include such further information as the Council thinks fit.

5   General duty to inform the public of the provisions of provisional maps

(1) The Council must consider and give effect to such steps as are reasonable in order to inform the public of the contents of provisional maps and must in particular consider the desirability of –

(a) making available during the provisional period, so far as is practicable, information published on any website they maintain on the internet which –
   (i) is equivalent to that shown on provisional maps, but shown by means of smaller scale maps; and
   (ii) includes that contained in any draft map modification statements which relate to them; and
(b) bringing to the attention of those appearing to have an interest in land shown as section 4(2) land on a provisional map, by whatever means are appropriate, the fact that such map has been issued and where it can be inspected.

(2) The duty imposed by paragraph (1) is to be without prejudice to the duties of the Council under regulation 4 but any failure on the part of the Council to discharge the duty imposed by paragraph (1) in relation to a provisional map is not to invalidate the issue of that provisional map by the Council or any other action required to be taken by the Council or the National Assembly under these Regulations.

6   Appeals by persons having an interest in land included on a provisional map

(1) Subject to paragraphs (2) and (3), an appeal may only be brought by sending or delivering to the National Assembly a completed appeal form which is received before the end of the appeal period.

(2) Subject to paragraph (3), an appeal may also be brought by sending or delivering to the National Assembly a completed appeal form which is received after the end of the appeal period if the National Assembly considers that it was not reasonably practicable for the appellant to comply with the requirements of paragraph (1) and provided the completed appeal form is received within such further period after the end of the appeal period as the National Assembly considers reasonable in the circumstances.

(3) Paragraph (2) does not apply to an appeal form received by the National Assembly after the National Assembly has given notice to the Council under regulation 7(1) in relation to the provisional map or part of a provisional map which includes the land to which the appeal form relates.

(4) If a person who wishes to bring an appeal sends or delivers to the National Assembly written notice of that intention which is received before the end of the appeal period then, provided that person sends or delivers to the National Assembly a completed appeal form within such further period as the National Assembly may; by giving written notice to that person, require, that appeal form is to be treated as if it had been received before the end of the appeal period.

(5) The information which a completed appeal form must contain is –

(a) the name, address and postcode of the appellant;
(b) sufficient particulars of the land to which the appeal relates as to enable that land to be identified, including a copy of the provisional map or an extract from it on which the boundaries of that land are clearly marked;
(c) such particulars as will enable the National Assembly and the Council to understand the grounds, being grounds which fall within section 6(3)(a) or (b) of the Act, on which the appeal is brought;
(d) the nature of the interest of the appellant in the land which is subject to the appeal;
(e) whether the appellant wishes to be heard by a person appointed by the National Assembly in connection with the appeal (rather than that the appeal be determined on the basis of written representations) and, if so, whether the appellant wishes to be heard at a local inquiry or, alternatively, at a hearing.

(6) An appeal form may be in either the English language or the Welsh language but if the appellant wishes the appeal to be dealt with in whole or in part through the medium of the language other than that in which the appeal form is expressed, the appeal form should incorporate or be accompanied by a request to that effect.

7   Preparation of maps to be issued as conclusive maps

(1) If, in respect of –

(a) a provisional map; or,
(b) if the National Assembly proposes to direct the Council under section 9(3) or 9(4) of the Act to issue as a map in conclusive form a part of a provisional map, such part of a provisional map,

all appeals under section 6 of the Act which have been brought in accordance with regulation 6 have either been determined or have been withdrawn, the National Assembly must give notice of that fact to the Council.

(2) The Council must, when it has received notice under paragraph (1), and in accordance with –

(a) any modification required by the National Assembly to be made to a provisional map in accordance with section 6(4)(a) of the Act;
(b) any direction by the National Assembly under section 9(3) or 9(4) of the Act that a map which covers part of the area of a provisional map is to be issued as a conclusive map; and
(c) any decision by the Council under section 9(1) or 9(2) of the Act that a map which covers part of the area of a provisional map is to be issued as a conclusive map;

prepare a map or maps based on that provisional map or any part of it to which the notice under paragraph (1) relates for issue in accordance with the provisions of section 9(1), (2), (3) or (4) (as the case may be) as a conclusive map or maps.

8   Issue of conclusive maps

(1) The Council is to be taken to have discharged its duty under section 9(1), (2), (3) or (4) of the Act (as the case may be) to issue a conclusive map when it first publishes a notice of issue of that conclusive map in accordance with paragraph (2)(d) of this regulation.

(2) The Council must not publish a notice of issue of a conclusive map until it has –

(a) made arrangements for the preservation at its head office of a printed copy of the conclusive map endorsed with a statement that it is the copy of the provisional map preserved for the purposes of this sub-paragraph;

(b) made such arrangements as are within its power for a copy of the conclusive map to be made available for inspection in printed form and, where possible in electronic form, by members of the public at all reasonable times (subject, in the case of inspection at offices other than its own, to such requirements for the making of appointments to do so as the relevant authority may require) at –

   (i) the head office of the Council and the local office of the Council, not including any office which is not open during normal office hours, which is nearest to the area to which the conclusive map relates; and

   (ii) during the period of one year beginning on the date on which the conclusive map was issued, the head office of each relevant local authority and relevant National Park authority, if any;

(c) despatched a copy of the conclusive map either in printed form to a scale of not less than 1:25,000 or, if the Council and the recipient agree, in electronic form, together with a notice containing the same information as that required to be contained in the notice of issue of the conclusive map to each of the organisations specified in Schedule 1 to these Regulations and to such other persons as it considers appropriate;

(d) published the notice of issue of the conclusive map, complying with the requirements of paragraph (3), in at least one daily newspaper circulating throughout that part of Wales which includes the area to which that map relates and such other newspapers or publications circulating in that part of Wales as the Council thinks fit;

(e) sent a copy of the notice of issue of the conclusive map, to each of the public libraries listed in Schedule 2, accompanied by a request that it be displayed to the public at that library; and

(f) sent the National Assembly a copy (or if not sent by electronic means, two copies) of the conclusive map together with a copy of the notice of issue relating to it.

(3) A notice of issue of a conclusive map must –

(a) identify the area to which the conclusive map relates;

(b) state that the effect of the conclusive map is to show the areas of section 4(2) land over which the public will, subject to such exceptions and restrictions as the Act provides, be entitled to exercise a right of access under section 2 of the Act when that section comes into force;

(c) give particulars of the means by which members of the public may inspect a copy of the conclusive map and state that if they wish to do so after the expiry of the period of one year beginning on the date when the conclusive map was issued, they may only do so by prior appointment;

(d) state that any person may, by a request in writing to the Council, require the Council to provide that person with one copy of the conclusive map or of an extract from the conclusive map relating to an identified part of the map to which the request relates, which copy or copies must be in printed form or, if the Council and that person agree, in electronic form;

(e) state that the Council's duty to provide a copy of the documents set out in sub-paragraph (d) is a duty –

  (i) in the case of a request in writing by a person who has an interest in any land shown on the conclusive map as section 4(2) land, whose request identifies the nature of that interest and the land to which it relates, and provided that person has not previously made such a request relating to that land, to provide one copy of the map or extract from it free of charge; and

  (ii) in all other cases, to provide such copy on payment of such fee as the Council may reasonably require;

(f) state the address to which any request under sub-paragraph (d) should be sent; and

(g) state the date on which the conclusive map was issued.

(4) Any notice published in accordance with paragraph (2)(d) or sent in accordance with paragraph (2)(e) may, in addition to such information as is required to be included under paragraph (3), include such further information as the Council shall think fit.

9   General duty to inform the public of the provisions of conclusive maps

(1) The Council must consider and give effect to such steps as are reasonable in order to inform the public of the contents of conclusive maps and must in particular consider the desirability of –

(a) making available, so far as is practicable, information equivalent to that shown on conclusive maps by means of smaller scale maps, published on any website they maintain on the internet; and

(b) bringing to the attention of those appearing to have an interest in land shown as section 4(2) land on a conclusive map, by whatever means are appropriate, the fact that such map has been issued and where it can be inspected.

(2) The duty imposed by paragraph (1) is to be without prejudice to the duties of the Council under regulation 8, but any failure on the part of the Council to discharge the duty imposed by paragraph (1) in relation to a conclusive map is not to invalidate the issue of that conclusive map by the Council or any other action required to be taken by the Council or the National Assembly under these Regulations.

10   Rights to inspect and receive copies

Where, under any provision of these Regulations, the Council is required to give notice to any person that a document may be inspected by that person or that a document is required to be supplied to that person then, if the person in question has complied with any condition to which that requirement is subject, the Council must give effect to that requirement.

11   Documents in electronic form and the use of communication by electronic means

(1) Any map or other document authorised or required by these Regulations to be prepared, issued or made available for inspection in electronic form must be capable of being reproduced in printed form.

(2) Subject to any provisions of these Regulations prescribing the method by which a copy of a map or other document is required or authorised to be sent by one person to another, any such document, including one which these Regulations require to be in written form, may, as an alternative to any other method, be sent by means of an electronic communication, provided the person who sends the document has reasonable grounds for believing that the document will come to the attention of the person to whom it is sent, in legible form, within a reasonable time.

12   Amendment of the Draft Maps Regulations

(1), (2) (*Amend Countryside Access (Draft Maps) (Wales) Regulations 2001, SI 2001/4001, above*)

(3) The amendment made by paragraph (2) is to have effect only in relation to a draft map issued on or after the day on which these Regulations come into force.

SCHEDULE 1

ORGANISATIONS TO BE NOTIFIED PURSUANT TO REGULATIONS 4(2)(B) AND 8(2)(C)

Regulations 4(2)(b) and 8(2)(c)

British Association for Shooting and Conservation

British Mountaineering Council

Country Land and Business Association

The Countryside Agency (where land included in the provisional or conclusive map has a border with England)

The Crown Estate

The Environment Agency

Farmers' Union of Wales

Forestry Commission

Local Access Forums whose area of responsibility covers land included in the provisional or conclusive map

The Ministry of Defence

National Farmers' Union Wales

National Trust Wales

Open Spaces Society

Ramblers' Association

Relevant Archaeological Trusts

Relevant local authorities

Relevant National Park authorities

Town and Community Councils in Wales whose area of responsibility covers land included in the provisional or conclusive map

SCHEDULE 2

PUBLIC LIBRARIES TO WHICH NOTICE IS TO BE SENT PURSUANT TO REGULATIONS 4(2)(D) AND 8(2)(E)

Regulations 4(2)(d) and 8(2)(e)

Aberdare

Aberystwyth

Bangor

Barry

Blackwood

Brecon

Bridgend

Brynmawr

Caernarfon

Cardiff Central

Cardigan

Carmarthen

Chepstow

Colwyn Bay

Cwmbran

Dolgellau

Flintshire

Grangetown

Haverfordwest

Llandrindod Wells

Llandudno

Llanelli

Llangefni

Llanwrst

Maesteg

Merthyr Tydfil

Neath

Newport Central

Newtown

Pembroke Dock

Penarth

Pontypridd

Port Talbot

Pwllheli

Rhuthin

Rhymney

Rhyl

Swansea East

Treorchy

Wrexham

LOCAL ACCESS FORUMS (ENGLAND) REGULATIONS 2002, SI 2002/1836

1 Citation, commencement and extent

(1) These Regulations may be cited as the Local Access Forums (England) Regulations 2002 and shall come into force on 7th August 2002.

(2) These Regulations extend to England only.

2 Interpretation

In these Regulations references to sections are references to sections of the Countryside and Rights of Way Act 2000.

3 Establishment of a local access forum

(1) Subject to regulation 13, where an appointing authority is required, by section 94(1), to establish a local access forum, that authority shall establish the forum by appointing the members of the forum before 8th August 2003.

(2) Before establishing any local access forum an appointing authority which is a local highway authority shall consult –

    (a) any district council in their area, and
    (b) such other persons as they consider appropriate,

as to the area for which the forum is to be established.

(3) Before establishing any local access forum an appointing authority which is a National Park authority shall consult –

    (a) any district or county council for any part of the area of the National Park for which the National Park authority is the appointing authority, and
    (b) such other persons as they consider appropriate,

as to the area for which the forum is to be established.

4 Membership of a local access forum

(1) A local access forum shall consist of no fewer than 10 and not more than 22 members.

(2) In the case of a local access forum –

    (a) consisting of not more than 16 members, not more than two members of such forum may also be members of a district or county council or National Park authority for any part of the area of the forum,
    (b) consisting of no fewer than 17 members, not more than three members of such forum may also be members of a district or county council or National Park authority for any part of the area of the forum.

(3) The members shall be persons who appear to the appointing authority to be representative of –

(a) users of local rights of way or the right conferred by section 2(1) (rights of public in relation to access land),

(b) owners and occupiers of access land or land over which local rights of way subsist, or

(c) any other interests especially relevant to the authority's area.

(4) The appointing authority shall ensure a reasonable balance is maintained between the number of members appointed in accordance with sub-paragraph (a) and in accordance with sub-paragraph (b) of paragraph (3).

(5) Subject to paragraph (6), before appointing any member the appointing authority shall –

(a) advertise the vacancy –
  (i) in such local or regional newspapers circulating in the authority's area as they consider appropriate, and
  (ii) if they maintain a website on the internet, on such a website, and
(b) consult such persons as they consider appropriate.

(6) The requirements in paragraph (5) to advertise and consult shall not apply to the appointment to a local access forum of any person who is a member of a district or county council or National Park authority for any part of the area of the forum.

5 Terms of membership

(1) Subject to the following paragraphs of this regulation, the terms of appointment of a member of a local access forum shall be determined by the appointing authority and notified to him in writing.

(2) A member of a local access forum shall be appointed for not less than one and not more than three years.

(3) A member of a local access forum may resign by notice in writing to the appointing authority which appointed him.

(4) An appointing authority –

(a) shall terminate the appointment of a member of a local access forum if they are satisfied that he has become a member of a district or county council or National Park authority and, as a result, regulation 4(2) is not complied with, and
(b) may terminate the appointment of a member of a forum if –
  (i) without the consent of the appointing authority, he has been absent from all meetings of the forum during a period of one year, or
  (ii) he has failed to comply with regulation 6(7).

(5) An appointing authority may re-appoint a person who ceases to be a member of a local access forum.

6 Proceedings of a local access forum

(1) Subject to the following paragraphs of this regulation and to regulations 7, 8 and 9, the proceedings (including the quorum) relating to the meetings of a local access forum shall be such as it may determine.

(2) A local access forum shall hold no fewer than two meetings every year.

(3) A local access forum shall have a chairman and a vice-chairman, who shall be appointed by election from amongst the members of the forum.

(4) The first chairman and vice-chairman of a local access forum shall be appointed at the first meeting of the forum.

(5) The period of appointment of the chairman and vice-chairman shall be determined by the local access forum, but in each case it may not exceed the period of appointment as a member of the forum.

(6) With a view to maintaining a reasonable balance between the interests of which the chairman and vice-chairman are respectively representative, a local access forum shall take such steps (as regards the selection of candidates for election as chairman and vice-chairman, determining the order in which they are appointed or the duration of their appointments as such, any combination of these or otherwise) as may be necessary to ensure that so far as practicable the chairman or the vice-chairman or each of them is a person who on his appointment as a member of the forum was eligible to be so appointed –

    (a) on any basis mentioned in regulation 4(3) other than any on which the other was eligible to be so appointed, or
    (b) (where each was appointed in accordance with regulation 4(3)(c)) on the basis of an interest other than any which was the basis on which the other was eligible to be so appointed.

(7) A member of a local access forum who is directly or indirectly interested in any matter brought up for consideration at a meeting of the forum shall disclose the nature of his interest to the meeting.

7 Access to meetings and documents of a local access forum

(1) A meeting of a local access forum shall be open to the public.

(2) The right of admission of the public conferred by paragraph (1) is without prejudice to any power of exclusion to suppress or prevent disorderly conduct or other misbehaviour at a meeting.

(3) Copies of the agenda for a meeting of a local access forum and copies of any report for the meeting shall be open to inspection by members of the public at the offices of the appointing authority in accordance with paragraph (4).

(4) Any document which is required by paragraph (3) to be open to inspection shall be so open at least three clear days before the meeting, except that –

    (a) where the meeting is convened at shorter notice, the copies of the agenda and reports shall be open to inspection from the time the meeting is convened, and
    (b) where an item is added to an agenda, copies of the document adding the item to the agenda (or of the revised agenda), and the copies of any report for the meeting relating to the item, shall be open to inspection from the time the item is added to the agenda,

but nothing in this paragraph requires copies of any agenda, document or report to be open to inspection by the public until copies are available to members of the local access forum.

(5) An item of business may not be considered at a meeting of a local access forum unless either –

(a) paragraph (4) has been complied with, or
(b) by reason of special circumstances, which shall be specified in the minutes, the chairman of the meeting is of the opinion that the item should be considered at the meeting as a matter of urgency.

8   Inspection of minutes and other documents after meetings of a local access forum

(1) After a meeting of a local access forum the following documents shall be open to inspection by members of the public at the offices of the appointing authority until the expiration of the period of two years beginning with the date of the meeting, namely –

(a) the minutes, or a copy of the minutes, of the meeting,
(b) a copy of the agenda for the meeting, and
(c) a copy of any report for the meeting.

(2) If and so long as copies of a report for a meeting of a local access forum are required by paragraph (3) of regulation 7 or paragraph (1) of this regulation to be open to inspection by members of the public –

(a) copies of a list, compiled by the secretary to the forum, of any background papers for the report, and
(b) at least one copy of each of the documents included in that list,

shall also be open to their inspection at the offices of the appointing authority.

(3) Any document required by paragraph (1) or (2) to be open to inspection by members of the public shall be taken to be so open if arrangements exist for its production to members of the public as soon as is reasonably practicable after the making of a request to inspect it.

(4) For the purposes of paragraph (2) the background papers for a report are those documents relating to the subject matter of the report which –

(a) disclose any facts or matters on which, in the opinion of the secretary to the local access forum, the report or an important part of the report is based, and
(b) have, in his opinion, been relied on to a material extent in preparing the report,

but do not include any published works.

9   Supplemental provisions about access to documents of a local access forum

(1) A document required by regulation 7 or 8 to be open to inspection shall be so open at all reasonable hours.

(2) Where a document is open to inspection by a person under regulation 7 or 8, the person may, subject to paragraph (3) –

(a) make copies of or extracts from the document, or
(b) require the person having custody of the document to supply to him a copy of or extracts from the document,

upon payment to the appointing authority providing the facility of such reasonable fee as may be required in respect of any expenses thereby incurred.

(3) Paragraph (2) does not require or authorise the doing of any act which infringes the copyright in any work.

10   Secretary to a local access forum

(1) The appointing authority shall employ a secretary for each local access forum which they establish.

(2) The secretary shall be responsible for the administration of the local access forum.

(3) The secretary may not be –

  (a) a member of the local access forum in relation to which he is employed as secretary, or
  (b) a member of the appointing authority in question.

11   Financial provisions

(1) Subject to paragraph (2), an appointing authority shall meet any reasonable expenses incurred by a local access forum which they establish or by the members of that forum.

(2) For the purposes of paragraph (1), reasonable expenses incurred by the members of a local access forum are such expenses as are incurred by them in connection with their attendance at meetings of the forum and any other activities relating to the discharge of the functions of the forum, but only in respect of –

  (a) travel and subsistence costs, and
  (b) any expenses of arranging for the care of their children or dependants.

12   Annual report

(1) A local access forum shall prepare an annual report on the discharge of its functions.

(2) The report shall be published by the local access forum's appointing authority.

13   Joint local access forums

(1) Two or more appointing authorities may establish a joint local access forum for their areas or for any parts of their areas by appointing the members of the forum before 8th August 2003, and where they propose to establish such a forum, references in regulation 3(2) and (3) to a local access forum shall be construed as references to a joint local access forum.

(2) Paragraph (1) shall not apply in relation to any appointing authority which has established a local access forum under regulation 3(1).

(3) Where a joint local access forum is established these Regulations shall have effect in relation to that forum with the following modifications –

  (a) any reference in these Regulations to a local access forum shall, unless a contrary intention appears, have effect as if for the words 'local access forum' there were substituted the words 'joint local access forum',
  (b) regulation 4 (membership of a local access forum) has effect as if –
    (i)   in paragraph (3), for the words 'appointing authority' there were substituted the words 'the appointing authorities', and for the words 'the authority's area' there were substituted the words 'the authorities' areas',

(ii) in paragraph (4), for the words 'The appointing authority' there were substituted the words 'The appointing authorities', and

(iii) in paragraph (5), for the words 'the appointing authority' there were substituted the words 'the appointing authorities', for the words 'the authority's area' there were substituted the words 'their respective areas', and for the words 'such a website' there were substituted the words 'their respective websites',

(c) regulation 5 (terms of membership) has effect as if –

(i) in paragraph (1), for the words 'the appointing authority' there were substituted the words 'the appointing authorities',

(ii) in paragraph (3), for the words 'the appointing authority' there were substituted the words 'one of the appointing authorities',

(iii) in paragraph (4), for the words 'An appointing authority' there were substituted the words 'Appointing authorities', and in sub-paragraph (b)(i) of that paragraph, for the words 'the appointing authority' there were substituted the words 'one of the appointing authorities', and

(iv) in paragraph (5), for the words 'An appointing authority' there were substituted the words 'Appointing authorities',

(d) regulation 7 (access to meetings and documents of a local access forum) has effect as if, in paragraph (3), for the words 'the appointing authority' there were substituted the words 'the appointing authorities',

(e) regulation 8 (inspection of minutes and other documents after meetings of a local access forum) has effect as if, in paragraphs (1) and (2), for the words 'the appointing authority' there were substituted the words 'the appointing authorities',

(f) regulation 10 (secretary to a local access forum) has effect as if –

(i) in paragraph (1), for the words 'The appointing authority' there were substituted the words 'One of the appointing authorities', and

(ii) in paragraph (3), for the words 'the appointing authority' there were substituted the words 'any of the appointing authorities',

(g) regulation 11 (financial provisions) has effect as if, in paragraph (1), for the words 'an appointing authority' there were substituted the words 'appointing authorities', and at the end of that paragraph there were inserted the words 'in such shares as may be agreed or failing agreement, equally', and

(h) regulation 12 (annual report) has effect as if, in paragraph (2), for the words 'by the local access forum's appointing authority' there were substituted the words 'jointly by the local access forum's appointing authorities'.

14 Application of these Regulations to London borough councils

(1) Where a council of a London borough resolve that section 94(1) applies to the council or to any part of their area, these Regulations shall, subject to the following paragraphs of this regulation, apply to the council of a London borough or to the part of their area to which the resolution relates.

(2) Regulations 3 (establishment of a local access forum) and 13 (joint local access forums) shall apply as if for the date mentioned in regulations 3(1) and 13(1) there were substituted a date one year after the date of the resolution.

(3) Regulation 4 (membership of a local access forum) shall have effect as if, in paragraphs (2)(a) and (b) and (6), for the words 'district or county council' there were substituted the words 'district, county or London borough council'.

(4) Regulation 5 (terms of membership) shall have effect as if, in paragraph (4)(a), for the words 'district or county council' there were substituted the words 'district, county or London borough council'.

COUNTRYSIDE AND RIGHTS OF WAY ACT 2000 (COMMENCEMENT NO 3) (WALES) ORDER 2002, SI 2002/2615

1 Citation and application

(1) This Order may be cited as the Countryside and Rights of Way Act 2000 (Commencement No 3) (Wales) Order 2002.

(2) This order applies to Wales.

2 Appointed day

The day appointed for the coming into force in relation to Wales of sections 60 and 61 of the Countryside and Rights of Way Act 2000 (rights of way improvement plans) is 1st November 2002.

COUNTRYSIDE AND RIGHTS OF WAY ACT 2000 (COMMENCEMENT NO 2) ORDER 2002, SI 2002/2833

1 Citation and extent

(1) This Order may be cited as the Countryside and Rights of Way Act 2000 (Commencement No 2) Order 2002.

(2) This Order applies in relation to England only.

2 Appointed day

21st November 2002 is the day appointed for the coming into force of sections 60 to 62 of the Countryside and Rights of Way Act 2000.

Appendix 4

DETR CIRCULAR 04/2001: COUNTRYSIDE AND RIGHTS OF WAY ACT 2000

29 January 2001

Contents

- Introduction

- Part I: Access to the countryside
- Part II: Rights of way and common land
  - Restricted byways
  - Public path creation orders for purposes of Part I of the Act
  - Effect of Part I of the Act on powers to stop up or divert highways
  - Wilful obstruction of a highway
  - Vegetation overhanging bridleways
  - Traffic regulation orders for purposes of conserving natural beauty
  - Unauthorised Driving of Mechanically Propelled Vehicles elsewhere than on Roads
  - Vehicular access over common land
  - Provisions in Part II to be brought into force by commencement order
  - Section 70
  - Section 72 and Schedule 16

- Part III: Nature conservation and wildlife protection
  - ...

- Part IV: Areas of outstanding natural beauty
  - ...

- Part V: Miscellaneous and supplementary
  - Local access forums
  - Management agreements
  - Norfolk and Suffolk Broads
  - Town and Village Greens
  - Isles of Scilly

Introduction

1. The Countryside and Rights of Way Act received Royal Assent on 30 November 2000. Some of its provisions (those specified in section 103(1)) came into force on that day while certain others will automatically come into force on 30 January 2001 (those set out in section 103(2)). Section 103(3) of the Act provides a power for the Secretary of State to commence, as respects England, the other provisions in the Act. An order has

been made[1] bringing into force several other provisions on either 30 January or 1 April 2001. This circular provides guidance to local authorities on these sets of provisions, and also gives brief details of other provisions in the Act which will affect local authorities on which more detailed guidance will be issued in due course.

2. Copies of the Act and the accompanying Explanatory Notes may be obtained from The Stationery Office or accessed at their web site.[2]

Part I: Access to the countryside

3. Part I introduces a new right of access for open-air recreation to mountain, moor, heath, down (collectively described as open country) and registered common land. There will be restrictions on the new right, including restrictions on dogs and provisions for landowners to exclude or restrict access for any reason for up to 28 days a year without seeking permission. There is also provision for further restrictions on access for reasons of land management, conservation, fire prevention and to avoid danger to the public. The Act also includes a power to extend the right to coastal land by order, and enables landowners voluntarily to dedicate irrevocably any land to public access.

4. The Act provides for certain functions in respect of access land to be exercised by 'access authorities', ie National Park Authorities for their areas and local highway authorities elsewhere. These functions include powers to make byelaws (section 17), appoint wardens (section 18) and to erect and maintain notices indicating boundaries etc (section 19). Access authorities will have the power under section 35 of the Act to negotiate agreements to provide means of access and to undertake the necessary works themselves if agreement cannot be reached.

5. District councils which are not access authorities also have powers to appoint wardens under section 18.

6. The right of access will be brought into effect in relation to any land by a commencement order and may be commenced at different times in different areas. It is intended that such commencement orders will not be made until all necessary regulations have been made and other preparatory work has been completed. The Department has a Public Service Agreement to implement the right of access by 2005. However, the Act enables access to land over 600 metres and registered common land (which can already be identified from existing maps) to be introduced earlier, ahead of the Countryside Agency publishing statutory maps of open country and registered common land. The Secretary of State will look to commons registration authorities to assist the Countryside Agency in fulfilling its statutory mapping duties by providing the Agency with data from the common land registers and commenting on maps of common land produced by the Agency.

7. Although most of the provisions mentioned in paragraph 4 (except the power to appoint wardens) come into force on 30 January, local authorities are advised that they need to take no action under them at this stage. This is because the powers can only be exercised in relation to land which is access land for the purposes of section 1(1) of the Act. Whilst some land will qualify as access land from 30 January (land over 600 metres and registered common land), most land will not qualify as access land until it has been shown on conclusive maps issued by the Countryside Agency. The Secretary of State

---

1   The Countryside and Rights of Way Act 2000 (Commencemet No. 1) Order 2001 (S.I. 2001/114 (C4)).
2   www.hmso.gov.uk/acts/acts2000/20000037.htm

does not consider it will be necessary for access authorities to use the powers available to them in Part I until the right of access to access land is commenced by Ministerial Order, or in anticipation of the right being commenced. We shall issue further guidance to access authorities before any such commencement Order is made.

8. The function of determining applications for restrictions and exclusions of access falls to the 'relevant authorities', ie National Park Authorities as regards their areas and the Countryside Agency elsewhere. Where land which is dedicated to access under section 16 is woodland, the Forestry Commission is the relevant authority.

Part II: Rights of way and common land

9. The provisions contained in Part II of the Act change the law on rights of way in a number of respects and will affect local authorities' functions in relation to rights of way. Most of these provisions, for example the requirement in sections 60–61 to prepare rights of way improvement plans (see also paragraph 16 below), will be brought into force when the necessary regulations have been made and further guidance issued.

10. Guidance is given in paragraphs 11 to 45 below on those provisions in Part II which come into force on 30 January 2001 under section 103(2) of the Act, or which will be commenced by order on 30 January or 1 April 2001. Authorities should continue to refer to Department of the Environment Circular 2/93 for matters not affected by the provisions which come into force on these dates.

Restricted byways

11. The Act creates a new category of highway – restricted byways – carrying a public right of way on foot, on horseback or leading a horse, and for vehicles other than mechanically propelled vehicles. On commencement of sections 47 and 48 of the Act, highways which are shown in definitive maps as roads used as public paths (RUPPs) will instead be treated as being shown as restricted byways and will have restricted byway rights created over them. Supplementary provisions are contained in sections 49 to 51. All of these provisions are to be brought into force by commencement orders at a later date.

12. However, section 52 of the Act, which enables the Secretary of State to amend by regulations existing legislation in relation to restricted byways, takes effect automatically on 30 January. This will enable the Department to scrutinise the large body of legislation relating to highways and determine which provisions should or should not apply to restricted byways or how they should be modified.

13. The Act requires that regulations made by the Secretary of State under section 52 be approved by both Houses of Parliament. In addition, the Secretary of State is required to consult the National Assembly for Wales before making provision which affects Wales and to obtain the Assembly's consent before expressly amending or revoking secondary legislation which the Assembly has made. The Assembly is also entitled to submit proposals to the Secretary of State on how his regulation making power might be exercised.

14. The Assembly itself has the power to make regulations under section 52 amending certain classes of legislation relating to Wales. These are: any local or private Act passed before or in the same session as the 2000 Act and relating only to Wales; and any secondary legislation made before enactment of the 2000 Act which the Assembly has the power to amend or revoke as respects Wales.

15. When section 47 of the Act is brought into force, section 54 of the Wildlife and Countryside Act 1981 will cease to have effect and so surveying authorities will no longer be under the duty in that section to reclassify RUPPs. Until then, however, the duty under section 54 continues to apply and authorities should continue to review their RUPPs and make reclassification orders. Any such orders, or applications for orders modifying the status of a RUPP, which are made before section 47 of the 2000 Act is brought into force are to be processed to a final determination. Section 48(9) of the Act requires that provision is made for this in the relevant commencement orders to be made under section 103(3).

Public path creation orders for purposes of Part I of the Act

16. Section 58 of the Act enables the Countryside Agency to apply to the Secretary of State (or the Countryside Council for Wales to apply to the National Assembly for Wales) to make a public path creation order. This is to facilitate access to land to which the public are to be given access under Part I of the Act. For example, there may be no practicable means for the public to gain access to some areas of access land (sometimes described as 'inaccessible islands'). Before making such an application, the countryside bodies are required to have regard to any rights of way improvement plan prepared under section 60 of the Act by the local highway authority for the area.

17. If requested by the Countryside Agency to use his reserve powers to make a public path creation order, the Secretary of State would not be obliged to do so but would consider carefully whether the circumstances warranted his taking action. Before making an order, the Secretary of State would be required by section 26 of the Highways Act 1980 to consult with local authorities in whose area the new path would be situated. Generally, it will be for local authorities, where necessary, to provide new means for the public to reach access land, either by negotiating permissive access with landowners or by using their existing powers under the Highways Act 1980 to create rights of way by agreement or by order.

Effect of Part I of the Act on powers to stop up or divert highways

18. Section 59 relates to powers, whether or not by order, to stop up or divert highways. It prevents an authority, when exercising such powers from regarding the existence of the new right of access to open countryside under Part I of the Act as, for example, reducing the need for the highway, the need for an alternative highway or the need to reserve a public right of way. In addition, when deciding whether to stop up or divert a highway, it may be necessary for an authority to consider the extent (if any) to which that highway is likely to be used apart from the exercise of the power. The section requires, when assessing that use in relation to a highway situated on or in the vicinity of access land, that particular regard be had to when the right of access would not be exercisable.

19. The purpose of section 59 is to prevent the new right of access from being used to support a case for stopping up or diverting highways, except, for example, where a diversion may be required to help people reach access land.

Wilful obstruction of a highway

20. Section 64 of the Act inserts a new section 137ZA into the Highways Act 1980. The new section empowers a magistrates' court, when convicting a person under section 137 of that Act of wilfully obstructing a highway, to order that person to remove the obstruction. Under new section 137ZA(3), failure to comply with an order, without

reasonable excuse, is an offence punishable by a fine not exceeding level 5 on the standard scale (currently £5,000). Further fines, not exceeding ¹⁄₂₀th of level 5, may be imposed for each day the offence continues after conviction under section 137ZA.

21. A person who has been ordered to remove an obstruction may not be prosecuted again under section 137 of the Highways Act 1980 in respect of that obstruction during the period set by the court under section 137ZA for removing it. Neither may they be similarly prosecuted during any period set under section 311(1) of the Highways Act 1980 for complying with directions of the court.

22. Highway authorities have powers at common law to remove unlawful obstructions in certain circumstances. Where authorities choose to exercise these powers after a person has been convicted under new section 137ZA(3), then subsection (4) in conjunction with section 305 of the Highways Act 1980 allows authorities to recover their costs through the magistrates' court.

Vegetation overhanging bridleways

23. Section 154 of the Highways Act 1980 enables highway authorities and certain local authorities to require owners and occupiers of land whose trees, shrubs or hedges overhang highways to the extent of endangering or obstructing the passage of vehicles or pedestrians, to cut the vegetation back. Section 65 of the 2000 Act extends section 154 to apply to vegetation which endangers or obstructs the passage of horse-riders. Authorities will, therefore, be able to require that vegetation overhanging bridleways or carriageways is cut back to a height which is suitable for horse-riders.

Traffic regulation orders for purposes of conserving natural beauty

24. Local traffic authorities have powers under the Road Traffic Regulation Act 1984 to make traffic regulation orders to prohibit, restrict or regulate traffic using particular highways. The Secretary of State has similar powers as respects trunk roads. Circular 2/93 sets out one of the purposes for which traffic regulation orders may be made.

25. Section 22 of the 1984 Act enables authorities to make traffic regulation orders in respect of the use of roads in certain areas for the purpose of conserving or enhancing the natural beauty of the area, or of affording better opportunities for the public to enjoy the amenities of the area. In England and Wales the areas concerned include:

- National Parks
- Areas of outstanding natural beauty
- Country parks
- Areas where the Countryside Agency or the Countryside Council for Wales are undertaking experimental projects
- Nature reserves
- National Trails
- Land belonging to, and held inalienably by, the National Trust.

26. Section 66 of the 2000 Act extends section 22 to include Sites of Special Scientific Interest and removes the restriction in that section which prevented orders being made in relation to Greater London.

27. The section also inserts a new section 22A into the 1984 Act. The new section enables traffic authorities to make orders to control vehicular traffic on unclassified roads and byways in areas not covered by section 22 of that Act for the purposes of conserving or enhancing the natural beauty of the area.

28. A definition in sections 22 and 22A makes it clear that conserving the natural beauty of an area is to be construed as including the conservation of flora, fauna, geological and physiographical features of the area.

29. The Secretary of State will consider whether further advice on the making of traffic regulation orders is necessary when other provisions in Part II of the Act are brought into force.

Unauthorised Driving of Mechanically Propelled Vehicles elsewhere than on Roads

30. Schedule 7 to the 2000 Act makes a number of changes to the prohibition of driving motor vehicles elsewhere than on roads contained in section 34 of the Road Traffic Act 1988. The Schedule substitutes a new section 34. It also inserts a new section 34A into the 1988 Act. The latter provision is to be brought into force at a date still to be determined. In part, these provisions address issues brought to attention by various cases in recent years.

31. Section 34 currently relates to the driving of a 'motor vehicle', a term which is defined in section 185(1) of the 1988 Act. The Act extends the offence to cover mechanically propelled vehicles which may not fall within the current offence because they are not intended or adapted for use on roads – ie they do not fall within the definition of 'motor vehicle'. Schedule 7 makes similar amendments to section 21 of the 1988 Act which relates to the offence of driving or parking 'motor vehicles' on cycle tracks.

32. The new offenes under section 34 and section 21 do not apply to certain classes of vehicles such as invalid carriages, mechanically propelled vehicles controlled by pedestrians used for cutting grass and electrically assisted pedal cycles.

33. As before, the new section 34(1)(b) prohibits driving on footpaths and bridleways. However, the offence is also extended to the new category of highway, restricted byways.

34. The recording of a way in a definitive map as a footpath or bridleway (or, when the relevant provisions are in force, a restricted byway) does not mean that higher rights do not exist over the way in question. In other words, it does not mean that there are no public rights of way to drive mechanically propelled vehicles over the way. However, section 34(2), which is a new provision, specifies that for the purposes of the offence where a way is shown in a definitive map as a footpath, bridleway, or restricted byway, it is to be presumed to be a way of the kind shown unless the contrary is proved. It is, accordingly, presumed to carry only those public rights of way which a footpath, bridleway or restricted byway carry. Therefore, once the prosecution have proved that a highway is shown in a definitive map as a footpath, bridleway or restricted byway, the burden of proof would be on the defence to prove on the balance of probabilities that there are full public vehicular rights of way.

35. Section 34(2) will be subject to the new section 34A of the 1988 Act when that latter provision is brought into force. However, until then the presumption under section 34(2) applies without being subject to section 34A.

36. Section 34A provides for the presumption in section 34(2) to be rebuttable only in those circumstances which are expressly set out in it or in regulations made under it. This means that, except where those circumstances apply or the defences in section 34 are made out, the offence under section 34(1)(b) is committed where the way being

driven on is shown in a definitive map as a footpath, bridleway or restricted byway. This is irrespective of whether there are public rights of way to drive mechanically propelled vehicles.

Vehicular access over common land

37. Section 68 deals with problems relating to vehicular access across common, and other, land over which it is an offence to drive. Despite the fact that many property owners, or their predecssors, have been using a vehicular access to their property across such land unhindered for many years, they have recently found that they have not acquired a legal right to do so. This is because a prescriptive right through long use cannot be acquired where the activity being undertaken is a criminal offence. To compound the problem, such property owners are sometimes faced with having to pay a substantial sum of money to acquire a legal right of vehicular access, without which the property would probably be unsaleable.

38. This section provides that where a person has used a vehicular access to property across land over which it is an offence to drive, regulations can be made to provide for the creation of a statutory easement, providing certain qualifying criteria are met. Although section 68 itself will be brought into effect by commencement order, the statutory easement scheme will only come into effect when the regulations provided for in section 68(2) are agreed by Parliament. These regulations will specify such matters as the criteria to be met in order to apply for an easement, the method of applying, the methodology for calculating the price to be paid by the property owner to the owner of the land over which the access is sought, the conditions to which the easement will be subject; dispute resolution procedures and how the easement will be recorded by the Land Registry.

39. This section will have particular relevance to local authorities that own land over which it is an offence to drive. However, where such an authority wish to grant an easement for less than the price due in accordance with the provisions to be set out in the regulations, it will still be open to them to consider whether, in accordance with the provisions of section 123 or 127 of the Local Government Act 1972, they wish to seek the Secretary of State's consent for such a disposal at less than the best consideration reasonably obtainable. Specific consent would only be required if the undervalue exceeded that permitted by paragraph 6 of the Local Government Act 1972 General Disposal Consents 1998.

Provisions in Part II to be brought into force by commencement order

40. The Secretary of State has made an order under section 103(3) of the Act to bring certain other provisions in Part II into force.

Section 70

41. Section 70(2) and (4) will come into force on 1 April 2001.

42. Section 70(2) amends section 134 of the Highways Act 1980. Section 134 confers a right to plough or otherwise disturb the surface of a footpath or bridleway which crosses agricultural land, but subject to a duty to make good the surface of the highway and to mark out its width. Failure to comply with that duty is an offence under subsection (4). Currently, subsection (5) restricts who may bring proceedings for that offence to highway authorities and certain councils. Section 70 removes that restriction by causing subsection (5) to be repealed. This means that any person will be able to

prosecute the offence under section 134(4) of the 1980 Act but under the terms of the commencement order, only in respect of offences committed on or after 1 April 2001.

43. Section 70(4) amends section 21(2)(b) of the Road Traffic Act 1988. The amendment provides highway authorities with a defence against prosecution for driving or parking mechanically propelled vehicles on cycle tracks when this is done to prevent or remove obstructions or in the prevention or abatement of any other interferences with the highway. The amendment arises out of a judgment by the House of Lords (*Goodes v East Sussex County Council* [2000] 3 All ER 603) which would appear to mean that the current provisions in section 300 of the 1980 Act and section 21(2)(b) of the 1988 Act do not cover the removal of obstructions or the abatement of nuisances. This is because a narrow interpretation was given to the meaning of 'maintenance' that appears to exclude the removal of obstructions and the such like.

44. Subsection (3) of section 70 amends section 300 of the Highways Act 1980 and similarly provides highway authorities with immunity from prosecution for driving mechanically propelled vehicles on footpaths and bridleways. However, the operation of the amended section 300 depends upon amendments being made to secondary legislation and section 70(3) will be brought into force at a later date when those amendments have been made.

Section 72 and Schedule 16

45. Section 72 provides a number of definitions for the Interpretation of Part II. Section 72 and the repeal in Schedule 16 to the Act relating to section 22 of the Road Traffic Regulation Act 1984 are brought into force on 30 January 2001.

Part V: Miscellaneous and supplementary

Local access forums

76. Section 94 places a duty on highway authorities and national park authorities to establish local access forums to advise on the improvement of public access for open-air recreation and the enjoyment of the area. Relevant decision-making authorities will have to have regard to forums' views in reaching decisions, for example in relation to draft maps, the imposition of byelaws, and proposals for long term closures of access land (under Part I), as well as on wider access issues contained in new rights of way improvement plans (under Part II). The duty will not arise until regulations are made setting out the constitution and functions of the forums. The regulations are expected to be issued later this year and will be subject to public consultation. The regulations must provide that membership of forums will include users of rights of way and the new right of access, landowners and occupiers, together with any other interests especially relevant to the area. The duty does not apply to London boroughs, but any such council will have the power to set up a forum if it wishes to do so. The Secretary of State may exclude the duty in respect of any other local authority – for example, if there is little or no access land and an insignificant network of recreational rights of way in the area.

Management agreements

77. Section 39 of the Wildlife and Countryside Act 1981 enables local authorities to enter into management agreements with the owner of land in the countryside for its conservation (and for other related purposes). Section 96 of the 2000 Act amends section 39 in order that the Countryside Agency, the Countryside Council for Wales, and conservation boards in areas of outstanding natural beauty, may also enter into

such agreements, and to enable agreements to be made in respect of any land, whether or not it is in the countryside. These amendments will allow these bodies, for example, to make agreements with the owner of land both for its dedication to access, and the long term conservation of access (by ensuring that dedicated land cannot become excepted land for the purposes of Schedule 1).

Norfolk and Suffolk Broads

78. Section 97 of the Act places a duty on any relevant authority, in exercising or performing any functions in relation to land in the Norfolk and Suffolk Broads, to have regard to the purposes for which the Broads have been designated (conserving and enhancing natural beauty, promoting public enjoyment and protecting the interests of navigation). This brings the treatment of the Broads into line with that for National Parks and AONBs.

Town and Village Greens

79. Section 98 of the Act revises and clarifies the third limb of the definition of town and village greens contained in section 22(1) of the Commons Registration Act 1965.

80. Under the first part of the revised definition the land will be regarded as village green provided that it is land on which for not less than 20 years a significant number of the inhabitants of any locality, or of any neighbourhood within a locality, have indulged in lawful sports and pastimes as of right. The implications of this are that the commons registration authority will need to be satisfied only that a significant number of local inhabitants have used the land in a qualifying manner. Use by people not from the locality will therefore be irrelevant. Furthermore, the use of the words '. . . any locality, or neighbourhood within a locality . . .' is intended to clarify that a locality does not necessarily equate to an administrative area, eg an entire parish, but rather to a suitable area which the land in question might reasonably be expected to serve as a green.

81. The second part of the revised definition provides that the local inhabitants must either continue to use the land in a qualifying manner or must have ceased to use the land within any period prescribed in regulations. These regulations may also require that specific procedures relating to the process of applying to register land as a green are followed.

82. The revised defintions contained in this section come into effect on 30 January 2001. The Government is still considering what provisions should be contained in subsequent regulations.

Isles of Scilly

83. The commencement order referred to in paragraph 1 above brings into force certain parts of section 100 of the Act which deals with the application of various provisions to the Isles of Scilly. Section 100 prevents Part I and sections 58 to 61 and 71 from applying to the Isles of Scilly except by order made by the Secretary of State after consultation with the Council of the Isles. Section 100 also amends the Highways Act 1980 to make similar provision in respect of certain provisions in Schedule 6 that will be inserted into the 1980 Act and in respect of the power for highway authorities to recover the costs of removing certain obstructions which is described in paragraph 22 above. Finally, section 100 empowers the Secretary of State, after consultation with the Council of the Isles, to make an order modifying the application of Part IV of the Act to the Isles of Scilly.

84. Section 100, with the exception of subsections (3) and (5)(a) will be brought into force on 30 January 2001. Subsection (3), which relates to Part IV of the Act, will be brought into force on 1 April 2001. Subsection (5)(a) will be brought into force when the new provisions in the Highways Act 1980 to which it relates are also brought into force.

CLL BRAUN
Assistant Secretary

The Chief Executive:
  County Councils in England
  District Councils in England
  Unitary Authorities in England
  London Borough Councils
  Council of the Isles of Scilly
The Town Clerk, City of London
The National Park Officer, National Park Authorities in England
The Chief Executive, The Broads Authority
Head of Paid Services, Greater London Authority

Appendix 5

HIGHWAYS ACT 1980

PART III

CREATION OF HIGHWAYS

24 Construction of new highways and provision of road-ferries

(1) The Minister may, with the approval of the Treasury, construct new highways; but where he proposes to construct a new highway other than –

(a) a trunk road,

(b) a special road,

(c) a highway the construction of which is authorised by an order relating to a trunk road under section 14 above or an order under section 18 above, or

(d) a highway to be constructed for purposes connected with any function exercisable by him under an agreement made under section 4 above,

he shall give notice of his proposals to, and consider any representations by, every council through whose area the highway will pass.

(2) A local highway authority may construct new highways; but –

(a) where a new highway to be constructed by such an authority will communicate with a highway for which the Minister is the highway authority; . . .

(b) . . .

the communication shall not be made unless the manner in which it is to be made has been approved by the Minister . . .

(3) . . .

(4) The Minister or a local highway authority may provide and maintain new road-ferries.

Amendment – Local Government Act 1985, s 102, Sch 17.

Explanatory text – see **4.10.1**.

---

25 Creation of footpath or bridleway by agreement

(1) A local authority may enter into an agreement with any person having the necessary power in that behalf for the dedication by that person of a footpath or bridleway over land in their area.

An agreement under this section is referred to in this Act as a 'public path creation agreement'.

(2) For the purposes of this section 'local authority' –

    (a) in relation to land outside Greater London means a county council, a district council ... ; and

    (b) in relation to land in Greater London means ... a London borough council or the Common Council.

(3) Before entering into an agreement under this section, a local authority shall consult any authority or authorities in whose area the land concerned is situated.

(4) An agreement under this section shall be on such terms as to payment or otherwise as may be specified in the agreement and may, if it is so agreed, provide for the dedication of the footpath or bridleway subject to limitations or conditions affecting the public right of way over it.

(5) Where a public path creation agreement has been made it shall be the duty of the local authority who are a party to it to take all necessary steps for securing that the footpath or bridleway is dedicated in accordance with it.

[(6) As soon as may be after the dedication of a footpath or bridleway in accordance with a public path creation agreement, the local authority who are party to the agreement shall give notice of the dedication by publication in at least one local newspaper circulating in the area in which the land to which the agreement relates is situated.]

Amendments – Environment Act 1995, s 120(3), Sch 24; Local Government Act 1985, s 102, Sch 17; Wildlife and Countryside Act 1981, s 64.

Explanatory text – see **3.3.1**.

---

26   Compulsory powers for creation of footpaths and bridleways

(1) Where it appears to a local authority that there is need for a footpath or bridleway over land in their area and they are satisfied that, having regard to –

    (a) the extent to which the path or way would add to the convenience or enjoyment of a substantial section of the public, or to the convenience of persons resident in the area, and

    (b) the effect which the creation of the path or way would have on the rights of persons interested in the land, account being taken of the provisions as to compensation contained in section 28 below,

it is expedient that the path or way should be created, the authority may by order made by them and submitted to and confirmed by the Secretary of State, or confirmed by them as an unopposed order, create a footpath or bridleway over the land.

An order under this section is referred to in this Act as a 'public path creation order'; and for the purposes of this section 'local authority' has the same meaning as in section 25 above.

(2) Where it appears to the Secretary of State in a partiuclar case that there is need for a footpath or bridleway as mentioned in subsection (1) above, and he is satisfied as mentioned in that subsection, he may, after consultation with each body which is a local authority for the purposes of this section in relation to the land concerned, make a public path creation order creating the footpath or bridleway.

(3) A local authority shall, before exercising any power under this section, consult any other local authority or authorities in whose area the land concerned is situated.

(4) A right of way created by a public path creation order may be either unconditional or subject to such limitations or conditions as may be specified in the order.

(5) A public path creation order shall be in such form as may be prescribed by regulations made by the Secretary of State, and shall contain a map, on such scale as may be so prescribed, defining the land over which a footpath or bridleway is thereby created.

(6) Schedule 6 to this Act shall have effect as to the making, confirmation, validity and date of operation of public path creation orders.

Prospective amendment – Subsection prospectively inserted by the CROW Act 2000, s 57, Sch 6, Pt I, para 1:

'(3A) The considerations to which –

(a) the Secretary of State is to have regard in determining whether or not to confirm or make a public path creation order, and
(b) a local authority are to have regard in detemrining whether or not to confirm such an order as an unopposed order,

include any material provision of a rights of way improvement plan prepared by any local highway authority whose area includes land over which the proposed footpath or bridleway would be created.'

Explanatory text – see **3.4**.

---

27   Making up of new footpaths and bridleways

(1) On the dedication of a footpath or bridleway in pursuance of a public path creation agreement, or on the coming into operation of a public path creation order, being –

(a) an agreement or order made by a local authority who are not the highway authority for the path in question, or
(b) an order made by the Secretary of State under section 26(2) above in relation to which he directs that this subsection shall apply,

the highway authority shall survey the path or way and shall certify what work (if any) appears to them to be necessary to bring it into a fit condition for use by the public as a footpath or bridleway, as the case may be, and shall serve a copy of the certificate on the local authority mentioned in paragraph (a) above or, where paragraph (b) applies, on such local authority as the Secretary of State may direct.

(2) It shall be the duty of the highway authority to carry out any works specified in a certificate under subsection (1) above, and where the authority have carried out the work they may recover from the authority on whom a copy of the certificate was served any expenses reasonably incurred by them in carrying out that work, including any expenses so incurred in the discharge of any liability for compensation in respect of the carrying out thereof.

(3) Notwithstanding anything in the preceding provisons of this section, where an agreement or order is made as mentioned in subsection (1)(a) above, the local authority making the agreement or order may –

(a) with the consent of the highway authority carry out (in place of the highway authority) the duties imposed by that subsection on the highway authority; and

(b) carry out any works which, apart from this subsection, it would be the duty of the highway authority to carry out under subsection (2) above.

(4) Where the Secretary of State makes a public path creation order under section 26(2) above, he may direct that subsection (5) below shall apply.

(5) Where the Secretary of State gives such a direction –

(a) the local authority who, on the coming into force of the order, became the highway authority for the path or way in question shall survey the path or way and shall certify what work (if any) appears to them to be necessary to bring it into a fit condition for use by the public as a footpath or bridleway, as the case may be, and shall furnish the Secretary of State with a copy of the certificate;

(b) if the Secretary of State is not satisfied with a certificate made under the foregoing paragraph, he shall either cause a local inquiry to be held or shall give to the local authority an opportunity of being heard by a person appointed by him for the purpose and, after considering the report of the person appointed to hold the inquiry or the person so appointed as aforesaid, shall make such order either confirming or varying the certificate as he may think fit; and

(c) subject to the provisions of the last foregoing paragraphs, it shall be the duty of the highway authority to carry out the work specified in a certificate made by them under paragraph (a) above.

(6) In this section 'local authority' means any council . . . .

Amendment – Environment Act 1995, s 120(3), Sch 24.

Explanatory text – see **3.4.1**.

---

28   Compensation for loss caused by public path creation order

(1) Subject to the following provisions of this section, if, on a claim made in accordance with this section, it is shown that the value of an interest of a person in land is depreciated, or that a person has suffered damage by being disturbed in his enjoyment of land, in consequence of the coming into operation of a public path creation order, the authority by whom the order was made shall pay to that person compensation equal to the amount of the depreciation or damage.

(2) A claim for compensation under this section shall be made within such time and in such manner as may be prescribed by regulations made by the Secretary of State, and shall be made to the authority by whom the order was made.

(3) For the purposes of the application of this section to an order made by the Secretary of State under section 26(2) above, references in this section to the authority by whom the order was made are to be construed as references to such one of the authorities referred to in that subsection as may be nominated by the Secretary of State for the purposes of this subsection.

(4) Nothing in this section confers on any person, in respect of a footpath or bridleway created by a public path creation order, a right to compensation for depreciation of the value of an interest in land, or for disturbance in his enjoyment of land, not being in either case land over which the path or way was created or land held therewith, unless

the creation of the path or way would have been actionable at his suit if it had been effected otherwise than in the exercise of statutory powers.

(5) In this section 'interest', in relation to land, includes any estate in land and any right over land, whether the right is exercisable by virtue of the ownership of an interest in land or by virtue of a licence or agreement, and in particular includes sporting rights.

Explanatory text – see **4.6.5**.

29 Protection for agriculture and forestry

In the exercise of their functions under this Part of this Act relating to the making of public path creation agreements and public path creation orders it shall be the duty of councils . . . to have due regard to the needs of agriculture and forestry.

Amendments – Environment Act 1995, s 120(3), Sch 24.

Prospective amendment – Section prospectively substituted by the CROW Act 2000, s 57, Sch 6, Pt I, para 2:

'29 Duty to have regard to agriculture, forestry and nature conservation

(1) In the exercise of their functions under this Part of this Act relating to the making of public path creation agreements and public path creation orders it shall be the duty of councils to have due regard to –

(a) the needs of agriculture and forestry, and
(b) the desirability of conserving flora, fauna and geological and physiographical features.

(2) In this section, "agriculture" includes the breeding or keeping of horses.'

Explanatory text – see **3.3.1, 3.4.1, 4.5.1, 4.6.1**.

30 Dedication of highway by agreement with parish or community council

(1) The council of a parish or community may enter into an agreement with any person having the necessary power in that behalf for the dedication by that person of a highway over land in the parish or community or an adjoining parish or community in any case where such a dedication would in the opinion of the council be beneficial to the inhabitants of the parish or community or any part thereof.

(2) Where the council of a parish or community have entered into an agreement under subsection (1) above for the dedication of a highway they may carry out any works (including works of maintenance or improvement) incidental to or consequential on the making of the agreement or contribute towards the expense of carrying out such works, and may agree or combine with the council of any other parish or community to carry out such works or to make such a contribution.

Explanatory text – see **3.3.2**.

31 Dedication of way as highway presumed after public use for 20 years

(1) Where a way over land, other than a way of such a character that use of it by the public could not give rise at common law to any presumption of dedication, has been

actually enjoyed by the public as of right and without interruption for a full period of 20 years, the way is to be deemed to have been dedicated as a highway unless there is sufficient evidence that there was no intention during that period to dedicate it.

(2) The period of 20 years referred to in subsection (1) above is to be calculated retrospectively from the date when the right of the public to use the way is brought into question, whether by a notice such as is mentioned in subsection (3) below or otherwise.

(3) Where the owner of the land over which any such way as aforesaid passes –

(a) has erected in such manner as to be visible to persons using the way a notice inconsistent with the dedication of the way as a highway, and

(b) has maintained the notice after the 1st January 1934, or any later date on which it was erected,

the notice, in the absence of proof of a contrary intention, is sufficient evidence to negative the intention to dedicate the way as a highway.

(4) In the case of land in the possession of a tenant for a term of years, or from year to year, any person for the time being entitled in reversion to the land shall, notwithstanding the existence of the tenancy, have the right to place and maintain such a notice as is mentioned in subsection (3) above, so, however, that no injury is done thereby to the business or occupation of the tenant.

(5) Where a notice erected as mentioned in subsection (3) above is subsequently torn down or defaced, a notice given by the owner of the land to the appropriate council that the way is not dedicated as a highway is, in the absence of proof of a contrary intention, sufficient evidence to negative the intention of the owner of the land to dedicate the way as a highway.

(6) An owner of land may at any time deposit with the appropriate council –

(a) a map of the land on a scale of not less than 6 inches to 1 mile, and

(b) a statement indicating what ways (if any) over the land he admits to have been dedicated as highways;

and, in any case in which such a deposit has been made, statutory declarations made by that owner or by his successors in title and lodged by him or them with the appropriate council at any time –

(i) within six years from the date of the deposit, or

(ii) within six years from the date on which any previous declaration was last lodged under this section,

to the effect that no additional way (other than any specifically indicated in the declaration) over the land delineated on the said map has been dedicated as a highway since the date of the deposit, or since the date of the lodgment of such previous declaration, as the case may be, are, in the absence of proof of a contrary intention, sufficient evidence to negative the intention of the owner or his successors in title to dedicate any such additional way as a highway.

(7) For the purposes of the foregoing provisions of this section 'owner', in relation to any land, means a person who is for the time being entitled to dispose of the fee simple in the land; and for the purposes of subsections (5) and (6) above 'the appropriate council' means the council of the county[, metropolitan district] or London borough in which the way (in the case of subsection (5)) or the land (in the case of subsection (6)) is situated or, where the way or land is situated in the City, the Common Council.

(8) Nothing in this section affects any incapacity of a corporation or other body or person in possession of land for public or statutory purposes to dedicate a way over the land as a highway if the existence of a highway would be incompatible with those purposes.

(9) Nothing in this section operates to prevent the dedication of a way as a highway being presumed on proof of user for any less period than 20 years, or being presumed or proved in any circumstances in which it might have been presumed or proved immediately before the commencement of this Act.

(10) Nothing in this section or section 32 below affects [section 56(1) of the Wildlife and Countryside Act 1981 (which provides that a definitive map and statement] are conclusive evidence as to the existence of the highways shown on the map and as to certain particulars contained in the statement), . . .

(11) For the purposes of this section 'land' includes land covered with water.

Amendments – Local Government Act 1985, s 8, Sch 4, Pt I, para 7; Wildlife and Countryside Act 1981, ss 72(11), 73, Sch 17, Pt II.

Prospective amendment – Word 'six' prospectively substituted in subs (6)(i), (ii), by the CROW Act 2000, s 57, Sch 6, Pt I, para 3:

'ten'.

Prospective amendment – Section prospectively inserted by the CROW Act 2000, s 57, Sch 6, Pt I, para 4:

'31A Register of maps, statements and declarations

(1) The appropriate council shall keep, in such manner as may be prescribed, a register containing such information as may be prescribed with respect to maps and statements deposited and declarations lodged with that council under section 31(6) above.

(2) Regulations may make provision for the register to be kept in two or more parts, each containing such information as may be prescribed with respect to such maps, statements and declarations.

(3) Regulations may make provision as to circumstances in which an entry relating to a map, statement or declaration, or anything relating to it, is to be removed from the register or from any part of it.

(4) Every register kept under this section shall be available for inspection free of charge at all reasonable hours.

(5) In this section –

"appropriate council" has the same meaning as in section 31(6) above;

"prescribed" means prescribed by regulations;

"regulations" means regulations made by the Secretary of State.'

Explanatory text – see **3.5.7(4), 3.5.8**.

---

32 Evidence of dedication of way as highway

A court or other tribunal, before determining whether a way has or has not been dedicated as a highway, or the date on which such dedication, if any, took place, shall take into consideration any map, plan or history of the locality or other relevant document which is tendered in evidence, and shall give such weight thereto as the court or tribunal considers justified by the circumstances, including the antiquity of the tendered document, the status of the person by whom and the purpose for which it was made or compiled, and the custody in which it has been kept and from which it is produced.

Explanatory text – see **7.4.1**.

33 Protection of rights of reversioners

The person entitled to the remainder or reversion immediately expectant upon the determination of a tenancy for life, or pour autre vie, in land shall have the like remedies by action for trespass or an injunction to prevent the acquisition by the public of a right of way over that land as if he were in possession thereof.

Explanatory text – see **3.5.8**.

34 Conversion of private street into highway

Without prejudice to the foregoing provisions of this Part of this Act, a street which is not a highway and land to which section 232 below applies may become a highway by virtue of a declaration made by a county council, [a metropolitan district council,] a London borough council or the Common Council in accordance with the provisions in that behalf contained in Part XI of this Act.

Amendment – Local Government Act 1985, s 8, Sch 4, Pt I, para 8.

Explanatory text – see **3.1**.

. . .

PART IV

MAINTENANCE OF HIGHWAYS

Highways maintainable at public expense

36 Highways maintainable at public expense

(1) All such highways as immediately before the commencement of this Act were highways maintainable at the public expense for the purposes of the Highways Act 1959 continue to be so maintainable (subject to this section and to any order of a magistrates'court under section 47 below) for the purposes of this Act.

(2) Without prejudice to any other enactment (whether contained in this Act or not) whereby a highway may become for the purposes of this Act a highway maintainable at the public expense, and subject to this section and section 232(7) below, and to any order of a magistrates' court under section 47 below, the following highways (not falling within subsection (1) above) shall for the purposes of this Act be highways maintainable at the public expense –

    (a) a highway constructed by a highway authority, otherwise than on behalf of some other person who is not a highway authority;

(b) a highway constructed by a council within their own area under [Part II of the Housing Act 1985], other than one in respect of which the local highway authority are satisfied that it has not been properly constructed, and a highway constructed by a council outside their own area under the said Part V, being, in the latter case, a highway the liability to maintain which is, by virtue of [the said Part II], vested in the council who are the local highway authority for the area in which the highway is situated;

(c) a highway that is a trunk road or a special road; . . .

(d) a highway, being a footpath or bridleway, created in consequence of a public path creation order or a public path diversion order or in consequence of an order made by the Minister of Transport or the Secretary of State under [section 247 of the Town and Country Planning Act 1990 or by a competent authority under section 257 of that Act], or dedicated in pursuance of a public path creation agreement;

[(e) a highway, being a footpath or bridleway, created in consequence of a rail crossing diversion order, or of an order made under section 14 or 16 of the Harbours Act 1964, or of an order made under section 1 or 3 of the Transport and Works Act 1992.]

(3) Paragraph (c) of subsection (2) above is not to be construed as referring to a part of a trunk road or special road consisting of a bridge or other part which a person is liable to maintain under a charter or special enactment, or by reason of tenure, enclosure or prescription.

[(3A) Paragraph (e) of subsection (2) above shall not apply to a footpath or bridleway, or to any part of a footpath or bridleway, which by virtue of an order of a kind referred to in that subsection is maintainable otherwise than at the public expense.]

(4) Subject to subsection (5) below, where there occurs any event on the occurrence of which, under any rule of law relating to the duty of maintaining a highway by reason of tenure, enclosure or prescription, a highway would, but for the enactment which abrogated the former rule of law under which a duty of maintaining highways fell on the inhabitants at large (section 38(1) of the Highways Act 1959) or any other enactment, become, or cease to be, maintainable by the inhabitants at large of any area, the highway shall become, or cease to be, a highway which for the purposes of this Act is a highway maintainable at public expense.

(5) A highway shall not by virtue of subsection (4) above become a highway which for the purposes of this Act is a highway maintainable at the public expense unless either –

(a) it was a highway before 31st August 1835; or

(b) it became a highway after that date and has at some time been maintainable by the inhabitants at large of any area or a highway maintainable at the public expense;

and a highway shall not by virtue of that subsection cease to be a highway maintainable at the public expense if it is a highway which under any rule of law would become a highway maintainable by reason of enclosure but is prevented from becoming such a highway by section 51 below.

(6) The council of every county[, metropolitan district] and London borough and the Common Council shall cause to be made, and shall keep corrected up to date, a list of the streets within their area which are highways maintainable at the public expense.

(7) Every list made under subsection (6) above shall be kept deposited at the offices of the council by whom it was made and may be inspected by any person free of charge at

all reasonable hours and in the case of a list made by the council of a county [in England], the county council shall supply to the council of each district in the county an up to date list of the streets within the area of the district that are highways maintainable at the public expense, and the list so supplied shall be kept deposited at the office of the district council and may be inspected by any person free of charge at all reasonable hours.

Amendments – Housing (Consequential Provisions) Act 1985, s 4, Sch 2, para 47; Transport and Works Act 1992, ss 64 (post), 68(1), Sch 4, Pt I; Planning (Consequential Provisions) Act 1990, s 4, Sch 2, para 43(3); Local Government Act 1985, s 8, Sch4, Pt I, para 7; Local Government (Wales) Act 1994, s 22(1), Sch 7, Pt I, para 4.

Prospective amendment – Paragraph prospectively inserted after subs (2)(e) by the CROW Act 2000, s 57, Sch 6, Pt I, para 5:

> '(f) a highway, being a footpath, a bridleway, a restricted byway or a way over which the public have a right of way for vehicular and all other kinds of traffic, created in consequence of a special diversion order or an SSSI diversion order.'

Explanatory text – see **8.3.4, 8.3.7**.

Methods whereby highways may become maintainable at public expense

37 Provisions whereby highway created by dedication may become maintainable at public expense

(1) A person who proposes to dedicate a way as a highway and who desires that the proposed highway shall become maintainable at the public expense by virtue of this section shall give notice of the proposal, not less than 3 months before the date of the proposed dedication, to the council who would, if the way were a highway, be the highway authority therefor, describing the location and width of the proposed highway and the nature of the proposed dedication.

(2) If the council consider that the proposed highway will not be of sufficient utility to the public to justify its being maintained at the public expense, they may make a complaint to a magistrates' court for an order to that effect.

(3) If the council certify that the way has been dedicated in accordance with the terms of the notice and has been made up in a satisfactory manner, and if –

  (a) the person by whom the way was dedicated or his successor keeps it in repair for a period of 12 months from the date of the council's certificate, and
  (b) the way has been used as a highway during that period,

then, unless an order has been made in relation to the highway under subsection (2) above, the highway shall, at the expiration of the period specified in paragraph (a) above, become for the purposes of this Act a highway maintainable at the public expense.

(4) If the council, on being requested by the person by whom the way was dedicated or his successor to issue a certificate under subsection (3) above, refuse to issue the certificate, that person may appeal to a magistrates' court against the refusal, and the court, if satisfied that the certificate ought to have been issued, may make an order to the effect that subsection (3) above shall apply as if the certificate had been issued on a date specified in the order.

(5) Where a certificate has been issued by a council under subsection (3) above, or an order has been made under subsection (4) above, the certificate or a copy of the order, as the case may be, shall be deposited with the proper officer of the council and may be inspected by any person free of charge at all reasonable hours.

Explanatory text – see **8.1.4, 8.2.1, 8.3.3**.

38   Power of highway authorities to adopt by agreement

(1) Subject to subsection (2) below, where any person is liable under a special enactment or by reason of tenure, enclosure or prescription to maintain a highway, the Minister, in the case of a trunk road, or a local highway authority, in any other case, may agree with that person to undertake the maintenance of that highway; and where an agreement is made under this subsection the highway to which the agreement relates shall, on such date as may be specified in the agreement, become for the purposes of this act a highway maintainable at the public expense and the liability of that person to maintain the highway shall be extinguished.

(2) A local highway authority shall not have power to make an agreement under subsection (1) above with respect to a highway with respect to which they or any other highway authority have power to make an agreement under Part V or Part XII of this Act.

[(3) A local highway authority may agree with any person to undertake the maintenance of a way –

(a) which that person is willing and has the necessary power to dedicate as a highway, or
(b) which is to be constructed by that person, or by a highway authority on his behalf, and which he proposes to dedicate as a highway;

and where an agreement is made under this subsection the way to which the agreement relates shall, on such date as may be specified in the agreement, become for the purposes of this Act a highway maintainable at the public expense.

(3A) The Minister may agree with any person to undertake the maintenance of a road –

(a) which that person is willing and has the necessary power to dedicate as a highway, or
(b) which is to be constructed by that person, or a highway authority on his behalf, and which he proposes to dedicate as a highway,

and which the Minister proposes should become a trunk road; and where an agreement is made under this subsection the road shall become for the purposes of this Act a highway maintainable at the public expense on the date on which an order comes into force under section 10 directing that the road become a trunk road or, if later, the date on which the road is opened for the purposes of through traffic.]

(4) Without prejudice to the provisions of subsection (3) above and subject to the following provisions of this section, a local highway authority may, by agreement with railway, canal or tramway undertakers, undertake to maintain as part of a highway maintainable at the public expense a bridge or viaduct which carries the railway, canal or tramway of the undertakers over such a highway or which is intended to carry such a railway, canal or tramway over such a highway and is to be constructed by those undertakers or by the highway authority on their behalf.

(5) ...

(6) An agreement under this section may contain such provisions as to the dedication as a highway of any road or way to which the agreement relates, the bearing of the expenses of the construction, maintenance or improvement of any highway, road, bridge or viaduct to which the agreement relates and other relevant matters as the authority making the agreement think fit.

Amendments – New Roads and Street Works Act 1991, s22(1); Local Government Act 1985, s 102, Sch 17.

Explanatory text – see **3.1, 8.9**.

...

Maintenance of highways maintainable at public expense

41   Duty to maintain highways maintainable at public expense

(1) The authority who are for the time being the highway authority for a highway maintainable at the public expense are under a duty, subject to subsections (2) and (4) below, to maintain the highway.

(2) An order made by the Minister under section 10 above directing that a highway proposed to be constructed by him shall become a trunk road may, as regards –

   (a) a highway to which this subsection applies which becomes a trunk road by virtue of the order, or

   (b) a part of a highway to which this subsection applies, being a part which crosses the route of the highway to be so constructed,

contain such a direction as is specified in subsection (4) below.

(3) Subsection (2) above applies to –

   (a) any highway maintainable at the public expense by a local highway authority, and

   (b) any highway other than a highway falling within paragraph (a) above or a highway maintainable under a special enactment or by reason of tenure, enclosure or prescription.

(4) The direction referred to in subsection (2) above is –

   (a) in a case where the highway or part of a highway falls within subsection (3)(a) above, a direction that, notwithstanding subsection (1) above, it shall be maintained by the highway authority for the highway until such date, not being later than the date on which the new route is opened for the purposes of through traffic, as may be specified in a notice given by the Minister to that authority; and

   (b) in a case where the highway or part of a highway falls within subsection (3)(b) above, a direction that, notwithstanding subsection (1) above, the Minister is to be under no duty to maintain it until such date as aforesaid.

(5) Where an order under section 10 above contains a direction made in pursuance of subsections (2) to (4) above, then, until the date specified in the notice given by the Minister pursuant to the direction, in accordance with subsection (4) above, the powers of a highway authority under sections 97, 98, 270 and 301 below as respects the

highway to which the direction relates are exercisable by the highway authority to whom the notice is required to be given, as well as by the Minister.

Explanatory text – see **8.6.1, 8.8.2**.

42 Power of district councils to maintain certain highways

(1) Subject to Part I of Schedule 7 to this Act, the council of a [non-metropolitan] district may undertake the maintenance of any eligible highway in the district which is a highway maintainable at the public expense.

(2) For the purposes of subsection (1) above the following are eligible highways –

(a) footpaths,
(b) bridleways, and
(c) roads (referred to in Schedule 7 to this Act as 'urban roads') which are neither trunk roads nor classified roads and which –

(i) are restricted roads for the purposes of [section 81 of the Road Traffic Regulation Act 1984] (30mph speed limit), or
(ii) are subject to an order [made by virtue of section 84(1)(a) of that Act imposing a speed limit] not exceeding 40 mph, or
(iii) are otherwise streets in an urban area.

(3) The county council who are the highway authority for a highway which is for the time being maintained by a [non-metropolitan] district council by virtue of this section shall reimburse to the district council any expenses incurred by them in carrying out on the highway works of maintenance necessary to secure that the duty to maintain the highway is performed, and Part II of Schedule 7 to this Act shall have effect for this purpose.

Amendments – Local Government Act 1985, s 8, Sch 4, Pt I, para 11; Road Traffic Regulation Act 1984, s 146, Sch 13, para 40; Road Traffic Act 1991, s 48, Sch 4, para 11.

Explanatory text – see **8.6.2**.

43 Power of parish and community councils to maintain footpaths and bridleways

(1) The council of a parish or community may undertake the maintenance of any footpath or bridleway within the parish or community which is, in either case, a highway maintainable at the public expense; but nothing in this subsection affects the duty of any highway authority or other person to maintain any such footpath or bridleway.

(2) The highway authority for any footpath or bridleway which a parish or community council have power to maintain under subsection (1) above, and a [non-metropolitan] district council for the time being maintaining any such footpath or bridleway by virtue of section 42 above, may undertake to defray the whole or part of any expenditure incurred by the parish or community council in maintaining the footpath or bridleway.

(3) The power of a parish or community council under subsection (1) above is subject to the restrictions for the time being imposed by any enactment on their expenditure,

but for the purposes of any enactment imposing such a restriction their expenditure is to be deemed not to include any expenditure falling to be defrayed by a highway authority or district council by virtue of subsection (2) above.

Amendment – Local Government Act 1985, s 8, Sch 4, Pt I, para 12.

Explanatory text – see **8.6.3**.

44 Person liable to maintain highway may agree to maintain publicly maintainable highway

Where any person is liable under a special enactment or by reason of tenure, enclosure or prescription to maintain a highway, he may enter into an agreement with the highway authority for that highway for the maintenance by him of any highway maintainable at the public expense by the highway authority; but nothing in this section affects the duty of a highway authority to maintain a highway as respects which any such agreement is made.

Explanatory text – see **8.2.2, 8.2.3, 8.2.4, 8.2.5**.

...

47 Power of magistrates' court to declare unnecessary highway to be not maintainable at public expense

(1) Where a highway authority are of opinion that a highway maintainable at the public expense by them is unnecessary for public use and therefore ought not to be maintained at the public expense, they may, subject to subsections (2) to (4) below, apply to a magistrates' court for an order declaring that the highway shall cease to be so maintained.

(2) No application shall be made under this section for an order relating to a trunk road, special road, metropolitan road, footpath or bridleway.

(3) Where a county council, as highway authority, propose to make an application under this section for an order relating to any highway [in England], they shall give notice of the proposal to the council of the district in which the highway is situated, and the application shall not be made if, within 2 months from the date of service of the notice by the county council, notice is given to the county council by the district council that the district council have refused to consent to the making of the application.

(4) If a highway authority propose to make an application under this section for an order relating to a highway situated in a parish or a community they shall give notice of the proposal –

(a) to the council of the parish or community, or
(b) in the case of a parish not having a separate parish council, to the chairman of the parish meeting,

and the application shall not be made if, within 2 months from the date of service of the notice by the highway authority, notice is given to the highway authority by the council of the parish or community or the chairman of the parish meeting, as the case may be, that the council or meeting have refused to consent to the making of the application.

(5) Where an application is made to a magistrates' court under this section, 2 or more justices of the peace acting for the petty sessions area for which the court acts shall together view the highway to which the application relates, and no further proceedings shall be taken on the application unless they are of opinion, after viewing the highway, that there was ground for making the application.

(6) The [chief executive] to the justices who view a highway in accordance with the provision of subsection (5) above shall, as soon as practicable after the view, notify the highway authority by whom an application under this section relating to the highway was made of the decision of the justices and, if the justices decide that there was ground for making the application, of the time, not being less than 6 weeks from the date of the notice, and place, at which the application is to be heard by a magistrates' court.

(7) A magistrates' court shall not hear an application under this section unless it is satisfied that the highway authority making the application have –

(a) not less than one month before the date on which the application is to be heard by the court, given notice to the owners and the occupiers of all lands adjoining the highway to which the application relates of the making of the application, and the purpose of it, and of the time and place at which the application is to be heard by the court, and

(b) given public notice in the terms and manner required by subsection (8) below.

(8) A highway authority making an application under this section shall publish, once at least in each of the 4 weeks immediately preceding the week in which the application is to be heard, in a local newspaper circulating in the area in which the highway to which the application relates is situated, a notice –

(a) stating that an application has been made to a magistrates' court under this section and the purpose of the application,

(b) describing the highway, and

(c) specifying the time and place at which the application is to be heard,

and shall cause a copy of the notice to be fixed, at least 14 days before the date on which the application is to be heard by the court, to the principal doors of every church and chapel in the parish or community in which the highway is situated, or in some conspicuous position near the highway.

(9) On the hearing of an application for an order under this section, a magistrates' court shall hear any person who objects to the order being made and may either dismiss the application or make an order declaring that the highway to which the application relates shall cease to be maintained at the public expense.

(10) Where an order is made under this section the highway to which the order relates shall cease to be a highway maintainable at the public expense.

(11) The highway authority on whose application an order is made under this section shall give notice of the making of the order to any public utility undertakers having apparatus under, in, upon, over, along or across the highway to which the order relates.

Amendment – Local Government (Wales) Act 1994, s 22(1), Sch 7, Pt I, para 5; Access to Justice Act 1999, s 90(1), Sch 13, para 118.

Explanatory text – see **8.9**.

48   Power of magistrates' court to order a highway to be again maintainable at public expense

(1) Subject to subsection (2) below, if it appears to a magistrates' court that, in consequence of any change of circumstances since the time at which an order was made under section 47 above, the highway to which the order relates has again become of public use and ought to be maintained at the public expense, the court may by order direct that the highway shall again become for the purposes of this Act a highway maintainable at the public expense.

(2) An order under this section shall not be made except on the application of a person interested in the maintenance of the highway to which the application relates, and on proof that not less than 1 month before making the application he gave notice to the highway authority for the highway of his intention to make application under this section.

Explanatory text – see **8.9**.

Maintenance of privately maintainable highways

49   Maintenance of approaches to certain privately maintainable bridges

Where a person is liable to maintain the approaches to a bridge by reason of the fact that he is liable to maintain the bridge by reason of tenure or prescription, his liability to maintain the approaches extends to 100 yards from each end of the bridge.

50   Maintenance of privately maintainable footpaths and bridleways

(1) Where apart from section 41 above a person would under a special enactment or by reason of tenure, enclosure or prescription be under an obligation to maintain a footpath or bridleway, the operation of section 41(1) does not release him from the obligation.

(2) The council of a [non-metropolitan] district, parish or community may undertake by virtue of this subsection the maintenance of any footpath or bridleway within the district, parish or community (other than a footpath or bridleway the maintenance of which they have power to undertake under section 42 or, as the case may be, section 43 above) whether or not any other person is under a duty to maintain the footpath or bridleway; but nothing in this subsection affects the duty of any other person to maintain any such footpath or bridleway.

(3) The power of a district council under subsection (2) above is subject to Part I of Schedule 7 to this Act; and the power of a parish or community council under that subsection is subject to the restrictions for the time being imposed by any enactment on their expenditure.

Amendment – Local Government Act 1985, s 8, Sch 4, Pt I, para 14.

Explanatory text – see **8.2.7, 8.6.2, 8.6.3**.

51 No liability to maintain by reason of enclosure if highway fenced with consent of highway authority

(1) If a person across whose land there is a highway maintainable at public expense erects a fence between the highway and the adjoining land, and the fence is erected with the consent of the highway authority for the highway, he does not thereby become liable to maintain the highway by reason of enclosure.

(2) Nothing in subsection (1) above is to be construed as imposing on any person a liability to maintain a highway by reason of enclosure.

Explanatory text – see 8.2.5.

. . .

53 Power of magistrates' court to extinguish liability to maintain privately maintainable highway

(1) Where a person is liable by reason of tenure, enclosure or prescription to maintain a highway, a magistrates' court may, on a complaint made either by that person or by the highway authority for the highway, make an order that the liability of that person to maintain the highway shall be extinguished, and on the extinguishment of that liability the highway, if it is not then a highway maintainable at the public expense, shall become for the purposes of this Act a highway maintainable at the public expense.

(2) Where a complaint is made to a magistrates' court under this section by a person liable as aforesaid to maintain a highway –

    (a) the highway authority for the highway have a right to be heard by the court at the hearing of the complaint, and

    (b) the court shall not make an order on the complaint unless it is satisfied that not less than 21 days before the date on which the complaint is heard by the court the complainant gave notice to the highway authority for the highway of the making of the complaint and of the time and place at which it was to be heard by the court.

(3) Where by virtue of an order under this section the liability of a person to maintain a highway is extinguished, that person is liable to pay to the highway authority for the highway such sum as may be agreed between him and that authority or, in default of agreement, as may be determined by arbitration to represent the value to him of the extinguishment of his liability.

(4) A sum payable by any person under subsection (3) above shall, at his option, be paid –

    (a) as a lump sum, or

    (b) by annual payments of such amount, and continuing for such number of years, as may be agreed between him and the highway authority or, in default of agreement, as may be determined by arbitration.

(5) Any matter which by virtue of subsection (3) or (4) above is to be determined by arbitration shall be determined by a single arbitrator appointed, in default of agreement between the parties concerned, by the Minister.

(6) Nothing in this section affects any exemption from rating under any enactment as continued by section 117 of the General Rate Act 1967.

Explanatory text – see **8.9**.

---

54   Extinguishment of liability to maintain privately maintainable highway diverted by order of magistrates' court

(1) Where a highway which a person is liable to maintain under a special enactment or by reason of tenure, enclosure or prescription is diverted in accordance with an order made under section 116 below, then –

  (a) the substituted highway becomes for the purposes of this Act a highway maintainable at the public expense, and
  (b) the person liable as aforesaid to maintain the highway so diverted is liable to pay to the highway authority for the substituted highway such sum as may be agreed between him and that authority or, in default of agreement, as may be determined by arbitration to represent the value to him of the extinguishment of his liability.

(2) A sum payable by any person under subsection (1) above shall, at his option, be paid –

  (a) as a lump sum, or
  (b) by annual payments of such amount, and continuing for such number of years, as may be agreed between him and the highway authority or, in default of agreement, as may be determined by arbitration.

(3) Any matter which by virtue of subsection (1) or (2) above is to be determined by arbitration shall be determined by a single arbitrator appointed, in default of agreement between the parties concerned, by the Minister.

Explanatory text – see **8.9**.

. . .

Enforcement of liability for maintenance

56   Proceedings for an order to repair highway

(1) A person ('the complainant') who alleges that a way or bridge –

  (a) is a highway maintainable at the public expense or a highway which a person is liable to maintain under a special enactment or by reason of tenure, enclosure or prescription, and
  (b) is out of repair,

may serve a notice on the highway authority or other person alleged to be liable to maintain the way or bridge ('the respondent') requiring the respondent to state whether he admits that the way or bridge is a highway and that he is liable to maintain it.

(2) If, within 1 month from the date of service on him of a notice under subsection (1) above, the respondent does not serve on the complainant a notice admitting both that

the way or bridge in question is a highway and that the respondent is liable to maintain it, the complainant may apply to the Crown Court for an order requiring the respondent, if the court finds that the way or brige is a highway which the respondent is liable to maintain and is out of repair, to put it in proper repair within such reasonable period as may be specified in the order.

(3) The complainant for an order under subsection (2) above shall give notice in writing of the application to the appropriate officer of the Crown Court and the notice shall specify –

   (a) the situation of the way or bridge to which the application relates,
   (b) the name of the respondent,
   (c) the part of the way or bridge which is alleged to be out of repair, and
   (d) the nature of the alleged disrepair;

and the complainant shall serve a copy of the notice on the respondent.

(4) If, within 1 month from the date of service on him of a notice under subsection (1) above, the respondent serves on the complainant a notice admitting both that the way or bridge in question is a highway and that the respondent is liable to maintain it, the complainant may, within 6 months from the date of service on him of that notice, apply to a magistrates' court for an order requiring the respondent, if the court finds that the highway is out of repair, to put it in proper repair within such reasonable period as may be specified in the order.

(5) A court in determining under this section whether a highway is out of repair shall not be required to view the highway unless it thinks fit, and any such view may be made by any 2 or more of the members of the court.

(6) If at the expiration of the period specified in an order made under subsection (2) or (4) above a magistrates' court is satisfied that the highway to which the order relates has not been put in proper repair, then, unless the court thinks fit to extend the period, it shall by order authorise the complainant (if he has not the necessary power in that behalf) to carry out such works as may be necessary to put the highway in proper repair.

(7) Any expenses which a complainant reasonably incurs in carrying out works authorised by an order under subsection (6) above are recoverable from the respondent summarily as a civil debt.

(8) Where any expenses recoverable under subsection (7) above are recovered from the respondent, then, if the respondent would have been entitled to recover from some other person the whole or part of the expenses of repairing the highway in question if he had repaired it himself, he is entitled to recover from that other person the whole or the like part, as the case may be, of the expenses recovered from him.

(9) Where an application is made under this section for an order requiring the respondent to put in proper repair a footpath or bridleway which, in either case, is a highway maintainable at the public expense and some other person is liable to maintain the footpath or bridleway under a special enactment or by reason of tenure, enclosure or prescription, that other person has a right to be heard by the court which hears the application, but only on the question whether the footpath or bridleway is in proper repair.

Explanatory text – see **8.7**.

57   Default powers of highway authorities in respect of non-repair of privately maintainable highways

(1) Where a person is liable under a special enactment or by reason of tenure, enclosure or prescription to maintain a footpath or bridleway which, in either case, is a highway maintainable at the public expense, and the highway authority for the highway repair it in the performance of their duty to maintain it, they may, subject to subsection (3) below, recover the necessary expenses of doing so from that person in any court of competent jurisdiction.

(2) Where a person is liable as aforesaid to maintain a highway other than such a footpath or bridleway as is referred to in subsection (1) above the highway authority for the highway may, if in their opinion the highway is not in proper repair, repair it and, subject to subsection (3) below, recover the necessary expenses of doing so from that person in any court of competent jurisdiction.

(3) The right of recovery conferred by the foregoing provisions of this section is not exercisable –

  (a) in a case where a highway authority repair a footpath or bridleway in obedience to an order of a court made under section 56 above, unless not less than 21 days before the date on which the application was heard by the court the authority gave notice to the person liable to maintain the path or way of the making of an application with respect to it and of the time and place at which the application was to be heard by the court (so however that there is no obligation to give notice to him under this paragraph if he was the person on whose application the order of the court was made);

  (b) in any other case, unless the highway authority, before repairing the highway, have given notice to the person liable to maintain it that the highway is not in proper repair, specifying a reasonable time within which he may repair it, and he has failed to repair it within that time.

(4) Where a highway authority exercise a right of recovery from any person under the foregoing provisions of this section, then, if that person would have been entitled to recover from some other person the whole or part of the expenses of repairing the highway if he had repaired it himself, he is entitled to recover from that other person the whole or the like part, as the case may be, of the expenses recovered from him by the highway authority.

Explanatory text – see **8.2.7**.

58   Special defence in action against a highway authority for damages for non-repair of highway

(1) In an action against a highway authority in respect of damage resulting from their failure to maintain a highway maintainable at the public expense it is a defence (without prejudice to any other defence or the application of the law relating to contributory negligence) to prove that the authority had taken such care as in all the

circumstances was reasonably required to secure that the part of the highway to which the action relates was not dangerous for traffic.

(2) For the purposes of a defence under subsection (1) above, the court shall in particular have regard to the following matters –

(a) the character of the highway, and the traffic which was reasonably to be expected to use it;
(b) the standard of maintenance appropriate for a highway of that character and used by such traffic;
(c) the state of repair in which a reasonable person would have expected to find the highway;
(d) whether the highway authority knew, or could reasonably have been expected to know, that the condition of the part of the highway to which the action relates was likely to cause danger to users of the highway;
(e) where the highway authority could not reasonably have been expected to repair that part of the highway before the cause of action arose, what warning notices of its condition had been displayed;

but for the purposes of such a defence it is not relevant to prove that the highway authority had arranged for a competent person to carry out or supervise the maintenance of the part of the highway to which the action relates unless it is also proved that the authority had given him proper instructions with regard to the maintenance of the highway and that he had carried out the instructions.

(3) This section binds the Crown.

(4) ...

Amendment – New Roads and Street Works Act 1991, s 168(2), Sch 9.

Explanatory text – see **8.8.3**.

Recovery by highway authorities etc of certain expenses incurred in maintaining highways

59   Recovery of expenses due to extraordinary traffic

(1) Subject to subsection (3) below, where it appears to the highway authority for a highway maintainable at the public expense, by a certificate of their proper officer, that having regard to the average expense of maintaining the highway or other similar highways in the neighbourhood extraordinary expenses have been or will be incurred by the authority in maintaining the highway by reason of the damage caused by excessive weight passing along the highway, or other extraordinary traffic thereon, the highway authority may recover from any person ('the operator') by or in consquence of whose order the traffic has been conducted the excess expenses.

(2) In subsection (1) above 'the excess expenses' means such expenses as may be proved to the satisfaction of the court having cognizance of the case to have been or to be likely to be incurred by the highway authority by reason of the damage arising from the extraordinary traffic; and for the purposes of that subsection the expenses incurred by a highway authority in maintaining a highway are (without prejudice to the application of this section to a by-pass provided under this Act for use in connection with a cattle-grid) to be taken to include expenses incurred by them in maintaining a cattle-grid provided for the highway under this Act.

(3) If before traffic which may cause such damage commences the operator admits liability in respect of such traffic, then –

  (a) the operator and the highway authority may agree for the payment by the operator to the highway authority of a sum by way of a composition of such liability, or
  (b) either party may require that the sum to be so paid shall be determined by arbitration;

and where a sum has been so agreed or determined the operator is liable to pay that sum to the highway authority and is not liable to proceedings for the recovery of the excess expenses under subsection (1) above.

(4) [The county court with jurisdiction to hear and determine a claim for a sum recoverable under this section is] the county court in the district in which the highway or any part of it is situated.

(5) Proceedings for the recovery of any sums under this section shall be commenced within 12 months from the time at which the damage has been done or, where the damage is the consequence of any particular building contract or work extending over a long period, not later than 6 months from the date of completion of the contract or work.

(6) In the application of this section to highways for which the Minister is the highway authority the words 'by a certificate of their proper officer' in subsection (1) are to be omitted.

Amendment – Administration of Justice Act 1982, s 37, Sch 3, Pt IV, para 8(2).

Explanatory text – see **8.5.3**.

. . .

PART V

IMPROVEMENT OF HIGHWAYS

General power of improvement

Explanatory text for Part V – see **10.4**.

---

62   General power of improvement

(1) The provisions of this Part of this Act have effect for the purpose of empowering or requiring highway authorities and other persons to improve highways.

(2) Without prejudice to the powers of improvement specifically conferred on highway authorities by the following provisions of this Part of this Act, any such authority may, subject to subsection (3) below, carry out, in relation to a highway maintainable at the public expense by them, any work (including the provision of equipment) for the improvement of the highway.

(3) Notwithstanding subsection (2) above, but without prejudice to any enactment not contained in this Part of this Act, work of any of the following descriptions shall be

carried out only under the powers specifically conferred by the following provisions of this Part of this Act, and not under this section –

(a) the division of carriageways, provision of roundabouts and variation of the relative widths of carriageways and footways;

(b) the construction of cycle tracks;

(c) the provision of subways, refuges, pillars, walls, barriers, rails, fences or posts for the use or protection of persons using a highway;

(d) the construction and reconstruction of bridges and alteration of level of highways;

(e) the planting of trees, shrubs and other vegetation and laying out of grass verges;

(f) the provision, maintenance, alteration, improvement or other dealing with cattle-grids, by-passes, gates and other works for use in connection with cattle-grids;

[(ff) the construction, maintenance and removal of road humps;]

[(fg) the construction and removal of such traffic calming works as may be specially authorised by the Secretary of State under section 90G below or prescribed by regulations made by him under section 90H below;]

(g) the execution of works for the purpose of draining a highway or of otherwise preventing surface water from flowing on to it;

(h) the provision of barriers or other works for the purpose of affording to a highway protection against hazards of nature.

(4) A highway authority may alter or remove any works executed by them under this section.

(5) . . .

Amendments – Transport Act 1981, s 32(1), Sch 10, Pt I, para 1; Traffic Calming Act 1992, s 1(1); Local Government Act 1985, s 102, Sch 17.

. . .

Dual carriageways, roundabouts and cycle tracks

. . .

65   Cycle tracks

(1) Without prejudice to section 24 above, a highway authority may, in or by the side of a highway maintainable at the public expense by them which consists of or comprises a made-up carriageway, construct a cycle track as part of the highway; and they may light any cycle track constructed by them under this section.

(2) A highway authority may alter or remove a cycle track constructed by them under this section.

Safety provisions

66   Footways and guard-rails etc for publicly maintainable highways

(1) It is the duty of a highway authority to provide in or by the side of a highway maintainable at the public expense by them which consists of or comprises a made-up carriageway, a proper and sufficient footway as part of the highway in any case where

they consider the provision of a footway as necessary or desirable for the safety or accommodation of pedestrians; and they may light any footway provided by them under this subsection.

(2) A highway authority may provide and maintain in a highway maintainable at the public expense by them which consists of or comprises a carriageway, such raised paving, pillars, walls, rails or fences as they think necessary for the purpose of safeguarding persons using the highway.

(3) A highway authority may provide and maintain in a highway maintainable at the public expense by them which consists of a footpath, such barriers, rails or fences as they think necessary for the purpose of safeguarding persons using the highway.

(4) The powers conferred by the foregoing provisions of this section to provide any works include power to alter or remove them.

(5) The power conferred by subsection (3) above, and the power to alter or remove any works provided under that subsection, shall not be exercised so as to obstruct any private access to any premises or interfere with the carrying out of agricultural operations.

(6) The powers of a highway authority under subsections (2) and (3) above may, with the consent of the Minister, be exercised by the council of a county or metropolitan district in relation to any part within the county [or metropolitan district] but outside Greater London of a highway for which the Minister is the highway authority.

(7) The powers of a highway authority under subsections (2) and (3) above may, with the consent of the highway authority, be exercised by the council of a London borough or, as the case may require, by the Common Council in relation to any part within the borough, or the City, of a highway for which the council, or the Common Council, are not the highway authority.

(8) A highway authority or council shall pay compensation to any person who sustains damage by reason of the execution by them of works under subsection (2) or (3) above.

Amendment – Local Government Act 1985, s 8, Sch 4, Pt I, para 17.

Prospective amendments – Words prospectively inserted after word 'footpath' in subs (3) by the CROW Act 2000, s 70(1)(a):

'or bridleway'.

Word prospectively inserted after word 'barriers,' in subs (3) by the CROW Act 2000, s 70(1)(b):

'posts,'

Explanatory text – see **10.3**.

. . .

71   Margins for horses and livestock

(1) It is the duty of a highway authority to provide in or by the side of a highway maintainable at the public expense by them which consists of or comprises a made-up carriageway adequate grass or other margins as part of the highway in any case where they consider the provision of margins necessary or desirable for the safety or

accommodation of ridden horses and driven livestock; and a highway authority may light a margin provided by them under this section.

(2) A highway authority may alter or remove a margin provided by them under this section.

Widths

72 Widening of highways

(1) A highway authority may widen any highway for which they are the highway authority and may for that purpose agree with a person having power in that behalf for the dedication of adjoining land as part of a highway.

(2) A council ... have the like power to enter into a public path creation agreement under section 25 above, or to make a public path creation order under section 26 above, for the purpose of securing the widening of an existing footpath or bridleway as they have for the purpose of securing the creation of a footpath or bridleway, and references in those sections to the dedication or creation of a footpath or bridleway are to be construed accordingly.

(3) The council of a parish or community have the like power to enter into an agreement under section 30 above for the purpose of securing the widening of an existing highway in the parish or community or an adjoining parish or community as they have for the purpose of securing the dedication of a highway, and references in that section to the dedication of a highway are to be construed accordingly.

Amendment – Environment Act 1995, s 120(3), Sch 24.

. . .

Levels

76 Levelling of highways

A highway authority may execute works for levelling a highway maintainable at the public expense by them.

77 Alteration of levels

(1) Without prejudice to section 76 above, a highway authority may raise or lower or otherwise alter, as they think fit, the level of a highway maintainable at the public expense by them.

(2) A highway authority shall pay compensation to any person who sustains damage by reason of the execution by them of works under this section.

. . .

Miscellaneous improvements

. . .

99 Metalling of highways

A highway authority may, in relation to a highway maintainable at the public expense by them, execute works for the conversion of the highway into a metalled highway.

100 Drainage of highways

(1) The highway authority for a highway may, for the purpose of draining it or of otherwise preventing surface water from flowing on to it, do all or any of the following –

    (a) construct or lay, in the highway or in land adjoining or lying near to the highway, such drains as they consider necessary;

    (b) erect barriers in the highway or in such land as aforesaid to divert surface water into or through any existing drain;

    (c) scour, cleanse and keep open all drains situated in the highway or in such land as aforesaid.

(2) Where under subsection (1) above a drain is constructed or laid, or barriers are erected, for the purpose of draining surface water from a highway or, as the case may, diverting it into an existing drain, the water may be discharged into or through that drain and into any inland waters, whether natural or artificial, or any tidal waters.

(3) A highway authority shall pay compensation to the owner or occupier of any land who suffers damage by reason of the exercise by the authority of any power under subsection (1) or (2) above.

(4) If a person, without the consent of the highway authority, alters, obstructs or interferes with a drain or barrier which has been constructed, laid or erected by the authority in exercise of their powers under subsection (1) above, or which is under their control, then –

    (a) the authority may carry out any work of repair or reinstatement necessitated by his action and may recover from him the expenses reasonably incurred by them in so doing, and

    (b) without prejudice to their right to exercise that power, he is guilty of an offence and liable to a fine not exceeding three times the amount of those expenses.

(5) Without prejudice to their powers under the foregoing provisions of this section, a highway authority may, for the purpose of the drainage of a highway or proposed highway for which they are or, as the case may be, will be the highway authority, exercise any powers exercisable by a [sewerage undertaker under [sections 158, 159, 163, 165 and 168 of the Water Industry Act 1991] for the purposes of the drainage of highways within the area of that undertaker].

(6) Where the highway authority are a county council they shall, before exercising any powers [under [sections 158, 159, 163, 165 and 168 of the Water Industry Act 1991]] by virtue of subsection (5) above, give notice of their intention to do so to the district council, and the [sewerage undertaker], within whose area the powers are proposed to be exercised[; and where the highway authority are a metropolitan district council they shall, before so exercising any powers under that Act, give such notice to the [sewerage undertaker] within whose area the powers are proposed to be exercised].

[(6A) In subsection (6) above, 'the district council' shall be read, in relation to Wales, as 'the Welsh council'.

(6B) Where the highway authority are a Welsh council –

    (a) subsection (6) above does not apply; but

    (b) before exercising any powers under sections 158, 159, 163, 165 and 168 of the Water Industry Act 1991 by virtue of subsection (5) above, they shall give notice of their intention to do so –

        (i)   to the sewerage undertaker; and

(ii) where they propose to exercise those powers outside the county or county borough, to the Welsh council or, as the case may be, to the district council

within whose area the powers are proposed to be exercised.]

(7) A person who is liable to maintain a highway by reason of tenure, enclosure or prescription shall, for the purpose of draining it, have the like powers as are conferred on a highway authority by subsections (1) and (2) above for that purpose, and subsections (3) and (4) above shall have effect in relation to a highway so maintainable as if references therein to a highway authority and to subsection (1) or (2) above included references to the person liable to maintain that highway and to this subsection respectively.

(8) This section is without prejudice to any enactment the purpose of which is to protect water against pollution.

(9) In this section –

'drain' includes a ditch, gutter, watercourse, soak-away, bridge, culvert, tunnel and pipe; and

'owner', in relation to any land, means a person, other than a mortgagee not in possession, who is for the time being entitled to dispose of the fee simple in the land, whether in possession or in reversion, and includes also a person holding or entitled to the rents and profits of the land under a lease the unexpired term of which exceeds 3 years.

Amendments – Water Act 1989, s 190(1), Sch 25, para 62(4); Water Consolidation (Consequential Provisions) Act 1991, s 2(1), Sch 1, para 36; Local Government Act 1985, s 8, Sch 4, Pt I, para 21; Local Government (Wales) Act 1994, s 22(1), Sch 7, Pt I, para 9.

Explanatory text – see **8.4.7**.

PART VIII

STOPPING UP AND DIVERSION OF HIGHWAYS AND STOPPING UP OF MEANS OF ACCESS TO HIGHWAYS

Stopping up and diversion of highways

116 Power of magistrates' court to authorise stopping up or diversion of highway

(1) Subject to the povisions of this section, if it appears to a magistrates' court, after a view, if the court thinks fit, by any two or more of the justices composing the court, that a highway (other than a trunk road or a special road) as respects which the [highway] authority have made an application under this section –

(a) is unnecessary, or
(b) can be diverted so as to make it nearer or more commodious to the public,

the court may by order authorise it to be stopped up or, as the case may be, to be so diverted.

(2) ...

(3) If an authority propose to make an application under this section for an order relating to any highway (other than a classified road) they shall give notice of the proposal to –

  [(a) if the highway is in a non-metropolitan district, the council of that district; and]
  [(aa) if the highway is in Wales, the Welsh council for the area in which it is situated if they are not the highway authority for it; and]
  (b) if the highway is in England, the council of the parish (if any) in which the highway is situated or, if the parish does not have a separate parish council, to the chairman of the parish meeting; and
  (c) if the highway is in Wales, the council (if any) of the community in which the highway is situated;

and the application shall not be made if within 2 months from the date of service of the notice by the authority notice is given to the authority by the district council [or Welsh council] or by the parish or community council or, as the case may be, by the chairman of the parish meeting that the council or meeting have refused to consent to the making of the application.

(4) An application under this section may be made, and an order under it may provide, for the stopping up or diversion of a highway for the purposes of all traffic, or subject to the reservation of a footpath or bridleway.

(5) An application or order under this section may include 2 or more highways which are connected with each other.

(6) A magistrates' court shall not make an order under this section unless it is satisfied that the applicant authority have given the notices required by Part I of Schedule 12 to this Act.

(7) On the hearing of an application under this section the applicant authority, any person to whom notice is required to be given under paragraph 1 of Schedule 12, any person who uses the highway and any other person who would be aggrieved by the making of the order applied for, have a right to be heard.

(8) An order under this section authorising the diversion of a highway –

  (a) shall not be made unless the written consent of every person having a legal interest in the land over which the highway is to be diverted is produced to and deposited with the court; and
  (b) except in so far as the carrying out of the diversion may necessitate temporary interference with the highway, shall not authorise the stopping up of any part of the highway until the new part to be substituted for the part to be stopped up (including, where a diversion falls to be carried out under orders of 2 different courts, any necessary continuation of the new part in the area of the other court) has been completed to the satisfaction of 2 justices of the peace acting for the same petty sessions area as the court by which the order was made and a certificate to that effect signed by them has been transmitted to the clerk of the applicant authority.

(9) Every order under this section shall have annexed to it a plan signed by the chairman of the court and shall be transmitted by the clerk of the court to the proper officer of the applicant authority, together with any written consents produced to the court under subsection (8) above.

(10) Part II of Schedule 12 to this Act applies where, in pursuance of an order under this section, a highway is stopped up or diverted and, immediately before the order is made,

there is under, in, upon, over, along or across the highway any apparatus belonging to or used by any statutory undertakers for the purpose of their undertaking.

[(11) In this section 'statutory undertakers' includes operators of driver information systems.]

Amendments – Local Government Act 1985, ss 8, 102, Sch 4, Pt I, para 24, Sch 17; Road Traffic (Driver Licensing and Information Systems) Act 1989, s 13(1), Sch 4, para 3(1), (3); Local Government (Wales) Act 1994, s 22(1), Sch 7, Pt I, para 11.

Prospective amendment – Words 'or bridleway' in subs (4) prospectively substituted by the CROW Act 2000, s 51, Sch 5, para 15:

'‚ bridleway or restricted byway'

Explanatory text – see **4.4**.

117 Application for order under section 116 on behalf of another person

A person who desires a highway to be stopped up or diverted but is not authorised to make an application for that purpose under section 116 above may request the highway authority ... to make such an application; and if the authority grant the request they may, as a condition of making the application, require him to make such provision for any costs to be incurred by them in connection with the matter as they deem reasonable.

Amendment – Local Government Act 1985, s 102, Sch 17.

Explanatory text – see **4.4.4**.

118 Stopping up of footpaths and bridleways

(1) Where it appears to a council as respects a footpath or bridleway in their area (other than one which is a trunk road or a special road) that it is expedient that the path or way should be stopped up on the ground that it is not needed for public use, the council may by order made by them and submitted to and confirmed by the Secretary of State, or confirmed as an unopposed order, extinguish the public right of way over the path or way.

An order under this section is referred to in this Act as a 'public path extinguishment order'.

(2) The Secretary of State shall not confirm a public path extinguishment order, and a council shall not confirm such an order as an unopposed order, unless he or, as the case may be, they are satisfied that it is expedient so to do having regard to the extent (if any) to which it appears to him or, as the case may be, them that the path or way would, apart from the order, be likely to be used by the public, and having regard to the effect which the extinguishment of the right of way would have as respects land served by the path or way, account being taken of the provisions as to compensation contained in section 28 above as applied by section 121(2) below.

(3) A public path extinguishment order shall be in such form as may be prescribed by regulations made by the Secretary of State and shall contain a map, on such scale as may

be so prescribed, defining the land over which the public right of way is thereby extinguished.

(4) Schedule 6 to this Act has effect as to the making, confirmation, validity and date of operation of public path extinguishment orders.

(5) Where, in accordance with regulations made under paragraph 3 of the said Schedule 6, proceedings preliminary to the confirmation of the public path extinguishment order are taken concurrently with proceedings preliminary to the confirmation of a public path creation order[, public path diversion order or rail crossing diversion order] then, in considering –

(a) under subsection (1) above whether the path or way to which the public path extinguishment order relates is needed for public use, or
(b) under subsection (2) above to what extent (if any) that path or way would apart from the order be likely to be used by the public,

the council or the Secretary of State, as the case may be, may have regard to the extent to which the public path creation order, public path diversion order or rail crossing diversion order would provide an alternative path or way.

(6) For the purposes of subsections (1) and (2) above, any temporary circumstances preventing or diminishing the use of a path or way by the public shall be disregarded.

(7) . . .

Amendments – Transport and Works Act, s 47(1), Sch 2, paras 1, 2(1), (2); Environment Act 1995, s 120(3), Sch 24.

Prospective amendments – Subsection prospectively inserted after subs (6) by the CROW Act 2000, s 57, Sch 6, Pt I, para 6:

'(6A) The considerations to which –

(a) the Secretary of State is to have regard in determining whether or not to confirm a public path extinguishment order, and
(b) a council are to have regard in determining whether or not to confirm such an order as an unopposed order,

include any material provision of a rights of way improvement plan prepared by any local highway authority whose area includes land over which the order would extinguish a public right of way.'

Section prospectively inserted after section 118 by the CROW Act 2000, s 57, Sch 6, Pt I, para 7:

'118ZA   Application for a public path extinguishment order

(1) The owner, lessee or occupier of any land used for agriculture, forestry or the breeding or keeping of horses may apply to a council for the area in which the land is situated for the making of a public path extinguishment order in relation to any footpath or bridleway which crosses the land.

(2) An application under this section shall be in such form as may be prescribed and shall be accompanied by a map, on such scale as may be prescribed, showing the land over which it is proposed that the public right of way should be extinguished, and by such other information as may be prescribed.

(3) Regulations may provide –

(a) that a prescribed charge is payable on the making of an application under this section, and
(b) that further prescribed charges are payable by the applicant if the council make a public path extinguishment order on the application.

(4) An application under this section is not to be taken to be received by the council until the requirements of regulations under section 121A below have been satisfied in relation to it.

(5) A council which receives an application under this section shall determine the application as soon as reasonably practicable.

(6) Before determining to make a public path extinguishment order on an application under this section, the council may require the applicant to enter into an agreement with them to defray, or to make such contribution as may be specified in the agreement towards, any compensation which may become payable under section 28 above as applied by section 121(2) below.

(7) Where –

(a) an application under this section has been made to a council, and
(b) the council have not determined the application within four months of receiving it,

the Secretary of State may, at the request of the applicant and after consulting the council, by direction require the council to determine the application before the end of such period as may be specified in the direction.

(8) As soon as practicable after determining an application under this section, the council shall –

(a) give to the applicant notice in writing of their decision and the reasons for it, and
(b) give a copy of the notice to such other persons as may be prescribed.

(9) The council to whom an application under this section has been made may make a public path extinguishment order on the application only if the land over which the public right of way is to be extinguished by the order is that shown for the purposes of subsection (2) above on the map accompanying the application.

(10) Any reference in this Act to the map accompanying an application under this section includes a reference to any revised map submitted by the applicant in prescribed circumstances in substitution for that map.

(11) This section has effect subject to the provisions of sections 121A and 121C below.

(12) In this section –

"prescribed" means prescribed by regulations;

"regulations" means regulations made by the Secretary of State.'

[118A   Stopping up of footpaths and bridleways crossing railways

(1) This section applies where it appears to a council expedient in the interests of the safety of members of the public using it or likely to use it that a footpath or bridleway in their area which crosses a railway, otherwise than by tunnel or bridge, should be stopped up.

(2) Where this section applies, the council may by order made by them and submitted to and confirmed by the Secretary of State, or confirmed as an unopposed order, extinguish the public right of way over the path or way –

(a) on the crossing itself, and
(b) for so much of its length as they deem expedient from the crossing to its intersection with another highway over which there subsists a like right of way (whether or not other rights of way also subsist over it).

(3) An order under this section is referred to in this Act as a 'rail crossing extinguishment order'.

(4) The Secretary of State shall not confirm a rail crossing extinguishment order, and a council shall not confirm such an order as an unopposed order, unless he or, as the case may be, they are satisfied that it is expedient to do so having regard to all the circumstances, and in particular to –

    (a) whether it is reasonably practicable to make the crossing safe for use by the public, and

    (b) what arrangements have been made for ensuring that, if the order is confirmed, any appropriate barriers and signs are erected and maintained.

(5) Before determining to make a rail crossing extinguishment order on the representations of the operator of the railway crossed by the path or way, the council may require him to enter into an agreement with them to defray, or to make such contribution as may be specified in the agreement towards, any expenses which the council may incur in connection with the erection or maintenance of barriers and signs.

(6) A rail crossing extinguishment order shall be in such form as may be prescribed by regulations made by the Secretary of State and shall contain a map, on such scale as may be so prescribed, defining the land over which the public right of way is thereby extinguished.

(7) Schedule 6 to this Act has effect as to the making, confirmation, validity and date of operation of rail crossing extinguishment orders.

(8) In this section –

    'operator', in relation to a railway, means any person carrying on an undertaking which includes maintaining the permanent way;

    'railway' includes tramway but does not include any part of a system where rails are laid along a carriageway.]

Amendment – Inserted by Transport and Works Act 1992, s 47(1), Sch 2, paras 1, 3.

Prospective amendments – Sections prospectively inserted after section 118A by the CROW Act 2000, s 57, Sch 6, Pt I, para 8:

'118B   Stopping up of certain highways for purposes of crime prevention, etc

(1) This section applies where it appears to a council –

    (a) that, as respects any relevant highway for which they are the highway authority and which is in an area designated by the Secretary of State by order for the purposes of this section, the conditions in subsection (3) below are satisfied and it is expedient, for the purpose of preventing or reducing crime which would otherwise disrupt the life of the community, that the highway should be stopped up, or

    (b) that, as respects any relevant highway for which they are the highway authority and which crosses land occupied for the purposes of a school, it is expedient, for the purpose of protecting the pupils or staff from –

        (i) violence or the threat of violence,

        (ii) harassment,

        (iii) alarm or distress arising from unlawful activity, or

        (iv) any other risk to their health or safety arising from such activity,

that the highway should be stopped up.

(2) In subsection (1) above "relevant highway" means –

    (a) any footpath, bridleway or restricted byway,

(b) any highway which is shown in a definitive map and statement as a footpath, a bridleway, or a restricted byway, but over which the public have a right of way for vehicular and all other kinds of traffic, or

(c) any highway which is shown in a definitive map and statement as a byway open to all traffic,

but does not include a highway that is a trunk road or a special road.

(3) The conditions referred to in subsection (1)(a) above are –

(a) that premises adjoining or adjacent to the highway are affected by high levels of crime, and

(b) that the existence of the highway is facilitating the persistent commission of criminal offences.

(4) Where this section applies, the council may by order made by them and submitted to and confirmed by the Secretary of State, or confirmed as an unopposed order, extinguish the public right of way over the highway.

(5) An order under subsection (4) above is in this Act referred to as a "special extinguishment order".

(6) Before making a special extinguishment order, the council shall consult the police authority for the area in which the highway lies.

(7) The Secretary of State shall not confirm a special extinguishment order made by virtue of subsection (1)(a) above, and a council shall not confirm such an order as an unopposed order, unless he or, as the case may be, they are satisfied that the conditions in subsection (3) above are satisfied, that the stopping up of the highway is expedient as mentioned in subsection (1)(a) above and that it is expedient to confirm the order having regard to all the circumstances, and in particular to –

(a) whether and, if so, to what extent the order is consistent with any strategy for the reduction of crime and disorder prepared under section 6 of the Crime and Disorder Act 1998,

(b) the availability of a reasonably convenient alternative route or, if no reasonably convenient alternative route is available, whether it would be reasonably practicable to divert the highway under section 119B below rather than stopping it up, and

(c) the effect which the extinguishment of the right of way would have as respects land served by the highway, account being taken of the provisions as to compensation contained in section 28 above as applied by section 121(2) below.

(8) The Secretary of State shall not confirm a special extinguishment order made by virtue of subsection (1)(b) above, and a council shall not confirm such an order as an unopposed order unless he or, as the case may be, they are satisfied that the stopping up of the highway is expedient as mentioned in subsection (1)(b) above and that it is expedient to confirm the order having regard to all the circumstances, and in particular to –

(a) any other measures that have been or could be taken for improving or maintaining the security of the school,

(b) whether it is likely that the coming into operation of the order will result in a substantial improvement in that security,

(c) the availability of a reasonably convenient alternative route or, if no reasonably convenient alternative route is available, whether it would be reasonably practicable to divert the highway under section 119B below rather than stopping it up, and

(d) the effect which the extinguishment of the right of way would have as respects land served by the highway, account being taken of the provisions as to compensation contained in section 28 above as applied by section 121(2) below.

(9) A special extinguishment order shall be in such form as may be prescribed by regulations made by the Secretary of State and shall contain a map, on such scale as may be prescribed, defining the land over which the public right of way is thereby extinguished.

(10) Schedule 6 to this Act has effect as to the making, confirmation, validity and date of operation of special extinguishment orders.

118C   Application by proprietor of school for special extinguishment order

(1) The proprietor of a school may apply to a council for the making by virtue of section 118B(1)(b) above of a special extinguishment order in relation to any highway for which the council are the highway authority and which –

    (a) crosses land occupied for the purposes of the school, and
    (b) is a relevant highway as defined by section 118B(2) above.

(2) Subsections (2) to (11) of section 118ZA above shall apply to applications under this section as they apply to applications under that section, with the substitution for references to a public path extinguishment order of references to a special extinguishment order; and regulations made under that section by virtue of this subsection may make different provision for the purposes of this section and for the purposes of that section.'.

Explanatory text – see **4.5**.

---

119   Diversion of footpaths and bridleways

(1) [Where it appears to a council as respects a footpath or bridleway in their area (other than one that is a trunk road or a special road) that, in the interests of the owner, lessee or occupier of land crossed by the path or way or of the public, it is expedient that the line of the path or way, or part of that line, should be diverted (whether on to land of the same or] of another owner, lessee or occupier), the council may, subject to subsection (2) below, by order made by them and submitted to and confirmed by the Secretary of State, or confirmed as an unopposed order, –

    (a) create, as from such date as may be specified in the order, any such new footpath or bridleway as appears to the council requisite for effecting the diversion, and
    (b) extinguish, as from such date as may be so specified in accordance with the provisions of subsection (3) below, the public right of way over so much of the path or way as appears to the council requisite as aforesaid.

An order under this section is referred to in this Act as a 'public path diversion order'.

(2) A public path diversion order shall not alter a point of termination of the path or way –

    (a) if that point is not on a highway, or
    (b) (where it is on a highway) otherwise than to another point which is on the same highway, or a highway connected with it, and which is substantially as convenient to the public.

(3) Where it appears to the council that work requires to be done to provide necessary facilities for the convenient exercise of any such new public right of way as is mentioned in subsection (1)(a) above, the date specified under subsection (1)(b) above shall be later than the date specified under subsection (1)(a) by such time as appears to the council requisite for enabling the work to be carried out.

(4) A right of way created by a public path diversion order may be either unconditional or (whether or not the right of way extinguished by the order was subject to limitations or conditions of any description) subject to such limitations or conditions as may be specified in the order.

(5) Before determining to make a public path diversion order [on the representations of an owner, lessee or occupier of land crossed by the path or way, the council may require him] to enter into an agreement with them to defray, or to make such contribution as may be specified in the agreement towards, –

(a) any compensation which may become payable under section 28 above as applied by section 121(2) below, or

(b) where the council are the highway authority for the path or way in question, any expenses which they may incur in bringing the new site of the path or way into fit condition for use for the public, or

(c) where the council are not the highway authority, any expenses which may become recoverable from them by the highway authority under the provisions of section 27(2) above as applied by subsection (9) below.

(6) The Secretary of State shall not confirm a public path diversion order, and a council shall not confirm such an order as an unopposed order, unless he or, as the case may be, they are satisfied that the diversion to be effected by it is expedient as mentioned in subsection (1) above, and further that the path or way will not be substantially less convenient to the public in consequence of the diversion and that it is expedient to confirm the order having regard to the effect which –

(a) the diversion would have on public enjoyment of the path or way as a whole,

(b) the coming into operation of the order would have as respects other land served by the existing public right of way, and

(c) any new public right of way created by the order would have as respects the land over which the right is so created and any land held with it,

so, however, that for the purposes of paragraphs (b) and (c) above the Secretary of State or, as the case may be, the council shall take into account the provisions as to compensation referred to in subsection (5)(a) above.

(7) A public path diversion order shall be in such form as may be prescribed by regulations made by the Secretary of State and shall contain a map, on such scale as may be so prescribed, –

(a) showing the existing site of so much of the line of the path or way as is to be diverted by the order and the new site to which it is to be diverted,

(b) indicating whether a new right of way is created by the order over the whole of the new site or whether some part of it is already comprised in a footpath or bridleway, and

(c) where some part of the new site is already so comprised, defining that part.

(8) Schedule 6 to this Act has effect as to the making, confirmation, validity and date of operation of public path diversion orders.

(9) Section 27 above (making up of new footpaths and bridleways) applies to a footpath or bridleway created by a public path diversion order with the substitution, for references to a public path creation order, of references to a public path diversion order and, for references to section 26(2) above, of references to section 120(3) below.

Amendment – Wildlife and Countryside Act 1981, s 63, Sch 16, para 5.

Prospective amendments – Words 'so specified' in subs (1)(b) prospectively substituted by the CROW Act 2000, s 47, Sch 6, Pt I, para 9(1), (2):

'specified in the order or determined'.

Subs (3) prospectively substituted by the CROW Act 2000, s57, Sch6, PtI, para9(1), (3):

'(3) Where it appears to the council that work requires to be done to bring the new site of the footpath or bridleway into a fit condition for use by the public, the council shall –

(a) specify a date under subsection (1)(a) above, and

(b) provide that so much of the order as extinguishes (in accordance with subsection (1)(b) above) a public right of way is not to come into force until the local highway authority for the new path or way certify that the work has been carried out.'

Words prospectively inserted after words 'diversion order' in subs (5) by Countryside and Rights of Way Act 2000, s 57, Sch 6. Pt I, para 9(1), (4)(a):

'on an application under section 119ZA below or'.

Word 'him' in subs (5) prospectively substituted by Countryside and Rights of Way Act 2000, s 57, Sch 6, Pt I, para 9(1), (4)(b):

'the person who made the application or representations'.

Subsection prospectively inserted after subs (6) by Countryside and Rights of Way Act 2000, s 57, Sch 6, Pt I, para 9(1), (5):

'(6A) The considerations to which –

(a) the Secretary of State is to have regard in determining whether or not to confirm a public path diversion order, and

(b) a council are to have regard in determining whether or not to confirm such an order as an unopposed order,

include any material provision of a rights of way improvement plan prepared by any local highway authority whose area includes land over which the order would create or extinguish a public right of way.'

Section prospectively inserted after section 119 by Countryside and Rights of Way Act 2000, s 57, Sch 6, Pt I, para 10:

'119ZA　Application for a public path diversion order

(1) Subject to subsection (2) below, the owner, lessee or occupier of any land used for agriculture, forestry or the breeding or keeping of horses may apply to a council for the area in which the land is situated for the making of a public path diversion order in relation to any footpath or bridleway which crosses the land, on the ground that in his interests it is expedient that the order should be made.

(2) No application may be made under this section for an order which would create a new footpath or bridleway communicating with –

(a) a classified road,

(b) a special road,

(c) a GLA road, or

(d) any highway not falling within paragraph (a) or (b) above for which the Minister is the highway authority,

unless the application is made with the consent of the highway authority for the way falling within paragraph (a), (b), (c) or (d) above.

(3) No application under this section may propose the creation of a new right of way over land covered by works used by any statutory undertakers for the purposes of their undertaking or the curtilage of such land, unless the application is made with the consent of the statutory undertakers; and in this subsection "statutory undertakers" and "statutory undertaking" have the same meaning as in Schedule 6 to this Act.

(4) An application under this section shall be in such form as may be prescribed and shall be accompanied by a map, on such scale as may be prescribed –

(a) showing the existing site of so much of the line of the path or way as it is proposed to divert and the new site to which it is proposed to be diverted,

    (b) indicating whether it is proposed to create a new right of way over the whole of the new site or whether some of it is already comprised in a footpath or bridleway, and

    (c) where some part of the new site is already so comprised, defining that part,

and by such other information as may be prescribed.

(5) Regulations may provide –

    (a) that a prescribed charge is payable on the making of an application under this section, and

    (b) that further prescribed charges are payable by the applicant if the council make a public path diversion order on the application.

(6) An application under this section is not to be taken to be received by the council until the requirements of regulations under section 121A below have been satisfied in relation to it.

(7) A council which receives an application under this section shall determine the application as soon as reasonably practicable.

(8) Where –

    (a) an application under this section has been made to a council, and

    (b) the council have not determined the application within four months of receiving it,

the Secretary of State may, at the request of the applicant and after consulting the council, by direction require the council to determine the application before the end of such period as may be specified in the direction.

(9) As soon as practicable after determining an application under this section, the council shall –

    (a) give to the applicant notice in writing of their decision and the reasons for it, and

    (b) give a copy of the notice to such other persons as may be prescribed.

(10) The council to whom an application under this section has been made may make a public path diversion order on the application only if –

    (a) the land over which the public right of way is to be extinguished by the order, and

    (b) the new site to which the path or way is to be diverted,

are those shown for the purposes of subsection (4) above on the map accompanying the application.

(11) Any reference in this Act to the map accompanying an application under this section includes a reference to any revised map submitted by the applicant in prescribed circumstances in substitution for that map.

(12) This section has effect subject to the provisions of section 121A and 121C below.

(13) In this section –

"prescribed" means prescribed by regulations;

"regulations" means regulations made by the Secretary of State.'

[119A Diversion of footpaths and bridleways crossing railways

(1) This section applies where it appears to a council expedient in the interests of the safety of members of the public using it or likely to use it that a footpath or bridleway in their area which crosses a railway, otherwise than by tunnel or bridge, should be diverted (whether on to land of the same or of another owner, lessee or occupier).

(2) Where this section applies, the council may by order made by them and submitted to and confirmed by the Secretary of State, or confirmed as an unopposed order –

   (a) create, as from such date as may be specified in the order, any such new path or way as appears to the council requisite for effecting the diversion, and

   (b) extinguish, as from such date as may be so specified, the public right of way over the crossing and over so much of the path or way of which the crossing forms part as appears to the council requisite as aforesaid.

(3) An order under this section is referred to in this Act as a 'rail crossing diversion order'.

(4) The Secretary of State shall not confirm a rail crossing diversion order, and a council shall not confirm such an order as an unopposed order, unless he or, as the case may be, they are satisfied that it is expedient to do so having regard to all the circumstances, and in particular to –

   (a) whether it is reasonably practicable to make the crossing safe for use by the public, and

   (b) what arrangements have been made for ensuring that, if the order is confirmed, any appropriate barriers and signs are erected and maintained.

(5) A rail crossing diversion order shall not alter a point of termination of a path or way diverted under the order –

   (a) if that point is not on a highway over which there subsists a like right of way (whether or not other rights of way also subsist over it), or

   (b) (where it is on such a highway) otherwise than to another point which is on the same highway, or another such highway connected with it.

(6) A rail crossing diversion order may make provision requiring the operator of the railway to maintain all or part of the footpath or bridleway created by the order.

(7) Where it appears to the council that work requires to be done to provide necessary facilities for the convenient exercise of any such new right of way as is mentioned in subsection (2)(a) above, the date specified under subsection (2)(b) shall be later than the date specified under subsection (2)(a) by such time as appears to the council requisite for enabling the work to be carried out.

(8) Before determining to make a rail crossing diversion order on the representations of the operator of the railway crossed by the path or way the council may require him to enter into an agreement with them to defray, or make such contribution as may be specified in the agreement towards, –

   (a) any compensation which may become payable under section 28 above as applied by section 121(2) below;

   (b) any expenses which the council may incur in connection with the erection or maintenance of barriers and signs;

   (c) where the council are the highway authority for the path or way in question, any expenses which they may incur in bringing the new site of the path or way into fit condition for use by the public;

   (d) where the council are not the highway authority, any expense which may become recoverable from them by the highway authority under the provisions of section 27(2) above as applied by subsection (11) below.

(9) A rail crossing diversion order shall be in such form as may be prescribed by regulations made by the Secretary of State and shall contain a map, on such scale as may be so prescribed –

(a) showing the existing site of so much of the line of the path or way as is to be diverted by the order and the new site to which it is to be diverted,

(b) indicating whether a new right of way is created by the order over the whole of the new site or whether some part of it is already comprised in a footpath or bridleway, and

(c) where some part of the new site is already so comprised, defining that part.

(10) Schedule 6 to this Act has effect as to the making, confirmation, validity and date of operation of rail crossing diversion orders.

(11) Section 27 above (making up of new footpaths and bridleways) applies to a footpath or bridleway created by a rail crossing diversion order with the substitution, for references to a public path creation order, of references to a rail crossing diversion order and, for references to section 26(2) above, of references to section 120(3) below.

(12) In this section and in section 120 below –

'operator', in relation to a railway, means any person carrying on an undertaking which includes maintaining the permanent way;

'railway' includes tramway but does not include any part of a system where rails are laid along a carriageway.]

Amendment – Inserted by Transport and Works Act 1992, s 47(1), Sch 2, paras 1, 4.

Prospective amendment – Words 'so specified' in subs (2)(b) prospectively substituted by the CROW Act 2000, s 57, Sch 6, Pt I, para 11(1), (2):

'specified in the order or determined under subsection (7) below'.

Subsection (7) prospectively substituted by Countryside and Rights of Way Act 2000, s 57, Sch 6, Pt I, para 11(1), (3):

'(7) Where it appears to the council that work requires to be done to bring the new site of the footpath or bridleway into a fit condition for use by the public, the council shall –

(a) specify a date under subsection (2)(a) above, and

(b) provide that so much of the order as extinguishes (in accordance with subsection (2)(b) above) a public right of way is not to come into force until the local highway authority for the new path or way certify that the work has been carried out.'

Sections prospectively inserted after section 119A by Countryside and Rights of Way Act 2000, s 57, Sch 6, Pt I, para 12:

'119B Diversion of certain highways for purposes of crime prevention, etc

(1) This section applies where it appears to a council –

(a) that, as respects any relevant highway for which they are the highway authority and which is in an area designated by the Secretary of State by order under section 118B(1)(a) above, the conditions in subsection (3) below are satisfied and it is expedient, for the purpose of preventing or reducing crime which would otherwise disrupt the life of the community, that the line of the highway, or part of that line should be diverted (whether on to land of the same or another owner, lessee or occupier), or

(b) that, as respects any relevant highway for which they are the highway authority and which crosses land occupied for the purposes of a school, it is expedient, for the purpose of protecting the pupils or staff from –

(i) violence or the threat of violence,

(ii) harassment,

    (iii) alarm or distress arising from unlawful activity, or

    (iv) any other risk to their health or safety arising from such activity,

that the line of the highway, or part of that line, should be diverted (whether on to land of the same or another owner, lessee or occupier).

(2) In subsection (1) above "relevant highway" means –

    (a) any footpath, bridleway or restricted byway,

    (b) any highway which is shown in a definitive map and statement as a footpath, a bridleway, or a restricted byway, but over which the public have a right of way for vehicular and all other kinds of traffic, or

    (c) any highway which is shown in a definitive map and statement as a byway open to all traffic,

but does not include a highway that is a trunk road or a special road.

(3) The conditions referred to in subsection (1)(a) above are –

    (a) that premises adjoining or adjacent to the highway are affected by high levels of crime, and

    (b) that the existence of the highway is facilitating the persistent commission of criminal offences.

(4) Where this section applies, the council may by order made by them and submitted to and confirmed by the Secretary of State, or confirmed as an unopposed order –

    (a) create, as from such date as may be specified in the order, any such – (i) new footpath, bridleway or restricted byway, or (ii) in a case falling within subsection (2)(b) or (c) above, new highway over which the public have a right of way for vehicular and all other kinds of traffic, as appears to the council requisite for effecting the diversion, and

    (b) extinguish, as from such date as may be specified in the order or determined in accordance with the provisions of subsection (8) below, the public right of way over so much of the highway as appears to the council to be requisite for the purpose mentioned in paragraph (a) or (b) of subsection (1) above.

(5) An order under subsection (4) above is in this Act referred to as a "special diversion order".

(6) Before making a special diversion order, the council shall consult the police authority for the area in which the highway is situated.

(7) A special diversion order shall not alter a point of termination of the highway –

    (a) if that point is not on a highway, or

    (b) (where it is on a highway) otherwise than to another point which is on the same highway, or a highway connected with it.

(8) Where it appears to the council that work requires to be done to bring the new site of the highway into a fit condition for use by the public, the council shall –

    (a) specify a date under subsection (4)(a) above, and

    (b) provide that so much of the order as extinguishes (in accordance with subsection (4)(b) above) a public right of way is not to come into force until the local highway authority for the new highway certify that the work has been carried out.

(9) A right of way created by a special diversion order may be either unconditional or (whether or not the right of way extinguished by the order was subject to limitations or conditions of any description) subject to such limitations or conditions as may be specified in the order.

(10) The Secretary of State shall not confirm a special diversion order made by virtue of subsection (1)(a) above, and a council shall not confirm such an order as an unopposed order unless he or, as the case may be, they are satisfied that the conditions in subsection (3) above are satisfied, that the diversion of the highway is expedient as mentioned in subsection (1)(a) above and that it is expedient to confirm the order having regard to all the circumstances, and in particular to –

(a) whether and, if so, to what extent the order is consistent with any strategy for the reduction of crime and disorder prepared under section 6 of the Crime and Disorder Act 1998,

(b) the effect which the coming into operation of the order would have as respects land served by the existing public right of way, and

(c) the effect which any new public right of way created by the order would have as respects the land over which the right is so created and any land held with it,

so, however, that for the purposes of paragraphs (b) and (c) above the Secretary of State or, as the case may be, the council shall take into account the provisions as to compensation contained in section 28 above as applied by section 121(2) below.

(11) The Secretary of State shall not confirm a special diversion order made by virtue of subsection (1)(b) above, and a council shall not confirm such an order as an unopposed order unless he or, as the case may be, they are satisfied that the diversion of the highway is expedient as mentioned in subsection (1)(b) above and that it is expedient to confirm the order having regard to all the circumstances, and in particular to –

(a) any other measures that have been or could be taken for improving or maintaining the security of the school,

(b) whether it is likely that the coming into operation of the order will result in a substantial improvement in that security,

(c) the effect which the coming into operation of the order would have as respects land served by the existing public right of way, and

(d) the effect which any new public right of way created by the order would have as respects the land over which the right is so created and any land held with it,

so, however, that for the purposes of paragraphs (c) and (d) above the Secretary of State or, as the case may be, the council shall take into account the provisions as to compensation contained in section 28 above as applied by section 121(2) below.

(12) A special diversion order shall be in such form as may be prescribed by regulations made by the Secretary of State and shall contain a map, on such scale as may be so prescribed –

(a) showing the existing site or so much of the line of the highway as is to be diverted by the order and the new site to which it is to be diverted,

(b) indicating whether a new right of way is created by the order over the whole of the new site or whether some part of it is already comprised in a highway, and

(c) where some part of the new site is already so comprised, defining that part.

(13) Schedule 6 to this Act has effect as to the making, confirmation, validity and date of operation of special diversion orders.

(14) Section 27 above (making up of new footpaths and bridleways) applies to a highway created by a special diversion order with the substitution –

(a) for references to a footpath or bridleway of references to a footpath, a bridleway, a restricted byway or a highway over which the public have a right of way for vehicular and all other kinds of traffic,

(b) for references to a public path creation order of references to a special diversion order, and

(c) for references to section 26(2) above of references to section 120(3) below.

(15) Neither section 27 nor section 36 above is to be regarded as obliging a highway authority to provide on any highway created by a special diversion order a metalled carriage-way.

119C   Application by proprietor of school for special diversion order

(1) The proprietor of a school may apply to a council for the making by virtue of section 119B(1)(b) above of a special diversion order in relation to any highway for which the council are the highway authority and which –

(a) crosses land occupied for the purposes of the school, and

(b) is a relevant highway as defined by section 119B(2) above.

(2) No application may be made under this section for an order which would create a new highway communicating with –

(a) a classified road,
(b) a special road,
(c) a GLA road, or
(d) any highway not falling within paragraph (a) or (b) above for which the Minister is the highway authority,

unless the application is made with the consent of the highway authority for the way falling within paragraph (a), (b), (c) or (d) above.

(3) Before determining to make a special diversion order on an application under this section, the council may require the applicant to enter into an agreement with them to defray, or to make such contribution as may be specified in the agreement towards –

(a) any compensation which may become payable under section 28 above as applied by section 121(2) below, or
(b) to the extent that the council are the highway authority for the highway in question, any expenses which they may incur in bringing the new site of the highway into fit condition for use by the public, or
(c) to the extent that the council are not the highway authority, any expensess which may become recoverable from them by the highway authority under the provisions of section 27(2) above as applied by section 119B(14) above.

(4) Subsections (3) to (12) of section 119ZA above shall apply to applications under this section as they apply to applications under that section, with the substitution –

(a) for references to a public path diversion order of references to a special diversion order, and
(b) for references to a footpath or bridleway of references to a highway,

and regulations made under that section by virtue of this subsection may make different provision for the purposes of this section and for the purposes of that section.

119D   Diversion of certain highways for protection of sites of special scientific interest

(1) Subsection (3) below applies where, on an application made in accordance with this section by the appropriate conservation body, it appears to a council, as respects any relevant highway for which they are the highway authority and which is in, forms part of, or is adjacent to or contiguous with, a site of special scientific interest –

(a) that public use of the highway is causing, or that continued public use of the highway is likely to cause, significant damage to the flora, fauna or geological or physiographical features by reason of which the site of special scientific interest is of special interest, and
(b) that it is expedient that the line of the highway, or part of that line should be diverted (whether on to land of the same or another owner, lessee or occupier) for the purpose of preventing such damage.

(2) In subsection (1) "relevant highway" means –

(a) a footpath, bridleway or restricted byway,
(b) a highway which is shown in a definitive map and statement as a footpath, a bridleway or a restricted byway but over which the public have a right of way for vehicular and all other kinds of traffic, or
(c) any highway which is shown in a definitive map and statement as a byway open to all traffic,

but does not include any highway that is a trunk road or special road.

(3) Where this subsection applies, the council may, by order made by them and submitted to and confirmed by the Secretary of State, or confirmed as an unopposed order, –

(a) create, as from such date as may be specified in the order, any such – (i) new footpath, bridleway or restricted byway, or (ii) in a case falling within subsection (2)(b) or (c) above, new highway over which the public have a right of way for vehicular and all other kinds of traffic, as appears to the council requisite for effecting the diversion, and

(b) extinguish, as from such date as may be specified in the order or determined in accordance with the provisions of subsection (6) below, the public right of way over so much of the way as appears to the council to be requisite for the purpose mentioned in subsection (1)(b) above.

(4) An order under this section is referred to in this Act as an "SSSI diversion order".

(5) An SSSI diversion order shall not alter a point of termination of the highway –

(a) if that point is not on a highway, or

(b) (where it is on a highway) otherwise than to another point which is on the same highway, or a highway connected with it.

(6) Where it appears to the council that work requires to be done to bring the new site of the highway into a fit condition for use by the public, the council shall –

(a) specify a date under subsection (3)(a) above, and

(b) provide that so much of the order as extinguishes (in accordance with subsection (3)(b) above) a public right of way is not to come into force until the local highway authority for the new highway certify that the work has been carried out.

(7) A right of way created by an SSSI diversion order may be either unconditional or (whether or not the right of way extinguished by the order was subject to limitations or conditions of any description) subject to such limitations or conditions as may be specified in the order.

(8) Before determining to make an SSSI diversion order, the council may require the appropriate conservation body to enter into an agreement with them to defray, or to make such contribution as may be specified in the agreement towards, –

(a) any compensation which may become payable under section 28 above as applied by section 121(2) below,

(b) to the extent that the council are the highway authority for the highway, any expenses which they may incur in bringing the new site of the highway into fit condition for use for the public, or

(c) to the extent that the council are not the highway authority, any expenses which may become recoverable from them by the highway authority under the provisions of section 27(2) above as applied by section 119E(6) below.

(9) The Secretary of State shall not confirm an SSSI diversion order, and a council shall not confirm such an order as an unopposed order, unless he, or as the case may be, they are satisfied that the conditions in subsection (1)(a) and (b) are satisfied, and that it is expedient to confirm the order having regard to the effect which –

(a) the diversion would have on public enjoyment of the right of way as a whole;

(b) the coming into operation of the order would have as respects other land served by the existing public right of way; and

(c) any new public right of way created by the order would have as respects the land over which the right is so created and any land held with it,

so, however, that for the purposes of paragraphs (b) and (c) above the Secretary of State or, as the case may be, the council shall take into account the provisions as to compensation referred to in subsection (8)(a) above.

(10) Schedule 6 to this Act has effect as to the making, confirmation, validity and date of operation of SSSI diversion orders.

(11) This section has effect subject to section 119E below.

(12) In this section –

"the appropriate conservation body" means –

(a) as respects England, English Nature, and
(b) as respects Wales, the Countryside Council for Wales;

"site of special scientific interest" has the same meaning as in the Wildlife and Countryside Act 1981.

119E   Provisions supplementary to section 119D

(1) An application under section 119D above shall be in such form as may be prescribed and shall be accompanied by –

(a) a map, of such scale as may be prescribed, –
  (i)   showing the existing site of so much of the line of the highway as would be diverted if the order were made and the new site to which it would be diverted,
  (ii) indicating whether a new right of way would be created by the order over the whole of the new site or whether some of it is already comprised in a highway, and
  (iii) where some part of the new site is already so comprised, defining that part,
(b) by an assessment in the prescribed form of the effects of public use of the right of way on the site of special scientific interest, and
(c) by such other information as may be prescribed.

(2) At least fourteen days before making an application under section 119D above, the appropriate conservation body shall give a notice in the prescribed form of their intention to do so –

(a) to any owner, lessee or occupier of land over which the proposed order would create or extinguish a public right of way;
(b) to such other persons as may be prescribed; and
(c) in the case of English Nature, to the Countryside Agency.

(3) A council, in determining whether it is expedient to make or confirm an SSSI diversion order, and the Secretary of State, in determining whether to confirm such an order, shall, in particular, have regard to the following questions –

(a) whether the council would be able to prevent damage of the kind referred to in section 119D(1) above by making a traffic regulation order, and
(b) if so, whether the making of a traffic regulation order would cause less inconvenience to the public than that which would be caused by the diversion of the highway.

(4) The Secretary of State, in determining whether it is expedient to make an SSSI diversion order under section 120(3) below in a case where by virtue of section 22(4) of the Road Traffic Regulation Act 1984 he has power to make a traffic regulation order shall, in particular, have regard to the following questions –

(a) whether he would be able to prevent damage of the kind referred to in section 119D(1) above by making a traffic regulation order, and
(b) if so, whether the making of a traffic regulation order would cause less inconvenience to the public than that which would be caused by the diversion of the highway.

(5) An SSSI diversion order shall be in such form as may be prescribed and shall contain a map, on such scale as may be prescribed, –

(a) showing the existing site of so much of the line of the highway as is to be diverted by the order and the new site to which it is to be diverted,
(b) indicating whether a new right of way is created by the order over the whole of the new site or whether some part of it is already comprised in a highway, and
(c) where some part of the new site is already so comprised, defining that part.

(6) Section 27 above (making up of new footpaths and bridleways) applies to a highway created by an SSSI diversion order with the substitution –

(a) for references to a footpath or bridleway of references to a footpath, a bridleway, a restricted byway or a highway over which the public have a right of way for vehicular and all other kinds of traffic,

(b) for references to a public path creation order, of references to an SSSI diversion order, and

(c) for references to section 26(2) above, of references to section 120(3) below.

(7) Neither section 27 nor section 36 above is to be regarded as obliging a highway authority to provide on any highway created by an SSSI diversion order a metalled carriage-way.

(8) In this section –

"the appropriate conservation body" has the same meaning as in section 119D above;

"prescribed" means prescribed by regulations made by the Secretary of State;

"site of special scientific interest" has the same meaning as in the Wildlife and Countryside Act 1981;

"traffic regulation order" means an order under section 1 or 6 of the Road Traffic Regulation Act 1984.'

Explanatory text – see **4.6.**

---

120 Exercise of powers of making public path extinguishment and diversion orders

(1) Where a footpath or bridleway lies partly within and partly outside the area of a council the powers conferred by sections 118 [to 119A] above on the council extend, subject to subsection (2) below, to the whole of the path or way as if it lay wholly within their area.

(2) The powers of making [orders under sections 118 to 119A] above are not exercisable by a council –

(a) with respect to any part of a footpath or bridleway which is within their area, without prior consultation with [any] other council in whose area that part of the footpath or bridleway is situated;

(b) with respect to any part of a footpath or bridleway which is outside their area, without the consent of every council in whose area it is; and

(c) with respect to any part of a footpath or bridleway in a National Park, withour prior consultation with the [Countryside Agency] [(if the National Park is in England) or the Countryside Council for Wales (if the National Park is in Wales)].

(3) Where it appears to the Secretary of State as respects a footpath or bridleway that it is expedient as mentioned in section 118(1) [or 118A(1) or 119A(1)] above that the path or way should be stopped up [or diverted], or where an owner, lessee or occupier of land crossed by a footpath or bridleway satisfies the Secretary of State that a diversion of it is expedient as mentioned in section 119(1) above, then if –

(a) no council having power to do so have made and submitted to him a public path extinguishment order[, a rail crossing extinguishment order, a rail crossing diversion order] or a public path diversion order, as the case may be, and

(b) the Secretary of State is satisfied that, if such an order were made and submitted to him, he would have power to confirm the order in accordance with the provisions in that behalf of sections 118 [to 119A] above,

he may himself make the order after consultation [(subject to subsection (3A) below)] with the appropriate authority.

[(3A) Where –

    (a) the operator of a railway makes a request to a council to make an order under section 118A or 119A above in respect of a crossing over the railway,

    (b) the request is in such form and gives such particulars as are prescribed by regulations made by the Secretary of State, and

    (c) the council have neither confirmed the order nor submitted it to the Secretary of State within 6 months of receiving the request,

the power conferred on the Secretary of State by subsection (3) above may be exercised without consultation with the council.]

(4) A council proposing to make a public path diversion order or a rail crossing diversion order such that the authority who will be the highway authority for a part of the path or way after the diversion will be a different body from the authority who before the diversion are the highway authority for it shall, before making the order, notify the first mentioned authority.

(5) Where under subsection (3) above the Secretary of State decides to make a public path diversion order, [or, on the representations of the operator of the railway concerned, a rail crossing diversion order, he may require the person] on whose representations he is acting to enter into an agreement with such council as he may specify [for that person] to defray, or to make such contribution as may be specified in the agreement towards any such compensation or expenses as are specified in paragraphs (a), (b) and (c) of section 119(5)[, or as the case may be 119A(8),] above.

Amendments – Environmental Protection Act 1990, s 130, Sch 8, para 5(1), (3); Transport and Works Act 1992, s 47(1), Sch 2, paras 1, 5; Local Government (Wales) Act 1994, s 22(1), Sch 7, Pt I, para 12; Development Commission (Transfer of Functions and Miscellaneous Provisions) Order 1999, SI 1999/416.

Prospective amendments – The words 'to 119A' in subs (1) are prospectively substituted by the CROW Act 2000, s 57, Sch 6, Pt I, para 13(1), (2):

    ', 118A, 119 and 119A'.

Subsection prospectively inserted after subs (1) by the CROW Act 2000, s57, Sch 6, Pt I, para 13(1), (3):

    '(1A) Where a council are the highway authority for only part of a highway, the powers conferred on the council by sections 118B, 119B and 119D above are exercisable with respect to the whole of the highway, but subject to subsection (2) and only with the consent of every other council which is a highway authority for any other part with respect to which the powers are exercised.'

The words 'to 119A' in subs (2) are prospectively substituted by the CROW Act 2000, s 57, Sch 6, Pt I, para 13(1), (4)(a):

    'to 119D'.

The words 'footpath or bridleway', wherever occurring in subs (2), are prospectively substituted by the CROW Act 2000, s 57, Sch 6, Pt I, para 13(1), (4)(b):

    'highway'.

Words prospectively inserted after words 'or diverted' in subs (3) by the CROW Act 2000, s 57, Sch 6, Pt I, para 13(1), (5)(a):

    'or where it appears to the Secretary of State as respects a relevant highway as defined by section 118B(2), 119B(2) or 119D(2) that it is expedient as mentioned in section 118B(1)(a) or (b), 119B(1)(a) or (b) or 119D(1)(b) that the highway should be stopped up or diverted'.

The words 'a rail crossing diversion order or a public path diversion order' in subs (3)(a) are prospectively substituted by the CROW Act 2000, s 57, Sch 6, Pt I, para 13(1), (5)(b):

'a special extinguishment order, a public path diversion order, a rail crossing diversion order, a special diversion order or an SSSI diversion order'.

The words 'to 119A' in subs (3)(b) are prospectively substituted by the CROW Act 2000, s 57, Sch 6, Pt I, para 13(1), (5)(c):

'to 119D'.

The words '(subject to subsection (3A) below)' in subs (3) are prospectively substituted by the CROW Act 2000, s 57, Sch 6, Pt I, para 13(1), (5)(d):

'(subject to the following provisions of this section)'.

Words prospectively inserted at the end of subs (3) by the CROW Act 2000, s 57, Sch 6, Pt I, para 13(1), (5)(e):

'and, in the case of an SSSI diversion order, with the appropriate conservation body'.

Subsection prospectively inserted after subs (3) by the CROW Act 2000, s 57, Sch 6, Pt I, para 13(1), (6):

'(3ZA) Where an appeal to the Secretary of State is brought under section 121D(1) below, paragraph (a) of subsection (3) above does not apply, and the power conferred on him by that subsection may be exercised without consultation with the appropriate authority.'

Subsections prospectively inserted after subs (3A) by the CROW Act 2000, s 57, Sch 6, Pt I, para 13(1), (7):

'(3B) Unless an appeal to the Secretary of State is brought under section 121D(1) below, the power conferred on the Secretary of State by subsection (3) above to make a special extinguishment order or a special diversion order is exercisable only after consultation with the police authority in whose area the highway lies.

(3C) The power conferred on the Secretary of State by subsection (3) above to make an SSSI diversion order may be exercised even though the appropriate conservation body has not made an application under section 119D above to the council who are the highway authority for the highway.

(3D) Where –

    (a) the appropriate conservation body has made an application under section 119D above to a council in respect of a highway for which the council are the highway authority, and
    (b) the council have neither confirmed the order nor submitted it to the Secretary of State for confirmation within 6 months of receiving the application,

the power conferred on the Secretary of State by subsection (3) above to make an SSSI diversion order may be exercised without consultation with the council.'

The words 'or a rail crossing diversion order' in subs (4) are prospectively substituted by the CROW Act 2000, s57, Sch6, PtI, para13(1), (8)(a):

', a rail crossing diversion order, a special diversion order or an SSSI diversion order'.

The words 'path or way' in subs (4) are prospectively substituted by the CROW Act 2000, s 57, Sch 6, Pt I, para 13(1), (8)(b):

'highway'.

Subsection (5) is prospectively substituted by the CROW Act 2000, s 57, Sch 6, Pt I, para 13(1), (9):

'(5) The Secretary of State may, before determining –

(a) under subsection (3) above, to make a public path diversion order,

(b) under subsection (3) above, to make a public path extinguishment order, special extinguishment order, public path diversion order or special diversion order on an appeal under section 121D(1)(a) below,

(c) to confirm a public path extinguishment order, special extinguishment order, public path diversion order or special diversion order in respect of which an appeal under section 121D(1)(b) or (c) below has been brought, or

(d) under subsection (3) above, to make a rail crossing diversion order on the representations of the operator of the railway concerned,

require the appropriate person to enter into such agreement as he may specify with such council as he may specify for that person to defray, or to make such contribution as may be specified in the agreement towards, any such compensation or expenses as are specified in paragraphs (a), (b) and (c) of section 119(5), or as the case may be, section 118ZA(6), 119(8) or 119C(3) above.

(6) In subsection (5) above "the appropriate person" means –

(a) in a case falling within paragraph (a) of that subsection –
  (i) where an appeal under section 121D(1)(a) below has been brought, the appellant, or
  (ii) in any other case, the person on whose representations the Secretary of State is acting,

(b) in a case falling within paragraph (b) or (c) of that subsection, the appellant, and

(c) in a case falling within paragraph (d) of that subsection, the operator of the railway concerned.'

Subsections prospectively inserted after subs (6) by the CROW Act 2000, s 57, Sch 6, Pt I, para 13(1), (10):

'(7) Where under subsection (3) above the Secretary of State decides to make an SSSI diversion order he may require the appropriate conservation body to enter into an agreement with such council as he may specify for the body to defray, or to make such contribution as may be specified in the agreement towards, any such compensation or expenses as are specified in paragraphs (a), (b) and (c) of section 119D(8) above.

(8) In this section "the appropriate conservation body" has the same meaning as in section 119D above.'

Explanatory text – see **4.8**.

---

121 Supplementary provisions as to public path extinguishment and diversion orders

(1) A public path extinguishment order[, a rail crossing extinguishment order, a public path diversion order or a rail crossing diversion order] affecting in any way the area of more than one council may contain provisions requiring one of the councils to defray, or contribute towards, expenses incurred in consequence of the order by another of the councils; and a public path diversion order [or a rail crossing diversion order] diverting a part of the line of a path or way from a site in the area of one local highway authority to a site in the area of another may provide that the first mentioned authority are to continue to be the highway authority for that part of the path or way after the diversion.

(2) Section 28 above (compensation for loss caused by public path creation order) applies in relation to public path extinguishment orders[, rail crossing extinguishment orders, public path diversion orders and rail crossing diversion orders] as it applies in relation to public path creation orders but as if the references in it to section 26(2) above were references to section 120(3) above.

(3) Section 29 above (protection for agriculture and forestry) applies in relation to the making of public path extinguishment orders[, rail crossing extinguishment orders, public path diversion orders and rail crossing diversion orders] as it applies in relation to the making of public path creation agreements and public path creation orders.

(4) The Secretary of State shall not make or confirm a public path extinguishment order[, a rail crossing extinguishment order, a public path diversion order or a rail crossing diversion order] and a council shall not confirm such an order as an unopposed order, if the order extinguishes a right of way over land under, in, upon, over, along or across which there is any apparatus belonging to or used by any statutory undertakers for the purpose of their undertaking unless the undertakers have consented to the making or, as the case may be, confirmation of the order.

(5) A consent under subsection (4) above may be given subject to the condition that there are included in the order such provisions for the protection of the undertakers as they reasonably require, but a consent under that subsection shall not be unreasonably withheld, and any question whether the withholding of such a consent is unreasonable or whether any requirement is reasonable shall be determined by the appropriate Minister.

(6) In subsection (5) above the 'appropriate Minister' means –

  (a) in relation to statutory undertakers carrying on an undertaking for the supply of . . ., [or hydraulic power], the Secretary of State; and
  (b) in relation to any other statutory undertakers, the Minister.

Amendments – Gas Act 1986, s 67(4), Sch 9, Pt I; Electricity Act 1989, s 112(4), Sch 18; Water Act 1989, s 190(1), Sch 25, para 62(6); Transport and Works Act 1992, s 47(1), Sch 2, paras 1, 6.

Prospective amendments – Words prospectively inserted after words 'rail crossing extinguishment order,' in subs (1) by the CROW Act 2000, s 57, Sch 6, Pt I, para 14(1), (2)(a):

  'a special extinguishment order'.

The words 'or a rail crossing diversion order', wherever occurring in subs (1), are prospectively substituted by the CROW Act 2000, s 57, Sch 6, Pt I, para 14(1), (2)(b):

  ', a rail crossing diversion order, a special diversion order or an SSSI diversion order'.

The words 'path or way', wherever occurring in subs (1), are prospectively substituted by the CROW Act 2000, s 57, Sch 6, Pt I, para 14(1), (2)(c):

  'highway'.

Words prospectively inserted after the words 'rail crossing extinguishment orders,' in subs (2) by the CROW Act 2000, s 57, Sch 6, Pt I, para 14(1), (3)(a):

  'special extinguishment orders'.

The words 'and rail crossing diversion orders' in subs (2) are prospectively substituted by the CROW Act 2000, s 57, Sch 6, Pt I, para 14(1), (3)(b):

  ', rail crossing diversion orders, special diversion orders and SSSI diversion orders'.

The words from 'but' onwards in subs (2) are prospectively substituted by the CROW Act 2000, s 57, Sch 6, Pt I, para 14(1), (3)(b):

  'but as if –

    (a) the references in it to section 26(2) above were references to section 120(3) above, and

(b) in relation to special extinguishment orders, special diversion orders and SSSI diversion orders, the reference in section 28(4) to a footpath or bridleway included a reference to a restricted byway or a highway over which the public have a right of way for vehicular and all other kinds of traffic.'

The words '(protection for agriculture and forestry)' in subs (3) are prospectively substituted by the CROW Act 2000, s 57, Sch 6, Pt I, para 14(1), (4)(a):

'(duty to have regard to agriculture, forestry and nature conservation)'.

Words prospectively inserted after the words 'rail crossing extinguishment orders,' in subs (3) by the CROW Act 2000, s 57, Sch 6, Pt I, para 14(1), (4)(b):

'special extinguishment orders'.

The words 'and rail crossing diversion orders' in subs (3) are prospectively substituted by the CROW Act 2000, s 57, Sch 6, Pt I, para 14(1), (4)(c):

', rail crossing diversion orders, special diversion orders and SSSI diversion orders'.

Words prospectively inserted after the words 'rail crossing extinguishment order,' in subs (4) by the CROW Act 2000, s 57, Sch 6, Pt I, para 14(1), (5)(a):

'a special extinguishment order'.

The words 'or a rail crossing diversion order' in subs (4) are prospectively substituted by the CROW Act 2000, s 57, Sch 6, Pt I, para 14(1), (5)(b):

', a rail crossing diversion order, a special diversion order or an SSSI diversion order'.

Subsections prospectively inserted after subs (5) by the CROW Act 2000, s 57, Sch 6, Pt I, para 14(1), (6):

'(5A) Before making a determination under subsection (5) above the appropriate Minister may, if he thinks fit, give any person an opportunity to be heard on the question, and he must either give such an opportunity or cause a local inquiry to be held if a request to be heard with respect to the question to be determined is made –

(a) by the statutory undertakers,
(b) in the case of an order made on an application under section 118ZA, 118C, 119ZA or 119C above, by the person who made the application, and
(c) in the case of an order to be made on an appeal under section 121D(1)(a) below, by the appellant.

(5B) The appropriate Minister may appoint any person to exercise on his behalf, with or without payment, the function of determining a question falling to be determined under subsection (5) above.

(5C) Schedule 12ZA to this Act shall have effect with respect to appointments under subsection (5B) above; and subsection (5A) above has effect subject to the provisions of that Schedule.

(5D) Subsections (2) to (5) of section 250 of the Local Government Act 1972 (giving of evidence at, and defraying of costs of, inquiries) shall apply in relation to hearings or local inquiries which the appropriate Minister causes to be held under subsection (5A) above as they apply (by virtue of section 302(1) of this Act) to local inquiries which the Secretary of State causes to be held under this Act.

(5E) Section 322A of the Town and Country Planning Act 1990 (orders as to costs where no hearing or inquiry takes place) applies in relation to a hearing or inquiry under subsection (5A) above as it applies in relation to a hearing or local inquiry for the purposes referred to in that section, but as if references to the Secretary of State were references to the appropriate Minister.'

The words 'subsection (5)' in subs (6) are prospectively substituted by the CROW Act 2000, s 57, Sch 6, Pt I, para 14(1), (7):

'subsections (5) to (5E)'.

Sections prospectively inserted after s 121 by the CROW Act 2000, s 57, Sch 6, Pt I, para 15:

'121A   Regulations with respect to applications for orders

(1) The Secretary of State may by regulations make provision as respects applications under section 118ZA, 118C, 119ZA or 119C above –

- (a) requiring the applicant to issue a certificate as to the interests in, or rights in or over, the land to which the application relates and the purpose for which the land is used,
- (b) requiring the applicant to give notice of the application to such persons as may be prescribed,
- (c) requiring the applicant to certify that any requirement of regulations under this section has been complied with or to provide evidence that any such requirement has been complied with,
- (d) as to the publicising of any application,
- (e) as to the form, content and service of such notices and certificates, and
- (f) as to the remission or refunding in prescribed circumstances of the whole or part of any prescribed charge.

(2) If any person –

- (a) issues a certificate which purports to comply with any requirement imposed by virtue of subsection (1) above and contains a statement which he knows to be false or misleading in a material particular; or
- (b) recklessly issues a certificate which purports to comply with any such requirement and contains a statement which is false or misleading in a material particular,

he shall be guilty of an offence.

(3) A person guilty of an offence under this section shall be liable on summary conviction to a fine not exceeding level 5 on the standard scale.

(4) Notwithstanding section 127 of the Magistrates' Courts Act 1980 (limitation of time for taking proceedings) summary proceedings for an offence under this section may be instituted at any time within three years after the commission of the offence.

121B   Register of applications

(1) Every council shall keep, in such manner as may be prescribed, a register containing such information as may be prescribed with respect to applications under section 118ZA, 118C, 119ZA or 119C above.

(2) The register shall contain such information as may be prescribed with respect to the manner in which such applications have been dealt with.

(3) Regulations may make provision for the register to be kept in two or more parts, each part containing such information relating to applications under section 118ZA, 118C, 119ZA or 119C above as may be prescribed.

(4) Regulations may make provision –

- (a) for a specified part of the register to contain copies of applications and of the maps submitted with them, and
- (b) for the entry relating to any application, and everything relating to it, to be removed from any part of the register when the application (including any appeal to the Secretary of State) has been finally disposed of (without prejudice to the inclusion of any different entry relating to it in another part of the register).

(5) Every register kept under this section shall be available for inspection by the public free of charge at all reasonable hours.

(6) In this section –

"prescribed" means prescribed by regulations;

"regulations" means regulations made by the Secretary of State.

121C   Cases where council may decline to determine applications

(1) A council may decline to determine an application under section 118ZA, 118C, 119ZA or 119C above if, within the period of three years ending with the date on which the application is received, the Secretary of State –

(a) has refused to make an order on an appeal under section 121D(1)(a) below in respect of a similar application, or

(b) has refused to confirm an order which is similar to the order requested.

(2) Before declining under subsection (1) above to determine an application under section 118C or 119C above, the council shall consider whether since the previous decision of the Secretary of State was made the risks referred to in subsection (1)(b)(i) to (iv) of section 118B or of section 119B have substantially increased.

(3) A council may decline to determine an application under section 118ZA, 118C, 119ZA or 119C above if –

(a) in respect of an application previously made to them under that section which is similar to the current application or relates to any of the land to which the current application relates, the council have not yet determined whether to make a public path extinguishment order, special extinguishment order, public path diversion order or special diversion order, or

(b) the council have made a similar order or an order which relates to any of the land to which the current application relates but no final decision as to the confirmation of the order has been taken.

(4) For the purposes of this section an application or order is similar to a later application or order only if they are, in the opinion of the council determining the later application, the same or substantially the same, but an application or order may be the same or substantially the same as a later application or order even though it is made to or by a different council.

121D   Right of appeal to Secretary of State in respect of applications for orders

(1) Subject to the provisions of this section, where, in relation to an application made under section 118ZA, 118C, 119ZA or 119C above, the council to which the application was made –

(a) refuse to make an order on the application,

(b) refuse to confirm as an unopposed order an order made on the application, or

(c) refuse to submit to the Secretary of State an order which is made on the application and against which any representation or objection has been duly made and not withdrawn,

the applicant may, by giving notice to the Secretary of State, appeal to the Secretary of State.

(2) Subsection (1)(a) above does not confer any right to appeal to the Secretary of State where –

(a) the council have no power to make the order requested without the consent of another person and that consent has not been given, or

(b) the reason, or one of the reasons, for the refusal to make the order is that the applicant has refused to enter into an agreement required by the council –

   (i)   in the case of a public path extinguishment order, under subsection (6) of section 118ZA above,

   (ii) in the case of a special extinguishment order, under the subsection as applied by section 118C(2) above,

   (iii) in the case of a public path diversion order, under section 119(5) above,

   (iv) in the case of a special diversion order, under section 119C(3) above.

(3) Paragraph (b) of subsection (1) above does not confer any right to appeal to the Secretary of State in a case where the council has no power to confirm the order without the consent of another person and that consent has not been given; and paragraph (c) of that subsection does not confer

any right to appeal to the Secretary of State in a case where, if the order had been unopposed, the council would have had no power to confirm it without the consent of another person and that consent has not been given.

121E   Determination of appeals

(1) Where an appeal to the Secretary of State is brought under section 121D(1)(a) above, the Secretary of State shall –

  (a) prepare a draft of a public path extinguishment order, special extinguishment order, public path diversion order or special diversion order under section 120(3) above giving effect to the application and containing such other provisions as, after consultation with such persons as he thinks fit, the Secretary of State may determine,

  (b) give notice of the draft order in accordance with paragraph 1(2) of Schedule 6 to this Act, and

  (c) subject to subsection (6) below and to paragraph 2 of that Schedule, determine whether to make the order (with or without modifications) under section 120(3) above.

(2) Where an appeal to the Secretary of State is brought under section 121D(1)(b) or (c) above, the order made on the application shall be treated as having been submitted to him for confirmation (with or without modifications).

(3) Where an appeal to the Secretary of State is brought under section 121D(1) above, the Secretary of State may not make or confirm a public path diversion order or special diversion order if it appears to him that –

  (a) work is necessary to bring the new highway created by the order into a fit condition for use by the public,

  (b) if the order were made, the work could not be carried out by the highway authority without –
    (i)   the consent of another person, or
    (ii) any authorisation (however described) which is required by or under any enactment, and

  (c) the consent or authorisation has not been obtained.

(4) Where an appeal to the Secretary of State is brought under section 121D(1) above, the Secretary of State may not –

  (a) make a public path diversion order or special diversion order so as to create a public right of way over land covered by works used for the purposes of a statutory undertaking or the curtilage of such land, or

  (b) modify such an order so as to create such a public right of way,

unless the statutory undertaker has consented to the making or modification of the order.

(5) In subsection (4) above "statutory undertaker" and "statutory undertaking" have the same meaning as in Schedule 6 to this Act.

(6) Subsection (1)(c) above does not apply where any consent required by section 121(4) above has not been obtained.

(7) The Secretary of State may by regulations make further provision with respect to appeals under section 121D(1) above.

(8) Regulations under subsection (7) above may, in particular, make provision –

  (a) as to the manner in which, and time within which, notice of an appeal is to be given,

  (b) as to the provision of information to the Secretary of State by the council to which the application to which the appeal relates was made,

  (c) for the payment by the applicant of any expenses incurred by the Secretary of State –
    (i)   in preparing a draft order,
    (ii) in giving any notice required by subsection (1)(b) above or Schedule 6 to this Act,

(d) requiring the production by the council to whom the application was made of any certificates required by regulations under section 121A(1)(a) above,

(e) requiring the applicant to give notice of the appeal to such persons as may be prescribed,

(f) requiring the applicant to certify that any requirement of regulations under this section has been complied with or to provide evidence that any such requirement has been complied with,

(g) as to the publicising of any appeal,

(h) as to the form, content and service of such notices and certificates,

(i) modifying the provisions of Schedule 6 to this Act in their application to the procedure on appeals under section 121D(1) above, and

(j) as to the remission or refunding in prescribed circumstances of any prescribed charge.

(9) The Secretary of State may by regulations provide that section 28 above, as applied by section 121(2) above, is to have effect in cases where a public path extinguishment order, special extinguishment order, public path diversion order or special diversion order is made under section 120(3) above on an appeal under section 121D(1)(a) above, as if the reference to such one of the authorities referred to as may be nominated by the Secretary of State were a reference to such one of those authorities as may be specified in or determined in accordance with, the regulations.

(10) Subsections (2) to (4) of section 121A above shall apply in relation to any certificate purporting to comply with a requirement imposed by virtue of this section as they apply to a certificate purporting to comply with a requirement imposd by virtue of subsection (1) of that section.

(11) For the purposes of this section –

(a) a draft public path extinguishment order or special extinguishment order gives effect to an application under section 118ZA or 118C above only if the land over which the public right of way is to be extinguished by the order is that shown for the purposes of subsection (2) of section 118ZA above (or that subsection as applied by section 118C(2) above) on the map accompanying the application, and

(b) a draft public path diversion order or draft special diversion order gives effect to an application made to a council under section 119ZA or 119C above only if –
  (i) the land over which the public right of way is to be extinguished by the order, and
  (ii) the new site to which the highway is to be diverted, are those shown for the purposes of subsection (4) of section 119ZA above (or that subsection as applied by section 119C(4) above) on the map accompanying the application.

(12) In this section "prescribed" means prescribed by regulations made by the Secretary of State.'

Explanatory text – see 4.8.

---

122   Power to make temporary diversion where highway about to be repaired or widened

(1) A highway authority who are about to repair or widen a highway, and a person who is about to repair or widen a highway maintainable by him by reason of tenure, enclosure or prescription, may, subject to the provisions of this section, construct on adjoining land a temporary highway for use while the work is in progress.

(2) Where any damage is sustained by the owner or occupier of any land in consequence of the construction of a highway on that land in exercise of a power conferred by this section the owner or occupier of the land may recover compensation in respect of that damage from the authority or other person by whom the highway was constructed.

(3) Nothing in this section authorises interference with land which is part of the site of a house, or is a garden, lawn, yard, court, park, paddock, plantation, planted walk or avenue to a house, or is inclosed land set apart for building or as a nursery for trees.

Explanatory text – see **4.11.2**.

123 Saving and interpretation

(1) The provisions of any enactment contained in the foregoing provisions of this Part of this Act do not prejudice any power conferred by any other enactment (whether contained in this Part of this Act or not) to stop up or divert a highway, and do not otherwise affect the operation of any enactment not contained in this Part of this Act relating to the extinguishment, suspension, diversion or variation of public rights of way.

(2) Unless the context otherwise requires, expressions in the foregoing provisions of this Part of this Act, other than expressions to which meanings are assigned by sections 328 and 329 below, have the same meanings respectively as in [the Town and Country Planning Act 1990].

Amendment – Planning (Consequential Provisions) Act 1990, s 4, Sch 2, para 45(7).

. . .

PART IX

LAWFUL AND UNLAWFUL INTERFERENCE WITH HIGHWAYS AND STREETS

Protection of public rights

130 Protection of public rights

(1) It is the duty of the highway authority to assert and protect the rights of the public to the use and enjoyment of any highway for which they are the highway authority, including any roadside waste which forms part of it.

(2) Any council may assert and protect the rights of the public to the use and enjoyment of any highway in their area for which they are not the highway authority, including any roadside waste which forms part of it.

(3) Without prejudice to subsections (1) and (2) above, it is the duty of a council who are a highway authority to prevent, as far as possible, the stopping up or obstruction of –

(a) the highways for which they are the highway authority, and
(b) any highway for which they are not the highway authority, if, in their opinion, the stopping up or obstruction of that highway would be prejudicial to the interests of their area.

(4) Without prejudice to the foregoing provisions of this section, it is the duty of a local highway authority to prevent any unlawful encroachment on any roadside waste comprised in a highway for which they are the highway authority.

(5) Without prejudice to their powers under section 222 of the Local Government Act 1972, a council may, in the performance of their functions under the foregoing

provisions of this section, institute legal proceedings in their own name, defend any legal proceedings and generally take such steps as they deem expedient.

(6) If the council of a parish or community or, in the case of a parish or community which does not have a separate parish or community council, the parish meeting or a community meeting, represent to a local highway authority –

(a) that a highway as to which the local highway authority have the duty imposed by subsection (3) above has been unlawfully stopped up or obstructed, or

(b) that an unlawful encroachment has taken place on a roadside waste comprised in a highway for which they are the highway authority,

it is the duty of the local highway authority, unless satisfied that the representations are incorrect, to take proper proceedings accordingly and they may do so in their own name.

(7) Proceedings or steps taken by a council in relation to an alleged right of way are not to be treated as unauthorised by reason only that the alleged right is found not to exist.

Prospective amendments – Sections prospectively inserted by the CROW Act 2000, s 63(1):

'130A   Notices to enforce duty regarding public paths

(1) Any person who alleges, as respects any highway for which a local highway authority other than an inner London authority are the highway authority –

(a) that the highway falls within subsection (2) below, and

(b) that it is obstructed by an obstruction to which this section applies,

may serve on the highway authority notice requesting them to secure the removal of the obstruction from the highway.

(2) A highway is within this subsection if it is –

(a) a footpath, bridleway, or restricted byway, or

(b) a way shown in a definitive map and statement as a restricted byway or a byway open to all traffic.

(3) Subject to subsection (4) below, this section applies to an obstruction of the highway if the obstruction is without lawful authority and either –

(a) the powers conferred by section 143, 149 or 154 below are exercisable in respect of it, or

(b) it is of a description prescribed by regulations made by the Secretary of State and the authority have power (otherwise than under any of those sections) to secure its removal.

(4) This section does not apply to an obstruction if –

(a) it is or forms part of –
    (i) a building (whether temporary or permanent) or works for the construction of a building, or
    (ii) any other structure (including a tent, caravan, vehicle or other temporary or movable structure) which is designed, adapted or used for human habitation,

(b) an order may be made in respect of it under section 56 above, or

(c) the presence of any person constitutes the obstruction.

(5) A person serving a notice under subsection (1) above must include in the notice the name and address, if known to him, of any person who it appears to him may be for the time being responsible for the obstruction.

(6) A highway authority on whom a notice under subsection (1) above is served shall, within one month from the date of service of the notice, serve –

  (a) on every person whose name and address is, pursuant to subsection (5) above, included in the notice and, so far as reasonably practicable, on every other person who it appears to them may be for the time being responsible for the obstruction, a notice informing that person that a notice under subsection (1) above has been served in relation to the obstruction and stating what, if any, action the authority propose to take, and

  (b) on the person who served the notice under subsection (1) above, a notice containing the name and address of each person on whom notice is served under paragraph (a) above and stating what, if any, action the authority propose to take in relation to the obstruction.

(7) For the purposes of this section the persons for the time being responsible for an obstruction include the owner and any other person who for the time being –

  (a) has possession or control of it, or
  (b) may be required to remove it.

(8) A notice under subsection (1) or (6) above shall be in such form and contain such information as may be prescribed by regulations made by the Secretary of State.

(9) In this section 'inner London authority' means Transport for London, the council of an inner London borough or the Common Council of the City of London.

(10) Subsection (2) above has effect until the commencement of section 47 of the Countryside and Rights of Way Act 2000 with the substitution for the references to a restricted byway and to a way shown in a definitive map and statement as a restricted byway of a reference to a way shown in a definitive map and statement as a road used as a public path.

130B Orders following notice under section 130A

(1) Where a notice under section 130A(1) above has been served on a highway authority in relation to any obstruction, the person who served it, if not satisfied that the obstruction has been removed, may apply to a magistrates' court in accordance with section 130C below for an order under this section.

(2) An order under this section is an order requiring the highway authority to take, within such reasonable period as may be fixed by the order, such steps as may be specified in the order for securing the removal of the obstruction.

(3) An order under this section shall not take effect –

  (a) until the end of the period of twenty-one days from the day on which the order is made; or
  (b) if an appeal is brought in respect of the order within that period (whether by way of appeal to the Crown Court or by way of case stated for the opinion of the High Court), until the final determination or withdrawal of the appeal.

(4) Subject to subsection (5) below, the court may make an order under this section if it is satisfied –

  (a) that the obstruction is one to which section 130A above applies or, in a case falling within subsection (4)(a)(ii) of that section, is one to which that section would apply but for the obstruction having become used for human habitation since service of the notice relating to it under subsection (1) of that section,

  (b) that the way obstructed is a highway within subsection (2) of that section, and

  (c) that the obstruction significantly interferes with the exercise of public rights of way over that way.

(5) No order shall be made under this section if the highway authority satisfy the court –

  (a) that the fact that the way obstructed is a highway within section 130A(2) above is seriously disputed,

  (b) on any other grounds, that they have no duty under section 130(3) above to secure the removal of the obstruction, or

(c) that, under arrangements which have been made by the authority, its removal will be secured within a reasonable time, having regard to the number and seriousness of obstructions in respect of which they have such a duty.

(6) A highway authority against whom an order is made under this section shall, as soon as practicable after the making of the order, cause notice of the order and of the right to appeal against it to be displayed in such manner and at such places on the highway concerned as may be prescribed by regulations made by the Secretary of State, and the notice shall be in such form and contain such information as may be so prescribed.

(7) An order under this section may be varied on the application of the highway authority to whom it relates.

130C   Section 130B: procedure

(1) A person proposing to make an application under section 130B above shall before making the application serve notice of his intention to do so on the highway authority concerned.

(2) A notice under subsection (1) above shall be in such form and contain such information as may be prescribed by regulations made by the Secretary of State.

(3) The notice may not be served before the end of two months beginning with the date of service on the highway authority of the notice under section 130A(1) above ('the request notice').

(4) An application in respect of which notice has been served under subsection (1) above may be made at any time –

(a) after the end of five days beginning with the date of service of that notice, and
(b) before the end of six months beginning with the date of service on the highway authority of the request notice.

(5) On making the application the applicant must give notice to the court of the names and addresses of which notice was given to the applicant under section 130A(6)(b) above.

(6) On the hearing of the application any person who is, within the meaning of section 130A above, a person for the time being responsible for the obstruction to which the application relates has a right to be heard as respects the matters mentioned in section 130B(4) above.

(7) Notice of the hearing, of the right to be heard under subsection (6) above and of the right to appeal against a decision on the application shall be given by the court to each person whose name and address is notified to the court under subsection (5) above.

130D   Section 130B: costs

Where an application under section 130B above is dismissed by virtue of paragraph (a), (b) or (c) of subsection (5) of that section, the court, in determining whether and if so how to exercise its power under section 64(1) of the Magistrates' Courts Act 1980 (costs), shall have particular regard to any failure by the highway authority to give the applicant appropriate notice of, and information about, the grounds relied on by the authority under that paragraph.'

Explanatory text – see **9.2**.

Damage to highways, streets etc

131   Penalty for damaging highway etc

(1) If a person, without lawful authority or excuse –

(a) makes a ditch or excavation in a highway which consists of or comprises a carriageway, or
(b) removes any soil or turf from any part of a highway, except for the purpose of improving the highway and with the consent of the highway authority for the highway, or

(c) deposits anything whatsoever on a highway so as to damage the highway, or

(d) lights any fire, or discharges any firearm or firework, within 50 feet from the centre of a highway which consists of or comprises a carriageway, and in consequence thereof the highway is damaged,

he is guilty of an offence.

(2) If a person without lawful authority or excuse pulls down or obliterates a traffic sign placed on or over a highway, or a milestone or direction post (not being a traffic sign) so placed, he is guilty of an offence; but it is a defence in any proceedings under this subsection to show that the traffic sign, milestone or post was not lawfully so placed.

(3) A person guilty of an offence under this section is liable to a fine not exceeding [level 3 on the standard scale].

Amendment – Criminal Justice Act 1982, ss 38, 46.

Explanatory text – see **9.6.7**.

[131A   Disturbance of surface of certain highways

(1) A person who, without lawful authority or excuse, so disturbs the surface of –

(a) a footpath,

(b) a bridleway, or

(c) any other highway which consists of or comprises a carriageway other than a made-up carriageway,

to render it inconvenient for the exercise of the public right of way is guilty of an offence and liable to a fine not exceeding level 3 on the standard scale.

(2) Proceedings for an offence under this section shall be brought only by the highway authority or the council of the non-metropolitan district, parish or community in which the offence is committed; and, without prejudice to section 130 (protection of public rights) above, it is the duty of the highway authority to ensure that where desirable in the public interest such proceedings are brought.]

Amendment – Inserted by Rights of Way Act 1990, s 1(2).

Explanatory text – see **9.6.7**.

132   Unauthorised marks on highways

(1) A person who, without either the consent of the highway authority for the highway in question or an authorisation given by or under an enactment or a reasonable excuse, paints or otherwise inscribes or affixes any picture, letter, sign or other mark upon the surface of a highway or upon any tree, structure or works on or in a highway is guilty of an offence and liable to a fine not exceeding [level 4 on the standard scale].

(2) The highway authority for a highway may, without prejudice to their powers apart from this subsection and whether or not proceedings in respect of the matter have been taken in pursuance of subsection (1) above, remove any picture, letter, sign or other mark which has, without either the consent of the authority or an authorisation given by or under an enactment, been painted or otherwise inscribed or affixed upon the surface of the highway or upon any tree, structure or works on or in the highway.

Amendment – Criminal Justice Act 1982, ss 38, 46.

Explanatory text – see **9.6.3**.

. . .

[134   Ploughing etc of footpath or bridleway

(1) Where in the case of any footpath or bridleway (other than a field-edge path) which passes over a field or enclosure consisting of agricultural land, or land which is being brought into use for agriculture –

(a) the occupier of the field or enclosure desires in accordance with the rules of good husbandry to plough, or otherwise disturb the surface of, all or part of the land comprised in the field or enclosure, and

(b) it is not reasonably convenient in ploughing, or otherwise disturbing the surface of, the land to avoid disturbing the surface of the path or way so as to render it inconvenient for the exercise of the public right of way,

the public right of way shall be subject to the condition that the occupier has the right so to plough or otherwise disturb the surface of the path or way.

(2) Subsection (1) above does not apply in relation to any excavation or any engineering operation.

(3) Where the occupier has disturbed the surface of a footpath or bridleway under the right conferred by subsection (1) above he shall within the relevant period, or within an extension of that period granted under subsection (8) below –

(a) so make good the surface of the path or way to not less than its minimum width as to make it reasonably convenient for the exercise of the right of way; and

(b) so indicate the line of the path or way on the ground to not less than its minimum width that it is apparent to members of the public wishing to use it.

(4) If the occupier fails to comply with the duty imposed by subsection (3) above he is guilty of an offence and liable to a fine not exceeding level 3 on the standard scale.

(5) . . .

(6) Without prejudice to section 130 (protection of public rights) above, it is the duty of the highway authority to enforce the provisions of this section.

(7) For the purposes of this section 'the relevant period' –

(a) where the disturbance of the surface of the path or way is the first disturbance for the purposes of the sowing of a particular agricultural crop, means fourteen days beginning with the day on which the surface of the path or way was first disturbed for those purposes; or

(b) in any other case, means twenty-four hours beginning with the time when it was disturbed.

(8) On an application made to the highway authority before the disturbance or during the relevant period, the authority may grant an extension of that period for an additional period not exceeding twenty-eight days.

(9) In this section 'minimum width', in relation to a highway, has the same meaning as in Schedule 12A to this Act.]

Amendments – Substituted by Rights of Way Act 1990, s 1(3). Amended by CROW Act 2000, ss 70(2), 102, Sch 16, Pt II.

Explanatory text – see **9.3.2**.

[135   Authorisation of other works disturbing footpath or bridleway

(1) Where the occupier of any agricultural land, or land which is being brought into use for agriculture, desires to carry out in relation to that land an excavation or engineering operation, and the excavation or operation –

(a) is reasonably necessary for the purposes of agriculture, but
(b) will so disturb the surface of a footpath or bridleway which passes over that land as to render it inconvenient for the exercise of the public right of way,

he may apply to the highway authority for an order that the public right of way shall be subject to the condition that he has the right to disturb the surface by that excavation or operation during such period, not exceeding three months, as is specified in the order ('the authorisation period').

(2) The highway authority shall make an order under subsection (1) above if they are satisfied either –

(a) that it is practicable temporarily to divert the path or way in a manner reasonably convenient to users; or
(b) that it is practicable to take adequate steps to ensure that the path or way remains sufficiently convenient, having regard to the need for the excavation or operation, for temporary use while it is being carried out.

(3) An order made by a highway authority under subsection (1) above –

(a) may provide for the temporary diversion of the path or way during the authorisation period, but shall not divert it on to land not occupied by the applicant unless written consent to the making of the order has been given by the occupier of that land, and by any other person whose consent is needed to obtain access to it;
(b) may include such conditions as the authority reasonably think fit for the provision, either by the applicant or by the authority at the expense of the applicant, of facilities for the convenient use of any such diversion, including signposts and other notices, stiles, bridges and gates;
(c) shall not affect the line of a footpath or bridleway on land not occupied by the applicant;

and the authority shall cause notices of any such diversion, together with a plan showing the effect of the diversion and the line of the alternative route provided, to be prominently displayed throughout the authorisation period at each end of the diversion.

(4) An order made by a highway authority under subsection (1) above may include such conditions as the authority reasonably think fit –

(a) for the protection and convenience during the authorisation period of users of the path or way;
(b) for making good the surface of the path or way to not more than its minimum width before the expiration of the authorisation period;

(c) for the recovery from the applicant of expenses incurred by the authority in connection with the order.

(5) An order under this section shall not authorise any interference with the apparatus or works of any statutory undertakers.

(6) If the applicant fails to comply with a condition imposed under subsection (3)(b) or (4)(a) or (b) above he is guilty of an offence and liable to a fine not exceeding level 3 on the standard scale.

(7) Proceedings for an offence under this section in relation to a footpath or bridleway shall be brought only by the highway authority or (with the consent of the highway authority) the council of the non-metropolitan district, parish or community in which the offence is committed.

(8) Without prejudice to section 130 (protection of public rights) above it is the duty of the highway authority to enforce the provisions of this section.

(9) In this section 'minimum width', in relation to a highway, has the same meaning as in Schedule 12A to this Act.]

Amendment – Substituted by Rights of Way Act 1990, s 1(4).

Prospective amendment – Sections prospectively inserted by the CROW Act 2000, s 57, Sch 6, Pt I, para 16:

'135A Temporary diversion for dangerous works

(1) Where works of a prescribed description are likely to cause danger to users of a footpath or bridleway which passes over any land, the occupier of the land may, subject to the provisions of this section, temporarily divert –

(a) so much of the footpath or bridleway as passes over that land, and
(b) so far as is requisite for effecting that diversion, so much of the footpath or bridleway as passes over other land occupied by him.

(2) A person may not under this section divert any part of a footpath or bridleway if –

(a) the period or periods for which that part has been diverted under this section, and
(b) the period or periods for which any other part of the same footpath or bridleway passing over land occupied by him has been diverted under this section,

amount in aggregate to more than fourteen days in any one calendar year.

(3) Where a person diverts a footpath or bridleway under this section –

(a) he shall do so in a manner which is reasonably convenient for the exercise of the public right of way, and
(b) where the diversion is by means of a temporary footpath or bridleway, he shall so indicate the line of the temporary footpath or bridleway on the ground to no less than the minimum width that it is apparent to members of the public wishing to use it.

(4) This section does not authorise a person –

(a) to divert a footpath or bridleway on to land not occupied by him without the consent of the occupier of that land and of any other person whose consent is needed to obtain access to it,
(b) to divert a footpath onto a highway other than a footpath or bridleway, or
(c) to divert a bridleway onto a highway other than a bridleway.

(5) The person by whom a footpath or bridleway is diverted under this section shall –

(a) at least fourteen days before the commencement of the diversion, give notice of the diversion in accordance with subsection (6) below,

(b) at least seven days before the commencement of the diversion, publish notice of the diversion in a local newspaper circulating in the area in which the footpath or bridleway is situated, and

(c) display such notices as may be prescribed at such places, in such manner and at such times before or during the diversion as may be prescribed.

(6) Notice under subsection (5)(a) above shall be given –

(a) to the highway authority for the footpath or bridleway,

(b) if the footpath or bridleway is on or contiguous with access land in England, to the Countryside Agency, and

(c) if the footpath or bridleway is on or contiguous with access land in Wales, to the Countryside Council for Wales.

(7) A notice under subsection (5)(a), (b) or (c) above shall be in such form and contain such information as may be prescribed.

(8) If a person –

(a) in a notice which purports to comply with the requirements of subsection (5)(a) or (b) above, makes a statement which he knows to be false in a material particular,

(b) by a notice displayed on or near a footpath or bridleway, falsely purports to be authorised under this section to divert the footpath or bridleway, or

(c) in diverting a footpath or bridleway under this section, fails to comply with subsection (3) above,

he shall be guilty of an offence and liable to a fine not exceeding level 3 on the standard scale.

(9) In this section –

"access land" has the same meaning as in Part I of the Countryside and Rights of Way Act 2000;

"minimum width" in relation to a temporary footpath or bridleway, means the minimum width, within the meaning of Schedule 12A to this Act, of the footpath or bridleway diverted;

"prescribed" means prescribed by regulations made by the Secretary of State.

135B   Temporary diversion for dangerous works: supplementary

(1) The person by whom a footpath or bridleway is diverted under section 135A above shall, before the diversion ceases to be authorised by that section, make good any damage to the footpath or bridleway resulting from the works mentioned in subsection (1) of that section, and remove from the footpath or bridleway any obstruction resulting from those works.

(2) Any person who fails to comply with the duty imposed on him by subsection (1) above is guilty of an offence and liable to a fine not exceeding level 3 on the standard scale.

(3) The highway authority may make good any damage, or remove any obstruction, in respect of which any person has failed to comply with that duty and recover from that person the amount of any expenses reasonably incurred by them in or in connection with doing so.

(4) Paragraph 3(1) of Schedule 12A to this Act does not apply in relation to any disturbance of the surface of a footpath or bridleway which subsection (1) above requires any person to make good; but paragraphs 7 and 8 of that Schedule apply for the purpose of subsection (3) above as if –

(a) references to the authority were references to the highway authority,

(b) references to the work were references to work carried out under subsection (3) above in relation to a footpath or bridleway, and

(c) references to the relevant land were references to the land over which the footpath or bridleway passes.

(5) The diversion of a footpath or bridleway under section 135A above does not –

(a) affect the liability of any person for anything done in relation to the path or way otherwise than for the purposes of or in consequence of the works mentioned in subsection (1) of that section, or

(b) authorise any interference with the apparatus or works of any statutory undertakers.

(6) Without prejudice to section 130 (protection of public rights of way) above, it is the duty of the highway authority to enforce the provisions of section 135A and this section.'

Explanatory text – see 4.11.4, 9.3.4.

---

136   Damage to highway consequent on exclusion of sun and wind

(1) If a highway which consists of or comprises a carriageway is being damaged in consequence of the exclusion from it of the sun and wind by a hedge or tree (other than a tree planted for ornament or for shelter to a building, courtyard or hop ground), a magistrates' court may by order require the owner or occupier of the land on which the hedge or tree is growing, so to cut, prune or plash the hedge or prune or lop the tree as to remove the cause of damage.

(2) The power of a magistrates' court to make an order under subsection (1) above is exercisable on a complaint made by the highway authority for the highway, or, in the case of a highway maintainable by reason of tenure, enclosure or prescription, by the person liable to maintain the highway.

(3) If a person against whom an order under subsection (1) above is made fails to comply with it within 10 days from such date as may be specified in the order, he is guilty of an offence and liable to a fine not exceeding [level 1 on the standard scale], and the highway authority or other person on whose complaint the order was made may carry out the work required by the order and may recover the expenses reasonably incurred by them or him in so doing from the person in default.

(4) No person shall be required by an order made under this section, nor is any person permitted by subsection (3) above, to cut or prune a hedge at any time [except] between the last day of September and the first day of April.

Amendments – Criminal Justice Act 1982, ss 37, 46; Wildlife and Countryside Act 1981, s 72(13).

Obstruction of highways and streets

137   Penalty for wilful obstruction

(1) If a person, without lawful authority or excuse, in any way wilfully obstructs the free passage along a highway he is guilty of an offence and liable to a fine not exceeding [level 3 on the standard scale].

(2) . . .

Amendments – Criminal Justice Act 1982, ss 38, 46; Police and Criminal Evidence Act 1984, ss 26(1), 119(2), Sch 7, Pt I.

Explanatory text – see **9.2.3**.

[137ZA Power to order offender to remove obstruction

(1) Where a person is convicted of an offence under section 137 above in respect of the obstruction of a highway and it appears to the court that –

(a) the obstruction is continuing, and
(b) it is in that person's power to remove the cause of the obstruction,

the court may, in addition to or instead of imposing any punishment, order him to take, within such reasonable period as may be fixed by the order, such steps as may be specified in the order for removing the cause of the obstruction.

(2) The time fixed by an order under subsection (1) above may be extended or further extended by order of the court on an application made before the end of the time as originally fixed or as extended under this subsection, as the case may be.

(3) If a person fails without reasonable excuse to comply with an order under subsection (1) above, he is guilty of an offence and liable to a fine not exceeding level 5 on the standard scale; and if the offence is continued after conviction he is guilty of a further offence and liable to a fine not exceeding one-twentieth of that level for each day on which the offence is so continued.

(4) Where, after a person is convicted of an offence under subsection (3) above, the highway authority for the highway concerned exercise any power to remove the cause of the obstruction, they may recover from that person the amount of any expenses reasonably incurred by them in, or in connection with, doing so.

(5) A person against whom an order is made under subsection (1) above is not liable under section 137 above in respect of the obstruction concerned –

(a) during the period fixed under that subsection or any extension under subsection (2) above, or
(b) during any period under section 311(1) below by a court before whom he is convicted of an offence under subsection (3) above in respect of the order.]

Amendment – Inserted by the CROW Act 2000, s 64(1).

Explanatory text – see **9.2.3**.

[137A Interference by crops

(1) Where a crop other than grass has been sown or planted on any agricultural land the occupier of the land shall from time to time take such steps as may be necessary –

(a) to ensure that the line on the ground of any relevant highway on the land is so indicated to not less than its minimum width as to be apparent to members of the public wishing to use the highway; and
(b) to prevent the crop from so encroaching on any relevant highway, whether passing over that or adjoining land, as to render it inconvenient for the exercise of the public right of way.

(2) For the purposes of subsection (1) above, a crop shall be treated as encroaching on a highway if, and only if, any part of the crop grows on, or otherwise extends onto or over,

the highway in such a way as to reduce the apparent width of the highway to less than its minimum width.

(3) For the purposes of the application of subsection (1) above in the case of a particular crop, the crop shall be treated as grass if, and only if –

(a) it is of a variety or mixture commonly used for pasture, silage or haymaking, whether or not it is intended for such a use in that case; and
(b) it is not a cereal crop.

(4) If the occupier fails to comply with the duty imposed by subsection (1) above he is guilty of an offence and liable to a fine not exceeding level 3 on the standard scale.

(5) Without prejudice to section 130 (protection of public rights) above, it is the duty of the highway authority to enforce the provisions of this section.

(6) In this section –

'minimum width', in relation to a highway, has the same meaning as in Schedule 12A to this Act; and

'relevant highway' means –

(a)   a footpath,
(b)   a bridleway, or
(c)   any other highway which consists of or comprises a carriageway other than a made-up carriageway.]

Amendment – Inserted by Rights of Way Act 1990, s 1(5).

Explanatory text – see **9.3.3**.

. . .

143   Power to remove structures from highways

(1) Where a structure has been erected or set up on a highway otherwise than under a provision of this Act or some other enactment, a competent authority may by notice require the person having control or possession of the structure to remove it within such time as may be specified in the notice.

For the purposes of this section the following are competent authorities –

(a) in the case of a highway which is for the time being maintained by a [non-metropolitan] district council by virtue of section 42 or 50 above, that council and also the highway authority, and
(b) in the case of any other highway, the highway authority.

(2) If a structure in respect of which a notice is served under this section is not removed within the time specified in the notice, the competent authority serving the notice may, subject to subsection (3) below, remove the structure and recover the expenses reasonably incurred by them in so doing from the person having control or possession of the structure.

(3) The authority shall not exercise their power under subsection (2) above until the expiration of one month from the date of service of the notice.

(4) In this section 'structure' includes any machine, pump, post or other object of such a nature as to be capable of causing obstruction, and a structure may be treated for the purposes of this section as having been erected or set up notwithstanding that it is on wheels.

Amendment – Local Government Act 1985, s 8, Sch 4, Pt I, para 25.

Explanatory text – see **9.6.5**.

...

145   Powers as to gates across highways

(1) Where there is a gate of less than the minimum width across so much of a highway as consists of a carriageway, or across a highway that is a bridleway, the highway authority for the highway may by notice to the owner of the gate require him to enlarge the gate to that width or remove it.

In this subsection 'the minimum width' means, in relation to a gate across so much of a highway as consists of a carriageway, 10 feet and, in relation to a gate across a bridleway, 5 feet, measured in either case between the posts of the gate.

(2) If a person on whom a notice under subsection (1) above is served fails to comply, within 21 days from the date of service of the notice on him, with a requirement of the notice, he is guilty of an offence and liable to a fine not exceeding 50p for each day during which the failure continues.

Explanatory text – see **9.2.4**.

---

146   Duty to maintain stiles etc on footpaths and bridleways

(1) Any stile, gate or other similar structure across a footpath or bridleway shall be maintained by the owner of the land in a safe condition, and to the standard of repair required to prevent unreasonable interference with the rights of the persons using the footpath or bridleway.

(2) If it appears to the appropriate authority that the duty imposed by subsection (1) above is not being complied with, they may, after giving to the owner and occupier not less than 14 days' notice of their intention, take all necessary steps for repairing and making good the stile, gate or other works.

For the purposes of this section the appropriate authority is –

(a) in the case of a footpath or bridleway which is for the time bing maintained by a [non-metropolitan] district council by virtue of section 42 or 50 above, that council, and

(b) in the case of any other footpath or bridleway, the highway authority.

(3) The appropriate authority may recover from the owner of the land the amount of any expenses reasonably incurred by the authority in and in connection with the exercise of their powers under subsection (2) above, or such part of those expenses as the authority think fit.

(4) The appropriate authority shall contribute not less than a quarter of any expenses shown to their satisfaction to have been reasonably incurred in compliance with

subsection (1) above, and may make further contributions of such amount in each case as, having regard to all the circumstances, they consider reasonable.

(5) Subsection (1) above does not apply to any structure –

(a) if any conditions for the maintenance of the structure are for the time being in force under section 147 below, or
(b) if and so long as, under an agreement in writing with any other person, there is a liability to maintain the structure on the part of the appropriate authority or, where the appropriate authority are a [non-metropolitan] district council, on the part of either the appropriate authority or the highway authority.

Amendment – Local Government Act 1985, s 8, Sch 4, Pt I, para 25.

Prospective amendment – Paragraph prospectively inserted before the word 'or' at the end of para (a) in subs (5) by the CROW Act 2000, s 69(4):

'(aa) if any conditions for the maintenance of the structure imposed by virtue of subsection (4) of section 147ZA below are for the time being in force under that section,'

Explanatory text – see **9.2.4**.

---

147 Power to authorise erection of stiles etc on footpath or bridleway

(1) The following provisions of this section apply where the owner, lessee or occupier of agricultural land, or of land which is being brought into use for agriculture, represents to a competent authority, as respects a footpath or bridleway that crosses the land, that for securing that the use, or any particular use, of the land for agriculture shall be efficiently carried on, it is expedient that stiles, gates or other works for preventing the ingress or egress of animals should be erected on the path or way.

For the purposes of this section the following are competent authorities –

(a) in the case of a footpath or bridleway which is for the time being maintained by a [non-metropolitan] district council by virtue of section 42 or 50 above, that council and also the highway authority, and
(b) in the case of any other footpath or bridleway, the highway authority.

(2) Where such a representation is made the authority to whom it is made may, subject to such conditions as they may impose for maintenance and for enabling the right of way to be exercised without undue inconvenience to the public, authorise the erection of the stiles, gates or other works.

(3) Where an authorisation in respect of a footpath or bridleway is granted under this section the public right of way is to be deemed to be subject to a condition that the stiles, gates or works may be erected and maintained in accordance with the authorisation and so long as the conditions attached to it are complied with.

(4) For the purposes of section 143 above, any stile, gate or works erected in pursuance of an authorisation under this section is to be deemed to be erected under this section only if the provisions of the authorisation and any conditions attached to it are complied with.

(5) In this section references to agricultural land and to land being brought into use for agriculture include references to land used or, as the case may be, land being brought into use, for forestry.

(6) Nothing in this section prejudices any limitation or condition having effect apart from this section.

Amendment – Local Government Act 1985, s 8, Sch 4, Pt I, para 25.

Prospective amendments – Subsections prospectively inserted after subs(2) by the CROW Act 2000, s 69(1):

'(2A) In exercising their powers under subsection (2) above a competent authority shall have regard to the needs of persons with mobility problems.

(2B) The Secretary of State may issue guidance to competent authorities as to matters to be taken into account for the purposes of subsection (2) above; and in exercising their powers under subsection (2) above competent authorities shall have regard to any such guidance issued to them.'

Words prospectively inserted at the end of subs(5) by the CROW Act 2000, s 69(2):

'or for the breeding or keeping of horses.'

Section prospectively inserted after s 147 by the CROW Act 2000, s 69(3):

'147ZA Agreements relating to improvements for benefit of persons with mobility problems

(1) With respect to any relevant structure, a competent authority may enter into an agreement with the owner, lessee or occupier of the land on which the structure is situated which provides –

   (a) for the carrying out by the owner, lessee or occupier of any qualifying works and the payment by the competent authority of the whole or any part of the costs incurred by him in carrying out those works, or

   (b) for the carrying out by the competent authority of any qualifying works at their own expense or subject to the payment by the owner, lessee or occupier of the whole or any part of the costs incurred in carrying out those works.

(2) In this section –

   (a) "competent authority" has the same meaning as in section 147 above,

   (b) "relevant structure" means a stile, gate or other structure which –

      (i) is authorised by a condition or limitation subject to which the public right of way over the footpath or bridleway was created, or

      (ii) is authorised under section 147 above, but does not include a structure to which an agreement falling within section 146(5)(b) above relates, and

   (c) "qualifying works", in relation to a relevant structure, means works for replacing or improving the structure which will result in a structure that is safer or more convenient for persons with mobility problems.

(3) An agreement under this section may include such conditions as the competent authority thinks fit.

(4) Those conditions may in particular include conditions expressed to have enduring effect –

   (a) for the maintenance of the structure as replaced or improved, and

   (b) for enabling the public right of way to be exercised without undue inconvenience to the public.

(5) Where an agreement under this section has been entered into in relation to any structure –

   (a) the public right of way is to be deemed to be subject to a condition that the structure as replaced or improved may be erected and maintained in accordance with the agreement so long as any conditions included by virtue of subsection (4) above are complied with,

   (b) in a case falling within subsection (2)(b)(i) above, as from the effective date the previous condition or limitation relating to the relevant structure shall cease to have effect, and

(c) in a case falling within subsection (2)(b)(ii) above, as from the effective date the previous authorisation under section 147 above shall cease to have effect in relation to the relevant structure.

(6) In subsection (5) above 'the effective date' means –

(a) the first anniversary of the day on which the agreement was entered into, or
(b) such earlier date as may be specified for the purposes of this subsection in the agreement.

(7) For the purposes of section 143 above, any stile, gate or other structure replaced or improved in pursuance of an agreement under this section is to be deemed to be erected under this section only if any conditions included by virtue of subsection (4) above are complied with.

(8) A competent authority may not enter into an agreement under this section except with the consent of every owner, lessee or occupier of the land on which the relevant structure is situated who is not a party to the agreement.

(9) The Secretary of State may issue guidance to competent authorities as to matters to be taken into account for the purposes of this section; and in exercising their powers under this section competent authorities shall have regard to any such guidance issued to them.'

Explanatory text – see **9.2.4**.

. . .

148   Penalty for depositing things or pitching booths etc on highway

If, without lawful authority or excuse –

(a) a person deposits on a made-up carriageway any dung, compost or other material for dressing land, or any rubbish, or
(b) a person deposits on any highway that consists of or comprises a made-up carriageway any dung, compost or other material for dressing land, or any rubbish, within 15 feet from the centre of that carriageway, or
(c) a person deposits any thing whatsoever on a highway to the interruption of any user of the highway, or
(d) a hawker or other itinerant trader pitches a booth, stall or stand, or encamps, on a highway,

he is guilty of an offence and liable to a fine not exceeding [level 3 on the standard scale].

Amendment – Criminal Justice Act 1982, ss 38, 46.

Explanatory text – see **9.6.4**.

149   Removal of things so deposited on highways as to be a nuisance etc

(1) If any thing is so deposited on a highway as to constitute a nuisance, the highway authority for the highway may by notice require the person who deposited it there to remove it forthwith and if he fails to comply with the notice the authority may make a complaint to a magistrates' court for a removal and disposal order under this section.

(2) If the highway authority for any highway have reasonable grounds for considering –

(a) that any thing unlawfully deposited on the highway constitutes a danger (including a danger caused by obstructing the view) to users of the highway, and

(b) that the thing in question ought to be removed without the delay involved in giving notice or obtaining a removal and disposal order from a magistrates' court under this section,

the authority may remove the thing forthwith.

(3) The highway authority by whom a thing is removed in pursuance of subsection (2) above may either –

(a) recover from the person by whom it was deposited on the highway, or from any person claiming to be entitled to it, any expenses reasonably incurred by the authority in removing it, or
(b) make a complaint to a magistrates' court for a disposal order under this section.

(4) A magistrates' court may, on a complaint made under this section, make an order authorising the complainant authority –

(a) either to remove the thing in question and dispose of it or, as the case may be, to dispose of the thing in question, and
(b) after payment out of any proceeds arising from the disposal of the expenses incurred in the removal and disposal, to apply the balance, if any, of the proceeds to the maintenance of highways maintainable at the public expense by them.

(5) If the thing in question is not of sufficient value to defray the expenses of removing it, the complainant authority may recover from the person who deposited it on the highway the expenses, or the balance of the expenses, reasonably incurred by them in removing it.

(6) A magistrates' court composed of a single justice may hear a complaint under this section.

Explanatory text – see 9.6.4, 10.11.

---

150   Duty to remove snow, soil etc from highway

(1) If an obstruction arises in a highway from accumulation of snow or from the falling down of banks on the side of the highway, or from any other cause, the highway authority shall remove the obstruction.

(2) If a highway authority fail to remove an obstruction which it is their duty under this section to remove, a magistrates' court may, on a complaint made by any person, by order require the authority to remove the obstruction within such period (not being less than 24 hours) from the making of the order as the court thinks reasonable, having regard to all the circumstances of the case.

(3) In considering whether to make an order under this section and, if so, what period to allow for the removal of the obstruction, the court shall in particular have regard to –

(a) the character of the highway to which the complaint relates, and the nature and amount of the traffic by which it is ordinarily used,
(b) the nature and extent of the obstruction, and
(c) the resources of manpower, vehicles and equipment for the time being available to the highway authority for work on highways and the extent to which those resources are being, or need to be, employed elsewhere by that authority on such work.

(4) Where they are under a duty to remove an obstruction under subsection (1) above, a highway authority may –

  (a) take any reasonable steps (including the placing of lights, signs and fences on the highway) for warning users of the highway of the obstruction;
  (b) sell any thing removed in carrying out the duty, unless the thing is claimed by its owner before the expiration of 7 days from the date of its removal;
  (c) recover from the owner of the thing which caused or contributed to the obstruction, or where the thing has been sold under paragraph (b) above, from its previous owner, the expenses reasonably incurred as respects the obstruction in carrying out the duty and in exercising any powers conferred by this subsection, but so that no such expenses are recoverable from a person who proves that he took reasonable care to secure that the thing in question did not cause or contribute to the obstruction.

(5) Where a highway authority sell any thing in exercise of their powers under subsection (4) above, then –

  (a) if any expenses are recoverable under that subsection by the authority from the previous owner of the thing, they may set off the expenses against the proceeds of sale (without prejudice to the recovery of any balance of the expenses from the previous owner) and shall pay over any balance of the proceeds to the previous owner; and
  (b) if no expenses are so recoverable, they shall pay over the whole of the proceeds of sale to the previous owner.

(6) The foregoing provisions of this section apply to a person liable to maintain a highway by reason of tenure, enclosure or prescription as they apply to the highway authority for that highway, and references in those provisions to a highway authority are to be construed accordingly.

Explanatory text – see **9.6.6**.

---

151   Prevention of soil etc being washed on to street

(1) A competent authority may, by notice to the owner or occupier of any land adjoining a street which is a highway maintainable at the public expense, require him, within 28 days from the date of service of the notice, to execute such works as will prevent soil or refuse from that land from falling, or being washed or carried, on to the street or into any sewer or gully in it in such quantities as to obstruct the street or choke the sewer or gully.

  For the purposes of this section the following are competent authorities –

  (a) in relation to a street outside Greater London, the highway authority for the street and[, if the street is situated in a non-metropolitan district, the council of that district; and]
  (b) in relation to a street within Greater London, the council of the London borough in which the street is situated or, if it is situated in the City of London, the Common Council ...

[(1A) In relation to a street in Wales, the competent authorities for the purposes of this section are the highway authority for the street and, if different, the Welsh council in whose area the street is situated.]

(2) A person aggrieved by a requirement under this section may appeal to a magistrates' court.

(3) Subject to any order made on appeal, if a person on whom a notice is served under this section fails to comply with it within the period specified in subsection (1) above, he is guilty of an offence and liable to a fine not exceeding [level 3 on the standard scale]; and if the offence is continued after conviction, he is guilty of a further offence and liable to a fine not exceeding £1 for each day on which the offence is so continued.

Amendments – Local Government Act 1985, ss 8, 102, Sch 4, Pt I, para 26, Sch 17; Local Government (Wales) Act 1994, s 22(1), Sch 7, Pt I, para 13; Criminal Justice Act 1982, ss 38, 46.

Explanatory text – see **9.6.6**.

. . .

154 Cutting or felling etc trees etc that overhang or are a danger to roads or footpaths

(1) Where a hedge, tree or shrub overhangs a highway or any other road or footpath to which the public has access so as to endanger or obstruct the passage of vehicles or pedestrians, or obstructs or interferes with the view of drivers of vehicles or the light from a public lamp, [or overhangs a highway so as to endanger or obstruct the passage of horse-riders,] a competent authority may, by notice either to the owner of the hedge, tree or shrub or to the occupier of the land on which it is growing, require him within 14 days from the date of service of the notice so to lop or cut it as to remove the cause of the danger, obstruction or interference.

For the purposes of this section the following are competent authorities –

(a) in relation to a highway for which the Minister is the highway authority and which is in a district or London borough, the Minister and also the council of the district or, as the case may be, borough;
(b) in relation to a highway for which a local highway authority are the highway authority, that authority and[, if the highway is situated in a non-metropolitan district, the council of that district;]
(c) in relation to a road or footpath that is not a highway, the local authority in whose area the road or footpath is situated;

and 'hedge, tree or shrub' includes vegetation of any description.

[(1A) In subsection (1)(a) above, any reference to a district includes a reference to a Welsh county or county borough.]

(2) Where it appears to a competent authority for any highway, or for any other road or footpath to which the public has access –

(a) that any hedge, tree or shrub is dead, diseased, damaged or insecurely rooted, and
(b) that by reason of its condition it, or part of it, is likely to cause danger by falling on the highway, road or footpath,

the authority may, by notice either to the owner of the hedge, tree or shrub or to the occupier of the land on which it is situated, require him within 14 days from the date of service of the notice so to cut or fell it as to remove the likelihood of danger.

(3) A person aggrieved by a requirement under subsection (1) or (2) above may appeal to a magistrates' court.

(4) Subject to any order made on appeal, if a person on whom a notice is served under subsection (1) or (2) above fails to comply with it within the period specified in those subsections, the authority who served the notice may carry out the work required by the notice and recover the expenses reasonably incurred by them in so doing from the person in default.

Amendments – Local Government Act 1985, s 8, Sch 4, Pt I, para 27; Local Government (Wales) Act 1994, s 22(1), Sch 7, Pt I, para 14; CROW Act 2000, s 65.

Explanatory text – see **9.2.5**.

---

155   Penalties in connection with straying animals

(1) If any horses, cattle, sheep, goats or swine are at any time found straying or lying on or at the side of a highway their keeper is guilty of an offence, but this subsection does not apply in relation to a part of a highway passing over any common, waste or unenclosed ground.

In this section 'keeper', in relation to any animals, means a person in whose possession they are.

(2) A person guilty of an offence under this section is liable to a fine not exceeding [level 3 on the standard scale].

(3) A person guilty of an offence under this section is also liable to pay the reasonable expenses of removing any animal so found straying or lying to the premises of their keeper, or to the common pound, or to such other place as may have been provided for the purpose, and any person who incurs such expenses is entitled to recover them summarily as a civil debt.

For the purposes of this subsection 'expenses', in a case where an animal has been removed to the common pound, includes the usual fees and charges of the authorised keeper of the pound.

(4) If a person, without lawful authority or excuse, releases any animal seized for the purpose of being impounded under this section from the pound or other place where it is impounded, or on the way to or from any such place, or damages any such place, he is guilty of an offence and liable to a fine not exceeding [level 2 on the standard scale].

(5) Nothing in this section prejudices or affects any right of pasture on the side of a highway.

Amendment – Criminal Justice Act 1982, ss 38, 46.

Explanatory text – see **9.7.5**.

. . .

160A   Further powers of highway authorities and district councils in relation to highways

Schedule 12A to this Act shall have effect.

Amendment – Inserted by Rights of Way Act 1990, s 1(6).

Explanatory text – see **9.3.5, 9.3.6**.

Danger or annoyance to users of highways and streets

161 Penalties for causing certain kinds of danger or annoyance

(1) If a person, without lawful authority or excuse, deposits any thing whatsoever on a highway in consequence of which a user of the highway is injured or endangered, that person is guilty of an offence and liable to a fine not exceeding [level 3 on the standard scale].

[(2) If a person without lawful authority or excuse –

(a) lights any fire on or over a highway which consists of or comprises a carriageway; or
(b) discharges any firearm or firework within 50 feet of the centre of such a highway,

and in consequence a user of the highway is injured, interrupted or endangered, that person is guilty of an offence and liable to a fine not exceeding level 3 on the standard scale.]

(3) If a person plays at football or any other game on a highway to the annoyance of a user of the highway he is guilty of an offence and liable to a fine not exceeding [level 1 on the standard scale].

(4) If a person, without lawful authority or excuse, allows any filth, dirt, litter or other offensive matter or thing to run or flow on to a highway from any adjoining premises, he is guilty of an offence and liable to a fine not exdeeding [level 1 on the standard scale].

Amendment – Criminal Justice Act 1982, ss 38, 46; Highways (Amendment) Act 1986, s 1(2).

Explanatory text – see **9.5.5., 9.5.6**.

[161A Danger or annoyance caused by fires lit otherwise than on highways

(1) If a person –

(a) lights a fire on any land not forming part of a highway which consists of or comprises a carriageway; or
(b) directs or permits a fire to be lit on any such land,

and in consequence a user of any highway which consists of or comprises a carriageway is injured, interrupted or endangered by, or by smoke from, that fire or any other fire caused by that fire, that person is guilty of an offence and liable to a fine not exceeding level 5 on the standard scale.

(2) In any proceedings for an offence under this section it shall be a defence for the accused to prove –

(a) that at the time the fire was lit he was satisfied on reasonable grounds that it was unlikely that users of any highway consisting of or comprising a carriageway would be injured, interrupted or endangered by, or by smoke from, that fire or any other fire caused by that fire; and

(b) either –
(i) that both before and after the fire was lit he did all he reasonably could to prevent users of any such highway from being so injured, interrupted or endangered, or
(ii) that he had a reasonable excuse for not doing so.]

Amendment – Inserted by Highways (Amendment) Act 1986, s 1(3).

Explanatory text – see **9.5.6**.

---

162   Penalty for placing rope etc across highway

A person who for any purpose places any rope, wire or other apparatus across a highway in such a manner as to be likely to cause danger to persons using the highway is, unless he proves that he had taken all necessary means to give adequate warning of the danger, guilty of an offence and liable to a fine not exceeding [level 3 on the standard scale].

Amendment – Criminal Justice Act 1982, ss 38, 46.

Explanatory text – see **9.2.4**.

---

163   Prevention of water falling on or flowing on to highway

(1) A competent authority may, by notice to the occupier of premises adjoining a highway, require him within 28 days from the date of service of the notice to construct or erect and thereafter to maintain such channels, gutters or downpipes as may be necessary to prevent –

(a) water from the roof or any other part of the premises falling upon persons using the highway, or
(b) so far as is reasonably practicable, surface water from the premises flowing on to, or over, the footway of the highway.

For the purposes of this section the competent authorities, in relation to any highway, are the highway authority and also (where they are not the highway authority) the local authority for the area in which the highway is situated.

(2) A notice under subsection (1) above may, at the option of the authority, be served on the owner of the premises in question instead of on the occupier or may be served on both the owner and the occupier of the premises.

(3) A person aggrieved by a requirement under this section may appeal to a magistrates' court.

(4) Subject to any order made on appeal, if a person on whom a notice is served under this section fails to comply with the requirement of the notice within the period specified in subsection (1) above he is guilty of an offence and liable to a fine not exceeding [level 1 on the standard scale]; and if the offence is continued after conviction he is guilty of a further offence and liable to a fine not exceeding £2 for each day on which the offence is so continued.

Amendment – Criminal Justice Act 1982, ss 38, 46.

---

164   Power to require removal of barbed wire

(1) Where on land adjoining a highway there is a fence made with barbed wire, or having barbed wire in or on it, and the wire is a nuisance to the highway, a competent authority may by notice served on the occupier of the land require him to abate the nuisance within such time, not being less than one month nor more than 6 months from the date of service of the notice, as may be specified in it.

For the purposes of this section –

(a) the competent authorities, in relation to any highway, are the highway authority and also (where they are not the highway authority) the local authority for the area in which the highway is situated;
'barbed wire' means wire with spikes or jagged projections, and barbed wire is to be deemed to be a nuisance to a highway if it is likely to be injurious to persons or animals lawfully using the highway.

(2) If at the expiration of the time specified in the notice the occupier has failed to comply with the notice, a magistrates' court, if satisfied on complaint made by the authority that the wire is a nuisance to the highway, may order the occupier to abate the nuisance and, if he fails to comply with the order within a reasonable time, the authority may do whatever may be necessary in execution of the order and recover from him the expenses reasonably incurred by them in so doing.

(3) If the local authority who are a competent authority in relation to the highway concerned are the occupiers of the land in question proceedings under this section may be taken against them by any ratepayer within the area of that local authority and the foregoing provisions apply accordingly in relation to him and to the authority as they apply in relation to an authority and to an occupier of land.

Explanatory text – see **9.2.4**.

---

165   Dangerous land adjoining street

(1) If, in or on any land adjoining a street, there is an unfenced or inadequately fenced source of danger to persons using the street, the local authority in whose area the street is situated may, by notice to the owner or occupier of that land, require him within such time as may be specified in the notice to execute such works of repair, protection, removal or enclosure as will obviate the danger.

(2) A person aggrieved by a requirement under subsection (1) above may appeal to a magistrates' court.

(3) Subject to any order made on appeal, if a person on whom a notice is served under this section fails to comply with the notice within the time specified in it, the authority by whom the notice was served may execute such works as are necessary to comply with the notice and may recover the expenses reasonably incurred by them in so doing from that person.

(4) Where the power conferred by subsection (1) above is exercisable in relation to land adjoining a street and has not been exercised by the local authority empowered to exercise it, then, if that authority are not the highway authority for the street, the highway authority for the street may request the local authority to exercise the power.

(5) If the local authority refuse to comply with a request made under subsection (4) above or fail within a reasonable time after the request is made to them to do so, the highway authority may exercise the power (and where they do so subsections (2) and (3) above apply accordingly).

Explanatory text – see **9.5.7**.

. . .

[175A   Duty to have regard to needs of disabled and blind in executing works, etc

(1) In executing works in a street which may impede the mobility of disabled persons or blind persons highway authorities, local authorities and any other person exercising a statutory power to execute works on a highway shall have regard to the needs of such persons.

(2) Any such authority or person as is mentioned in subsection (1) above shall have regard to the needs of disabled persons and blind persons when placing lamp-posts, bollards, traffic-signs, apparatus or other permanent obstructions in a street.

(3) Highway authorities shall have regard to the needs of disabled persons when considering the desirability of providing ramps at appropriate places between carriageways and footways.

(4) In executing in a street any such works as are mentioned in subsection (1) above, any such authority or person as is mentioned in that subsection shall have regard to the need of blind persons to have any openings, whether temporary or permanent, in the street, properly protected.

(5) Section 28 of the Chronically Sick and Disabled Persons Act 1970 (power to define certain expressions for the purposes of provisions of that Act) shall have effect as if any reference in it to a provision of that Act included a reference to this section.]

Amendments – Inserted by Disabled Persons Act 1981, s 1(1).

Explanatory text – see **9.2.4, 10.4**.

. . .

Vesting of highways etc

263   Vesting of highways maintainable at public expense

(1) Subject to the provision of this section, every highway maintainable at the public expense, together with the materials and scrapings of it, vests in the authority who are for the time being the highway authority for the highway.

(2) Subsection (1) above does not apply –

    (a) to a highway with respect to the vesting of which, on its becoming or ceasing to be a trunk road, provision is made by section 265 below, or

    (b) to a part of a trunk road with respect to the vesting of which provision is made by section 266 below, or

    (c) to a part of a special road with respect to the vesting of which provision is made by section 267 below.

(3) Where a scheme submitted to the Minister jointly by two or more local highway authorities under section 16 above determines which of those authorities are to be the special road authority for the special road or any part of it ('the designated authority') and the designated authority are not the highway authority for the road or that part of it, the road or that part of its vests in the designated authority.

(4) Where –

    (a) the responsibility for the maintenance of a bridge or other part of a highway is transferred to a highway authority by means of an order under section 93 above, but the property in it is not so transferred, or

    (b) the responsibility for the maintenance of a part of a highway is transferred to a highway authority in pursuance of an agreement made under section 94 above, but the property in that part is not so transferred,

the part of the highway in question does not by virtue of subsection (1) above vest in that highway authority.

(5) Notwithstanding anything in subsection (1) above, any such material as is referred to in that subsection which is removed from a highway by a [non-metropolitan] district council in exercise of their powers under sections 42, 50 or 230(7) above vests in the district council and not in the highway authority.

Amendments – Local Government Act 1985, s 8, Sch 4, Pt I, para 37.

Explanatory text – see **2.2.1.**

. . .

293 Powers of entry for purposes connected with certain orders relating to footpaths and bridleways

(1) A person duly authorised in writing by the Secretary of State or other authority having power under this Act to make a public path creation order, a public path extinguishment order[, a rail crossing extinguishment order, a public path diversion order or a rail crossing diversion order] may enter upon any land for the purpose of surveying it in connection with the making of the order.

(2) For the purpose of surveying land, or of estimating its value, in connection with a claim for compensation payable by an authority in respect of that or any other land under section 28 above, or under that section as applied by section 121(2) above, a person who is an officer of the Valuation Office or who has been duly authorised in writing by the authority from whom the compensation is claimed may enter upon the land.

(3) A person authorised under this section to enter upon any land shall, if so required, produce evidence of his authority before entering; and a person shall not under this

section demand admission as of right to any land which is occupied unless at least 7 days' notice in writing of the intended entry has been given to the occupier.

(4) A person who wilfully obstructs a person acting in the exercise of his powers under this section is guilty of an offence and liable to a fine not exceeding [level 3 on the standard scale].

Amendments – Transport and Works Act 1992, s 47(1), Sch 2, paras 1, 7; Criminal Justice Act 1982, ss 38, 46.

Prospective amendment – Words prospectively inserted after 'rail crossing extinguishment order' in subs (1) by the CROW Act 2000, Sch 6, para 17:

'a special extinguishment order'

and, in place of 'or a rail crossing diversion order', prospectively substituted:

', a rail crossing diversion order, a special diversion order or an SSSI diversion order'.

Explanatory text – see **4.8.1**.

. . .

297   Power of highway authority or council to require information as to ownership of land

(1) A highway authority or a council may, for the purpose of enabling them to discharge or exercise any of their functions under this Act, require the occupier of any premises and any person who, either directly or indirectly, receives rent in respect of any premises, to state in writing the nature of his own interest therein and the name and address of any other person known to him as having an interest therein, whether as freeholder, mortgagee, lessee or otherwise.

(2) Any person who, having been required in pursuance of this section to give any information, fails to give that information is guilty of an offence and liable to a fine not exceeding [level 3 on the standard scale].

(3) Any person who, having been so required to give any information, knowingly makes any mis-statement in respect thereof is guilty of an offence and liable –

   (a) on summary conviction to a fine not exceeding the prescribed sum within the meaning of section 32(9) of the Magistrates' Courts Act 1980 (£1,000 or such other sum as may be fixed by order under section 143(1) of that Act); or
   (b) on conviction on indictment to imprisonment for a term not exceeding 2 years or to a fine, or both.

Amendments – Criminal Justice Act 1982, ss 38, 46.

Explanatory text – see **9.11.2**.

. . .

300   Right of local authorities to use vehicles and appliances on footways and bridleways

(1) No statutory provision prohibiting or restricting the use of footpaths, footways or bridleways shall affect the use by a competent authority of appliances or vehicles,

whether mechanically operated or propelled or not, for cleansing, maintaining or improving footpaths, footways or bridleways or their verges, or for maintaining or altering structures or other works situated therein.

For the purposes of this section –

(a) the following are competent authorities, namely, the council of any county, district or London borough, the Common Council, the Council of the Isles of Scilly, any parish or community council, or parish meeting, the Sub-Treasurer of the Inner Temple and the Under-Treasuer of the Middle Temple; and

(b) 'statutory provision' means a provision contained in, or having effect under, any enactment.

(2) The Minister of Transport and the Secretary of State acting jointly may make regulations prescribing the conditions under which the rights conferred by this section may be exercised, and such regulations may in particular make provision as to –

(a) the construction of any appliances or vehicles used under this section,

(b) the maximum weight of any such appliances or vehicles, or the maximum weight borne by any wheel or axle,

(c) the maximum speed of any such appliances or vehicles,

(d) the hours during which the appliances or vehicles may be used, and

(e) the giving by the Minister of Transport or the Secretary of State of directions dispensing with or relaxing any requirement of the regulations as it applies to a particular authority or in any particular case.

Explanatory text – see **9.8.4**.

. . .

Inquiries

302 Provisions as to inquiries

(1) Subject to subsection (2) below, the Minister and the Secretary of State may each cause such inquiries to be held as he may consider necessary or desirable for the purposes of his functions under this Act, and subsections (2) to (5) of section 250 of the Local Government Act 1972 (giving of evidence at, and defraying of costs, of inquiries) apply, subject to subsection (2) below, in relation to any inquiry which either of the said Ministers may cause to be held under this section, or in compliance with any requirement of this Act, with the substitution in the case of an inquiry held by the Secretary of State, for references to a Minister, of references to the Secretary of State.

(2) Subsection (4) of the said section 250 (costs of the Minister holding the inquiry to be defrayed by the parties) does not apply in relation to –

(a) an inquiry caused to be held by the Minister for the purposes of his functions under section 93 above, or

(b) an inquiry held in compliance with paragraph 3 of Schedule 10 to this Act, or with paragraph 9 of Schedule 11 to this Act,

in so far as the Minister is of opinion, having regard to the object and result of the inquiry, that the Minister's costs should be defrayed by him.

Explanatory text – see **4.8.12, 6.6.1**.

. . .

Determination of disputes as to compensation

307   Disputes as to compensation which are to be determined by Lands Tribunal and related provisions

(1) Any dispute arising on a claim for compensation under any provision of this Act to which this section applies shall be determined by the Lands Tribunal.

The provisions of this Act to which this section applies are sections 21, 22, 28, 73, 74, 109, 110, 121(2), 126, . . . and 292.

(2) For the purposes of any reference to the Lands Tribunal under this section, section 4 of the Land Compensation Act 1961 (costs) has effect with the substitution, for references to the acquiring authority, of references to the authority from whom the compensation in question is claimed.

(3) Rules 2 to 4 of the Rules in section 5 of the said Act of 1961 (rules for valuation on a compulsory acquisition) apply to the calculation of compensation under any provision of this Act to which this section applies, in so far as it is calculated by reference to the depreciation of the value of an interest in land.

(4) In determining the amount of compensation payable under sections 109, 110 or 126 above the Lands Tribunal shall have regard to any new means of access to the premises of the claimant or, as the case may be, any new right of access to a watercourse from the premises of the claimant, provided by the highway authority from whom the compensation is claimed.

(5) In determining the amount of compensation payable under section 73 above in respect of injurious affection, the Land Tribunal –

(a)   shall take into account any benefit accruing to the claimant by reason of the improvement of the street in relation to which an improvement line has been prescribed under that section, and

(b)   may take into account and embody in their award any undertaking with regard to the exercise of the powers of a highway authority under that section in relation to the property affected which the authority have offered to give to the claimant;

and the terms of any undertaking so embodies in the award are binding on and enforceable against the authority.

(6) In determining the amount of compensation payable under section 74 above, the Lands Tribunal shall take into account any benefit accruing to the claimant by reason of any improvement made or about to be made to the highway in relation to which a building line has been prescribed under that section.

(7) In determining the amount of compensation payable under section 193 or section 200(2) above, the Land Tribunal shall take into account any benefit accruing to the claimant by reason of the widening of a street under the said section 193 or the said section 200(2), as the case may be.

Amendments – Planning and Compensation Act 1991, s 84(6), Sch 19, Pt V.

Explanatory text – see **4.6.5**.

. . .

311   Continuing offences

(1) Where by virtue of any provision of this Act, or of byelaws made under it, a person convicted of an offence is, if the offence in respect of which he was convicted is continued after conviction, guilty of a further offence and liable to a fine for each day on which the offence is so continued, the court before whom the person is convicted of the original offence may fix a reasonable period from the date of conviction for compliance by the defendant with any directions given by the court.

(2) Where a court fixes such a period the defendant is not liable to a fine in respect of the further offence for any day before the expiration of that period.

. . .

315   Notice to be given of right of appeal

Where an appeal lies under this Act to the Crown Court or a magistrates' court against a requirement, order, refusal or other decision of a highway authority or a council, the notice given by the authority or council to the person concerned of the making of the requirement or order or of the refusal or other decision against which such an appeal lies shall state the right of appeal to the Crown Court or a magistrates' court, as the case may be, and the time within which such an appeal may be brought.

. . .

316   Appeals and applications to magistrates' courts

(1) Where any provision of this Act provides –

   (a) for an appeal to a magistrates' court against a requirement, order, refusal or other decision of a highway authority or a council, or

   (b) for any other matter to be determined by, or an application in respect of any matter to be made to, a magistrates' court,

the procedure shall be by way of complaint for an order.

(2) The time within which an appeal such as is mentioned in subsection (1)(a) above may be brought is 21 days from the date on which notice of the decision of the highway authority or council is served on the person wishing to appeal, and for the purpose of this subsection the making of the complaint is to be deemed to be the bringing of the appeal.

. . .

317   Appeals to the Crown Court from decisions of magistrates' courts

(1) Where a person aggrieved by an order, determination or other decision of a magistrates' court under this Act is not by any other enactment authorised to appeal to the Crown Court he may appeal to that court.

(2) The applicant for an order under section 116 above or any person who was entitled under subsection (7) of that section to be, and was, or claimed to be, heard on the application may appeal to the Crown Court against the decision made by the magistrates' court on the application.

Prospective amendment – Text prospectively inserted after subsection (2) by CROW Act 2000, s 63(2):

'(3) Any person who, in relation to the decision of a magistrates' court on an application under section 130B above does not fall within subsection (1) above but –

  (a) is, within the meaning of section 130A above, a person for the time being responsible for the obstruction to which the application related, or
  (b) when the application was heard, was such a person and was, or claimed to be, heard on the application,

may appeal to the Crown Court against the decision on any ground relating to the matters mentioned in section 130B(4) above.'

Explanatory text – see **4.4.6, 9.2.2**.

. . .

Crown application

327 Application of Act to Crown land

(1) The provisions of this section apply in relation to any land belonging to Her Majesty in right of the Crown or of the Duchy of Lancaster, or belonging to the Duchy of Cornwall, or belonging to a government department, or held in trust for Her Majesty for the purposes of a government department.

(2) The appropriate authority in relation to any land and a highway authority may agree that any provisions of this Act specified in the agreement shall apply to that land and, while the agreement is in force, those provisions shall apply to that land accordingly, subject however to the terms of the agreement.

(3) Any such agreement as is mentioned in subsection (2) above may contain such consequential and incidental provisions, including provisions of a financial character, as appear to the appropriate authority to be necessary or equitable, but provisions of a financial character shall not be included in an agreement made by a government department without the approval of the Treasury.

(4) In this section 'the appropriate authority' means –

  (a) in the case of land belonging to Her Majesty in right of the Crown, the Crown Estate Commissioners or other government department having the management of the land in question;
  (b) in the case of land belonging to Her Majesty in right of the Duchy of Lancaster, the Chancellor of the Duchy;
  (c) in the case of land belonging to the Duchy of Cornwall, such person as the Duke of Cornwall, or the possessor for the time being of the Duchy of Cornwall, appoints;
  (d) in the case of land belonging to a government department or held in trust for Her Majesty for the purposes of a government department, that department;

and, if any question arises as to what authority is the appropriate authority in relation to any land, that question shall be referred to the Treasury, whose decision shall be final.

Interpretation

328   Meaning of 'highway'

(1) In this Act, except where the context otherwise requires, 'highway' means the whole or a part of a highway other than a ferry or waterway.

(2) Where a highway passes over a bridge or through a tunnel, that bridge or tunnel is to be taken for the purposes of this Act to be a part of the highway.

(3) In this Act, 'highway maintainable at the public expense' and any other expression defined by reference to a highway is to be construed in accordance with the foregoing provisions of this section.

329   Further provision as to interpretation

(1) In this Act, except where the context otherwise requires –

> . . .
> [*definition not reproduced*]
> 'adjoining' includes abutting on, and 'adjoins' is to be construed accordingly;
> [*definition not reproduced*]
> 'agriculture' includes horticulture, fruit growing, seed growing, dairy farming, the breeding and keeping of livestock (including any creature kept for the production of food, wool, skins or fur, or for the purpose of its use in the farming of land), the use of land as grazing land, meadow land, osier land, market gardens and nursery grounds, and the use of land for woodlands where that use is ancillary to the farming of land for other agricultural purposes, and 'agricultural' is to be construed accordingly;
> 'apparatus' includes any structure constructed for the lodging therein of apparatus;
> [*definitions not reproduced*]
> 'bridleway' means a highway over which the public have the following, but no other, rights of way, that is to say, a right of way on foot and a right of way on horseback or leading a horse, with or without a right to drive animals of any description along the highway;
> [*definitions not reproduced*]
> 'carriageway' means a way constituting or comprised in a highway, being a way (other than a cycle track) over which the public have a right of way for the passage of vehicles;
> [*definitions not reproduced*]
> 'council' means a county council ... or a local authority;
> 'cycle track' means a way constituting or comprised in a highway, being a way over which the public have the following, but no other, rights of way, that is to say, a right of way on pedal cycles (other than pedal cycles which are motor vehicles within the meaning of the Road Traffic Act 1988) with or without a right of way on foot;
> [*definitions not reproduced*]
> 'enactment' includes an enactment in a local or private Act of Parliament and a provision of an order, scheme, regulations or other instrument made under or confirmed by a public general, local or private Act of Parliament;

['field-edge path' means a footpath or bridleway that follows the sides or headlands of a field or enclosure;]

[*definition not reproduced*]

'footpath' means a highway over which the public have a right of way on foot only, not being a footway;

[*definition not reproduced*]

'functions' includes powers and duties;

[*definitions not reproduced*]

'highway maintainable at the public expense' means a highway which by virtue of section 36 above or of any other enactment (whether contained in this Act or not) is a highway which for the purposes of this Act is a highway maintainable at the public expense;

'horse' includes pony, ass and mule, and 'horseback' is to be construed accordingly;

[*definitions not reproduced*]

'land' includes land covered by water and any interest or right in, over or under land;

[*definitions not reproduced*]

'local authority' means the council of a district or London borough or the Common Council but, in relation to Wales, means a Welsh council;

[*definition not reproduced*]

'made-up carriageway' means a carriageway, or a part thereof, which has been metalled or in any other way provided with a surface suitable for the passage of vehicles;

'maintenance' includes repair, and 'maintain' and 'maintainable' are to be construed accordingly;

[*definitions not reproduced*]

'owner', in relation to any premises, means a person, other than a mortgage not in possession, who, whether in his own right or as trustee or agent for any other person, is entitled to receive the rack rent of the premises or, where the premises are ot let at a rack rent, would be so entitled if the premises were so let;

. . .

'premises' includes land and buildings;

[*definitions not reproduced*]

'public path creation agreement' means an agreement under section 25 above;

'public path creation order' means an order under section 26 above;

'public path diversion order' means an order under section 119 above;

'public path extinguishment order' means an order under section 118 above;

[*definitions not reproduced*]

['rail crossing diversion order' means an order under section 119A above;

'rail crossing extinguishment order' means an order under section 118A above;]

[*definitions not reproduced*]

'statutory undertakers' means persons authorised by any enactment to carry on any of the following undertakings: –

(a) a railway, tramway, road transport, water transport, canal, inland navigation, dock, harbour, pier or lighthouse undertaking, or

(b) an undertaking for the supply of ... or hydraulic power,

and 'statutory undertaking' is to be construed accordingly;

['street' has the same meaning as in Part III of the New Roads and Street Works Act 1991;]

[*definitions not reproduced*]

(2) A highway at the side of a river, canal or other inland navigation is not excluded from the definition in subsection (1) above of either 'bridleway' or 'footpath', by reason only that the public have a right to use the highway for purposes of navigation, if the highway would fall within that definition if the public had no such right thereover. [*subsections not reproduced*]

Amendments – Acquisition of Land Act 1981, s 34, Sch 6; Transport Act 1981, s 32, Sch 10, Pt I, para 1; SI 1981/238; Cycle Tracks Act 1984, s 1 ; London Regional Transport Act 1984, s 71(3), Sch 6, para 21; Sch 7; Road Traffic Regulation Act 1984, s 146, Sch 13; Telecommunications Act 1984, s 109, Sch 4, para 76; Local Government Act 1985, s 102, Sch 17; Gas Act 1986, s 67(4), Sch 9, Pt I; Road Traffic (Consequential Provisions) Act 1988, s 4, Sch 3, para 21(2); Electricity Act 1989, s 112(4), Sch 18; Road Traffic (Driver Licensing and Information Systems) Act 1989, s 13(1), Sch 4, para 3(13); Statute Law (Repeals) Act 1989; Water Act 1989, s 190(1), (3), Sch 25, para 62(12), Sch 27, Pt I; Planning (Consequential Provisions) Act 1990, s 4, Sch 2, para 45(17); Rights of Way Act 1990, s 2; New Roads and Street Works Act 1991, s 168(1), Sch 8, Pt I, para 15; Traffic Calming Act 1992, s 1(3); Transport and Works Act 1992, s 47, Sch 2, para 9; Statute Law (Repeals) Act 1993; Local Government (Wales) Act 1994, s 22(1), Sch 7, para 27(2)–(4); SI 1996/593; Access to Justice Act 1999, s 106, Sch 15, Pt V(1); Greater London Authority Act 1999, s 263(6); SI 2001/1149.

Prospective amendments – Definitions prospectively inserted at various places in subs (1) by the CROW Act 2000, ss 51, 57, Sch 5, Pt II, para 16(a), Sch 6, Pt I, para 20(a)–(f):

"definitive map and statement" has the same meaning as in Part III of the Wildlife and Countryside Act 1981;';
"proprietor", in relation to a school, has the same meaning as in the Education Act 1996;';
"restricted byway" has the same meaning as in Part II of the Countryside and Rights of Way Act 2000;';
"school" has the same meaning as in the Education Act 1996;';
"special diversion order" means an order under section 119B(4) above;';
"special extinguishment order" means an order under section 118B(4) above;';
"SSSI diversion order" means an order under section 119D above;'.

Words either "bridleway" or "footpath" in subs (2) prospectively substituted by the CROW Act 2000, s 51, Sch 5, Pt II, para 16(b):

"bridleway", "footpath" or "restricted byway"'.

. . .

Savings, etc

333 Saving for rights and liabilities as to interference with highways

[(1)] No provision of this Act relating to obstruction of or other interference with highways is to be taken to affect any right of a highway authority or other person under any enactment not contained in this Act, or under any rule of law, to remove an obstruction from a highway or otherwise abate a nuisance or other interference with the highway, or to affect the liability of any person under such an enactment or rule to proceedings (whether civil or criminal) in respect of any such obstruction or other interference.

[(2) Nothing in section 134 or 135 above relating to disturbance of the surface of a highway in any manner is to be taken as affecting any right existing apart from this Act to disturb its surface in that manner.]

Amendments – Rights of Way Act 1990, s 3.

. . .

SCHEDULE 6

PROVISIONS AS TO MAKING, CONFIRMATION, VALIDITY AND DATE OF
OPERATION OF CERTAIN ORDERS RELATING TO FOOTPATHS AND
BRIDLEWAYS

PART I

PROCEDURE FOR MAKING AND CONFIRMING CERTAIN ORDERS RELATING
TO FOOTPATHS AND BRIDLEWAYS

1.–(1) Before a public path creation order, a public path extinguishment order[, a rail crossing extinguishment order, a public path diversion order or a rail crossing diversion order] is submitted to the Secretary of State for confirmation or confirmed as an unopposed order, the authority by whom the order was made shall give notice in the prescribed form –

(a) stating the general effect of the order and that it has been made and is about to be submitted for confirmation or to be confirmed as an unopposed order,

(b) naming a place in the area in which the land to which the order relates is situated where a copy of the order and of the map referred to therein may be inspected free of charge [and copies thereof may be obtained at a reasonable charge] at all reasonable hours, and

(c) specifying the time (which shall not be less than 28 days from the date of the first publication of the notice) within which, and the manner in which, representations or objections with respect to the order may be made.

(2) Before the Secretary of State makes a public path creation order, a public path extinguishment order[, a rail crossing extinguishment order, a public path diversion order or a rail crossing diversion order], he shall prepare a draft of the order and shall give notice –

(a) stating that he proposes to make the order and the general effect of it,

(b) naming a place in the area in which the land to which the draft order relates is situated where a copy of the draft order and of the map referred to in it may be inspected free of charge [and copies thereof may be obtained at a reasonable charge] at all reasonable hours, and

(c) specifying the time (which shall not be less than 28 days from the date of the first publication of the notice) within which, and the manner in which, representations or objections with respect to the draft order may be made.

[(3) The notices to be given under sub-paragraph (1) or (2) above shall be given –

(a) by publication in at least one local newspaper circulating in the area in which the land to which the order relates is situated;

(b) by serving a like notice on –

(i) every owner, occupier and lessee (except tenants for a month or any period less than a month and statutory tenants within the meaning of the Rent (Agriculture) Act 1976 or the Rent Act 1977 [and licensees under an assured agricultural occupancy within the meaning of Part I of the Housing Act 1988] of any of that land;

(ii) every council, the council of every parish or community and the parish meeting of every parish not having a separate parish council being a council, parish or community whose area includes any of that land;

(iii) every person on whom notice is required to be served in pursuance of sub-paragraph (3A) or (3B) below; and

(iv) such other persons as may be prescribed in relation to the area in which that land is situated or as the authority or, as the case may be, the Secretary of State may consider appropriate; and

(c) by causing a copy of the notice to be displayed in a prominent position –

(i) at the ends of so much of any footpath or bridleway as is created, stopped up or diverted by the order;

(ii) at council offices in the locality of the land to which the order relates; and

(iii) at such other places as the authority or, as the case may be, the Secretary of State may consier appropriate.]

[(3A) Any person may, on payment of such reasonable charge as the authority may consider appropriate, require an authority to give him notice of all such public path creation orders, public path extinguishment orders[, rail crossing extinguishment orders, public path diversion orders and rail crossing diversion orders] as are made by the authority during a specified period, are of a specified description and relate to land comprised in a specified area; and in this sub-paragraph 'specified' means specified in the requirement.

(3B) Any person may, on payment of such reasonable charge as the Secretary of State may consider appropriate, require the Secretary of State to give him notice of all such draft public path creation orders, draft public path extinguishment orders[, draft rail crossing extinguishment orders, draft public path diversion orders and draft rail crossing diversion orders] as are prepared by the Secretary of State during a specified period, are of a specified description and relate to land comprised in a specified area; and in this sub-paragraph 'specified' means specified in the requirement.

(3C) The Secretary of State may, in any particular case, direct that it shall not be necessary to comply with sub-paragraph (3)(b)(i) above; but if he so directs in the case of any land, then in addition to publication the notice shall be addressed to 'The owner and any occupiers' of the land (describing it) and a copy or copies of the notice shall be affixed to some conspicuous object or objects on the land.]

(4) Where under this paragraph a notice is required to be served on an owner of land and the land belongs to an ecclesiastical benefice, a like notice shall be served on the Church Commissioners.

[(4A) Sub-paragraph (3)(b) and (c) and, where applicable, sub-paragraphs (3C) and (4) above shall be complied with not less than 28 days before the expiration of the time specified in the notice.

(4B) A notice required to be served by sub-paragraph (3)(b)(i), (ii) or (iv) above shall be accompanied by a copy of the order.

(4C) A notice required to be displayed by sub-paragraph (3)(c)(i) above at the ends of so much of any way as is affected by the order shall be accompanied by a plan showing the general effect of the order so far as it relates to that way.

(4D) In sub-paragraph (3)(c)(ii) above 'council offices' means offices or buildings acquired or provided by a council or by the council of a parish or community or the parish meeting of a parish not having a separate parish council.]

2.–(1) If no representations or objections are duly made, or if any so made are withdrawn, then –

   (a) the Secretary of State may, if he thinks fit, confirm or make the order, as the case may be, with or without modifications;
   (b) the authority by whom the order was made (where not the Secretary of State) may, instead of submitting the order to the Secretary of State, themselves confirm the order (but without any modification).

(2) If any representation or objection duly made is not withdrawn, the Secretary of State shall, before confirming or making the order, as the case may be, if the objection is made by a local authority cause a local inquiry to be held, and in any other case either –

   (a) cause a local inquiry to be held, or
   (b) afford to any person by whom any representation or objection has been duly made and not withdrawn an opportunity of being heard by a person appointed by him for the purpose,

and, after considering the report of the person appointed to hold the inquiry or to hear representations or objections, may, subject as provided below, confirm or make the order, as the case may be, with or without modifications.

In the case of a public path creation order or a public path diversion order, if objection is made by statutory undertakers on the ground that the order provides for the creation of a public right of way over land covered by works used for the purposes of their undertaking or the curtilage of such land, and the objection is not withdrawn, the order is subject to special parliamentary procedure.

(3) Notwithstanding anything in the foregoing provisions of this paragraph, the Secretary of State shall not confirm or make an order so as to affect land not affected by the order as submitted to him or the draft order prepared by him, as the case may be, except after –

   (a) giving such notice as appears to him requisite of his proposal so to modify the order, specifying the time (which shall not be less than 28 days from the date of the first publication of the notice) within which, and the manner in which, representations or objections with respect to the proposal may be made,
   (b) holding a local inquiry or affording to any person by whom any representation or objection has been duly made and not withdrawn an opportunity of being heard by a person appointed by him for the purpose, and
   (c) considering the report of the person appointed to hold the inquiry or to hear representations or objections, as the case may be,

and, in the case of a public path creation order or a public path diversion order, if objection is made by statutory undertakers on the ground that the order as modified would provide for the creation of a public right of way over land covered by works used for the purposes of their undertaking or the curtilage of such land, and the objection is not withdrawn, the order is subject to special parliamentary procedure.

[2A.–(1) A decision of the Secretary of State under paragraph 2 above as respects an order made by an authority other than the Secretary of State shall, except in [the case of a rail crossing extinguishment order, the case of a rail crossing diversion order and] such classes of case as may for the time being be prescribed or as may be specified in directions given by the Secretary of State, be made by a person appointed by the Secretary of State for the purpose instead of by the Secretary of State; and a decision made by a person so appointed shall be treated as a decision of the Secretary of State.

(2) The Secretary of State may, if he thinks fit, direct that a decision which, by virtue of sub-paragraph (1) above and apart from this sub-paragraph, falls to be made by a person appointed by the Secretary of State shall instead be made by the Secretary of State; and a direction under this sub-paragraph shall state the reasons for which it is given and shall be served on the person, if any, so appointed, the authority and any person by whom a representation or objection has been duly made and not withdrawn.

(3) Where the Secretary of State has appointed a person to make a decision under paragraph 2 above the Secretary of State may, at any time before the making of the decision, appoint another person to make it instead of the person first appointed to make it.

(4) Where by virtue of sub-paragraph (2) or (3) above a particular decision falls to be made by the Secretary of State or any other person instead of the person first appointed to make it, anything done by or in relation to the latter shall be treated as having been done by or in relation to the former.

(5) Provision may be made by regulations of the Secretary of State for the giving of publicity to any directions given by the Secretary of State under this paragraph.

3.–(1) The Secretary of State may, subject to the provisions of this Part of this Schedule, by regulations make such provision as to the procedure on the making, submission and confirmation of orders to which this Schedule applies as appears to him to be expedient.

(2) Provision may be made by regulations of the Secretary of State for enabling proceedings preliminary to the confirmation of a public path extinguishment order or a rail crossing extinguishment order [or a rail crossing extinguishment order] to be taken concurrently with proceedings preliminary to the confirmation of a public path creation order[, a public path diversion order or a rail crossing diversion order].

(3) In this Part of this Schedule –

    (a) 'local authority' means –

        [[(i) a billing authority or a precepting authority, as defined in secion 69 of the Local Government Finance Act 1992;
        (ia) ... a combined fire authority, as defined in section 144 of the Local Government Finance Act 1988;]
        (ii) a levying body within the meaning of section 74 of that Act; and
        (iii) a body as regards which section 75 of that Act applies]
        and includes any drainage authority and any joint board or joint committee if all the constituent authorities are such local authorities as aforesaid;
    (b) 'prescribed' means prescribed by regulations made by the Secretary of State;

and for the purposes of this Schedule the Civil Aviation Authority[, a person who holds a licence under Chapter I of Part I of the Transport Act 2000 (to the extent that the person is carrying out activities authorised by the licence)] and [a universal service provider in connection with the provision of a universal postal service] are to be deemed to be statutory undertakers and their undertakings statutory undertakings.

[(3ZA) For the purposes of sub-paragraph (3) above the undertaking of a person who holds a licence under Chapter I of Part I of the Transport Act 2000 shall not be considered to be a statutory undertaking except to the extent that it is the person's undertaking as licence holder.]

[(3A) For the purposes of sub-paragraph (3) above the undertaking of a universal service provider shall be taken to be his undertaking so far as it relates to the provision of a universal postal service.]

Amendments – Transport and Works Act 1992, s 47(1), Sch 2, paras 1, 10; Wildlife and Countryside Act 1981, s 63, Sch 16, para 6; Housing Act 1988, ss 63, 140(1), Sch 16, para 7, Sch 17, Pt I, para 30; Local Government Finance (Repeals, Savings and Consequential Amendments) Order 1990, SI 1990/776, art 8, Sch 3, para 21; Local Government Finance Act 1992, s 117(1), Sch 13, para 50; Police and Magistrates' Courts Act 1984, s 93, Sch 9, Pt I; Postal Services Act 2000 (Consequential Modifications No 1) Order 2001, SI 2001/1149; Transport Act 2000 (Consequential Amendments) Order 2001, SI 2001/4050.

Prospective amendments – By CROW Act 2000, Sch, para 23, in para 1(1) and (2), after 'rail crossing extinguishment order', are prospectively inserted the words:

', a special extinguishment order'

and the words 'or a rail crossing diversion order' are prospectively substituted by:

', a rail crossing diversion order, a special diversion order or an SSSI diversion order';

in para 1(3A), after 'rail crossing extinguishment orders' are prospectively inserted the words:

', special extinguishment orders'

and the words 'and rail crossing diversion orders' are prospectively substituted by:

', rail crossing diverison orders, special diversion orders and SSSI diversion orders';

in para 1(3B), after ', draft rail crossing extinguishment orders' are prospectively inserted the words:

', draft special extinguishment orders'

and the words 'and draft rail crossing diversion orders' are prospectively substituted by:

', draft rail crossing diversion orders, draft special diversion orders and draft SSSI diversion orders';

at the beginning of para(2)1)(a) are prospectively substituted the words:

'subject to sub-paragraph (2A)';

in para 2(2) and (3), the words 'or a public path diversion order' are prospectively substituted by:

', a public path diversion order, a special diversion order or as an SSI diversion ofder';

after para 2(2), there is prospectively inserted:

'(2A) Before making or confirming an order on an appeal under section 121D(1) of this Act, the Secretary of State shall –

(a) if requested by the authority who made an order to which the appeal relates to cause a local inquiry to be held, cause such an inquiry to be held, and
(b) if a request to be heard with respect to the question to be determined is made by the appellant, either afford to the appellant an opportunity of being heard by a person appointed by the Secretary of State for the purpose or cause a local inquiry to be held,

whether or not he would be required to do so apart from this sub-paragraph.'

After para 2 there is prospectively inserted:

'2ZA.–(1) Where a public path extinguishment order, a special extinguishment order, a public path diversion order or a special diversion order is made by an authority other than the Secretary of

State on an application under section 118ZA, 118C, 119ZA or 119C of this Act, that authority shall, as soon as reasonably practicable after the expiry of the time for representations, determine –

(a) whether, in the case of an unopposed order, to confirm it under paragraph 2(1)(b) above, or

(b) whether to submit the order to the Secretary of State.

(2) The authority making a determination required by sub-paragraph (1) above shall, as soon as practicable after making it, give to the applicant notice in writing of their determination and the reasons for it and give a copy of the notice to such other person as may be prescribed.

(3) Where –

(a) an authority other than the Secretary of State have made a public path extinguishment order, a special extinguishment order, a public path diversion order or a special diversion order on an application under section 118ZA, 118C, 119ZA or 119C of this Act, and

(b) at the end of the period of two months beginning with the expiry of the time for representations, that authority have not determined –

(i) whether, in the case of an unopposed order, to confirm it under paragraph 2(1)(b) above, or

(ii) whether to submit the order to the Secretary of State,

the Secretary of State may, at the request of the person on whose application the order was made, by direction require the authority to determine that question before the end of such period as may be specified in the direction.

(4) In this paragraph "the time for representations" means the time specified by the authority in accordance with paragraph 1(1)(c) above.

2ZB. Where, in relation to any public path extinguishment order, special extinguishment order, public path diversion order or special diversion order which was made by an authority other than the Secretary of State on an application under section 118ZA, 118C, 119ZA or 119C of this Act, no representations or objections are duly made or any representations or objections so made are withdrawn, that authority may not submit the order to the Secretary of State for confirmation with any modification of the map in the order.'

in para 2A(1), from the beginning to the word 'shall', there is prospectively substituted:

'The following decisions –

(a) a decision of the Secretary of State under paragraph 2 above as respects an order made by an authority other than the Secretary of State including any related decision under section 120(5) of this Act, and

(b) a decision of the Secretary of State under section 121E(1)(c) of this Act, including any related decision under section 120(5) of this Act,

shall';

after para 2A, there is prospectively inserted:

'2B.–(1) Subject to sub-paragraph (2), subsections (2) to (5) of section 250 of the Local Government Act 1972 (giving of evidence at, and defraying of costs of, inquiries) apply to a haring which the Secretary of State causes to be held under paragraph 2 above as they apply (by virtue of section 302(1) of this Act) to a local inquiry which he causes to be held under this Act.

(2) In its application to a hearing or local inquiry held under paragraph 2 above by a person appointed under paragraph 2A(1) above, subsection (5) of section 250 of that Act shall have effect as if the reference to the Minister causing the inquiry to be held were a reference to the person so appointed or the Secretary of State.

(3) Section 322A of the Town and Country Planning Act 1990 (orders as to costs where no hearing or inquiry takes place) appies in relation to a hearing or inquiry under paragraph 2 above as it applies in relation to a hearing or local inquiry for the purposes referred to in that section.';

in para 3(2), the words 'or a rail crossing extinguishment order' are prospectively substituted by:

', a rail crossing extinguishment order or a special extinguishment order'

and the words 'or a rail crossing diversion order' are prospectively substituted by:

', a rail crossing diversion order, a special diversion order or an SSSI diversion order'.

PART II

VALIDITY AND DATE OF OPERATION OF CERTAIN ORDERS RELATING TO FOOTPATHS AND BRIDLEWAYS

4.–[(1)] As soon as may be after an order to which this Schedule applies has been confirmed or made by the Secretary of State or confirmed as an unopposed order, the authority by whom the order was made or, in the case of an order made by the Secretary of State, the Secretary of State, shall publish, in the manner required in relation to the class of order in question by paragraph 1(3) above, a notice in the prescribed form describing the general effect of the order, stating that it has been confirmed or made, and naming a place where a copy of it as confirmed or made may be inspected free of charge [and copies thereof may be obtained at a reasonable charge] at all reasonable hours, and –

[(a) serve a like notice on any persons on whom notices were required to be served under paragraph 1(3)(b), (3C) or (4) above; and
(b) cause like notices to be displayed in the like manner as the notices caused to be displayed under paragraph 1(3)(c) above;]

but no such notice or copy need be served on a person unless he has sent to the authority or the Secretary of State (according as the notice or copy would require to be served by an authority or by the Secretary of State) a request in that behalf specifying an address for service.

[(2) A notice required to be served by sub-paragraph (1)(a) above, on –

(a) a person on whom notice was required to be served by paragraph 1(3)(b)(i) or (ii) above; or
(b) in the case of an order which has been confirmed or made with modifications, a person on whom notice was required to be served by paragraph 193)(b)(iv) above,

shall be accompanied by a copy of the order as confirmed or made.

(3) As soon as may be after a decision not to confirm an order to which this Schedule applies, the authority by whom the order was made shall give notice of the decision by serving a copy of it on any persons on whom notices were required to be served under paragraph 1(3)(b), (3C) or (4) above.]

[4A. As soon as may be after an order to which this Schedule applies has come into operation otherwise than –

(a) on the date on which it was confirmed or made by the Secretary of State or confirmed as an unopposed order; or
(b) at the expiration of a specified period beginning with that date,

the authority by whom the order was made or, in the case of an order made by the Secretary of State, the Secretary of State shall give notice of its coming into operation by publication in at least one local newspaper circulating in the area in which the land to which the order relates is situated.]

5. Schedule 2 to this Act (except paragraph 1 thereof) applies in relation to an order to which this Schedule applies as it applies in relation to a scheme or order to which that Schedule applies, but with the following modifications –

(a) for references to a scheme or order to which that Schedule applies substitute references to an order to which this Schedule applies;

(b) for the references in paragraphs 2, 4 and 5 thereof to the date on which the notice required by paragraph 1 thereof is first published substitute references to the date on which the notice required by paragraph 4 above is first published; and

(c) paragraph 4 of that Schedule has effect as if the words 'or on such later date, if any, as may be specified in the scheme or order' were omitted.

6. In this Part of this Schedule 'prescribed' means prescribed by regulations made by the Secretary of State.

Amendments – Wildlife and Countryside Act, s 63, Sch 16, paras 8(1)(2), 9.

Prospective amendments – By CROW Act 2000, Sch 6, para 23, at the end of para 4(3) are prospectively inserted the words:

'other than any person on whom notice of the decision is required to be served under paragraph 2ZA(2) above'

. . .

SCHEDULE 12

PROVISIONS AS TO ORDERS UNDER SECTION 116 AND CONVEYANCES UNDER SECTION 256

PART I

NOTICES TO BE GIVEN BY APPLICANT FOR ORDER UNDER SECTION 116

1. At least 28 days before the day on which an application for an order under section 116 of this Act is made in relation to a highway the applicant authority shall give notice of their intention to apply for the order, specifying the time and place at which the application is to be made and the terms of the order applied for (embodying a plan showing what will be the effect thereof) –

(a) to the owners and occupiers of all lands adjoining the highway;

(b) to any statutory undertakers having apparatus under, in, upon, over, along or across the highway;

(c) if the highway is a classified road, to the Minister;

(d) if the highway is a classified [road in a non-metropolitan district, to the district council [if the highway is a classified road in a Welsh county or county borough and the council of that county or county borough is not the highway authority, to the council of that county or county borough], and if the highway is a classified road] in, or partly in, a parish or community which has a separate parish council or community council, to the parish or community council, as the case may require or, in the case of a parish which does not have a separate parish council, to the chairman of the parish meeting.

2. Not later than 28 days before the day on which the application is made the applicant authority shall cause a copy of the said notice to be displayed in a prominent position at the ends of the highway.

3. At least 28 days before the day on which the application is made the applicant authority shall publish in the London Gazette and in at least one local newspaper circulating in the area in which the highway is situated a notice containing the particulars specified in paragraph 1 above, except that there may be substituted for the plan a statement of a place in the said area where the plan may be inspected free of charge at all reasonable hours.

Amendments – Local Government Act 1985, s 8, Sch 4, Pt I, para 43; Local Government (Wales) Act 1994, s 22(1), Sch 7, Pt I, para 29.

PART II

APPARATUS OF STATUTORY UNDERTAKERS

4. Where this Part of this Schedule applies in relation to a highway, the statutory undertakers whose apparatus is under, in, upon, over, along or across the highway have the same powers and rights in respect of that apparatus, subject to the provisions of this Schedule, as if the order authorising the highway to be stopped up or diverted had not been made or, as the case may be, as if the conveyance of land pursuant to section 256 of this Act had not been made.

5. Where a highway is stopped up or diverted in pursuance of an order under section 116 or land is conveyed pursuant to section 256, the statutory undertakers whose apparatus is under, in, upon, over, along or across the highway may, and, if reasonably requested so to do by the authority on whose application the order was made, or who conveyed the land, as the case may be, shall –

    (a) remove the apparatus and place it or other apparatus provided in substitution for it in such other position as they may reasonably determine and have power to place it; or

    (b) provide other apparatus in substitution for the existing apparatus and place it in such position as aforesaid.

Any works executed under this paragraph (including the provision of apparatus thereunder) are hereafter in this Part of this Schedule referred to as 'undertakers' works'.

6. Subject to the following provisions of this Part of this Schedule, the authority on whose application an order under section 116 stopping up or diverting a highway was made or, as the case may be, the authority who conveyed the land pursuant to section 256, shall pay to any statutory undertakers an amounmt equal to the cost reasonably incurred by them in or in connection with –

    (a) the execution of undertakers' works required in consequence of the stopping up or diversion of that highway or, as the case may be, the conveyance of the land, and

    (b) the doing of any other work or thing rendered necessary by the execution of undertakers' works.

7. If in the course of the execution of undertakers' works under paragraph 5 above –

    (a) apparatus of better type, of greater dimensions or of greater capacity is placed in substitution for existing apparatus of worse type, of smaller dimensions or of smaller capacity, or

(b) apparatus (whether existing apparatus or apparatus substituted for existing apparatus) is placed at a depth greater than the depth at which the existing apparatus was,

and the placing of apparatus of that type, dimensions or capacity, or the placing of apparatus at that depth, as the case may be, is not agreed by the authority concerned, or, in default of agreement, is not determined by arbitration to be necessary, then, if it involves cost in the execution of the undertakers' works exceeding that which would have been involved if the apparatus placed had been of the existing type, dimensions or capacity, or at the existing depth, as the case may be, the amount which apart from this paragraph would be payable to the undertakers by virtue of paragraph 6 above shall be reduced by the amount of that excess.

8. For the purposes of paragraph 7 above –

(a) an extension of apparatus to a length greater than the length of existing apparatus shall not be treated as a placing of apparatus of greater dimensions than those of the existing apparatus;
(b) where the provision of a joint in a cable is agreed, or is determined to be necessary, the consequential provision of a jointing chamber or of a manhole shall be treated as if it also had been agreed or had been so determined.

9. An amount which apart from this paragraph would be payable to undertakers in respect of works of theirs by virtue of paragraph 6 above (and having regard, where relevant, to paragraph 7 above) shall, if the works include the placing of apparatus provided in substitution for apparatus placed more than $7\frac{1}{2}$ years earlier so as to confer on the undertakers any financial benefit by deferment of the time for renewal of the apparatus in the ordinary course, be reduced by the amount which represents that benefit.

10. Any question arising under this Part of this Schedule shall, in default of agreement between the parties concerned, be determined by arbitration.

[PART IIII

INTERPRETATION

11. In this Schedule, 'statutory undertakers' includes operators of driver informaton systems.]

Amendments – Part inserted by Road Traffice (Driver Licensing and Information Systems) Act 1989, s 13(1), Sch 4, para 3(1), (14).

Prospective amendments – By CROW Act 2000, Sch 6, para 24, after Sch 12 there is prospectively inserted:

'SCHEDULE 12ZA

DELEGATION OF FUNCTION OF MAKING DETERMINATION

Interpretation

1. In this Schedule –

"appointed person" means a person appointed under section 121(5B) of this Act;
"appropriate Minister" has the same meaning as in section 121(5) of this Act;
"appointment", in the case of any appointed person, means appointment under section 121(5B) of this Act.

2. An appointment under section 121(5B) of this Act must be in writing and –

(a) may relate to a particular question specified in the appointment or to questions of a description so specified,

(b) may provide for any function to which it relates to be exercisable by the appointed person either uconditionally or subject to the fulfilment of such conditions as may be specified in the appointment, and

(c) may, by notice in writing given to the appointed person, be revoked at any time by the appropriate Minister in respect of any question which has not been determined by the appointed person before that time.

Powers of appointed person

3. Subject to the provisions of this Schedule, an appointed person shall, in relation to the determination of any question to which his appointment relates, have the same powers and duties as the appropriate Minister, other than –

(a) any function of holding an inquiry or other hearing or of causing an inquiry or other hearing to be held; or

(b) any function of appointing a person for the purpose –
    (i) of enabling persons to appear before and be heard by the person so appointed; or
    (ii) of referring any question or matter to that person.

Holding of inquiries and other hearings by appointed persons

4.–(1) If either of the following persons –

(a) the statutory undertakers to which the question relates, and

(b) in the case of an order to be made on an application under section 118ZA, 118C, 119Za or 119C of this Act, the person who made the application,

express a wish to appear before and be heard by the appointed person, the appointed person shall give them an opportunity of appearing and being heard.

(2) Whether or not sub-paragraph (1) above applies, the appointed person –

(a) may hold an inquiry or other hearing in connection with the determination of the question, and

(b) shall, if the appropriate Minister so directs, hold an inquiry in conneciton with that determination.

(3) Where an appointed person holds an inquiry or other hearing by virtue of this Schedule, an assessor may be appointed by the appropriate Minister to sit with the appointed person at the inquiry or hearing and advise him on any matters arising, notwithstanding that the appointed person is to determine the question.

(4) Subject to paragraph 7 below, the costs of an inquiry or other hearing held under this Schedule shall be defrayed by the appropriate Minister.

Revocation of appointments and making of new appointments

5.–(1) Where under paragraph 2(c) above the appointment of the appointed person is revoked in respect of any question, the appropriate Minister shall, unless he proposes to determine the question himself, appoint another person under section 121(5B) of this Act to determine the question instead.

(2) Where such a new appointment is made, the consideration of the question, or any hearing in connection with it, shall be begun afresh.

(3) Nothing in sub-paragraph (2) above shall require any person to be given an opportunity of making fresh representations or modifying or withdrawing any representations already made.

Certain acts and omissions of appointed person to be treated as those of appropriate Minister

6.–(1) Anything done or omitted to be done by an appointed person in, or in connection with, the exercise or purported exercise of any function to which the appointment relates shall be treated for all purposes as done or omitted to be done by the appropriate Minister.

(2) Sub-paragraph (1) above does not apply –

    (a) for the purposes of so much of any contract made between the appropriate Minister and the appointed person as relates to the exercise of the function, or

    (b) for the purposes of any criminal proceedings brought in respect of anything done or omitted to be done as mentioned in that sub-paragraph.

Local inquiries and hearings: evidence and costs

7. Subsections (2) to (5) of section 250 of the Local Government Act 1972 (local inquiries: evidence and costs) shall apply to local inquiries or other hearings held under this Schedule by an appointed person as they apply to inquiries caused to be held under that section by a Minister, but as if –

    (a) in subsection (2) (evidence) the reference to the person appointed to hold the inquiry were a reference to the appointed person,

    (b) in subsection (4) (recovery of costs of holding inquiry) references to the Minister causing the inquiry to be held were references to the appropriate Minister, and

    (c) in subsection (5) (orders as to the costs of the parties) the reference to the Minister causing the inquiry to be held were a reference to the appointed person or the appropriate Minister.'

[SCHEDULE 12A

FURTHER POWERS OF HIGHWAY AUTHORITIES AND COUNCILS IN RELATION TO INTERFERENCE WITH HIGHWAYS

Interpretation

1.–(1) For the purposes of this Schedule the 'minimum width' and 'maximum width' of a highway shall be determined in accordance with sub-paragraphs 92) and (3) below.

(2) In any case where the width of the highway is proved, that width is both the 'minimum width' and the 'maximum width'.

(3) In any other case –

    (a) the 'minimum width' is –
        (i)   as respects a footpath which is not a field-edge path, 1 metre,
        (ii) as respects a footpath which is a field-edge path, 1.5 metres,
        (iii) as respects a bridleway which is not a field-edge path, 2 metres, or
        (iv) as respects any other highway, 3 metres; and
    (b) the 'maximum width' is –
        (i)   as respcts a footpath, 1.8 metres,
        (ii) as respects a bridleway, 3 metres, or
        (iii) as respects any other highway, 5 metres.

Competent authorities

2. For the purposes of this Schedule each of the following shall be a competent authority in relation to a highway –

    (a) the highway authority; and

(b) in the case of a highway maintained by a district council under section 42 or 50 of this Act, that council.

Power to carry out works

3.–(1) Where the surface of –

(a) a footpath,
(b) a bridleway, or
(c) any other highway wihch consists of or comprises a carriageway other than a made-up carriageway,

has been so disturbed as to render it inconvenient for the exercise of the public right of way, a competent authority may make good the surface to an extent not less than the minimum width nor greater than the maximum width.

(2) Where the surface of a footpath or bridleway was disturbed under the right conferred by section 134(1) of this Act, the power conferred by sub-paragraph (1) above shall not become exercisable until the expiration of the period which is the relevant period for the purposes of section 134 or an extension of that period granted under subsection (8) of that section.

(3) Where the surface of a footpath or bridleway was disturbed under an order made by virtue of section 135 of this Act, the power conferred by sub-paragraph (1) above shall not become exercisable until the expiration of the period which is the authorisation period for the purposes of section 135.

4.–(1) Where the occupier of any land fails to carry out the duty imposed on him by section 134(3)9b) or 137A(1) of this Act in relation to a highway, a competent authority may carry out such works as may be necessary or expedient for the purpose of rectifying the default.

(2) Sub-paragraph (1) above does not authorise the carrying out of works to an extent greater than the maximum width of the highway.

(3) Where the surface of a footpath or bridleway, was disturbed under the right conferred by section 134(1) of this Act, the power conferred by sub-paragraph (1) above shall not become exercisable until the expiration of the period which is the relevant period for the purposes of section 134, or an extension of that period granted under subsection (8) of that section.

5. If the applicant fails to comply with a condition imposed under section 135(3)9b) or (4)(a) or (b) of this Act, a competent authority may carry out such works as may be necessary or expedient for the purpose of rectifying the default.

6. Paragraphs 7 to 9 below have effect in relation to the carrying out by a competent authority of work under paragraphs 3 to 5 above in relation to a highway which passes over any land ('the relevant land').

Entry on land

7. Subject to paragraph 8 below, any person duly authorised in writing by the authority may enter on the relevant land, or any other land the authority reasonably believe to be in the same occupation, for any purpose connected with the carrying out of the work; and may take with him on to the land such vehicles, machinery and other equipment as may be requisite.

8.–(1) Except in the case of entry, solely for the purpose of obtaining information, on land other than a building or structure, before entering on any land the authority shall give the occupier not less than twenty-four hours' notice of their intention to do so; and the notice shall –

(a) identify the highway to which it relates; and

(b) specify the work to be carried out and the equipment to be used for that purpose; and

(c) identify the line or lines of passage over the land in question, if any, that may need to be used for access to the site of the work; and

(d) state the date and time when the power to enter on the land becomes exercisable.

(2) Without prejudice to section 322 (service of notices etc) of this Act, if after reasonable enquiry the authority are satisfied that it is not practicable to ascertain the name and address of the occupier, a notice under this paragraph may be given by addressing it to him as 'The Occupier' of the land (describing it) and affixing copies of the notice to some conspicuous object –

(a) at each end of so much of the highway as is referred to in the notice; and

(b) at such other points in the vicinity of that highway as the authority may consider suitable; and

(c) if appropriate, at a point adjacent to a highway comprising made-up carriageway from which access is required for equipment.

(3) A notice shall not be given under this paragraph before the power referred to in paragraph 3, 4 or 5 above has become exercisable.

Financial

9.–(1) Subject to sub-paragraph (2) below, a competent authority may recover the amount of any expenses reasonably incurred by the authority in, or in connection with, the carrying out of the work–

(a) in a case falling within paragraph 3(1) above, from the occupier of the relevant land or the person who disturbed the surface of the highway; and

(b) in any other case, from the occupier of the relevant land.

(2) A person –

(a) is not liable under paragraph (a) of sub-paragraph (1) above if he shows that he had any lawful authority or excuse for disturbing the surface of the highway; and

(b) is not liable under that paragraph as an occupier of land if he shows that the surface of the highway was not disturbed by him or with his consent.]

Amendment – Schedule inserted by Rights of Way Act 1990, s 4.

Appendix 6

WILDLIFE AND COUNTRYSIDE ACT 1981

(1981 c 69)

. . .

Countryside

39 Management agreements with owners and occupiers of land

(1) A relevant authority may, for the purpose of conserving or enhancing the natural beauty or amenity of any land which is . . . within their area or promoting its enjoyment by the public, make an agreement (in the section referred to as a 'management agreement') with any person having an interest in the land with respect to the management of the land during a specified term or without limitation of the duration of the agreement.

(2) Without prejudice to the generality of subsection (1), a management agreement –

(a) may impose on the person having an interest in the land restrictions as respects the method of cultivating the land, its use for agricultural purposes or the exercise of rights over the land and may impose obligations on that person to carry out works or agricultural or forestry operations or do other things on the land;

(b) may confer on the relevant authority power to carry out works for the purpose of performing their functions under the 1949 Act and the 1968 Act; and

(c) may contain such incidental and consequential provisions (including provisions for the making of payments by either party to the other) as appear to the relevant authority to be necessary or expedient for the purposes of the agreement.

(3) The provisions of a management agreement with any person interested in the land shall, unless the agreement otherwise provides, be binding on persons deriving title under or from that person and be enforceable by the relevant authority against those persons accordingly.

(4) Schedule 2 to the Forestry Act 1967 (powers for tenant for life and others to enter into forestry dedication covenants) shall apply to management agreements as it applies to forestry dedication covenants.

(5) In this section 'the relevant authority' means –

(a) . . .
(aa) as respects land within the Broads, the Broads Authority;
(b) . . .
(c) as respects any other land, the local planning authority.
[(d) as respects any land in England, the Countryside Agency;
(e) as respects any land in Wales, the Countryside Council for Wales;

(f) as respects land in any area of outstanding natural beauty designated under section 82 of the Countryside and Rights of Way Act 2000 for which a conservation board has been established under section 86 of that Act, that board].

(6) The powers conferred by this section on a relevant authority shall be in addition to and not in derogation of any powers conferred on such an authority by or under any enactment.

Amendments – Local Government Act 1985, ss 7, 102(2), Sch 3, para 7(3), (5)(b), Sch 17; Norfolk and Suffolk Broads Act 1988, s 2(5), Sch 3, Pt I, para 31(2); Environment Act 1995, s 120, Sch 24; CROW Act 2000, ss 96(a), 102, Sch 16, Pt VI.

Explanatory text – see **11.3.2**.

. . .

PART III

PUBLIC RIGHTS OF WAY

Ascertainment of public rights of way

53 Duty to keep definitive map and statement under continuous review

(1) In this Part 'definitive map and statement', in relation to any area, means, subject to section 57(3), –

(a) the latest revised map and statement prepared in definitive form for that area under section 33 of the [National Parks and Access to the Countryside Act 1949]; or
(b) where no such map and statement have been so prepared, the original definitive map and statement prepared for that area under section 32 of that Act; or
(c) where no such map and statement have been so prepared, the map and statement prepared for that area under section 55(3).

(2) As regards every definitive map and statement, the surveying authority shall –

(a) as soon as reasonably practicable after the commencement date, by order make such modifications to the map and statement as appear to them to be requisite in consequence of the occurrence, before that date, of any of the events specified in subsection (3); and
(b) as from that date, keep the map and statement under continuous review and as soon as reasonably practicable after the occurrence, on or after that date, of any of those events, by order make such modifications to the map and statement as appear to them to be requisite in consequence of the occurrence of that event.

(3) The events referred to in subsection (2) are as follows –

(a) the coming into operation of any enactment or instrument, or any other event, whereby –
(i) a highway shown or required to be shown in the map and statement has been authorised to be stopped up, diverted, widened or extended;
(ii) a highway shown or required to be shown in the map and statement as a highway of a particular description has ceased to be a highway of that description; or

    (iii) a new right of way has been created over land in the area to which the map relates, being a right of way such that the land over which the right subsists is a public path;

(b) the expiration, in relation to any way in the area to which the map relates, of any period such that the enjoyment by the public of the way during that period raises a presumption that the way has been dedicated as a public path;

(c) the discovery by the authority of evidence which (when considered with all other relevant evidence available to them) shows –

    (i) that a right of way which is not shown in the map and statement subsists or is reasonably alleged to subsist over land in the area to which the map relates, being a right of way to which this Part applies;

    (ii) that a highway shown in the map and statement as a highway of a particular description ought to be there shown as a highway of a different description; or

    (iii) that there is no public right of way over land shown in the map and statement as a highway of any description, or any other particulars contained in the map and statement require modification.

(4) The modifications which may be made by an order under subsection (2) shall include the addition to the statement of particulars as to –

(a) the position and width of any public path or byway open to all traffic which is or is to be shown on the map; and

(b) any limitations or conditions affecting the public right of way thereover.

(5) Any person may apply to the authority for an order under subsection (2) which makes such modifications as appear to the authority to be requisite in consequence of the occurrence of one or more events falling within paragraph (b) or (c) of subsection (3); and the provisions of Schedule 14 shall have effect as to the making and determination of applications under this subsection.

(6) Orders under subsection (2) which make only such modifications as appear to the authority to be requisite in consequence of the occurrence of one or more events falling within paragraph (a) of subsection (3) shall take effect on their being made; and the provisions of Schedule 15 shall have effect as to the making, validity and date of coming into operation of other orders under subsection (2).

Prospective amendments – Words prospectively inserted after the words 'subject to section 57(3)' in subs (1) by the CROW Act 2000, s 51, Sch 5, Pt I, para 1 (1), (2):

   'and 57A(1)'.

Words prospectively inserted after the words 'public path' in subs (a)(iii) by the CROW Act 2000, s 51 Sch 5, Pt I, para 1(1), (3):

   'or a restricted byway'.

The words 'a right of way to which this Part applies' in subs (3)(c)(i) are prospectively substituted by the CROW Act 2000, s 51, Sch 5, Pt I, para 1(1), (4):

   'a right of way such that the land over which the right subsists is a public path or, subject to section 54A, a byway open to all traffic'.

Words prospectively inserted after the words 'public path' in subs(4) by the CROW Act 2000, s 51, Sch 5, Pt I, para 1(1), (5):

   ', restricted byway'.

Subsections prospectively inserted after subs (4) by the CROW Act 2000, s 51, Sch 5, Pt I, para 1(1), (6):

'(4A) Subsection (4B) applies to evidence which, when considered with all other relevant evidence available to the surveying authority, shows as respects a way shown in a definitive map and statement as a restricted byway that the public have, and had immediately before the commencement of section 47 of the Countryside and Rights of Way Act 2000, a right of way for vehicular and all other kinds of traffic over that way.

(4B) For the purposes of subsection (3)(c)(ii), such evidence is evidence which, when so considered, shows that the way concerned ought, subject to section 54A, to be shown in the definitive map and statement as a byway open to all traffic.'

Subsection prospectively inserted after subs (5) by the CROW Act 2000, s 51, Sch 5, Pt I, para 1(1), (7):

'(5A) Evidence to which subsection (4B) applies on the commencement of section 47 of the Countryside and Rights of Way Act 2000 shall for the purposes of subsection (5) and any application made under it be treated as not having been discovered by the surveying authority before the commencement of that section.'

Sections prospectively inserted after s 53 by the CROW Act 2000, s 51, Sch 5, Pt I, para 2:

'53A   Power to include modifications in other orders

(1) This section applies to any order –

    (a) which is of a description prescribed by regulations made by the Secretary of State,
    (b) whose coming into operation would, as regards any definitive map and statement, be an event within section 53(3)(a),
    (c) which is made by the surveying authority, and
    (d) which does not affect land outside the authority's area.

(2) The authority may include in the order such provision as it would be required to make under section 53(2)(b) in consequence of the coming into operation of the other provisions of the order.

(3) An authority which has included any provision in an order by virtue of subsection (2) –

    (a) may at any time before the order comes into operation, and
    (b) shall, if the order becomes subject to special parliamentary procedure,

withdraw the order and substitute for it an order otherwise identical but omitting any provision so included.

(4) Anything done for the purposes of any enactment in relation to an order withdrawn under subsection (3) shall be treated for those purposes as done in relation to the substituted order.

(5) No requirement for the confirmation of an order applies to provisions included in the order by virtue of subsection (2), but any power to modify an order includes power to make consequential modifications to any provision so included.

(6) Provisions included in an order by virtue of subsection (2) shall take effect on the date specified under section 56(3A) as the relevant date.

(7) Where any enactment provides for questioning the validity of an order on any grounds, the validity of any provision included by virtue of subsection (2) may be questioned in the same way on the grounds –

    (a) that it is not within the powers of this Part, or
    (b) that any requirement of this Part or of regulations made under it has not been complied with.

(8) Subject to subsections (5) to (7), the Secretary of State may by regulations provide that any procedural requirement as to the making or coming into operation of an order to which this section applies shall not apply, or shall apply with modifications prescribed by the regulations, to so much of the order as contains provision included by virtue of subsection (2).

(9) Regulations under this section shall be made by statutory instrument which shall be subject to annulment in pursuance of a resolution of either House of Parliament.

53B Register of applications under section 53

(1) Every surveying authority shall keep, in such manner as may be prescribed, a register containing such information as may be prescribed with respect to applications under section 53(5).

(2) The register shall contain such information as may be prescribed with respect to the manner in which such applications have been dealt with.

(3) Regulations may make provision for the register to be kept in two or more parts, each part containing such information relating to applications under section 53(5) as may be prescribed.

(4) Regulations may make provision –

  (a) for a specified part of the register to contain copies of applications and of the maps submitted with them, and

  (b) for the entry relating to any application, and everything relating to it, to be removed from any part of the register when –

    (i) the application (including any appeal to the Secretary of State) has been finally disposed of, and

    (ii) if an order is made, a decision has been made to confirm or not to confirm the order, (without prejudice to the inclusion of any different entry relating to it in another part of the register).

(5) Every register kept under this section shall be available for inspection free of charge at all reasonable hours.

(6) In this section –

'prescribed' means prescribed by regulations;
'regulations' means regulations made by the Secretary of State by statutory instrument;

and a statutory instrument containing regulations under this section shall be subject to annulment in pursuance of a resolution of either House of Parliament.'

Explanatory text – see Chapter 5.

---

54 Duty to reclassify roads used as public paths

(1) As regards every definitive map and statement, the surveying authority shall, as soon as reasonably practicable after the commencement date –

  (a) carry out a review of such of the particulars contained in the map and statement as relate to roads used as public paths; and

  (b) by order make such modifications to the map and statement as appear to the authority to be requisite to give effect to subsections (2) and (3);

and the provisions of Schedule 15 shall have effect as to the making, validity and date of coming into operation of orders under this subsection.

(2) A definitive map and statement shall show every road used as a public path by one of the three following descriptions, namely –

  (a) a byway open to all traffic;
  (b) a bridleway;
  (c) a footpath,

and shall not employ the expression 'road used as a public path' to describe any way.

(3) A road used as a public path shall be shown in the definitive map and statement as follows –

   (a) if a public right of way for vehicular traffic has been shown to exist, as a byway open to all traffic;

   (b) if paragraph (a) does not apply and public bridleway rights have not been shown not to exist, as a bridleway; and

   (c) if neither paragraph (a) nor paragraph (b) applies, as a footpath.

(4) Each way which, in pursuance of an order under subsection (1), is shown in the map and statement by any of the three descriptions shall, as from the coming into operation of the order, be a highway maintainable at the public expense; and each way which, in pursuance of paragraph 9 of Part III of Schedule 3 to the [Countryside Act 1968] is so shown shall continue to be so maintainable.

(5) In this section 'road used as a public path' means a way which is shown in the definitive map and statement as a road used as a public path.

(6) In subsections (2)(a) and (5) of section 51 of the 1949 Act (long distance routes) references to roads used as public paths shall include references to any way shown in a definitive map and statement as a byway open to all traffic.

(7) Nothing in this section or section 53 shall limit the operation of traffic orders under the Road Traffic Regulation Act 1984 or oblige a highway authority to provide, on a way shown in a definitive map and statement as a byway open to all traffic, a metalled carriage-way or a carriage-way which is by any other means provided with a surface suitable for the passage of vehicles.

Amendment – Road Traffic Regulation Act 1984, s 146, Sch 13, para 53.

Prospective amendments – Section prospectively repealed by CROW Act 2000, ss 57(1), 102, Sch 16, Pt II.

Until the coming into force of the CROW Act 2000, s 47(1), the words from the beginning of subs (2) to 'by' are prospectively substituted by the CROW Act 2000, s 51, Sch 5, Pt I, para 3(1), (2)(a):

> 'Where the particulars relating to any road used as a public path have been reviewed under subsection (1)(a), the definitive map and statement shall be modified so as to show that way by'.

Until the coming into force of the CROW Act 2000, s 47(1), the words from 'and shall not' in subs(2) to the end of subs(2) are prospectively repealed by the CROW Act 2000, s 51, Sch 5, Pt I, para 3(1), (2)(b).

The words 'A road used as a public path' in subs (3) are prospectively substituted by the CROW Act 2000, s 51, Sch 5, Pt I, para 3(1), (3):

> 'Such a way'.

Subsection prospectively inserted after subs (5) by the CROW Act 2000, s 51, Sch 5, Pt I, para 3(1), (4):

> '(5A) No order under this Part modifying a definitive map and statement, and no provision included by virtue of section 53A(2) in any order, shall use the expression "road used as a public path" to describe any way not already shown as such in the map and statement.'

Section prospectively inserted after s 54 by the CROW Act 2000, s 51, Sch 5, Pt I, para 4:

> **'54A BOATs not to be added to definitive maps**
>
> (1) No order under this Part shall, after the cut-off date, modify a definitive map and statement so as to show as a byway open to all traffic any way not shown in the map and statement as a highway of any description.

(2) In this section "the cut-off date" means, subject to regulations under subsection (3), 1st January 2026.

(3) The Secretary of State may make regulations –

(a) substituting as the cut-off date a date later than the date specified in subsection (2) or for the time being substituted under this paragraph;

(b) containing such transitional provisions or savings as appear to the Secretary of State to be necessary or expedient in connection with the operation of subsection (1), including in particular its operation in relation to –

(i) an order under section 53(2) for which on the cut-off date an application is pending,

(ii) an order under this Part which on that date has been made but not confirmed,

(iii) an order under section 55 made after that date, or

(iv) an order under this Part relating to any way as respects which such an order, or any provision of such an order, has after that date been to any extent quashed.

(4) Regulations under subsection (3)(a) –

(a) may specify different dates for different areas; but

(b) may not specify a date later than 1st January 2031, except as respects an area within subsection (5).

(5) An area is within this subsectoin if it is in –

(a) the Isles of Scilly, or

(b) an area which, at any time before the repeal by section 73 of this Act of sections 27 to 34 of the 1949 Act –

(i) was excluded from the operation of those sections by virtue of any provision of the 1949 Act, or

(ii) would have been so excluded but for a resolution having effect under section 35(2) of that Act.

(6) Where by virtue of regulations under subsection (3) there are different cut-off dates for areas into which different parts of any way extend, the cut-off date in relation to that way is the later or latest of those dates.

(7) Where it appears to the Secretary of State that any provision of this Part can by virtue of subsection (1) have no further application he may by order make such amendments or repeals in this Part as appear to him to be, in consequence, necessary or expedient.

(8) An order or regulations under this section shall be made by statutory instrument which shall be subject to annulment in pursuance of a resolution of either House of Parliament.'

Explanatory text – see **5.3.3, 5.3.4, 5.7.2**.

55　No further surveys or reviews under the 1949 Act

(1) No survey under sections 27 to 32 of the 1949 Act, or review under section 33 of that Act, shall be begun after the commencement date; and where on that date a surveying authority have not completed such survey or review begun earlier, the Secretary of State may, after consultation with the authority, direct the authority –

(a) to complete the survey or review; or

(b) to abandon the survey or review to such extent as may be specified in the direction.

(2) Where such a survey or review so begun is abandoned, the Secretary of State shall give such notice of the abandonment as appears to him requisite.

(3) Where, in relation to any area, no such survey has been so begun or such a survey so begun is abandoned, the surveying authority shall prepare for that area a map and statement such that, when they have been modified in accordance with the provisions of this Part, they will serve as the definitive map and statement for that area.

(4) Where such a survey so begun is abandoned after a draft map and statement have been prepared and the period for making representations or objections has expired, the authority shall by order modify the map and statement prepared under subsection (3) so as –

(a) to give effect to any determination or decision of the authority under section 29(3) or (4) of the 1949 Act in respect of which either there is no right of appeal or no notice of appeal has been duly served;

(b) to give effect to any decision of the Secretary of State under section 29(6) of that Act; and

(c) to show any particulars shown in the draft map and statement with respect to which no representation or objection has been duly made, or in relation to which all such representations or objections had been withdrawn.

(5) Where such a review so begun is abandoned after a draft map and statement have been prepared and the period for making representations or objections has expired, the authority shall by order modify the map and statement under review so as –

(a) to give effect to any decision of the Secretary of State under paragraph 4(4) of Part II of Schedule 3 to the 1968 Act; and

(b) to show any particulars shown in the draft map and statement but not in the map and statement under review, and to omit any particulars shown in the map and statement under review but not in the draft map and statement, being (in either case) particulars with respect to which no representation or objection has been duly made, or in relation to which all such representations or objections have been withdrawn.

(6) Orders under subsection (4) or (5) shall take effect on their being made.

Prospective amendment – Subsections prospectively inserted after subs (6) by the CROW Act 2000, s 51, Sch 5, Pt I, para 5:

'(7) Every way which –

(a) in pursuance of an order under subsection (5) is shown in a definitive map and statement as a byway open to all traffic, a bridleway or a footpath, and

(b) before the making of the order, was shown in the map and statement under review as a road used as a public path,

shall be a highway maintainable at the public expense.

(8) Subsection (7) does not oblige a highway authority to provide, on a way shown in a definitive map and statement as a byway open to all traffic, a metalled carriage-way or a carriage-way which is by any other means provided with a surface suitable for the passage of vehicles.'

Explanatory text – see **5.2.7, 5.3.1, 8.3.5.**

---

56   Effect of definitive map and statement

(1) A definitive map and statement shall be conclusive evidence as to the particulars contained therein to the following extent, namely –

(a) where the map shows a footpath, the map shall be conclusive evidence that there was at the relevant date a highway as shown on the map, and that the public had thereover a right of way on foot, so however that this paragraph shall be without prejudice to any question whether the public had at that date any right of way other than that right;

(b) where the map shows a bridleway, the map shall be conclusive evidence that there was at the relevant date a highway as shown on the map, and that the public had thereover at that date a right of way on foot and a right of way on horseback or leading a horse, so however that this paragraph shall be without prejudice to any question whether the public had at that date any right of way other than those rights;

(c) where the map shows a byway open to all traffic, the map shall be conclusive evidence that there was at the relevant date a highway as shown on the map, and that the public had thereover at that date a right of way for vehicular and all other kinds of traffic;

(d) where the map shows a road used as a public path, the map shall be conclusive evidence that there was at the relevant date a highway as shown on the map, and that the public had thereover at that date a right of way on foot and a right of way on horseback or leading a horse, so however that this paragraph shall be without prejudice to any question whether the public had at that date any right of way other than those rights; and

(e) where by virtue of the foregoing paragraphs the map is conclusive evidence, as at any date, as to a highway shown thereon, any particulars contained in the statement as to the position or width thereof shall be conclusive evidence as to the position or width thereof at that date, and any particulars so contained as to limitation or conditions affecting the public right of way shall be conclusive evidence that at the said date the said right was subject to those limitations or conditions, but without prejudice to any question whether the right was subject to any other limitations or conditions at that date.

(2) For the purposes of this section 'the relevant date' –

(a) in relation to any way which is shown on the map otherwise than in pursuance of an order under the foregoing provisions of this Part means the date specified in the statement as the relevant date for the purposes of the map;

(b) in relation to any way which is shown on the map in pursuance of such an order, means the date which, in accordance with subsection (3), is specified in the order as the relevant date for the purposes of the order.

(3) Every order under the foregoing provisions of this Part shall specify, as the relevant date for the purposes of the order, such date, not being earlier than six months before the making of the order, as the authority may determine.

(4) A document purporting to be certified on behalf of the surveying authority to be a copy of or of any part of a definitive map or statement as modified in accordance with the provisions of this Part shall be receivable in evidence and shall be deemed, unless the contrary is shown, to be such a copy.

(5) Where it appears to the Secretary of State that paragraph (d) of subsection (1) can have no further application, he may by order made by statutory instrument repeal that paragraph.

Prospective amendments – The words 'road used as a public path' in subs(1)(d) are provisionally substituted by the CROW Act 2000, s 51, Sch 5, Pt I, para 6(1), (2)(a):

'restricted byway'.

Words prospectively inserted after the words 'the map shall' in subs (1)(d) by the CROW Act 2000, s 51, Sch 5, Pt I, para 6(1), (2)(b):

', subject to subsection (2A),'.

Words prospectively inserted after the words 'leading a horse' in subs(1)(d) by the CROW Act 2000, s 51, Sch 5, Pt I, para 6(1), (2)(c):

'together with a right of way for vehicles other than mechanically propelled vehicles'.

Subsection prospectively inserted after subs(1) by the CROW Act 2000, s 51, Sch 5, Pt I, para 6(1), (3):

'(1A) In subsection (1)(d) "mechanically propelled vehicle" does not include an electrically assisted pedal cycle of a class prescribed for the purposes of section 189(1)(c) of the Road Traffic Act 1988.'

Words prospectively inserted after the words 'this Part' in subs (2)(a) by the CROW Act 2000, s 51, Sch 5, Pt I, para 6(1), (4)(a)(i):

'or an order to which section 53A applies which includes provision made by virtue of subsection (2) of that section'.

Words prospectively inserted after the word 'means' in subs(2)(a) by the CROW Act 2000, s 51, Sch 5, Pt I, para 6(1), (4)(a)(ii):

', subject to subsection (2A),'.

Words prospectively inserted after figure '(3)' in subs (2)(b) by the CROW Act 2000, s 51, Sch 5, Pt I, para 6(1), (4)(b):

'or (3A)'.

Subsection prospectively inserted after subs (2) by the CROW Act 2000, s 51, Sch 5, Pt I, para 6(1), (5):

'(2A) In the case of a map prepared before the date of the coming into force of section 47 of the Countryside and Rights of Way Act 2000 –

(a) subsection (1)(d) and (e) have effect subject to the operation of any enactment or instrument, and to any other event, whereby a way shown on the map as a restricted byway has, on or before that date –
(i)   been authorised to be stopped up, diverted or widened, or
(ii) become a public path, and
(b) subsection (2)(a) has effect in relation to any way so shown with the substitution of that date for the date mentioned there.'

Subsection prospectively inserted after subs(3) by the CROW Act 2000, s51, Sch5, Pt I, para6(1), (6):

'(3A) Every order to which section 53A applies which includes provision made by virtue of subsection (2) of that section shall specify, as the relevant date for the purposes of the order, such date as the authority may in accordance with regulations made by the Secretary of State determine.'

Subsection prospectively inserted after subs (4) by the CROW Act 2000, s 51, Sch 5, Pt I, para 6(1), (7):

'(4A) Regulations under this section shall be made by statutory instrument which shall be subject to annulment in pursuance of a resolution of either House of Parliament.'

Subsection (5) prospectively repealed by the CROW Act 2000, ss 51, 102, Sch 5, Pt I, para 6(1), (8), Sch 16, Pt II.

Explanatory text – see **5.5**.

57 Supplementary provisions as to definitive maps and statements

(1) An order under the foregoing provisions of this Part shall be in such form as may be prescribed by regulations made by the Secretary of State, and shall contain a map, on such scale as may be so prescribed, showing the modifications to which the order relates.

(2) Regulations made by the Secretary of State may prescribe the scale on which maps are to be prepared under section 55(3), and the method of showing in definitive maps and statements anything which is required to be so shown.

(3) Where, in the case of a definitive map and statement for any area which have been modified in accordance with the foregoing provisions of this Part, it appears to the surveying authority expedient to do so, they may prepare a copy of that map and statement as so modified; and where they do so, the map and statement so prepared, and not the map and statement so modified, shall be regarded for the purposes of the foregoing provisions of this Part as the definitive map and statement for that area.

(4) The statement prepared under subsection (3) shall specify, as the relevant date for the purposes of the map, such date, not being earlier than six months before the preparation of the map and statement, as the authority may determine.

(5) As regards every definitive map and statement, the surveying authority shall keep –

    (a) a copy of the map and statement; and
    (b) copies of all orders under this Part modifying the map and statement,

available for inspection free of charge at all reasonable hours at one or more places in each district comprised in the area to which the map and statement relate and, so far as appears practicable to the surveying authority, a place in each parish so comprised; and the authority shall be deemed to comply with the requirement to keep such copies available for inspection in a district or parish if they keep available for inspection there a copy of so much of the map and statement and copies of so many of the orders as relate to the district or parish.

(5A) Subsection (5) shall apply in relation to land in Wales as if 'in each district comprised' were omitted.

(6) Notwithstanding anything in subsection (5), an authority shall not be required to keep available for inspection more than one copy of –

    (a) any definitive map and statement; or
    (b) each order under this Part modifying the map and statement,

if, as respects the area to which that map and statement relate, a subsequent map and statement have been prepared under subsection (3); and the said single copies may be kept in such place in the area of the authority as they may determine.

(7) Every surveying authority shall take such steps as they consider expedient for bringing to the attention of the public the provisions of this Part including in particular, section 53(5) and subsection (5).

(8) Regulations under this section shall be made by statutory instrument which shall be subject to annulment in pursuance of a resolution of either House of Parliament.

Amendment – Local Government (Wales) Act 1994, s 66, Sch 16, para 65(7).

Prospective amendments – The words 'on such scale as may be so prescribed,' in subs (1) are prospectively repealed by the CROW Act 2000, ss 51, 102, Sch 5, Pt I, para 7(1), (2), Sch 16, Pt II.

The words 'section 55(3)' in subs (2) are prospectively substituted by the CROW Act 2000, s 51, Sch 5, Pt I, para 7(1), (3):

'subsection (1) or any other provision of this Part'.

Words prospectively inserted after the words 'for the purposes of the foregoing provisions of this Part' in subs (3) by the CROW Act 2000, s 51, Sch 5, Pt I, para 7(1), (4):

', and for the purposes of section 57A(1),'.

Subsection prospectively inserted after subs (3) by the CROW Act 2000, s 51, Sch 5, Pt I, para 7(1), (5):

'(3A) Where as respects any definitive map and statement the requirements of section 53(2), and of section 55 so far as it applies, have been complied with, the map and statement are to be regarded for the purposes of subsection (3) as having been modified in accordance with the foregoing provisions of this Part whether or not, as respects the map and statement, the requirements of section 54 have been complied with.'

Subsections prospectively inserted after subs (6) by the CROW Act 2000, s 51, Sch 5, Pt I, para 7(1), (6):

'(6A) In subsection (1), the reference to an order under the foregoing provisions of this Part includes a reference to so much of an order to which section 53A applies as contains provision made by virtue of subsection (2) of that section; and subsections (5) and (6) apply to –

    (a) orders to which section 53A applies modifying the map and statement, and
    (b) such documents relating to them as may be prescribed by regulations made by the Secretary of State,

as those subsections apply to orders under this Part modifying the map and statement.

(6B) Regulations under paragraph (b) of subsection (6A) may require any document to be prepared by a surveying authority for the purposes of that paragraph, and any such document shall be in such form as may be prescribed by the regulations.

(6C) Regulations made by the Secretary of State may require any surveying authority –

    (a) to keep such other documents as may be prescribed by the regulations available for inspection at such times and places and in such manner as may be so prescribed, or
    (b) to provide to any other surveying authority any document so prescribed which that authority is, by regulations under paragraph (a), required to keep available for inspection.'

Section prospectively inserted after s 57 by the CROW Act 2000, s 51, Sch 5, Pt I, para 8:

'57A   Consolidation of definitive maps and statements

(1) Where –

    (a) different definitive maps and statements relate to different parts of a surveying authority's area,
    (b) as respects so much of each definitive map and statement as relates to that area the requirements of section 53(2), and of section 55 so far as it applies, have been complied with, and
    (c) there is no part of that area to which no definitive map and statement relate,

the authority may, if it appears to them expedient to do so, prepare a map and statement comprising copies of so much of each definitive map and statement as relates to the authority's area; and where they do so the map and statement so prepared and not, so far as copied, the earlier maps and statements shall be regarded for the purposes of sections 53 to 56 and 57(2) and (3) as the definitive map and statement for the area to which they relate.

(2) The power conferred by subsection (1) is not exercisable by a surveying authority if the definitive map and statement relating to any part of the authority's area is a map and statement in respect of which a review under section 33 of the 1949 Act was begun before the commencement date but has been neither abandoned in pursuance of a direction under section 55(1) nor completed.

(3) References in subsection (1) to a definitive map and statement are, in the case of a map and statement modified in accordance with any of the foregoing provisions of this Part, references to the map and statement as modified.

(4) The statement prepared under subsection (1) shall specify, as the relevant date for the purposes of the map, such date, not being earlier than six months before the preparation of the map and statement, as the authority may determine.

(5) Every surveying authority shall take such steps as they consider expedient for bringing to the attention of the public the preparation by them of any map and statement under subsection (1).'.

Explanatory text – see **5.1.2, 5.2.5**.

58   Application of ss 53 to 57 to inner London

(1) Subject to subsection (2), the foregoing provisions of this Part shall not apply to any area to which this subsection applies; and this subsection applies to any area which, immediately before 1st April 1965, formed part of the administrative county of London.

(2) A London borough council may by resolution adopt the said foregoing provisions as respects any part of their area specified in the resolution, being a part to which subsection (1) applies, and those provisions shall thereupon apply accordingly.

(3) Where by virtue of a resolution under subsection (2), the said foregoing provisions apply to any area, those provisions shall have effect in relation thereto as if for references to the commencement date there were substituted references to the date on which the resolution comes into operation.

Explanatory text – see **5.2.6**.

Miscellaneous and supplemental

59   Prohibition on keeping bulls on land crossed by public rights of way

(1) If, in a case not falling within subsection (2), the occupier of a field or enclosure crossed by a right of way to which this Part applies permits a bull to be at large in the field or enclosure, he shall be liable on summary conviction to a fine not exceeding [level 3 on the standard scale].

(2) Subsection (1) shall not apply to any bull which –

   (a)   does not exceed the age of ten months; or
   (b)   is not of a recognised dairy breed and is at large in any field or enclosure in which cows or heifers are also at large.

(3) Nothing in any byelaws, whenever made, shall make unlawful any act which is, or but for subsection (2) would be, made unlawful by subsection (1).

(4) In this section 'recognised dairy breed' means one of the following breeds, namely, Ayrshire, British Friesian, British Holstein, Dairy Shorthorn, Guernsey, Jersey and Kerry.

(5) The Secretary of State may by order add any breed to, or remove any breed from, subsection (4); and an order under this subsection shall be made by statutory instrument which shall be subject to annulment in pursuance of a resolution of either House of Parliament.

Amendment – Criminal Justice Act 1982, s 46.
Explanatory text – see **9.7.2**.

. . .

62   Appointment of wardens for public rights of way

A local authority may appoint such number of persons as appears to the authority to be necessary or expedient to act as wardens as respects a footpath, bridleway or byway open to all traffic which is both in the countryside and in the area of the authority, and the purpose for which the wardens may be so appointed is to advise and assist the public in connection with the use of the path or way.

63   Orders creating, extinguishing or diverting footpaths and bridleways

The enactments mentioned in Schedule 16 (which relate to the making and confirmation of certain orders creating, extinguishing or diverting footpaths and bridleways) shall have effect subject to the amendments provided for in that Schedule.

Explanatory text – see **Chapters 3 and 4**.

. . .

66   Interpretation of Part III

(1) In this Part –

'bridleway' means a highway over which the public have the following, but no other, rights of way, that is to say, a right of way on foot and a right of way on horseback or leading a horse, with or witout a right to drive animals of any description along the highway;

'byway open to all traffic' means a highway over which the public have a right of way for vehicular and all other kinds of traffic, but which is used by the public mainly for the purpose for which footpaths and bridleways are so used;

'definitive map and statement' has the meaning given by section 53(1);

'footpath' means a highway over which the public have a right of way on foot only, other than such a highway at the side of a public road;

'horse' includes a pony, ass and mule, and 'horseback' shall be construed accordingly;

'public path' means a highway being either a footpath or a bridleway;

'right of way to which this Part applies' means a right of way such that the land over which the right subsists is a public path or a byway open to all traffic;

['surveying authority', in relation to any area, means the county council, [county borough council,] metropolitan district council or London borough council whose area includes that area.]

(2) A highway at the side of a river, canal or other inland navigation shall not be excluded from any definition contained in subsection (1) by reason only that the public have a right to use the highway for purposes of navigation, if the highway would fall within that definition if the public had no such right thereover.

(3) The provisions of section 30(1) of the 1968 Act (riding of pedal cycles on bridleways) shall not affect the definition of bridleway in subsection (1) and any rights exercisable by virtue of those provisions shall be disregarded for the purposes of this Part.

Amendment – Local Government Act 1985, s 7, Sch 3, para 7(6); Local Government (Wales) Act 1994, s 66(6), Sch 16, para 65(8).

Prospective amendment – Definition prospectively inserted after the definition 'public path' in subs (1) by the CROW Act 2000, s 51, Sch 5, Pt I, para 9:

'"restricted byway" has the same meaning as in Part II of the Countryside and Rights of Way Act 2000;'.

PART IV

MISCELLANEOUS AND GENERAL

67   Application to Crown

(1) Subject to the following provisions of this section, Part II, except section 51, and Part III shall apply to Crown land, that is to say, land an interest in which belongs to Her Majesty in the right of the Crown or the Duchy of Lancaster or to the Duchy of Cornwall, and land an interest in which belongs to a Government department or is held in trust for Her Majesty for the purposes of a Government department.

(1A) An interest in Crown land, other than one held by or on behalf of the Crown, may be acquired under section 28N, but only with the consent of the appropriate authority.

(1B) Byelaws made by virtue of section 28R may apply to Crown land if the appropriate authority consents.

(2)–(4) (*not reproduced*).

Amendment – CROW Act 2000, s 75(1), Sch 9, para 6.

---

68   Application to the Isles of Scilly

The Secretary of State may, after consultation with the Council of the Isles of Scilly, by order made by statutory instrument provide for the application of the provisions of Part II or III to the Isles of Scilly as if those Isles were a separate county; and any such order may provide for the application of those provisions to those Isles subject to such modifications as may be specified in the order.

. . .

SCHEDULE 14

APPLICATIONS FOR CERTAIN ORDERS UNDER PART III

Form of applications

1. An application shall be made in the prescribed form and shall be accompanied by –

   (a) a map drawn to the prescribe scale and showing the way or ways to which the application relates; and
   (b) copies of any documentary evidence (including statements of witnesses) which the applicant wishes to adduce in support of the application.

Notice of applications

2.–(1) Subject to sub-paragraph (2), the applicant shall serve a notice stating that the application has been made on every owner and occupier of any land to which the application relates.

(2) If, after reasonable inquiry has been made, the authority are satisfied that it is not practicable to ascertain the name or address of an owner or occupier of any land to which the application relates, the authority may direct that the notice required to be served on him by sub-paragraph (1) may be served by addressing it to him by the description 'owner' or 'occupier' of the land (describing it) and by affixing it to some conspicuous object or objects on the land.

(3) When the requirements of this paragraph have been complied with, the applicant shall certify that fact to the authority.

(4) Every notice or certificate under this paragraph shall be in the prescribed form.

Determination by authority

3.–(1) As soon as reasonably practicable after receiving a certificate under paragraph 2(3), the authority shall –

   (a) investigate the matters stated in the application; and
   (b) after consulting with every local authority whose area includes the land to which the application relates, decide whether to make or not to make the order to which the application relates.

(2) If the authority have not determined the application within twelve months of their receiving a certificate under paragraph 2(3), then, on the applicant making representations to the Secretary of State, the Secretary of State may, after consulting with the authority, direct the authority to determine the application before the expiration of such period as may be specified in the direction.

(3) As soon as practicable after determining the application, the authority shall give notice of their decision by serving a copy of it on the applicant and any person on whom notice of the application was required to be served under paragraph 2(1).

Appeal against a decision not to make an order

4.–(1) Where the authority decide not to make an order, the applicant may, at any time within 28 days after service on him of notice of the decision, serve notice of appeal against that decision on the Secretary of State and the authority.

(2) If on considering the appeal the Secretary of State considers that an order should be made, he shall give to the authority such directions as appear to him necessary for the purpose.

Interpretation

5.–(1) In this Schedule –

'application' means an application under section 53(5);

'local authority' means [a non-metropolitan district council], a parish . . . council or the parish meeting of a parish not having a separate parish council [but, in relation to Wales, means a community council];

'prescribed' means prescribed by regulations made by the Secretary of State.

(2) Regulations under this Schedule shall be made by statutory instrument which shall be subject to annulment in pursuance of a resolution of either House of Parliament.

Amendments – Local Government Act 1985, s 7, Sch 3, para 7; Local Government (Wales) Act 1994, s 66(6), (8), Sch 16, para 65(11), Sch 18.

Prospective Amendment – Words prospectively inserted at the end of para 4(2) by the CROW Act 2000, s 51, Sch 5, Pt I, para 10:

'(which may include a direction as to the time within which an order is to be made)'.

Explanatory text – see **5.8.2**, **5.8.7**.

SCHEDULE 15

PROCEDURE IN CONNECTION WITH CERTAIN ORDERS UNDER PART III

Consultation

1. Before making an order, the authority shall consult with every local authority whose area includes the land to which the order relates.

Coming into operation

2. An order shall not take effect until confirmed either by the authority or the Secretary of State under paragraph 6 or by the Secretary of State under paragraph 7.

Publicity for orders

3.–(1) On making an order, the authority shall give notice in the prescribed form –

   (a) describing the general effect of the order and stating that it has been made and requires confirmation;
   (b) naming a place in the area in which the land to which the order relates is situated where a copy of the order may be inspected free of charge, and copies thereof may be obtained at a reasonable charge, at all reasonable hours; and
   (c) specifying the time (not being less than 42 days from the date of the first publication of the notice) within which, and the manner in which, representations or objections with respect to the order may be made.

(2) Subject to sub-paragraph (4), the notice to be given under sub-paragraph (1) shall be given –

    (a) by publication in at least one local newspaper circulating in the area in which the land to which the order relates is situated;

    (b) by serving a like notice on –
        (i)   every owner and occupier of any of that land;
        (ii) every local authority whose area includes any of that land;
        (iii) every person on whom notice is required to be served in pursuance of sub-paragraph (3); and
        (iv) such other persons as may be prescribed in relation to the area in which that land is situated or as the authority may consider appropriate; and

    (c) by causing a copy of the notice to be displayed in a prominent position –
        (i)   at the ends of so much of any way as is affected by the order;
        (ii) at council offices in the locality of the land to which the order relates; and
        (iii) at such other places as the authority may consider appropriate.

(3) Any person may, on payment of such reasonable charge as the authority may consider appropriate, require an authority to give him notice of all such orders as are made by the authority during a specified period, are of a specified description and relate to land comprised in a specified area; and in this sub-paragraph 'specified' means specified in the requirement.

(4) The Secretary of State may, in any particular case, direct that it shall not be necessary to comply with sub-paragraph (2)(b)(i); but if he so directs in the case of any land, then in addition to publication the notice shall be addressed to 'The owners and any occupiers' of the land (describing it) and a copy or copies of the notice shall be affixed to some conspicuous object or objects on the land.

(5) Sub-paragraph (2)(b) and (c) and, where applicable, sub-paragraph (4) shall be complied with not less than 42 days before the expiration of the time specified in the notice.

(6) A notice required to be served by sub-paragraph (2)(b) on the owner or occupier of any land, or on a local authority, shall be accompanied by a copy of so much of the order as relates to that land or, as the case may be, the area of that authority; and a notice required to be served by that sub-paragraph on such other persons as may be prescribed or as the authority may consider appropriate shall be accompanied by a copy of the order.

(7) A notice required to be displayed by sub-paragraph (2)(c) at the ends of so much of any way as is affected by the order shall be accompanied by a plan showing the general effect of the order so far as it relates to that way.

(8) At any time after the publication of a notice under this paragraph and before the expiration of the period specified in the notice for the making of representations and objections, any person may require the authority to inform him what documents (if any) were taken into account in preparing the order and –

    (a) as respects any such documents in the possession of the authority, to permit him to inspect them and take copies; and

    (b) as respects any such documents not in their possession, to give him any information the authority have as to where the documents can be inspected;

and on any requirement being made under this sub-paragraph the authority shall comply therewith within 14 days of the making of the requirement.

(9) Nothing in sub-paragraph (8) shall be construed as limiting the documentary or other evidence which may be adduced at any local inquiry or hearing held under paragraph 7 or 8.

Representations or objections made with respect to abandoned surveys or reviews

4.–(1) This paragraph applies where a survey begun under sections 27 to 32 of the 1949 Act, or a review begun under section 33 of that Act, is abandoned after a draft map and statement have been prepared.

(2) If an order modifies the definitive map and statement so as –

  (a) to show any particulars shown in the draft map and statement but not in the definitive map and statement; or
  (b) to omit any particulars shown in the definitive map and statement but not in the draft map and statement,

any representation or objection duly made with respect to the showing in or omission from the draft map and statement of those particulars shall be treated for the purposes of paragraphs 6 and 7 as a representation or objection duly made with respect to the corresponding modification made by the order.

Severance of orders

5.–(1) Where at any time representations or objections duly made and not withdrawn relate to some but not all of the modifications made by an order, the authority may, by notice given to the Secretary of State, elect that, for the purposes of the following provisions of this Schedule, the order shall have effect as two separate orders –

  (a) the one comprising the modifications to which the representations or objections relate; and
  (b) the other comprising the remaining modifications.

(2) Any reference in sub-paragraph (1) to an order includes a reference to any part of an order which, by virtue of one or more previous elections under that sub-paragraph, has effect as a separate order.

Unopposed orders

6.–(1) If so representations or objections are duly made, or if any so made are withdrawn, the authority may –

  (a) confirm the order without modification; or
  (b) if they require any modification to be made, submit the order to the Secretary of State for confirmation by him.

(2) Where an order is submitted to the Secretary of State under sub-paragraph (1), the Secretary of State may confirm the order with or without modifications.

Opposed orders

7.–(1) If any representation or objection duly made is not withdrawn the authority shall submit the order to the Secretary of State for confirmation by him.

(2) Where an order is submitted to the Secretary of State under sub-paragraph (1), the Secretary of State shall either –

(a) cause a local inquiry to be held; or

(b) afford any person by whom a representation or objection has been duly made and not withdrawn an opportunity of being heard by a person appointed by the Secretary of State for the purpose.

(3) On considering any representations or objections duly made and the report of the person appointed to hold the inquiry or hear representations or objections, the Secretary of State may confirm the order with or without modifications.

Restriction on power to confirm orders with modifications

8.–(1) The Secretary of State shall not confirm an order with modifications so as –

(a) to affect land not affected by the order;

(b) not to show any way shown in the order or to show any way not so shown; or

(c) to show as a highway of one description a way which is shown in the order as a highway of another description,

except after complying with the requirements of sub-paragraph (2).

(2) The said requirements are that the Secretary of State shall –

(a) give notice as appears to him requisite of his proposal so to modify the order, specifying the time (which shall not be less than 28 days from the date of the first publication of the notice) within which, and the manner in which, representations or objections with respect to the proposal may be made;

(b) hold a local inquiry or afford any person by whom any representation or objection has been duly made and not withdrawn an opportunity of being heard by a person appointed by the Secretary of State for the purpose; and

(c) consider the report of the person appointed to hold the inquiry or to hear representations or objections.

Local inquiries

9. The provisions of subsections (2) to (5) of section 250 of the Local Government Act 1972 (which relate to the giving of evidence at, and defraying the cost of, local inquiries) shall apply in relation to any inquiry held under paragraph 7 or 8 as they apply in relation to a local inquiry which a Minister causes to be held under sub-section (1) of that section.

Appointment of inspectors etc

10.–(1) A decision of the Secretary of State under paragraph 6, 7 or 8 shall, except in such classes of case as may for the time being be prescribed or as may be specified in directions given by the Secretary of State, be made by a person appointed by the Secretary of State for the purpose instead of by the Secretary of State; and a decision made by a person so appointed shall be treated as a decision of the Secretary of State.

(2) The Secretary of State may, if he thinks fit, direct that a decision which, by virtue of sub-paragraph (1) and apart from this sub-paragraph, falls to be made by a person appointed by the Secretary of State shall instead be made by the Secretary of State; and a direction under this sub-paragraph shall state the reasons for which it is given and shall be served on the person, if any, so appointed, the authority and any person by whom a representation or objection has been duly made and not withdrawn.

(3) Where the Secretary of State has appointed a person to make a decision under paragraph 6, 7 or 8 the Secretary of State may, at any time before the making of the

decision, appoint another person to make it instead of the person first appointed to make it.

(4) Where by virtue of sub-paragraph (2) or (3) a particular decision falls to be made by the Secretary of State or any other person instead of the person first appointed to make it, anything done by or in relation to the latter shall be treated as having been done by or in relation to the former.

(5) Regulations under this paragraph may provide for the giving of publicity to any directions given by the Secretary o State under this paragraph.

Notice of final decisions on orders

11.–(1) As soon as practicable after a decision to confirm an order is made or, in the case of a decision by the Secretary of State, as soon as practicable after receiving notice of his decision, the authority shall give notice –

  (a) describing the general effect of the order as confirmed and stating that it has been confirmed (with or without modification) and the date on which it took effect; and
  (b) naming a place in the area in which the land to which the order relates is situated where a copy of the order as confirmed may be inspected free of charge, and copies thereof may be obtained at a reasonable charge, at all reasonable hours.

(2) A notice under sub-paragraph (1) shall be given –

  (a) by publication in the manner required by paragraph 3(2)(a);
  (b) by serving a like notice on any persons on whom notices were required to be served under paragraph 3(2)(b) or (4); and
  (c) by causing like notices to be displayed in the like manner as the notices required to be displayed under paragraph 3(2)(c).

(3) A notice required to be served by sub-paragraph (2)(b) on the owner or occupier of any land, or on a local authority, shall be accompanied by a copy of so much of the order as confirmed as relates to that land or, as the case may be, the area of that authority;

and, in the case of an order which has been confirmed with modifications, a notice required to be served by that sub-paragraph on such other persons as may be prescribed or as the authority may consider appropriate shall be accompanied by a copy of the order as confirmed.

(4) As soon as practicable after a decision not to confirm an order or, in the case of a decision by the Secretary of State, as soon as practicable after receiving notice of his decision, the authority shall give notice of the decision by serving a copy of it on any persons on whom notices were required to be served under paragraph 3(2)(b) or (4).

Proceedings for questioning validity of orders

12.–(1) If any person is aggrieved by an order which has taken effect and desires to question its validity on the ground that it is not within the powers of section 53 and 54 or that any of the requirements of this Schedule have not been complied with in relation to it, he may within 42 days from the date of publication of the notice under paragraph 11 make an application to the High Court under this paragraph.

(2) On any such application the High Court may, if satisfied that the order is not within those powers or that the interests of the applicant have been substantially prejudiced by

a failure to comply with those requirements, quash the order, or any provision of the order, either generally or in so far as it affects the interests of the applicant.

(3) Except as provided by this paragraph, the validity of an order shall not be questioned in any legal proceedings whatsoever.

Supplemental

13.–(1) The Secretary of State may, subject to the provisions of this Schedule, by regulations make such provision as to the procedure on the making, submission and confirmation of orders as appears to him to be expedient.

(2) In this Schedule –

'council offices' means offices or buildings acquired or provided by the authority or by a local authority;

'local authority' means [a non-metropolitan district council], a parish . . . council or the parish meeting of a parish not having a separate parish council [but, in relation to Wales, means a community council];

'order' means an order to which the provisions of this Schedule apply;

'prescribed' means prescribed by regulations made by the Secretary of State.

(3) Regulations under this Schedule shall be made by statutory instrument which shall be subject to annulment in pursuance of a resolution of either House of Parliament.

Amendments – Local Government Act 1985, s 7, Sch 3, para 7; Local Government (Wales) Act 1994, s 66(6), (8), Sch 16, para 65(12), Sch 18.

Prospective Amendments – Words prospectively inserted after the words 'with respect to the order' in para 3(1)(c) by the CROW Act 2000, s 51, Sch 5, Pt I, para 11(1), (2):

', which must include particulars of the grounds relied on,'

Words prospectively inserted after the words 'Nothing in sub-paragraph' in para 3(9) by the CROW Act 2000, s 51, Sch 5, Pt I, para 11(1), (3)(a):

'(1)(c) or'

Words prospectively inserted after the words 'construed as limiting' in para 3(9) by the CROW Act 2000, s 51, Sch 5, Pt I, para 11(1), (3)(b):

'the grounds which may be relied on or'

Words prospectively inserted after the words 'the Secretary of State shall' in para 7(2) by the CROW Act 2000, s 51, Sch 5, Pt I, para 11(1), (4):

', subject to sub-paragraph (2A),'

Subparagraph prospectively inserted in para 7 by the CROW Act 2000, s 51, Sch 5, Pt I, para 11(1), (5):

'(2A) The Secretary of State may, but need not, act as mentioned in sub-paragraph (2)(a) or (b) if, in his opinion, no representation or objection which has been duly made and not withdrawn relates to an issue which would be relevant in determining whether or not to confirm the order, either with or without modifications.'

Paragraph 7(3) words 'the person appointed to hold the inquiry' prospectively substituted by the CROW Act 2000, s 51, Sch 5, Pt I, para 11(1), (6):

'any person appointed to hold an inquiry'

Words prospectively inserted after the words 'requisite of his proposal' in para 8(2)(a) by the CROW Act 2000, s 51, Sch 5, Pt I, para 11(1), (7)(a):

', which must include particulars of the grounds relied on,'

Paragraphs 8(2)(b), (c) prospectively substituted by the CROW Act 2000, s 51, Sch 5, Pt I, para 11(1), (7)(b):

'(b) if any representation or objection duly made is not withdrawn (but subject to sub-paragraph (3)), hold a local inquiry or afford any person by whom any such representation or objection has been made an opportunity of being heard by a person appointed by the Secretary of State for the purpose; and

(c) consider the report of any person appointed to hold an inquiry or to hear representations or objections.

(3) The Secretary of State may, but need not, act as mentioned in sub-paragraph (2)(b) if, in his opinion, no representation or objection which has been duly made and not withdrawn relates to an issue which would be relevant in determining whether or not to confirm the order in accordance with his proposal.

(4) Sub-paragraph (2)(a) shall not be construed as limiting the grounds which may be relied on at any local inquiry or hearing held under this paragraph.'

Paragraph 9 prospectively repealed by the CROW Act 2000, ss 51, 102, Sch 5, Pt I, paras 11(1), (8), Sch 16, Pt II.

Paragraph 10A prospectively inserted by the CROW Act 2000, s 51, Sch 5, Pt I, para 11(1), (8):

'Hearings and local inquiries

10A.–(1) Subject to sub-paragraph (2), subsections (2) to (5) of section 250 of the Local Government Act 1972 (giving of evidence at, and defraying of costs of, inquiries) shall apply in relation to any hearing or local inquiry held under paragraph 7 or 8 as they apply in relation to a local inquiry which a Minister causes to be held under subsection (1) of that section.

(2) In its application to a hearing or inquiry held under paragraph 7 or 8 by a person appointed under paragraph 10(1), subsection (5) of that section shall have effect as if the reference to the Minister causing the inquiry to be held were a reference to the person so appointed or the Secretary of State.

(3) Section 322A of the Town and Country Planning Act 1990 (orders as to costs where no hearing or inquiry takes place) shall apply in relation to a hearing or local inquiry under paragraph 7 or 8 as it applies in relation to a hearing or local inquiry for the purposes referred to in that section.'

Explanatory text – see **5.8**.

INDEX

References are to paragraph numbers.